Chronic Pain: Clinical Updates and Perspectives

Chronic Pain: Clinical Updates and Perspectives

Editors

Carmen M. Galvez-Sánchez
Casandra Isabel Montoro Aguilar
Markus W. Hollmann

MDPI

Basel • Beijing • Wuhan • Barcelona • Belgrade • Novi Sad • Cluj • Manchester

Editors
Carmen M. Galvez-Sánchez
University of Jaén
Jaén, Spain

Casandra Isabel Montoro Aguilar
University of Jaén
Jaén, Spain

Markus W. Hollmann
Amsterdam University
Medical Center (AUMC)
Amsterdam,
The Netherlands

Editorial Office
MDPI
St. Alban-Anlage 66
4052 Basel, Switzerland

This is a reprint of articles from the Special Issue published online in the open access journal *Journal of Clinical Medicine* (ISSN 2077-0383) (available at: https://www.mdpi.com/journal/jcm/special_issues/chronic_pain_research).

For citation purposes, cite each article independently as indicated on the article page online and as indicated below:

Lastname, A.A.; Lastname, B.B. Article Title. *Journal Name* **Year**, *Volume Number*, Page Range.

ISBN 978-3-0365-8644-1 (Hbk)
ISBN 978-3-0365-8645-8 (PDF)
doi.org/10.3390/books978-3-0365-8645-8

Contents

Journal of
Clinical Medicine

MDPI

Editorial

Chronic Pain: Clinical Updates and Perspectives

Carmen M. Galvez-Sánchez * and Casandra I. Montoro *

Department of Psychology, University of Jaén, 23071 Jaén, Spain
* Correspondence: cgalvez@ujaen.es (C.M.G.-S.); imontoro@ujaen.es (C.I.M.)

Citation: Galvez-Sánchez, C.M.; Montoro, C.I. Chronic Pain: Clinical Updates and Perspectives. *J. Clin. Med.* **2022**, *11*, 3474. https://doi.org/10.3390/jcm11123474

Received: 12 June 2022
Accepted: 15 June 2022
Published: 16 June 2022

The International Association for the Study of Pain (IASP) has defined pain as an unpleasant sensory and emotional experience associated with actual or potential tissue damage, or described in terms of such damage, which also comprises a subjective component [1]. Pain is characterized by a multidimensional nature in which three dimensions are usually differentiated: sensory-discriminative, emotional-affective, and cognitive-evaluative [1]. Furthermore, pain can be classified according to different aspects, for example the duration, the explaining cause, or the anatomical location [1]. Depending on the duration and the main classification, it is possible to differentiate between acute pain (less than 6 months) or chronic pain (more than 6 months) [1].

Regarding chronic pain, it entails a serious health burden, and a high comorbidity with other disorders such as anxiety, depression, insomnia, and cognitive impairments [2–11]. Given its high comorbidity with the above-reported disorders, chronic pain generates important socio-health expenses related to its management, as well as numerous indirect economic costs as a result of high rates of absenteeism, reduced labor productivity, and disability [12,13]. The prevalence of chronic pain in the general population of developing countries is estimated at 18% [14], and it is expected to increase with population growing and aging which in turn will require more effective prevention, diagnosis, and pain treatment strategies due to the higher associated socio-health and personal costs [15]. Chronic pain negatively affects both the patient and relatives' quality of life [16,17]. Based on the aforementioned, chronic pain has been recognized as a bioethical issue [18] and different international organizations have declared the access to an adequate pain therapy as a human right [17,19,20].

The principal chronic pain disorders include headache, migraine, and local and generalized musculoskeletal diseases. The last may be further divided into those with inflammatory (i.e., autoimmune or infectious), mechanical (i.e., chronic low back pain), or unknown origin [21]. These disorders have in common the tendency to exhibit periods of remission of symptoms and phases of exacerbation [21].

Fibromyalgia, chronic tension-type headache, migraine, and the temporomandibular disorder are some examples of chronic pain disorders without a clear physiological cause. In all of these disorders, the pain intensity is found not to be proportional to the reported injury [22–25]. Nonetheless, the most empirically supported hypothesis is the presence of an alteration at central nervous system level [3,26]. The central pain processing mechanisms are proposed to be altered and produce a phenomenon called central sensitization. This phenomenon consists of a great sensitization to pain and excitability of the neurons of the posterior horns of the spinal cord and the reticulo-thalamic-cortical system [27,28]. Additionally, central sensitization implies a neuronal reorganization along with a deficient descending pain modulation system leading to an extreme sensitivity to touch, cold, or heat [29–31].

The intervention of chronic pain should be considered from a biopsychosocial perspective. As pointed out before, chronic pain is a condition characterized by physiological and biological correlates, in turn modulated by emotions (including negative beliefs) [4,32–35], personality factors [36–40], and coping styles [8,41], and related to different psychological behaviors [42]. In addition to these factors, the evolution and prognosis of chronic pain is not only affected by social but also by cultural factors (i.e., socio-economics, social support, educational level, work-related situation, etc.) [37,43]. Consequently, the treatment based on a multidisciplinary approach is shown to be the most effective in chronic pain management [44]. Anesthesiologists, psychiatrists, neurosurgeons, psychologists, and physiotherapists are frequently integrated into multidisciplinary pain teams [42]. Despite the benefits of the multidisciplinary approach in the treatment of chronic pain, it is not fully effective [45]. The treatment of chronic pain is still a current social and sanitary challenge [42], which also require personalized care to improve the health-related quality of the lives of these patients [46,47]. Personalized pain medicine remains a gap which needs to be overcome [48]. The person-centered medicine and personalized medicine in the areas of chronic pain research and management (including the cognitive, physical, affective, and behavioral domains) are necessary [46,49]. Authors point out the need for the fusion of these paradigms into a single new approach with the objective to avoid possible miscommunication, duplication of efforts, and ineffective treatment of chronic pain patients [47].

In general, to contribute to the effectiveness of chronic pain treatment, patients must be informed of the characteristics of the treatment. Thus, they are capable of committing to the treatment and can achieve better results [50]. It is crucial: (1) to establish clear and realistic therapeutic goals to motivate patients and increase their adherence to treatment, (2) to promote a good therapeutic alliance or rapport between the patient and the therapist, (3) to help patients to understand their responsibility in the treatment process, and (4) to ensure they are aware of the relevance of their implication to change the perspective from helplessness and despair to self-efficacy and personal self-control over the disorder [49]. Indeed, the perception of control and self-efficacy are issues to be addressed in any of the chronic pain treatments, because patients usually perceive pain as something uncontrollable, which generates low self-efficacy and hopelessness [51]. By contrast, patients with a higher perception of self-efficacy tend to have less pain, negative emotions, and disability and react better to treatment [51,52]. Therefore, active coping strategies must be promoted. Other elements such as postural and sleep hygiene, a proper diet, and regular and adapted physical exercise are further necessary to include in chronic pain treatment [5,49,53]. In addition, the involvement of patients´ relatives is vital for the success of the intervention, and the reinforcement of new, healthier behaviors and lifestyles on patients [54].

In sum, the chronic pain field requires continuous research in order to improve its prevention, diagnosis, and treatment. Considering the worldwide incidence, and prevalence of chronic pain in developing countries [14], scientists, clinicians, and governments must move forward together to overcome the great treatment challenge that chronic pain entails. This will markedly contribute to improving the health-related quality of life of patients and relatives, as well as to decreasing its socio-economic costs.

Funding: This research received no external funding.

Conflicts of Interest: The authors declare no conflict of interest.

References

1. International Association for the Study of Pain (IASP). Pain IASP Taxonomy. 2015. Available online: http://www.iasp-pain.org/Education/Content.aspx?ItemNumber=1698&navItemNumber=576 (accessed on 12 May 2022).
2. Montoro, C.I.; Duschek, S.; Muñoz Ladrón de Guevara, C.; Fernández-Serrano, M.J.; Reyes del Paso, G.A. Aberrant cerebral blood flow responses during cognition: Implications for the understanding of cognitive deficits in fibromyalgia. *Neuropsychology* **2015**, *29*, 173. [CrossRef]
3. Montoro, C.I.; Duschek, S.; de Guevara, C.M.L.; Reyes del Paso, G.A. Patterns of cerebral blood flow modulation during painful stimulation in fibromyalgia: A transcranial doppler sonography study. *Pain Med.* **2016**, *17*, 2256–2267. [CrossRef] [PubMed]
4. Amaro-Díaz, L.; Montoro, C.I.; Fischer-Jbali, L.R.; Galvez-Sánchez, C.M. Chronic Pain and Emotional Stroop: A Systematic Review. *J. Clin. Med.* **2022**, *11*, 3259. [CrossRef]
5. Veehof, M.M.; Oskam, M.J.; Schreurs, K.M.; Bohlmeije, E.T. Acceptance-based interventions for the treatment of chronic pain: A systematic review and meta-analysis. *Pain* **2011**, *152*, 533–542. [CrossRef] [PubMed]

6. Galvez-Sánchez, C.M.; de la Coba, P.; Colmenero, J.M.; Reyes Del Paso, G.A.; Duschek, S. Attentional function in fibromyalgia and rheumatoid arthritis. *PLoS ONE* **2021**, *16*, e0246128. [CrossRef]
7. Galvez-Sánchez, C.M.; Montoro, C.I.; Duschek, S.; Reyes Del Paso, G.A. Depression and trait-anxiety mediate the influence of clinical pain on health-related quality of life in fibromyalgia. *J. Affect Disord.* **2020**, *265*, 486–495. [CrossRef] [PubMed]
8. Galvez-Sánchez, C.M.; Montoro, C.I.; Duschek, S.; Del Paso, G. Pain catastrophizing mediates the negative influence of pain and trait-anxiety on health-related quality of life in fibromyalgia. *Qual. Life Res.* **2020**, *29*, 1871–1881. [CrossRef]
9. Galvez-Sánchez, C.M.; Reyes Del Paso, G.A.; Duschek, S. Cognitive Impairments in Fibromyalgia Syndrome: Associations with Positive and Negative Affect, Alexithymia, Pain Catastrophizing and Self-Esteem. *Front. Psychol.* **2018**, *9*, 377. [CrossRef]
10. Galvez-Sánchez, C.M.; Muñoz Ladrón de Guevara, C.; Montoro, C.I.; Fernández-Serrano, M.J.; Duschek, S.; Reyes Del Paso, G.A. Cognitive deficits in fibromyalgia syndrome are associated with pain responses to low intensity pressure stimulation. *PLoS ONE* **2018**, *13*, e0201488. [CrossRef]
11. Reyes del Paso, G.A.; Montoro, C.I.; Duschek, S. Reaction time, cerebral blood flow, and heart rate responses in fibromyalgia: Evidence of alterations in attentional control. *J. Clin. Exp. Neuropsychol.* **2015**, *37*, 414–428. [CrossRef]
12. Societal Impact of Pain (SIP). Policy Recommendations 207. 2017. Available online: https://www.sip-platform.eu/resources/details/SIP_2017_Policy_Recommendations (accessed on 12 May 2022).
13. Patel, A.S.; Farquharson, R.; Carroll, D.; Moore, A.; Phillips, C.J.; Taylor, R.S.; Barden, J. The impact and burden of chronic pain in the workplace: A qualitative systematic review. *Pain Pract.* **2012**, *12*, 578–589. [CrossRef] [PubMed]
14. Sá, K.N.; Moreira, L.; Baptista, A.F.; Yeng, L.T.; Teixeira, M.J.; Galhardoni, R.; de Andrade, D.C. Prevalence of chronic pain in developing countries: Systematic review and meta-analysis. *Pain Rep.* **2019**, *4*, e779. [CrossRef] [PubMed]
15. Breivik, H.; Collett, B.; Ventafridda, V.; Cohen, R.; Gallacher, D. Survey of chronic pain in Europe: Prevalence, impact on daily life, and treatment. *Eur. J. Pain* **2006**, *10*, 287–333. [CrossRef] [PubMed]
16. Pereira, M.G.; Carvalho, C.; Costa, E.; Leite, Â.; Almeida, V. Quality of life in chronic pain patients: Illness- and wellness-focused coping as moderators. *PsyCh J.* **2021**, *10*, 283–294. [CrossRef] [PubMed]
17. Domenichiello, A.F.; Ramsden, C.E. The silent epidemic of chronic pain in older adults. *Prog. Neuropsychopharmacol. Biol. Psychiatry* **2019**, *93*, 284–290. [CrossRef] [PubMed]
18. Christopher, M.J. It's time for bioethics to see chronic pain as an ethical issue. *Am. J. Bioeth.* **2011**, *11*, 3–4. [CrossRef]
19. World Medical Association (WMA). WMA Resolution on the Access to Adequate Pain Treatment, Adopted by the 62nd WMA General Assembly, Montevideo, Uruguay. 2011. Available online: https://www.wma.net/policies-post/wma-resolution-on-the-access-to-adequate-pain-treatment/ (accessed on 12 May 2022).
20. International Pain Summit of The International Association for The Study of Pain (IASP). Declaration of Montréal: Declaration that access to pain management is a fundamental human right. *J. Pain Palliat. Care Pharmacother.* **2011**, *25*, 29–31. [CrossRef]
21. Breivik, H.; Eisenberg, E.; O'Brien, T. The individual and societal burden of chronic pain in Europe: The case for strategic prioritization and action to improve knowledge and availability of appropriate care. *BMC Public Health* **2013**, *13*, 1229–1243. [CrossRef]
22. Yunus, M.B. Central sensitivity syndromes: An overview. *J. Musculoskelet. Pain* **2009**, *17*, 400–408. [CrossRef]
23. Cernuda-Morollón, E.; Larrosa, D.; Ramón, C.; Vega, J.; Martínez-Camblor, P.; Pascual, J. Interictal increase of CGRP levels in peripheral blood as a biomarker for chronic migraine. *Neurology* **2013**, *81*, 1191–1196. [CrossRef]
24. Yu, S.; Han, X. Update of chronic tension-type headache. *Curr. Pain Headache Rep.* **2015**, *19*, 469. [CrossRef] [PubMed]
25. Sarlani, E.; Greenspan, J. Evidence for generalized hyperalgesia in temporo-mandibular disorders patients. *Pain* **2003**, *10*, 221–226. [CrossRef]
26. Clauw, D.J. Fibromyalgia: A clinical review. *JAMA* **2014**, *311*, 1547–1555. [CrossRef] [PubMed]
27. Latremoliere, A.; Woolf, C.J. Central sensitization: A generator of pain hypersensitivity by central neural plasticity. *J. Pain* **2009**, *10*, 895–926. [CrossRef]
28. Kindler, L.L.; Bennett, R.M.; Jones, K.D. Central sensitivity syndromes: Mounting pathophysiologic evidence to link fibromyalgia with other common chronic pain disorders. *Pain Manag. Nurs.* **2011**, *12*, 15–24. [CrossRef]
29. Woolf, C.J.; Salter, M.W. Neuronal plasticity: Increasing the gain in pain. *Science* **2000**, *288*, 1765–1768. [CrossRef]
30. Woolf, C.J. Central sensitization: Implications for the diagnosis and treatment of pain. *Pain* **2011**, *152*, S2–S15. [CrossRef]
31. De la Coba, P.; Montoro, C.I.; Reyes Del Paso, G.A.; Galvez-Sánchez, C.M. Algometry for the assessment of central sensitisation to pain in fibromyalgia patients: A systematic review. *Ann. Med.* **2022**, *54*, 1403–1422. [CrossRef]
32. Montoro, C.I.; Duschek, S.; Schuepbach, D.; Gandarillas, M.; Reyes del Paso, G.A. Cerebral blood flow variability in fibromyalgia syndrome: Relationships with emotional, clinical and functional variables. *PLoS ONE* **2018**, *13*, e0204267. [CrossRef]
33. Fischer-Jbali, L.R.; Montoro, C.I.; Montoya, P.; Halder, W.; Duschek, S. Central nervous activity during an emotional Stroop task in fibromyalgia syndrome. *Int. J. Psychophysiol.* **2022**, *177*, 133–144. [CrossRef]
34. Fischer-Jbali, L.R.; Montoro, C.I.; Montoya, P.; Halder, W.; Duschek, S. Central nervous activity during implicit processing of emotional face expressions in fibromyalgia syndrome. *Brain Res.* **2021**, *1758*, 147333. [CrossRef]
35. Fischer-Jbali, L.R.; Montoro, C.I.; Montoya, P.; Halder, W.; Duschek, S. Central Nervous Activity during a Dot Probe Task with Facial Expressions in Fibromyalgia. *Biol. Psychol.* **2021**, 108361. [CrossRef] [PubMed]
36. Montoro, C.I.; del Paso, G.A.R. Personality and fibromyalgia: Relationships with clinical, emotional, and functional variables. *Pers. Individ. Differ.* **2015**, *85*, 236–244. [CrossRef]

37. Galvez-Sánchez, C.M.; Duschek, S.; Reyes Del Paso, G.A. Psychological impact of fibromyalgia: Current perspectives. *Psychol. Res. Behav. Manag.* **2019**, *12*, 117–127. [CrossRef] [PubMed]
38. Galvez-Sánchez, C.M.; Reyes Del Paso, G.A.; Duschek, S.; Montoro, C.I. The Link between Fibromyalgia Syndrome and Anger: A Systematic Review Revealing Research Gaps. *J. Clin. Med.* **2022**, *11*, 844. [CrossRef]
39. Galvez-Sánchez, C.M.; Montoro Aguilar, C.I. Migraine and Neuroticism: A Scoping Review. *Behav. Sci.* **2022**, *12*, 30. [CrossRef]
40. Montoro Aguilar, C.I.; Duschek, S.; Reyes del Paso, G.A. An exploratory analysis of the influence of personality and emotional factors on cerebral blood flow responses during painful stimulation in fibromyalgia. *Scand. J. Psychol.* **2018**, *59*, 301–310. [CrossRef]
41. Montoro, C.I.; Reyes del Paso, G.A.; Duschek, S. Alexithymia in fibromyalgia syndrome. *Pers. Individ. Differ.* **2016**, *102*, 170–179. [CrossRef]
42. Kanner, R. *Secretos En El Tratamiento Del Dolor*; McGraw-Hill Interamericana: Mexico City, Mexico, 2006.
43. Duschek, S.; Nassauer, L.; Montoro, C.I.; Bair, A.; Montoya, P. Dispositional empathy is associated with experimental pain reduction during provision of social support by romantic partners. *Scand. J. Pain* **2019**, *20*, 205–209. [CrossRef]
44. Warfield, C.A.; Fausett, H.J. *Manual De Diagnóstico y De Tratamiento Del Dolor*; Masson: Barcelona, Spain, 2004.
45. Siracusa, R.; Paola, R.D.; Cuzzocrea, S.; Impellizzeri, D. Fibromyalgia: Pathogenesis, Mechanisms, Diagnosis and Treatment Options Update. *Int. J. Mol. Sci.* **2021**, *22*, 3891. [CrossRef]
46. Davydov, D.M.; Galvez-Sánchez, C.M.; Montoro, C.I.; de Guevara, C.; Reyes Del Paso, G.A. Personalized behavior management as a replacement for medications for pain control and mood regulation. *Sci. Rep.* **2021**, *11*, 20297. [CrossRef] [PubMed]
47. Braš, M.; Đorđević, V.; Milunović, V.; Brajković, L.; Miličić, D.; Konopka, L. Person-centered medicine versus personalized medicine: Is it just a sophism? A view from chronic pain management. *Psychiatr. Danub.* **2011**, *23*, 246–250. [PubMed]
48. Bruehl, S. Personalized pain medicine: Pipe dream or reality? *Anesthesiology* **2015**, *122*, 967–968. [CrossRef] [PubMed]
49. Muñoz Ladrón de Guevara, C.; Reyes del Paso, G.A.; Fernández Serrano, M.J.; Montoro, C.I. Fibromyalgia Syndrome and Cognitive Decline: The Role of Body Mass Index and Clinical Symptoms. *J. Clin. Med.* **2022**, *11*, 3404. [CrossRef]
50. Galvez-Sánchez, C.M.; Montoro, C.I.; Moreno-Padilla, M.; Reyes Del Paso, G.A.; de la Coba, P. Effectiveness of Acceptance and Commitment Therapy in Central Pain Sensitization Syndromes: A Systematic Review. *J. Clin. Med.* **2021**, *10*, 2706. [CrossRef]
51. Mirsharifa, S.M.; Mirzaian, B.; Dousti, Y. The efficacy of Acceptance and Commitment Therapy (ACT) Matrix on depression and psychological capital of the patients with irritable bowel syndrome. *Open Access Maced. J. Med. Sci.* **2019**, *7*, 421. [CrossRef]
52. Wicksell, R.K.; Kemani, M.; Jensen, K.; Kosek, E.; Kadetoff, D.; Sorjonen, K.; Ingvar, M.; Olsson, G.L. Acceptance and commitment therapy for fibromyalgia: A randomized controlled trial. *Eur. J. Pain* **2013**, *17*, 599–611. [CrossRef]
53. Otis, J.D. *Managing Chronic Pain. A Cognitive-Behavioral Therapy Approach*; Oxford University Press: New York, NY, USA, 2007.
54. Cooper, S.; Gilbert, L. The role of 'social support' in the experience of fibromyalgia—Narratives from South Africa. *Health Soc. Care Community* **2017**, *25*, 1021–1030. [CrossRef]

Journal of
Clinical Medicine

MDPI

Review

Chronic Pain and Emotional Stroop: A Systematic Review

Lidia Amaro-Díaz [1], Casandra I. Montoro [1,*], Laura R. Fischer-Jbali [2] and Carmen M. Galvez-Sánchez [1,*]

1 Department of Psychology, University of Jaén, 23071 Jaén, Spain; lamaro@ujaen.es
2 Institute of Psychology, University of Health Sciences, Medical Informatics and Technology, 6060 Hall in Tirol, Austria; laura.fischer-jbali@umit.at
* Correspondence: imontoro@ujaen.es (C.I.M.); cgalvez@ujaen.es (C.M.G.-S.)

Abstract: Chronic pain is an unpleasant sensory and emotional experience that persists for more than 3 months and is often accompanied by symptoms such as depression, fatigue, sleep disturbances, and cognitive impairment. Emotional dysregulation may also be involved in its etiology. Emotions are known to modulate the experience of pain by influencing cognition and behavior (emotional awareness, emotional expression and experience, and verbalizations). A useful task to explore emotional processing and emotional dysregulation is the emotional Stroop task. Despite the large number of studies using this task, their objectives are diverse; it is necessary to integrate them. The main objective of the present systematic review was to determine the extent of the abnormalities in behavioral performance (including attentional biases) and/or brain alterations in patients with chronic pain during the emotional Stroop task. This systematic review was conducted in accordance with the Cochrane Collaboration guidelines and Preferred Reporting Items for Systematic Reviews and Meta-Analysis (PRISMA) statement. The protocol was previously registered in the Prospective Register of Systematic Reviews (PROSPERO) international database. The selected articles were extracted from the PubMed, Scopus, and Web of Science databases. Fifteen studies were identified as eligible for systematic review. The studies reported alterations in brain regions related to pain and emotional regulation, as well as attentional bias and higher response time latencies (related to the words' emotional load) in patients with chronic pain. The results confirm the validity of the emotional Stroop task to measure emotions and selective attention. As attentional bias towards negative information is often seen in chronic pain patients, and given the relation between selective attention and greater activation of the brain areas associated with pain and emotional processing, this type of task plays a crucial role in research on emotional and attentional processes among chronic pain patients. Further, attentional bias towards negative information has been associated with higher levels of pain. Taken together, the results suggest the need for cognitive training and an emotional approach to chronic pain therapies, especially targeting attentional biases and negative mood.

Keywords: chronic pain; emotional Stroop task; brain regions; emotional regulation; attentional bias

Citation: Amaro-Díaz, L.; Montoro, C.I.; Fischer-Jbali, L.R.; Galvez-Sánchez, C.M. Chronic Pain and Emotional Stroop: A Systematic Review. *J. Clin. Med.* **2022**, *11*, 3259. https://doi.org/10.3390/jcm11123259

Academic Editor: Stefan Evers

Received: 26 March 2022
Accepted: 5 June 2022
Published: 7 June 2022

1. Introduction

1.1. Emotional Stroop Task

The emotional Stroop task is a well-established paradigm based on the classic Stroop task [1–3]. The aim of this task is to evaluate the interference between emotional stimuli and cognitive processes [4]. Different to the classic Stroop task, in the emotional Stroop task the words presented are emotionally loaded [1,2,5,6]. There are two trial types in both tasks, i.e., incongruent (read the written word and de-code the semantic content; inhibition of an automated action) and congruent (focus on the color of the presented words; activation of a voluntary action) [5,6]. In the emotional Stroop task, the colors of words describing typical chronic pain symptoms (emotionally relevant words) must typically be specified, as well as non-disease-related words with positive, neutral, or negative connotations [2]. These words should be read as quickly as possible, ignoring the affective content of the stimuli presented [7]. This paradigm measures the cognitive interference that occurs when the processing of one stimulus (word) prevents simultaneous processing of a second stimulus (color) [1,8]. According to the emotional Stroop task, the magnitude of the interference effect depends on the extent to which the words are related to the individual's emotional concerns [1].

The emotional Stroop task is a valuable tool to assess attentional bias in people with chronic pain, and can establish the extent to which patients preferentially attend to pain-related information over neutral or positive information [1,9–11]. Therefore, the pain hypervigilance hypothesis pertaining to chronic pain conditions can be investigated by the emotional Stroop task [2,11,12]. This hypothesis suggests that involuntary attention to pain-related information is relevant to the development of these disorders [2,11,12]. Different versions of the task have been applied.

1.2. Chronic Pain

Chronic pain is defined by the International Association for the Study of Pain (2020) as a pain condition that lasts for longer than 3 months. It is characterized as a complex sensory and emotional experience that varies according to the context, as well as the meaning of pain, and the psychological state of the individual [13]. Chronic pain has a significant impact on the individual and society [14]. Furthermore, it is considered a standalone condition, rather than a concomitant symptom of other ailments [15]; it causes sleep disruption, depression, and fatigue, as well as limitations in everyday activities and professional work [16]. Furthermore, it is associated with negative emotions and psychological distress [16]. Patients with chronic pain may experience, in certain situations, excessive emotional, cognitive, and behavioral responses [17]. However, the most important clinical symptom of chronic pain is the pain itself [18]. There is a positive correlation between the severity of chronic pain and the intensity of pain and the related phenomenon of outbreaks [18]. Chronic pain has a major impact on the quality of life of those who suffer from it [17,19,20].

Chronic pain is more common in women, elderly people, and the relatively deprived (e.g., those with lower socioeconomic status, disadvantaged geographical and cultural backgrounds, certain employment statuses and occupational factors, or a history of abuse or interpersonal violence) [21]. Several studies of chronic pain reported an inverse relationship between the occurrence of pain and the patient's socioeconomic status [22,23]. More disadvantaged economic circumstances increase the likelihood of experiencing chronic pain [24]. About 1710 million people have this disease worldwide, including around 20% of the European population [16,21]. The best-known chronic pain diseases are fibromyalgia syndrome (FMS) [2,25,26], migraine [7], temporomandibular disorders (TMDs) [27], chronic musculoskeletal pain (CLBP) [1,28], and chronic neuropathic pain (CNP) [28].

FMS is a chronic widespread pain disorder characterized by generalized musculoskeletal pain and numerous other symptoms, such as morning stiffness, fatigue, sleep disturbance (insomnia), anxiety, depression, mental decline, cognitive deficits, and reduced health-related quality of life [19,20,29–31]. FMS affects about 2–4% of the general population [32,33], with women being more predisposed to it than men [34]. However, the diagnosis of FMS seems to be gender biased, i.e., there is a tendency to overdiagnose FMS in women, even without applying the official criteria [34]. It is thought that overdiagnosis may be mainly due to a lack of knowledge, and a negotiated decision between the patient and doctor to satisfy certain psychosocial needs [34,35]. Although the etiology of FMS is unknown, central sensitization of pain (reflected in hyperalgesia and diffuse allodynia) seems to be the most plausible explanation [36,37]. This is probably due to the fact that FMS involves abnormal processing of pain in the central nervous system and inhibition of antinociceptive inhibitory mechanisms [36,37].

Migraine is an intense pulsing or throbbing pain in one area of the head lasting between 4 and 72 h, and associated with symptoms such as nausea, vomiting, sensitivity to light and sound, preceding neurological symptoms, etc. [38,39]. If migraine persists for more than 15 days a month, for at least 3 consecutive months, it is considered as chronic migraine. Migraine affects 10% of the population, and is more prevalent in women [39,40]. According to Ibrahimi et al. [41], in some women, migraine may be related to changes in hormone levels during the menstrual cycle. Chronic migraine is associated with several comorbidities such as obesity, obstructive sleep apnea, depression, and anxiety, and is also related to excessive use of caffeine and medications (e.g., opioids, barbiturates, and anti-inflammatory drugs) [38]. Pathological neurological and psychological aspects (e.g., a tendency toward perfectionism, rigid and obsessive personality, anxiety, and stress) seem to play a crucial role in the etiology of migraine [39].

TMDs are a group of diseases (temporomandibular joint disorders, masticatory muscle disorders, and disorders affecting associated structures) that affect the oral and maxillofacial region, involve the masticatory muscles and the temporomandibular joint, and can cause chronic pain [42]. The most common symptoms are generalized pain, psychological discomfort, orofacial pain, joint sounds, physical disability, and limitation of mandibular movements [42,43]. The prevalence of this disorder in the general population is between 30–50% [44], and it is more common in women [45]. TMDs have several comorbidities (sleep apnea, migraine, bruxism, neck pain, and biopsychosocial distress) that contribute to the development or persistence of symptoms [46,47]. However, it is not clear whether these comorbidities increase the risk of TMDs or simply coexist with them [48]. Currently, the frequency of somatic symptoms is considered to be the strongest predictor of TMD incidence [48].

Among the different types of chronic pain, CLBP lasts for at least 12 weeks [49], and affects the regions below the costal margin and above the inferior gluteal folds, with or without leg pain [50]. Patients with this disease mainly experience pain in the lower back [50]. Additionally, they exhibit impaired movement and coordination [51]. These disturbances affect the control of voluntary movements [51]. CLBP is the leading cause of disability and the most common of all non-communicable diseases [51,52]. This type of chronic pain has a worldwide prevalence of around 5–10% [16,53]; the prevalence is higher in females, people with less schooling, and smokers [54]. The overall prevalence has doubled over time due to changes in the workplace industry and lifestyles (it is associated with a higher prevalence of obesity, for example) [55]. CLBP is associated with functional cortical, neurochemical, and structural changes in several brain regions, including the somatosensory cortex [56].

CNP can be conceptualized as a pain caused by a lesion or disease of the somatosensory system [57,58]. The painful sensations that accompany CNP (e.g., burning, shooting, tingling, etc.) can be debilitating [59] and long-lasting, even with optimal medical treatment [60,61]. The most common conditions associated with this kind of pain are amputation, leprosy, painful radiculopathy, and trigeminal and postherpetic neuralgia [57]. The most frequent causes of CNP are lumbar and cervical painful radiculopathies [57]. About 6.9–10% of the general population suffers from CNP [21,59,62] and it is more frequent in women [59].

Chronic pain involves physical, psychological, and social factors [15]. The development of chronic pain is associated with risk factors, which are classified as "modifiable" and "non-modifiable" [15]. These include biological, sociodemographic, clinical, and psychological factors [15]. Cognitive and emotional factors strongly influence the connectivity of brain regions that modulate pain perception, emotional states, attention, and expectations [63].

According to imaging studies, the activity of afferent and descendent pain pathways is altered by the attentional state, and by positive and negative emotions [13]. The brain areas most involved in chronic pain are the somatosensory cortex, anterior cingulate gyrus, insula, and the prefrontal and inferior parietal cortices [64]. In addition to these areas, the regions most related to emotions (e.g., the insula, amygdala, and periaqueductal grey) are also involved in this disease [65].

In support of the above, there is considerable evidence of the importance of interventions targeting thoughts, emotions, and behaviors in chronic pain patients [66]. This is due to their associations with distress, the ability to effectively cope with pain, and the perceived intensity of pain [66]. From a physical and psychological point of view, chronic pain is a highly stressful condition that can lead to anger and frustration with both oneself and others [67]. Techniques and therapies concerned with mental and emotional well-being are important to enhance pain resilience [67]. Emotions are involved in the conceptualization, assessment, and treatment of chronic pain [68]. Emotions modulate the experience of pain by influencing cognitions and behaviors (emotional awareness, emotional expression and experience, and verbalizations) [68].

1.3. Previous Reviews on the Emotional Stroop Task and Chronic Pain

According to the reviewed literature, and as previously reported, the emotional Stroop task is a valuable and suitable technique to measure the alterations in emotional and cerebral activation areas that characterize chronic pain conditions (i.e., FMS, migraine, CNP, CLBP, and TMDs) [2,9,69]. Other reviews related to chronic pain and the emotional Stroop task assessed the attentional bias of patients with chronic pain [11,70], as well as the origins thereof [71]. However, each review used the emotional Stroop task for different objectives, such as to characterize cognitive inhibition mechanisms and attentional control functions in patients with FMS [25], assess attentional biases for negative affective stimuli related to migraine [7], test the hypothesis of generalized hypervigilance in FMS and explore the possible mediating role of anxiety [26], and investigate attentional bias in patients with chronic pain [9,70]. Furthermore, it seems that findings related to the emotional Stroop task and chronic pain are equivocal. Although in the majority of studies attentional bias in people with chronic pain was demonstrated [1,2,11], other studies, such as Andersson et al. [9], did not observe significant effects in terms of inhibition or increased interference during color naming in chronic pain.

Given the modulatory effect of emotions on pain, the importance of exploring and integrating all of the previous results, especially those addressing pain and emotional processing, should not be overlooked. Accordingly, the main objective of the present systematic review was, for the first time, to perform an integrated analysis of all studies using an emotional Stroop task to assess the associations of alterations in specific brain regions with the behavioral performance (e.g., attentional biases) of patients with chronic pain.

2. Materials and Methods

2.1. Search Strategy

This systematic review was conducted based on the guidelines of the Cochrane Collaboration, and in accordance with the Preferred Reporting Items for Systematic Reviews and Meta-Analyses (PRISMA) [72]. As a first step, the inclusion and exclusion criteria, as well as the analyses, were specified. Subsequently, the protocol was registered in the Prospective Register of Systematic Reviews (PROSPERO) international database (Registration ID: CRD42021279615). The following terms, extracted by MeSH (Medical Subject Headings), were used for the search: chronic pain and emotional Stroop. The last search was carried out on 1 March 2022.

Independent searches of the Scopus, PubMed, and Web of Science (WOS) databases were conducted by three researchers (L.A.-D., C.I.M.-A., and L.R.F.-J.). All of the identified articles were reviewed, and those that did not meet the criteria for subsequent analysis of the full text were discarded. First, in order to eliminate irrelevant studies, the titles and abstracts of each study were analyzed. In a second step, the remaining articles were screened in detail for eligibility. All full texts of the selected articles were checked and analyzed based on the inclusion and exclusion criteria. Any discrepancies found during the review of these articles were reviewed by the fourth author (C.M.G.-S.). The PRISMA flowchart (Figure 1) shows the screening and selection process for the inclusion of studies. In addition, C.M.G.-S. examined all articles for eligibility for the study prior to data extraction and quality assessment. The PICO question was as follows: How do patients with chronic pain perform in the emotional Stroop task?

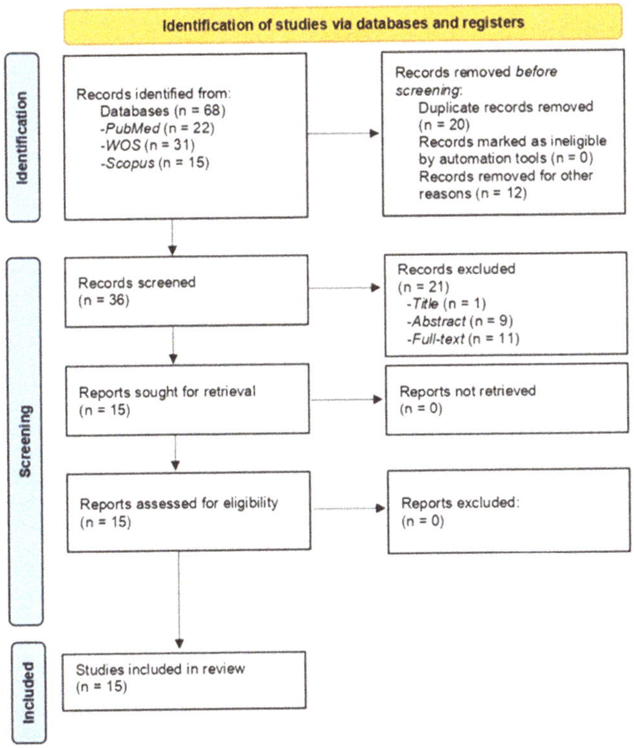

Figure 1. Flow diagram of Chronic Pain and Emotional Stroop (PRISMA).

2.2. Eligibility Criteria

The following study inclusion criteria were applied: (1) written in English or Spanish; (2) original, peer-reviewed study; (3) adult patients (≥18 years old); and (4) focused on chronic pain and the emotional Stroop task.

The exclusion criteria were as follows: (1) written in languages other than English or Spanish; (2) review article or meta-analysis; (3) inclusion of non-adult patients (≤18 years old); and (4) commentary, report, letter, editorial, meeting, and/or congress abstract or case report.

2.3. Data Extraction and Quality Assessment

L.A.-D., C.I.M.-A., and L.R.F.-J. independently extracted study characteristics, methodologies and results, and assessed the limitations of each study. Discrepancies were reviewed by C.M.G.-S. The sequence for data extraction was as follows: first author, study name, country, year of publication, study design, sample size, number of participants in each study group, and age and sex of the participants. The characteristics of the study are shown in Table 1. C.M.G.-S. reviewed all data to ensure the accuracy of the data extraction.

Table 1. Characteristics of selected studies on Chronic Pain and Emotional Stroop.

Chronic Pain and Emotional Stroop					
First Author (Publication Year), Study Name, Country	**Objective**	**Study Design/Diagnostic Technique**	**Sample Size, Age (Mean ± SD)**	**Emotional Stroop**	**Results**
Hatchard et al. [73] Reduced emotional reactivity in breast cancer survivors with chronic neuropathic pain following mindfulness-based stress reduction (MBSR): an fMRI pilot investigation. Canada.	To analyze the impact of MBSR on the emotional reactivity of breast cancer survivors with CNP (8 weeks).	Randomized controlled trial (pilot study). MBSR program: pain disability, psychological well-being, and overall quality of life.	N = 21 women. MBSR treatment group = 11 (48.36 ± 11.37). WL control group = 10 (56.50 ± 8.11).	Modified Stroop task. Stimuli: 8 blocks (each block 16 words and 33 s long): 4 pain-related sensory and negative affective words and 4 neutral words. Total duration: 7 min.	MBSR treatment group: less BOLD activity post-MBSR across several brain regions (pain processing and visual attention). Reduced pain interference following MBSR.
Taylor et al. [69] Neural responses to a modified Stroop paradigm in patients with complex chronic musculoskeletal pain compared to matched controls: an experimental functional magnetic resonance imaging study. United Kingdom *.	To investigate the general deficit in attentional control and specific attentional bias for pain-related stimuli and BOLD signal differences in pain and emotion related brain regions.	Experimental fMRI study. Patients with CMSKP: BOLD fMRI.	N = 29 (25–83 years). CMSKP group = 15. HC group = 14.	Modified Stroop task. Stimuli (16 from each word group): pain-related, positive-emotional, and neutral control words. 16 blocks: 2 word-type, 2 control word set, and 4 fixation-cross (the rest in each run). Total duration: less than 15 min (with a short break).	CMSKP group: less accurate in responses (all word types). BOLD fMRI responses: increases in neural activation in CMSKP group (anterior cingulate cortex, insula, and primary and secondary somatosensory cortex).
Duschek et al. [2] Attentional bias toward negative information in patients with fibromyalgia syndrome. Austria.	To investigate the contribution of specific features (FMS) to expected attentional bias.	Experimental study. FMS diagnosis: ACR (Wolfe et al., 1990).	N = 61 women. FMS group = 27 (52.70 ± 9.20). HC group = 34 (53.90 ± 8.40).	Modified emotional Stroop task. Stimuli: 40 positive, 40 negative, and 40 neutral adjectives. Color word: below adjective printed in black (500 ms after stimuli) **.	FMS: attentional bias, delayed response (negative words), and reaction times longer (negative words). Association with interference scores for positive and negative words (severity of FMS and attentional bias toward affectively negative information).
Mercado et al. [25] Brain correlates of cognitive inhibition in fibromyalgia: emotional intrusion of symptom-related words. Spain.	To characterize cognitive inhibition mechanisms and attentional control functions (FMS).	Experimental study. FMS diagnosis: ACR (Wolfe et al., 1990).	N = 50 women. FMS group = 25 (47.80 ± 8.34). HC group = 25 (48.00 ± 7.48).	An emotional variant of the Stroop task. Stimuli (4 categories): linguistic words (300 ms); FMS SF, arousing; negative and positive; and neutral (32 words: red, blue, yellow, and green) **.	SF words: part of their own symptoms (FMS). RT: faster in SF words. Number of errors: smaller for SF words.

Table 1. *Cont.*

Chronic Pain and Emotional Stroop					
First Author (Publication Year), Study Name, Country	**Objective**	**Study Design/Diagnostic Technique**	**Sample Size, Age (Mean ± SD)**	**Emotional Stroop**	**Results**
Puschmann et al. [7] Hypervigilance or avoidance of trigger related cues in migraineurs?—A case-control study using the emotional stroop task. Germany.	To assess attentional biases for negative affective stimuli related to migraine.	Case-control study. Migraine diagnosis: IHS (2004).	N = 53. EM group = 17 (41.35 ± 11.87) (85% women). FM group = 16 women (43.40 ± 13.30). HC group = 20 (39.80 ± 10.50) (90.5% women).	Computerized version of the modified emotional Stroop task. Task 1: General affective words: 36 nouns (Berlin Affective Word List); 12 for each valence (negative, neutral, and positive). Time words: 2000 ms. Time between words: 500 ms **. Task 2: 81 affective face pictures (Karolinska Directed Emotional Faces). 3 stimuli (each category 27 pictures): positive, negative, and neutral. Maximum response: 2000 ms **.	FM group: responded faster to negative stimuli and learned avoidance mechanism away from affective migraine triggers.
Weissman-Fogel et al. [27] Abnormal cortical activity in patients with temporomandibular disorder evoked by cognitive and emotional tasks. Canada.	To test if patients with TMD perform poorly in cognitive and emotion tasks and abnormal task-evoked brain activity.	Experimental study. TMD diagnosis: specialist dentists (Pain Unit of the Mount Sinai Hospital Dental Clinic), standard clinical criteria, and involvement of myofascial and/or temporomandibular joint (clinical testing).	N = 34 women. TMD group = 17 (35.20 ± 11.6). HC group = 17 (34.00 ± 9.90).	nStroop: common household items. ncStroop: number words (cognitive interference). ecStroop: TMD-related emotional words (emotional interference). Stroop block: 12 sets of words (1250 ms) **.	Each Stroop task activated brain areas (attention, cognition, and motor planning). TMD patients: sluggish reaction times for all Stroop tasks and decoupling of the normally positively associated activity between prefrontal—cingulate cortices and between amygdala—cingulate cortex.
González et al. [26] Generalized hypervigilance in fibromyalgia patients: an experimental analysis with the emotional Stroop paradigm. Spain.	To test the hypothesis of generalized hypervigilance in FMS and explore the possible mediating role of anxiety.	Experimental analysis. FMS diagnosis: (Wolfe, Smith, Yunus et al.).	N = 50 women. Final sample = 49. FMS group = 25 (50.56 ± 8.66). HC group = 24 (48.04 ± 7.55).	Emotional Stroop task. 4 stimuli (32 words): fibromyalgia symptoms and neutral, positive, and negative arousal. Stimuli: 300 ms (interval 1.5–2 s) **. 4 colors: red, green, yellow, and blue. 32 trials (128 randomized trials).	Possible presence of generalized hypervigilance response in FMS patients (significant slowness in the color naming).

Table 1. *Cont.*

Chronic Pain and Emotional Stroop					
First Author (Publication Year), Study Name, Country	**Objective**	**Study Design/Diagnostic Technique**	**Sample Size, Age (Mean ± SD)**	**Emotional Stroop**	**Results**
Asmundson et al. [74] Hypervigilance and attentional fixedness in chronic musculoskeletal pain: consistency of findings across modified stroop and dot-probe tasks. Canada.	To investigate attentional biases for sensory and affect pain stimuli in CMSKP patients.	Experimental analysis. CMSKP diagnosis: (rehabilitation program—Regina urban area).	N = 75. Final sample = 65. CMSKP group = 36 (women = 22 (36.27 ± 11.76); men = 14 (40.79 ± 9.38)). HC group = 29 (women = 18 (42.00 ± 10.64; men = 11 (35.91 ± 10.30)).	Computerized modified Stroop task. Stimuli: 15 sensory pain, 15 health catastrophe and 15 neutral words. 4 colors: red, blue, yellow, and green. 10 blocks: 30 trials per block **.	CMSKP group: initial attention to the threat positively associated with vigilance for that particular threat, and negatively associated with disengagement from the threat.
Roelofs et al. [28] An examination of word relevance in a modified stroop task in patients with chronic low back pain. Netherlands.	To examine the role of personal relevance of sensory pain-related words in selective attentional processing in low back pain patients.	Experimental study. Chronic low back pain diagnosis: Belgian pain clinics (University of Ghent and University Hospital of Leuven at 'Pellenberg').	N = 30. CLBP group = 30 (41.20 ± 11.60) (19 women).	Computerized version of modified Stroop task. Stimuli: 33 sensory pain-related words. Colors: red, blue, yellow, and green. 132 trials. Total duration: 8 min.	No significant results. No support for the hypothesis that sensory pain-related words interact with Fear of Pain scores in accounting for reaction times (naming the color of sensory pain-related words). Modified Stroop task not a robust measure of selective attentional processing in chronic low back pain patients.
Andersson et al. [9] Personalized pain words and Stroop interference in chronic pain patients. Sweden.	To investigate attentional bias in patients with chronic pain.	Mixed design. One between-group factor and one within-group factor in a 2 × 2 design. Chronic pain diagnosis: local pain clinic.	N = 40. Chronic pain group = 20 (44.50 ± 9.82) (16 women). HC group = 20 (45.60 ± 9.45) (16 women).	Computerized modified version of emotional Stroop task with personalized words. 6 trials: Color-naming pain and control words (99 words each trial). 5 colors: blue, red, yellow, white, and green. Total duration: 15–23 min.	Pain group: slower on pain words and longer on color-name pain words. 11 chronic pain patients: Stroop interference effect. Repeated measure effect: threat word category and Stroop color naming.
Snider et al. [75] Automatic and strategic processing of threat cues in patients with chronic pain: a modified stroop evaluation. Canada.	To determine if chronic back and/or neck pain patients exhibit delayed color-naming latencies for syndrome-specific cues (strategic and automatic levels of processing).	Experimental study. Back and/or neck pain diagnosis (minimum 3 months). Rehabilitation program in Regina Health District.	N = 66. Chronic back and/or neck pain group = 33 (35.50 ± 10.30). HC = 33 (35.00 ± 10.10).	A modified Stroop evaluation. Stimuli: 10 affect pain, 10 physical threat, 10 social threat, and 10 neutral words. 200 trials. 50 words, 2 times: unmasked and masked conditions. 4 colors: red, blue, yellow, and green. 10 blocks: 5 unmasked and 5 masked (20 trials for each one) **.	Chronic pain patients: selectively process pain-related cues at the strategic level. Delayed color-naming latencies (sensory and affect pain words; unmasked condition). Delayed color-naming latencies (pain words; unmasked condition) positively associated with high pain-specific cognitive anxiety and interference and lower levels of anxiety sensitivity.

Table 1. *Cont.*

Chronic Pain and Emotional Stroop					
First Author (Publication Year), Study Name, Country	**Objective**	**Study Design/Diagnostic Technique**	**Sample Size, Age (Mean ± SD)**	**Emotional Stroop**	**Results**
Crombez et al. [1] The emotional stroop task and chronic pain: what is threatening for chronic pain sufferers? Belgium.	To investigate chronic pain patients display an involuntary attentional shift towards pain-related information.	Experimental study. CLBP diagnosis: pain clinic —physical rehabilitation unit (university clinic).	N = 25. CLBP group = 25 (48.36 ± 14.12).	Computer version of emotional Stroop task. 5 experimental stimuli: 7 sensory pain, 7 affect pain, 7 related back disorder, 7 other disorder, and 7 general negative valence words (5 neutral words in each category). Total words: 70 **. 4 colors: blue, yellow, green, and red.	Attentional bias: sensory pain words. Current pain intensity predictive of the effect.
Pincus et al. [76] Do chronic pain patients 'stroop' on pain stimuli? United Kingdom *.	To investigate the presence of information processing biases on tasks of attention and memory in relation to mood states in chronic pain patients.	Experiment 1: 2 × 4 factorial design. Chronic pain diagnosis: hospital pain clinic. Experiment 2: 2 × 8 factorial design. Chronic pain diagnosis: hospital pain clinic.	Experiment 1: N = 40. Chronic pain group = 20 (18 women). HC group = 20 (12 women). Experiment 2: N = 34. Chronic pain group = 17 (12 women). HC group = 17 (11 women).	Experiment 1: classical Stroop and congruent color naming. 10 blocks. Stimuli (10 words for each one): sensory, affective, positive, and neutral words. 5 colors: red, brown, blue, orange, and green. 50 trials **. Experiment 2: classical stroop, color naming. Stimuli (10 words for each one): sensory, affective, positive, physical threat, social threat, and household objects. 50 trials. 3 colors: pink, yellow, and green. Interval between words: 500 ms **.	Memory recall bias. Interference effect for emotionally salient stimuli related to anxiety and depression.
Duckworth et al. [77] Information processing in chronic pain disorder: a preliminary analysis. United States of America.	To establish the comparative usefulness of selective attention, impaired stimulus filtering, and affective language deficiency models for explaining somatic focus in a chronic pain population.	Experimental study. Chronic pain diagnosis: interdisciplinary facility (Athens, Georgia).	N = 29. HSF group = 10 (43.10 ± 12.00). LSF group = 9 (38.20 ± 12.20). HC group = 10 (39.30 ± 11.10).	Modified Stroop task. Stimuli (105 words): 35 somatic pain-content, 35 depression-content, and 35 neutral-content (5 s for each one). 5 colors: red, yellow, green, blue, and white. Total duration: 15 min.	Chronic pain patients misinterpret bodily sensations.

Table 1. *Cont.*

Chronic Pain and Emotional Stroop					
First Author (Publication Year), Study Name, Country	**Objective**	**Study Design/Diagnostic Technique**	**Sample Size, Age (Mean ± SD)**	**Emotional Stroop**	**Results**
Pearce et al. [78] An experimental investigation of the construct validity of the McGill Pain Questionnaire. United Kingdom.	To avoid problems with self-report measures of pain.	Experimental study. Chronic pain diagnosis: pain clinic.	N = 32. Chronic pain group = 16 (53.50 ± 14.10). HC group = 16 (52.60 ± 14.50).	Stroop task. Stimuli: negative emotional, sensory pain, affect pain, and neutral words. 4 tasks: conflicting color, negative emotional, sensory pain, and affect pain **.	Chronic pain group: high score on affective/evaluative and miscellaneous scales. Greater interference effect (chronic pain group): standard conflicting color Stroop.

Note: * Mean age and standard deviation of participating subjects not reported. ** Total duration of task not reported. **Abbreviations:** ACR = American College of Rheumatology; BOLD fMRI = Blood Oxygenation Level Dependent Functional Magnetic Resonance Imaging; BOLD = Blood Oxygenation Level Dependent; CLBP = Chronic Low Back Pain; CMSKP = Chronic Musculoskeletal Pain; CNP = Chronic Neuropathic Pain; ecStroop = emotional counting Stroop Task; EM = Episodic Migraine; FM = Frequent Migraine; fMRI = Functional Magnetic Resonance Imaging; FMS = Fibromyalgia Syndrome; HC = Healthy Controls; IHS = International Headache Society; HSF = High-Somatic Focus; LSF = Low-Somatic Focus; MBSR = Mindfulness-Based Stress Reduction; ncStroop = number counting Stroop Task; nStroop = neutral Stroop Task; NW = Neutral Words; RT = Reaction Time; SF = Symptom-related; TMD = Temporomandibular Disorder; WL = Waitlist.

2.4. Data Synthesis

Our review focuses on studies of patients over 18 years of age, suffering from any chronic pain condition (FMS, CLBP, CNP, migraine, or TMD). In addition, all of the studies used the emotional Stroop task (or any variant thereof), and the performance of patients with chronic pain was compared (in most cases) with a control group composed by healthy participants. Attention was also paid to the activation of brain areas responsible for emotional and pain processing during the application of the emotional Stroop task, as well as to possible attentional biases towards certain types of stimuli presented in the task.

According to the objectives of this review, the type of the Stroop task performed in each study (and whether the sample had a control group) and the study design (e.g., randomized controlled trial, experimental, or case-control study) were determined. In addition, the target population, as well as the proportion of male and female participants, and their mean and standard deviation age, were ascertained. Furthermore, the main results of each study, which are shown in Table 1 (first author, study name and country, objective, diagnostic technique, sample size and age, type of emotional Stroop task, and results), were analyzed. Finally, the limitations of each study were assessed.

3. Results

3.1. Literature Search and Study Characteristics

After a comprehensive search, 68 relevant articles were identified in the databases. After eliminating duplicates, a total of 36 articles were selected for this review. The PRISMA flow diagram (for details, see Section 2.1. Search strategy) shows the exclusion of studies at each screening stage (Figure 1). Finally, 15 full-text articles were included; they were checked for suitability according to the predefined inclusion criteria, and then subjected to data extraction (Table 1) and quality assessment.

Regarding the characteristics of the selected studies, the year of publication rangedfrom 1989 to 2021. Most of the studies included a control group of healthy participants [2,7,9,25,26,28,73–78], although two were uncontrolled clinical trials [1,28]. The location of the studies varied widely: 11 were conducted in Europe (Spain [25,26], United Kingdom [69,76,78], Sweden [9], Germany [7], Austria [2], Netherlands [28], and Belgium [1]), 1 in the United States [77], and 4 in Canada [27,73–75]. Further details of the characteristics of the selected studies can be found in Table 1.

In terms of the study designs, an experimental design was used in the majority of cases [1,2,25–28,69,74,75,77,78], although two studies used a factorial design [9,76], one used a case-control design [7], and one used a pilot randomized controlled trial design [73].

Regarding the results of the studies (Table 1) related to performance on the emotional Stroop task, longer reaction times and delayed responses to negative emotional words (associated with pain) were observed in patients with chronic pain, especially those with FMS [7,9,25,26,74–78]. Most studies revealed an emotional interference effect in FMS patients [25,79,80]. Greater processing of negative and/or positive words was also observed in patients with FMS [79,81]. Moreover, greater responses were observed in regions related to pain and emotional regulation (the somatosensory region, and the cingulate and prefrontal cortices, among other regions) compared to healthy controls [27,69,73]. Specifically, in the presence of negative stimuli with emotional content, patients with chronic pain showed greater activation in the aforementioned brain regions, indicating greater processing of pain and negative emotions in these patients [27,69,73]. Previous evidence indicates that patients with CLBP and FMS have an attentional bias towards negative words with emotional content [1,2,9,74].

3.2. Participants

Among the 15 selected articles, 7 used the Stroop task for patients with general chronic pain [9,69,74–78], while 3 used it for FMS patients [2,25,26], 2 for CLBP patients [1,28], 1 for migraine patients [7], 1 for TMD patients [27], and 1 for CNP patients [73].

The total study sample (n = 677) was divided into two main groups: a clinical group (n = 386) and a control group (with slightly fewer participants; n = 291). The clinical group included 11 women with CNP (age range: 48–57 years) [73] and 17 with TMDs (age range: 34–36 years) [27], 17 participants with migraine (85% women) [7], 19 women, 11 men and 25 participants of unspecified gender with CLBP (age range: 35–49 years) [69,74], 77 women with FMS (age range: 47–54 years) [2,25,26], 33 participants of unspecified gender with chronic back and/or neck pain (age range: 30–36 years), and 94 women, 50 men and 33 participants of unspecified gender with general chronic pain (age range: 38–83 years) [9,69,74–78].

It should be noted that two of the studies did not have a control group [1,28]. Regarding subjects' sex, there were more female than male participants [2,7,9,25–28,73,74,76]. Nevertheless, five studies included both men and women [7,9,28,74,76]. Notably, none of the reviewed studies included a sample composed entirely of men. Further, five studies did not provide information about the sex of the participants [1,69,75,77,78].

In the selected articles, the majority of the chronic pain participants did not have comorbid psychiatric illnesses (e.g., depression or anxiety) [1,7,9,25–28,74,75,77]. Furthermore, some of them used these conditions as exclusion criteria [7,25–27,69,74,76,77]. Other studies considered these conditions as a symptom of chronic pain, especially in FMS [2,25]. However, these conditions could negatively influence emotional Stroop task responses [76,82].

3.3. *Quality of Selected Studies*

The quality assessment was conducted independently by two researchers (L.A.-D. and C.I.M.-A.), and the initial agreement was 93%. To achieve a consensus, the interpretation and monitoring of the criteria was discussed with a third reviewer (C.M.S.-G.). This quality assessment was focused on the analysis of the limitations of the selected studies.

The authors of the reviewed studies indicated various limitations of their research, such as small sample and effect sizes [2,7,9,26,73–75,77], an absence of a neutral category of words [28], issues with the methods and/or criteria used for the diagnosis of chronic pain (e.g., ACR criteria for FMS and IHS criteria for migraine) [2,75], and with pharmacological treatments [2,25,69,75], non-control of the medication status (pharmacological) of the patients and healthy controls [75], low statistical power and non-inclusion of an additional experimental condition for the Stroop task [26], non-inclusion of a masked version of the test and failure to record each participant's pain level at the time of the test [74], use of non-specific stimuli [1,7,9,28,73,74], non-inclusion of additional measures of psychological distress to improve construct validity [77], a non-pragmatic approach to the study patients [69], failure to assess sensitivity to anxiety or fear of pain, failure to screen for psychiatric disturbances through screening interviews, and non-inclusion of a pain comparison group [9], and failure to control for the effect of some variables (e.g., time since surgery, dose of chemotherapy received, type of chemotherapy drugs, current medications and menopausal) [73].

Additional limitations were identified during this review, including non-randomization of participants to different groups in most studies [1,2,7,9,25–28,69,74–78], the absence of a control group to compare the results [1,28], non-blinding of participants, personnel and outcome assessments [1,2,7,9,25–28,69,74–78], non-specification of the criteria used to diagnose the disease [69,73,74,77], failure to report effect size measures [1,7,25,27,28,69,73,75–78], failure to indicate the sex ratio in some studies [1,69,75,77,78], and failure to report analyses by sex [69,76]. Moreover, some studies did not report the mean age [7,69,76] or standard deviation of their sample [69,76], and provided incomplete data on the task performed (e.g., failure to disclose the total duration of the task) [1,7,9,27,28,69,77].

4. Discussion

The present systematic review aimed to analyze studies that used an emotional Stroop task in patients with chronic pain, and assessed associated alterations of specific brain regions and behavioral performance (e.g., attentional biases). In general, and as reported in the literature, the emotional Stroop task proved to be a valid tool to assess emotional and pain processing in patients with chronic pain [2,9,69]. Most studies reported the activation of certain brain regions (the somatosensory region, and cingulate and prefrontal cortices, among other regions) during the emotional Stroop task; these regions are related to pain and emotional regulation in patients with chronic pain [27,69,73].

First, patients' performance in the emotional Stroop task, as well as the presence of attentional biases, will be discussed, followed by a brief overview of the brain areas showing neural activation in relation to the performance of the emotional Stroop task. Finally, the benefits and effects of psychological therapies that can reduce the neural activation observed in patients with chronic pain will be discussed.

Regarding performance on the emotional Stroop task, greater processing of negative and/or positive words was observed in patients with FMS, suggesting the existence of an underlying interference process, triggered by events capable of immediately capturing attention (i.e., those conveying affective meaning) [78,81]. Studies such as that of Algom et al. [83] indicate that this interference effect in the emotional Stroop task is mediated by pre-attentive inhibition, associated with the threat of negative emotional stimuli presented during the task. However, this inhibition mechanism is considered to be independent from that of selective attention [83]. In FMS patients, delayed responses to pain words were associated with pain-specific anxiety and cognitive interference, as well as low sensitivity to anxiety [75]. Some studies indicated that the slowness in color naming during the emotional Stroop task seen in FMS patients is associated with the presence of a generalized hypervigilance response [12,26]. This response is associated with a tendency for FMS subjects to be slower with respect to the color naming of symptomatic (pain-related words) and arousing negative words, depending on the degree of perceived unpleasantness [9,26]. However, it is suggested that, in larger samples, more significant interactions between patient and control groups would be seen, and that it is necessary to compare these findings with those for other diseases [9,12,26,69]. In patients with CLBP and FMS, attentional bias to sensory pain words was associated with the emotional load of the words presented in the emotional Stroop task [1,2,9,74]. This provides clear evidence of the presence of emotion-driven selective attention in FMS and CLBP [1,2,30,84]. In fact, the existence of attentional bias towards negative information seems to play an important mediating role in the relationship between a negative affective state and heightened pain [2,30,84]. In the study by Duschek et al. [2], such attentional bias was also observed in patients with FMS; they showed a specific bias towards negative information, which led to an increase in pain intensity. This further supports the findings of the literature reviewed herein. In CLBP, attentional bias was even greater in the context of words related to back pathology, and in association with increased pain intensity [1,76]. However, the causal nature of the relationship between attentional bias and pain could not be established, as most of the included studies used a cross-sectional design. On the other hand, there are data showing that individuals with greater attentional bias towards negative affective stimuli (i.e., words associated with pain) may be more prone to chronic pain symptoms [85]. In fact, attentional bias in these individuals may be a risk factor for the development of chronic pain and could also serve as a prognostic factor [71]. Attentional bias has been consistently linked to individuals' anticipation and/or experience of pain across different chronic pain conditions [70,85].

In terms of neuronal activation, in patients with chronic pain in general, greater activation was observed when performing the emotional Stroop task [69]. Compared to the healthy group, greater activation in the anterior cingulate cortex, insula, and the primary and secondary somatosensory cortex was seen [69]. More specifically, pain-related words in the Stroop task were associated with significant differences between chronic pain patients and healthy controls, in terms of activation of the pain-processing centers of the brain (i.e., the anterior cingulate cortex, insula, parietal operculum, and the primary and secondary somatosensory cortices) [11,69]. Greater activation of brain areas related to attention, cognition, and motor planning in patients with TMDs compared to controls was also found [27]. TMD subjects showed increased task-evoked responses in prefrontal, lateral, and inferior parietal areas, as well as in the amygdala, pregenual anterior cingulate, primary motor areas, and the medial prefrontal and posterior cingulate areas [27,86]. In addition, patients also showed dissociations with respect to the activity of the prefrontal cortex and cingulate, and of the amygdala and cingulate, which are normally correlated [27,86–88]. Hence, the prominence of chronic pain (which requires attention) and slow behavioral responses may be explained by attenuated, or slow and/or desynchronized, recruitment of attentional processing areas [27,86–88].

Some of the studies reviewed herein focused on specific psychological therapies, such as the mindfulness-based stress reduction technique, which yielded a significant reduction in brain activity in regions related to pain, emotional regulation, and cognitive processing (i.e., regions in the left somatosensory cortex, left precuneus, and left dorsolateral prefrontal cortex) in patients with CNP, using the emotional Stroop task as a measure of emotional reactivity [73]. This demonstrates the impact of psychological therapy on the neural correlates of pain processing and attention [73]. Mindfulness-based psychological therapies seem to be a viable complementary treatment for people suffering from CNP [73,89]. Indeed, the reduction in cerebral activity observed after mindfulness treatment suggested that the emotionally charged words presented during the task had a diminished capacity to capture attention after the therapy compared to before the therapy [90,91]. Thus, the application of this technique reduces brain activation and pain perception, where trait mindfulness is a major component of the therapy [90,91]. However, to draw firm conclusions, longitudinal studies regarding the effect of this type of psychological therapy on patients with chronic pain are needed. Moreover, other therapies, such as cognitive behavioral therapy, have been used in patients with TMDs to effectively reduce the abnormal neuronal and brain activation seen in patients after performing the emotional Stroop task [27]. Likewise, in patients with FMS, cognitive therapy for chronic pain has focused on reducing the negative attentional bias exhibited by these patients [2]. The self-control strategies involved in this therapy promote conscious withdrawal of attention from dysfunctional cognitions and possible stressors, such as emotionally charged negative words, after the application of the Emotional Stroop task [2]. Similarly, techniques such as attention training, focusing, and exposure (cognitive behavioral therapy) have proven useful in patients with FMS, to reduce the activation of emotional and pain processing areas after the application of the emotional Stroop task [26]. This therapy also reduces the hypervigilance exhibited by patients with FMS, and attentional bias to negative emotions [26].

An important limitation of the present review is that the majority of the sample was female [2,7,9,25–28,73,74,76], where the overall gender ratio of the studies was not equal. However, as previously noted, chronic pain is more prevalent in females, in whom it also tends to be overdiagnosed [34], and so studies frequently include a larger female sample. Another limitation is the lack of information on effect sizes [2,7,9,26,73–75,77]; this lack of information on the magnitude of the differences found limited the interpretability of the results. In addition, some of the studies did not specify the clinical criteria used to diagnose the different types of chronic pain [2,75], which calls into question whether the diagnoses were made on the basis of valid criteria. Furthermore, only one of the selected studies did not obtain statistically significant results [77]. A possible explanation for this may be insufficient sample sizes, which tend to preclude large variability in the results. In addition, a more accurate study quality assessment tool will be necessary for future studies. To further elaborate on the results obtained by each study, future reviews could perform a meta-analysis and also compare the findings with those of other emotional tasks, such as the dot-probe or spatial cueing task. Finally, to overcome the absence of effect sizes in the studies [1,7,25,27,28,69,73–78], calculation (and pooling) of Cohen's d or standardized measures of means would be useful (although this is more crucial and typical for meta-analyses).

The main strength of the present review was that it strictly followed a systematic methodological approach in accordance with the study protocol, which was previously registered in PROSPERO, and was prepared in accordance with the updated PRISMA guidelines [72]. Further, in terms of the thematic focus of the systematic review, this is the first review to relate the emotional Stroop task to chronic pain.

In light of the findings of the present review and the analyzed literature, continuing to examine the efficacy of the emotional Stroop task in patients with chronic pain is of high clinical relevance. Future research on chronic pain and the emotional Stroop task should aim to uncover neurobiological correlates in chronic pain patients during performance of the task. Once the precise neuroanatomical correlates underlying the disease are known, specific and integrated research and/or intervention protocols can be established to improve health-related quality of life. Given the negative attentional biases that chronic pain patients exhibit during the performance of the emotional Stroop task, a treatment aimed at the conscious redirection of attention against negative aspects could be implemented, along with relaxation techniques, modification of beliefs about pain, enhancement of coping skills, and targeted treatment of anxiety and/or depression [66]. Future research aiming to establish a relationship between attentional bias and the anticipation and/or experience of pain would be also useful to identify individuals at risk of developing chronic pain, as well as prognostic factors. Psychological treatments can be as effective as surgery for alleviating chronic pain symptoms, by altering the central processing of pain sensation [66]. In this sense, another therapy suitable for chronic pain patients is Acceptance and Commitment Therapy (ACT), the mindfulness component of which is the basis of mindfulness therapy. This therapy has proven effective for people with chronic pain [92–95]. In addition, chronic pain patients with a history of psychosocial trauma may benefit from exposure and emotional processing techniques, which have proven effective [96]. Following the application of the emotional Stroop task, studies suggest that the use of other psychological therapies may be beneficial in reducing brain activation (e.g., the cingulate, amygdala, and medial prefrontal cortex) [2,26,27]. Specifically, Weissman-Fogel et al. [27] suggested that cognitive behavioral therapy could be effective for reducing brain activation after the application of the emotional Stroop task in patients with TMDs. Unfortunately, there are currently no studies that have evaluated the effectiveness of the aforementioned techniques in reducing activation in these areas (i.e., the cingulate, amygdala, and medial prefrontal cortex). Nonetheless, such therapy (e.g., self-control, focusing, exposure, and attentional training) and cognitive therapy in patients with FMS can reduce hypervigilance towards negative stimuli with emotional content [2,26].

Numerous models of the development and/or maintenance of chronic pain suggest that attentional biases are important therein [97,98]. These models support the findings of the present systematic review. Furthermore, each model attributes different roles to attentional processes [97,98]. However, they all make the same assumption; people pay excessive attention to painful stimuli when they experience pain and feel fearful of, or threatened by, pain [97,99]. Indeed, as it was mentioned above, there is an attentional bias towards negative stimuli in people with chronic pain [2]. Furthermore, increased attention to threat/negative cues has been observed in patients with other conditions apart from chronic pain (e.g., anxiety disorders and post-traumatic stress disorder) [9,73]. This bias might be explained by the Threat Interpretation Model [100], which suggests a relationship between threat, threat interpretation, and stimuli, through the vigilance–avoidance hypothesis [100]. This hypothesis states that individuals usually pay more attention to threat stimuli and this attentional bias is usually accompanied by an avoidance of negative/threat stimuli [100]. This pattern of vigilance–avoidance may be variable across individuals, as the interpretation of stimuli may differ according to the degree of importance assigned to the perceived stimuli [100]. Furthermore, this model may generate verifiable predictions about the role of attentional processes, and how they are influenced by interpretations [100], which would have a positive impact on clinical practice (i.e., the development and improvement of chronic pain treatments).

In conclusion, after performing the emotional Stroop task, specific brain areas (e.g., the prefrontal cortex, somatosensory cortex, cingulum, and amygdala) related to emotional and pain processing are activated in patients with chronic pain (FMS, migraine, CNP, TMDS, and CLBP). During the task, chronic pain patients showed longer reaction times and delayed responses to words with negative emotional content. They also showed attentional biases towards pain sensory words. Therefore, the use of psychological therapies (e.g., mindfulness, cognitive, and cognitive behavioral therapies) will help reduce the brain activation and attentional bias produced by the emotional Stroop task in these patients.

Author Contributions: Conceptualization, L.A.-D., C.I.M. and C.M.G.-S.; methodology, L.A.-D., C.I.M. and C.M.G.-S.; formal analysis, L.A.-D., C.I.M. and C.M.G.-S.; resources, L.A.-D., C.I.M., L.R.F.-J. and C.M.G.-S.; data curation, L.A.-D., C.I.M. and C.M.G.-S.; writing—original draft preparation, L.A.-D., C.I.M. and C.M.G.-S.; writing—review and editing, L.A.-D., C.I.M., L.R.F.-J. and C.M.G.-S.; visualization, L.A.-D., C.I.M., L.R.F.-J. and C.M.G.-S.; supervision, C.I.M. and C.M.G.-S. All authors have read and agreed to the published version of the manuscript.

Funding: This research received no external funding.

Institutional Review Board Statement: Not applicable.

Informed Consent Statement: Not applicable.

Data Availability Statement: Not applicable.

Conflicts of Interest: The authors declare no conflict of interest.

References

1. Crombez, G.; Hermans, D.; Adriaensen, H. The emotional stroop task and chronic pain: What is threatening for chronic pain sufferers? *Eur. J. Pain* **2000**, *4*, 37–44. [CrossRef] [PubMed]
2. Duschek, S.; Werner, N.S.; Limbert, N.; Winkelmann, A.; Montoya, P. Attentional Bias Toward Negative Information in Patients with Fibromyalgia Syndrome. *Pain Med.* **2014**, *15*, 603–612. [CrossRef] [PubMed]
3. Stroop, J.R. Studies of interference in serial verbal reactions. *J. Exp. Psychol.* **1935**, *18*, 643–662. [CrossRef]
4. Straub, E.R.; Schmidts, C.; Kunde, W.; Zhang, J.; Kiesel, A.; Dignath, D. Limitations of cognitive control on emotional distraction—Congruency in the Color Stroop task does not modulate the Emotional Stroop effect. *Cogn. Affect. Behav. Neurosci.* **2022**, *22*, 21–41. [CrossRef]
5. Imbir, K.K.; Duda-Goławska, J.; Pastwa, M.; Jankowska, M.; Żygierewicz, J. Event-Related Potential Correlates of Valence, Arousal, and Subjective Significance in Processing of an Emotional Stroop Task. *Front. Hum. Neurosci.* **2021**, *15*, 617861. [CrossRef] [PubMed]
6. Larsen, R.J.; Mercer, K.A.; Balota, D.A. Lexical characteristics of words used in emotional Stroop experiments. *Emotion* **2006**, *6*, 62–72. [CrossRef]
7. Puschmann, A.-K.; Sommer, C. Hypervigilance or avoidance of trigger related cues in migraineurs?—A case-control study using the emotional stroop task. *BMC Neurol.* **2011**, *11*, 141. [CrossRef]
8. Derbyshire, S.W.G.; Vogt, B.A.; Jones, A.K. Pain and Stroop interference tasks activate separate processing modules in anterior cingulate cortex. *Exp. Brain Res.* **1998**, *118*, 52–60. [CrossRef]
9. Andersson, G.; Haldrup, D. Personalized pain words and Stroop interference in chronic pain patients. *Eur. J. Pain* **2003**, *7*, 431–438. [CrossRef]
10. Beck, J.G.; Freeman, J.B.; Shipherd, J.C.; Hamblen, J.L.; Lackner, J.M. Specificity of Stroop interference in patients with pain and PTSD. *J. Abnorm. Psychol.* **2001**, *110*, 536–543. [CrossRef]
11. Roelofs, J.; Peters, M.L.; Zeegers, M.P.A.; Vlaeyen, J.W.S. The modified Stroop paradigm as a measure of selective attention towards pain-related stimuli among chronic pain patients: A meta-analysis. *Eur. J. Pain* **2002**, *6*, 273–281. [CrossRef] [PubMed]
12. Crombez, G.; Van Damme, S.; Eccleston, C. Hypervigilance to pain: An experimental and clinical analysis. *Pain* **2005**, *116*, 4–7. [CrossRef] [PubMed]
13. Bushnell, M.C.; Ceko, M.; Low, L.A. Cognitive and emotional control of pain and its disruption in chronic pain. *Nat. Rev. Neurosci.* **2013**, *14*, 502–511. [CrossRef] [PubMed]
14. Fayaz, A.; Croft, P.; Langford, R.M.; Donaldson, L.J.; Jones, G.T. Prevalence of chronic pain in the UK: A systematic review and meta-analysis of population studies. *BMJ Open* **2016**, *6*, e010364. [CrossRef]
15. Mills, S.E.E.; Nicolson, K.P.; Smith, B.H. Chronic pain: A review of its epidemiology and associated factors in population-based studies. *Br. J. Anaesth.* **2019**, *123*, e273–e283. [CrossRef]
16. Cieza, A.; Causey, K.; Kamenov, K.; Hanson, S.W.; Chatterji, S.; Vos, T. Global estimates of the need for rehabilitation based on the Global Burden of Disease study 2019: A systematic analysis for the Global Burden of Disease Study 2019. *Lancet* **2020**, *396*, 2006–2017. [CrossRef]

17. Hawker, G.A. The assessment of musculoskeletal pain. *Clin. Exp. Rheumatol.* **2017**, *35* (Suppl. S107), 8–12.
18. Smith, B.H.; Elliot, A.M.; Hannaford, P.C.; Chamber, W.A.; Smith, W.C. Factors Related to the Onset and Persistence of Chronic Back Pain in the Community: Results from a general population follow-up study. *Spine* **2004**, *29*, 1032–1040. [CrossRef]
19. Galvez-Sánchez, C.M.; Montoro, C.I.; Duschek, S.; del Paso, G.A.R. Pain catastrophizing mediates the negative influence of pain and trait-anxiety on health-related quality of life in fibromyalgia. *Qual. Life Res.* **2020**, *29*, 1871–1881. [CrossRef]
20. Galvez-Sánchez, C.M.; Montoro, C.I.; Duschek, S.; del Paso, G.A.R. Depression and trait-anxiety mediate the influence of clinical pain on health-related quality of life in fibromyalgia. *J. Affect. Disord.* **2020**, *265*, 486–495. [CrossRef]
21. van Hecke, O.; Torrance, N.; Smith, B. Chronic pain epidemiology and its clinical relevance. *Br. J. Anaesth.* **2013**, *111*, 13–18. [CrossRef] [PubMed]
22. Blyth, F.M. Chronic pain–is it a public health problem? *Pain* **2008**, *137*, 465–466. [CrossRef] [PubMed]
23. Poleshuck, E.L.; Green, C.R. Socioeconomic disadvantage and pain. *Pain* **2008**, *136*, 235–238. [CrossRef] [PubMed]
24. Brekke, M.; Hjortdahl, P.; Kvien, T.K. Severity of musculoskeletal pain: Relationship to socioeconomic inequality. *Soc. Sci. Med.* **2022**, *54*, 221–228. [CrossRef]
25. Mercado, F.; González, J.L.; Barjola, P.; Fernández-Sánchez, M.; López-López, A.; Alonso, M.; Gómez-Esquer, F. Brain correlates of cognitive inhibition in fibromyalgia: Emotional intrusion of symptom-related words. *Int. J. Psychophysiol.* **2013**, *88*, 182–192. [CrossRef]
26. González, J.L.; Mercado, F.; Barjola, P.; Carretero, I.; López-López, A.; Bullones, M.A.; Fernández-Sánchez, M.; Alonso, M. Generalized hypervigilance in fibromyalgia patients: An experimental analysis with the emotional Stroop paradigm. *J. Psychosom. Res.* **2010**, *69*, 279–287. [CrossRef]
27. Weissman-Fogel, I.; Moayedi, M.; Tenenbaum, H.C.; Goldberg, M.B.; Freeman, B.V.; Davis, K.D. Abnormal cortical activity in patients with temporomandibular disorder evoked by cognitive and emotional tasks. *Pain* **2011**, *152*, 384–396. [CrossRef]
28. Roelofs, J.; Peters, M.L.; Crombez, G.; Verschuere, B.; Vlaeyen, J.W.S. An Examination of Word Relevance in a Modified Stroop Task in Patients with Chronic Low Back Pain. *Percept. Mot. Ski.* **2005**, *100*, 955–963. [CrossRef]
29. Clauw, D.J. Fibromyalgia: An Overview. *Am. J. Med.* **2009**, *122*, S3–S13. [CrossRef]
30. del Paso, G.A.R.; Pulgar, Á.; Duschek, S.; Garrido, S. Cognitive impairment in fibromyalgia syndrome: The impact of pain, emotional disorders, medication, and cardiovascular regulation. *Eur. J. Pain* **2012**, *16*, 421–429. [CrossRef]
31. Wolfe, F.; Clauw, D.J.; Fitzcharles, M.-A.; Goldenberg, D.L.; Katz, R.S.; Mease, P.; Russell, A.S.; Russell, I.J.; Winfield, J.B.; Yunus, M.B. The American College of Rheumatology Preliminary Diagnostic Criteria for Fibromyalgia and Measurement of Symptom Severity. *Arthritis Care Res.* **2010**, *62*, 600–610. [CrossRef] [PubMed]
32. Cabo-Meseguera, A.; Cerdá-Olmedo, G.; Trillo-Mata, J.L. Fibromialgia: Prevalencia, perfiles epidemiológicos y costes económicos. *Med. Clin.* **2017**, *149*, 441–448. [CrossRef] [PubMed]
33. Marques, A.P.; Santo, A.D.S.D.E.; Berssaneti, A.A.; Matsutani, L.A.; Yuan, S.L.K. Prevalence of fibromyalgia: Literature review update. *Rev. Bras. Reumatol. Engl. Ed.* **2016**, *57*, 356–363. [CrossRef]
34. Srinivasan, S.; Maloney, E.; Wright, B.; Kennedy, M.; Kallail, K.J.; Rasker, J.J.; Häuser, W.; Wolfe, F. The Problematic Nature of Fibromyalgia Diagnosis in the Community. *ACR Open Rheumatol.* **2019**, *1*, 43–51. [CrossRef]
35. Wolfe, F.; Walitt, B.; Perrot, S.; Rasker, J.J.; Häuser, W. Fibromyalgia diagnosis and biased assessment: Sex, prevalence and bias. *PLoS ONE* **2018**, *13*, e0203755. [CrossRef]
36. Loggia, M.L.; Berna, C.; Kim, J.; Cahalan, C.M.; Gollub, R.L.; Wasan, A.D.; Harris, R.E.; Edwards, R.R.; Napadow, V. Disrupted Brain Circuitry for Pain-Related Reward/Punishment in Fibromyalgia. *Arthritis Rheumatol.* **2014**, *66*, 203–212. [CrossRef]
37. Sumpton, J.E.; Moulin, D.E. Chapter 33—Fibromyalgia. *Handb. Clin. Neurol.* **2014**, *119*, 513–527. [CrossRef]
38. Walter, K. What Is Migraine? *JAMA* **2022**, *327*, 93. [CrossRef]
39. Rainero, I.; Govone, F.; Gai, A.; Vacca, A.; Rubino, E. Is Migraine Primarily a Metaboloendocrine Disorder? *Curr. Pain Headache Rep.* **2018**, *22*, 36. [CrossRef]
40. Arnold, M. Headache Classification Committee of the International Headache Society (IHS) the International Classification of Headache Disorders, 3rd edition. *Cephalalgia* **2018**, *38*, 1–211. [CrossRef]
41. Ibrahimi, K.; van Oosterhout, W.P.J.; van Dorp, W.; Danser, A.H.J.; Garrelds, I.M.; Kushner, S.A.; Lesaffre, E.M.; Terwindt, G.M.; Ferrari, M.D.; Van den Meiracker, A.H.; et al. Reduced trigeminovascular cyclicity in patients with menstrually related migraine. *Neurology* **2015**, *84*, 125–131. [CrossRef] [PubMed]
42. Xiang, T.; Tao, Z.-Y.; Liao, L.-F.; Wang, S.; Cao, D.-Y. Animal Models of Temporomandibular Disorder. *J. Pain Res.* **2021**, *14*, 1415–1430. [CrossRef] [PubMed]
43. Takashima, M.; Arai, Y.; Kawamura, A.; Hayashi, T.; Takagi, R. Quantitative evaluation of masseter muscle stiffness in patients with temporomandibular disorders using shear wave elastography. *J. Prosthodont. Res.* **2017**, *61*, 432–438. [CrossRef] [PubMed]
44. Guerrero, L.; Coronado, L.; Maulén, M.; Meeder, W.; Henríquez, C.; Lovera, M. Prevalencia de trastornos temporomandibulares en la población adulta beneficiaria de Atención Primaria en Salud del Servicio de Salyd Valparaíso, San Antonio. *Av. Odontoestomatol.* **2017**, *33*, 113–120.
45. LeResche, L. Epidemiology of Temporomandibular Disorders: Implications for the Investigation of Etiologic Factors. *Crit. Rev. Oral Biol. Med.* **1997**, *8*, 291–305. [CrossRef]
46. De Oliveira-Souza, A.I.S.; de O Ferro, J.K.; Barros, M.M.M.B.; de Oliveira, D.A. Cervical musculoskeletal disorders in patients with temporomandibular dysfunction: A systematic review and meta-analysis. *J. Bodyw. Mov. Ther.* **2020**, *24*, 84–101. [CrossRef]

47. Prodoehl, J.; Kraus, S.; Buros, S.A. Predicting the number of physical therapy visits and patient satisfaction in individuals with temporomandibular disorder: A cohort study. *J. Oral Rehabil.* **2022**, *49*, 22–36. [CrossRef]
48. Slade, G.D.; Ohrbach, R.; Greenspan, J.D.; Fillingim, R.B.; Bair, E.; Sanders, A.E.; Dubner, R.; Diatchenko, L.; Meloto, C.B.; Smith, S.; et al. Painful Temporomandibular Disorder: Decade of discovery from OPPERA studies. *J. Dent. Res.* **2016**, *95*, 1084–1092. [CrossRef]
49. Koes, B.W.; van Tulder, M.; Lin, C.-W.C.; Macedo, L.G.; McAuley, J.; Maher, C. An updated overview of clinical guidelines for the management of non-specific low back pain in primary care. *Eur. Spine J.* **2010**, *19*, 2075–2094. [CrossRef]
50. van Tulder, M.; Becker, A.; Bekkering, T.; Breen, A.; Gil del Real, M.T.; Hutchinson, A.; Koes, B.; Laerum, E.; Malmivaara, A.; On behalf of the COST B13 Working Group on Guidelines for the Management of Acute Low Back Pain in Primary Care. Chapter 3 European guidelines for the management of acute nonspecific low back pain in primary care. *Eur. Spine J.* **2006**, *15* (Suppl. S2), S169–S191. [CrossRef]
51. Dal Farra, F.; Risio, R.G.; Vismara, L.; Bergna, A. Effectiveness of osteopathic interventions in chronic non-specific low back pain: A systematic review and meta-analysis. *Complement. Ther. Med.* **2020**, *56*, 102616. [CrossRef] [PubMed]
52. Owen, P.J.; Miller, C.T.; Mundell, N.L.; Verswijveren, S.; Tagliaferri, S.D.; Brisby, H.; Bowe, S.J.; Belavy, D.L. Which specific modes of exercise training are most effective for treating low back pain? Network meta-analysis. *Br. J. Sports. Med.* **2020**, *54*, 1279–1287. [CrossRef] [PubMed]
53. Melloh, M.; Röder, C.; Elfering, A.; Theis, J.C.; Müller, U.; Staub, L.P.; Aghayev, E.; Zweig, T.; Barz, T.; Kohlmann, T.; et al. Differences across health care systems in outcome and cost-utility of surgical and conservative treatment of chronic low back pain: A study protocol. *BMC Musculoskelet. Disord.* **2008**, *9*, 81. [CrossRef]
54. Fujii, T.; Matsudaira, K. Prevalence of low back pain and factors associated with chronic disabling back pain in Japan. *Eur. Spine J.* **2012**, *22*, 432–438. [CrossRef]
55. Aure, O.F.; Nilsen, J.H.; Vasseljen, O. Manual Therapy and Exercise Therapy in Patients with Chronic Low Back Pain: A randomized, controlled trial with 1-year follow-up. *Spine* **2003**, *28*, 525–531. [CrossRef] [PubMed]
56. Kälin, S.; Rausch-Osthoff, A.-K.; Bauer, C.M. What is the effect of sensory discrimination training on chronic low back pain? A systematic review. *BMC Musculoskelet. Disord.* **2016**, *17*, 143. [CrossRef]
57. Colloca, L.; Ludman, T.; Bouhassira, D.; Baron, R.; Dickenson, A.H.; Yarnitsky, D.; Freeman, R.; Truini, A.; Attal, N.; Finnerup, N.; et al. Neuropathic pain. *Nat. Rev. Dis. Primers* **2017**, *3*, 17002. [CrossRef]
58. Finnerup, N.B.; Haroutounian, S.; Kamerman, P.; Baron, R.; Bennett, D.L.H.; Bouhassira, D.; Cruccu, G.; Freeman, R.; Hansson, P.; Nurmikko, T.; et al. Neuropathic pain: An updated grading system for research and clinical practice. *Pain* **2016**, *157*, 1599–1606. [CrossRef] [PubMed]
59. Bouhassira, D.B.; Attal, N.; Fermanian, J.; Alchaar, H.; Gautron, M.; Masquelier, E.; Rostaing, S.; Lanteri-Minet, M.; Collin, E.; Grisart, J.; et al. Development and validation of the Neuropathic Pain Symptom Inventory. *Pain* **2004**, *108*, 248–257. [CrossRef]
60. Bredal, I.S.; Smeby, N.A.; Ottesen, S.; Warncke, T.; Schlichting, E. Chronic Pain in Breast Cancer Survivors: Comparison of Psychosocial, Surgical, and Medical Characteristics Between Survivors with and Without Pain. *J. Pain Symptom Manag.* **2014**, *48*, 852–862. [CrossRef]
61. Carlson, L.E.; Speca, M.; Patel, K.D.; Goodey, E. Mindfulness-Based Stress Reduction in Relation to Quality of Life, Mood, Symptoms of Stress, and Immune Parameters in Breast and Prostate Cancer Outpatients. *Psychosom. Med.* **2003**, *65*, 571–581. [CrossRef] [PubMed]
62. Torrance, N.; Smith, B.H.; Bennett, M.I.; Lee, A.J. The Epidemiology of Chronic Pain of Predominantly Neuropathic Origin. Results from a General Population Survey. *J. Pain* **2006**, *7*, 281–289. [CrossRef] [PubMed]
63. Crofford, L.J. Chronic Pain: Where the Body Meets the Brain. *Trans. Am. Clin. Climatol. Assoc.* **2015**, *126*, 167–183. [PubMed]
64. Pérez, C. El dolor crónico desde el punto de vista de la neurociencia. *NPunto* **2021**, *41*, 4–33.
65. van de Riet, W.A.C.; Grèzes, J.; de Gelder, B. Specific and common brain regions involved in the perception of faces and bodies and the representation of their emotional expressions. *Soc. Neurosci.* **2009**, *4*, 101–120. [CrossRef] [PubMed]
66. American Psychological Association. Managing Chronic Pain: How Psychologists Can Help with Pain Management. 15 December 2013. Available online: http://www.apa.org/topics/pain/management (accessed on 17 January 2022).
67. American Psychological Association. Coping with Chronic Pain. 1 January 2011. Available online: http://www.apa.org/topics/pain/chronic (accessed on 24 January 2022).
68. Lumley, M.A.; Cohen, J.L.; Borszcz, G.S.; Cano, A.; Radcliffe, A.M.; Porter, L.S.; Schubiner, H.; Keefe, F.J. Pain and emotion: A biopsychosocial review of recent research. *J. Clin. Psychol.* **2011**, *67*, 942–968. [CrossRef]
69. Taylor, A.M.; Harris, A.D.; Varnava, A.; Phillips, R.; Hughes, O.; Wilkes, A.R.; Hall, J.E.; Wise, R.G. Neural responses to a modified Stroop paradigm in patients with complex chronic musculoskeletal pain compared to matched controls: An experimental functional magnetic resonance imaging study. *BMC Psychol.* **2016**, *4*, 5. [CrossRef]
70. Crombez, G.; Van Ryckeghem, D.; Eccleston, C.; Van Damme, S. Attentional bias to pain-related information: A meta-analysis. *Pain* **2013**, *154*, 497–510. [CrossRef]
71. Todd, J.; Van Ryckeghem, D.; Sharpe, L.; Crombez, G. Attentional bias to pain-related information: A meta-analysis of dot-probe studies. *Health Psychol. Rev.* **2018**, *12*, 419–436. [CrossRef]

72. Page, M.J.; McKenzie, J.E.; Bossuyt, P.M.; Boutron, I.; Hoffmann, T.C.; Mulrow, C.D.; Shamseer, L.; Tetzlaff, J.M.; Akl, E.A.; Brennan, S.E.; et al. The PRISMA 2020 statement: An updated guideline for reporting systematic reviews. *BMJ* **2021**, *372*, 71. [CrossRef]
73. Hatchard, T.; Mioduszewski, O.; Khoo, E.-L.; Romanow, H.; Shergill, Y.; Tennant, E.; Leeming, A.; Fang, Z.; Poulin, P.; Smith, A.M. Reduced Emotional Reactivity in Breast Cancer Survivors with Chronic Neuropathic Pain Following Mindfulness-Based Stress Reduction (MBSR): An fMRI Pilot Investigation. *Mindfulness* **2020**, *12*, 751–762. [CrossRef]
74. Asmundson, G.J.; Wright, K.D.; Hadjistavropoulos, H.D. Hypervigilance and Attentional Fixedness in Chronic Musculoskeletal Pain: Consistency of Findings Across Modified Stroop and Dot-probe Tasks. *J. Pain* **2005**, *6*, 497–506. [CrossRef] [PubMed]
75. Snider, B.S.; Asmundson, G.J.G.; Wiese, K.C. Automatic and Strategic Processing of Threat Cues in Patients with Chronic Pain: A Modified Stroop Evaluation. *Clin. J. Pain* **2000**, *16*, 144–154. [CrossRef]
76. Pincus, T.; Fraser, L.; Pearce, S. Do chronic pain patients 'Stroop' on pain stimuli? *Br. J. Clin. Psychol.* **1998**, *37*, 49–58. [CrossRef]
77. Duckworth, M.P.; Iezzi, A.; Adams, H.E.; Hale, D. Information processing in chronic pain disorder: A preliminary analysis. *J. Psychopathol. Behav. Assess.* **1997**, *19*, 239–245. [CrossRef]
78. Pearce, J.; Morley, S. An experimental investigation of the construct validity of the McGill Pain Questionnaire. *Pain* **1989**, *39*, 115–121. [CrossRef]
79. McNeely, H.E.; Lau, M.A.; Christensen, B.K.; Alain, C. Neurophysiological evidence of cognitive inhibition anomalies in persons with major depressive disorder. *Clin. Neurophysiol.* **2008**, *199*, 1578–1589. [CrossRef]
80. Taake, I.; Jaspers-Fayer, F.; Liotti, M. Early frontal responses elicited by physical threat words in an emotional Stroop task: Modulation by anxiety sensitivity. *Biol. Psychol.* **2009**, *81*, 48–57. [CrossRef]
81. Vanhooff, J.; Dietz, K.; Sharma, D.; Bowman, H. Neural correlates of intrusion of emotion words in a modified Stroop task. *Int. J. Psychophysiol.* **2008**, *67*, 23–34. [CrossRef]
82. Joyal, M.; Wensing, T.; Levasseur-Moreau, J.; Leblond, J.; Sack, A.; Fecteau, S. Characterizing emotional Stroop interference in posttraumatic stress disorder, major depression and anxiety disorders: A systematic review and meta-analysis. *PLoS ONE* **2019**, *14*, e0214998. [CrossRef]
83. Algom, D.; Chajut, E.; Lev, S. A Rational Look at the Emotional Stroop Phenomenon: A Generic Slowdown, Not a Stroop Effect. *J. Exp. Psychol. Gen.* **2004**, *133*, 323–338. [CrossRef] [PubMed]
84. Walteros, C.; Sánchez-Navarro, J.P.; Muñoz, M.A.; Martínez-Selva, J.M.; Chialvo, D.; Montoya, P. Altered associative learning and emotional decision making in fibromyalgia. *J. Psychosom. Res.* **2011**, *70*, 294–301. [CrossRef] [PubMed]
85. Sharpe, L.; Haggman, S.; Nicholas, M.; Dear, B.F.; Refshauge, K. Avoidance of affective pain stimuli predicts chronicity in patients with acute low back pain. *Pain* **2014**, *155*, 45–52. [CrossRef] [PubMed]
86. Neugebauer, V.; Galhardo, V.; Maione, S.; Mackey, S.C. Forebrain pain mechanisms. *Brain Res. Rev.* **2009**, *60*, 226–242. [CrossRef]
87. Tracey, I.; Mantyh, P.W. The Cerebral Signature for Pain Perception and Its Modulation. *Neuron* **2007**, *55*, 377–391. [CrossRef]
88. Wiech, K.; Tracey, I. The influence of negative emotions on pain: Behavioral effects and neural mechanisms. *NeuroImage* **2009**, *47*, 987–994. [CrossRef]
89. Alomar, S.; Bakhaidar, M. Neuroimaging of neuropathic pain: Review of current status and future directions. *Neurosurg. Rev.* **2018**, *41*, 771–777. [CrossRef]
90. Harrison, R.; Zeidan, F.; Kitsaras, G.; Ozcelik, D.; Salomons, T.V. Trait Mindfulness Is Associated with Lower Pain Reactivity and Connectivity of the Default Mode Network. *J. Pain* **2018**, *20*, 645–654. [CrossRef]
91. Zeidan, F.; Salomons, T.; Farris, S.R.; Emerson, N.M.; Adler-Neal, A.; Jung, Y.; Coghill, R.C. Neural mechanisms supporting the relationship between dispositional mindfulness and pain. *Pain* **2018**, *159*, 2477–2485. [CrossRef]
92. McCracken, L.M.; Vowles, K.E.; Eccleston, C. Acceptance-based treatment for persons with complex, long standing chronic pain: A preliminary analysis of treatment outcome in comparison to a waiting phase. *Behav. Res. Ther.* **2005**, *43*, 1335–1346. [CrossRef]
93. Vowles, K.E.; McCracken, L.M. Acceptance and values-based action in chronic pain: A study of treatment effectiveness and process. *J. Consult. Clin. Psychol.* **2008**, *76*, 397–407. [CrossRef] [PubMed]
94. Wicksell, R.K.; Melin, L.; Olsson, G.L. Exposure and acceptance in the rehabilitation of adolescents with idiopathic chronic pain—A pilot study. *Eur. J. Pain* **2007**, *11*, 267–274. [CrossRef] [PubMed]
95. Wicksell, R.K.; Melin, L.; Lekander, M.; Olsson, G.L. Evaluating the effectiveness of exposure and acceptance strategies to improve functioning and quality of life in longstanding pediatric pain—A randomized controlled trial. *Pain* **2009**, *141*, 248–257. [CrossRef] [PubMed]
96. Leserman, J. Sexual Abuse History: Prevalence, Health Effects, Mediators, and Psychological Treatment. *Psychosom. Med.* **2005**, *67*, 906–915. [CrossRef] [PubMed]
97. Crombez, G.; Eccleston, C.; Van Damme, S.; Vlaeyen, J.W.; Karoly, P. Fear-Avoidance Model of Chronic Pain: The next generation. *Clin. J. Pain* **2012**, *28*, 475–483. [CrossRef]
98. Eccleston, C.; Crombez, G. Pain demands attention: A cognitive–affective model of the interruptive function of pain. *Psychol. Bull.* **1999**, *125*, 356–366. [CrossRef]
99. Vlaeyen, J.W.S.; Linton, S.J. Fear-avoidance and its consequences in chronic musculoskeletal pain: A state of the art. *Pain* **2000**, *85*, 317–332. [CrossRef]
100. Todd, J.; Sharpe, L.; Johnson, A.; Perry, K.; Colagiuri, B.; Dear, B.F. Towards a new model of attentional biases in the development, maintenance and management of pain. *Pain* **2015**, *156*, 1589–1600. [CrossRef]

Journal of *Clinical Medicine*

MDPI

Article

Do Men and Women Have a Different Association between Fear-Avoidance and Pain Intensity in Chronic Pain? An Experience Sampling Method Cohort-Study

Sophie Waardenburg [1,2], Lars Visseren [3,4], Elke van Daal [1], Brigitte Brouwer [1], Jan van Zundert [1,5], Sander M. J. van Kuijk [2], Richel Lousberg [4], Ellen M. M. Jongen [6], Carsten Leue [7] and Nelleke de Meij [1,*]

1 Department of Anesthesiology and Pain Management, Maastricht University Medical Centre MUMC+, 6229 HX Maastricht, The Netherlands
2 Department of Clinical Epidemiology and Medical Technology Assessment, Maastricht University Medical Centre MUMC+, 6229 HX Maastricht, The Netherlands
3 Faculty of Health, Medicine and Life Sciences, Maastricht University, 6229 ER Maastricht, The Netherlands
4 Department of Psychiatry and Neuropsychology, Maastricht University, 6229 ER Maastricht, The Netherlands
5 Department of Anesthesiology, Multidisciplinary Pain Centre Ziekenhuis Oost Limburg, 3600 Genk, Belgium
6 Faculty of Psychology, Open University, 6419 DJ Heerlen, The Netherlands
7 Department of Psychiatry, Maastricht University Medical Centre MUMC+, 6229 HX Maastricht, The Netherlands
* Correspondence: p.de.meij@mumc.nl

Abstract: Background: Fear-avoidance is one of the factors associated with chronic pain. However, it remains unclear whether the association between fear-avoidance and pain depends on sex. The present study aimed to investigate whether the association between fear-avoidance and pain intensity differed between men and women in chronic pain patients. Additionally, the potential confounding effect of affective experiences on the association between fear-avoidance and pain intensity was analyzed. Method: This cohort study included hospital referred chronic pain patients (n = 45). Short momentary assessment questions according to the experience sampling method (ESM) were used to repeatedly assess patients' pain intensity, level of fear-avoidance and positive as well as negative affect during their daily life. Linear mixed-effects models were applied in the statistical analysis. Unadjusted and adjusted models were made, in which the latter corrected for statistically significant affective experiences and baseline variables, taking the Aikake Information Criterion into account to assess a better model of fit. Results: The results demonstrated an association between fear-avoidance and pain intensity that differed for men and women. In men (n = 13), no association between these variables was found (−0.04 (95% CI: −0.14, 0.06) with a p-value of 0.48), whereas in women (n = 32), an increase in fear-avoidance was associated with a (slight) increase in pain intensity (0.18 (95% CI 0.06, 0.30) with a p-value of 0.003). Affect did not confound the above-mentioned findings. Conclusion: Our data supports previous research highlighting the importance of sex differences in pain experience. These findings may be relevant for clinicians to consider more personalized (i.e., gender specific) pain management in chronic pain patients.

Keywords: chronic pain; pain intensity; fear-avoidance; positive affect; negative affect; experience sampling method; momentary assessment; anxiety; depression

Citation: Waardenburg, S.; Visseren, L.; van Daal, E.; Brouwer, B.; van Zundert, J.; van Kuijk, S.M.J.; Lousberg, R.; Jongen, E.M.M.; Leue, C.; de Meij, N. Do Men and Women Have a Different Association between Fear-Avoidance and Pain Intensity in Chronic Pain? An Experience Sampling Method Cohort-Study. *J. Clin. Med.* **2022**, *11*, 5515. https://doi.org/10.3390/jcm11195515

Academic Editor: Carmen María Galvez Sánchez

Received: 18 August 2022
Accepted: 16 September 2022
Published: 20 September 2022

1. Introduction

Chronic pain affects more than 30% of people worldwide and has a large impact on both patients and society [1]. Due to the complex interactions between biological, psychological and social factors [1,2], it is difficult to manage chronic pain. One of these factors is fear-avoidance, which refers to the avoidance of movements or activities resulting from fear of pain [3]. According to the fear-avoidance model, pain may be interpreted as threatening (i.e., pain catastrophizing), which can lead to avoidant behaviors and hypervigilance to bodily sensations. Conversely, fear-avoidance and hypervigilance may induce physical disuse and disability, contributing to long-term consequences, including maintenance of chronic pain disability or an increase in the pain experience [3]. Although the association between fear-avoidance and chronic pain has been well-established, only sparse research has been conducted on potential sex differences regarding this association. As a growing number of articles suggests the importance of sex differences in relation to pain, and specifically in pain catastrophizing [4–6], it is important to further investigate whether the association between fear-avoidance and pain also depends on sex.

Furthermore, the biopsychosocial model of pain shows that emotional distress or affective states may influence pain intensity [1] and may, therefore, also confound the association between sex and fear-avoidance. It is known that dynamic fluctuations regarding positive and negative affect are observed in various mental disorders [7], such as depression. Given that depression and pain share pathways [8], fluctuations in emotion regulation as observed in depression and other mental disorders may also be found in chronic pain patients. However, the effect of affective states, such as happiness, anxiety and irritation on the association between fear-avoidance and pain has not been adequately studied. The cross-sectional design of studies that have investigated the association between affective states and chronic pain could not capture the fluctuations of emotional distress over time.

Hence, the present study aimed to investigate whether the association between fear-avoidance and pain intensity in chronic pain patients differs between men and women. Additionally, the potential confounding effect of specific affective experiences on the association between fear-avoidance and pain intensity was analyzed by using the experience sampling method (ESM).

2. Methods

2.1. Study Design

This cohort study used questionnaires administered according to ESM. Experience sampling is a structured digital diary technique to appraise subjective experiences in daily life, often applied in patients with psychiatric disorders or somatic illnesses [9]. Patients are repeatedly asked to complete short questionnaires during the day, which allows for the assessment of moment-to-moment changes in both symptoms and mental states, aiming to map daily functioning [10]. This study was approved by the local medical ethical committee (METC-number: 2018-0955).

2.2. Study Population

The cohort of the present study consisted of chronic pain patients who were referred to the University Hospital Pain Centre of the Maastricht University Medical Centre+ (MUMC+). The patients were recruited from March 2019 until July 2021 while performing their digital intake at the pain center, during which they were asked whether they wanted to be approached for participation in this study. If their answer was positive, patients were contacted by a research nurse for a more extensive explanation about the ESM-procedures. Patients with any type of pain at any location were eligible for participation. To be included, patients had to be 18 years or older and to have experienced pain complaints for at least three months. Additionally, the patient had to be in possession of a smartphone and able to use the ESM application named Psymate. Patients who were interested in participation also received all required information by an information letter, complemented with a consent form. Before the start of the study, all patients who wanted to participate provided informed consent.

2.3. Experience Sampling

Both outcome (pain intensity), predictor (fear-avoidance) and potential confounders (affect) were measured by repeated ESM assessments. These ESM assessments consisted of 18 questions and were completed through a smartphone application (Psymate). The items in the Psymate application illustrate adequate psychometric properties, and sensitivity to change over time [11]. Patients were asked to answer the questions 10 times a day, for six consecutive days. The questionnaires were completed in semi-random time blocks of 112.5 min from 7:30 a.m. until 10:30 p.m. during the patients' daily life, whenever patients received a notification ('beep') from the Psymate-app on their smartphone [12,13]. Fear-avoidance was assessed by the statement 'due to fear for (more) pain I did not make unnecessary movements since the last beep', asking the participants about their fear-avoidance behavior since the last beep. The items of positive and negative affect come originally from the validated PANAS questionnaire [14–16] and were assessed thoroughly before the application in the ESM. Positive affect was assessed by the following statements 'I feel cheerful', 'I feel relaxed', 'I feel satisfied', and 'I feel enthusiastic', whereas negative affect was measured by the statements 'I feel insecure', 'I feel irritated', 'I feel lonely', 'I feel anxious', 'I feel guilty' and 'I am worrying'. The 10 different items concerning the affective state, as well as the item assessing the level of fear-avoidance, were answered on a 7-point Likert scale, ranging from 1 (not at all) to 7 (very much). The outcome variable 'pain intensity' was assessed by the statement 'I am in pain', and could be answered on an 11-point scale, ranging from 0 (no pain) to 10 (worst pain possible).

2.4. Baseline Variables

As part of the standard digital intake at the MUMC+, patients were asked to complete a set of questionnaires that reflected the pain complaints, quality of life, anxiety and depressive symptoms. These questionnaires consisted of the Hospital Anxiety and Depression Scale (HADS), Numeric Rating Scale (NRS) for pain intensity, Pain Catastrophizing Scale (PCS), Brief Pain Inventory (BPI) and the 12-item Short-Form Health Survey (SF-12) [17–21]. An explanation of how these measurement instruments were assessed is provided in more detail by the article of Brouwer et al. [22]. During intake, patients also had to indicate how long they had been experiencing pain and at which location(s). Moreover, demographic variables including sex, age, marital status, education level and employment were collected. In addition to the intake questionnaires, patients had to complete one additional questionnaire that assessed the level of fear-avoidance at baseline. The 'TAMPA Scale for Kinesiophobia' (TSK) (Dutch translated), which includes 17 questions on a 4-point scale, was used for this. TSK-scores range from 17 to 68, and scores greater than 37 indicate a high degree of fear-avoidance [23]. Similar to the ESM-measurements, the TSK was completed through the Psymate-app once before the start of the ESM-examination period.

2.5. Statistical Analysis

Baseline characteristics of the cohort are described as mean and standard deviation for continuous variables, and as count and percentage for categorical variables. Sex differences in baseline characteristics were tested using the independent-samples t-test for continuous variables, and Pearson's chi-square test or Fisher's exact test for categorical variables. ESM-data were analyzed using linear mixed-effects models with random intercept and slope on three levels; patients, days, and beeps. The model was built in several steps. First, the crude association between fear-avoidance and pain was assessed as fixed and as random effect. Second, the interaction of fear avoidance and sex was added. The third and fourth model assessed for potential confounders concerning baseline variables and affect. Consequently, two backward stepwise elimination processes were applied. The third model assessed the first backward stepwise elimination of the baseline variables (patients sociodemographic variables, pain characteristics and PROMs of Table 1). The fourth model assessed the items of negative and positive affect ('I feel cheerful, 'I feel relaxed', 'I feel satisfied', 'I feel enthusiastic', 'I feel insecure', 'I feel irritated', 'I feel lonely', 'I feel anxious', 'I feel guilty' and 'I am worrying') as being potential confounders by the backward stepwise elimination process. Autocorrelation by using a first-order continuous time covariate autoregressive structure was added in the fifth model. The stipulated models are presented in Figure 1. Analyses were performed using R, version 4.1.2, with the function lme (linear mixed effects models) from the statistical package nlme (3.1–153). All tests were investigated two-sided against a significance level (α) of 0.05.

Table 1. Baseline description of the chronic pain patient cohort.

Patient Baseline Characteristics	Total Cohort, n = 45	Men, n = 13	Women, n = 32	p-Value
	Demographic Characteristics			
Age in years, *mean (SD)*	47.6 (12.8)	52.8 (13.8)	45.5 (12.0)	0.086
Marital status, *n (%)*				0.411
Relationship	36 (80.0)	9 (69.2)	27 (84.4)	
No relationship	9 (20.0)	4 (30.8)	5 (15.6)	
Education, *n (%)*				0.287
Low (*<9 years of education*)	32 (71.1)	11 (84.6)	21 (65.6)	
High (*≥9 years of education*)	13 (28.9)	2 (15.4)	11 (34.4)	
Employment, *n (%)*				1.000
Unemployed (*no paid job*)	29 (64.4)	8 (61.5)	21 (65.6)	
Employed (*paid job*)	16 (35.6)	5 (38.5)	11 (34.4)	
	Pain Characteristics			
Pain duration in months, *mean (SD)*	73.2 (81.1)	45.9 (55.5)	84.3 (87.8)	0.088
Pain location, *n (%)*				
Head	5 (11.1)	1 (7.7)	4 (12.5)	1.000
Neck	15 (33.3)	3 (23.1)	12 (37.5)	0.492
Arm	7 (15.6)	1 (7.7)	6 (18.8)	0.654
Lower back	25 (55.6)	10 (76.9)	15 (46.9)	0.066
Upper leg	19 (42.2)	5 (38.5)	14 (43.8)	0.745
Lower leg	12 (26.7)	3 (23.1)	9 (28.1)	1.000
Chest/abdomen	4 (8.9)	2 (15.4)	2 (6.3)	0.567
Other	10 (22.2)	2 (15.4)	8 (25.0)	0.698
	PROMs Scores			
NRS, *mean (SD)*	7.1 (1.7)	6.8 (1.9)	7.3 (1.6)	0.391
PCS, *mean (SD)*	23.2 (11.9)	26.8 (14.1)	21.8 (10.9)	0.207
BPI REM *mean (SD)*	11.6 (8.1)	14.2 (9.6)	10.5 (7.2)	0.095
BPI WAW, *mean (SD)*	24.7 (10.0)	25.6 (9.2)	24.3 (10.5)	0.440
TSK, *mean (SD)*	36.2 (6.0)	39.6 (6.5)	34.8 (5.2)	0.013 *
TSK > 37, *n (%)*	21 (46.7)	9 (69.2)	12 (37.5)	0.053
HADS-A, *mean (SD)*	6.8 (3.8)	8.2 (4.2)	6.2 (3.6)	0.125
HADS-D, *mean (SD)*	7.5 (4.9)	9.2 (5.2)	6.8 (4.7)	0.127
PHS, *mean (SD)*	29.4 (6.8)	29.6 (6.4)	29.2 (7.0)	0.862
MHS, *mean (SD)*	45.7 (12.1)	43.1 (12.5)	46.8 (12.0)	0.367

Abbreviations: NRS, Numerical Rating Scale for pain intensity; PCS, Pain Catastrophizing Scale; BPI-REM, Affective Subscale of the Brief Pain Inventory; BPI-WAW, Active Subscale of the Brief Pain Inventory; TSK, Tampa Scale of Kinesiophobia; HADS-A, Hospital Anxiety and Depression Scale-Anxiety subscale; HADS-D, Hospital Anxiety and Depression Scale-Depression subscale; PHS, Physical Health Score; MHS, Mental Health Score; PROM, Patient Reported Outcome Measure. * p-value < 0.05.

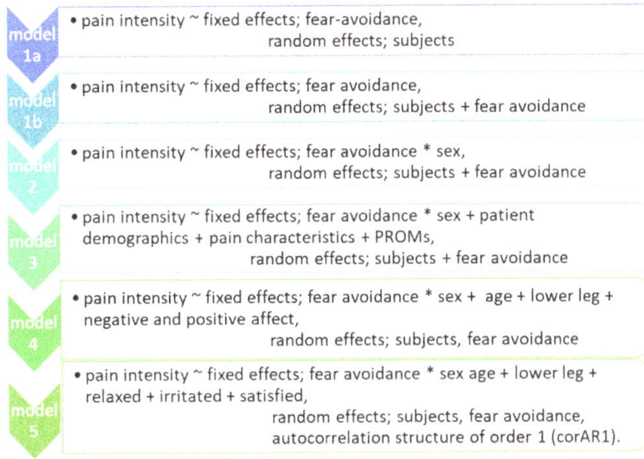

Figure 1. Construction of linear mixed-effects model applied to the data. ~ Separation of the dependent and independent variables. * Indicative of an interaction term and the original variables themselves.

3. Results

3.1. Description of the Sample

Initially, 217 patients indicated they were interested in the study and were therefore approached. Out of these 217 patients, 168 patients (77%) declined to participate after receiving all the information about the study procedures, whereas 49 patients (23%) provided informed consent. Three patients were excluded from analysis because their pain complaints were present for less than three months, and one patient was excluded due to missing data on sex at baseline. This resulted in a sample of 45 chronic pain patients, from which 13 (21%) were men and 32 (71%) women (Figure 2). The mean level of fear-avoidance (TSK) at baseline was significantly (p = 0.013) higher for men (39.6; SD ± 6.5) than for women (34.8; SD ± 5.2). Moreover, a high degree of fear-avoidance (TSK-score > 37) was also more frequently present in men (69%) than in women (38%), although not significantly different (p = 0.053). Mean pain intensity (NRS) was 6.8 (SD ± 1.9) for men and 7.3 (SD ± 1.6) for women (p = 0.391), indicating no statistically significant sex difference in pain intensity at baseline. Other baseline variables, as well as the p-values of the differences between men and women, are presented in Table 1.

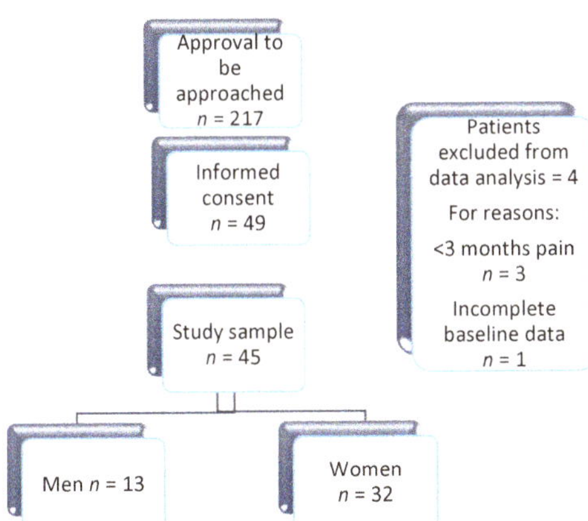

Figure 2. Flowchart of the study sample.

3.2. Sex Differences in the Association between Fear-Avoidance and Pain Intensity and the Influence of Affective States

The crude association between fear-avoidance and pain intensity had a coefficient of 0.17 (95% CI: 0.12, 0.22), $p = 0.000$, indicating that an increase in fear-avoidance of 1 unit was associated with an average pain increase of 0.17. The model that also included the interaction between fear-avoidance and sex showed that the association differed between men and women: the interaction term had a coefficient of 0.18 (95% CI: 0.05, 0.31), $p = 0.005$ (Table 2; model 2). For men, a 1-point increase in fear-avoidance was associated with a −0.02 decrease in pain intensity, whereas for women a 1-point increase in fear-avoidance was associated with a 0.18 increase in pain intensity (Table 2 and Figure 3).

Table 2. Unadjusted and adjusted model regarding sex differences in the association between fear-avoidance and pain intensity.

	Model 2 AIC = 4476.42			Model 5 [a] AIC = 4376.42		
	Estimate	CI	Sig.	Estimate	CI	Sig.
Intercept	9.08	6.47, 11.7	0.000 ***	9.52	6.86, 12,18	<0.001 ***
Fear-avoidance	−0.02	−0.12, 0.09	0.78	−0.04	−0.14, 0.06	0.48
Sex (men = 0; women = 1)	−0.53	−1.96, 0.89	0.45	−0.4	−1.82, 1.02	0.57
Fear-avoidance x sex	0.18	0.05,0.31	0.005 **	0.18	0.06, 0.30	0.003 **

Dependent variable: pain intensity; CI = confidence intervals; [a] Adjusted for baseline variables: age, lower leg and the emotions: relaxed ***, irritated *** and satisfied ***; ** p-value < 0.01; *** p-value < 0.001.

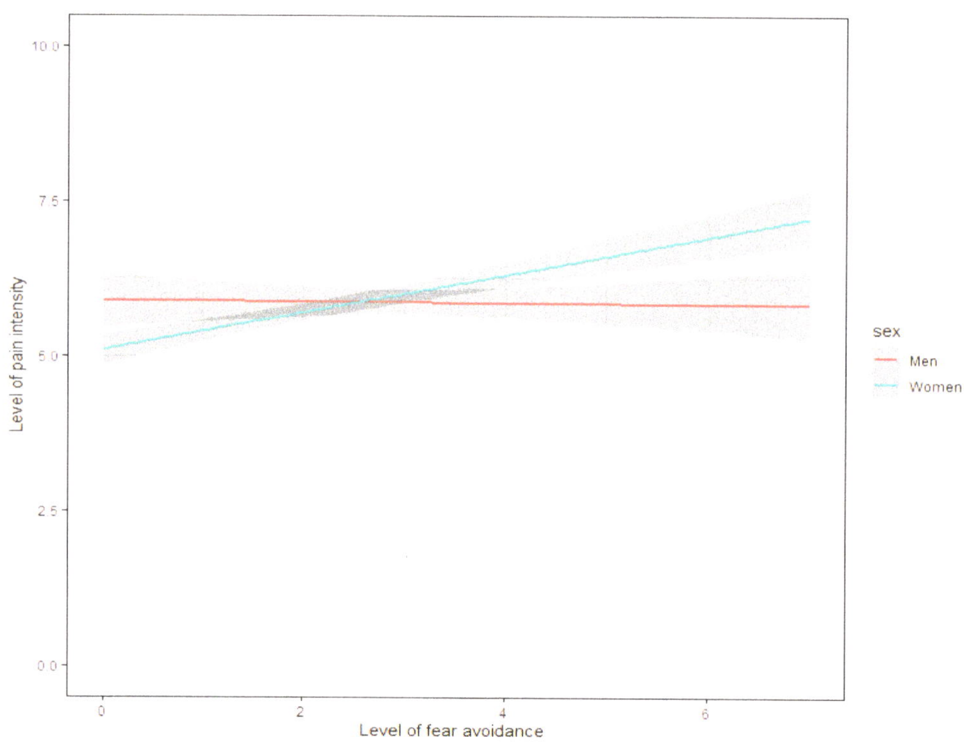

Figure 3. Visualization of the interaction between fear-avoidance and sex in relation to pain intensity. Note: the grey area is the 95% confidence interval of the estimates.

In the subsequent model, potential confounders were added. Backward stepwise elimination resulted in a model with the baseline variables 'age' and 'lower leg' and affective experiences 'relaxed', 'irritated', and 'satisfied' included (Table 2; model 5, and Figure 4). By adding the confounders, the association between fear-avoidance and pain intensity in the model with the interaction did not change considerably from a coefficient of −0.02 (95% CI: −0.12, 0.09) with a p-value of 0.78 to a coefficient of −0.04 (95% CI:−0.14, 0.05) with a p-value of 0.48. Although these three affective experiences all had a significant association with pain intensity, the estimate of the interaction term between fear-avoidance and sex did not change by adding affect to the model (Table 2; model 5).

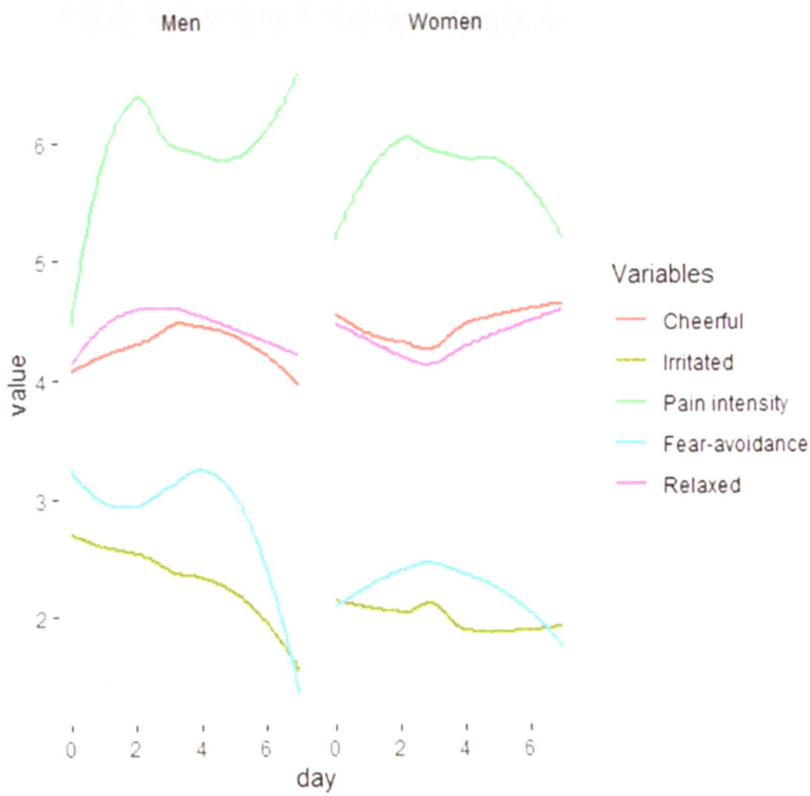

Figure 4. Visualization of the fluctuation of pain intensity, fear avoidance and affective experiences for men and women separately. Note: fear-avoidance and the affective experiences are measured on a 7-point Likert scale and pain intensity is measure on the eleven-point numeric rating scale. Each line represents the average of the 10 beeps per day per variable.

4. Discussion

4.1. Summary of Main Findings

To our knowledge, this is the first study using the experience sampling method to investigate sex differences in the association between fear-avoidance and pain intensity in chronic pain patients, including the potential confounding effect of affective experiences. Cross-sectional results demonstrated that men had on average more fear-avoidance than women. However, results from the longitudinal data of the ESM suggest that no association between fear-avoidance and pain intensity was found in men, whereas in women, an increase in fear-avoidance was associated with a (slight) increase in pain intensity. Nonetheless, affect did not confound these findings.

4.2. Differences in the Association of Fear-Avoidance and Pain Intensity

The fact that men had a higher mean TSK-score than women in the present study is consistent with the literature from previous cross-sectional studies that investigated sex differences in TSK-scores concerning chronic pain patients [24,25]. It remains debatable why male chronic pain patients tend to have more fear-avoidance than female patients, although it has been suggested that this could depend upon social norms, higher expectations or a deeper concern about losing work capacity or productivity as a result of re-injury [25]. However, the results of our study indicate that the tendency of having more fear-avoidance does not seem to influence pain intensity in men. Moreover, whether the increase in fear-avoidance in men at baseline influences (negatively) pain treatment outcomes remains unanswered.

4.3. Sex Differences in the Association between Fear-Avoidance and Pain Intensity

Both the unadjusted and adjusted model concerning the interaction between fear-avoidance and sex in relation to pain intensity showed that this interaction was significant, and hence, the association between fear avoidance and pain differs between men and women. The adjusted model was corrected for the affective experiences 'relaxed', 'irritated', and 'satisfied', but did not lead to a different conclusion. In the unadjusted and adjusted models, the association between fear-avoidance and pain intensity for men was negligible (0.02 and −0.04, respectively). In contrast, for women, the model demonstrated that the association between fear-avoidance and pain intensity was equal to a coefficient of 0.18 in both models (Table 2), indicating that increases in fear-avoidance were associated with (slight) increases in pain intensity. Whether this (small) association was clinically significant, it may yet be debated. We propose to further investigate if this association holds when applied to other pain populations, preferably with larger sample sizes and equal percentage of both sexes.

Ramirez et al. in 2014 [26] analyzed differences in pain experience between men and women in patients with spinal chronic pain and found a contrasting result, in that fear-avoidance was associated with pain intensity in men, but not in women. However, because of the cross-sectional design of the study the strength of the evidence is limited. Moreover, previous studies suggest that women are more sensitive to threat-related stimuli than men, and this would generally lead to an increased pain perception [6,27] and have greater catastrophic thoughts than men, which would generally lead to an increased pain perception. The results found in the present study are in line with these suggestions.

No previous studies have investigated the potential confounding effect of affective states on the association between fear-avoidance and pain intensity with the ESM. In a review by Baets et al. in 2019 the predictive moderating and mediating roles of emotional factors were examined on pain and disability following shoulder treatment [28]. A predictive role was found for fear-avoidance of pain and disability when surgical treatment was given, yet not when receiving physiotherapy. Moreover, this study indicated a moderating role for optimism in the relationship between catastrophizing and shoulder disability in patients receiving physiotherapy. However, this role was not found in the relationship between fear-avoidance and disability of the shoulder. The results of our ESM study specified that affect has a moderating effect on pain intensity itself, but not on the relationship between fear-avoidance and pain intensity. The statistically significant effect of positive affective experiences, such as feeling relaxed (−0.15, $p \leq 0.001$) and satisfied (−0.10, $p \leq 0.001$), on pain intensity itself may indicate that there is a potential role for positive affect, such as optimism, self-efficacy and positive expectations in future research and treatment [28,29].

4.4. Strengths and Limitations

The present study has a few important advantages. First, due to the use of the ESM, symptoms were assessed in the actual moment, eliminating the potential influence of recall and contextual biases, which is a common problem with traditional retrospective questionnaires [30,31]. Moreover, symptoms such as pain and fear, as well as affect, are likely to fluctuate over time [7]. Due to the many repeated measurements in ESM, these fluctuations could be captured, in contrast to cross-sectional studies. Because of these advantages and the low cost of the ESM method, it might be an attractive and effective method to use more often in future (clinical) studies, or even treatment trajectories, since ESM is feasible due to the widespread use of smartphones. Moreover, ESM may be applied as an additional tool in clinical practice to provide feedback as part of personalized pain intervention [32].

On the other hand, this study has a few limitations. First, seventy-two percent of the participants completed the full 6 days from the ESM examination-period, which resulted in 28% missing data. As experience sampling is time-consuming, these missed assessments were expected beforehand, and the repeating character of ESM accounts for, and decreases, the influence of missing data [33]. However, missed assessments might be a concern, as a sub-group of pain patients might have missed assessments as a consequence of their current mood or level of pain. This may have resulted in overestimation of functioning [9]. Moreover, the sample size in this study was rather small, with an especially low number of men. The percentage of 29% of men deviates from the 40% of men in the overall pain registry cohort DATA*PAIN* [22]. Accordingly, a lack of power could explain why no significant association was found between fear-avoidance and pain intensity for men. Many patients who initially indicated to be interested in the study chose not to participate after receiving all information about the study procedures (Figure 1). This indicates that ESM may be (too) burdensome, at least with the current number of questions and repeated measures. As the usability of ESM in chronic pain patients has not yet been validated, it remains difficult to conclude whether this method is suitable for the chronic pain population. Although momentary assessment is recommended in different somatic and psychiatric conditions, and the benefits of the ESM are becoming more and more apparent [34], it is important to perform more research about ESM and to evaluate its validity and reliability in chronic pain patients.

Fear-avoidance was assessed by the statement 'due to fear for (more) pain I did not make unnecessary movements since the last beep', asking the participant how the behavior of fear has influenced the level of movement since the last beep. As a result, a time frame is assessed between the afore-appointed beep until the actual beep, representing a lagged item. This was the main reason why we did not add a lagged model, as in our case that would be regressing two time points in time instead of one. Moreover, as mentioned before, no intention of causality was intended, meaning that the direction of predictor and outcome could have been reversed: an analysis we want to recommend for future research.

Furthermore, even though the dataset covered a vast number of relevant factors for chronic pain, some factors such as pain etiology were not accounted for at baseline, and other important factors such as pain catastrophizing were missing in the daily assessments, which could explain the sex differences found in our results.

5. Conclusions

The results in this study indicate that the association between fear-avoidance and pain intensity differs between men and women. For men, no association between these variables was found, whereas for women, an increase in fear-avoidance was associated with a (slight) increase in pain intensity. Affective experiences, however, did not confound the association between fear-avoidance and pain intensity in either men or women. Our findings support research highlighting the importance of sex differences in pain experience, which may be important for clinicians to consider for a more personalized pain management approach in chronic pain patients. Nevertheless, further research with a larger sample and equal numbers of sexes is needed to confirm these findings and their clinical implication.

Author Contributions: Conceptualization, N.d.M., B.B., C.L., R.L. and E.M.M.J.; methodology, N.d.M., B.B., R.L. and C.L.; formal analysis, S.M.J.v.K., S.W. and E.v.D.; investigation N.d.M., S.M.J.v.K., S.W. and E.v.D.; resources, N.d.M., B.B., C.L., R.L. and E.M.M.J.; data curation, S.M.J.v.K. and S.W.; writing—original draft preparation, E.v.D., S.W., S.M.J.v.K., N.d.M. and B.B.; writing—review and editing, E.v.D., S.W., S.M.J.v.K., N.d.M., B.B., R.L., C.L. and L.V.; visualization, S.W.; supervision, J.v.Z.; project administration, N.d.M.; funding acquisition, N.d.M. and B.B. All authors have read and agreed to the published version of the manuscript.

Funding: This research received no external funding.

Institutional Review Board Statement: The study was conducted in accordance with the Declaration of Helsinki, and approved by the Institutional Review Board of METC azM/UM (protocol code 2018-0955 and 19 January 2019).

Informed Consent Statement: Informed consent was obtained from all subjects involved in the study.

Data Availability Statement: All data relevant to the study are included in the article. Data can only be obtained by contacting the corresponding author.

Conflicts of Interest: The authors declare no conflict of interest.

References

1. Cohen, S.P.; Vase, L.; Hooten, W.M. Chronic pain: An update on burden, best practices, and new advances. *Lancet* **2021**, *397*, 2082–2097. [CrossRef]
2. Nugraha, B.; Gutenbrunner, C.; Barke, A.; Karst, M.; Schiller, J.; Schäfer, P.; Falter, S.; Korwisi, B.; Rief, W.; Treede, R.-D.; et al. The IASP classification of chronic pain for ICD-11: Functioning properties of chronic pain. *Pain* **2019**, *160*, 88–94. [CrossRef] [PubMed]
3. Vlaeyen, J.W.S.; Linton, S.J. Fear-avoidance and its consequences in chronic musculoskeletal pain: A state of the art. *Pain* **2000**, *85*, 317–332. [CrossRef]
4. Fillingim, R.B.; King, C.D.; Ribeiro-Dasilva, M.C.; Rahim-Williams, B.; Riley, J.L., III. Sex, Gender, and Pain: A Review of Recent Clinical and Experimental Findings. *J. Pain* **2009**, *10*, 447–485. [CrossRef] [PubMed]
5. Mogil, J.S. Sex differences in pain and pain inhibition: Multiple explanations of a controversial phenomenon. *Nat. Rev. Neurosci.* **2012**, *13*, 859–866. [CrossRef] [PubMed]
6. Rhudy, J.L.; Williams, A.E. Gender differences in pain: Do emotions play a role? *Gend. Med.* **2005**, *2*, 208–226. [CrossRef]
7. Myin-Germeys, I.; Kasanova, Z.; Vaessen, T.; Vachon, H.; Kirtley, O.; Viechtbauer, W.; Reininghaus, U. Experience sampling methodology in mental health research: New insights and technical developments. *World Psychiatry* **2018**, *17*, 123–132. [CrossRef]
8. Bair, M.J.; Robinson, R.L.; Katon, W.; Kroenke, K. Depression and pain comorbidity: A literature review. *Arch. Intern. Med.* **2003**, *163*, 2433–2445. [CrossRef]
9. Verhagen, S.J.W.; Hasmi, L.; Drukker, M.; van Os, J.; Delespaul, P.A.E.G. Use of the experience sampling method in the context of clinical trials: Table 1. *Évid. Based Ment. Health* **2016**, *19*, 86–89. [CrossRef]
10. Csikszentmihalyi, M. *Handbook of Research Methods for Studying Daily Life*; Guilford Press: New York, NY, USA, 2011.
11. Verhagen, S.J.W.; Berben, J.A.; Leue, C.; Marsman, A.; Delespaul, P.A.E.G.; van Os, J.; Lousberg, R. Demonstrating the reliability of transdiagnostic mHealth Routine Outcome Monitoring in mental health services using experience sampling technology. *PLoS ONE* **2017**, *12*, e0186294. [CrossRef]
12. Daniëls, N.E.M.; Hochstenbach, L.M.J.; van Bokhoven, M.A.; Beurskens, A.J.H.M.; Delespaul, P.A.E.G. Implementing Experience Sampling Technology for Functional Analysis in Family Medicine—A Design Thinking Approach. *Front. Psychol.* **2019**, *10*, 2782. [CrossRef] [PubMed]
13. Verhagen, S.J.W.; Daniëls, N.E.M.; Bartels, S.L.; Tans, S.; Borkelmans, K.W.H.; de Vugt, M.E.; Delespaul, P.A.E.G. Measuring within-day cognitive performance using the experience sampling method: A pilot study in a healthy population. *PLoS ONE* **2019**, *14*, e0226409. [CrossRef]
14. Crawford, J.R.; Henry, J.D. The Positive and Negative Affect Schedule (PANAS): Construct validity, measurement properties and normative data in a large non-clinical sample. *Br. J. Clin. Psychol.* **2004**, *43 Pt 3*, 245–265. [CrossRef] [PubMed]
15. Peeters, F.P.R. Affectiviteit en zelfbeoordeling van depressie en angst. *Tijdschr. Voor Psychiatr.* **1996**, *38*, 240–250.
16. Watson, D.; Clark, L.A.; Tellegen, A. Development and validation of brief measures of positive and negative affect: The PANAS scales. *J. Pers. Soc. Psychol.* **1988**, *54*, 1063–1070. [CrossRef]
17. Cleeland, C.S. *The Brief Pain Inventory User Guide*; The University of Texas MD Anderson Cancer Center: Houston, TX, USA, 2009; pp. 1–11.
18. Dworkin, R.H.; Turk, D.C.; Farrar, J.T.; Haythornthwaite, J.A.; Jensen, M.P.; Katz, N.P.; Kerns, R.D.; Stucki, G.; Allen, R.R.; Bellamy, N.; et al. Core outcome measures for chronic pain clinical trials: IMMPACT recommendations. *Pain* **2005**, *113*, 9–19. [CrossRef]

19. Hays, R.D.; Morales, L.S. The RAND-36 measure of health-related quality of life. *Ann. Med.* **2001**, *33*, 350–357. [CrossRef]
20. Stern, A.F. The Hospital Anxiety and Depression Scale. *Occup. Med.* **2014**, *64*, 393–394. [CrossRef]
21. Sullivan, M.J. *The Pain Catastrophizing Scale: User Manual*; McGill University: Montreal, QC, Canada, 2009; pp. 1–36.
22. Brouwer, B.; Waardenburg, S.; Jacobs, C.; Overdijk, M.; Leue, C.; Köke, A.; van Kuijk, S.; van Kleef, M.; Van Zundert, J.; de Meij, N. Biopsychosocial baseline values of 15,000 patients suffering from chronic pain: Dutch Data Pain study. *Reg. Anesth. Pain Med.* **2020**, *45*, 774–782. [CrossRef]
23. Vlaeyen, J.W.; Kole-Snijders, A.M.; Boeren, R.G.; van Eek, H. Fear of movement/(re)injury in chronic low back pain and its relation to behavioral performance. *Pain* **1995**, *62*, 363–372. [CrossRef]
24. Bränström, H.; Fahlström, M. Kinesiophobia in patients with chronic musculoskeletal pain: Differences between men and women. *J. Rehabil. Med.* **2008**, *40*, 375–380. [CrossRef] [PubMed]
25. Rovner, G.S.; Sunnerhagen, K.S.; Björkdahl, A.; Gerdle, B.; Börsbo, B.; Johansson, F.; Gillanders, D. Chronic pain and sex-differences; women accept and move, while men feel blue. *PLoS ONE* **2017**, *12*, e0175737. [CrossRef] [PubMed]
26. Ramírez-Maestre, C.; Esteve, R. The Role of Sex/Gender in the Experience of Pain: Resilience, Fear, and Acceptance as Central Variables in the Adjustment of Men and Women with Chronic Pain. *J. Pain* **2014**, *15*, 608–618.e1. [CrossRef] [PubMed]
27. Ramírez-Maestre, C.; Martínez, A.E.L.; Zarazaga, R.E. Personality characteristics as differential variables of the pain experience. *J. Behav. Med.* **2004**, *27*, 147–165. [CrossRef] [PubMed]
28. De Baets, L.; Matheve, T.; Meeus, M.; Struyf, F.; Timmermans, A. The influence of cognitions, emotions and behavioral factors on treatment outcomes in musculoskeletal shoulder pain: A systematic review. *Clin. Rehabil.* **2019**, *33*, 980–991. [CrossRef]
29. Huber, M.; van Vliet, M.; Giezenberg, M.; Winkens, B.; Heerkens, Y.; Dagnelie, P.C.; Knottnerus, J.A. Towards a 'patient-centred' operationalisation of the new dynamic concept of health: A mixed methods study. *BMJ Open* **2016**, *6*, e010091. [CrossRef]
30. Mujagic, Z.; Leue, C.; Vork, L.; Lousberg, R.; Jonkers, D.M.A.E.; Keszthelyi, D.; Hesselink, M.A.; Van Schagen, T.J.C.; Van Os, J.; Masclee, A.A.M.; et al. The Experience Sampling Method—A new digital tool for momentary symptom assessment in IBS: An exploratory study. *Neurogastroenterol. Motil.* **2015**, *27*, 1295–1302. [CrossRef]
31. Shiffman, S.; Stone, A.A.; Hufford, M.R. Ecological momentary assessment. *Annu. Rev. Clin. Psychol.* **2008**, *4*, 1–3. [CrossRef]
32. van Os, J.; Verhagen, S.; Marsman, A.; Peeters, F.; Bak, M.; Marcelis, M.; Drukker, M.; Reininghaus, U.; Jacobs, N.; Lataster, T.; et al. The experience sampling method as an mHealth tool to support self-monitoring, self-insight, and personalized health care in clinical practice. *Depress. Anxiety* **2017**, *34*, 481–493. [CrossRef]
33. Vork, L.; Mujagic, Z.; Drukker, M.; Keszthelyi, D.; Conchillo, J.M.; Hesselink, M.A.M.; Van Os, J.; Masclee, A.A.M.; Leue, C.; Kruimel, J.W. The Experience Sampling Method—Evaluation of treatment effect of escitalopram in IBS with comorbid panic disorder. *Neurogastroenterol. Motil.* **2019**, *31*, e13515. [CrossRef]
34. Stone, A.A.; Obbarius, A.; Junghaenel, D.U.; Wen, C.K.; Schneider, S. High-resolution, field approaches for assessing pain: Ecological Momentary Assessment. *Pain* **2021**, *162*, 4–9. [CrossRef] [PubMed]

Journal of
Clinical Medicine

MDPI

Review

The Importance of Nutrition as a Lifestyle Factor in Chronic Pain Management: A Narrative Review

Ömer Elma [1,2], Katherine Brain [3,4,†] and Huan-Ji Dong [5,*,†]

1 Pain in Motion International Research Group, Department of Physiotherapy, Human Physiology and Anatomy, Faculty of Physical Education & Physiotherapy, Vrije Universiteit Brussel, 1090 Brussels, Belgium
2 Department of Physical Medicine and Physiotherapy, University Hospital Brussels, 1090 Brussels, Belgium
3 School of Health Science, College of Health, Medicine and Wellbeing, University of Newcastle, Callaghan, NSW 2308, Australia
4 Hunter Integrated Pain Service, Newcastle, NSW 2300, Australia
5 Pain and Rehabilitation Centre, Department of Health, Medicine and Caring Sciences, Linköping University, SE-581 85 Linköping, Sweden
* Correspondence: huanji.dong@liu.se
† These authors contributed equally to this work.

Abstract: In everyday clinical practice, healthcare professionals often meet chronic pain patients with a poor nutritional status. A poor nutritional status such as malnutrition, unhealthy dietary behaviors, and a suboptimal dietary intake can play a significant role in the occurrence, development, and prognosis of chronic pain. The relationship between nutrition and chronic pain is complex and may involve many underlying mechanisms such as oxidative stress, inflammation, and glucose metabolism. As such, pain management requires a comprehensive and interdisciplinary approach that includes nutrition. Nutrition is the top modifiable lifestyle factor for chronic non-communicable diseases including chronic pain. Optimizing one's dietary intake and behavior needs to be considered in pain management. Thus, this narrative review reports and summarizes the existing evidence regarding (1) the nutrition-related health of people experiencing pain (2) the underlying potential mechanisms that explain the interaction between nutrition and chronic pain, and (3) the role of nutrition screening, assessment and evaluation for people experiencing pain and the scope of nutrition practice in pain management. Future directions in the nutrition and chronic pain field are also discussed.

Keywords: diet; nutrition; nutrition recommendation; chronic pain

Citation: Elma, Ö.; Brain, K.; Dong, H.-J. The Importance of Nutrition as a Lifestyle Factor in Chronic Pain Management: A Narrative Review. *J. Clin. Med.* **2022**, *11*, 5950. https://doi.org/10.3390/jcm11195950

Academic Editors: Carmen María Galvez Sánchez, Casandra I. Montoro Aguilar and Markus W. Hollmann

Received: 18 August 2022
Accepted: 5 October 2022
Published: 9 October 2022

1. Introduction

Chronic pain, as defined by The International Association for the Study of Pain (IASP), is pain that persists or recurs for more than 3 months [1]. Chronic pain is a serious health issue, affecting approximately 20% of adults worldwide and it is anticipated that this will continue to increase alongside the growing and ageing population [1]. There is also a significant socioeconomic burden associated with chronic pain, including high health care use and costs, high absenteeism, loss of productivity, functional impairment, and disability [2]. Due to the complexity of chronic pain and its comorbidities, both evidence and clinical practice have guided the development of integrative pain management, from monodisciplinary to multidisciplinary treatments and from multidisciplinary treatments to interdisciplinary programs, based on a biopsychosocial approach [3–5].

An accumulating body of evidence suggests that poor nutrition, such as malnutrition, unhealthy dietary behaviors, and a poor dietary intake can play a significant role in the occurrence, prognosis, and maintenance of chronic non-cancer pain, hereafter described as chronic pain [4,6,7]. Unhealthy dietary behaviors and a poor dietary intake is characterized by the limited intake of core nutrient-rich foods and an excessive intake of energy-dense nutrient poor foods [8]. The role of nutrition as an important lifestyle factor in pain management is gaining more attention. Over the past two decades, nutrition has occasionally been acknowledged by pain organizations, health care professionals, and consumers, and the interest in the role of nutrition in pain management has grown significantly. In a submission to the European Parliament in 2001, poor appetite and nutrition were listed, amongst others, as a burden associated with chronic pain [9]. In 2013, a qualitative study conducted by Chronic Pain Australia, an organization representing consumers experiencing pain, reported that individuals wanted more information on nutrition and pain management [10]. In 2015, Australia's Faculty of Pain Management acknowledged that dietitians should provide input into patient care, where necessary [11]. Nutrition was also a major focus in the Consortium Pain Task Force White Paper, in 2018 [12]. More recently, in 2020, the IASP recognized the importance of optimizing one's dietary intake in pain management strategies based on a large body of evidence, which indicated the significant effect of nutrition-based interventions on pain reduction [13,14].

Despite the growing evidence regarding the role and integration of nutrition in chronic pain management, it is still unclear how nutritional factors interact with chronic pain, the exact nature of the underlying mechanisms of this interaction, and how the nutritional care process can be implemented in chronic pain management. Thus, the aim of this narrative review is to summarize the existing evidence regarding (1) the nutrition-related health of people experiencing pain (2) the underlying potential mechanisms that explain the interaction between nutrition and chronic pain, and (3) the role of nutrition screening, assessment and evaluation for people experiencing pain, and the scope of nutrition practice in pain management.

2. Searching Methods and Results

2.1. Searching Methods

To answer the three aims of this narrative review, the existing literature was screened in an unsystematic way by three reviewers (O.E., K.B., and H.-J.D.). Each author used three online databases; PubMed, Web of Science, and Google Scholar and ensured the search was conducted no later than the 1 August 2022. Three different groups of search terms were used for each of the three study aims. Search terms can be found in Table 1. Additionally, the authors conducted forward and backward tracking of the included articles to identify studies via the reference lists or citations. Both experimental and observational studies published in English were included in the review. Studies published prior to 2000, abstracts, posters and flyers, conference proceedings, and unpublished papers were not included in the study. Studies where the full text was unavailable were also excluded.

In addition, an unsystematic search of two databases: Medline and CINAHL, as well as the European Society of Clinical Nutrition and Metabolism (ESPEN) guidelines and Practice-based Evidence in Nutrition (PEN), was conducted in July 2022 by K.B. The aim of this search was to identify the existing guidelines relating to the nutritional management of chronic pain. Search terms included the following MESH headings ("practice guideline or guideline"; "diet, food and nutrition") and key words ("chronic pain, fibromyalgia, arthritis, back pain, musculoskeletal pain, and migraine disorders").

2.2. Searching Results

Once the search on the PubMed, Web of Science, and Google Scholar databases was completed, a total of 1400 articles were identified. In total 112 eligible articles were identified and included in the paper. The full texts of two eligible studies were not available and the corresponding authors did not respond to the request for the full text [15,16]. The findings were analyzed based on the three study aims: the nutrition-related health of people experiencing pain, the underlying potential mechanisms that explain the interaction between nutrition and chronic pain, and the role of nutrition screening, assessment, and evaluation for people experiencing pain, and the scope of nutrition practice in pain management.

Table 1. Search Terms.

Search Terms for the "The Nutrition-Related Health of People Experiencing Pain"	
Pain	"Chronic Pain"; "Myalgia"; "Fibromyalgia"; "Arthritis"; "Osteoarthritis"; "Headache"; "Migraine"
Nutrition	"Diet"; "Dietary Pattern"; "Eating Behavior"; "Nutrition"; "Malnutrition"; "Underweight"; "Obesity"; "Overweight"; "Fat Mass"
Search terms for the "The underlying potential mechanisms that explain the interaction between nutrition and chronic pain"	
Pain	"Chronic Pain"; "Myalgia"; "Fibromyalgia"; "Arthritis"; "Osteoarthritis"; "Headache"; "Migraine"
Nutrition	"Diet"; "Dietary Pattern"; "Eating Behavior"; "Nutrition"; "Obesity"; "Overweight"; "Fat Mass"
Mechanism	"Metabolism"; "Inflammation"; "Oxidative Stress"; "* genetics"
Search terms for the "The role of nutrition screening, assessment, and evaluation of chronic pain patients and the scope of nutrition practice in the pain management process	
Pain	"Chronic Pain"; "Myalgia"; "Fibromyalgia"; "Arthritis"; "Osteoarthritis"; "Headache"; "Migraine"
Nutrition	"Diet"; "Nutrition"; "Food"; "Dietary Pattern"; "Eating Behavior"; "Dietary Assessment"; "Gastrointestinal Symptoms"

* Wildcard represents unknown characters and identify word combinations by filling in automatically.

Following the searches on Medline and CINAHL for the guidelines related to nutrition and pain management, 112 articles were identified. None of the identified articles provided relevant information about the guidelines related to nutrition and pain. One article provided conditional recommendations and an evidence based decision aid for the use of specific dietary ingredients in chronic musculoskeletal pain [17]. However, the population of interest in this article was the United States military, which limits the generalizability of the findings to the general population. The search results from Practice-based Evidence in Nutrition (PEN) identified 32 practice guideline toolkits, of which seven corresponded to pain-related conditions such as osteoarthritis, musculoskeletal/connective tissue disorders, irritable bowel syndrome, rheumatoid arthritis, interstitial cystitis, inflammatory bowel disease, and spinal cord injury but there were no guidelines for chronic pain [18]. Of the 54 ESPEN guidelines, none were related to chronic pain [19].

3. The Nutrition-Related Health of People Experiencing Pain

Identifying the nutrition-related health and clinical features of people experiencing chronic pain is important for effective pain management. Malnutrition, or poor nutrition, is a health condition that occurs when an adequate nutrition cannot be acquired. An insufficient supply or consumption of nutrition (undernutrition) can lead to a person becoming underweight, while an oversupply or excessive consumption of nutrition (overnutrition) can lead to a person becoming overweight or obese. In this section, the associations between malnutrition, weight, dietary habits, and chronic pain will be discussed.

3.1. Underweight, Overweight, and Obesity

Population-based studies suggest that there is a higher prevalence of chronic pain amongst people with an unhealthy weight (i.e., underweight, overweight, or obese), compared to those who are of a healthy weight [20–22]. Underweight is defined as a body weight below the healthy weight range, while overweight and obesity are defined as an excessive and abnormal increase in white adipose tissue. The body mass index (BMI) is a weight-for-height index (kg/m^2), which is commonly used to classify the weight status in adults. A BMI of less than 18.5 kg/m^2 is defined as underweight, between 25.0 kg/m^2 and 29.9 kg/m^2 is defined as overweight and over 30 kg/m^2 is considered obese. Obesity also consists of three subclasses: class I (30–34.9 kg/m^2), class II (35–39.9 kg/m^2), and class III ($\geq$40 kg/m^2). There are limitations associated with the BMI as it does not take into account ethnicity or body composition such as fat and muscle mass. It also does not factor in the biological, physical, economic, psychological, and social aspects that contribute to weight status. Therefore, it is important to ensure that health professionals use a holistic approach to measuring health and do not rely on weight and the BMI alone.

There is a significant focus on excessive weight and chronic pain, but it is essential to highlight that being underweight is also associated with chronic pain. The electronic Persistent Pain Outcome Collaboration (ePPOC), an Australian initiative, synthesises a standard set of data from participating chronic pain services in Australia and New Zealand. In 2020, the ePPOC reported that 2% of the 20,000 patients seeking pain management were underweight, 32% were overweight, and 39% were obese [23]. Undernutrition may also occur amongst adolescents with chronic pain and eating disorders, especially those who experience gastrointestinal issues, anxiety, and a greater functional disability [24,25]. Importantly, malnutrition and frailty are common contributors and are consequences of chronic pain. Malnutrition occurs when, over time, a person consumes too many or too few nutrients to meet their nutritional needs. This can cause adverse effects on the body, how it functions, and lead to poor health outcomes, such as a reduced life expectancy and quality of life [26]. Malnutrition may occur by not eating enough, not eating the right foods, or being unable to absorb nutrients. In Australia, up to 50% of older adults (>65 years) are malnourished or at an increased risk of malnutrition [27]. A moderate-high risk of malnutrition has also been reported by other studies conducted in different countries [28–30]. The evidence suggests that those experiencing hip and knee pain are at an increased risk of sarcopenia (a form of malnutrition where the loss of muscle mass occurs) and falls [31–33]. Pain can also impact the sensory pleasure related to food which may lead to a decrease in satiety and an increased risk of malnutrition [34]. Frailty is characterised by a decline in physical, mental, and multisystem functions and can be described as a multidimensional state of depleted physiological and psychosocial conditions [35]. A serious consequence of frailty is the increased risk of disability and death from minor external stresses, such as a mild infection or facing a stressful event [36,37]. For older adults in particular, frailty is a severe consequence related to malnutrition and chronic pain [30,38], which can predict future adverse health outcomes, such as falls and physical disability, as well as hospitalization and even mortality [36]. A recent systematic review pooled the findings from 12 cross-sectional and 12 longitudinal studies in a meta-analysis and found that older people (>60 years) with chronic pain were almost two times more likely to develop frailty after an average follow up of 5.8 years, compared to those without chronic pain [39].

The western lifestyle and diet are contributing factors impacting the global development of overnutrition, or excess weight (overweight and obesity) [40]. At the population level, overweight and obesity may explain the rising trends in chronic pain amongst middle-aged adults [41]. An Australian longitudinal study of an elderly cohort reported a relationship between fat mass, the BMI, and pain [42]. This trend has also been confirmed in the clinical populations. For example, it was found that over 25% of chronic pain patients had a comorbidity of obesity [43], much higher than the general population in Sweden [44]. The prevalence was even higher in Australia. Up to 45% of patients from a tertiary pain clinic were classed as obese [45]. Undernutrition, on the other hand, is most common among older patients [30,38,46] as well as patients with orofacial pain [47] or functional gastrointestinal disorders [48,49]. Large clinical cohort studies identified that obese patients had, in general, a worse pain profile than the normal weight patients, for example, a higher pain intensity, an increased pain interference, and more constant pain [43,50].

Recent evidence has acknowledged the importance of nutritional factors affecting specific pain conditions. For example, studies exploring fibromyalgia have demonstrated that overweight or obese patients experienced more pain, impaired function, had higher levels of depression, and medication use than patients who were normal weight [51,52].

Underweight, overweight, and obesity coexist with chronic pain due to the nutrition-related underlying mechanisms. There is an interrelationship between the nutritional status, chronic pain pathophysiology, and eating behaviors. Diet profoundly impacts the body and has a complex relationship with the pain experience [4,13]. Dietary intervention (i.e., diet patterns and eating behaviors) has also been identified as one of the integrative treatments to alleviate chronic pain [4,53]. According to the existing evidence, common chronic pain conditions have been associated with nutritional factors, such as osteoarthritis [54], rheumatic arthritis [55], fibromyalgia [56], back pain [57], irritable bowel syndrome (IBS) [49], pelvic pain (e.g., endometriosis) [58], diabetic neuropathy [59], migraine headache [60], post-herpetic neuralgia [61], and carpal tunnel syndrome [62]. A summary of common pain locations related to over- and undernutrition are shown in Figure 1. Multiple site pain conditions and spreading pain conditions, such as myofascial pain syndrome and fibromyalgia are not illustrated in the figure. Based on the IASP classification of chronic pain [63], these pain conditions may not always belong to one category (nociceptive, nociplastic, or neuropathic pain), depending on the grading of the predominant central sensitization [64,65].

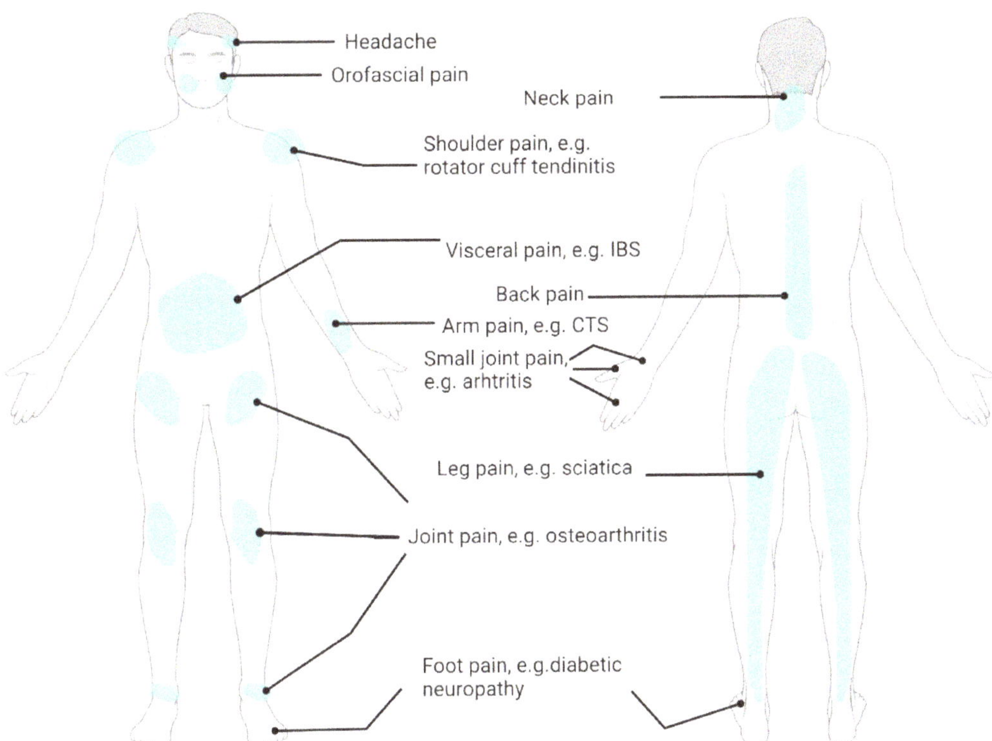

Figure 1. Pain Sites Related to Poor Nutrition. IBS: Irritable Bowel Syndrome; CTS: Carpal Tunnel Syndrome.

Poor nutrition not only impacts chronic pain pathophysiology, but also impacts other health outcome measures. For instance, compared with non-obese patients, obese patients with chronic pain had more physical limitations [66,67], a lower psychological wellbeing [68], more sleep disturbances [69,70], a poor health-related quality of life (HRQoL) [71], and a function dependence [72,73]. Multiple physical and/or mental diseases also frequently coexist with chronic pain, such as type 2 diabetes, cardiovascular disease or metabolic syndrome, anxiety (or post-traumatic stress syndrome), and depression [21,74]. These conditions can be modified using nutrition-related treatments.

3.2. Eating Behaviors and Dietary Preferences in People Experiencing Chronic Pain

Optimal dietary and nutrient intake are essential elements of musculoskeletal health. In addition to weight changes, a suboptimal nutrient intake and poor eating behaviors can cause altered serum nutrient levels, which can be observed among the patients with chronic pain. For instance, high levels of serum glutamate and aspartate were reported in patients with chronic migraine, orofacial pain, fibromyalgia, and complex regional pain syndrome [75–78]. Low levels of nutrients are also commonly recognized, such as vitamin D, omega-3 polyunsaturated fatty acid, vitamin B12, magnesium, zinc, ferritin, selenium, and folic acid [56,79]. Although, these studies do not draw conclusive and direct links with the aetiology of chronic pain, it is anticipated that chronic pain patients may have altered eating behaviors, either before the onset of pain or during the development of pain.

There is also an association between a suboptimal dietary intake and some pain conditions, such as irritable bowel syndrome (IBS) and pelvic pain syndromes [80,81]. Some special but diverse dietary triggers have been reported by headache patients (particularly migraines) [60]. It is also suggested that people experiencing pain generally consume more calories, added sugars, saturated fatty acids, sodium, and caffeine. This association has been demonstrated in a cross-sectional study that found one third of males and approximately half of female participants were consuming more than the recommended daily caloric intake, moderate fat intake, and a high saturated fat intake [82]. This study also showed that the intake of vitamin D, vitamin E, and magnesium, in people experiencing chronic pain, was lower than the recommended daily intake. Data from the British Birth Cohort Study has been analyzed and showed that women with chronic pain were more likely to decrease their intake of fruit and vegetables, and increase their high fatty foods consumption over time, compared to women without chronic pain [83]. The low intake of micronutrients has also been reported in another patient population with rheumatoid arthritis [84]. Another study observed that obese osteoarthritis patients had an increased calorie, fat, and sugar intake and this impacted on their pain severity [85]. Additionally, for patients with undernutrition, pain experiences could be accompanied by a loss of appetite and a decreased food intake [24,25,86,87]. This could lead to a poor dietary intake or absorption of nutrients (i.e., medications that affect gastrointestinal functions [87]) and subsequently a decreased fat free mass and impaired physical and mental functions (i.e., daily functioning and cognitive functions [86]).

4. The Underlying Potential Mechanisms That Explain the Interaction between Nutrition and Chronic Pain

The interaction between nutrition and chronic pain is bidirectional. However, it is not clear how nutritional factors interact with the pain generating mechanisms and the potential mechanisms that contribute to this relationship. Identifying and understanding these mechanisms can potentially increase the effectiveness of nutrition assessments and treatments in chronic pain management. The potential action mechanisms of the nutritional factors in chronic pain management have been identified and illustrated in Figure 2.

4.1. Inflammation and Oxidative Stress

Oxidative stress is defined as an increase in the reactive oxygen species produced as a byproduct of oxygen metabolism and a decrease in the ability of antioxidative compounds to detoxify cells and tissues. In addition to other factors (e.g., radiation, smoking, air pollution), dietary induced oxidative stress is one factor that can initiate and contribute to the immune cell activation and inflammation [88]. The immune cell activation, followed by a rise in oxygen consumption, also raises the amount of reactive oxygen species which can create an oxidative stress—inflammation cycle [88]. Thus, it is possible to say that the consequence of oxidative stress becomes its cause. The decreased antioxidative and detoxifying ability of the body can play a role in inflammation induced pain mechanisms [89]. Inversely, there is some evidence that an increased dietary antioxidant intake and the increased detoxifying ability of the body can alleviate pain among a chronic musculoskeletal pain population [90]. In the latest pain research, it is known that inflammation can interact with various pain mechanisms including nociceptive (pain arising due to activation of nociceptors), neuropathic (pain arising due to direct damage to the peripheral and central nervous system), and nociplastic (altered nociceptive system despite the absence of a clear nociceptive and neuropathic input) pain mechanisms [91].

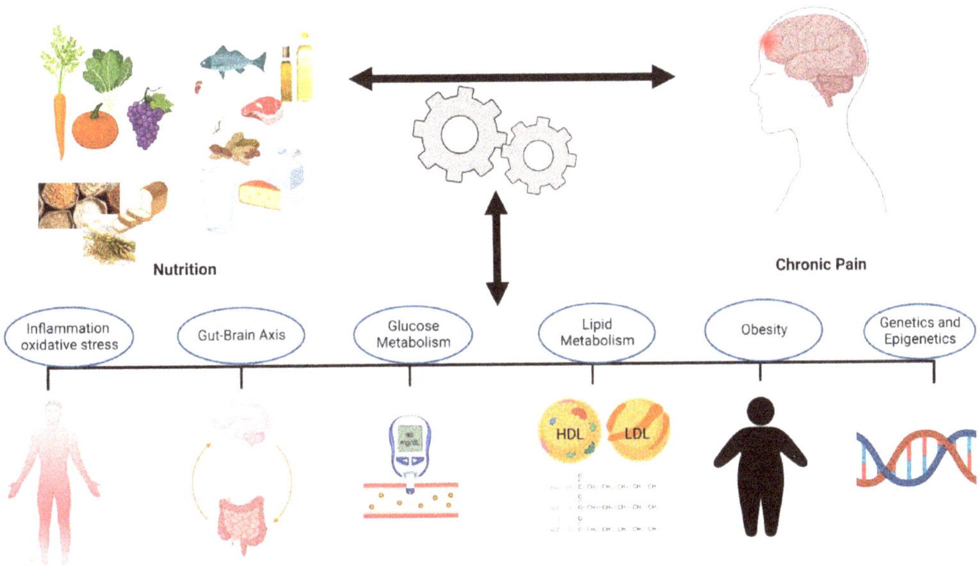

Figure 2. Potential Mechanisms of the Interaction Between Nutrition and Chronic Pain.

Inflammation is the body's immediate, natural, and protective response against infections and injuries. Physiologically, inflammatory processes, as a part of the immune reactions, are regulated by time. A late or prolonged inflammatory response might lose its protective effectiveness. A persistent proinflammatory state has been identified as an important risk factor for several pathophysiological conditions, including atherosclerosis, cardiovascular diseases, diabetes mellitus, obesity, cancer, and chronic pain [92]. Chronic and uncontrolled inflammation can be harmful and can lead to many acute and chronic diseases, including maintenance, occurrence, and prognosis of chronic pain [92]. This finding is supported by several pain studies on the immune system. To exemplify, immune cells evoke pain via the stimulation of nociceptors, changes in neuronal structures, and sensitization of the peripheral and central nervous systems via the release of inflammatory biomarkers [91,93].

Neuroinflammation is a localized inflammatory response that occurs in the peripheral and central nervous system [91]. In chronic pain conditions, neuroinflammation is characterized with the glial cell activation and an increased production of inflammatory biomarkers which can lead to peripheral and central nervous system sensitization [91]. Abnormal central nervous system glial cell activity has been reported in chronic pain conditions, especially nociplastic-related conditions, such as chronic non-specific low back pain, fibromyalgia, migraine, and spinal radiculopathy [94].

4.2. Microbiota-Gut-Brain Axis

Gut microbiota plays an important role in the human body and contributes to many structural, protective, and metabolic functions [95]. Thus, gut health constitutes an essential place in the maintenance of general health. The gut and brain have a bidirectional communication pathway and the intestinal microbiota has a modulating effect on this gut-brain axis [96]. The evidence shows that this link occurs through the connection between the vagus nerve and brainstem, via spinal afferents to the spinal cord [96]. Diversity of the gut microbiota is influenced by various factors, including medication use, mental health, infection, and nutrition which can lead to the dysregulation of the gut microbiota [97,98]. Dysregulation of the microbiota-gut-brain axis has been identified among various pathologic conditions, such as inflammatory bowel disease, diabetes, obesity, autism, depression, and chronic pain [97,98]. The accumulating evidence shows that the interrelation between nutrition and the microbiota-gut-brain axis can have a modulating effect in acute and chronic pain pathophysiology [97,98].

Microbes residing in the gut can be modified by nutritional factors. Thus, the microbiota-gut-brain axis has been identified as a target for nutritional interventions [99]. The differences in the diversity of the microbiome among the various populations that follow certain dietary patterns, such as vegetarian, vegan, and omnivorous diets, has been well documented [100]. Energy dense, unhealthy, proinflammatory dietary patterns that are nutrient poor and high in unsaturated fats, refined carbohydrates, and low in fruits and vegetables can cause a diet induced inflammation in the gut [94]. Proinflammatory cytokines released in response to unhealthy dietary patterns, activate the vagus nerve receptors located in the gastrointestinal tract. Upon activation, the vagus nerve can trigger the glial cell activation and the neuroinflammation process in the central nervous system [94]. Peripheral and central proinflammatory responses, including the aberrant glial cell activity, contribute to the maintenance, occurrence, and prognosis of chronic pain [94]. Targeting the gut microbiota with nutritional interventions in chronic pain populations is a promising approach for pain management.

4.3. Disturbed Glucose Metabolism

Diabetes has been reported as an important risk factor for chronic pain. In addition to neuropathic pain, chronic non-neuropathic pain conditions, such as fibromyalgia, chronic wide-spread pain, chronic low back, and neck pain are more common among people with diabetes, compared to people without diabetes, especially amongst those who have poorly controlled diabetes [101,102]. Patients with chronic musculoskeletal pain have been identified as having a disturbed glucose metabolism, including an increased fasting glucose level, an increased insulin resistance, a higher postprandial glycemic response, and a higher prevalence of type-2 diabetes mellitus [103]. A well-known antihyperglycemic medicine, metformin, which is commonly used to treat type-2 diabetes has also shown it can significantly alleviate pain in chronic pain populations and thus could be a potential treatment for people experiencing chronic pain [104].

An excessive carbohydrate intake and a decrease in glucose metabolism efficiency can increase reactive oxygen species and evoke an oxidative stress response [105]. The oxidative stress response is an endogenous factor that can activate toll like receptors and initiate inflammatory reactions in the peripheral and central nervous systems [105]. Thus, the identification of a disrupted glucose metabolism and targeting glucose regulation constitute significant places in chronic pain management [105]. Studies exploring the effect of low-carbohydrate diets, including the ketogenic diet, have revealed promising results including improvements in the glucose metabolism [106]. In another study, people with chronic musculoskeletal pain, who followed a low carbohydrate diet, had a decrease in serum inflammatory biomarkers and pain sensitivity [107]. Studies that explored the action mechanism of a ketogenic diet on chronic pain suggested that the carbohydrate intake played a role in neuroinflammation and central sensitization [108]. However, it is also important to consider the weight reducing effect of low-carbohydrate diets. A decrease in adipose tissue may also improve pain sensitivity in chronic pain populations and therefore, obesity requires special attention in terms of its role in the interaction between nutrition and pain generating mechanisms [6,109].

4.4. Disrupted Lipid Metabolism

Lipids are essential for several bodily functions, and are one of the body's main energy sources. Nutrition strategies, including the modification of single nutrients, supplements, or overall eating patterns, can affect serum lipid profiles in both positive and negative ways. To exemplify, an excessive intake of saturated fats, dietary fructose, and an overall western style of eating increases low-density lipoprotein (LDL), triglycerides, and decreases high-density lipoprotein (HDL). A high LDL cholesterol level increases the risk of cardiovascular disease (CVD) and is commonly known as "bad cholesterol", while a high HDL cholesterol level is protective, reduces the risk of CVD, and is often referred to as "good cholesterol". Omega-3 unsaturated fatty acids, antioxidants, intermittent fasting, and adherence to the Mediterranean diet, can have the reverse effects on the same lipid biomarkers [110–114].

A disrupted lipid metabolism also plays a role in various health conditions, such as atherosclerosis, diabetes, cardiovascular diseases, metabolic syndrome, and obesity. [115]. The role of a disrupted lipid metabolism in chronic pain is gaining more attention and targeting this mechanism via dietary factors is a promising approach for chronic pain management. For instance, low back pain has been found to be prevalent among individuals with a decreased lumbar blood supply [116]. The relationship between the decreased lumbar blood supply and spinal pain constitutes a base for the atherosclerosis theory of the persistent non-specific low back pain. Prevalence of low back pain has been found inversely associated with the serum HDL cholesterol and positively associated with serum triglycerides and LDL cholesterol, which overall contribute to the atherosclerosis hypothesis [116,117]. Additionally, compared to healthy controls, fibromyalgia patients have shown a disrupted serum lipid profile and this disruption was found to be positively associated with pain sensitivity [118]. In a systematic review, the biomarkers of the serum lipid metabolism, including the decreased serum HDL cholesterol, the increased serum LDL cholesterol, and triglycerides, was found to be strongly associated with musculoskeletal pain arising from tendinopathy [119].

4.5. Obesity/Overweight

Obesity is associated with a proinflammatory state and is an important risk factor for various metabolic changes and chronic diseases, including cardiovascular diseases, cancer, diabetes mellitus, and chronic pain [109,120,121]. The existing evidence suggests that there is a concurrence and bidirectional relationship between obesity and chronic pain [109]. Obesity has been associated with several chronic musculoskeletal pain conditions including osteoarthritis, fibromyalgia, pelvic pain, and chronic low back pain [122]. It has been hypothesized that overweight/obesity play an important role in chronic pain by two main mechanisms; first increasing the mechanical load on neuromusculoskeletal structures and second, initiating or contributing to neuroimmune reactions, namely chronic low grade systemic inflammation [123].

Increased adipocytes and adipose tissue are positively associated with increased macrophages and promote inflammatory responses such as an increase in inflammatory cytokines (IL-6, TNF-alpha) and acute phase proteins (CRP) [124]. Excessive adipose tissue also increases the relocation of inflammatory cytokines into the central nervous system and promotes the activation of glial cells which can eventually play a role in nociplastic pain [125].

Exposure to high saturated fat and energy dense dietary patterns increase the circulated inflammatory cytokine levels. An in vivo study using an animal model suggests that exposure to a diet rich in saturated fat for one day causes the glial cell activation for two weeks in rats [126]. Dietary patterns that restrict the caloric intake have been shown to relieve pain in people with chronic musculoskeletal pain [127].

4.6. Epigenetic Factors

Epigenetics can be explained as a change in the gene expression without any change in the deoxyribonucleic acid (DNA) sequence. Epigenetic mechanisms are divided into three main categories, namely DNA methylation, histone modifications, and non-coding ribonucleic acid (RNA) interference [128]. Almost every cell in the body has the same DNA. However, each cell has different activated or highlighted genes in the DNA. Epigenetics explains the interaction between nature (genes) and nurture (environment), and how the genes we inherit interact with environmental factors including diet [128]. Many epigenetic mechanisms are reversible and modifiable which make them an attractive therapeutic target.

Nutrition is a major modifiable lifestyle factor that has the ability to alter the epigenetic regulation and can cause an epigenetic dysregulation. Additionally, epigenetic markers also have the ability to alter the body's response to certain dietary intake and patterns [129,130]. Dysregulation of the epigenetic markers can alter the gene expression, protein synthesis, cell function, and metabolism and can lead to chronic diseases [131,132].

Recent findings show that epigenetic changes can alter the expression of nociceptive or antinociceptive genes [133]. Moreover, the epigenetic dysregulation can play a role in the transition from acute to chronic pain [134]. Preclinical studies have shown an increase in inflammatory responses after the consumption of a diet rich in saturated fats and a high-carbohydrate diet via DNA methylation [135]. The DNA methylation level of genes that promote inflammatory cytokines, especially TNF-alpha, has been associated with obesity and an omega-6 polyunsaturated fatty acids intake [136]. Saturated fatty acids are known for their inflammatory characteristics and a higher intake of saturated fatty acids has been associated with the DNA methylation level of the genes that play an essential role in the inflammatory biomarker synthesis and insulin resistance [137]. Alternatively, nutrients and foods with anti-inflammatory properties, such as omega-3 polyunsaturated fatty acids, extra virgin olive oil, curcumin, and polyphenols showed anti-inflammatory effects via its effects on the DNA methylation processes in immune cells [138]. Early findings show that there is an interaction between nutrition and the epigenetic factors and this has an important role in chronic pain and the associated mechanisms, such as obesity, a disturbed glucose metabolism, and gut microbiota diversity. Although the use of genetic and epigenetic data in chronic pain management is still in a very early phase, the potential for the development of personalized pain medicine, or precision pain medicine is both promising and innovative [139].

5. Implementation and Scope of Nutrition in Chronic Pain Management

The relationship between nutrition and chronic pain is important and complex, yet traditionally, nutrition has been underrepresented in the evidence-based biopsychosocial and lifestyle approach to pain management. Pain management is multifaceted and must include an interdisciplinary approach. As such, health professionals need to be aware of, and be able to identify nutrition-related risk factors associated with chronic pain, provide basic nutrition-based treatment strategies, and know when and how to refer to a dietitian for more complex issues and advice. A thorough nutrition assessment and treatment plan should be included in all pain management programs. Dietitians can be a valuable part of a multidisciplinary team and can provide comprehensive assessments and treatments.

5.1. Nutrition Assessment for Chronic Pain

There is growing evidence to show that there is an association between diet and health outcomes that are important for people experiencing chronic pain. Therefore, a nutrition assessment should be conducted early in treatment. This may be through a brief, opportunistic intervention that a health professional (e.g., general practitioner (GP), nurse or allied health professional) may provide to a patient, a structured nutrition screening process at a pain clinic, or a comprehensive dietary assessment conducted by a dietitian. There are several nutrition-related risk factors associated with chronic pain and these should be addressed in a dietary assessment. The factors include malnutrition, weight change, the presence of other comorbidities, abnormal biochemistry results, appetite or gastrointestinal complaints, and a poor dietary intake.

5.1.1. Malnutrition Screening

Malnutrition screening is a vital component to consider when conducting a nutrition assessment for people experiencing pain. It is essential for those at an increased risk of malnutrition, such as older adults, those with orofacial pain or functional gastrointestinal conditions [30,38,46–49]. The process should include the use of a validated malnutrition screening tool. There are several validated malnutrition screening tools, such as the Malnutrition Universal Screening Tool, Malnutrition Screening Tool, Mini Nutritional Assessment-Short Form, and the Nutrition Risk Screening Tool [140,141]. These tools use similar parameters and are reliable in identifying people who are malnourished or at risk of malnutrition. Most health services or facilities use a specific screening tool based on their population, the complexity, and sensitivity of the tool. This serves as guide for health professionals when choosing the tool. People who fall into the malnutrition or in the at risk of malnutrition categories, should be referred to a dietitian.

5.1.2. Monitoring Weight Changes

Measuring weight can be confronting for patients and given that the BMI is not always an accurate measurement of weight, it is important to discuss weight measurements with patients to ensure they are comfortable. Monitoring changes in weight over time, (i.e., monthly) can be a useful indication of under- or overnutrition. It can also be useful in identifying serious illnesses associated with sudden and unplanned weight loss, such as cancer [142] and inflammatory bowel disease [143]. The BMI or a waist circumference can help to identify changes in weight over time. However, as previously stated, the BMI must be used with caution. A visual assessment or asking a patient if their clothes are tighter or looser can be less confronting and still obtain the same information. Dietary strategies for pain management are likely to result in improvements in overall health and potentially weight loss. For a successful and sustained nutrition-related change, focusing on pain is more likely to resonate with a patient, compared to weight loss [144]. Patients are more likely to feel validated and motivated which will assist with behavior changes [144,145].

5.1.3. Identifying Other Comorbidities

Several studies have shown that people experiencing chronic pain also have multiple comorbidities [45,146]. Many of these comorbidities can be influenced by nutrition, such as cardiovascular disease (CVD), diabetes, and depression [147–149]. Recent studies have found that people with musculoskeletal pain were twice as likely to have CVD than those without [150], people with diabetes were 1.4 times more likely to report lower back pain and 1.2 times more likely to report neck pain [102], and people with depression were three times more likely to experience non-neuropathic pain and six times more likely to experience neuropathic pain [151]. Globally, a poor diet is the top modifiable risk factor for morbidity [152]. Chronic pain and chronic health conditions share a relationship with inflammation, oxidative stress and a poor diet quality [153]. As such, many of the nutrition recommendations in Table 2 may not only improve pain experiences but may also improve the severity and impact of other chronic health conditions [53]. A referral to a dietitian should also be considered so a detailed and tailored assessment and relevant advice can be provided.

Table 2. Nutrition recommendations for people experiencing chronic pain.

Food Group/Nutrient	Recommendation	Rationale	Practical Tips
Fruit and vegetables	Encourage the consumption of fruit and vegetables. Aim for a variety and wide range of bright colors.	Fruit and vegetables contain phytonutrients which reduce oxidative stress and inflammation.	Choose frozen fruits and vegetables options to reduce preparation time and effort, food waste, and increase variety. Nutrients are retained through freezing.
Breads, cereals, and grains	Choose wholegrain and fiber-rich options. Aim for foods with a low glycemic index. *	Provides slow but sustained energy. Fiber & prebiotics—improves gut health and feeds the gutmicrobiome which may play a role in pain and inflammation.	Swap bread, pasta, and rice for wholegrain options. Swap high GI foods for low GI options.
Meat and meat alternatives	Choose lean meats (e.g., chicken, fish, and small amounts of red meat). Prioritize oily fish, legumes, nuts, and seeds.	Contain healthy fats which reduce inflammation. Build strength to address deconditioning associated with chronic pain.	Swap processed meats for lean meats. Choose tinned fish and legumes to save time and effort with meal preparation.
Dairy and dairy alternatives	Choose high quality dairy foods (e.g., milk, cheese, and yoghurt).	Contains protein to build strength, variety of fats, and important vitamins and minerals.	Choose reduced fat options where possible. Pre-sliced or grated cheese will reduce energy and time needed to prepare meals. Individual tubs of natural or Greek yoghurt (no added sugar) are an easy snack
Healthy fats and oils	Omega-3 and monounsaturated fats.	Reduces inflammation.	Swap cooking oil for olive or canola oil.
Drinks	Consume 2–3 L water/day. Limit caffeine.	Dehydration increases sensitivity to pain [154–156].	Carry a water bottle with you and set a goal to consume it all within a set time period. Swap sugar-sweetened beverages and energy drinks for mineral water.
Added sugar and ultra-processed food	Reduce and limit intake.	Increases inflammation and oxidative stress.	Choose healthy snack options, e.g., fruit, nuts, wholegrain crackers, and cheese or popcorn. Utilize minimally processed foods to facilitate home cooking rather than convenience/takeaway options, e.g., pre-cut vegetables, tinned fish and legumes, tomato based sauces, and microwave rice.

* Glycemic index is a ranking system for carbohydrate foods and is based on the speed of digestion and impact on the blood glucose levels over a period of time. Glucose has a GI of 100 and this is the reference used for other foods. Carbohydrates that breakdown quickly and lead to a sharp increase in blood glucose levels are high GI foods. Carbohydrates that breakdown slowly and lead to a gradual and sustained increase of the blood glucose levels are low GI foods.

5.1.4. Identifying Abnormal Biochemistry Results

As outlined in Section 3.2, there are several micronutrient deficiencies that are commonly associated with chronic pain, such as the B-group vitamins and Vitamin D [56,79,82,157]. These can be identified through routine pathology tests. Dietitians can also identify these deficiencies through comprehensive dietary assessment methods. While it is unclear what the exact relationship is between chronic pain and micronutrient deficiencies, evidence suggests that some vitamins, especially the B-group vitamins, play a role in maintaining the health of the nervous system and pain-signaling pathways [121,158]. Additionally, this paper also outlines several underlying mechanisms associated with chronic pain, including a disrupted lipid and glucose metabolism. Abnormal serum lipids, glucose, and insulin can be used to identify issues with metabolism that may be present and contributing to pain experiences in people with pain [94].

5.1.5. Identifying Gastrointestinal Complaints

Gastrointestinal complaints are common in people experiencing chronic pain. A recent systematic review found that people with irritable bowel syndrome were 1.8 times more likely to have fibromyalgia and that 50% of those with fibromyalgia had a least one functional gastrointestinal disorder [159]. Functional gastrointestinal disorders (FGIDs) comprise a variety of chronic and recurrent gastrointestinal symptoms that cannot be explained by structure or biochemical abnormalities [160]. While the exact nature of FGIDs is still unclear, it has been linked with an altered gut-brain communication and a hypersensitivity of the enteric nervous system [161]. People experiencing chronic pain should be screened for symptoms associated with FGIDs, such as abdominal pain, dysphagia, dyspepsia, diarrhea, constipation, and bloating [161]. There are several strategies (e.g., medication, exercise, cognitive behavior therapy, and nutritional strategies) that are used to manage symptoms using an interdisciplinary approach. From a nutrition perspective, there are a variety of options. These include a diet that is low in fermentable oligosaccharides, disaccharides, monosaccharides and polyols (FODMAPs), modifying the fiber intake, or restricting certain foods, such as caffeine, alcohol, spicy foods, and foods high in fat [162,163]. Given the variety in dietary strategies, it is important to refer patients to a dietitian to ensure a comprehensive dietary assessment is undertaken before trialing these strategies. Some of these dietary strategies can result in an inadequate nutrient intake. For example, a low FODMAP diet is an elimination diet and removing foods and food groups from the diet leads to a nutritional inadequacy [164]. Thus, it is vital that dietitians work with patients to ensure they can meet their nutritional needs while trialing these strategies.

5.1.6. Assessing the Dietary Intake

A poor dietary intake is another risk factor for chronic pain. Many people experiencing pain are likely to have a limited intake of the core nutrient-rich foods and an excessive intake of energy-dense nutrient-poor foods [82,83]. Health professionals can measure the dietary intake by assessing the diet quality. Diet quality can be defined as a varied nutritious diet, which provides individuals with adequate amounts of essential nutrients needed to support overall health and wellbeing [165]. Optimizing the diet quality will address several risk factors in one strategy. Diet quality can be measured using a diet quality index or diet score such as the Diet Quality Index-International [166], the Healthy Eating Index [167] or the Dietary Inflammatory Index [168]. Some can be automatically calculated, such as the Australian Recommended Food Score (ARFS), which can be determined by completing an online questionnaire called the Healthy Eating Quiz [169]. Every country also has a set of dietary guidelines and health professionals can compare a patient's intake against these guidelines to determine areas for improvement. However, as acknowledged in Philpott (2019), chronic pain services would significantly benefit from including dietitians and their skills in the assessment, medication, and support of diets specific to chronic pain [170]. Dietitians can conduct detailed and tailored dietary assessments which provide more insight into a patient's dietary intake and can identify more areas for improvement.

5.2. Nutrition Treatments for Chronic Pain

Evidence suggests that following a predominately plant-based eating pattern (e.g., vegetarian, vegan, or flexitarian eating pattern) or a Mediterranean eating pattern (characterized by a high consumption of fruit, vegetables, legumes, wholegrains, dairy, olive oil, moderate consumption of fish, and small amounts of red meat) or an optimizing diet quality are most effective at reducing pain experiences [53]. The evidence available in the scientific literature is also supported by practice guidance toolkits [18]. However, these guidelines are limited to specific chronic pain conditions such as osteoarthritis, rheumatoid arthritis, and fibromyalgia. These toolkits also recommend predominately plant-based eating patterns, healthy fats and oils, and consuming a wide variety of nutritious foods. The evidence presented in the literature and toolkits can be synthesized into dietary recommendations that health professionals can provide to people experiencing pain (Table 2).

The evidence also indicates that reducing and limiting the intake of added sugar and energy-dense, nutrient poor, or ultra-processed foods will reduce the underlying mechanisms such as inflammation and oxidative stress that contribute to chronic pain experiences [94,171]. Ultra-processed foods undergo several industrial food processes and contain high amounts of sugar, chemically modified protein (e.g., hydrolyzed proteins), oil products (e.g., hydrogenated oils), and food additives [172]. They also contribute to a poor diet quality, metabolic health, and the development of chronic health conditions [173]. Examples of these foods include soft drinks, sweet or savory packaged snacks, and processed meats. National dietary guidelines recommend limiting the consumption of these foods, both in the amount consumed and in the frequency of consumption. In addition, the World Health Organization (WHO) recommends that adults limit their added sugar intake to less than 10% of their total caloric intake [174]. This includes foods such as table sugar, syrups, sweet packaged snacks and baked products, and sugar-sweetened beverages.

It is also important to consider the barriers or practical implications to adhering to a particular eating pattern. These include: ability and access to shop, prepare and cook food, pain flare-ups, cost, culinary skills, sleep, gastrointestinal symptoms, food intolerances, environment, motivation, and mood [53,175]. As part of a multidisciplinary team, a dietitian can work with the patient and their health care team to develop a sustainable plan that improves pain experiences, other health outcomes, and that can be adhered to over a long period of time [175].

Social determinants of health, such as education, socioeconomic status, access and quality of essential services, and the social environment, also play a role in an individual's ability to access nutritious and affordable food. Food insecurity is the inability to reliably access adequate and affordable nutritious food and it is associated with chronic pain and poor mental health. Findings from a recent survey of 200 adult food bank users in the United States, found that 53% of respondents reported experiencing chronic pain [176]. In this study, after controlling for age and gender, depression, and chronic pain significantly predicted food insecurity. A study which analyzed data from approximately 80,000 Canadians aged $\geq$12 years found that those who were food-insecure were 1.3 times more likely to experience chronic pain and almost 2.7 times more likely to have used prescription opioids in the last year [177]. This demonstrates that multidisciplinary teams must explore barriers, practical implications, and social determinants of health when it comes to nutrition and pain.

Other health professionals, such as psychologists, occupational therapists, and physiotherapists can also provide valuable advice and guidance that will work, in combination with the advice and guidance provided by the dietitian, to address some of these practical implications. For example, a psychologist can help address mood and motivation, an occupational therapist can undertake a functional assessment and provide advice on how to participate in nutrition and food-related activities, such as cooking, and physiotherapists can assist by facilitating people to build their strength and mobility which will help with accessing food.

A common denominator for all health professionals is behavior change. These practical implications can also be considered barriers that may make behavior change difficult. Behavior change is a fundamental part of the biopsychosocial and lifestyle approaches to pain management. Models and frameworks, such as the Behavior Change Model [178], can be used to understand and implement behavior change to overcome these barriers.

It is important that all health professionals in a multidisciplinary team are familiar with behavior change models and incorporate behavior change techniques in their practice.

5.3. Scope of Practice

Dietary changes vary in their simplicity and sustainability. Some changes are easy, and others are harder to implement and sustain over time. These changes can be categorized into general healthy eating, basic, or complex recommendations for chronic pain, and personalized medical nutrition therapy as outlined in Figure 3.

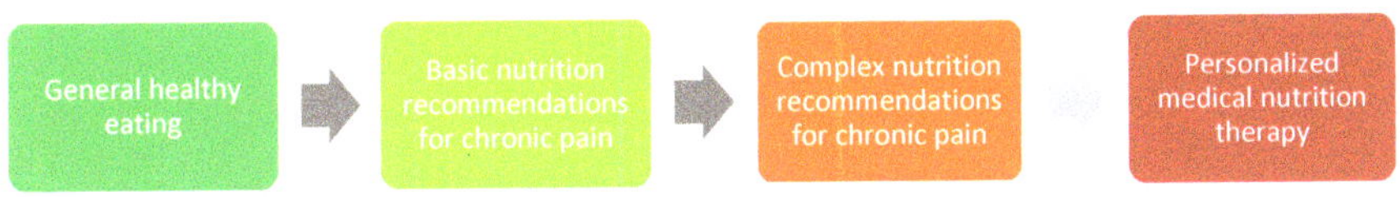

Figure 3. Nutrition and the chronic pain scope of practice.

In a multidisciplinary team, all health professionals should understand all of the components involved in pain management, including nutrition. However, it must be acknowledged that all health professionals have a particular area of expertise. Dietitians are experts qualified to provide medical nutrition therapy using the nutrition care process. In the nutrition and chronic pain scope of practice, all health professionals, should understand general healthy eating and have a basic understanding of nutrition-related recommendations for chronic pain. Pain management teams include medical, nursing, physiotherapy, psychology, and other allied health professionals and all have a significant role in providing relevant and appropriate health education to patients, including nutritional recommendations. However, a comprehensive understanding of nutrition-related recommendations for chronic pain and personalized medical nutrition therapy, should be provided by credentialed dietitians (e.g., Accredited Practising Dietitian or Registered Dietitian) who have undertaken approved study at university and registered with their respective national dietetic association (e.g., Dietitian's Australia or British Dietetic Association). Regardless of a patient's needs, whether it be advice on general healthy eating, basic or complex nutrition recommendations, or personalized medical nutrition therapy, a dietitian can provide valuable input at all stages.

5.3.1. General Healthy Eating

Each country has dietary guidelines for healthy eating. Dietary guidelines promote healthy eating and lifestyle behaviors, rather than treating nutrition-related diseases. They convey the big picture and encourage the consumption of a variety of nutrient-dense foods. While this is not specific to chronic pain, many people do not meet the recommendations in these guidelines, which will impact on their overall health and wellbeing. For example, in Australia, only 6% of adults met the recommended daily amount of fruit and vegetables in 2020–2021 [179]. This highlights that health professionals still need to support people to improve their dietary intake to align with the recommendations.

5.3.2. Basic Nutrition Recommendations for Chronic Pain

Basic recommendations for chronic pain, such as those provided in Table 2, are simple recommendations that all health professionals can support and help their clients to achieve. These are more specific to chronic pain as they address the underlying mechanisms, such as inflammation and oxidative stress.

5.3.3. Complex Recommendations for Chronic Pain

Some people have a more complicated relationship with nutrition and pain, this is often due to the multiple barriers and/or underlying mechanisms and/or comorbidities, such as FGIDs. As previously mentioned, FGIDs are often associated with chronic pain and nutrition-related strategies should be provided by a dietitian.

5.3.4. Personalized Medical Nutrition Therapy

Dietitians are trained to provide personalized medical nutrition therapy which acknowledges that a one-size fits all approach is not appropriate as individuals have different circumstances. Using the Nutrition Care Process [180], dietitians translate evidence-based nutrition information into tailored and practical dietary advice. Dietitians also participate in ongoing professional development to keep apprised of new or updated information. Patients who want to trial an elimination diet must do so with the support of a dietitian to ensure they maintain an adequate nutrition. Patients who have multiple comorbidities requiring multiple nutrition strategies should see a dietitian who can work with them to facilitate the appropriate dietary changes.

6. Future Perspectives

Nutrition interventions deserve to be an essential part of pain management [4,14]. Diet is a modifiable lifestyle factor that can be improved through nutrition interventions. At present, although nutrition is gaining more attention in pain management, current evidence mostly comes from preclinical studies, observational trials, or experimental studies that lack control groups or long-term follow up periods. Most of the available human trials are observational studies and explore the association between nutrition and pain, but do not clarify the causality behind the interactions between nutritional factors and pain. Future trials should consist of high-quality randomized controlled trials in more specific populations and on various chronic pain conditions. Studies in clinical settings need to be carefully designed to match patient characteristics due to the complexity of chronic pain. Clinical trials may explore both pain and nutritional-related comorbidities, such as patients with excess weight and vulnerable groups with somatic (i.e., frail elderly with multimorbidity) or psychiatric diseases (i.e., eating disorders). Additionally, it is of interest to explore more specific dietary patterns and dietary quality in the clinical populations so that real-world data may support the evidence of the appropriate dietary therapies in target patient populations. The latest research, however, is usually based on the general populations [57,181].

Current dietary guidelines provide advice for the general population to ensure people consume adequate nutrition and prevent chronic diseases [8]. However, as suggested in the observational studies, the needs of people experiencing pain differ from those who do not experience chronic pain. Thus, specific dietary guidelines need to be developed for chronic pain. These guidelines need to take into consideration the specific needs of people experiencing pain. They also need to be incorporated into the assessment and diagnosis procedures for chronic pain. Nutritional screening and assessments should be specific for people experiencing pain and be adapted, based on the evidence related to the pathophysiology and underlying mechanisms of chronic pain. The lack of clinical guidelines for nutrition and chronic pain indicates that the evidence needs to be synthesized into a clinical guideline for nutrition and chronic pain.

Investigating the relationship between nutritional factors and the physiological processes of the body are highly complex due to the difficulty of isolating the impacts of nutritional factors from the high number of confounding factors among individuals. As a starting point, developing general dietary guidelines for specific populations and subgroups constitutes an important place in pain medicine. However, based on novel and innovative technology and science, there will most likely be a shift from a "one size fits all" approach to personalized nutritional (pain) medicine. Improving technological development will allow researchers and clinicians to deal with large and more complex amounts of data which can be adapted to pain and nutrition. To exemplify, artificial intelligence and machine learning based software and applications have a great potential to collect real life and complex data from individuals and to capture meaningful insights for research and clinical purposes.

It is also important to explore the barriers people with chronic pain experience when adopting healthier eating patterns, to ensure successful and meaningful change. One perspective is to address other lifestyle factors in parallel to nutritional intervention. Strong associations were found between dietary habits, sedentary behaviors, and physical activity, especially among younger people [182,183]. Diet and sleep also have a bidirectional relationship [184]. Since sedentary behavior and sleep disturbances are extremely common among patients with chronic pain, future nutrition-based studies may consider the evaluation and combined effects of lifestyle interventions (physical activity, sedentary behavior, sleep, and dietary therapy).

7. Conclusions

The relationship between nutrition and chronic pain is complex but traditionally underrepresented despite the emerging evidence which indicates that poor nutrition and dietary intake may play a key role in the development and management of chronic pain [13,53]. This paper highlights that nutrition contributes to chronic pain patients' profiles; there is a strong link between the underlying mechanisms of chronic pain and nutrition and there is a place for a nutrition-related assessment and management in chronic pain management. Health professionals and chronic pain services need to be aware and understand the role nutrition plays in chronic pain management. With this growing evidence base, nutrition assessments and management plans should be incorporated into the care of people experiencing chronic pain.

Author Contributions: Conceptualization, Ö.E., K.B. and H.-J.D.; Methodology, Ö.E., K.B. and H.-J.D.; Investigation, Ö.E., K.B. and H.-J.D.; Writing—Original Draft Preparation, Ö.E., H.-J.D. and K.B.; Writing—Review & Editing, Ö.E., H.-J.D. and K.B.; Visualization, Ö.E., K.B. and H.-J.D. All authors have read and agreed to the published version of the manuscript.

Funding: This study was supported by grants from County Council of Östergötland (SC-2021), Sweden. The content is solely the responsibility of the authors and does not necessarily represent the official views of County Council of Östergötland.

Institutional Review Board Statement: Not applicable.

Informed Consent Statement: Not applicable.

Data Availability Statement: Not applicable.

Conflicts of Interest: The authors declare no conflict of interest.

References

1. Treede, R.D.; Rief, W.; Barke, A.; Aziz, Q.; Bennett, M.I.; Benoliel, R.; Cohen, M.; Evers, S.; Finnerup, N.B.; First, M.B.; et al. Chronic pain as a symptom or a disease: The IASP Classification of Chronic Pain for the International Classification of Diseases (ICD-11). *Pain* **2019**, *160*, 19–27. [CrossRef] [PubMed]
2. Galvez-Sánchez, C.M.; Montoro, C.I. Chronic Pain: Clinical Updates and Perspectives. *J. Clin. Med.* **2022**, *11*, 3474. [CrossRef] [PubMed]
3. Bonakdar, R.A. Integrative Pain Management. *Med. Clin. N. Am.* **2017**, *101*, 987–1004. [CrossRef] [PubMed]
4. Taekman, J.M.; Bonakdar, R. Integrative Pain Management Must Include Diet Considerations. *Anesth. Analg.* **2018**, *127*, 305. [CrossRef] [PubMed]
5. Gerdle, B.; Fischer, M.R.; Ringqvist, Å. Interdisciplinary Pain Rehabilitation Programs: Evidence and Clinical Real-World Results. In *Pain Management-From Pain Mechanisms to Patient Care*; IntechOpen: London, UK, 2022.
6. Elma, Ö.; Yilmaz, S.T.; Deliens, T.; Coppieters, I.; Clarys, P.; Nijs, J.; Malfliet, A. Do Nutritional Factors Interact with Chronic Musculoskeletal Pain? A Systematic Review. *J. Clin. Med.* **2020**, *9*, 702. [CrossRef] [PubMed]
7. Verdú, E.; Homs, J.; Boadas-Vaello, P. Physiological Changes and Pathological Pain Associated with Sedentary Lifestyle-Induced Body Systems Fat Accumulation and Their Modulation by Physical Exercise. *Int. J. Environ. Res. Public Health* **2021**, *18*, 13333. [CrossRef]
8. National Health and Medical Research Council. *Australian Dietary Guidelines*; National Health and Medical Research Council: Canberra, Australia, 2013.
9. Niv, D.; Devor, M. Chronic pain as a disease in its own right. *Pain Pract.* **2004**, *4*, 179–181. [CrossRef]
10. Nielsen, M. *A Focus Group Study of Consumer Priorities for Pain Management Resources in NSW*; Chronic Pain Association of Australia: Baulkham Hills, Australia, 2013.
11. Goodchild, C.S.; Cohen, M. The Faculty of Pain Medicine, Australian and New Zealand College of Anesthetists. *Pain Med.* **2005**, *6*, 275–276. [CrossRef] [PubMed]

12. Tick, H.; Nielsen, A.; Pelletier, K.R.; Bonakdar, R.; Simmons, S.; Glick, R.; Ratner, E.; Lemmon, R.L.; Wayne, P.; Zador, V. Evidence-Based Nonpharmacologic Strategies for Comprehensive Pain Care: The Consortium Pain Task Force White Paper. *Explore* **2018**, *14*, 177–211. [CrossRef]
13. Brain, K.; Burrows, T.L.; Rollo, M.E.; Chai, L.K.; Clarke, E.D.; Hayes, C.; Hodson, F.J.; Collins, C.E. A systematic review and meta-analysis of nutrition interventions for chronic noncancer pain. *J. Hum. Nutr. Diet.* **2019**, *32*, 198–225. [CrossRef]
14. The International Association for the Study of Pain (IASP). 2020 Global Year for the Prevention of Pain: Nutrition and Chronic Pain. Available online: https://www.iasp-pain.org/resources/fact-sheets/nutrition-and-chronic-pain/ (accessed on 30 July 2022).
15. Azad, K.A.; Alam, M.N.; Haq, S.A.; Nahar, S.; Chowdhury, M.A.; Ali, S.M.; Ullah, A.K. Vegetarian diet in the treatment of fibromyalgia. *Bangladesh Med. Res. Counc. Bull.* **2000**, *26*, 41–47. [PubMed]
16. Lee, K.C.; Khan, A.; Longworth, S.; Sell, P. Prevalence of vitamin D deficiency in patients presenting with low back pain in an outpatient setting. *Eur. Spine. J.* **2014**, *1*, S124–S125. [CrossRef]
17. Boyd, C.; Crawford, C.; Berry, K.; Deuster, P. Conditional Recommendations for Specific Dietary Ingredients as an Approach to Chronic Musculoskeletal Pain: Evidence-Based Decision Aid for Health Care Providers, Participants, and Policy Makers. *Pain Med.* **2019**, *20*, 1430–1448. [CrossRef]
18. Dietitians of Canada. Practice-Based Evidence in Nutrition–The Global Resource for Nutrition Practice. In Practice-based Evidence in Nutrition®. Available online: https://www.pennutrition.com/index.aspx (accessed on 26 September 2022).
19. The European Society for Clinical Nutrition and Metabolism. ESPEN Guidelines & Consensus Papers. 2022. Available online: https://www.espen.org/guidelines-home/espen-guidelines (accessed on 25 September 2022).
20. Stone, A.A.; Broderick, J.E. Obesity and pain are associated in the United States. *Obesity* **2012**, *20*, 1491–1495. [CrossRef] [PubMed]
21. Dong, H.J.; Larsson, B.; Levin, L.A.; Bernfort, L.; Gerdle, B. Is excess weight a burden for older adults who suffer chronic pain? *BMC Geriatr.* **2018**, *18*, 270. [CrossRef] [PubMed]
22. Yamada, K.; Kubota, Y.; Iso, H.; Oka, H.; Katsuhira, J.; Matsudaira, K. Association of body mass index with chronic pain prevalence: A large population-based cross-sectional study in Japan. *J. Anesth.* **2018**, *32*, 360–367. [CrossRef]
23. Tardif, H.; Blanchard, M.B.; Quinsey, K.; Bryce, M.P.; White, J.M.; Blacklock, J.A.; Eagar, K. *Electronic Persistent Pain Outcomes Collaboration Annual Data Report 2018*; The Australian Health Services Research Institute: Wollongong, Australia, 2019.
24. Pianucci, L.; Sonagra, M.; Greenberg, B.A.; Priestley, D.R.; Gmuca, S. Disordered eating among adolescents with chronic pain: The experience of a pediatric rheumatology subspecialty pain clinic. *Pediatr. Rheumatol.* **2021**, *19*, 16. [CrossRef]
25. Holstein, B.E.; Andersen, A.; Damsgaard, M.T.; Madsen, K.R.; Pedersen, T.P. Underweight among adolescents in Denmark: Prevalence, trends (1998–2018), and association of underweight with socioeconomic status. *Fam. Pract.* **2022**, *39*, 413–419. [CrossRef]
26. Agarwal, E.; Miller, M.; Yaxley, A.; Isenring, E. Malnutrition in the elderly: A narrative review. *Maturitas* **2013**, *76*, 296–302. [CrossRef]
27. Scholes, G. Protein-energy malnutrition in older Australians: A narrative review of the prevalence, causes and consequences of malnutrition, and strategies for prevention. *Health Promot. J. Austr.* **2022**, *33*, 187–193. [CrossRef]
28. Fraser, A.M. Malnutrition in Older Adults in the United States. In *Handbook of Famine, Starvation, and Nutrient Deprivation: From Biology to Policy*; Preedy, V., Patel, V.B., Eds.; Springer International Publishing: Cham, Switzerland, 2017; pp. 1–20. [CrossRef]
29. Murawiak, M.; Krzymińska-Siemaszko, R.; Kaluźniak-Szymanowska, A.; Lewandowicz, M.; Tobis, S.; Wieczorowska-Tobis, K.; Deskur-Śmielecka, E. Sarcopenia, Obesity, Sarcopenic Obesity and Risk of Poor Nutritional Status in Polish Community-Dwelling Older People Aged 60 Years and Over. *Nutrients* **2022**, *14*, 2889. [CrossRef] [PubMed]
30. Costa, A.B.P.; Machado, L.A.C.; Dias, J.M.D.; De Oliveira, A.K.C.; Viana, J.U.; Da Silva, S.L.A.; Couto, F.G.P.; Torres, J.L.; Mendes, L.; Dias, R.C. Nutritional Risk is Associated with Chronic Musculoskeletal Pain in Community-dwelling Older Persons: The PAINEL Study. *J. Nutr. Gerontol. Geriatr.* **2016**, *35*, 43–51. [CrossRef] [PubMed]
31. Iijima, H.; Aoyama, T. Increased recurrent falls experience in older adults with coexisting of sarcopenia and knee osteoarthritis: A cross-sectional study. *BMC Geriatr.* **2021**, *21*, 698. [CrossRef] [PubMed]
32. Lin, T.; Dai, M.; Xu, P.; Sun, L.; Shu, X.; Xia, X.; Zhao, Y.; Song, Q.; Guo, D.; Deng, C.; et al. Prevalence of Sarcopenia in Pain Patients and Correlation Between the Two Conditions: A Systematic Review and Meta-Analysis. *J. Am. Med. Dir. Assoc.* **2022**, *23*, 902.e1–902.e20. [CrossRef]
33. Maruya, K.; Fujita, H.; Arai, T.; Asahi, R.; Morita, Y.; Ishibashi, H. Sarcopenia and lower limb pain are additively related to motor function and a history of falls and fracture in community-dwelling elderly people. *Osteoporos. Sarcopenia* **2019**, *5*, 23–26. [CrossRef]
34. Geha, P.; deAraujo, I.; Green, B.; Small, D.M. Decreased food pleasure and disrupted satiety signals in chronic low back pain. *Pain* **2014**, *155*, 712–722. [CrossRef]
35. Fried, L.P.; Tangen, C.M.; Walston, J.; Newman, A.B.; Hirsch, C.; Gottdiener, J.; Seeman, T.; Tracy, R.; Kop, W.J.; Burke, G.; et al. Frailty in older adults: Evidence for a phenotype. *J. Gerontol. A Biol. Sci. Med. Sci.* **2001**, *56*, M146–M156. [CrossRef]
36. Vermeiren, S.; Vella-Azzopardi, R.; Beckwée, D.; Habbig, A.K.; Scafoglieri, A.; Jansen, B.; Bautmans, I. Frailty and the Prediction of Negative Health Outcomes: A Meta-Analysis. *J. Am. Med. Dir. Assoc.* **2016**, *17*, 1163.e1–1163.e17. [CrossRef]
37. Desrichard, O.; Vallet, F.; Agrigoroaei, S.; Fagot, D.; Spini, D. Frailty in aging and its influence on perceived stress exposure and stress-related symptoms: Evidence from the Swiss Vivre/Leben/Vivere study. *Eur. J. Ageing* **2018**, *15*, 331–338. [CrossRef]
38. Chen, C.; Winterstein, A.G.; Fillingim, R.B.; Wei, Y.-J. Body weight, frailty, and chronic pain in older adults: A cross-sectional study. *BMC Geriatr.* **2019**, *19*, 143. [CrossRef]

39. Lin, T.; Zhao, Y.; Xia, X.; Ge, N.; Yue, J. Association between frailty and chronic pain among older adults: A systematic review and meta-analysis. *Eur. Geriatr. Med.* **2020**, *11*, 945–959. [CrossRef] [PubMed]
40. Fox, A.; Feng, W.; Asal, V. What is driving global obesity trends? Globalization or "modernization"? *Glob. Health* **2019**, *15*, 32. [CrossRef]
41. Stokes, A.C.; Xie, W.; Lundberg, D.J.; Hempstead, K.; Zajacova, A.; Zimmer, Z.; Glei, D.A.; Meara, E.; Preston, S.H. Increases in BMI and chronic pain for US adults in midlife, 1992 to 2016. *SSM Popul. Health* **2020**, *12*, 100644. [CrossRef] [PubMed]
42. Pan, F.; Laslett, L.; Blizzard, L.; Cicuttini, F.; Winzenberg, T.; Ding, C.; Jones, G. Associations Between Fat Mass and Multisite Pain: A Five-Year Longitudinal Study. *Arthritis Care Res.* **2017**, *69*, 509–516. [CrossRef] [PubMed]
43. Dong, H.J.; Larsson, B.; Rivano Fischer, M.; Gerdle, B. Facing obesity in pain rehabilitation clinics: Profiles of physical activity in patients with chronic pain and obesity-A study from the Swedish Quality Registry for Pain Rehabilitation (SQRP). *PLoS ONE* **2020**, *15*, e0239818. [CrossRef]
44. Public Health Agency of Sweden. Overweight and Obesity. 2018. Available online: https://www.folkhalsomyndigheten.se/the-public-health-agency-of-sweden/living-conditions-and-lifestyle/obesity/ (accessed on 30 July 2022).
45. Brain, K.; Burrows, T.; Rollo, M.E.; Hayes, C.; Hodson, F.J.; Collins, C.E. Population Characteristics in a Tertiary Pain Service Cohort Experiencing Chronic Non-Cancer Pain: Weight Status, Comorbidities, and Patient Goals. *Healthcare* **2017**, *5*, 28. [CrossRef]
46. Bauer, S.; Hödl, M.; Eglseer, D. Association between malnutrition risk and pain in older hospital patients. *Scand. J. Caring Sci.* **2021**, *35*, 945–951. [CrossRef] [PubMed]
47. Durham, J.; Touger-Decker, R.; Nixdorf, D.R.; Rigassio-Radler, D.; Moynihan, P. Oro-facial pain and nutrition: A forgotten relationship? *J. Oral Rehabil.* **2015**, *42*, 75–80. [CrossRef]
48. Cuomo, R.; Andreozzi, P.; Zito, F.P.; Passananti, V.; De Carlo, G.; Sarnelli, G. Irritable bowel syndrome and food interaction. *World J. Gastroenterol.* **2014**, *20*, 8837–8845. [CrossRef] [PubMed]
49. Algera, J.; Colomier, E.; Simrén, M. The Dietary Management of Patients with Irritable Bowel Syndrome: A Narrative Review of the Existing and Emerging Evidence. *Nutrients* **2019**, *11*, 2162. [CrossRef] [PubMed]
50. Basem, J.I.; White, R.S.; Chen, S.A.; Mauer, E.; Steinkamp, M.L.; Inturrisi, C.E.; Witkin, L.R. The effect of obesity on pain severity and pain interference. *Pain Manag.* **2021**, *11*, 571–581. [CrossRef]
51. Gota, C.E.; Kaouk, S.; Wilke, W.S. Fibromyalgia and Obesity: The Association Between Body Mass Index and Disability, Depression, History of Abuse, Medications, and Comorbidities. *J. Clin. Rheumatol.* **2015**, *21*, 289–295. [CrossRef] [PubMed]
52. Atzeni, F.; Alciati, A.; Salaffi, F.; Di Carlo, M.; Bazzichi, L.; Govoni, M.; Biasi, G.; Di Franco, M.; Mozzani, F.; Gremese, E.; et al. The association between body mass index and fibromyalgia severity: Data from a cross-sectional survey of 2339 patients. *Rheumatol. Adv. Pract.* **2021**, *5*, rkab015. [CrossRef]
53. Brain, K.; Burrows, T.L.; Bruggink, L.; Malfliet, A.; Hayes, C.; Hodson, F.J.; Collins, C.E. Diet and chronic non-cancer pain: The state of the art and future directions. *J. Clin. Med.* **2021**, *10*, 5203. [CrossRef]
54. Thomas, S.; Browne, H.; Mobasheri, A.; Rayman, M.P. What is the evidence for a role for diet and nutrition in osteoarthritis? *Rheumatology* **2018**, *57*, iv61–iv74. [CrossRef] [PubMed]
55. Gioia, C.; Lucchino, B.; Tarsitano, M.G.; Iannuccelli, C.; Di Franco, M. Dietary Habits and Nutrition in Rheumatoid Arthritis: Can Diet Influence Disease Development and Clinical Manifestations? *Nutrients* **2020**, *12*, 1456. [CrossRef]
56. Bjorklund, G.; Dadar, M.; Chirumbolo, S.; Aaseth, J. Fibromyalgia and nutrition: Therapeutic possibilities? *Biomed. Pharmacother.* **2018**, *103*, 531–538. [CrossRef] [PubMed]
57. Zick, S.M.; Murphy, S.L.; Colacino, J. Association of chronic spinal pain with diet quality. *Pain Rep.* **2020**, *5*, e837. [CrossRef]
58. Nirgianakis, K.; Egger, K.; Kalaitzopoulos, D.R.; Lanz, S.; Bally, L.; Mueller, M.D. Effectiveness of Dietary Interventions in the Treatment of Endometriosis: A Systematic Review. *Reprod. Sci.* **2022**, *29*, 26–42. [CrossRef]
59. Storz, M.A.; Küster, O. Plant-based diets and diabetic neuropathy: A systematic review. *Lifestyle Med.* **2020**, *1*, e6. [CrossRef]
60. Hindiyeh, N.A.; Zhang, N.; Farrar, M.; Banerjee, P.; Lombard, L.; Aurora, S.K. The Role of Diet and Nutrition in Migraine Triggers and Treatment: A Systematic Literature Review. *Headache J. Head Face Pain* **2020**, *60*, 1300–1316. [CrossRef]
61. Julian, T.; Syeed, R.; Glascow, N.; Angelopoulou, E.; Zis, P. B12 as a Treatment for Peripheral Neuropathic Pain: A Systematic Review. *Nutrients* **2020**, *12*, 2221. [CrossRef]
62. Tonga, F.; Bahadir, S. The Factors Associated with Carpal Tunnel Syndrome Severity. *Turk. Neurosurg.* **2022**, *32*, 392–397. [CrossRef] [PubMed]
63. Nicholas, M.; Vlaeyen, J.W.S.; Rief, W.; Barke, A.; Aziz, Q.; Benoliel, R.; Cohen, M.; Evers, S.; Giamberardino, M.A.; Goebel, A.; et al. The IASP classification of chronic pain for ICD-11: Chronic primary pain. *Pain* **2019**, *160*, 28–37. [CrossRef] [PubMed]
64. Nijs, J.; Lahousse, A.; Kapreli, E.; Bilika, P.; Saraçoğlu, İ.; Malfliet, A.; Coppieters, I.; de Baets, L.; Leysen, L.; Roose, E.; et al. Nociplastic Pain Criteria or Recognition of Central Sensitization? Pain Phenotyping in the Past, Present and Future. *J. Clin. Med.* **2021**, *10*, 3203. [CrossRef]
65. Nijs, J.; George, S.Z.; Clauw, D.J.; Fernández-de-las-Peñas, C.; Kosek, E.; Ickmans, K.; Fernández-Carnero, J.; Polli, A.; Kapreli, E.; Huysmans, E.; et al. Central sensitisation in chronic pain conditions: Latest discoveries and their potential for precision medicine. *Lancet Rheumatol.* **2021**, *3*, e383–e392. [CrossRef]
66. Fowler-Brown, A.; Wee, C.C.; Marcantonio, E.; Ngo, L.; Leveille, S. The mediating effect of chronic pain on the relationship between obesity and physical function and disability in older adults. *J. Am. Geriatr. Soc.* **2013**, *61*, 2079–2086. [CrossRef]
67. Patel, K.V.; Guralnik, J.M.; Dansie, E.J.; Turk, D.C. Prevalence and impact of pain among older adults in the United States: Findings from the 2011 National Health and Aging Trends Study. *Pain* **2013**, *154*, 2649–2657. [CrossRef] [PubMed]

68. Zdziarski, L.A.; Wasser, J.G.; Vincent, H.K. Chronic pain management in the obese patient: A focused review of key challenges and potential exercise solutions. *J. Pain Res.* **2015**, *8*, 63–77. [CrossRef] [PubMed]
69. Okifuji, A.; Donaldson, G.W.; Barck, L.; Fine, P.G. Relationship between fibromyalgia and obesity in pain, function, mood, and sleep. *J. Pain Off. J. Am. Pain Soc.* **2010**, *11*, 1329–1337. [CrossRef] [PubMed]
70. Correa-Rodríguez, M.; Mansouri-Yachou, J.E.; Casas-Barragán, A.; Molina, F.; Rueda-Medina, B.; Aguilar-Ferrandiz, M.E. The Association of Body Mass Index and Body Composition with Pain, Disease Activity, Fatigue, Sleep and Anxiety in Women with Fibromyalgia. *Nutrients* **2019**, *11*, 1193. [CrossRef]
71. Heo, M.; Allison, D.B.; Faith, M.S.; Zhu, S.; Fontaine, K.R. Obesity and quality of life: Mediating effects of pain and comorbidities. *Obes. Res.* **2003**, *11*, 209–216. [CrossRef]
72. Arranz, L.I.; Rafecas, M.; Alegre, C. Effects of obesity on function and quality of life in chronic pain conditions. *Curr. Rheumatol. Rep.* **2014**, *16*, 390. [CrossRef]
73. Arreghini, M.; Manzoni, G.M.; Castelnuovo, G.; Santovito, C.; Capodaglio, P. Impact of fibromyalgia on functioning in obese patients undergoing comprehensive rehabilitation. *PLoS ONE* **2014**, *9*, e91392. [CrossRef]
74. Higgins, D.M.; Buta, E.; Dorflinger, L.; Masheb, R.M.; Ruser, C.B.; Goulet, J.L.; Heapy, A.A. Prevalence and correlates of painful conditions and multimorbidity in national sample of overweight/obese Veterans. *J. Rehabil. Res. Dev.* **2016**, *53*, 71–82. [CrossRef]
75. Park, C.G.; Chu, M.K. Interictal plasma glutamate levels are elevated in individuals with episodic and chronic migraine. *Sci. Rep.* **2022**, *12*, 6921. [CrossRef]
76. Terumitsu, M.; Takado, Y.; Fukuda, K.I.; Kato, E.; Tanaka, S. Neurometabolite Levels and Relevance to Central Sensitization in Chronic Orofacial Pain Patients: A Magnetic Resonance Spectroscopy Study. *J. Pain Res.* **2022**, *15*, 1421–1432. [CrossRef]
77. Clos-Garcia, M.; Andrés-Marin, N.; Fernández-Eulate, G.; Abecia, L.; Lavín, J.L.; van Liempd, S.; Cabrera, D.; Royo, F.; Valero, A.; Errazquin, N.; et al. Gut microbiome and serum metabolome analyses identify molecular biomarkers and altered glutamate metabolism in fibromyalgia. *eBioMedicine* **2019**, *46*, 499–511. [CrossRef]
78. Alexander, G.M.; Reichenberger, E.; Peterlin, B.L.; Perreault, M.J.; Grothusen, J.R.; Schwartzman, R.J. Plasma amino acids changes in complex regional pain syndrome. *Pain Res. Treat.* **2013**, *2013*, 742407. [CrossRef]
79. Haddad, H.W.; Jumonville, A.C.; Stark, K.J.; Temple, S.N.; Dike, C.C.; Cornett, E.M.; Kaye, A.D. The Role of Vitamin D in the Management of Chronic Pain in Fibromyalgia: A Narrative Review. *Health Psychol. Res.* **2021**, *9*, 25208. [CrossRef] [PubMed]
80. Black, C.J.; Staudacher, H.M.; Ford, A.C. Efficacy of a low FODMAP diet in irritable bowel syndrome: Systematic review and network meta-analysis. *Gut* **2022**, *71*, 1117–1126. [CrossRef] [PubMed]
81. Chen, X.; Hu, C.; Peng, Y.; Lu, J.; Yang, N.Q.; Chen, L.; Zhang, G.Q.; Tang, L.K.; Dai, J.C. Association of diet and lifestyle with chronic prostatitis/chronic pelvic pain syndrome and pain severity: A case-control study. *Prostate Cancer Prostatic Dis.* **2016**, *19*, 92–99. [CrossRef]
82. Meleger, A.L.; Froude, C.K.; Walker, J., 3rd. Nutrition and eating behavior in patients with chronic pain receiving long-term opioid therapy. *PM R* **2014**, *6*, 7–12.e11. [CrossRef]
83. VanDenKerkhof, E.G.; Macdonald, H.M.; Jones, G.T.; Power, C.; Macfarlane, G.J. Diet, lifestyle and chronic widespread pain: Results from the 1958 British Birth Cohort Study. *Pain Res. Manag.* **2011**, *16*, 87–92. [CrossRef] [PubMed]
84. Hejazi, J.; Mohtadinia, J.; Kolahi, S.; Bakhtiyari, M.; Delpisheh, A. Nutritional Status of Iranian Women with Rheumatoid Arthritis: An Assessment of Dietary Intake and Disease Activity. *Women's Health* **2011**, *7*, 599–605. [CrossRef]
85. Choi, K.W.; Somers, T.J.; Babyak, M.A.; Sikkema, K.J.; Blumenthal, J.A.; Keefe, F.J. The Relationship Between Pain and Eating among Overweight and Obese Individuals with Osteoarthritis: An Ecological Momentary Study. *Pain Res. Manag.* **2014**, *19*, e159–e163. [CrossRef]
86. Tański, W.; Wójciga, J.; Jankowska-Polańska, B. Association between Malnutrition and Quality of Life in Elderly Patients with Rheumatoid Arthritis. *Nutrients* **2021**, *13*, 1259. [CrossRef]
87. Bosley, B.N.; Weiner, D.K.; Rudy, T.E.; Granieri, E. Is chronic nonmalignant pain associated with decreased appetite in older adults? Preliminary evidence. *J. Am. Geriatr. Soc.* **2004**, *52*, 247–251. [CrossRef]
88. Chatterjee, S. Oxidative stress, inflammation, and disease. In *Oxidative Stress and Biomaterials*; Elsevier: Amsterdam, The Netherlands, 2016; pp. 35–58.
89. Kaushik, A.S.; Strath, L.J.; Sorge, R.E. Dietary interventions for treatment of chronic pain: Oxidative stress and inflammation. *Pain Ther.* **2020**, *9*, 487–498. [CrossRef]
90. Schell, J.; Scofield, R.H.; Barrett, J.R.; Kurien, B.T.; Betts, N.; Lyons, T.J.; Zhao, Y.D.; Basu, A. Strawberries improve pain and inflammation in obese adults with radiographic evidence of knee osteoarthritis. *Nutrients* **2017**, *9*, 949. [CrossRef]
91. Matsuda, M.; Huh, Y.; Ji, R.-R. Roles of inflammation, neurogenic inflammation, and neuroinflammation in pain. *J. Anesth.* **2019**, *33*, 131–139. [CrossRef] [PubMed]
92. Chen, Y.; Liu, S.; Leng, S.X. Chronic low-grade inflammatory phenotype (CLIP) and senescent immune dysregulation. *Clin. Ther.* **2019**, *41*, 400–409. [CrossRef] [PubMed]
93. Gerdle, B.; Ghafouri, B.; Ernberg, M.; Larsson, B. Chronic musculoskeletal pain: Review of mechanisms and biochemical biomarkers as assessed by the microdialysis technique. *J. Pain Res.* **2014**, *7*, 313–326. [CrossRef] [PubMed]
94. Nijs, J.; Yilmaz, S.T.; Elma, Ö.; Tatta, J.; Mullie, P.; Vanderweeën, L.; Clarys, P.; Deliens, T.; Coppieters, I.; Weltens, N.; et al. Nutritional intervention in chronic pain: An innovative way of targeting central nervous system sensitization? *Expert Opin. Ther. Targets* **2020**, *24*, 793–803. [CrossRef]

95. De Gregori, M.; Belfer, I.; de Giorgio, R.; Marchesini, M.; Muscoli, C.; Rondanelli, M.; Martini, D.; Mena, P.; Arranz, L.I.; Lorente-Cebrián, S.; et al. of SIMPAR's "Feed Your Destiny" workshop: The role of lifestyle in improving pain management. *J. Pain Res.* **2018**, *11*, 1627–1636. [CrossRef]
96. Mayer, E.A. Gut feelings: The emerging biology of gut–brain communication. *Nat. Rev. Neurosci.* **2011**, *12*, 453–466. [CrossRef]
97. Guo, R.; Chen, L.-H.; Xing, C.; Liu, T. Pain regulation by gut microbiota: Molecular mechanisms and therapeutic potential. *Br. J. Anaesth.* **2019**, *123*, 637–654. [CrossRef]
98. Santoni, M.; Miccini, F.; Battelli, N. Gut microbiota, immunity and pain. *Immunol. Lett.* **2021**, *229*, 44–47. [CrossRef]
99. Pimentel, G.D.; Micheletti, T.O.; Pace, F.; Rosa, J.C.; Santos, R.V.; Lira, F.S. Gut-central nervous system axis is a target for nutritional therapies. *Nutr. J.* **2012**, *11*, 22. [CrossRef]
100. Tomova, A.; Bukovsky, I.; Rembert, E.; Yonas, W.; Alwarith, J.; Barnard, N.D.; Kahleova, H. The effects of vegetarian and vegan diets on gut microbiota. *Front. Nutr.* **2019**, *6*, 47. [CrossRef]
101. Mäntyselkä, P.; Miettola, J.; Niskanen, L.; Kumpusalo, E. Glucose regulation and chronic pain at multiple sites. *Rheumatology* **2008**, *47*, 1235–1238. [CrossRef]
102. Pozzobon, D.; Ferreira, P.H.; Dario, A.B.; Almeida, L.; Vesentini, G.; Harmer, A.R.; Ferreira, M.L. Is there an association between diabetes and neck and back pain? A systematic review with meta-analyses. *PLoS ONE* **2019**, *14*, e0212030. [CrossRef]
103. Pappolla, M.A.; Manchikanti, L.; Candido, K.D.; Grieg, N.; Seffinger, M.; Ahmed, F.; Fang, X.; Andersen, C.; Trescot, A.M. Insulin resistance is associated with central pain in patients with fibromyalgia. *Pain Physician* **2021**, *24*, 175–184.
104. Baeza-Flores, G.D.C.; Guzmán-Priego, C.G.; Parra-Flores, L.I.; Murbartián, J.; Torres-López, J.E.; Granados-Soto, V. Metformin: A prospective alternative for the treatment of chronic pain. *Front. Pharmacol.* **2020**, *11*, 558474. [CrossRef]
105. Elma, Ö.; Lebuf, E.; Marnef, A.Q.; Tümkaya Yilmaz, S.; Coppieters, I.; Clarys, P.; Nijs, J.; Malfliet, A.; Deliens, T. Diet can exert both analgesic and pronociceptive effects in acute and chronic pain models: A systematic review of preclinical studies. *Nutr. Neurosci.* **2021**, *25*, 2195–2217. [CrossRef]
106. Yuan, X.; Wang, J.; Yang, S.; Gao, M.; Cao, L.; Li, X.; Hong, D.; Tian, S.; Sun, C. Effect of the ketogenic diet on glycemic control, insulin resistance, and lipid metabolism in patients with T2DM: A systematic review and meta-analysis. *Nutr. Diabetes* **2020**, *10*, 38. [CrossRef]
107. Field, R.; Pourkazemi, F.; Rooney, K. Effects of a Low-Carbohydrate Ketogenic Diet on Reported Pain, Blood Biomarkers and Quality of Life in Patients with Chronic Pain: A Pilot Randomized Clinical Trial. *Pain Med.* **2022**, *23*, 326–338. [CrossRef]
108. Field, R.; Field, T.; Pourkazemi, F.; Rooney, K. Low-carbohydrate and ketogenic diets: A scoping review of neurological and inflammatory outcomes in human studies and their relevance to chronic pain. *Nutr. Res. Rev.* **2022**, 1–71. [CrossRef]
109. Okifuji, A.; Hare, B.D. The association between chronic pain and obesity. *J. Pain Res.* **2015**, *8*, 399–408. [CrossRef]
110. Santos, H.O.; Macedo, R.C. Impact of intermittent fasting on the lipid profile: Assessment associated with diet and weight loss. *Clin. Nutr. ESPEN* **2018**, *24*, 14–21. [CrossRef]
111. Higuera-Hernández, M.F.; Reyes-Cuapio, E.; Gutiérrez-Mendoza, M.; Budde, H.; Blanco-Centurión, C.; Veras, A.B.; Rocha, N.B.; Yamamoto, T.; Monteiro, D.; Zaldívar-Rae, J.; et al. Blueberry intake included in hypocaloric diet decreases weight, glucose, cholesterol, triglycerides and adenosine levels in obese subjects. *J. Funct. Foods* **2019**, *60*, 103409. [CrossRef]
112. Taskinen, M.-R.; Packard, C.J.; Borén, J. Dietary fructose and the metabolic syndrome. *Nutrients* **2019**, *11*, 1987. [CrossRef] [PubMed]
113. Zupo, R.; Lampignano, L.; Lattanzio, A.; Mariano, F.; Osella, A.R.; Bonfiglio, C.; Giannelli, G.; Pergola, G.D. Association between adherence to the Mediterranean Diet and circulating Vitamin D levels. *Int. J. Food Sci. Nutr.* **2020**, *71*, 884–890. [CrossRef] [PubMed]
114. Welty, F.K. Dietary treatment to lower cholesterol and triglyceride and reduce cardiovascular risk. *Curr. Opin. Lipidol.* **2020**, *31*, 206–231. [CrossRef]
115. Chen, L.; Chen, X.-W.; Huang, X.; Song, B.-L.; Wang, Y.; Wang, Y. Regulation of glucose and lipid metabolism in health and disease. *Sci. China Life Sci.* **2019**, *62*, 1420–1458. [CrossRef]
116. Yoshimoto, T.; Ochiai, H.; Shirasawa, T.; Nagahama, S.; Kobayashi, M.; Minoura, A.; Miki, A.; Chen, Y.; Hoshino, H.; Kokaze, A. Association between serum lipids and low back pain among a middle-aged Japanese population: A large-scale cross-sectional study. *Lipids Health Dis.* **2018**, *17*, 266. [CrossRef]
117. Heuch, I.; Heuch, I.; Hagen, K.; Zwart, J.-A. Brief Report: Associations Between Serum Lipid Levels and Chronic Low Back Pain. *Epidemiology* **2010**, *21*, 837–841. [CrossRef]
118. Cordero, M.D.; Alcocer-Gómez, E.; Cano-García, F.J.; Sánchez-Domínguez, B.; Fernández-Riejo, P.; Moreno Fernández, A.M.; Fernández-Rodríguez, A.; de Miguel, M. Clinical symptoms in fibromyalgia are associated to overweight and lipid profile. *Rheumatol. Int.* **2014**, *34*, 419–422. [CrossRef]
119. Tilley, B.J.; Cook, J.L.; Docking, S.I.; Gaida, J.E. Is higher serum cholesterol associated with altered tendon structure or tendon pain? A systematic review. *Br. J. Sport. Med.* **2015**, *49*, 1504–1509. [CrossRef]
120. Avgerinos, K.I.; Spyrou, N.; Mantzoros, C.S.; Dalamaga, M. Obesity and cancer risk: Emerging biological mechanisms and perspectives. *Metabolism* **2019**, *92*, 121–135. [CrossRef]
121. Kachur, S.; Lavie, C.J.; de Schutter, A.; Milani, R.V.; Ventura, H.O. Obesity and cardiovascular diseases. *Minerva Med.* **2017**, *108*, 212–228. [CrossRef] [PubMed]
122. Elma, Ö.; Yilmaz, S.T.; Deliens, T.; Clarys, P.; Nijs, J.; Coppieters, I.; Polli, A.; Malfliet, A. Chronic musculoskeletal pain and nutrition: Where are we and where are we heading? *PM R* **2020**, *12*, 1268–1278. [CrossRef] [PubMed]

123. Chin, S.-H.; Huang, W.-L.; Akter, S.; Binks, M. Obesity and pain: A systematic review. *Int. J. Obes.* **2020**, *44*, 969–979. [CrossRef] [PubMed]
124. Bianchi, V.E. Weight loss is a critical factor to reduce inflammation. *Clin. Nutr. ESPEN* **2018**, *28*, 21–35. [CrossRef]
125. Buckman, L.B.; Hasty, A.H.; Flaherty, D.K.; Buckman, C.T.; Thompson, M.M.; Matlock, B.K.; Weller, K.; Ellacott, K.L. Obesity induced by a high-fat diet is associated with increased immune cell entry into the central nervous system. *Brain Behav. Immun.* **2014**, *35*, 33–42. [CrossRef] [PubMed]
126. Valdearcos, M.; Robblee, M.M.; Benjamin, D.I.; Nomura, D.K.; Xu, A.W.; Koliwad, S.K. Microglia dictate the impact of saturated fat consumption on hypothalamic inflammation and neuronal function. *Cell Rep.* **2014**, *9*, 2124–2138. [CrossRef] [PubMed]
127. Robson, E.K.; Hodder, R.K.; Kamper, S.J.; O'Brien, K.M.; Williams, A.; Lee, H.; Wolfenden, L.; Yoong, S.; Wiggers, J.; Barnett, C.; et al. Effectiveness of weight-loss interventions for reducing pain and disability in people with common musculoskeletal disorders: A systematic review with meta-analysis. *J. Orthop. Sport. Phys. Ther.* **2020**, *50*, 319–333. [CrossRef]
128. Tiffon, C. The impact of nutrition and environmental epigenetics on human health and disease. *Int. J. Mol. Sci.* **2018**, *19*, 3425. [CrossRef] [PubMed]
129. Polli, A.; Ickmans, K.; Godderis, L.; Nijs, J. When environment meets genetics: A clinical review of the epigenetics of pain, psychological factors, and physical activity. *Arch. Phys. Med. Rehabil.* **2019**, *100*, 1153–1161. [CrossRef]
130. Ramos-Lopez, O.; Milagro, F.I.; Allayee, H.; Chmurzynska, A.; Choi, M.S.; Curi, R.; De Caterina, R.; Ferguson, L.R.; Goni, L.; Kang, J.X.; et al. Guide for current nutrigenetic, nutrigenomic, and nutriepigenetic approaches for precision nutrition involving the prevention and management of chronic diseases associated with obesity. *Lifestyle Genom.* **2017**, *10*, 43–62. [CrossRef] [PubMed]
131. Bohacek, J.; Mansuy, I.M. Epigenetic inheritance of disease and disease risk. *Neuropsychopharmacology* **2013**, *38*, 220–236. [CrossRef]
132. Brookes, E.; Shi, Y. Diverse epigenetic mechanisms of human disease. *Annu. Rev. Genet.* **2014**, *48*, 237–268. [CrossRef]
133. Nugroho, M.; Kamilla, D.; Auerkari, E. Genetic and epigenetic of pain perception. *J. Phys. Conf. Ser.* **2021**, *1943*, 012088. [CrossRef]
134. Buchheit, T.; Van de Ven, T.; Shaw, A. Epigenetics and the transition from acute to chronic pain. *Pain Med.* **2012**, *13*, 1474–1490. [CrossRef]
135. Ding, Y.; Li, J.; Liu, S.; Zhang, L.; Xiao, H.; Chen, H.; Petersen, R.; Huang, K.; Zheng, L. DNA hypomethylation of inflammation-associated genes in adipose tissue of female mice after multigenerational high fat diet feeding. *Int. J. Obes.* **2014**, *38*, 198–204. [CrossRef]
136. Hermsdorff, H.; Mansego, M.; Campión, J.; Milagro, F.; Zulet, M.; Martínez, J. TNF-alpha promoter methylation in peripheral white blood cells: Relationship with circulating TNFα, truncal fat and n-6 PUFA intake in young women. *Cytokine* **2013**, *64*, 265–271. [CrossRef]
137. Wang, X.; Cao, Q.; Yu, L.; Shi, H.; Xue, B.; Shi, H. Epigenetic regulation of macrophage polarization and inflammation by DNA methylation in obesity. *JCI Insight* **2016**, *1*, e87748. [CrossRef]
138. Ramos-Lopez, O.; Milagro, F.I.; Riezu-Boj, J.I.; Martinez, J.A. Epigenetic signatures underlying inflammation: An interplay of nutrition, physical activity, metabolic diseases, and environmental factors for personalized nutrition. *Inflamm. Res.* **2021**, *70*, 29–49. [CrossRef] [PubMed]
139. Polli, A.; Ickmans, K.; Godderis, L.; Nijs, J. The emerging field of epigenetics and its relevance for the physiotherapy profession. *J. Physiother.* **2019**, *65*, 1–2. [CrossRef] [PubMed]
140. Miller, J.; Wells, L.; Nwulu, U.; Currow, D.; Johnson, M.J.; Skipworth, R.J.E. Validated screening tools for the assessment of cachexia, sarcopenia, and malnutrition: A systematic review. *Am. J. Clin. Nutr.* **2018**, *108*, 1196–1208. [CrossRef] [PubMed]
141. Skipper, A.; Coltman, A.; Tomesko, J.; Charney, P.; Porcari, J.; Piemonte, T.A.; Handu, D.; Cheng, F.W. Reprint of: Position of the Academy of Nutrition and Dietetics: Malnutrition (Undernutrition) Screening Tools for All Adults. *J. Acad. Nutr. Diet.* **2022**, *122*, S50–S54. [CrossRef] [PubMed]
142. Nicholson, B.D.; Hamilton, W.; O'Sullivan, J.; Aveyard, P.; Hobbs, F.R. Weight loss as a predictor of cancer in primary care: A systematic review and meta-analysis. *Br. J. Gen. Pract.* **2018**, *68*, e311–e322. [CrossRef] [PubMed]
143. Elsherif, Y.; Alexakis, C.; Mendall, M. Determinants of Weight Loss prior to Diagnosis in Inflammatory Bowel Disease: A Retrospective Observational Study. *Gastroenterol. Res. Pract.* **2014**, *2014*, 762191. [CrossRef]
144. Amy Janke, E.; Kozak, A.T. "The more pain I have, the more I want to eat": Obesity in the context of chronic pain. *Obesity* **2012**, *20*, 2027–2034. [CrossRef]
145. Janke, E.A.; Spring, B.; Weaver, F. The effect of message framing on self-management of chronic pain: A new perspective on intervention? *Psychol. Health* **2011**, *26*, 931–947. [CrossRef] [PubMed]
146. Barnett, K.; Mercer, S.W.; Norbury, M.; Watt, G.; Wyke, S.; Guthrie, B. Epidemiology of multimorbidity and implications for health care, research, and medical education: A cross-sectional study. *Lancet* **2012**, *380*, 37–43. [CrossRef]
147. Burrows, T.; Teasdale, S.; Rocks, T.; Whatnall, M.; Schindlmayr, J.; Plain, J.; Latimer, G.; Roberton, M.; Harris, D.; Forsyth, A. Effectiveness of dietary interventions in mental health treatment: A rapid review of reviews. *Nutr. Diet.* **2022**, *79*, 279–290. [CrossRef] [PubMed]
148. Evert, A.B.; Dennison, M.; Gardner, C.D.; Garvey, W.T.; Lau, K.H.K.; MacLeod, J.; Mitri, J.; Pereira, R.F.; Rawlings, K.; Robinson, S.; et al. Nutrition Therapy for Adults With Diabetes or Prediabetes: A Consensus Report. *Diabetes Care* **2019**, *42*, 731–754. [CrossRef] [PubMed]
149. Szczepańska, E.; Białek-Dratwa, A.; Janota, B.; Kowalski, O. Dietary Therapy in Prevention of Cardiovascular Disease (CVD)-Tradition or Modernity? A Review of the Latest Approaches to Nutrition in CVD. *Nutrients* **2022**, *14*, 2649. [CrossRef] [PubMed]

150. Oliveira, C.B.; Maher, C.G.; Franco, M.R.; Kamper, S.J.; Williams, C.M.; Silva, F.G.; Pinto, R.Z. Co-occurrence of chronic musculoskeletal pain and cardiovascular diseases: A systematic review with meta-analysis. *Pain Med.* **2020**, *21*, 1106–1121. [CrossRef]
151. Ohayon, M.M.; Stingl, J.C. Prevalence and comorbidity of chronic pain in the German general population. *J. Psychiatr. Res.* **2012**, *46*, 444–450. [CrossRef] [PubMed]
152. GBD 2017 Diet Collaborators. Health effects of dietary risks in 195 countries, 1990–2017: A systematic analysis for the Global Burden of Disease Study 2017. *Lancet* **2019**, *393*, 1958–1972. [CrossRef]
153. Bruggink, L.; Hayes, C.; Lawrence, G.; Brain, K.; Holliday, S. Chronic pain: Overlap and specificity in multimorbidity management. *Aust. J. Gen. Pr.* **2019**, *48*, 689–692. [CrossRef]
154. Bear, T.; Philipp, M.; Hill, S.; Mündel, T. A preliminary study on how hypohydration affects pain perception. *Psychophysiology* **2016**, *53*, 605–610. [CrossRef] [PubMed]
155. Ogino, Y.; Kakeda, T.; Nakamura, K.; Saito, S. Dehydration enhances pain-evoked activation in the human brain compared with rehydration. *Anesth. Analg.* **2014**, *118*, 1317–1325. [CrossRef]
156. Tan, B.; Philipp, M.C.; Muhamed, A.M.C.; Mündel, T. Hypohydration but not menstrual phase influences pain perception in healthy women. *J. Appl. Physiol.* **2022**, *132*, 611–621. [CrossRef]
157. Gunn, J.; Hill, M.M.; Cotten, B.M.; Deer, T.R. An Analysis of Biomarkers in Patients with Chronic Pain. *Pain Physician* **2020**, *23*, E41–E49. [CrossRef]
158. Paez-Hurtado, A.M.; Calderon-Ospina, C.A.; Nava-Mesa, M.O. Mechanisms of action of vitamin B1 (thiamine), B6 (pyridoxine), and B12 (cobalamin) in pain: A narrative review. *Nutr. Neurosci.* **2022**, 1–19. [CrossRef]
159. Erdrich, S.; Hawrelak, J.A.; Myers, S.P.; Harnett, J.E. A systematic review of the association between fibromyalgia and functional gastrointestinal disorders. *Ther. Adv. Gastroenterol.* **2020**, *13*, 1756284820977402. [CrossRef]
160. Drossman, D.A. Functional Gastrointestinal Disorders: History, Pathophysiology, Clinical Features, and Rome IV. *Gastroenterology* **2016**, *150*, 1262–1279.e1262. [CrossRef]
161. Fikree, A.; Byrne, P. Management of functional gastrointestinal disorders. *Clin. Med.* **2021**, *21*, 44–52. [CrossRef] [PubMed]
162. Van Lanen, A.S.; de Bree, A.; Greyling, A. Efficacy of a low-FODMAP diet in adult irritable bowel syndrome: A systematic review and meta-analysis. *Eur. J. Nutr.* **2021**, *60*, 3505–3522. [CrossRef] [PubMed]
163. Gibson, P.R. The evidence base for efficacy of the low FODMAP diet in irritable bowel syndrome: Is it ready for prime time as a first-line therapy? *J. Gastroenterol. Hepatol.* **2017**, *32* (Suppl. S1), 32–35. [CrossRef] [PubMed]
164. Hill, P.; Muir, J.G.; Gibson, P.R. Controversies and Recent Developments of the Low-FODMAP Diet. *Gastroenterol. Hepatol.* **2017**, *13*, 36–45.
165. Wirt, A.; Collins, C.E. Diet quality—What is it and does it matter? *Public Health Nutr.* **2009**, *12*, 2473–2492. [CrossRef] [PubMed]
166. Kim, S.; Haines, P.S.; Siega-Riz, A.M.; Popkin, B.M. The Diet Quality Index-International (DQI-I) Provides an Effective Tool for Cross-National Comparison of Diet Quality as Illustrated by China and the United States. *J. Nutr.* **2003**, *133*, 3476–3484. [CrossRef] [PubMed]
167. Kirkpatrick, S.I.; Reedy, J.; Krebs-Smith, S.M.; Pannucci, T.E.; Subar, A.F.; Wilson, M.M.; Lerman, J.L.; Tooze, J.A. Applications of the Healthy Eating Index for Surveillance, Epidemiology, and Intervention Research: Considerations and Caveats. *J. Acad. Nutr. Diet.* **2018**, *118*, 1603–1621. [CrossRef]
168. Shivappa, N.; Steck, S.E.; Hurley, T.G.; Hussey, J.R.; Hébert, J.R. Designing and developing a literature-derived, population-based dietary inflammatory index. *Public Health Nutr.* **2014**, *17*, 1689–1696. [CrossRef]
169. Williams, R.L.; Rollo, M.E.; Schumacher, T.; Collins, C.E. Diet Quality Scores of Australian Adults Who Have Completed the Healthy Eating Quiz. *Nutrients* **2017**, *9*, 880. [CrossRef]
170. Philpot, U.; Johnson, M.I. Diet therapy in the management of chronic pain: Better diet less pain? *Future Med.* **2019**, *9*, 335–338. [CrossRef]
171. Elizabeth, L.; Machado, P.; Zinöcker, M.; Baker, P.; Lawrence, M. Ultra-Processed Foods and Health Outcomes: A Narrative Review. *Nutrients* **2020**, *12*, 1955. [CrossRef] [PubMed]
172. Monteiro, C.A.; Cannon, G.; Levy, R.B.; Moubarac, J.C.; Louzada, M.L.; Rauber, F.; Khandpur, N.; Cediel, G.; Neri, D.; Martinez-Steele, E.; et al. Ultra-processed foods: What they are and how to identify them. *Public Health Nutr.* **2019**, *22*, 936–941. [CrossRef] [PubMed]
173. Monteiro, C.A.; Cannon, G.; Lawrence, M.; Costa Louzada, M.d.; Pereira Machado, P. *Ultra-Processed Foods, Diet Quality, and Health Using the NOVA Classification System*; FAO: Rome, Italy, 2019; p. 49.
174. *Guideline: Sugars Intake for Adults and Children*; World Health Organization: Geneva, Switzerland, 2015.
175. Glenn, A.; Kavanagh, M.; Bockus-Thorne, L.; McNeill, L.; Melina, V.; Jenkins, D.; Grant, S. Medical nutrition therapy for chronic pain management. In *Clinical Pain Management: A Practical Guide*, 2nd ed.; Wiley Blackwell: Hoboken, NJ, USA, 2022; pp. 147–159.
176. Bigand, T.L.; Dietz, J.; Gubitz, H.N.; Wilson, M. Chronic pain and depressive symptoms are related to food insecurity among urban food bank users. *J. Public Health* **2021**, *43*, 573–580. [CrossRef] [PubMed]
177. Men, F.; Fischer, B.; Urquia, M.L.; Tarasuk, V. Food insecurity, chronic pain, and use of prescription opioids. *SSM Popul. Health* **2021**, *14*, 100768. [CrossRef] [PubMed]
178. Michie, S.; Van Stralen, M.M.; West, R. The behaviour change wheel: A new method for characterising and designing behaviour change interventions. *Implement. Sci.* **2011**, *6*, 42. [CrossRef]
179. Dietary behaviour. Available online: https://www.abs.gov.au/statistics/health/health-conditions-and-risks/dietary-behaviour/latest-release (accessed on 26 September 2022).

180. Nutrition Care Process [Internet]: Academy of Nutrition and Dietetics Evidence Analysis Library. Available online: https://www.ncpro.org//default.cfm (accessed on 26 September 2022).
181. Pasdar, Y.; Hamzeh, B.; Karimi, S.; Moradi, S.; Cheshmeh, S.; Shamsi, M.B.; Najafi, F. Major dietary patterns in relation to chronic low back pain; a cross-sectional study from RaNCD cohort. *Nutr. J.* **2022**, *21*, 28. [CrossRef]
182. Leech, R.M.; McNaughton, S.A.; Timperio, A. The clustering of diet, physical activity and sedentary behavior in children and adolescents: A review. *Int. J. Behav. Nutr. Phys. Act.* **2014**, *11*, 4. [CrossRef]
183. Liberali, R.; Del Castanhel, F.; Kupek, E.; Assis, M.A.A. Latent Class Analysis of Lifestyle Risk Factors and Association with Overweight and/or Obesity in Children and Adolescents: Systematic Review. *Child. Obes.* **2021**, *17*, 2–15. [CrossRef]
184. Scoditti, E.; Tumolo, M.R.; Garbarino, S. Mediterranean Diet on Sleep: A Health Alliance. *Nutrients* **2022**, *14*, 2998. [CrossRef]

Journal of
Clinical Medicine

MDPI

Brief Report

Changes in Psychological Outcomes after Cessation of Full Mu Agonist Long-Term Opioid Therapy for Chronic Pain

Marcelina Jasmine Silva [1,*], Zhanette Coffee [2], Chong Ho Alex Yu [3] and Joshua Hu [4]

[1] The Focus on Opioid Transitions (FOOT Steps) Program, IPM Medical Group, Walnut Creek, CA 94598, USA
[2] College of Nursing, University of Arizona, Tucson, AZ 85721, USA
[3] Office of Institutional Research, Azusa Pacific University, Azusa, CA 91702, USA
[4] College of Osteopathic Medicine, Touro University, Vallejo, CA 94592, USA
* Correspondence: MJSilvaDO@gmail.com

Abstract: Improved understanding of psychological features associated with full mu agonist long-term opioid therapy (LTOT) cessation may offer advantages for clinicians. This preliminary study presents changes in psychological outcomes in patients with chronic, non-cancer pain (CNCP) after LTOT cessation via a 10-week multidisciplinary program which included treatment with buprenorphine. Paired *t*-tests pre- and post-LTOT cessation were compared in this retrospective cohort review of data from electronic medical records of 98 patients who successfully ceased LTOT between the dates of October 2017 to December 2019. Indicators of quality of life, depression, catastrophizing, and fear avoidance, as measured by the 36-Item Short Form Survey, the Patient Health Questionnaire-9-Item Scale, the Pain Catastrophizing Scale, and the Fear Avoidance Belief Questionnaires revealed significant improvement. Scores did not significantly improve for daytime sleepiness, generalized anxiety, and kinesiophobia, as measured by the Epworth Sleepiness Scale, the Generalized Anxiety Disorder 7-Item Scale, and the Tampa Scale of Kinesiophobia. The results suggest that successful LTOT cessation may be interconnected with improvements in specific psychological states.

Keywords: chronic pain; opioids; patient experiences; psychological outcomes; management; treatment; buprenorphine

Citation: Silva, M.J.; Coffee, Z.; Yu, C.H.A.; Hu, J. Changes in Psychological Outcomes after Cessation of Full Mu Agonist Long-Term Opioid Therapy for Chronic Pain. *J. Clin. Med.* **2023**, *12*, 1354. https://doi.org/10.3390/jcm12041354

Academic Editors: Carmen María Galvez Sánchez, Casandra I. Montoro Aguilar, Markus W. Hollmann and Tomoyuki Kawamata

Received: 3 December 2022
Revised: 20 January 2023
Accepted: 2 February 2023
Published: 8 February 2023

1. Introduction

The medical community was called to action by The Centers for Disease Control and Prevention (CDC) 2016 guidelines to decrease exposure to full mu agonist long-term opioid therapy (LTOT) for chronic, non-cancer pain (CNCP) in an effort to stem the resulting sequelae of the increasing incidence of opioid overdose [1]. Less severe, but still disturbing, adverse full mu agonist opioid medication effects are numerous and well documented, ranging from immediate (cognitive impairment, dry mucous membranes, slowed intestinal motility) [2] to long-term and insidious (hypogonadism [3], immune compromise [4], and hyperalgesia) [5,6]. Associations between opioid use and declining mood states have also been well documented, such as a decline in patient-perceived quality of life [7], and increased measures of depression [8–11], catastrophizing [10,12,13], fear avoidance [14], and anxiety [10,12,15,16]. However, unforeseen complications regarding efforts to reduce or discontinue opioid dosing within the patient population that utilizes LTOT are becoming apparent [17,18], with recent reports documenting associated overdose and suicide [19–21]. Improved understanding of psychological features associated with a cohort of patients who successfully ceased LTOT may offer useful directives for how to proceed effectively when LTOT cessation is desired.

One potential alternative to LTOT is buprenorphine. Buprenorphine is an opioid drug with partial mu agonist properties [22]. It can be a safer option than full mu agonist opioids for some patients [23,24], as the dangers of respiratory depression and overdose-related death associated with opioid use are thought to be conferred by full mu receptor agonism [24,25]. However, partial mu agonism, in the case of buprenorphine, confers potent analgesia [26–29].

The primary aim of this study was to identify changes between psychological assessment questionnaires, pre and post LTOT cessation, for patients with CNCP. We present findings from a retrospective analysis in a cohort of patients with CNCP who were successfully able to cease LTOT through participation in a group, multidisciplinary program [14,30] that offered therapeutic options that included buprenorphine. This study took place prior to reports of declining clinical outcomes after LTOT cessation, which notably did not include the option of buprenorphine in care planning [2–6]. Informed by multiple reports of declining mood with opioid initiation [8–16], the researchers hypothesized that LTOT cessation would result in improved mood outcomes.

2. Materials and Methods

2.1. Study Design

De-identified data were collected via a retrospective review of electronic medical records (EMR) from October 2017 to December 2019, comparing the pre- and post-psychological assessment questionnaire scores of 98 patients with CNCP who successfully ceased LTOT use through participation in a previously described, group multidisciplinary program [14,30]. Questionnaires were given to each patient at orientation and at graduation. Pre- and post-LTOT cessation scores were paired and used for analysis in this study.

2.2. Intervention

The multidisciplinary program [14,30,31] operated as a stand-alone intervention within a larger, multi-center, private practice specializing in CNCP in Northern California. Two centers and clinical teams participated in program administration under one medical director. Patients in the program met for approximately six hours once a week for ten weeks. The standardized curriculum entailed group cognitive behavioral therapy, group home exercise training utilizing complimentary care activities, and individualized medication management. Buprenorphine was offered to each patient as an alternative to LTOT. Extended panel urine drug screening was mandated at each meeting to corroborate participant compliance.

2.3. Participants

Study participants were comprised of the 98 successful graduates of a multidisciplinary LTOT cessation program that commenced between October of 2017 and December of 2019. A total of 109 patients started the program, and 11 either voluntarily left or were referred to a higher level of care due to high acuity comorbidities diagnosed after admittance. Program inclusion criteria were: adult-aged patients who voluntarily enrolled for the purpose of LTOT cessation due to lack of satisfaction with pain control, medication effects, and/or functional capacity while on LTOT. Participants were diagnosed with CNCP from any etiology; had used daily LTOT at the time of admission for a minimum of a year's duration (although most reported much longer use), or struggled to maintain recent opioid cessation after prolonged use; had previously tried and failed or plateaued in regards to opioid weaning. Program recruitment, exclusion criteria, and criteria for referral have been described elsewhere [14,30,31]. Long-term opioid therapy was defined as any form of prescribed oral or transdermal long- or short-acting pharmaceutical opioid obtained while under the care of a physician. At admission, participants used LTOT amounts as high as 600 daily oral morphine milligram equivalents (MME) (median, 60 MME; 25% quartile, 36.5 MME; 75% quartile, 90 MME; interquartile range, 53.5 MME) [30].

2.4. Measures

Standardized psychological questionnaires were given to each patient at the program orientation meeting and again at the program graduation. Each questionnaire was previously and independently validated. Table 1 lists and describes the application of the Epworth Sleepiness Scale (ESS) [32], the 36-Item Short Form Survey (SF-36) [33], the

Generalized Anxiety Disorder–7 Item Scale (GAD-7) [34], the Patient Health Questionnaire (PHQ) [35], the Fear Avoidance Belief Questionnaire-Physical Activity (FAB-PA) and Work (FAB-W) [36], the Tampa Kinesiophobia Scale (TSK) [37], the Pain Catastrophizing Scale (PCS) [38], and the Brief Pain Inventory-Pain Severity (BPI-Pain) and Impairment (BPI-Impairment) survey [39].

Table 1. Psychological assessment questionnaires.

Questionnaire	Application
Epworth Sleepiness Scale (ESS) [32]	Measures daytime sleepiness: 0 to 10 is normal; 11–12 is mild; 13–15 is moderate excessive; and 16–24 is severe excessive.
The 36-Item Short Form Survey (SF-36) [33]	A total of 8 categories are scored on a scale from 0 to 100, with 100 representing the highest level of functioning possible: physical functioning, bodily pain, role limitations due to physical health problems, role limitations due to personal or emotional problems, emotional well-being, social functioning, energy/fatigue, and general health perceptions.
Generalized Anxiety Disorder 7-Item Scale (GAD-7) [34]	Assesses anxiety: 0–5 is mild, 6–10 is moderate, and 11–15 is high.
Patient Health Questionnaire (PHQ) [35]	Assesses depression: 1–4 is minimal, 5–9 is mild, 10–14 is moderate, 15–19 is moderately severe, and 20–27 is severe.
Fear Avoidance Beliefs Questionnaire—Work and Physical Activity (FAB-Wand PA) [14,36,40]	Two subscales (FAB-W: 0-42; FAB-PA 0-24) in which higher scores indicate more severe pain and disability due to fear avoidance beliefs about work and physical activity. Various score thresholds have been documented as associated with clinical relevancy and specific negative chronicity of CNCP. Higher scores have been associated with poor physical and manual therapy results and low return to work rates after an injury.
Tampa Scale of Kinesiophobia (TKS) [37]	A measure of fear of movement and reinjury. Scores range from 17–68, with higher scores being of higher severity.
Pain Catastrophizing Scale (PCS) [14,38,41,42]	Assesses levels of catastrophizing. In initial validation, a score of 30 or more correlated with high unemployment, self-declared "total" disability, and clinical depression. However, various lower score thresholds have been documented as associated with clinical relevancy for specific negative chronicity of CNCP.
Brief Pain Inventory-Severity and Impairment (BPI-Pain and Impairment) [39,43]	Provides two scores which assess the severity of pain and pain-related impairment on daily functions using the mean of several Likert scales of 0–10, with 10 being the worst.

Of note, additional data were gathered throughout the program for the separate analyses of protective and hindering psychological and clinical features associated with LTOT cessation success, and these can be found in earlier publications [14,30].

2.5. Analysis

Descriptive statistics were derived from retrospective data found in the demographic section of the EMR for program graduates. Paired *t*-tests were used to compare dataset means from psychological questionnaires pre- and post-LTOT cessation. Prior to paired comparison, principal component analysis (PCA) was used to compare individual SF-36 subcategory results for the pre- and posttests. The SF-36 is typically reported as 8 individual scores—one for each category. However, since running multiple *t*-tests for all SF-36 subcategories might inflate the Type I error rate and result in false findings, dimension reduction was employed to minimize the number of variables to be tested. In PCA, data visualization techniques, including the loading plot [44,45] and the scree plot, were utilized in order to identify the proper number of principal components.

3. Results

3.1. Descriptive Statistics

The study began with 109 clinical program participants; 11 left the clinical program and were lost to the follow-up. Thus, 98 subjects (representing 90% of the program participants) remained under observation after the successful cessation of LTOT during the 10-week program [30] and were included in the present study. Of those who successfully graduated, 95 subjects (97%) chose to use buprenorphine as an LTOT cessation tool. Program participants were 27 to 88 years old; 69% were identified as female. A broad range of payer sources were noted: 30% Medicare, 25% industrial insurance, 10% Medicaid, 44% commercial insurance, and <1% no insurance.

3.2. Principal Component Analysis and Scree Plot for the SF-36

The reliability index, as measured by the standardized Cronbach's alpha of the pretest of SF-36 is 0.8899, compared with 0.846 at the posttest, implying that the response patterns to these questions are internally consistent. In the loading plot, the axes of the plots are the principal components, while the variables are symbolized by vectors radiating from the center. Vectors pointing in the same direction, with a small angle between them, implies a positive and close relationship between the variables. Due to this characteristic, they could be loaded into the same component. Figure 1a indicates that all observed variables in the pretest of SF-36, as depicted by the vectors, pointed in the same direction and are close to each other. Figure 1b suggests that the observed items in the posttest of SF-36 could be classified into two groups, based on the clustering patterns.

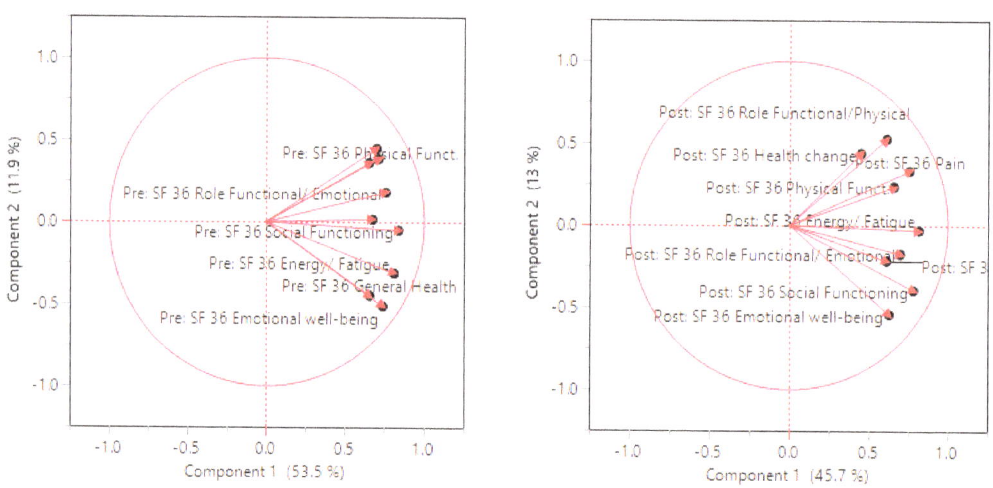

(**a**) Loading plot of pretest vectors. (**b**) Loading plot of posttest vectors.

Figure 1. Loading plots of SF-36 vectors.

In the scree plot (Figure 2a,b), the y-axis represents the eigenvalue, which is the sum of the squares of the loadings, whereas the x-axis denotes the number of potential components. Although the loading plot of the posttest indicates a 2-component model, both scree plots suggest that one single component is sufficient to yield the highest eigenvalue. Considering this finding, the average pretest and posttest scores of all SF-36 items were used for paired t-tests.

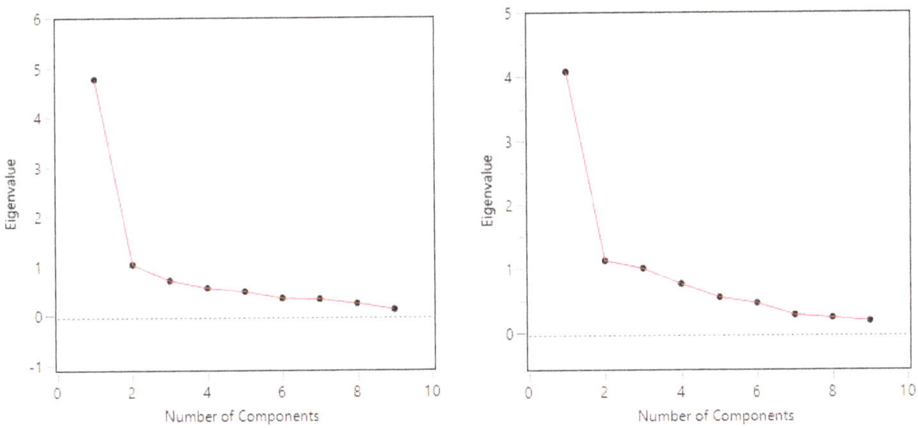

(**a**) Scree plot of pretest SF-36 variables.

(**b**) Scree plot of posttest SF-36 variables.

Figure 2. Scree plot of SF-36 variables.

3.3. Paired t-Tests

Paired *t*-tests were used to compare dataset means from psychological questionnaires pre- and post-LTOT cessation (Table 2). As indicated in the table, six out of ten paired *t*-tests yielded a significant *p*-value (<0.0001). Because multiple *t*-tests were conducted, the Type 1 error rate might be inflated. The Bonferroni correction rectifies the situation by dividing the alpha level by the number of tests. In this case, the adjusted alpha level is 0.05/10 = 0.005. Nevertheless, because the *p*-value of all significant results is <0.0001, which is far lower than 0.005, the conclusion remains the same.

Table 2. Paired *t*-tests of pre- and post-LTOT cessation psychological assessment questionnaires.

Variable	Pretest Mean	Posttest Mean	Std. Error	n	t-Ratio	*p*	Lower 95% CI	Upper 95% CI
SF-36	36.95	49.76	2.41	64	5.31	<0.0001 *	7.99	17.62
ESS	8.08	8.47	0.46	61	0.84	0.4058	−0.54	1.31
PHQ	11.82	7.91	0.81	57	−4.80	<0.0001 *	−5.53	−2.29
GAD7	7.71	7.43	0.94	58	−0.29	0.7692	−2.15	1.60
BPI-Pain	5.91	4.67	0.20	58	−6.19	<0.0001 *	−1.65	−0.84
BPI-Impairment	6.35	4.56	0.30	60	−5.88	<0.0001 *	−2.39	−1.18
PCS	21.6	13.32	1.39	56	−5.92	<0.0001 *	−11.09	−5.48
FAB-PA	12.95	11.18	1.03	55	−1.71	<0.0001 *	−3.83	0.31
FAB-W	24.02	23.8	1.31	45	−0.14	0.8867	−3.01	1.39
TSK	35.72	35.16	1.42	34	0.39	0.6967	−3.39	2.29

* Significant at the 0.01 Alpha level.

Data imputation was considered for this study for the inconsistent n value, but was ruled out because some participants deliberately chose to skip several questions or entire assessments. When data are missing due to inherent lack of randomness, it is impossible to account for systematic differences between the missing and the observed values based on the existing data, especially when the reference data are sparse. Further, when all or many responses in a group of questions are missing, multiple imputation will yield misleading results [46].

4. Discussion

4.1. Improved Psychological Assessment Scores Post-LTOT Cessation

This study found that the improvement between the pre- and post-cessation indicators of quality of life, depression, pain interference, catastrophizing, and fear avoidance (assessed via the SF-36, PHQ, BPI-Pain, BPI-Impairment, PCS, and FAB-PA, respectively) among subjects with CNCP who successfully ceased LTOT are significant at the level of $p < 0.001$. These findings are consistent with those in previous studies examining mood changes affiliated with problematic opioid use, which have described an intercorrelation between such use and increased depression [8–11,47], fear avoidance [43], catastrophizing [10,12,13,38,48], and decreased quality of life [7] with increased states of pain [12,14–16,47–60]. Interpretation of the present findings must consider not only the impact of LTOT cessation, but also that of buprenorphine introduction and concurrent participation in a group multidisciplinary program, or even a potential synergy between these factors.

Most subjects utilized buprenorphine for LTOT cessation. Buprenorphine acts as a partial mu agonist and as an antagonist at the delta [26,55] and kappa [24,26,55] opioid receptors [26,57–59]. These receptor dynamics have been theorized to confer anxiolytic [56] and anti-depressive effects [50,58–64] in opioid-dependent [56] and opioid-naïve [47,55,58,60] patients and to improve patient-reported scores regarding quality of life [28,50]. Perhaps the addition of buprenorphine can explain, at least in part, the discrepancy between the participants' mood improvements compared with recent studies documenting clinical deterioration with LTOT cessation [19–21]. This dynamic would be an interesting area of future study.

The effects of both partial and full mu agonist opioid exposure on quality of life have been previously studied. One study showed that full mu agonist opioid exposure lowered the SF-36 score initially, but no difference was found between patients with CNCP exposed to opioids vs. not exposed after 4 years duration [7]. Another reported that opioid-naïve patients exhibited improvements in SF-36 scores after 8 weeks of daily treatment with buprenorphine for the indication of treatment-resistant depression [50]. Similarly, a different study found that switching from LTOT to sublingual buprenorphine for at least 60 days resulted in improved quality of life scales, as measured using the QOLS [28]. Longer term follow-up studies would be helpful to better understand the relationship between LTOT, buprenorphine, and quality of life.

In the current dataset, the post-LTOT cessation depression scores (assessed via the PHQ) show a mean improvement from moderately severe to moderate depression, which trends consistently with the results in previous publications. The link between depression and problematic full mu agonist opioid use has been previously documented from a variety of angles. Higher depression scores have been correlated with opioid misuse in CNCP patients with no prior substance use disorder [10]. Depression has also been identified as a risk factor for prolonged post-surgical opioid use [11]. Similarly, researchers have found that opioid use is a risk factor for depression, independent of pain [8,9]. Buprenorphine's effect on depression has also been studied in patients with and without concurrent opioid use disorder and was shown to provide marked improvement in suicidal ideation and treatment-resistant depression after administration [47,58]. Similarly, in a meta-analysis conducted by Serafini et al., 13 studies concluded that buprenorphine alone, or in co-administration with other opioid antagonists, may significantly reduce depression [59]. The current data, supported by previous studies, strongly suggest that depression is an important target for assessment and therapy in the pursuit of LTOT cessation.

Previous reports regarding the PCS and FAB are nuanced. For the PCS, it is interesting to note that a score of 30 or higher was initially validated as clinically relevant [38,42]. However, lower scores have been documented to be associated with the chronicity of prolonged recovery and delayed return to work [45]. Therefore, the substantial improvement in the PCS score with LTOT cessation seen in this study can be argued to be clinically significant, despite being below 30 on the pretest, especially considering the scale of the improvement. Targeted psychosocial therapy to improve catastrophizing has been shown to significantly aid in returning to work after a period of disability [48]. Current results suggest that addressing catastrophizing may be an avenue worthy of future study for promoting LTOT cessation for patients with CNCP.

The optimal cut off for determining significant FAB scores has been studied in several contexts and varies respectively [36,40,61–64]. Higher FAB scores have been correlated with an increased probability of current and future work loss and disability [36,65,66], as well as social withdrawal [67] and increased LTOT reliance [14]. FAB analysis may also help determine which clinical interventions have an increased probability of a successful outcome to decrease patient-reported disability and pain [36,68,69]. Of note, some of the utility of the FAB, when correlated in these specific ways, has been validated only in industrially insured patients [69], and the FAB-W has been validated for currently—or recently—working patients [36,68,70]. Thus, the present FAB results are difficult to analyze based on previous validations, as the current study did not exclude participants who identified as disabled or retired, nor did it control for insurance payer type.

The BPI scores warrant notice in that their improvement implies a general lack of suffering among the participants, despite LTOT cessation.

4.2. Psychological Assessment Scores Lacking Significant Improvement Post-LTOT Cessation

Equally interesting is the lack of association seen between LTOT cessation and daytime sleepiness, generalized anxiety, and kinesiophobia (assessed via the ESS, GAD, and TSK, respectively). Nighttime sleep disturbance and daytime impaired cognition are common anecdotal complaints among patients on LTOT. Disturbed sleep architecture and increased obstructive and central sleep apnea have long been recognized as side effects of chronic opioid use [70,71]. Thus, it was surprising that LTOT cessation did not pair with improved daytime sleepiness. However, this outcome is consistent with previous studies documenting that sleep disturbance does not necessarily correlate with daytime sleepiness, as measured by the ESS, in chronic opioid users [70–72].

The improvement in anxiety (assessed via the GAD) between pre- and post-LTOT cessation was not significant. Previous studies have suggested that a self-medication model has been implicated in inciting, or exacerbating, opioid use disorder for patients with clinically significant anxiety [12,16,51], and higher anxiety scores have also been implicated in the increased length of post-operative opioid analgesic use [10]. Moreover, studies have found buprenorphine administration to be correlated with improvement in anxiety [47,56]. The relationship between anxiety and LTOT reliance warrants increased study to help reconcile present and previous findings.

Kinesiophobia (TSK) scores did not follow the significant improvement trajectory of the PCS and FAB- PA. These tools are often grouped together in the category of anxiety, or fear-based, belief and behavior assessments. However, previous investigation into their interchangeability has failed to show cross-over reliability [73]. Of note is the fact that many participants chose not to complete the TSK, for unknown reasons, and it was by far the most neglected of the tests by the participants, with an "n" of 34. Perhaps the smaller number of datasets affected the significance of this outcome.

4.3. Contribution to the Field

The present findings help to identify psychological improvements associated with successful LTOT cessation. While this study does not prove whether the intervention of the medication changes improved the mood outcomes, or whether the multidisciplinary program promoted a foundation of mood change that allowed for LTOT cessation, it is clear that specific mood improvements were associated with LTOT cessation. With further study, this dynamic may eventually suggest inroads to safer and more optimal treatments in the field of CNCP. Just as previous studies have shown that addressing high fear avoidance and catastrophizing beliefs improved disability measures [48,74], the current findings could provide the foundation to target specific psychological states for education and multidisciplinary support to aid in successful LTOT cessation in future trials.

4.4. Study Limitations

Studies that increase understanding of the clinical features that promote LTOT cessation are timely, yet scant, thus making the present findings relevant, despite the following design limitations: the data for this study were gathered retrospectively from a moderately-sized treatment cohort of non-randomized, non-blinded patients, who were treated in a private practice setting, and demographic subject data is limited. The lack of a long-term follow-up of mood status is also a limitation, and this follow-up would be especially interesting here, as an affiliated study showed prolonged cessation of LTOT in the current group [30].

5. Conclusions

This study found that improvements in indicators of quality of life, depression, pain interference, catastrophizing, and fear avoidance are associated with successful LTOT cessation in patients with chronic, non-cancer pain who participated in a multidisciplinary opioid cessation program that offered buprenorphine as a substitution. Further research is required to confirm the nature of this relationship. A better understanding of these potentially interdependent clinical phenomena may eventually help clarify and improve interventions for the cessation of LTOT in patients with CNCP.

Author Contributions: Conceptualization, M.J.S.; methodology, M.J.S., Z.C. and C.H.A.Y.; software, M.J.S., Z.C. and C.H.A.Y.; validation, C.H.A.Y.; formal analysis, M.J.S. and C.H.A.Y.; investigation, M.J.S. and Z.C.; resources, M.J.S., Z.C. and J.H.; data curation, M.J.S., Z.C. and C.H.A.Y.; writing—original draft preparation, M.J.S. and J.H.; writing—review and editing, M.J.S., Z.C., C.H.A.Y. and J.H.; visualization, M.J.S. and C.H.A.Y.; supervision, M.J.S.; project administration, M.J.S. All authors have read and agreed to the published version of the manuscript.

Funding: The researchers analyzed data through the course of routine, clinical, program-related quality assurance measures while under the employ of the IPM Medical Group. This research received no external funding.

Institutional Review Board Statement: This study was reviewed by Solutions IRB and was determined to be exempt from full review, according to 45CFR46.104(d)(4): (4) Secondary Research Uses of Data or Specimens, on 17 March 2020.

Informed Consent Statement: The IRB declared that consent was not required for this retrospective review of de-identified data or for publication of that data. However, participants were apprised of the nature of the intended use of their anonymous data, and provided consent at the time of data collection.

Data Availability Statement: The de-identified data can be retrieved from the authors, upon request.

Acknowledgments: The authors thank Jessica Goza, NP; Kelly Rumrill, NP; Tatiana Hernandez, CCA; and Julie Ginsburg, LAc, for their teamwork and assistance, as well as William George, Jr., for his encouragement.

Conflicts of Interest: The authors declare no conflict of interest.

References

1. Dowell, D.; Haegerich, T.M.; Chou, R. CDC Guideline for Prescribing Opioids for Chronic Pain—United States. *MMWR Recomm. Rep.* **2016**, *65*, 1–49. [CrossRef] [PubMed]
2. National Institute on Drug Abuse. Prescription Opioids DrugFacts. Available online: https://www.drugabuse.gov/publications/drugfacts/prescription-opioids (accessed on 19 October 2020).
3. Antony, T.; Alzaharani, S.Y.; El-Ghaiesh, S.H. Opioid-induced hypogonadism: Pathophysiology, clinical and therapeutics review. *Clin. Exp. Pharmacol. Physiol.* **2020**, *47*, 741–750. [CrossRef] [PubMed]
4. Eisenstein, T.K.; Rogers, T.J. Drugs of Abuse. In *Neuroimmune Pharmacology*; Ikezu, T., Gendelman, H.E., Eds.; Springer International Publishing: Cham, Switzerland, 2017; pp. 661–678. ISBN 978-3-319-44022-4.

5. Chu, L.F.; Angst, M.S.; Clark, D. Opioid-induced hyperalgesia in humans: Molecular mechanisms and clinical considerations. *Clin. J. Pain* **2008**, *24*, 479–496. [CrossRef] [PubMed]
6. Lee, M.; Silverman, S.M.; Hansen, H.; Patel, V.B.; Manchikanti, L. A comprehensive review of opioid-induced hyperalgesia. *Pain Physician* **2011**, *14*, 145–161. [CrossRef]
7. Radcliff, K.; Freedman, M.; Hilibrand, A.; Isaac, R.; Lurie, J.D.; Zhao, W.; Vaccaro, A.; Albert, T.; Weinstein, J. Does Opioid Pain Medication Use Affect the Outcome of Patients with Lumbar Disk Herniation? *Spine* **2013**, *38*, E849–E860. [CrossRef]
8. Scherrer, J.F.; Ahmedani, B.; Autio, K.; Debar, L.; Lustman, P.J.; Miller-Matero, L.R.; Salas, J.; Secrest, S.; Sullivan, M.D.; Wilson, L.; et al. The Prescription Opioids and Depression Pathways Cohort Study. *J. Psychiatr. Brain Sci.* **2020**, *5*, e200009. [CrossRef]
9. Scherrer, J.F.; Salas, J.; Schneider, F.D.; Bucholz, K.K.; Sullivan, M.D.; Copeland, L.A.; Ahmedani, B.K.; Burroughs, T.; Lustman, P.J. Characteristics of new depression diagnoses in patients with and without prior chronic opioid use. *J. Affect. Disord.* **2017**, *210*, 125–129. [CrossRef]
10. Helmerhorst, G.T.T.; Vranceanu, A.-M.; Vrahas, M.; Smith, M.; Ring, D. Risk Factors for Continued Opioid Use One to Two Months After Surgery for Musculoskeletal Trauma. *JBJS* **2014**, *96*, 495–499. [CrossRef]
11. Grattan, A.; Sullivan, M.D.; Saunders, K.W.; Campbell, C.I.; Von Korff, M.R. Depression and Prescription Opioid Misuse among Chronic Opioid Therapy Recipients with No History of Substance Abuse. *Ann. Fam. Med.* **2012**, *10*, 304–311. [CrossRef]
12. Arteta, J.; Cobos, B.; Hu, Y.; Jordan, K.; Howard, K. Evaluation of How Depression and Anxiety Mediate the Relationship between Pain Catastrophizing and Prescription Opioid Misuse in a Chronic Pain Population. *Pain Med.* **2016**, *17*, 295–303. [CrossRef]
13. Martel, M.O.; Jamison, R.N.; Wasan, A.D.; Edwards, R.R. The Association Between Catastrophizing and Craving in Patients with Chronic Pain Prescribed Opioid Therapy: A Preliminary Analysis. *Pain Med.* **2014**, *15*, 1757–1764. [CrossRef]
14. Silva, M.J.; Coffee, Z.; Yu, C.H.A.; Martel, M.O. Anxiety and Fear Avoidance Beliefs and Behavior May Be Significant Risk Factors for Chronic Opioid Analgesic Therapy Reliance for Patients with Chronic Pain—Results from a Preliminary Study. *Pain Med.* **2021**, *22*, 2106–2116. [CrossRef]
15. Martins, S.S.; Fenton, M.C.; Keyes, K.M.; Blanco, C.; Zhu, H.; Storr, C.L. Mood/Anxiety disorders and their association with non-medical prescription opioid use and prescription opioid use disorder: Longitudinal evidence from the National Epidemiologic Study on Alcohol and Related Conditions. *Psychol. Med.* **2012**, *42*, 1261–1272. [CrossRef]
16. Gros, D.F.; Milanak, M.E.; Brady, K.T.; Back, S.E. Frequency and Severity of Comorbid Mood and Anxiety Disorders in Prescription Opioid Dependence. *Am. J. Addict.* **2013**, *22*, 261–265. [CrossRef]
17. Manhapra, A.; Sullivan, M.D.; Ballantyne, J.C.; MacLean, R.R.; Becker, W.C. Complex Persistent Opioid Dependence with Long-term Opioids: A Gray Area That Needs Definition, Better Understanding, Treatment Guidance, and Policy Changes. *J. Gen. Intern. Med.* **2020**, *35*, 964–971. [CrossRef]
18. Process for Updating the Opioid Prescribing Guideline | CDC's Response to the Opioid Overdose Epidemic | CDC. Available online: https://www.cdc.gov/opioids/guideline-update/index.html (accessed on 25 February 2022).
19. Oliva, E.M.; Bowe, T.; Manhapra, A.; Kertesz, S.; Hah, J.M.; Henderson, P.; Robinson, A.; Paik, M.; Sandbrink, F.; Gordon, A.J.; et al. Associations between stopping prescriptions for opioids, length of opioid treatment, and overdose or suicide deaths in US veterans: Observational evaluation. *BMJ* **2020**, *368*, m283. [CrossRef]
20. James, J.R.; Scott, J.M.; Klein, J.W.; Jackson, S.; McKinney, C.; Novack, M.; Chew, L.; Merrill, J.O. Mortality After Discontinuation of Primary Care–Based Chronic Opioid Therapy for Pain: A Retrospective Cohort Study. *J. Gen. Intern. Med.* **2019**, *34*, 2749–2755. [CrossRef]
21. Mark, T.L.; Parish, W. Opioid medication discontinuation and risk of adverse opioid-related health care events. *J. Subst. Abuse Treat.* **2019**, *103*, 58–63. [CrossRef]
22. Lutfy, K.; Cowan, A. Buprenorphine: A Unique Drug with Complex Pharmacology. *Curr. Neuropharmacol.* **2004**, *2*, 395–402. [CrossRef]
23. Dahan, A.; Yassen, A.; Romberg, R.; Sarton, E.; Teppema, L.; Olofsen, E.; Danhof, M. Buprenorphine induces ceiling in respiratory depression but not in analgesia. *Br. J. Anaesth.* **2006**, *96*, 627–632. [CrossRef]
24. Walsh, S.L.; Preston, K.L.; Stitzer, M.L.; Cone, E.J.; Bigelow, G.E. Clinical pharmacology of buprenorphine: Ceiling effects at high doses. *Clin. Pharmacol. Ther.* **1994**, *55*, 569–580. [CrossRef] [PubMed]
25. Oral-MME-CFs-vFeb-2018.pdf. Available online: https://www.cms.gov/Medicare/Prescription-Drug-Coverage/PrescriptionDrugCovContra/Downloads/Oral-MME-CFs-vFeb-2018.pdf (accessed on 8 May 2020).
26. Gudin, J. A Narrative Pharmacological Review of Buprenorphine: A Unique Opioid for the Treatment of Chronic Pain. *Pain Ther.* **2020**, *9*, 41–54. [CrossRef]
27. Silva, M.J.; Rubinstein, A. Continuous Perioperative Sublingual Buprenorphine. *J. Pain Palliat. Care Pharmacother.* **2016**, *30*, 289–293. [CrossRef] [PubMed]
28. Daitch, D.; Daitch, J.; Novinson, M.D.; Frey, M.; Mitnick, A.C.; Pergolizzi, J.J. Conversion from High-Dose Full-Opioid Agonists to Sublingual Buprenorphine Reduces Pain Scores and Improves Quality of Life for Chronic Pain Patients. *Pain Med.* **2014**, *15*, 2087–2094. [CrossRef] [PubMed]
29. Karlsson, M.; Berggren, A.-C. Efficacy and safety of low-dose transdermal buprenorphine patches (5, 10, and 20 microg/h) versus prolonged-release tramadol tablets (75, 100, 150, and 200 mg) in patients with chronic osteoarthritis pain: A 12-week, randomized, open-label, controlled, parallel-group noninferiority study. *Clin. Ther.* **2009**, *31*, 503–513.

30. Silva, M.J.; Coffee, Z.; Yu, C.H. Prolonged Cessation of Chronic Opioid Analgesic Therapy: A Multidisciplinary Intervention. *Am. J. Manag. Care* **2022**, *28*, 60–65.
31. Silva, M.J.; Coffee, Z.; Goza, J.; Rumrill, K. Microinduction to Buprenorphine from Methadone for Chronic Pain: Outpatient Protocol with Case Examples. *J. Pain Palliat. Care Pharmacother.* **2022**, *36*, 40–48. [CrossRef]
32. Johns, M.W. A new method for measuring daytime sleepiness: The Epworth sleepiness scale. *Sleep* **1991**, *14*, 540–545. [CrossRef]
33. Ware, J.E.; Sherbourne, C.D. The MOS 36-item short-form health survey (SF-36). I. Conceptual framework and item selection. *Med. Care* **1992**, *30*, 473–483. [CrossRef]
34. Spitzer, R.L.; Kroenke, K.; Williams, J.B.W.; Löwe, B. A brief measure for assessing generalized anxiety disorder: The GAD-7. *Arch. Intern. Med.* **2006**, *166*, 1092–1097. [CrossRef]
35. Kroenke, K.; Spitzer, R.L.; Williams, J.B.W. The PHQ-9: Validity of a brief depression severity measure. *J. Gen. Intern. Med.* **2001**, *16*, 606–613. [CrossRef]
36. Waddell, G.; Newton, M.; Henderson, I.; Somerville, D.; Main, C.J. A Fear-Avoidance Beliefs Questionnaire (FABQ) and the role of fear-avoidance beliefs in chronic low back pain and disability. *Pain* **1993**, *52*, 157–168. [CrossRef]
37. Miller, R.P.; Kori, S.H.; Todd, D.D. The Tampa Scale: A Measure of Kinesiophobia. *Clin. J. Pain* **1991**, *7*, 51. [CrossRef]
38. Sullivan, M.J.L.; Bishop, S.R.; Pivik, J. The Pain Catastrophizing Scale: Development and Validation. *Psychol. Assess.* **1995**, *7*, 524–532. [CrossRef]
39. BPI_UserGuide.pdf. Available online: https://www.mdanderson.org/documents/Departments-and-Divisions/Symptom-Research/BPI_UserGuide.pdf (accessed on 8 October 2020).
40. George, S.Z.; Fritz, J.M.; Erhard, R.E. A comparison of fear-avoidance beliefs in patients with lumbar spine pain and cervical spine pain. *Spine* **2001**, *26*, 2139–2145. [CrossRef]
41. Adams, H.; Ellis, T.; Stanish, W.D.; Sullivan, M.J.L. Psychosocial factors related to return to work following rehabilitation of whiplash injuries. *J. Occup. Rehabil.* **2007**, *17*, 305–315. [CrossRef]
42. PCSManual_English.pdf. Available online: http://sullivan-painresearch.mcgill.ca/pdf/pcs/PCSManual_English.pdf (accessed on 8 May 2020).
43. Cleeland, C.S.; Ryan, K.M. Pain assessment: Global use of the Brief Pain Inventory. *Ann. Acad. Med. Singap.* **1994**, *23*, 129–138.
44. Jacoby, W.G. *Statistical Graphics for Visualizing Multivariate Data*; Sage Publications: Thousand Oaks, CA, USA, 1998.
45. Yan, W.; Kang, M. *GGE Biplot Analysis*; CRC Press: Boca Raton, FL, USA, 2003.
46. Sterne, J.A.C.; White, I.R.; Carlin, J.B.; Spratt, M.; Royston, P.; Kenward, M.G.; Wood, A.M.; Carpenter, J.R. Multiple imputation for missing data in epidemiological and clinical research: Potential and pitfalls. *BMJ* **2009**, *338*, b2393. [CrossRef]
47. Karp, J.F.; Butters, M.A.; Begley, A.; Miller, M.D.; Lenze, E.J.; Blumberger, D.; Mulsant, B.; Reynolds, C.F. Safety, Tolerability, and Clinical Effect of Low-Dose Buprenorphine for Treatment-Resistant Depression in Mid-Life and Older Adults. *J. Clin. Psychiatry* **2014**, *75*, e785–e793. [CrossRef]
48. Sullivan, M.J.L.; Adams, H.; Rhodenizer, T.; Stanish, W.D. A psychosocial risk factor–targeted intervention for the prevention of chronic pain and disability following whiplash injury. *Phys. Ther.* **2006**, *86*, 8–18. [CrossRef]
49. Brady, K.T.; Sinha, R. Co-occurring mental and substance use disorders: The neurobiological effects of chronic stress. *Am. J. Psychiatry* **2005**, *162*, 1483–1493. [CrossRef] [PubMed]
50. Weber, M.M.; Emrich, H.M. Current and historical concepts of opiate treatment in psychiatric disorders. *Int. Clin. Psychopharmacol.* **1988**, *3*, 255–266. [CrossRef]
51. Martins, S.S.; Keyes, K.M.; Storr, C.L.; Zhu, H.; Chilcoat, H.D. Pathways between nonmedical opioid use/dependence and psychiatric disorders: Results from the National Epidemiologic Survey on Alcohol and Related Conditions. *Drug Alcohol Depend.* **2009**, *103*, 16–24. [CrossRef] [PubMed]
52. Peciña, M.; Karp, J.F.; Mathew, S.; Todtenkopf, M.S.; Ehrich, E.W.; Zubieta, J.-K. Endogenous opioid system dysregulation in depression: Implications for new therapeutic approaches. *Mol. Psychiatry* **2019**, *24*, 576–587. [CrossRef] [PubMed]
53. Robinson, S.E. Buprenorphine: An Analgesic with an Expanding Role in the Treatment of Opioid Addiction. *CNS Drug Rev.* **2002**, *8*, 377–390. [CrossRef]
54. Bidlack, J.M.; Knapp, B.I.; Deaver, D.R.; Plotnikava, M.; Arnelle, D.; Wonsey, A.M.; Toh, M.F.; Pin, S.S.; Namchuk, M.N. In Vitro Pharmacological Characterization of Buprenorphine, Samidorphan, and Combinations Being Developed as an Adjunctive Treatment of Major Depressive Disorder. *J. Pharmacol. Exp. Ther.* **2018**, *367*, 267–281. [CrossRef]
55. Serafini, G.; Adavastro, G.; Canepa, G.; De Berardis, D.; Valchera, A.; Pompili, M.; Nasrallah, H.; Amore, M. The Efficacy of Buprenorphine in Major Depression, Treatment-Resistant Depression and Suicidal Behavior: A Systematic Review. *Int. J. Mol. Sci.* **2018**, *19*, 2410. [CrossRef]
56. Ahmadi, J.; Jahromi, M.S. Anxiety Treatment of Opioid Dependent Patients with Buprenorphine: A Randomized, Double-blind, Clinical Trial. *Indian J. Psychol. Med.* **2017**, *39*, 445–449. [CrossRef]
57. Zubieta, J.-K.; Ketter, T.A.; Bueller, J.A.; Xu, Y.; Kilbourn, M.R.; Young, E.A.; Koeppe, R.A. Regulation of Human Affective Responses by Anterior Cingulate and Limbic μ-Opioid Neurotransmission. *Arch. Gen. Psychiatry* **2003**, *60*, 1145–1153. [CrossRef]
58. Yovell, Y.; Bar, G.; Mashiah, M.; Baruch, Y.; Briskman, I.; Asherov, J.; Lotan, A.; Rigbi, A.; Panksepp, J. Ultra-Low-Dose Buprenorphine as a Time-Limited Treatment for Severe Suicidal Ideation: A Randomized Controlled Trial. *AJP* **2016**, *173*, 491–498. [CrossRef]

59. Pfeiffer, A.; Brantl, V.; Herz, A.; Emrich, H.M. Psychotomimesis mediated by kappa opiate receptors. *Science* **1986**, *233*, 774–776. [CrossRef]
60. Tenore, P.L. Psychotherapeutic Benefits of Opioid Agonist Therapy. *J. Addict. Dis.* **2008**, *27*, 49–65. Available online: https://www.tandfonline.com/doi/abs/10.1080/10550880802122646?journalCode=wjad20 (accessed on 3 February 2022). [CrossRef]
61. Fritz, J.M.; George, S.Z. Identifying psychosocial variables in patients with acute work-related low back pain: The importance of fear-avoidance beliefs. *Phys. Ther.* **2002**, *82*, 973–983. [CrossRef]
62. George, S.Z.; Fritz, J.M.; Childs, J.D. Investigation of Elevated Fear-Avoidance Beliefs for Patients with Low Back Pain: A Secondary Analysis Involving Patients Enrolled in Physical Therapy Clinical Trials. *J. Orthop. Sports Phys. Ther.* **2008**, *38*, 50–58. [CrossRef]
63. George, S.Z.; Fritz, J.M.; McNeil, D.W. Fear-avoidance beliefs as measured by the fear-avoidance beliefs questionnaire: Change in fear-avoidance beliefs questionnaire is predictive of change in self-report of disability and pain intensity for patients with acute low back pain. *Clin. J. Pain* **2006**, *22*, 197–203. [CrossRef]
64. Vlaeyen, J.W.; Linton, S.J. Fear-avoidance and its consequences in chronic musculoskeletal pain: A state of the art. *Pain* **2000**, *85*, 317–332. [CrossRef] [PubMed]
65. Linton, S.J.; Shaw, W.S. Impact of Psychological Factors in the Experience of Pain. *Phys. Ther.* **2011**, *91*, 700–711. [CrossRef]
66. Waddell, G.; Somerville, D.; Henderson, I.; Newton, M. Objective clinical evaluation of physical impairment in chronic low back pain. *Spine* **1992**, *17*, 617–628. [CrossRef]
67. Philips, H.; Jahanshahi, M. The components of pain behaviour report. *Behav. Res. Ther.* **1986**, *24*, 117–125. [CrossRef]
68. Flynn, T.; Fritz, J.; Whitman, J.; Wainner, R.; Magel, J.; Rendeiro, D.; Butler, B.; Garber, M.; Allison, S. A clinical prediction rule for classifying patients with low back pain who demonstrate short-term improvement with spinal manipulation. *Spine* **2002**, *27*, 2835–2843. [CrossRef]
69. Cleland, J.A.; Fritz, J.M.; Brennan, G.P. Predictive validity of initial fear avoidance beliefs in patients with low back pain receiving physical therapy: Is the FABQ a useful screening tool for identifying patients at risk for a poor recovery? *Eur. Spine J.* **2008**, *17*, 70–79. [CrossRef] [PubMed]
70. Hassamal, S.; Miotto, K.; Wang, T.; Saxon, A.J. A narrative review: The effects of opioids on sleep disordered breathing in chronic pain patients and methadone maintained patients. *Am. J. Addict.* **2016**, *25*, 452–465. [CrossRef] [PubMed]
71. Correa, D.; Farney, R.J.; Chung, F.; Prasad, A.; Lam, D.; Wong, J. Chronic opioid use and central sleep apnea: A review of the prevalence, mechanisms, and perioperative considerations. *Anesth. Analg.* **2015**, *120*, 1273–1285. [CrossRef]
72. Wang, D.; Teichtahl, H.; Goodman, C.; Drummer, O.; Grunstein, R.R.; Kronborg, I. Subjective Daytime Sleepiness and Daytime Function in Patients on Stable Methadone Maintenance Treatment: Possible Mechanisms. *J. Clin. Sleep Med.* **2008**, *4*, 557–562. [CrossRef]
73. Calley, D.Q.; Jackson, S.; Collins, H.; George, S.Z. Identifying Patient Fear-Avoidance Beliefs by Physical Therapists Managing Patients with Low Back Pain. *J. Orthop. Sports Phys. Ther.* **2010**, *40*, 774–783. [CrossRef]
74. Burton, A.K.; Waddell, G.; Tillotson, K.M.; Summerton, N. Information and advice to patients with back pain can have a positive effect. A randomized controlled trial of a novel educational booklet in primary care. *Spine* **1999**, *24*, 2484–2491. [CrossRef]

Journal of
Clinical Medicine

MDPI

Article

The Impact of Comorbid Chronic Pain on Pharmacotherapy for Veterans with Post-Traumatic Stress Disorder

Alessandra A. Pratt [1,*], Katherine Hadlandsmyth [1,2,3], Michelle A. Mengeling [1,2,4], Emily B. K. Thomas [2,5], Kelly Miell [1], Sonya B. Norman [6,7] and Brian C. Lund [1,2,8]

1 Center for Access & Delivery Research and Evaluation (CADRE), Iowa City VA Health Care System, 601 Highway 6 West, Building 42, Iowa City, IA 52246, USA
2 VA Office of Rural Health (ORH), Veterans Rural Health Resource Center-Iowa City (VRHRC-IC), Iowa City VA Health Care System, 601 Highway 6 West, Iowa City, IA 52246, USA
3 Department of Anesthesia, University of Iowa Carver College of Medicine, 200 Hawkins Drive, Iowa City, IA 52242, USA
4 Department of Internal Medicine, University of Iowa Carver College of Medicine, 200 Hawkins Drive, Iowa City, IA 52242, USA
5 Department of Psychological and Brain Sciences, University of Iowa College of Liberal Arts and Sciences, 340 Iowa Ave, Iowa City, IA 52246, USA
6 National Center for PTSD, 215 North Main Street, White River Junction, VT 05009, USA
7 Department of Psychiatry, University of California San Diego School of Medicine, 9500 Gilman Drive, La Jolla, CA 92093, USA
8 Department of Biostatistics, University of Iowa College of Public Health, 145 N Riverside Drive, Iowa City, IA 52242, USA
* Correspondence: alessandra.pratt@va.gov; Tel.: +1-(319)-338-0581 (ext. 63-7661)

Abstract: Objective: Chronic pain can worsen PTSD symptomatology and may increase the risk of the prescription of multiple central nervous system (CNS)-active medications. The objective is to determine the impact of chronic pain on the number of CNS medications, including psychiatric medications, as well as the amount of medication changes. Methods: Veterans Affairs (VA) administrative data were used to identify VA-served Veterans with PTSD (N = 637,428) who had chronic pain (50.3%) and did not have chronic pain (49.7%) in 2020. The outcomes included the number of changes in psychiatric medications and the number of currently prescribed CNS-active mediations during a one-year observation period. Results: The number of changes in psychiatric medications was significantly higher for those with chronic pain (mean (M) = 1.8) versus those without chronic pain (M = 1.6) (Z = 38.4, $p < 0.001$). The mean number of concurrent CNS-active medications were significantly higher for those with chronic pain (M = 2.7) versus those without chronic pain (M = 2.0) (Z = 179.7, $p < 0.001$). These differences persisted after adjustment for confounding factors using negative binomial regression. Conclusions: Veterans with comorbid chronic pain and PTSD are at increased risk for a higher number of medication changes and for receiving CNS-active polytherapy.

Keywords: PTSD; chronic pain; pharmacoepidemiology; Veterans

Citation: Pratt, A.A.; Hadlandsmyth, K.; Mengeling, M.A.; Thomas, E.B.K.; Miell, K.; Norman, S.B.; Lund, B.C. The Impact of Comorbid Chronic Pain on Pharmacotherapy for Veterans with Post-Traumatic Stress Disorder. *J. Clin. Med.* **2023**, *12*, 4763. https://doi.org/10.3390/jcm12144763

Academic Editors: Robert Barkin and Massimiliano Valeriani

Received: 18 April 2023
Revised: 22 June 2023
Accepted: 13 July 2023
Published: 19 July 2023

1. Introduction

Comorbid post-traumatic stress disorder (PTSD) and chronic pain are common among Veterans [1–3]. Chronic pain can amplify the symptoms of PTSD and complicate treatment, resulting in a greater use of healthcare services, which may be caused by poorer response to pain treatment [4–7]. Veterans with comorbid chronic pain and PTSD report having a poorer quality of life and have worse pain and psychological outcomes than those without concurrent disorders [8–10]. Specifically, Veterans with both PTSD and chronic pain have increased pain intensity or severity, can have pain-related disability, pain catastrophizing, and an increase in depressive and anxiety symptom severity [11–16]. Chronic pain can also result in greater psychiatric symptom instability among Veterans with PTSD [9,10]. As such, comorbid chronic pain and PTSD may result in an accumulation of multiple medications to treat these conditions [17]. Specifically, severe PTSD symptoms, magnified by chronic pain, may require more frequent psychotropic medication changes across time. However, it has not been clearly demonstrated whether those with comorbid chronic pain and PTSD receive more CNS medications or have more frequent psychotropic medication changes than those with PTSD but without chronic pain.

The siloed management for PTSD and chronic pain can result in the prescription of multiple concurrent central nervous system (CNS)-active medications [17,18]. Polytherapy with CNS-active medications can increase the risk of overdose mortality, suicide-related behaviors, and unintentional death [19]. Other effects of polytherapy can include the following: increased healthcare costs, adverse drug events, drug interactions, medication non-adherence, individual functional decline, cognitive impairment, falls, urinary incontinence, and change in nutritional status [20–22]. Polytherapy among Veterans with comorbid PTSD and chronic pain may result from an additive effect of multiple conditions, or it may be impacted by increased difficulties in managing psychiatric symptoms in the presence of comorbid chronic pain.

The current study aims to examine the impact of comorbid chronic pain on Veterans with PTSD via psychopharmacological prescription patterns. Specifically, this study aims to (1) determine the impact of chronic pain on a number of psychiatric medication changes across time (as an indicator of treatment instability) among Veterans with PTSD, and (2) determine the impact of comorbid chronic pain on the risk of multiple concurrent CNS-active medication prescriptions among Veterans with PTSD. We hypothesized that Veterans with chronic pain would have more psychiatric medication changes across time and have a higher number of concurrent CNS-active medications.

2. Methods

2.1. Data Sources

National Veterans Affairs (VA) administrative data from the VA Corporate Data Warehouse were used for this study. The presence of mental health and other medical comorbidities were determined using international classification of disease (ICD) codes from inpatient and outpatient encounters. Drug exposure was assessed using outpatient pharmacy dispensing data. The current study is an operations-supported quality improvement project determined not to constitute human subjects research by the local Institutional Review Board.

2.2. Patients

Veterans with PTSD were identified using ICD-9 and ICD-10 codes (309.81 and F43.1X) from inpatient and outpatient encounters. Patients were required to have at least one inpatient hospitalization coded for PTSD during 2020, or at least one PTSD-coded outpatient encounter during 2020 and a second PTSD-coded encounter within the past 730 days [23,24].

2.3. Outcomes

Exposure to two groups of medications was assessed. First, medications with CNS activity were identified using VA drug classification, as defined by Collett and colleagues [17,19]. Second, a subset of these medications typically used for psychiatric indications was examined, and was limited to antidepressants, antipsychotics, anticonvulsants, benzodiazepines, z-drug hypnotics, stimulants, and lithium (Supplemental Table S1). Three specific medications from these classes, gabapentin, topiramate, and duloxetine, were not considered in the psychiatric medication subset, as these agents are commonly used for the management of pain.

Drug exposure was assessed during the calendar year 2021, the year following patient selection, to ensure that diagnoses of PTSD and chronic pain preceded the outcome. The outcome measure for Aim 1 was the number of changes in psychiatric medication during the observation year. This was assessed by determining which psychiatric medications were active on the first day of the observation year, which were active on the last day of the observation year, and other psychiatric medications dispensed throughout the observation year. Medications present in the baseline regimen, but not in the follow-up regimen, were considered discontinued and counted as one change. Conversely, medications present at follow-up but not at baseline were considered new medications and counted as one change. Medications dispensed during the year, but not present in either regimen, were considered to have been started and then stopped and counted as two changes. The outcome measure for Aim 2 was the maximum number of CNS-active medications received concurrently at any point during the observation year, using previously established methodology [17]. Both outcome measures relied on longitudinal prescription histories, where medications were considered active on any given day during this period based on cabinet supply methodology [17,25]. Briefly, this approach estimates the day's supply on hand for each calendar day during a specified time interval, with adjustments for carrying forward oversupply for early refills and allowable nonadherence.

2.4. Analysis

The focus of the analysis was to determine whether the presence or absence of chronic pain was associated with two clinically relevant measures of drug exposure including (1) the number of psychiatric medication changes and (2) the maximum number of concurrent CNS-active medications over a one-year observation period. As both outcome measures were discrete counts with low frequencies and not expected to be normally distributed, bivariate associations with chronic pain were examined using the nonparametric Wilcoxon rank sum test. Chronic pain was identified using Tian's criteria [26], modified to include ICD-10 codes [27]. To meet criteria for chronic pain, patients were required to meet one of the following 3 criteria: 2 outpatient encounters separated by $\geq$30 days with a diagnosis code likely indicating chronic pain; at least 1 encounter coded with a diagnosis likely indicating chronic pain and at least 2 numeric pain rating scales $\geq$4; or long-term opioid use (>90 days) [26–28].

Negative binomial regression was then used to adjust the relationship between chronic pain and the outcome for potential confounders, including demographics, medical comorbidity using the Charlson index [29], a dichotomous indicator for any inpatient hospitalization during 2020, and psychiatric comorbidities [30]. Regression models involving the count of psychiatric medication changes were further adjusted for the number of psychiatric medications at baseline and whether an opioid or other pain medication was present at baseline. These variables were not included in models involving the number of concurrent CNS-active medications as they are intrinsically part of the outcome measure. A sensitivity analysis was conducted using the same patient selection criteria and outcome definitions but applied to Veterans with PTSD during the calendar year 2012. The purpose of the sensitivity analysis was to determine whether any relationships observed in the primary analysis were stable over time or had changed along with known changes in VA prescription patterns over this period, such as decreases in opioid and benzodiazepine prescription [31,32].

3. Results

3.1. Patient Selection

In 2020, a total of 637,428 Veterans received care at VA for PTSD, of whom 50.3% (n = 320,932) met the criteria for chronic pain. Veterans with PTSD and chronic pain were more likely to be older, female, and African American, relative to those without chronic pain (Table 1). Veterans with chronic pain also displayed higher rates of all psychiatric comorbidities examined, including depressive disorder, substance use disorder, anxiety disorder, bipolar disorder, and psychotic disorder. Veterans with chronic pain were also more likely to be prescribed more antidepressants, opioid analgesics, anticonvulsants, benzodiazepines, antipsychotics, sedative hypnotics, and antimigraine agents.

Table 1. Patient characteristics of Veterans with PTSD.

Characteristic	With Chronic Pain N = 320,932 *n* (%)	Without Chronic Pain N = 316,496 *n* (%)
Age		
<40	62,852 (19.6)	89,546 (28.3)
40–54	91,443 (28.5)	83,688 (26.4)
55–64	58,891 (18.4)	39,759 (12.6)
65+	107,746 (33.6)	103,503 (32.7)
Sex		
Male	265,065 (82.6)	272,656 (86.2)
Female	55,867 (17.4)	43,840 (13.9)
Race		
White	188,072 (58.6)	196,678 (62.1)
Black or African American	81,746 (25.5)	68,310 (21.6)
Other or unknown	51,114 (15.9)	51,508 (16.3)
Patient residence		
Urban	263,315 (82.1)	258,079 (81.5)
Rural	57,617 (17.9)	58,417 (18.5)
Comorbidities		
Depressive disorder	208,662 (65.0)	179,329 (56.7)
Substance use disorder	78,613 (24.5)	75,380 (23.8)
Anxiety disorder	46,731 (14.6)	40,999 (13.0)
Bipolar disorder	25,609 (8.0)	23,012 (7.3)
Psychotic disorder	12,640 (3.9)	11,664 (3.4)
CNS medication type		
Antidepressants	202,008 (62.9)	183,241 (57.9)
Anticonvulsants	78,788 (24.6)	43,713 (13.8)
Antipsychotics	38,937 (12.1)	33,547 (10.6)
Opioid analgesics	32,856 (10.2)	2552 (0.8)
Sedative hypnotics	33,852 (10.6)	26,095 (8.2)
Benzodiazepines	18,725 (5.8)	15,404 (4.9)
Anti-migraine agents	11,776 (3.7)	2843 (0.9)
Stimulants	8883 (2.8)	10,007 (3.2)
Anti-Parkinson's agents	8114 (2.5)	3647 (1.2)
Lithium salts	2737 (0.9)	2628 (0.8)
Non-opioid analgesics	1257 (0.4)	289 (0.1)
Anti-vertigo agents	1179 (0.4)	472 (0.2)
Other CNS-active medications	14,569 (0.9)	5334 (1.7)
Any inpatient hospitalization during 2020		
Yes	44,517 (13.9)	18,806 (5.9)
No	276,415 (86.1)	297,690 (94.1)

CNS = central nervous system; PTSD = post-traumatic stress disorder.

3.2. Medication Changes

From 1 January 2021 to 31 December 2021, the number of changes in psychiatric medications was significantly higher for those with chronic pain (mean (M) = 1.8, standard deviation (SD) = 2.0) compared to those without chronic pain (M = 1.6, SD = 1.9) (Z = 38.4, $p < 0.001$). This relationship was also observed with the 2012 sensitivity analysis, where Veterans with chronic pain (M = 2.3, SD = 2.4) had a higher mean number of changes than those without chronic pain (M = 1.9, SD = 2.2) (Z = 58.0, $p < 0.001$). Categorically, 8.9% of Veterans with chronic pain had five or more changes in their psychiatric medication prescriptions compared to 7.2% without chronic pain, and 26.1% of Veterans with chronic pain had three or more changes, compared to 22.7% without chronic pain (Figure 1).

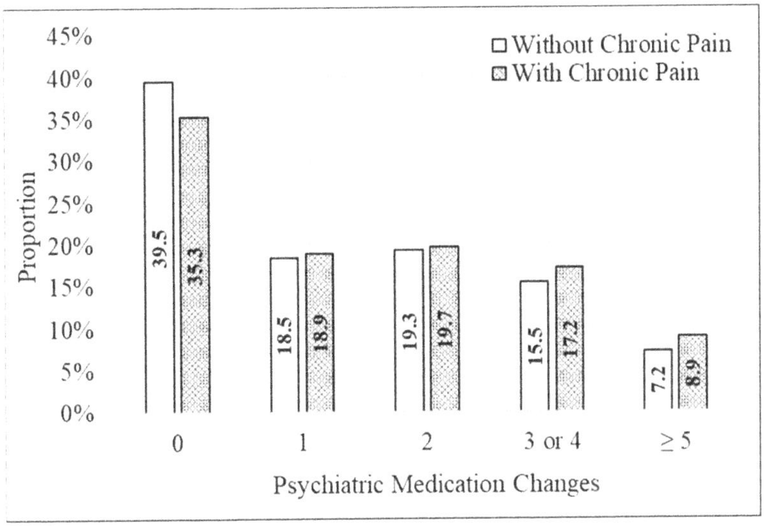

Figure 1. Distribution in the number of changes in CNS medications received by Veterans with PTSD, with and without chronic pain, during 2021.

Negative binomial regression was then used to determine whether the relationship between chronic pain and the number of psychiatric medication changes persisted after adjustment for potential confounding factors. The unadjusted IRR was 1.12 (95% CI: 1.11, 1.12), indicating that chronic pain was associated with a 12% greater risk for one additional psychiatric medication change, that is, 12% more likely to have one change than zero changes, 12% more likely to have two changes, relative to one change, etc. After adjustment for important confounding factors including demographics and psychiatric comorbidity, the association between chronic pain and the number of psychiatric medication changes remained significant, and the IRR point estimate was unchanged from the unadjusted model (aIRR = 1.11; 95% CI: 1.10, 1.11; Table 2).

Although not the primary focus of the analysis, several model covariates of note were found to be significantly associated with an elevated risk for changes in psychiatric medications, including female sex, Black or African American race, Charlson Comorbidity Index, recent inpatient hospitalization, and the presence of any examined psychiatric comorbidities. Conversely, covariates associated with a decreased risk for psychiatric medication changes included older age, rural residence, and the presence of at least one psychiatric medication at baseline. The association between chronic pain and an increased risk for the number of psychiatric medication changes was also observed in the 2012 sensitivity analysis (aIIR = 1.16; 95% CI: 1.15, 1.17; Supplemental Table S2).

Table 2. Clinical characteristics associated with the number of changes in psychiatric medications as a discrete count.

Characteristic	Multivariable Negative Binomial Regression aIRR (95% CI)
Chronic pain	
Not diagnosed	Reference
Diagnosed	1.11 (1.10, 1.11)
Age	
<40	Reference
40–54	0.94 (0.93, 0.94)
55–64	0.84 (0.83, 0.84)
65+	0.67 (0.67, 0.68)
Sex	
Male	Reference
Female	1.14 (1.13, 1.15)
Race	
White	Reference
Black or African American	1.07 (1.06, 1.08)
Other	1.03 (1.02, 1.04)
Patient residence	
Urban	Reference
Rural	0.96 (0.95, 0.97)
Charlson Comorbidity Index	
Per Point	0.99 (0.99, 0.99)
Inpatient hospitalization	
No	Reference
Yes	1.19 (1.17, 1.20)
Psychiatric medications	
0	Reference
1	0.77 (0.77, 0.78)
2	0.78 (0.77, 0.78)
≥3	0.83 (0.82, 0.84)
Comorbidities	
Depressive disorder	1.16 (1.16, 1.17)
Substance use disorder	1.11 (1.10, 1.12)
Anxiety disorder	1.17 (1.15, 1.17)
Psychotic disorder	1.27 (1.25, 1.29)
Bipolar disorder	1.33 (1.31, 1.34)
Pain medication present at baseline	
No pain medication	Reference
Opioid medication	0.97 (0.95, 0.98)
Non-opioid pain medication	0.98 (0.97, 0.99)

aIRR = adjusted incidence rate ratio; CI = confidence interval.

3.3. CNS Polytherapy

The number of concurrent CNS-active medications received during the observation period of 1 January 2021 to 31 December 2021 was M = 2.7 (SD = 1.6) for Veterans with chronic pain compared to M = 2.0 (SD = 1.3) for those without chronic pain (Z = 179.7, $p < 0.001$). Categorically, 12.9% of Veterans with chronic pain and PTSD had five or more concurrent CNS medications versus 4.3% without chronic pain (Figure 2). Differences were also found at four concurrent medications (15.3% with chronic pain versus 8.6% without chronic pain) and at three concurrent medications (23.4% with chronic pain and 19.4% without chronic pain). Cumulatively, 51.6% of Veterans with chronic pain were concurrently prescribed three or more CNS-active medications compared to 32.0% of Veterans without chronic pain.

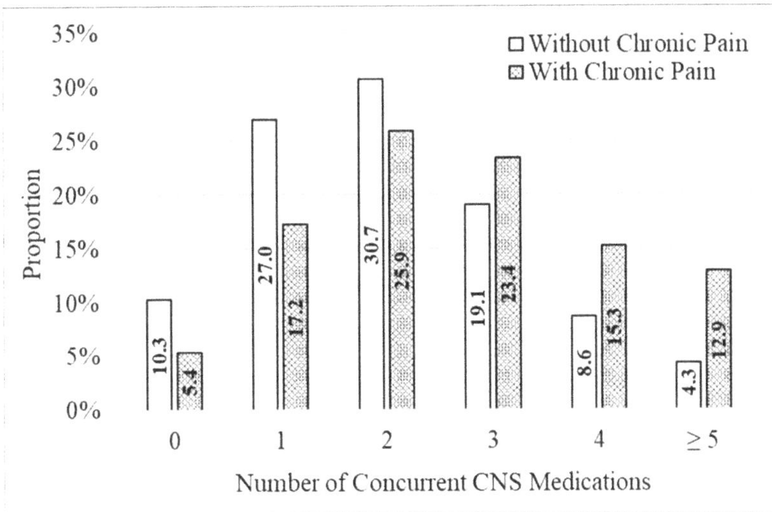

Figure 2. Distribution in the number of concurrent central nervous system (CNS) active medications received by Veterans with PTSD, with and without chronic pain, during 2021.

Negative binomial regression was then used to determine whether the relationship between chronic pain and the number of concurrent CNS medications persisted after adjusting for potential confounding factors. The adjusted IRR was 1.29 (95% CI: 1.28, 1.29; Supplemental Table S3), indicating that chronic pain was associated with a 29% greater risk for having one more CNS-active medication. However, when the number of concurrent CNS medications was restricted to just psychiatric medications, the relationship with chronic pain was substantially diminished (aIRR = 1.03; 95% CI: 1.02, 1.03; Supplemental Table S4).

Similar relationships were also observed with the 2012 sensitivity analysis. Veterans with chronic pain (M = 3.1, SD = 1.7) received more concurrent CNS-active medications than Veterans without chronic pain (M = 2.0, SD = 1.4) (Z = 219.1, $p < 0.001$). The association between chronic pain and the number of concurrent CNS medications was observed in the 2012 sensitivity analysis (aIIR = 1.46; 95% CI: 1.45, 1.46; Supplemental Table S5). As seen in the primary analysis, when the number of concurrent CNS medications was restricted to just psychiatric medications, the relationship with chronic pain was substantially diminished (aIRR = 1.07; 95% CI: 1.07, 1.08; Supplemental Table S6).

4. Discussion

Our findings, which demonstrate a greater number of psychiatric prescription changes when patients with PTSD also have chronic pain, are consistent with prior work, which demonstrated a magnifying effect of chronic pain on PTSD symptomology [4,5]. We found a moderate effect of a 12% higher risk for each additional medication change across a one-year timeframe among Veterans with PTSD and chronic pain, compared to those with PTSD alone. This higher likelihood of psychiatric medication changes may indicate instability in the patient's treatment regimen, reflecting a greater symptom burden, instability in symptoms, or greater difficulty in consistently managing symptoms. This finding is also consistent with prior work, which demonstrated an increased number of healthcare visits among Veterans with chronic pain and comorbid PTSD [6]. Veterans with this comorbidity may be seeking, or requiring, a greater number of visits and medication changes in an attempt to treat the heightened symptom load resulting from chronic pain comorbid to PTSD.

Adding to prior work [17], the current findings demonstrate higher rates of CNS polytherapy among Veterans with chronic pain and PTSD, relative to those with only PTSD. The higher rates of CNS-active polytherapy, resulting from the additive effect of psychopharmacologic and analgesic agents, may result, at least in part, from the siloed treatment of these two conditions. Veterans with both conditions may be seen by two different providers, each following a separate set of guidelines [1,33]. Both providers could be prescribing CNS-active medications without knowing the treatment course for the other condition, which could lead to an increased risk for polytherapy in Veterans with chronic pain that is comorbid to PTSD.

As such, providers may benefit from guidelines for treating Veterans with both chronic pain and PTSD. A coordinated cross-specialty treatment plan may result in Veterans having a more stable medication regimen (e.g., fewer medication changes) and lower risks associated with polytherapy [20]. Patients with comorbid chronic pain and PTSD may also benefit from combined behavioral interventions that simultaneously address both PTSD and chronic pain [34]. Because women, rural-dwelling people, and minoritized persons were at greater risk for psychiatric medication changes in our analyses, these populations may stand to benefit most from further research into integrated care for comorbid chronic pain and PTSD.

This study has some limitations. This work includes only Veterans receiving care from VA, so our findings may not generalize to Veterans or other patient populations receiving PTSD care outside of the VA healthcare system. In addition, we were not able to confidently distinguish newly diagnosed PTSD or chronic pain. It is unclear whether the relationships observed in this study would differ between newly diagnosed patients and patients with pre-existing conditions. Another limitation is that certain medications are indicated for both analgesia and psychiatric management (i.e., duloxetine, gabapentin, topiramate). Categorizing these medications as primarily analgesic medications may have impacted the models comparing psychiatric to analgesic prescribing patterns, though this conservative approach was taken to avoid overestimating differences. Finally, the process of prescribing medications in the VA system has been impacted by wide-reaching prescribing initiatives across the past decade, which has significantly reduced overall opioid and benzodiazepine prescriptions [35–37]. As such, to examine whether the patterns we identified reflected ongoing clinical phenomenon, as opposed to being in response to healthcare-system-specific initiatives, we conducted sensitivity analyses across time to determine whether the current findings (2021) remained significant a decade prior (2012). The continued significance of our findings supports the consistency of these findings across time. Our focus was to explore, as a proof of concept, the potential impact of chronic pain on the prescription of psychiatric and other CNS medications. Unfortunately, there is no defined value for what constitutes clinically meaningful in the prescribing metrics examined in this study.

In conclusion, the deleterious impact that chronic pain can have on PTSD symptomatology [4–7] is reflected in the differential prescribing patterns for Veterans with comorbid chronic pain compared to Veterans with PTSD alone. We found that Veterans with comorbid chronic pain and PTSD are at an increased risk for a higher number of medication changes and for receiving CNS-active polytherapy. Providers who treat Veterans with comorbid PTSD and chronic pain may benefit from guidelines to co-manage these conditions, avenues to coordinate care with cross-specialty colleagues, and the development of integrated behavioral interventions that address both conditions.

Supplementary Materials: The following supporting information can be downloaded at: https://www.mdpi.com/article/10.3390/jcm12144763/s1, Table S1: CNS active medications typically used for psychiatric indications and observed among dispensed medications. Table S2: Clinical characteristics associated with the number of changes in psychiatric medications as a discrete count for year 2012. Table S3: Clinical characteristics associated with CNS polytherapy medications as a discrete count for year 2021. Table S4: Clinical characteristics associated with psychiatric medications in the CNS polytherapy regimen, as a discrete count for year 2021.Table S5: Clinical characteristics associated with CNS polytherapy medications as a discrete count for year 2012. Table S6: Clinical characteristics associated with psychiatric medications in the CNS polytherapy regimen, as a discrete count for year 2012.

Author Contributions: Conceptualization, A.A.P., K.H., E.B.K.T., S.B.N. and B.C.L.; Methodology, A.A.P., K.H., M.A.M., E.B.K.T., K.M., S.B.N. and B.C.L.; Software, K.M. and B.C.L.; Validation, K.H., M.A.M., K.M. and B.C.L.; Formal analysis, A.A.P., K.H., M.A.M., K.M. and B.C.L.; Investigation, A.A.P., K.H. and B.C.L.; Resources, A.A.P., S.B.N. and B.C.L.; Data curation, K.M. and B.C.L.; Writing—original draft, A.A.P.; Writing—review & editing, K.H., M.A.M., E.B.K.T., K.M., S.B.N. and B.C.L.; Visualization, A.A.P. and B.C.L.; Supervision, K.H., M.A.M., E.B.K.T. and B.C.L.; Project administration, K.H., E.B.K.T., K.M. and B.C.L.; Funding acquisition, K.H., M.A.M., E.B.K.T., S.B.N. and B.C.L. All authors have read and agreed to the published version of the manuscript.

Funding: Funding was provided by the U.S. Department of Veterans Affairs (VA) Office of Rural Health (project number 03857). Visit https://www.ruralhealth.va.gov to learn more. The work reported here was also supported by the U.S. Department of Veterans Affairs Health Services Research and Development (HSR&D) Service through the Center for Access and Delivery Research and Evaluation (CADRE) (CIN 13-412). Pratt's time to develop and write this manuscript was supported by the Department of Veterans Affairs Office of Academic Affiliations Advanced Fellowship Program in Health Services Research, the Center for Access & Delivery Research and Evaluation, Iowa City VA Health Care System. The views expressed in this article are those of the authors and do not necessarily reflect the position or policy of the U.S. Department of Veterans Affairs or the United States Government.

Institutional Review Board Statement: Not applicable.

Informed Consent Statement: Not applicable.

Data Availability Statement: Not applicable.

Conflicts of Interest: The authors declare no conflict of interest.

References

1. Lew, H.L.; Otis, J.D.; Tun, C.; Kerns, R.D.; Clark, M.E.; Cifu, D.X. Prevalence of chronic pain, posttraumatic stress disorder, and persistent postconcussive symptoms in OIF/OEF veterans: Polytrauma clinical triad. *J. Rehabil. Res. Dev.* **2009**, *46*, 697–702. [CrossRef] [PubMed]
2. Beckham, J.C.; Crawford, A.L.; Feldman, M.E.; Kirby, A.C.; Hertzberg, M.A.; Davidson, J.; Moore, S.D. Chronic posttraumatic stress disorder and chronic pain in Vietnam combat veterans. *J. Psychosom. Res.* **1997**, *43*, 379–389. [CrossRef] [PubMed]
3. Shipherd, J.C.; Keyes, M.; Jovanovic, T.; Ready, D.J.; Baltzell, D.; Worley, V.; Gordon-Brown, V.; Hayslett, C.; Duncan, E. Veterans seeking treatment for posttraumatic stress disorder: What about comorbid chronic pain? *J. Rehabil. Res. Dev.* **2007**, *44*, 153–166. [CrossRef]
4. Noel, M.; Wilson, A.C.; Holley, A.L.; Durkin, L.; Patton, M.; Palermo, T.M. Posttraumatic stress disorder symptoms in youth with vs without chronic pain. *Pain* **2016**, *157*, 2277–2284. [CrossRef]
5. Asmundson, G.J.; Coons, M.J.; Taylor, S.; Katz, J. PTSD and the Experience of Pain: Research and Clinical Implications of Shared Vulnerability and Mutual Maintenance Models. *Can. J. Psychiatry* **2002**, *47*, 930–937. [CrossRef]
6. Outcalt, S.D.; Yu, Z.; Hoen, H.M.; Pennington, T.M.; Krebs, E.E. Health care utilization among veterans with pain and posttraumatic stress symptoms. *Pain Med.* **2014**, *15*, 1872–1879. [CrossRef] [PubMed]
7. Paylo, S.; Beck, J. Post-traumatic stress disorder symptoms, pain, and perceived control: Associations with psychosocial and physical functioning. *Pain* **2005**, *117*, 121–127. [CrossRef]
8. Morasco, B.J.; Lovejoy, T.I.; Lu, M.; Turk, D.C.; Lewis, L.; Dobscha, S.K. The relationship between PTSD and chronic pain: Mediating role of coping strategies and depression. *Pain* **2013**, *154*, 609–616. [CrossRef]
9. Bair, M.J.; Outcalt, S.D.; Ang, D.; Wu, J.; Yu, Z. Pain and psychological outcomes among Iraq and Afghanistan veterans with chronic pain and PTSD: ESCAPE trial longitudinal results. *Pain Med.* **2020**, *21*, 1369–1376. [CrossRef]
10. Benedict, T.M.; Keenan, P.G.; Nitz, A.J.; Moeller-Bertram, T. Post-traumatic stress disorder symptoms contribute to worse pain and health outcomes in veterans with PTSD compared to those without: A systematic review with meta-analysis. *Mil. Med.* **2020**, *185*, e1481–e1491. [CrossRef]
11. Vaegter, H.B.; Andersen, T.E.; Harvold, M.; Andersen, P.G.; Graven-Nielsen, T. Increased pain sensitivity in accident-related chronic pain patients with comorbid posttraumatic stress. *Clin. J. Pain* **2018**, *34*, 313–321. [CrossRef]
12. Gerrits, M.M.; Vogelzangs, N.; Van Oppen, P.; Van Marwijk, H.W.; van der Horst, H.; Penninx, B.W. Impact of pain on the course of depressive and anxiety disorders. *Pain* **2012**, *153*, 429–436. [CrossRef] [PubMed]

13. Carty, J.; O'Donnell, M.; Evans, L.; Kazantzis, N.; Creamer, M. Predicting posttraumatic stress disorder symptoms and pain intensity following severe injury: The role of catastrophizing. *Eur. J. Psychotraumatology* **2011**, *2*, 5652. [CrossRef]
14. Gilliam, W.P.; Schumann, M.E.; Craner, J.R.; Cunningham, J.L.; Morrison, E.J.; Seibel, S.; Sawchuk, C.; Sperry, J.A. Examining the effectiveness of pain rehabilitation on chronic pain and post-traumatic symptoms. *J. Behav. Med.* **2020**, *43*, 956–967. [CrossRef] [PubMed]
15. Herbert, M.S.; Malaktaris, A.L.; Dochat, C.; Thomas, M.L.; Wetherell, J.L.; Afari, N. Acceptance and commitment therapy for chronic pain: Does post-traumatic stress disorder influence treatment outcomes? *Pain Med.* **2019**, *20*, 1728–1736. [CrossRef]
16. Åkerblom, S.; Perrin, S.; Rivano Fischer, M.; McCracken, L.M. The relationship between posttraumatic stress disorder and chronic pain in people seeking treatment for chronic pain. *Clin. J. Pain* **2018**, *34*, 487–496. [CrossRef] [PubMed]
17. Hadlandsmyth, K.; Bernardy, N.C.; Lund, B.C. Central nervous system polytherapy among veterans with posttraumatic stress disorder: Changes across a decade. *Gen. Hosp. Psychiatry* **2022**, *74*, 46–50. [CrossRef]
18. Bernardy, N.C.; Lund, B.C.; Alexander, B.; Friedman, M.J. Increased Polysedative Use in Veterans with Posttraumatic Stress Disorder. *Pain Med.* **2014**, *15*, 1083–1090. [CrossRef]
19. Collett, G.A.; Song, K.; Jaramillo, C.A.; Potter, J.S.; Finley, E.P.; Pugh, M.J. Prevalence of central nervous system polypharmacy and associations with overdose and suicide-related behaviors in Iraq and Afghanistan war veterans in VA care 2010–2011. *Drugs-Real World Outcomes* **2016**, *3*, 45–52. [CrossRef]
20. Maher, R.L.; Hanlon, J.; Hajjar, E.R. Clinical consequences of polypharmacy in elderly. *Expert Opin. Drug Saf.* **2014**, *13*, 57–65. [CrossRef]
21. Weiner, D.K.; Hanlon, J.T.; Studenski, S.A. Effects of Central Nervous System Polypharmacy on Falls Liability in Community-Dwelling Elderly. *Gerontology* **1998**, *44*, 217–221. [CrossRef] [PubMed]
22. Wright, R.M.; Roumani, Y.F.; Boudreau, R.; Newman, A.B.; Ruby, C.M.; Studenski, S.A.; Shorr, R.I.; Bauer, D.C.; Simonsick, E.M.; Hilmer, S.N. Effect of central nervous system medication use on decline in cognition in community-dwelling older adults: Findings from the Health, Aging and Body Composition Study. *J. Am. Geriatr. Soc.* **2009**, *57*, 243–250. [CrossRef] [PubMed]
23. Gravely, A.A.; Cutting, A.; Nugent, S.; Grill, J.; Carlson, K.; Spoont, M. Validity of PTSD diagnoses in VA administrative data: Comparison of VA administrative PTSD diagnoses to self-reported PTSD Checklist scores. *J. Rehabil. Res. Dev.* **2011**, *48*, 21–30. [CrossRef]
24. Lund, B.C.; Bernardy, N.C. Rural differences in psychiatric medication prescribing in veterans with posttraumatic stress disorder. *J. Rural Health* **2022**, *38*, 764–772. [CrossRef]
25. Mosher, H.J.; Richardson, K.K.; Lund, B.C. The 1-year treatment course of new opioid recipients in Veterans Health Administration. *Pain Med.* **2016**, *17*, 1282–1291. [CrossRef] [PubMed]
26. Tian, T.Y.; Zlateva, I.; Anderson, D.R. Using electronic health records data to identify patients with chronic pain in a primary care setting. *J. Am. Med. Inform. Assoc.* **2013**, *20*, e275–e280. [CrossRef]
27. Mayhew, M.; DeBar, L.L.; Deyo, R.A.; Kerns, R.D.; Goulet, J.L.; Brandt, C.A.; Von Korff, M. Development and assessment of a crosswalk between ICD-9-CM and ICD-10-CM to identify patients with common pain conditions. *J. Pain* **2019**, *20*, 1429–1445. [CrossRef]
28. Mares, J.G.; Lund, B.C.; Adamowicz, J.L.; Burgess, D.J.; Rothmiller, S.J.; Hadlandsmyth, K. Differences in chronic pain care receipt among veterans from differing racialized groups and the impact of rural versus urban residence. *J. Rural Health* **2023**, *39*, 595–603. [CrossRef] [PubMed]
29. Quan, H.; Sundararajan, V.; Halfon, P.; Fong, A.; Burnand, B.; Luthi, J.-C.; Saunders, L.D.; Beck, C.A.; Feasby, T.E.; Ghali, W.A. Coding algorithms for defining comorbidities in ICD-9-CM and ICD-10 administrative data. *Med. Care* **2005**, *43*, 1130–1139. [CrossRef]
30. Hadlandsmyth, K.; Bernardy, N.C.; Lund, B.C. Gender differences in medication prescribing patterns for veterans with posttraumatic stress disorder: A 10-year follow-up study. *J Trauma Stress* **2022**, *35*, 1586–1597. [CrossRef]
31. Bernardy, N.C.; Friedman, M.J.; Lund, B.C. Deimplementation of Benzodiazepine Prescribing in Posttraumatic Stress Disorder in the Veterans Health Administration. *J. Clin. Psychiatry* **2022**, *83*, 40122. [CrossRef] [PubMed]
32. Hadlandsmyth, K.; Mosher, H.; Vander Weg, M.W.; Lund, B.C. Decline in prescription opioids attributable to decreases in long-term use: A retrospective study in the Veterans Health Administration 2010–2016. *J. Gen. Intern. Med.* **2018**, *33*, 818–824. [CrossRef] [PubMed]
33. Otis, J.D.; Keane, T.M.; Kerns, R.D.; Monson, C.; Scioli, E. The Development of an Integrated Treatment for Veterans with Comorbid Chronic Pain and Posttraumatic Stress Disorder. *Pain Med.* **2009**, *10*, 1300–1311. [CrossRef]
34. Mary Murphy, J.D.; Odom, A.; Hadlandsmyth, K. Posttraumatic Stress Disorder and Chronic Pain. In *PTSD Research Quarterly*; PTSD, NCF, Eds.; U.S. Department of Verterans Affairs: Washington, DC, USA, 2022.
35. Wells, D.L.; Popish, S.; Kay, C.; Torrise, V.; Christopher, M.L. VA Academic Detailing Service: Implementation and lessons learned. *Fed. Pract.* **2016**, *33*, 38. [PubMed]

36. Sandbrink, F.; Oliva, E.M.; McMullen, T.L.; Aylor, A.R.; Harvey, M.A.; Christopher, M.L.; Cunningham, F.; Minegishi, T.; Emmendorfer, T.; Perry, J.M. Opioid Prescribing and Opioid Risk Mitigation Strategies in the Veterans Health Administration. *J. Gen. Intern. Med.* **2020**, *35*, 927–934. [CrossRef]
37. Wiechers, I. *Program Focuses on Safe Psychiatric Medication*; Department of Veterans Affairs: Washington, DC, USA, 2021.

Journal of
Clinical Medicine

MDPI

Article

Self-Reported Practices and Emotions in Prescribing Opioids for Chronic Noncancer Pain: A Cross-Sectional Study of German Physicians

Erika Schulte [1,*], Frank Petzke [2], Claudia Spies [3], Claudia Denke [3], Michael Schäfer [3], Norbert Donner-Banzhoff [4], Ralph Hertwig [5] and Odette Wegwarth [3,5]

1 Department of Palliative Medicine, Universitätsmedizin Göttingen, 37075 Göttingen, Germany
2 Pain Clinic, Department of Anesthesiology, Universitätsmedizin Göttingen, 37075 Göttingen, Germany; frank.petzke@med.uni-goettingen.de
3 Department of Anesthesiology and Operative Intensive Care Medicine (CCM, CVK), Charité—Universitätsmedizin Berlin, Corporate Member of Freie Universität Berlin and Humboldt-Universität zu Berlin, and Berlin Institute of Health, 13353 Berlin, Germany; claudia.spies@charite.de (C.S.); claudia.denke@charite.de (C.D.); micha.schaefer@charite.de (M.S.); odette.wegwarth@charite.de (O.W.)
4 Department of Primary Care, Phillips-Universität Marburg, 35043 Marburg, Germany; norbert@staff.uni-marburg.de
5 Center for Adaptive Rationality, Max-Planck-Institut für Bildungsforschung, 14195 Berlin, Germany; hertwig@mpib-berlin.mpg.de
* Correspondence: erika.schulte@med.uni-goettingen.de; Tel.: +49-551-39-60222; Fax: +49-551-39-60505

Citation: Schulte, E.; Petzke, F.; Spies, C.; Denke, C.; Schäfer, M.; Donner-Banzhoff, N.; Hertwig, R.; Wegwarth, O. Self-Reported Practices and Emotions in Prescribing Opioids for Chronic Noncancer Pain: A Cross-Sectional Study of German Physicians. *J. Clin. Med.* **2022**, *11*, 2506. https://doi.org/10.3390/jcm11092506

Academic Editors: Markus W. Hollmann, Casandra I. Montoro Aguilar, Carmen María Galvez Sánchez and Patrice Forget

Received: 3 April 2022
Accepted: 25 April 2022
Published: 29 April 2022

Abstract: Background: The pressure on physicians when a patient seeks pain relief and their own desire to be self-effective may lead to the prescription of strong opioids for chronic noncancer pain (CNCP). This study, via physician self-reporting, aims to identify and measure (i) physician adherence to national opioid prescribing guidelines and (ii) physician emotions when a patient seeks a dosage increase of the opioid. Methods: Within a cross-sectional survey—conducted as part of a randomized controlled online intervention trial (ERONA)—600 German physicians were queried on their opioid prescribing behavior (choice and formulation of opioid, indications) for CNCP patients and their emotions to a case vignette describing a patient seeking an opioid dosage increase without signs of objective deterioration. Results: The prescription of strong opioids in this study was not always in accordance with current guidelines. When presented with a scenario in which a patient sought to have their opioid dose increased, some physicians reported negative feelings, such as either pressure (25%), helplessness (25%), anger (23%) or a combination. The risk of non-guideline-compliant prescribing behavior using the example of ultrafast-acting fentanyl for CNCP was increased when negative emotions were present (OR: 1.7; 95%-CI: 1.2–2.6; $p = 0.007$) or when sublingual buprenorphine was prescribed (OR: 15.4; 95%-CI: 10.1–23.3; $p < 0.001$). Conclusions: Physicians' emotional self-awareness represents the first step to identify such direct reactions to patient requests and to ensure a responsible, guideline-based opioid prescription approach for the long-term well-being of the patient.

Keywords: chronic noncancer pain; WHO III opioids; prescription; guideline adherence

1. Introduction

Strong opioids have been used for chronic noncancer pain (CNCP) since the 1980s [1]. While opioids show low-to-moderate improvements in pain relief and functionality, the administration of opioids in CNCP can have relevant side effects [2–7], including opioid use disorders [8–10]. Therefore, international and national guidelines have been brought into place [11–13] to help balance the benefits and risks, increase safety and inform prescribers about the evidence-based use of opioids in CNCP.

However, a current review shows that physicians' adherence to the North American Opioid Guidelines and their compliance with the recommendations has been low: treatment agreements, consented urine drug testing, consultations with drug monitoring programs, assessing the risk of aberrant medication-taking behavior and mental health screening [14]. To the best of our knowledge, we are not aware of any studies that have specifically focused on physicians' guideline adherence with regard to the indications for opioids and the individual opioid formulations. This gave rise to our motivation to investigate the extent to which physicians in Germany prescribe strong opioids for CNCP in line with the indication and the drug formulation.

Despite the lack of evidence for an opioid crisis in Germany comparable to the one in the US [15,16], there remains considerable uncertainty [13] as to when and for how long the types and formulations of opioids should be prescribed for CNCP, leaving ample responsibility with the treating physician. National guidelines have outlined recommendations to support the decision-making process prior to the initiation of opioid treatment that should integrate both the evaluation of risks and the potential benefits of opioids [17]. To date, opioid risk mitigation programs have focused primarily on the individual patient and on preventing addiction, misuse and overuse of opioids [18] and less on physicians' prescriptions habits and the challenges they may face when responding to a patient's desire for pain reduction through opioids and overall limited therapy options to treat chronic pain.

Studies focusing on the physician's decision process show, for example, that they prescribe more opioids to more psychologically stressed patients who express their suffering clearly [19]. In a qualitative study, opioid-prescribing general practitioners expressed substantial frustration and stress in managing chronic pain patients with opioids [20]. However, most studies focused on the patient characteristics (for example, consistent and objective information given by the patient, red flags, patient trustworthiness) that lead the provider to prescribe opioids for CNCP [21–24]. We could not find a single study investigating in depth the "inner conflict" of the opioid prescribing physician in Germany. Therefore, we tried to find phrases that describe this inner conflict and interviewed physicians regularly prescribing opioids for CNCP about whether they can identify themselves with these phrases of "inner conflict".

Taken together, the present analysis examined (I) the adherence of physicians in Germany to the national guideline recommendations for long-term opioid use with regard to indications and formulations of strong opioids in CNCP, (II) physicians' emotional reactions to patients' requests for an increased opioid dose without objective worsening of the underlying condition (presented as a case study vignette) and (III) possible prescriber-related factors that might be associated with non-guideline-compliant prescriptions.

2. Methods

The ERONA (experiencing the risk of overutilizing opioids among patients with chronic noncancer pain in ambulatory care) project—consisting of four prospective exploratory, randomized controlled online trials (RCT) with four independent study populations—aimed to investigate experiential versus text-based educational formats (DRKS00020358). The full peer-reviewed study protocol is published elsewhere [25]. The data reported here are based on survey questions that were included in the RCT prior to randomization of the physicians to one of two educational interventions addressing the benefit-to-harm ratio of strong opioids, defined as World Health Organization Step III opioids.

2.1. Study Population and Inclusion Criteria

Using a multi-layered strategy, IPSOS Health, an independent market research institution, recruited randomly selected potentially eligible physicians via its panels and business directories (e.g., directory of the National Association of Statutory Health Insurance Physicians). The first contact was made by e-mail. Interested physicians were then contacted by phone. The final intervention was online. All participants were reimbursed for participation by IPSOS Health. To detect a 15% difference in the randomized ERONA trial, 300 participants per intervention arm were recruited between April 2020 and August 2020, resulting in a sample of 600 physicians over a wide range of disciplines. Details of the sample size calculation were already published [25]. Only physicians prescribing strong opioids regularly for CNCP were included in the study and detected by the screener question: "Do you prescribe BtM (Betäubungsmittel)-based opioids to treat patients with chronic, non-tumor-related pain?". For strong opioids in Germany, it is necessary to make the prescription on a special prescription form, called *BtM*-prescription. Informed consent was obtained online prior to the study.

2.2. Survey Questionnaire

2.2.1. Baseline Characteristics

The following physician baseline characteristics were recorded in the online survey: age, gender, region of work (north, south, east, west of Germany), years of working experience, and workplace (doctor's office, medical care center, hospital, rehabilitation clinic/nursing home).

2.2.2. Opioid-Prescribing Behavior: Type and Formulation of Opioids, Indications

Physicians were asked about their opioid-prescribing behavior with two questions: (1) "Under which noncancer-related chronic pain conditions have you prescribed strong opioids for as the primary prescriber within the past 12 months?" and (2) "Which of the following strong opioid formulations are you currently prescribing for the treatment of chronic noncancer pain"? Regarding question 1, the list of suggested diagnoses was "chronic nonspecific low-back pain, osteoarthrosis, diabetic polyneuropathy, postherpetic neuralgia, phantom limb pain, disc prolapse, spinal stenosis, rheumatoid arthritis, fibromyalgia syndrome, secondary headaches, osteoporotic vertebral body fractures, chronic postsurgical pain, peripheral artery disease of the lower extremities, grade 3 and 4 pressure ulcers, chronic pain associated with fixed contractures, central neuropathic pain, chronic regional pain syndrome I and II, chronic pelvic pain associated with adhesions or endometriosis, chronic inflammatory bowel disease, primary headaches, functional disorders, chronic pancreatitis, craniomandibular dysfunction, persistent idiopathic facial pain, neuralgia (e.g., trigeminus) and multiple sclerosis" with the answer options "Yes/No/Does not apply". "Does not apply" was explained with "I haven't had a patient with this type of chronic pain condition.".

Regarding question 2, the list of selectable opioids included "morphine, buprenorphine, fentanyl, oxycodone, hydromorphone and tapentadol", each supplemented with the most common German trade names and the following prescribing options currently available in the German national formulary: "oral extended release/oral (or nasal or sublingual) immediate release/transdermal/or I do not prescribe this strong opioid at all". The opioids and their possible formulations were presented as a table with mandatory fields—excluding non-available combinations, such as transdermal and morphine. "Noncancer-related chronic pain condition" or "chronic noncancer pain" was printed in bold in question 1 and 2 of the survey, respectively. The answers to the indication questions were based on the German guideline recommendations for long-term use of opioids in chronic noncancer pain (LONTS) [13]. This guideline defines both evidence-based as well as consensus-based indications and contraindications for opioid therapy and was published in its current version prior to the survey.

2.2.3. Physicians' Emotional Response to Patients' Demands for Dose Escalation

Each physician was further presented a case vignette in which a patient with nonspecific low back pain and longstanding opioid therapy asked for an increase in opioid dose even though there was no evidence of objective somatic deterioration. The exact wording of the vignette and the respective question are given in Table 4. The five options for a response on an emotional level can also be found in Table 4. "Yes" or "no" was the possible answer for each statement. All statements needed to be affirmed or denied.

2.2.4. Risk Literacy

The physicians' medical risk literacy was assessed by administering an adapted version of the validated Critical Risk Interpretation Test (CRIT) [26]. The score of correct responses ranged from 0 to 5 with the latter being the highest possible degree of risk literacy.

2.2.5. Piloting

The questionnaire used in this study was piloted with 11 physicians that regularly treated CNCP patients: general practitioners and pain specialists with varying degrees of experience, both in the outpatient and in the hospital setting. They answered the questions as study participants, and they were also asked to give comments on the comprehensibility and quality of the questions. With their feedback, the framing and wording of the survey questions were revised and optimized. Both the German original version of the questions analyzed here and the English translation can be viewed in the Supplementary Materials.

2.3. Statistical Analysis

The survey did not permit any non-responses to the questionnaire items; thus, all datasets were complete. The data were descriptively analyzed by frequency distributions and percentages. A binary logistic regression model was used to explore potential associations between non-guideline compliant opioid prescription behavior—using the prescription of oral/nasal ultrafast acting fentanyl for CNCP as an example—and independent variables that may affect prescriptions, such as age, gender, work experience, prescription of other substances, such as buprenorphine, and the presence of negative emotions (at least one of the four possible suggested negative emotions). For the insertion of the independent variables into the model, the forward stepwise method was used. $p < 0.05$ was considered significant. Data were stored and analyzed with IBM SPSS Statistics (version 27) (Armonk, NY, USA).

3. Results

3.1. Recruitment of Participating Physicians

IPSOS contacted successfully contacted 8820 physicians. Of the 734 physicians who were interested in taking part in the survey, 7 did not meet the screener criterion, i.e., regularly prescribing opioids for CNCP; thus, 727 were recruited for the survey. A further 125 physicians, who had originally agreed to participate, eventually chose to not take part in the survey. Of the remaining 602 physicians who started the survey, 2 left the survey prematurely and 600 completed the survey. In the end, 6.8 percent of the contacted physicians answered the survey (Figure 1).

3.2. Demographic and Professional Characteristics

The proportion of men among the physicians surveyed was 69%. Most of the respondents (69%) were middle-aged (40–59 years of age), resulting in a huge group of participants (74%) with around 10–30 years of professional experience. The largest category of physicians who regularly prescribed opioids for CNCP according to this survey were general practitioners (60%), followed by specialist internists (25%), anesthetists (11%) and orthopedists (6%). All other specialist groups were equal to or less than 2% (Table 1). Most of the physicians worked in their own practice (Table 1).

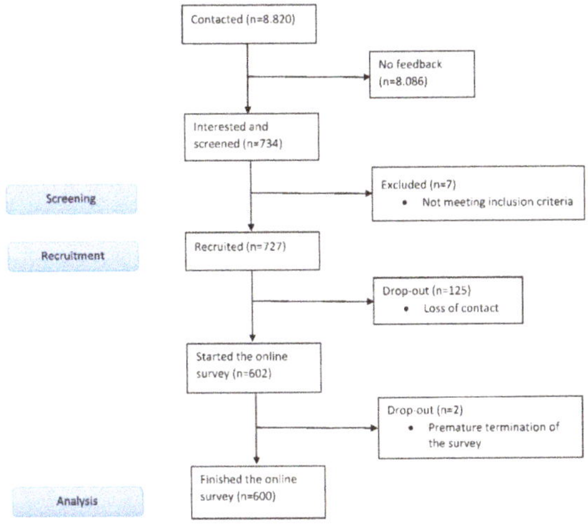

Figure 1. Flow chart of the study.

Table 1. Demographic and professional characteristics of the physicians surveyed.

	Total
	N = 600
	N (%)
Gender	
female	221 (36.8)
Age (years)	
20–39	51 (8.5)
40–59	413 (68.8)
60–79	136 (22.7)
Place of work in Germany	
North	133 (22.2)
South	133 (22.2)
East	160 (26.7)
West	174 (29.0)
Work experience (years)	
<10	46 (7.7)
10–19	199 (33.2)
20–29	247 (41.2)
>30	108 (18.0)
Type of workplace	
Doctor's office	386 (64.3)
Medical care center	149 (24.8)
Hospital	58 (9.7)
Rehabilitation clinic/nursing home	7 (1.2)
Areas of expertise [a]	
General medicine	360 (60.0)
Internal medicine	149 (24.8)
Anesthesiology	68 (11.3)
Orthopedic surgery	40 (6.7)
Psychiatry/psychotherapy/psychosomatic	12 (2.0)
Neurology	11 (1.8)
General surgery	11 (1.8)
Physical medicine	3 (0.5)
Gynecology	1 (0.2)
Urology	1 (0.2)

[a] Sum of expertise fields is >600 because some physicians have more than one specialization.

3.3. Self-Reports of the Opioid Ingredients and Galenics Prescribed

Transdermal fentanyl (99%), slow-release morphine (98%) and slow-release oxycodone (91%) were reported to be prescribed most frequently for CNCP in this survey. Of the 600 participants, 41% and 49% prescribed sublingual forms of buprenorphine and the ultrafast acting application of fentanyl (oral or nasal), respectively. The frequency of the other prescribed opioids for CNCP is shown in Table 2.

Table 2. Self-reported opioid prescribing behavior: opioid variant and formulations.

"Which of the following ***Strong Opioids*** *are you Currently Prescribing for the Treatment of* ***Chronic Noncancer Pain*** *and in which Dosage Form?"*	**Total** N = 600 N (%)
Morphine	
Oral extended release	587 (97.8)
Oral immediate release	517 (86.2)
No use	9 (1.5)
Buprenorphine	
Transdermal	482 (80.3)
Sublingual	245 (40.8)
No use	102 (17.0)
Fentanyl	
Transdermal	594 (99.0)
Oral/nasal immediate release	294 (49.0)
No use	2 (0.3)
Oxycodone	
Oral extended release	545 (90.8)
Oral immediate release	468 (78.0)
No use	5 (0.8)
Hydromorphone	
Oral extended release	473 (78.8)
Oral immediate release	207 (34.5)
No use	117 (19.5)
Tapentadol	
Oral extended release	515 (85.8)
Oral immediate release	354 (58.3)
no use	51 (8.5)

3.4. The Indications Detailed in the Self-Reported Opioid Prescribing Behavior

Physicians most often reported that their opioid prescription was for the following diagnoses: disc prolapse (62%) and grade 3 and 4 pressure ulcers (60%); the national LONTS guideline specifies an open recommendation for these (Table 3). Osteoarthritis was the most common indication (56%) that physicians reported prescribing strong opioids, for which the LONTS guideline provides an evidence-based positive recommendation for short-term (4–12 weeks) and immediate-term (13–26 weeks) use (Table 3). For chronic nonspecific low back pain, 38% of physicians reported prescription rates of strong opioids, for diabetic polyneuropathy 41% and for postherpetic neuralgia 38%, which follows positive (short-term use) or open guideline recommendations (long-term use) (Table 3). Although for the following diagnosis, the LONTS recommendations are negative (Table 3), 42% of physicians reported prescribing strong opioids in chronic inflammatory bowel disease, 30% in chronic pancreatitis, 26% in functional disorders, 25% in fibromyalgia syndrome and 20% in primary headaches.

Table 3. Indications of physician self-reported opioid prescribing behavior compared to guideline recommendations.

"For which ***noncancer-related diseases*** *have you prescribed strong opioids as the primary prescriber in the past 12 months?"*	Total N = 600 N (%)	Evidence Level According to LONTS [b] [13]
Chronic nonspecific low-back pain		
Yes	225 (37.5)	4–12 weeks: Ia, recommendation for
No	335 (55.8)	13–26 weeks: Ia, recommendation for
Does not apply [a]	40 (6.7)	>26 weeks: IIb, open recommendation
Osteoarthritis		
Yes	335 (55.8)	4–12 weeks: Ia, recommendation for
No	238 (39.7)	13–26 weeks: Ia, recommendation for
Does not apply [a]	27 (4.5)	>26 weeks: IIb, open recommendation
Diabetic polyneuropathy		
Yes	248 (41.3)	4–12 weeks: Ia, strong recommendation for
No	210 (35.0)	13–26 weeks: no data, open recommendation
Does not apply [a]	142 (23.7)	>26 weeks: IIb, open recommendation
Postherpetic neuralgia		
Yes	229 (38.2)	4–12 weeks: Ia, recommendation for
No	273 (45.5)	13–26 weeks: no data, open recommendation
Does not apply	98 (16.3)	>26 weeks: no data, open recommendation
Phantom limb pain		
yes	289 (48.2)	4–12 weeks: Ib, open recommendation for
no	186 (31.0)	13–26 weeks: no data, open recommendation
does not apply [a]	125 (20.8)	>26 weeks: no data, open recommendation
Disc prolapse [c]		
yes	370 (61.7)	4–12 weeks: Ib, open recommendation for
no	200 (33.3)	13–26 weeks: no data, open recommendation
does not apply [a]	30 (5.0)	>26 weeks: no data, open recommendation
Spinal stenosis		
yes	251 (41.8)	4–12 weeks: Ib, open recommendation for [c]
no	287 (47.8)	13–26 weeks: no data, open recommendation [c]
does not apply [a]	62 (10.3)	>26 weeks: no data, open recommendation [c]
Rheumatoid arthritis		
yes	263 (43.8)	4–12 weeks: Ib, open recommendation for
no	298 (49.7)	13–26 weeks: no data, open recommendation
does not apply [a]	39 (6.5)	>26 weeks: no data, open recommendation
Fibromyalgia syndrome		
yes	152 (25.3)	4–12 weeks: Ib, open recommendation for
no	252 (42.0)	13–26 weeks: no data, open recommendation
does not apply [a]	196 (32.7)	>26 weeks: no data, open recommendation
Secondary headaches		
yes	136 (22.7)	4–12 weeks: no data, open recommendation
no	380 (63.3)	13–26 weeks: no data, open recommendation
does not apply [a]	84 (14.0)	>26 weeks: no data, open recommendation
Vertebral body fractures in osteoporosis		
yes	231 (38.5)	4–12 weeks: no data, open recommendation
no	268 (44.7)	13–26 weeks: no data, open recommendation
does not apply [a]	101 (16.8)	>26 weeks: no data, open recommendation
Chronic postsurgical pain		
yes	336 (56.0)	4–12 weeks: no data, open recommendation
no	143 (23.8)	13–26 weeks: no data, open recommendation
does not apply [a]	121 (20.2)	>26 weeks: no data, open recommendation
Peripheral arterial disease of the lower extremities		
yes	171 (28.5)	4–12 weeks: no data, open recommendation
no	337 (56.2)	13–26 weeks: no data, open recommendation
does not apply [a]	92 (15.3)	>26 weeks: no data, open recommendation

Table 3. *Cont.*

"For which ***noncancer-related diseases*** *have you prescribed strong opioids as the primary prescriber in the past 12 months?"*	Total N = 600 N (%)	Evidence Level According to LONTS [b] [13]
Grade 3 and 4 pressure ulcers		
yes	362 (60.3)	4–12 weeks: no data, open recommendation
no	158 (26.3)	13–26 weeks: no data, open recommendation
does not apply [a]	80 (13.3)	>26 weeks: no data, open recommendation
Chronic pain associated with fixed contractures		
yes	231 (38.5)	4–12 weeks: no data, open recommendation
no	254 (42.3)	13–26 weeks: no data, open recommendation
does not apply [a]	115 (19.2)	>26 weeks: no data, open recommendation
Central neuropathic pain		
yes	112 (18.7)	4–12 weeks: no data, open recommendation
no	327 (54.5)	13–26 weeks: no data, open recommendation
does not apply [a]	161 (26.8)	>26 weeks: no data, open recommendation
Chronic regional pain syndrome I and II		
yes	274 (45.7)	4–12 weeks: no data, open recommendation
no	172 (28.7)	13–26 weeks: no data, open recommendation
does not apply [a]	154 (25.7)	>26 weeks: no data, open recommendation
Chronic pelvic pain		
yes	73 (12.2)	4–12 weeks: no data, open recommendation
no	217 (36.2)	13–26 weeks: no data, open recommendation
does not apply [a]	310 (51.7)	>26 weeks: no data, open recommendation
Chronic inflammatory bowel disease		
yes	252 (42.0)	
no	248 (41.3)	>26 weeks: IIIb, recommendation against
does not apply [a]	100 (16.7)	
Primary headaches		
yes	119 (19.8)	
no	406 (67.7)	>26 weeks: IIIb, strong recommendation against
does not apply [a]	75 (12.5)	
Functional disorders		
yes	158 (26.3)	
no	366 (61.0)	no data; independent of time: strong recommendation against
does not apply [a]	76 (12.7)	
Chronic pancreatitis		
yes	180 (30.0)	>26 weeks: IIIb, strong recommendation against
no	316 (52.7)	
does not apply [a]	104 (17.3)	
Craniomandibular dysfunction		
yes	86 (14.3)	
no	259 (43.2)	no recommendation
does not apply [a]	255 (42.5	
Persistent idiopathic facial pain		
yes	197 (32.8)	
no	264 (44.0)	no recommendation
does not apply [a]	139 (23.2)	
Neuralgia (e.g., trigeminus)		
yes	241 (40.2)	
no	295 (49.2)	no recommendation
does not apply [a]	64 (10.7)	
Multiple sclerosis		
yes	136 (22.7)	
no	295 (49.2)	No statement on this indication in LONTS [b]
does not apply [a]	169 (28.2)	

[a] does not apply = physician has not treated patients with this disease in the past 12 months; [b] German guideline for long-term use of opioids in chronic noncancer pain; [c] recommendation for radiculopathy.

3.5. Physicians' Self-Reported Emotional Reactions to Patient Requests to Increase Opioid Dosages

The feeling of being well-equipped to handle a patient's request of increasing the opioid dosage to treat unspecific low-back pain was reported by 59% of the physicians, whereas 43% of the physicians described negative feelings in such a situation. About one quarter of the physicians expressed feelings of either pressure (25%), helplessness (25%), anger, or a combination (23%) (Table 4). A smaller subgroup of physicians reported that despite negative feelings they can handle the situation quite well: 59 physicians reported anger and good management of the situation (10% of the whole group); helplessness and good management of the situation was reported by 32 physicians (5% of the whole group) (Figure 2).

Table 4. Physician self-reported emotional reactions to a patient's desire to increase opioid dosage in long-term opioid therapy of chronic unspecific low back pain.

Case Vignette: *"Please Imagine the Following Situation: A Patient with Chronic Noncancer Related Low-Back Pain who has Already been Prescribed an Opioid for a Long Time Comes to your Consultation with the Request to Increase the Opioid Dose. There are no Indications of a Finding that Requires Intervention, such as a New Neurological Disorder or Other red Flags.* ***Which of the Emotions Described below have you Already Observed in Yourself?"***	**Total** N = 600 N [a] (%)
"I can handle the situation ***quite well****."*	354 (59)
"I feel ***pressured*** *to increase the dose."*	148 (25)
"I feel ***helpless*** *because I don't have an easy solution."*	149 (25)
"I experience negative emotions such as ***anger****."*	135 (23)
"I have a ***bad feeling*** *about increasing the dose."*	258 (43)

[a] multiple answers were possible.

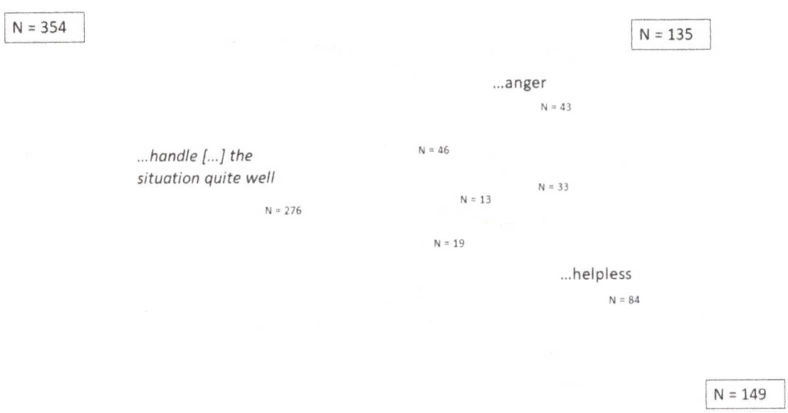

Figure 2. A selection of physician self-reported emotional reactions to a patient's desire to increase opioid dosage and their overlaps.

3.6. Covariate Analysis of Non-Guideline-Compliant Opioid Prescribing Behavior

Physicians prescribing ultrafast-acting fentanyl formulations were also highly likely to prescribe sublingual buprenorphine (OR: 15.4; 95%-CI: 10.1–23.3; $p < 0.001$). The presence of negative emotions in response to patients' demands for a dose escalation nearly doubled the likelihood of physicians to prescribe ultrafast-acting fentanyl to their patients (OR: 1.7; 95%-CI: 1.2–2.6; $p = 0.007$). Other aspects, such as work experience or risk literacy, were not found to be associated with physicians' prescription behavior. The final independent variables included in the binary logistic regression analysis (Table 5) increased the proportion of correctly predicted answers from 51.0% to 78.5%. The selected model explains 41% of the existing variance (Nagelkerkes R-Quadrat).

Table 5. Binary logistic regression analysis with non-guideline-compliant opioid prescribing (ultrafast-acting fentanyl for CNCP) as dependent variable.

	Non-Guideline-Compliant Opioid Prescribing Using the Example of Ultra-Fast-Acting Fentanyl for CNCP		
Independent Variables	**Odds Ratio**	**95% CI**	***p***
Buprenorphine, sublingual Prescribing for CNCP (reference class: no prescribing for CNCP)	15.4	10.1–23.3	<0.001
Negative emotions [a] present (reference class: not-present)	1.7	1.2–2.6	0.007

[a] as reaction to the case study vignette relating to a patient request for an opioid dose increase.

4. Discussion and Conclusions

This analysis of the ERONA study showed that physicians in Germany reported a prescribing behavior for strong opioids for CNCP that was not consistently compliant with current guidelines—both in terms of opioid indications and the opioid formulations selected. A bad feeling about increasing an opioid dose in a situation without objective signs of deterioration was reported by 43% of the physicians surveyed. Emotions such as pressure, helplessness and anger were reported by 25%, 25% and 23% of the physicians in this situation. Perceived negative feelings about an opioid increase were associated with more non-compliant prescribing behavior.

The LONTS guideline, based on controlled clinical studies, recommends opioid prescription at least for 4–12 weeks for the following four diagnoses: chronic nonspecific low back pain [27], osteoarthrosis [28], diabetic polyneuropathy and postherpetic neuralgia [29]. The prescribing behavior of the physicians surveyed in our study indicated that they prescribe strong opioids most frequently for osteoarthritis (OA) (56%), and less often for chronic nonspecific low back pain (CLBP) (38%) (Table 3). This corresponds to the recommendation of the National Guideline for CLBP [30], which specifies opioids may be a short-term option only for selected patients. Comparing treatment guidelines for OA and CLBP, psychosocial factors seem to be more prominent in CLBP than in OA, where they certainly also play a role, but the somatic pain component is usually in the foreground [31,32]. In addition, OA pain often affects older people, where other therapy options, such as NSAIDs, are often either contraindicated [33], exercise therapy is more limited [34], or both.

The opioid prescriptions by physicians in this study for functional disorders, fibromyalgia syndrome and primary headaches appeared problematic, and they were anticipated to have negative consequences for the patient, such as unwanted medication overuse, headache (MOH) [12] or problematic opioid use. Prevalence data on the use of opioids in functional disorders are difficult to define since various heterogeneous diseases are collated under this diagnosis.

Further, immediate-release opioids are seldom necessary for noncancer pain [13] and ultrafast-acting opioids are exclusively licensed for cancer pain [35]. The fact that we found 49% of physicians in our study prescribing ultrafast-acting fentanyl to CNCP can be considered highly problematic. The challenge of non-indicated "off-label-use" has been described previously [36,37] and has been observed in other cohorts, for instance among Italian patients with CNCP of which nearly 10% received ultrafast onset opioids [38].

Training, education and the implementation of prevention strategies—possibly including either medico-legal consequences, non-reimbursement by the health insurance companies or both—would be necessary measures to restrict such misuse [39].

The role of sublingual buprenorphine, on the other hand, must be seen in a differentiated manner. It has a significantly longer onset and action time than fast-acting fentanyl. It is also approved for non-cancer pain, unlike the rapid-acting fentanyl preparations. In this respect, we were surprised by the fact that physicians who prescribe sublingual buprenorphine, which can be indicated in CNCP, were 15 times more likely to also prescribe fast-acting fentanyl, which is not indicated in CNCP. Perhaps these figures expressed the fact that those physicians were well versed in handling a wide variety of preparations and galenics. However, even within this group, there were those who adhere to the indications and others that do not.

In our study, 43% of the physicians reported a negative emotion associated with their own responsibility to a dose elevation in response to a patient's demand to increase opioid dosage without any obvious deterioration. Our study documented—to the best of our knowledge, for the first time—that such negative emotions may significantly influence physicians' reaction to these demands: Physicians presenting with negative emotions tended to exemplify more non-guideline-compliant behavior than did those who did not report such negative emotions. Not having negative emotions appeared to protect physicians from prescribing and patients from receiving an opioid medication that is not indicated for noncancer chronic pain. These findings on the role of negative emotions on patients' potentially unwarranted demand for dosage increase has been seldom described until now. However, it was in line with the prescriber style described by Passik et al., which is, for example, characterized by "aggressive opioid titration [. . .] with intents to entirely eliminate pain." [40]. It is of course also conceivable that negative gut feelings warn against an unjustified prescription.

Considering the consequences of non-compliant prescriptions of potent but risky drugs for patients' safety, the currently rather under-studied influence of different negative emotional states on physicians' compliance to guidelines certainly requires more research on these aspects to inform curricula and continuing training programs on appropriate opioid prescriptions.

Our study had some limitations. A critical point of this study was the high non-response rate during the recruitment process because the remaining physician cohort may not be representative of physicians working in Germany. At first glance, for example, women seemed to be underrepresented. However, if one compares the proportion of women in our study with the data of the German Medical Association (GMA) [41] based on the six most frequently occurring groups of expertise in this study, the proportion is 37% compared to 40% (GMA), thus only a little bit lower. If it was considered that older and more experienced physicians answered this survey, our data appeared to be quite representative in this point since the proportion of women is lower in the group of older physicians. The external validity of this study of course remains a critical point. For example, physicians may have responded who are already more critical of their prescription of opioids or more aware of their feelings than others. However, the focus of this study should be to draw attention to the presence of emotional aspects of opioid prescription and not to claim that the numbers determined were absolutely correct.

Another limitation was that these data are only based on self-reports, which may invite inaccuracies due to social desirability. Questions may have been misunderstood, e.g., that the addition "for noncancer pain" was missed in the questions about opioid preparations. We hoped to have minimized such issues by piloting material with colleagues. A further limitation is that we did not know how frequently non-guideline-compliant prescriptions occurred, as we have no information about the patients actually seen in these practices and the rates of prescription. Another inherent limitation was that the current study showed only an association between negative emotions and prescribing behavior rather than a cause-and-effect relationship. It could be, for example, that physicians' overprescribing was leading to a feeling of helplessness and anger, but it could also be that their initial feeling of anger and helplessness was leading to overprescribing. Other study designs, especially either qualitative designs, longitudinal quantitative designs or a combination, should investigate these questions. Another important point is that the questions concerning the emotional reactions of the physicians are not a part of a validated questionnaire. This reduces the internal validity of the results. After a qualitative scientific examination of the topic "physicians' emotions and prescribing opioids" as suggested above, the goal should be to generate a validated questionnaire that serves both research purposes and routine use to sensitize physicians to this topic.

This analysis showed that in Germany strong opioids are largely prescribed in accordance with the existing guidelines. However, there were indications where the use of opioids should be viewed critically, e.g., in the case of primary headaches, fibromyalgia syndrome or other functional pain syndromes. Fast-acting fentanyl preparations should not be used in CNCP. Emotional aspects on the part of the prescribing physician could also play a role if opioids are not prescribed in accordance with the guidelines.

Supplementary Materials: The following supporting information can be downloaded at: https://www.mdpi.com/article/10.3390/jcm11092506/s1, Project: ERONA—Physicians.

Author Contributions: O.W. conceived the project and was involved in preparing the manuscript; E.S. and N.D.-B. were involved in planning the study; E.S. analyzed the data and drafted this manuscript; O.W., R.H. and C.S. secured the funding for the project; O.W., C.S. and R.H. supervised the project; F.P., C.D., N.D.-B., M.S., C.S. and O.W. reviewed and edited the manuscript. All authors have read and agreed to the published version of the manuscript.

Funding: This work is supported by the German Federal Ministry of Health (BMG) (grant number: 2519ATS001).

Institutional Review Board Statement: Institutional Ethics Board of the Max Planck Institute for Human Development, Berlin (Germany); Ethic Approval ID for pilot test: A 2019-32; for RCT and cross-sectional study: A 2020-05. Clinical trial number: DRKS00020358.

Informed Consent Statement: Informed consent was obtained before starting the survey.

Conflicts of Interest: See ICMJE form for Conflicts of Interests declared by CS. All other authors declare no competing interests.

References

1. Portenoy, R.K.; Foley, K.M. Chronic use of opioid analgesics in non-malignant pain: Report of 38 cases. *Pain* **1986**, *25*, 171–186. [CrossRef]
2. Bialas, P.; Maier, C.; Klose, P.; Häuser, W. Efficacy and harms of long-term opioid therapy in chronic non-cancer pain: Systematic review and metaanalysis of open-label extensions trials. *Eur. J. Pain* **2020**, *24*, 265–278. [CrossRef] [PubMed]
3. Chaparro, L.E.; Furlan, A.D.; Deshpande, A.; Mailis-Gagnon, A.; Atlas, S.; Turk, D.C. Opioids compared to placebo or other treatments for chronic low-back pain. *Cochrane Database Syst. Rev.* **2013**, *8*, CD004959. [CrossRef] [PubMed]
4. Chou, R.; Deyo, R.; Friedly, J.; Skelly, A.; Weimer, M.; Fu, R.; Dana, T.; Kraegel, P.; Griffin, J.; Grusing, S. Systemic Pharmacologic Therapies for Low Back Pain: A Systematic Review for an American College of Physicians Clinical Practice Guideline. *Ann. Intern. Med.* **2017**, *166*, 480–492. [CrossRef] [PubMed]
5. Furlan, A.D.; Sandoval, J.A.; Mailis-Gagnon, A.; Tunks, E. Opioids for chronic noncancer pain: A meta-analysis of effectiveness and side effects. *CMAJ* **2006**, *174*, 1589–1594. [CrossRef] [PubMed]
6. Moore, R.A.; McQuay, H.J. Prevalence of opioid adverse events in chronic non-malignant pain: Systematic review of randomised trials of oral opioids. *Arthritis Res. Ther.* **2005**, *7*, R1046–R1051. [CrossRef]
7. Nury, E.; Schmucker, C.; Nagavci, B.L.; Motschall, E.; Nitschke, K.; Schulte, E.; Wegwarth, O.; Meerpohl, J.J. The effectiveness and risk of long-term opioid therapy versus placebo and non-opioid therapy in patients with chronic non-cancer pain: A systematic review and meta-analysis. *Pain* **2022**, *163*, 610–636. [CrossRef]
8. Garland, E.L.; Froeliger, B.; Zeidan, F.; Partin, K.; Howard, M.O. The downward spiral of chronic pain, prescription opioid misuse, and addiction: Cognitive, affective, and neuropsychopharmacologic pathways. *Neurosci. Biobehav. Rev.* **2013**, *37*, 2597–2607. [CrossRef]
9. McDermott, K.A.; Griffin, M.L.; McHugh, R.K.; Fitzmaurice, G.M.; Jamison, R.N.; Provost, S.E.; Weiss, R.D. Long-term naturalistic follow-up of chronic pain in adults with prescription opioid use disorder. *Drug Alcohol Depend.* **2019**, *205*, 107675. [CrossRef]

10. Vowles, K.E.; McEntee, M.L.; Julnes, P.S.; Frohe, T.; Ney, J.P.; van der Goes, D.N. Rates of opioid misuses, abuse, and addiction in chronic pain: A systematic review and data synthesis. *Pain* **2015**, *156*, 569–576. [CrossRef]
11. Busse, J.W.; Craigie, S.; Juurlink, D.N.; Buckley, D.N.; Wang, L.; Couban, R.J.; Agoritsas, T.; Akl, E.A.; Carrasco-Labra, A.; Cooper, L.; et al. Guideline for opioid therapy and chronic noncancer pain. *CMAJ* **2017**, *189*, E659–E666. [CrossRef] [PubMed]
12. Dowell, D.; Haegerich, T.M.; Chou, R. CDC Guideline for Prescribing Opioids for Chronic Pain—United States. *JAMA* **2016**, *315*, 1624–1645. [CrossRef] [PubMed]
13. Häuser, W.; Bock, F.; Hüppe, M.; Nothacker, M.; Norda, H.; Radbruch, L.; Schiltenwolf, M.; Schuler, M.; Tölle, T.; Viniol, A.; et al. Koautoren für die Konsensusgruppe der 2. Aktualisierung der S3-Leitlinie LONTS. Empfehlungen der zweiten Aktualisierung der Leitlinie LONTS. Langzeitanwendung von Opioiden bei chronischen nicht-tumorbedingten Schmerzen. *Der Schmerz* **2020**, *34*, 204–244. [CrossRef] [PubMed]
14. Hossain, M.A.; Asamoah-Boaheng, M.; Badejo, O.A.; Bell, L.V.; Buckley, N.; Busse, J.W.; Campbell, T.S.; Corace, K.; Cooper, L.K.; Flusk, D.; et al. Prescriber adherence to guidelines for chronic noncancer pain management with opioids: Systematic review and meta-analysis. *Health Psychol.* **2020**, *39*, 430–451. [CrossRef]
15. Alenezi, A.; Yahyouche, A.; Paudyal, V. Current status of opioid epidemic in the United Kingdom and strategies for treatment optimisation in chronic pain. *Int. J. Clin. Pharm.* **2021**, *43*, 318–322. [CrossRef]
16. Pierce, M.; van Amsterdam, J.; Kalkman, G.A.; Schellekens, A.; van den Brink, W. Is Europe facing an opioid crisis like the United States? An analysis of opioid use and related adverse effects in 19 European countries between 2010 and 2018. *Eur. Psychiatry* **2021**, *64*, e47. [CrossRef]
17. Häuser, W.; Schug, S.; Furlan, A.D. The opioid epidemic and national guidelines for opioid therapy for chronic noncancer pain: A perspective from different continents. *Pain Rep.* **2017**, *2*, e599. [CrossRef]
18. Alford, D.P.; Lazure, P.; Murray, S.; Hardesty, I.; Krause, J.R.; White, J.L. National Trends in Prescription Opioid Risk Mitigation Practices: Implications for Prescriber Education. *Pain Med.* **2019**, *20*, 907–915. [CrossRef]
19. Turk, D.C.; Okifuji, A. What factors affect physicians' decisions to prescribe opioids for chronic noncancer pain patients? *Clin. J. Pain* **1997**, *13*, 330–336. [CrossRef]
20. Spitz, A.; Moore, A.A.; Papaleontiou, M.; Granieri, E.; Turner, B.J.; Reid, M.C. Primary care providers' perspective on prescribing opioids to older adults with chronic non-cancer pain: A qualitative study. *BMC Geriatr.* **2011**, *11*, 35. [CrossRef]
21. Bauer, S.R.; Hitchner, L.; Harrison, H.; Gerstenberger, J.; Steiger, S. Predictors of higher-risk chronic opioid prescriptions in an academic primary care setting. *Subst. Abus.* **2016**, *37*, 110–117. [CrossRef] [PubMed]
22. Harle, C.A.; Bauer, S.E.; Hoang, H.Q.; Cook, R.L.; Hurley, R.W.; Fillingim, R.B. Decision support for chronic pain care: How do primary care physicians decide when to prescribe opioids? a qualitative study. *BMC Fam. Pract.* **2015**, *16*, 48. [CrossRef]
23. Muench, J.; Fankhauser, K.; Voss, R.W.; Huguet, N.; Hartung, D.M.; O'Malley, J.; Bailey, S.R.; Cowburn, S.; Wright, D.; Barker, G.; et al. Assessment of Opioid Prescribing Patterns in a Large Network of US Community Health Centers, 2009 to 2018. *JAMA Netw. Open* **2020**, *3*, e2013431. [CrossRef] [PubMed]
24. Ramírez-Maestre, C.; Reyes-Pérez, Á.; Esteve, R.; López-Martínez, A.E.; Bernardes, S.; Jensen, M.P. Opioid Pain Medication Prescription for Chronic Pain in Primary Care Centers: The Roles of Pain Acceptance, Pain Intensity, Depressive Symptoms, Pain Catastrophizing, Sex, and Age. *Int. J. Environ. Res. Public Health* **2020**, *17*, 6428. [CrossRef] [PubMed]
25. Wegwarth, O.; Spies, C.; Schulte, E.; Meerpohl, J.J.; Schmucker, C.; Nury, E.; Brockmann, D.; Donner-Banzhoff, N.; Wind, S.; Goebel, E.; et al. Experiencing the risk of overutilising opioids among patients with chronic non-cancer pain in ambulatory care (ERONA): The protocol of an exploratory, randomised controlled trial. *BMJ Open* **2020**, *10*, e037642. [CrossRef] [PubMed]
26. Caverly, T.J.; Prochazka, A.V.; Combs, B.P.; Lucas, B.P.; Mueller, S.R.; Kutner, J.S.; Binswanger, I.; Fagerlin, A.; McCormick, J.; Pfister, S.; et al. Doctors and numbers: An assessment of the critical risk interpretation test. *Med. Decis. Mak.* **2015**, *35*, 512–524. [CrossRef] [PubMed]
27. Petzke, F.; Welsch, P.; Klose, P.; Sommer, C.; Häuser, W. Opioids for chronic low back pain. An updated systematic review and meta-analysis of efficacy, tolerability and safety in randomized placebo-controlled studies of at least four weeks double-blind duration. *Eur. J. Pain* **2020**, *24*, 497–517. [CrossRef]
28. Welsch, P.; Klose, P.; Petzke, F.; Häuser, W. Opioids for chronic osteoarthritis pain. An updated systematic review and metaanalysis of efficacy, tolerability and safety in randomized placebo-controlled studies of at least four weeks double-blind duration. *Eur. J. Pain* **2020**, *24*, 685–703. [CrossRef]
29. Sommer, C.; Klose, P.; Welsch, P.; Petzke, F.; Häuser, W. Opioids for chronic non-cancer neuropathic pain. An updated systematic review and metaanalysis of efficacy, tolerability and safety in randomized placebo-controlled studies of at least four weeks duration. *Eur. J. Pain* **2020**, *24*, 3–18. [CrossRef]
30. Bundesärztekammer (BÄK); Kassenärztliche Bundesvereinigung (KBV); Arbeitsgemeinschaft der Wissenschaftlichen Medizinischen Fachgesellschaften (AWMF). *Nationale VersorgungsLeitlinie Nicht-Spezifischer Kreuzschmerz—Langfassung*, 2nd ed.; Version 1; BÄK: Berlin, Germany; KBV: Berlin, Germany; AWMF: Frankfurt am Main, Germany, 2017; Available online: www.kreuzschmerz.versorgungsleitlinien.de (accessed on 24 June 2021). [CrossRef]
31. Katz, J.N.; Arant, K.R.; Loeser, R.F. Diagnosis and Treatment of Hip and Knee Osteoarthritis: A Review. *JAMA* **2021**, *325*, 568–578. [CrossRef]

32. Oliveira, C.B.; Maher, C.G.; Pinto, R.Z.; Traeger, A.C.; Lin, C.C.; Chenot, J.F.; van Tulder, M.; Koes, B.W. Clinical practice guidelines for the management of non-specific low back pain in primary care: An updated overview. *Eur. Spine J.* **2018**, *27*, 2791–2803. [CrossRef] [PubMed]
33. Nguyen, T.N.M.; Laetsch, D.C.; Chen, L.J.; Holleczek, B.; Meid, A.D.; Brenner, H.; Schöttker, B. Comparison of Five Lists to Identify Potentially Inappropriate Use of Non-Steroidal Anti-Inflammatory Drugs in Older Adults. *Pain Med.* **2021**, *22*, 1962–1969. [CrossRef] [PubMed]
34. Söderlund, A.; von Heideken Wågert, P. Adherence to and the Maintenance of Self-Management Behaviour in Older People with Musculoskeletal Pain-A Scoping Review and Theoretical Models. *J. Clin. Med.* **2021**, *10*, 303. [CrossRef] [PubMed]
35. WHO. *Guidelines for the Pharmacological and Radiotherapeutic Management of Cancer Pain in Adults and Adolescents 2018*; World Health Organization: Geneva, Switzerland, 2018.
36. Hughes, E. The Opioid That Made a Fortune for Its Maker—And for Its Prescribers. *New York Times*, 2 May 2018. Available online: https://nyti.ms/2Fz37rr (accessed on 27 March 2021).
37. Thomas, K. Doubts Raised about Off-Label Use of Subsys, a Strong Painkiller. *New York Times*, 13 May 2014. Available online: https://nyti.ms/1piOoWq (accessed on 27 March 2021).
38. Miceli, L.; Bednarova, R.; Di Cesare, M.; Santori, E.; Spizzichino, M.; DIMinco, L.; Botti, R.; Casciello, M.; Della Rocca, G. Outpatient therapeutic chronic opioid consumption in Italy: A one-year survey. *Minerva Anestesiol.* **2017**, *83*, 33–40. [CrossRef]
39. Fleischman, W.; Auth, D.; Shah, N.D.; Agrawal, S.; Ross, J.S. Association of a Risk Evaluation and Mitigation Strategy Program with Transmucosal Fentanyl Prescribing. *JAMA Netw. Open* **2019**, *2*, e191340. [CrossRef]
40. Passik, S.D.; Kirsh, K.L. The interface between pain and drug abuse and the evolution of strategies to optimize pain management while minimizing drug abuse. *Exp. Clin. Psychopharmacol.* **2008**, *16*, 400–404. [CrossRef]
41. Bundesärztekammer (BÄK). 2020. Available online: https://www.bundesaerztekammer.de/fileadmin/user_upload/downloads/pdf-Ordner/Statistik_2020/2020-Statistik.pdf (accessed on 17 April 2022).

Journal of
Clinical Medicine

MDPI

Review

Practical Considerations for the Use of Cannabis in Cancer Pain Management—What a Medical Oncologist Should Know

Alecsandra Gorzo [1], Andrei Havași [2], Ștefan Spînu [1], Adela Oprea [1], Claudia Burz [1,3] and Daniel Sur [1,2,*]

[1] Department of Medical Oncology, The Oncology Institute "Prof. Dr. Ion Chiricuţă", 400015 Cluj-Napoca, Romania
[2] Department of Medical Oncology, University of Medicine and Pharmacy "Iuliu Hațieganu", 400012 Cluj-Napoca, Romania
[3] Department of Allergology and Immunology, University of Medicine and Pharmacy "Iuliu Hațieganu", 400012 Cluj-Napoca, Romania
* Correspondence: dr.geni@yahoo.co.uk

Abstract: Pain is a highly debilitating emotional and sensory experience that significantly affects quality of life (QoL). Numerous chronic conditions, including cancer, are associated with chronic pain. In the setting of malignancy, pain can be a consequence of the tumor itself or of life-saving interventions, including surgery, chemotherapy, and radiotherapy. Despite significant pharmacological advances and awareness campaigns, pain remains undertreated in one-third of patients. To date, opioids have been the mainstay of cancer pain management. The problematic side effects and unsatisfactory pain relief of opioids have revived patients' and physicians' interest in finding new solutions, including cannabis and cannabinoids. The medical use of cannabis has been prohibited for decades, and it remains in Schedule 1 of the Misuse of Drugs Regulations. Currently, the legal context for its usage has become more permissive. Various preclinical and observational studies have aimed to prove that cannabinoids could be effective in cancer pain management. However, their clinical utility must be further supported by high-quality clinical trials.

Keywords: cancer pain; cannabis; Δ9-tetrahydrocannabinol; cannabidiol; opioids

Citation: Gorzo, A.; Havași, A.; Spînu, Ș.; Oprea, A.; Burz, C.; Sur, D. Practical Considerations for the Use of Cannabis in Cancer Pain Management—What a Medical Oncologist Should Know. *J. Clin. Med.* **2022**, *11*, 5036. https://doi.org/10.3390/jcm11175036

Academic Editors: Carmen María Galvez Sánchez, Casandra I. Montoro Aguilar and Markus W. Hollmann

Received: 25 July 2022
Accepted: 23 August 2022
Published: 27 August 2022

1. Introduction

Pain is an unpleasant emotional and sensory experience that is associated with potential or actual tissue damage. More than 70% of cancer patients experience pain, which impacts their emotional and physical dimensions [1]. The treatment of chronic cancer pain requires a comprehensive approach that includes both non-pharmacological and pharmacological modalities. Opioids are the foundation for managing moderate and severe cancer pain [2]. However, given the many side effects and risk of addiction, opioid-based pain management requires close monitoring [3]. According to epidemiological data, the rate of opioid overdoses has tripled since 2000, making the "opioid epidemic" one of the most challenging public health issues [4]. Although significant efforts have been made to elaborate recommendations and guidelines, many patients with cancer report inadequate pain relief using available therapeutic options. The main barriers to optimal pain management include inadequate pain assessment, fear of addiction, physicians' reluctance to prescribe strong opioids, and inadequate access to medications [5].

In recent years, alternative pharmacological interventions for cancer pain, including cannabis-based medicines, have been widely explored. There are a series of medications available, including plant-derived cannabinoids, synthetic cannabinoids, magistral preparations of cannabis plant derivatives, nutritional supplements and experimental medications. Cannabidiol (CBD) and Δ9-tetrahydrocannabinol (THC) are the most studied compounds in the cannabis family [6]. These compounds can be administered orally as capsules or oils, via inhalation, or as a spray under the tongue or on the buccal mucosa. However, the pharmacology of cannabinoids remains limited. The various delivery systems and routes, along with the different concentrations of cannabinoids, make predicting the efficacy very challenging [7]. A series of preclinical and observational studies have tried to bring to light the possible benefit of using cannabinoids in cancer pain management. However, their clinical efficacy is still to be supported by high-quality clinical trials [8,9].

This review aims to provide an update on the use of cannabis-based medicines for cancer pain management. In addition, the current study aims to inform the medical oncology community about the use of cannabis as a possible therapeutic option for pain relief.

2. Overview on Cancer Pain Management, and Related Issues

Pain affects 50–90% of cancer patients and is one of the most disabling symptoms [10]. Cancer pain is classified as neuropathic or nociceptive and has a complex pathophysiology. Nociceptive pain is described as visceral or somatic pain [11]. Malignant invasion of connective tissues, skin, or bone causes somatic cancer pain and is usually characterized as a localized painful sensation. In contrast, visceral pain is often poorly localized and is caused by organ inflammation, distention, or impaction [12]. Neuropathic cancer pain can result from direct tumor invasion of nervous tissues, post-irradiation plexopathies, or chemotherapy-induced peripheral neuropathy (CIPN) [13]. Patients describe it as an electric or burning sensation, and sometimes as muscle weakness. It often manifests as persistent background pain associated with acute exacerbations and is frequently unresponsive to opioids [14]. Pain assessment usually requires the use of a visual analog scale (VAS) from 0 to 100 mm, or a numerical rating scale (NRS) from 0 to 10. In most studies, a reduction in pain intensity of more than 30%, or 20 mm on the VAS, or 2 points on the NRS is considered a clinically significant improvement [15].

Strong opioids, including morphine, are the mainstay of moderate-to-severe cancer pain management.

It is generally agreed that cancer pain management needs a comprehensive approach, including non-pharmacological and pharmacological modalities [5]. The most widely acknowledged algorithm for treating cancer pain was developed by the World Health Organization (WHO). The algorithm recommends non-opioid analgesics (acetaminophen, non-steroidal anti-inflammatory drugs) as first-line treatment. In refractory patients, the therapy should be escalated to "weak opioids" (codeine) or "strong opioids" (morphine) [16]. For patients whose pain is partially responsive to opioids, adjuvant analgesic options are available, including antidepressants, anticonvulsants, local analgesics, and corticosteroids [17].

Despite the significant progress made in cancer pain management and awareness, pain is undertreated in one-third of patients, affecting the quality of life (QoL) [18]. More than eight million people worldwide die each year of advanced cancer [19]. About six million of these patients have no or inadequate access to strong opioids because of the poor availability of these substances in the world's most populated and impoverished countries [20].

A large study including 4707 cancer survivors showed that two-thirds of the patients reported at least one obstacle to cancer pain management. The most vulnerable groups included less-educated, non-white, and patients with more comorbidities [21]. Another prospective study including prostate, breast, colorectal, and lung cancer patients reported that minorities were twice as likely to be undertreated as white patients [22].

On the other hand, the aberrant use of opioids among patients is a serious concern in the U.S., and therefore, has led to discussions regarding epidemiological modeling and economic analysis to better allocate limited resources to attenuate the effects of the ongoing opioid epidemic. [23]. In a retrospective study, less than 50% of U.K. patients suffering from cancer received a strong opioid before their passing; however, the percentage was higher in Norway, reaching 60% [24,25]. Chronic opioid use is associated with significant side effects (constipation, nausea, vomiting, mental clouding, sleep disorders, effects on libido, and hyperalgesia), which are the main reasons for the discontinuation of analgesic treatment and QoL impairment [26]. Moreover, adverse effects often require further treatment for symptom management, leading to additional pill burden. Early provocative data from preclinical studies suggest that opioids could affect tumor progression and immune function; however, it is too premature to determine whether these data are clinically significant [27,28]. Through the endocannabinoid system, cannabis manages to regulate the immune response in different types of cells. More specifically, a series of changes appear, such as the alteration of cytokine secretion, the induction of apoptosis, and the activation of the innate and adaptive immune systems. Thus, it was observed that in patients receiving immunotherapy (immune checkpoint inhibitors), the time to tumor progression and overall survival decreased significantly [29].

Currently, an increasing number of patients with chronic cancer pain are seeking alternative treatment options. Therefore, interest in cannabis and cannabinoids has grown considerably in recent years. In addition, such products are increasingly available in many countries as the general attitude towards medical cannabis and cannabinoids has shifted [30].

3. Cannabis and Its Mechanisms of Action

Cannabis sativa L. has a long history of medicinal use. CBD and THC are the two components with the highest concentrations in *Cannabis* sp. (Figure 1) [31]. In recent years, especially since the endocannabinoid system was discovered, these compounds have received much attention [32]. The endocannabinoid system includes cannabinoid receptors (CB1 and CB2-G protein-coupled receptors), their endogenous ligands (endocannabinoids AEA—Anandamide and 2-AG—2-Arachidonoylglycerol), and the enzymes responsible for their degradation and synthesis [33]. The main enzyme involved in AEA production is N-acylphosphatidylethanolamine-specific phospholipase D (NAPE-PLD), whereas 2-AG synthesis is dependent on a specific phospholipase C followed by the sn-1-diacylglycerol lipase (DAGL) activity [34]. The AEA activity is terminated by a fatty acid amide hydrolase (FAAH) resulting in arachidonate and ethanolamine. 2-AG is hydrolyzed by a specific monoacylglycerol lipase (MAGL), as well as serine hydrolase alpha-beta-hydrolase domain 6 (ABHD6), resulting in arachidonate and glycerol [35,36]. Endocannabinoids act principally through the cannabinoid receptor (CB1 and CB2). Their implications were illustrated in several physiological and pathological conditions, including appetite, fertility, memory, immune system, cancer, and pain management [37].

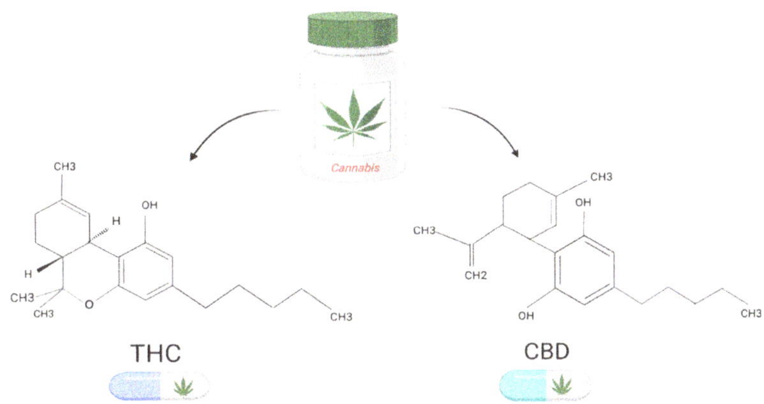

Figure 1. The main constituents of *Cannabis* sp. and their molecular formulas.

CB1 receptors are primarily expressed in the peripheral and central nervous systems, while CB2 receptors are highly expressed in the immune system. Both CB1 and CB2 receptors are negatively correlated with adenylate cyclase activity [38].

A large number of cannabinoid receptors have been described in the brain stem emetic centers and in regions involved in the behavioral effects of cannabinoids, including the hippocampus, basal ganglia, amygdala, and cerebellum. CB1 receptors are located predominantly in the presynaptic membrane and are therefore modulators of synaptic release [39].

It has been assumed that cannabinoids relieve pain by activating specific CB1 and CB2 receptors. However, the matter becomes more complex when plant-derived and endogenous cannabinoids influence multiple pain targets, including G protein-coupled receptor 55 (GPCR55), GPCR18, serotonin, and opioid receptors [40–43]. Moreover, cannabinoids can modulate transient receptor potential channels (TRPA, TRPV, and TRPM), Cys-loop ligand-gated ion channels, and nuclear receptors [44]. In addition, several studies have indicated multiple interactions at the molecular level between opioids, TRPV1, and cannabinoid receptors in pain modulation and perception.

The administration of cannabinoids has been shown to suppress all neurophysiological and behavioral responses to nociceptive stimuli. These compounds were found to exert their anti-nociceptive effect by an action on the peripheral nerves, direct activity in the brain, or direct spinal activity [45]. Therefore, rapidly after crossing the brain–blood barrier, the cannabinoids can interact with the rostral ventrolateral-medulla (RVM) and periaqueductal gray (PAG), inhibiting spinal nociceptive neurotransmission [46]. Other studies have demonstrated a potential peripheral site of action for cannabinoids [47]. Hence, in a tumor-bearing mouse model, the intraplantar administration of WIN 55,212-2, a non-selective cannabinoid receptor agonist, diminished the response produced by mechanical stimulation of C-fiber nociceptors [48]. These findings could further support new drug development with improved clinical efficacy and fewer side effects [49]. The general overview of the endocannabinoid system mechanism is depicted in (Figure 2).

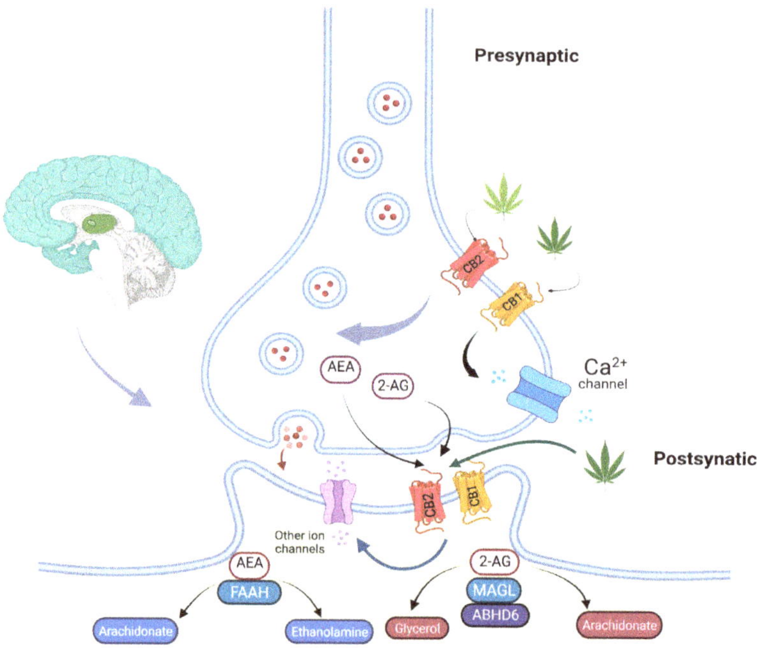

Figure 2. General overview of endocannabinoid system mechanism.

THC is the primary psychoactive ingredient of cannabis and can promote dependency among chronic users as it interacts with the dopaminergic system [50]. THC has an affinity for the CB1 and CB2 receptors similar to that of AEA. In addition to its psychoactive effect, THC is responsible for most of the pharmacological outcomes of cannabis, including analgesic, antioxidant, anti-inflammatory, bronchodilator, antipruritic, and anti-spastic activities [51].

CBD is the second most abundant component of cannabis and has broader medical applications than THC. However, CBD does not have THC-like or toxic drug effects but has been reported to reduce inflammation, muscle spasms, seizures, and anxiety [52]. There are studies in humans, non-human primates, and rodents that suggest the potential that CBD has in mitigating the effects of THC (mostly related to memory and behavior). There are also preclinical studies showing that CBD actually potentiates the effects of THC [53] The current state of knowledge suggests that CBD has a poor affinity for cannabinoid receptors, and its mechanism of action is different from that of the endocannabinoid system. The effects of CBD are often reported to be mediated by various orphan GPCRs and serotoninergic 5-HT1A receptors [54]. Moreover, studies have indicated that CBD can regulate pain perception by interacting with other G-coupled receptors, including δ-opioid, μ-opioid, and dopamine receptor D2 [55].

Cannabinoids are highly lipophilic substances that are stored in spleen and adipose tissues. After inhalation, peak plasma levels of CBD and THC are rapidly achieved within 3–10 min [56]. The bioavailability of inhaled THC varies considerably due to the differences between cannabis products and inhalation techniques, ranging between 10 and 35%, whereas inhaled CBD has an average bioavailability of 31%. In contrast, when administered orally, the peak plasma level of both compounds is obtained within approximately 1–2 h, and it is considerably lower than that obtained by smoking due to hepatic first-passage metabolism [57]. When inhaled by smoking, the analgesic effect of cannabinoids is experienced shortly after the first breath. However, the combustion products inhaled while smoking cannabis constitute a significant disadvantage and may negatively affect the respiratory tract [58]. On the other hand, the major limitation of oral cannabinoids is their poor pharmacokinetic profile, with highly variable absorption, slow onset of clinical effects, and unpredictable psychoactive effects [59].

The use of cannabis for recreational or medical purposes has been banned for decades. Several cannabinoid drugs have been developed to date. Nabiximols (Sativex®) is an almost 1:1 ratio of plant-based THC and CBD and is licensed for treating spasticity in multiple sclerosis [60]. Epidiolex, an oral CBD solution, was recently approved for the treatment of severe pediatric epilepsy, including Dravet and Lennox-Gastauld syndromes [61].

Dronabinol and nabilone are synthetic forms of THC licensed to treat chemotherapy-related nausea and vomiting in patients refractory to conventional antiemetics, and weight loss in patients with AIDS [62].

4. Cannabis-Based Medicines

The most documented reason for cannabinoid use is pain relief. Cancer pain is often chronic, with inflammatory, nociceptive, and neuropathic components [63]. Moreover, cancer pain is frequently challenging to control using the available therapeutic options because of its complexity. The available randomized controlled trials involving cannabinoids are limited, with equivocal results [64]. However, stimulated by the pain burden worldwide and the necessity for novel non-opioid and safer therapeutic options, interest in cannabinoids has increased in the scientific community (Table 1).

Table 1. Ongoing clinical trials investigating Cannabinoids for cancer pain.

Study Name	Phase	Status	Condition	Treatment	Primary Endpoint
NCT04808531	Phase 3	Not yet recruiting	Cancer-related pain	NanaBis™ Oxycodone Placebo Spray Placebo Tablet	Significant changes in responders with NanaBis™ spray over placebo Comparable efficacy in proportion of responders from NanaBis™ spray to the proportion of responders to Oxycodone
NCT04875286	N/A	Recruiting	Cancer-associated pain	Electronic health record review Questionnaire administration	Proportion of patients who prefer opioids + THC-marijuana and/or opioids with CBD to opioids alone for cancer pain relief
NCT03948074	Phase 2	Recruiting	Pain, nausea, anxiety, and sleep disturbance related to cancer	Cannabis	Average Patients' Global Impression of Change (PGIC) for overall cancer-related symptoms
NCT04042545	Phase 2	Recruiting	Cancer pain QoL	Cannabis Placebo	Uncontrolled cancer pain measured using a patient's self-administered questionnaire.

4.1. Preclinical Evidence

Behavioral studies have revealed that plant-based or synthetic cannabinoids may be effective in animal pain models [65]. However, the data obtained from human subjects are sometimes conflicting. Differences in methodologies and strains may explain the discrepancies observed. In humans, the perception of pain is influenced by numerous cognitive and emotional factors that can affect the results [66]. Animal studies have established cannabinoid-induced analgesia in a broad spectrum of pain models. When it comes to chronic pain, both neuropathic and inflammatory, cannabinoids have demonstrated greater potency compared to acute or physiological pain [67].

Up to 40% of the patients with cancer-related pain have neuropathic components. CB1 and CB2 receptors are both upregulated in nervous structures involved in the perception of pain caused by peripheral nerve damage, which could explain the positive effects of cannabinoid antagonists on neuropathic pain [68]. Various chemotherapeutic agents have been shown to induce CIPN in animal models, including platinum components, taxanes, vinca alkaloids, and proteasome inhibitors (bortezomib) [69]. In taxane-induced neuropathic pain, CB2-specific agonists (AM1714, R, S-AM1241, MDA7, MDA19, and AM1710) alleviate cold and mechanical allodynia via CB2 receptors. CBD has anti-nociceptive effects in paclitaxel models [70–72]. THC, CBD, and the CB2 agonist AM1241 alleviated vincristine-induced allodynia [73,74]. Moreover, CBD alleviated allodynia in a cisplatin model. In animal models, two endocannabinoids (AEA and 2-AG) reversed heat hyperalgesia and mechanical allodynia induced by cisplatin [75,76].

The peripheral anti-hyperalgesic effect was objectified in tissue-injury models, and it was shown that the nocifensive behavior was decreased by injecting 2-AG or AEA roughly to the injury site [77,78]. Several reports demonstrated the analgesic efficacy obtained from the pharmacological inhibition of FAAI, the main enzyme involved in AEA degradation, using carbamates, alpha-ketoheterocycle compounds, and analogs of N-arachidonoyl serotonin [79,80]. Other pre-clinical trials increased 2-AG levels by inhibiting MAGL activity and its degradation as an alternative approach [81,82]. Therefore, Khasabova et al. increased 2-AG levels mimicking its anti-hyperalgesic effect in bone cancer murine models, by administering JZL184, a selective inhibitor of MAGL [83].

4.2. Clinical Evidence

The first placebo-controlled trial published in 1975 reported that 15 and 20 mg THC oil provided more pain relief than placebo ($p < 0.025$) in a group of 10 patients with cancer treated with opioids (mainly methadone) [84]. A subsequent trial by the same researcher's group included 36 patients. They concluded that the amount of pain relief produced by 10 mg of THC oil was comparable to that produced by 60 mg of codeine. However, 20 mg of THC has been reported to cause side effects such as dizziness, ataxia, somnolence, and blurred vision [85].

In addition to oils, oromucosal sprays have been widely used in clinical trials to administer cannabis-based medicines. Johnson et al. investigated, for the first time, the analgesic efficacy of mixed cannabis extracts and nabiximols (Sativex®) (equimolar equivalents of THC and CBD) administered orally in 177 opioid-refractory, advanced pain cancer patients. The results showed a statistically significant improvement in the mean pain score in favor of nabiximols compared with placebo ($p < 0.024$). Moreover, patients treated with nabiximols required fewer doses of breakthrough pain medication [86].

The analgesic efficacy of nabiximols was further investigated in a double-blind, randomized, placebo-controlled trial on cancer patients suffering from severe pain (numerical rating scale (NRS) scores ≥ 4 and ≤ 8) poorly controlled by opioids. The design implied a two-week, self-titration and tolerability phase, followed by a three-week treatment period. However, the primary efficacy endpoint was not achieved. The negative outcome of this study could be explained by several contributing factors, including the high mortality rate reported in the study population and increased dropout rate. Furthermore, self-reported NRS scores could be significantly influenced by variations in day-to-day mood, especially in frail cancer patients. Moreover, a post hoc analysis showed that Sativex was effective only in U.S. cancer patients ($p = 0.037$). The U.S. subgroup of patients had a lower opioid baseline dose and increased exposure to cannabis in the past. These findings led to the hypothesis of reduced downregulation of opioid receptors, resulting in enhanced synergy between cannabinoids and opioid receptors and, therefore, a better outcome [87].

A long-term observational study conducted in Israel evaluated the safety and efficacy of medical cannabis in 3619 cancer patients. All participants received a mixture of 16 THC and CBD strains administered with various concentrations of oils and/or inflorescences (including capsules, flowers, and cigarettes). After one month, 19.5% of the active users (2082) reported a moderate improvement, and 66.3% reported a significant improvement in their general condition. In addition, 8.3% of the patients experienced side effects, including tiredness, cough, nausea, dizziness, confusion, and disorientation. After six months, among the active users (1211), 45.1% reported moderate, and 50.8% reported significant improvements. Moreover, the percentage of patients reporting good quality of life was 68.5% compared to 18.7% at baseline ($p < 0.001$). More importantly, 9.9% of the patients reported a decrease in opioid dose, 36% discontinued opioid use, and only 1.1% increased opioid dosage. Overall, 30% of the patients reported at least one side effect: dry mouth, dizziness, sleepiness, increased appetite, and psychoactive effects [88]. In a recent systematic review and meta-analysis, non-inhaled medical cannabis and cannabinoids showed little pain relief compared to placebo in patients with chronic non-cancer and cancer pain. In addition, these products lead to minor improvements in sleep quality and physical performance [89].

Regarding neuropathic pain, Lynch et al. conducted a placebo-controlled, double-blind pilot trial that addressed chemotherapy-induced neuropathy in 18 cancer patients. Nabiximols were reported to be beneficial, with an NNT (number needed to treat) of five [90].

5. Existing Concerns and Legal Considerations

In addition to the limited evidence for their efficacy, cannabinoids carry the risk of adverse events, similar to any other existing therapeutic agent. Over the past 40 years, almost 5000 adverse events associated with the medical use of cannabinoids have been reported [91]. The most common side effects were psychosis, cognitive impairment, dizziness, dysphoria, dry mouth, nausea, and vomiting. Moreover, using high doses for a long time was associated with memory and psychomotor speed impairments, particularly in adolescents and young adults [92]. Additionally, cannabis use raises the likelihood of car accidents, suicidal behavior, and partner and child violence. Cannabis use is a risk factor for a number of medical disorders, as well as adverse social consequences [93]. Another major issue with cannabis-based medicine is the lack of dosing guidelines. The optimal dose (producing effective pain management with tolerable adverse effects) was inconsistent among the studies due to inter-patient variability. Moreover, side effects are difficult to assess, especially in patients with advanced cancer, who are likely to take countless concomitant medications [30,85].

The use of cannabis has been extensively debated, based on the presumption that it can lead to dependence and addiction. Statistics show that approximately 9% (1 out of 11) of all people who have ever used cannabis will experience dependency at some point in their lives, and the percentage is almost double if the use begins during adolescence [94]. It is estimated that almost 22 million people worldwide are addicted to cannabis, which is considered one of the most frequent illicit-drug-use disorders [95]. Early research implied that U.S. states with medical cannabis regulations witnessed a slower increase in opioid analgesic overdose-related mortality. However, these associations were not significant when extended time frames were analyzed [96].

The medical use of cannabis has been prohibited for many years, and it is still listed in Schedule 1 of the Misuse of Drugs Regulations. Currently, the legal context of its use is becoming more permissive. Based on the expanding evidence regarding its medical applications, the WHO proposed that cannabis should be rescheduled within international laws. Therefore, in many European countries (Figure 3), Thailand, Canada, and almost three-quarters of the U.S., medical cannabis has become legal [97,98].

Figure 3. Legal framework for using medical cannabis in European countries.

6. Conclusions

Cancer pain is a highly debilitating syndrome that has a significant impact on QoL and is sometimes challenging to treat using the available therapeutic options. As life expectancy in cancer patients increases owing to remarkable improvements in therapies, cancer pain associated with life-saving interventions (surgery, chemotherapy, and radiotherapy) will become more prevalent. Although the results from preclinical trials are encouraging, there is a paucity of translatable evidence in clinical studies to support the use of cannabinoids for cancer pain management. Further clinical trials, more extensive and more rigorous, are needed to establish their clinical efficacy, dosing, and, not least, their potential interactions with other drugs. It is essential to carefully analyze the decision to use cannabinoids for cancer pain to avoid misuse, addiction, or dependency.

Author Contributions: Conceptualization, A.G., Ș.S. and D.S.; writing—original draft preparation, A.G.; writing—review and editing, A.G., A.H., Ș.S., A.O., C.B. and D.S.; supervision, D.S. All authors have read and agreed to the published version of the manuscript.

Funding: The research received no funding.

Institutional Review Board Statement: Not applicable.

Informed Consent Statement: Not applicable.

Data Availability Statement: Not applicable.

Acknowledgments: The authors want to acknowledge the support of the Romanian Society of Medical Oncology (SNOMR) for the payment of the APC.

Conflicts of Interest: The authors declare no conflict of interest.

References

1. Haroutounian, S.; Ratz, Y.; Ginosar, Y.; Furmanov, K.; Saifi, F.; Meidan, R.; Davidson, E. The Effect of Medicinal Cannabis on Pain and Quality-of-Life Outcomes in Chronic Pain. *Clin. J. Pain* **2016**, *32*, 1036–1043. [CrossRef] [PubMed]
2. Prommer, E.E. Pharmacological Management of Cancer-Related Pain. *Cancer Control* **2015**, *22*, 412–425. [CrossRef] [PubMed]
3. Candido, K.D.; Kusper, T.M.; Knezevic, N.N. New Cancer Pain Treatment Options. *Curr. Pain Headache Rep.* **2017**, *21*, 12. [CrossRef] [PubMed]
4. Bruera, E. Parenteral Opioid Shortage—Treating Pain during the Opioid-Overdose Epidemic. *N. Engl. J. Med.* **2018**, *379*, 601–603. [CrossRef]
5. Kwon, J.H. Overcoming Barriers in Cancer Pain Management. *J. Clin. Oncol.* **2014**, *32*, 1727–1733. [CrossRef]
6. Häuser, W.; Welsch, P.; Klose, P.; Radbruch, L.; Fitzcharles, M.-A. Efficacy, tolerability and safety of cannabis-based medicines for cancer pain. *Schmerz* **2019**, *33*, 424–436. [CrossRef]
7. Chayasirisobhon, S. Mechanisms of Action and Pharmacokinetics of Cannabis. *Perm. J.* **2020**, *25*, 1–4. [CrossRef]
8. Martín-Sánchez, E.; Furukawa, T.A.; Taylor, J.; Martin, J.L.R. Systematic Review and Meta-analysis of Cannabis Treatment for Chronic Pain. *Pain Med.* **2009**, *10*, 1353–1368. [CrossRef] [PubMed]
9. Nugent, S.M.; Morasco, B.J.; O'Neil, M.E.; Freeman, M.; Low, A.; Kondo, K.; Elven, C.; Zakher, B.; Motu'apuaka, M.; Paynter, R.; et al. The Effects of Cannabis Among Adults with Chronic Pain and an Overview of General Harms. *Ann. Intern. Med.* **2017**, *167*, 319–331. [CrossRef]
10. van den Beuken-van Everdingen, M.H.J.; Hochstenbach, L.M.J.; Joosten, E.A.J.; Tjan-Heijnen, V.C.G.; Janssen, D.J.A. Update on Prevalence of Pain in Patients with Cancer: Systematic Review and Meta-Analysis. *J. Pain Symptom Manag.* **2016**, *51*, 1070–1090.e9. [CrossRef]
11. Russo, M.M.; Sundaramurthi, T. An Overview of Cancer Pain: Epidemiology and Pathophysiology. *Semin. Oncol. Nurs.* **2019**, *35*, 223–228. [CrossRef] [PubMed]
12. Leppert, W.; Zajączkowska, R.; Wordliczek, J.; Dobrogowski, J.; Woroń, J.; Krzakowski, M. Pathophysiology and clinical characteristics of pain in most common locations in cancer patients. *J. Physiol. Pharmacol. Off. J. Pol. Physiol. Soc.* **2016**, *67*, 787–799.
13. Wordliczek, J.; Zajaczkowska, R. Mechanisms in Cancer Pain. In *Cancer Pain*; Hanna, M., Zylicz, Z., Eds.; Springer: London, UK, 2013; pp. 47–70. ISBN 978-0-85729-230-8.
14. Yoon, S.Y.; Oh, J. Neuropathic cancer pain: Prevalence, pathophysiology, and management. *Korean J. Intern. Med.* **2018**, *33*, 1058–1069. [CrossRef] [PubMed]
15. Fink, R.M.; Gallagher, E. Cancer Pain Assessment and Measurement. *Semin. Oncol. Nurs.* **2019**, *35*, 229–234. [CrossRef]
16. World Health Organization. *Cancer Pain Relief*; World Health Organization: Geneva, Switzerland, 1986.
17. Smith, T.J.; Saiki, C.B. Cancer Pain Management. *Mayo Clin. Proc.* **2015**, *90*, 1428–1439. [CrossRef]
18. Roberto, A.; Greco, M.T.; Uggeri, S.; Cavuto, S.; Deandrea, S.; Corli, O.; Apolone, G. Living systematic review to assess the analgesic undertreatment in cancer patients. *Pain Pract.* **2022**, *22*, 487–496. [CrossRef]

19. Stanic, J.; Perrenoud, B.; Rochat, E.; Ballabeni, P.; Jaques, C.; Schaer-Chaudhry, A.-C.; Zumstein-Shaha, M. Experiences of newly diagnosed cancer patients in confronting the finitudes of life: A qualitative systematic review protocol. *JBI Evid. Synth.* **2018**, *16*, 2288–2294. [CrossRef]
20. Clark, J.; Gnanapragasam, S.; Greenley, S.; Pearce, J.; Johnson, M. Perceptions and experiences of laws and regulations governing access to opioids in South, Southeast, East and Central Asia: A systematic review, critical interpretative synthesis and development of a conceptual framework. *Palliat. Med.* **2021**, *35*, 59–75. [CrossRef]
21. Stein, K.D.; Alcaraz, K.I.; Kamson, C.; Fallon, E.A.; Smith, T.G. Sociodemographic inequalities in barriers to cancer pain management: A report from the American Cancer Society's Study of Cancer Survivors-II (SCS-II). *Psycho-Oncol.* **2016**, *25*, 1212–1221. [CrossRef]
22. Paice, J.A. Cancer pain management and the opioid crisis in America: How to preserve hard-earned gains in improving the quality of cancer pain management. *Cancer* **2018**, *124*, 2491–2497. [CrossRef]
23. Patton, T.; Revill, P.; Sculpher, M.; Borquez, A. Using Economic Evaluation to Inform Responses to the Opioid Epidemic in the United States: Challenges and Suggestions for Future Research. *Subst. Use Misuse* **2022**, *57*, 815–821. [CrossRef] [PubMed]
24. Fredheim, O.M.S.; Brelin, S.; Hjermstad, M.J.; Loge, J.H.; Aass, N.; Johannesen, T.B.; Skurtveit, S. Prescriptions of analgesics during complete disease trajectories in patients who are diagnosed with and die from cancer within the five-year period 2005–2009. *Eur. J. Pain Lond. Engl.* **2017**, *21*, 530–540. [CrossRef]
25. Ziegler, L.; Mulvey, M.; Blenkinsopp, A.; Petty, D.; Bennett, M.I. Opioid prescribing for patients with cancer in the last year of life: A longitudinal population cohort study. *Pain* **2016**, *157*, 2445–2451. [CrossRef] [PubMed]
26. George, B.; Minello, C.; Allano, G.; Maindet, C.; Burnod, A.; Lemaire, A. Opioids in cancer-related pain: Current situation and outlook. *Supportive Care Cancer* **2019**, *27*, 3105–3118. [CrossRef]
27. Wall, T.; Sherwin, A.; Ma, D.; Buggy, D.J. Influence of perioperative anaesthetic and analgesic interventions on oncological outcomes: A narrative review. *Br. J. Anaesth.* **2019**, *123*, 135–150. [CrossRef] [PubMed]
28. Sekandarzad, M.W.; Doornebal, C.; Hollmann, M.W. Opiophobia in Cancer Biology-Justified?—The Role of Perioperative Use of Opioids in Cancer Recurrence. *Curr. Pharm. Des.* **2019**, *25*, 3020–3027. [CrossRef] [PubMed]
29. Bar-Sela, G.; Cohen, I.; Campisi-Pinto, S.; Lewitus, G.M.; Oz-Ari, L.; Jehassi, A.; Peer, A.; Turgeman, I.; Vernicova, O.; Berman, P.; et al. Cannabis Consumption Used by Cancer Patients during Immunotherapy Correlates with Poor Clinical Outcome. *Cancers* **2020**, *12*, 2447. [CrossRef]
30. Blake, A.; Wan, B.A.; Malek, L.; DeAngelis, C.; Diaz, P.; Lao, N.; Chow, E.; O'Hearn, S. A selective review of medical cannabis in cancer pain management. *Ann. Palliat. Med.* **2017**, *6*, S215–S222. [CrossRef]
31. Andre, C.M.; Hausman, J.-F.; Guerriero, G. Cannabis sativa: The Plant of the Thousand and One Molecules. *Front. Plant Sci.* **2016**, *7*, 19. [CrossRef]
32. Hill, K.P.; Palastro, M.D.; Johnson, B.; Ditre, J.W. Cannabis and Pain: A Clinical Review. *Cannabis Cannabinoid Res.* **2017**, *2*, 96–104. [CrossRef]
33. Mechoulam, R.; Parker, L.A. The Endocannabinoid System and the Brain. *Annu. Rev. Psychol.* **2013**, *64*, 21–47. [CrossRef] [PubMed]
34. Battista, N.; Di Tommaso, M.; Bari, M.; Maccarrone, M. The endocannabinoid system: An overview. *Front. Behav. Neurosci.* **2012**, *6*, 9. [CrossRef] [PubMed]
35. Ueda, N.; Tsuboi, K.; Uyama, T.; Ohnishi, T. Biosynthesis and degradation of the endocannabinoid 2-arachidonoylglycerol. *BioFactors Oxf. Engl.* **2011**, *37*, 1–7. [CrossRef]
36. Wang, J.; Ueda, N. Biology of endocannabinoid synthesis system. *Prostaglandins Other Lipid Mediat.* **2009**, *89*, 112–119. [CrossRef] [PubMed]
37. Ligresti, A.; Petrosino, S.; Di Marzo, V. From endocannabinoid profiling to 'endocannabinoid therapeutics. *Curr. Opin. Chem. Biol.* **2009**, *13*, 321–331. [CrossRef] [PubMed]
38. Zou, S.; Kumar, U. Cannabinoid Receptors and the Endocannabinoid System: Signaling and Function in the Central Nervous System. *Int. J. Mol. Sci.* **2018**, *19*, 833. [CrossRef]
39. Mackie, K. Distribution of Cannabinoid Receptors in the Central and Peripheral Nervous System. In *Cannabinoids*; Pertwee, R.G., Ed.; Handbook of Experimental Pharmacology; Springer: Berlin/Heidelberg, Germany, 2005; pp. 299–325.
40. Ye, L.; Cao, Z.; Wang, W.; Zhou, N. New Insights in Cannabinoid Receptor Structure and Signaling. *Curr. Mol. Pharmacol.* **2019**, *12*, 239–248. [CrossRef]
41. Lauckner, J.E.; Jensen, J.B.; Chen, H.-Y.; Lu, H.-C.; Hille, B.; Mackie, K. GPR55 is a cannabinoid receptor that increases intracellular calcium and inhibits M current. *Proc. Natl. Acad. Sci. USA* **2008**, *105*, 2699–2704. [CrossRef]
42. Bian, Y.; He, X.; Jing, Y.; Wang, L.; Wang, J.; Xie, X.-Q. Computational systems pharmacology analysis of cannabidiol: A combination of chemogenomics-knowledgebase network analysis and integrated in silico modeling and simulation. *Acta Pharmacol. Sin.* **2019**, *40*, 374–386. [CrossRef]
43. Da Fonseca Pacheco, D.; Klein, A.; De Castro Perez, A.; Da Fonseca Pacheco, C.M.; De Francischi, J.N.; Duarte, I.D.G. The μ-opioid receptor agonist morphine, but not agonists at δ- or κ-opioid receptors, induces peripheral antinociception mediated by cannabinoid receptors. *Br. J. Pharmacol.* **2008**, *154*, 1143–1149. [CrossRef]
44. Watkins, A.R. Cannabinoid interactions with ion channels and receptors. *Channels* **2019**, *13*, 162–167. [CrossRef] [PubMed]
45. Walker, J.M.; Huang, S.M. Cannabinoid analgesia. *Pharmacol. Ther.* **2002**, *95*, 127–135. [CrossRef]

46. Zogopoulos, P.; Vasileiou, I.; Patsouris, E.; Theocharis, S.E. The role of endocannabinoids in pain modulation. *Fundam. Clin. Pharmacol.* **2013**, *27*, 64–80. [CrossRef] [PubMed]
47. Potenzieri, C.; Brink, T.S.; Pacharinsak, C.; Simone, D.A. Cannabinoid Modulation of Cutaneous Aδ Nociceptors During Inflammation. *J. Neurophysiol.* **2008**, *100*, 2794–2806. Available online: https://journals.physiology.org/doi/full/10.1152/jn.90809.2008 (accessed on 17 August 2022). [CrossRef] [PubMed]
48. Uhelski, M.L.; Cain, D.M.; Harding-Rose, C.; Simone, D.A. The non-selective cannabinoid receptor agonist WIN 55,212-2 attenuates responses of C-fiber nociceptors in a murine model of cancer pain. *Neuroscience* **2013**, *247*, 84–94. [CrossRef]
49. Tijani, A.O.; Thakur, D.; Mishra, D.; Frempong, D.; Chukwunyere, U.I.; Puri, A. Delivering therapeutic cannabinoids via skin: Current state and future perspectives. *J. Control. Release* **2021**, *334*, 427–451. [CrossRef]
50. Bloomfield, M.A.P.; Ashok, A.H.; Volkow, N.D.; Howes, O.D. The effects of Δ9-tetrahydrocannabinol on the dopamine system. *Nature* **2016**, *539*, 369–377. [CrossRef]
51. Amin, M.R.; Ali, D.W. Pharmacology of Medical Cannabis. In *Recent Advances in Cannabinoid Physiology and Pathology*; Bukiya, A.N., Ed.; Advances in Experimental Medicine and Biology; Springer International Publishing: Cham, Germany, 2019; pp. 151–165.
52. Rock, E.M.; Parker, L.A. Constituents of Cannabis Sativa. In *Cannabinoids and Neuropsychiatric Disorders*; Murillo-Rodriguez, E., Pandi-Perumal, S.R., Monti, J.M., Eds.; Advances in Experimental Medicine and Biology; Springer International Publishing: Cham, Germany, 2021; pp. 1–13. ISBN 978-3-030-57369-0.
53. Boggs, D.L.; Nguyen, J.D.; Morgenson, D.; Taffe, M.A.; Ranganathan, M. Clinical and Preclinical Evidence for Functional Interactions of Cannabidiol and Δ9-Tetrahydrocannabinol. *Neuropsychopharmacol. Off. Publ. Am. Coll. Neuropsychopharmacol.* **2018**, *43*, 142–154. [CrossRef]
54. Ożarowski, M.; Karpiński, T.M.; Zielińska, A.; Souto, E.B.; Wielgus, K. Cannabidiol in Neurological and Neoplastic Diseases: Latest Developments on the Molecular Mechanism of Action. *Int. J. Mol. Sci.* **2021**, *22*, 4294. [CrossRef]
55. Mlost, J.; Bryk, M.; Starowicz, K. Cannabidiol for Pain Treatment: Focus on Pharmacology and Mechanism of Action. *Int. J. Mol. Sci.* **2020**, *21*, 8870. [CrossRef]
56. Lucas, C.J.; Galettis, P.; Schneider, J. The pharmacokinetics and the pharmacodynamics of cannabinoids. *Br. J. Clin. Pharmacol.* **2018**, *84*, 2477–2482. [CrossRef] [PubMed]
57. Reuter, S.E.; Martin, J.H. Pharmacokinetics of Cannabis in Cancer Cachexia-Anorexia Syndrome. *Clin. Pharmacokinet.* **2016**, *55*, 807–812. [CrossRef]
58. Biehl, J.R.; Burnham, E.L. Cannabis Smoking in 2015: A Concern for Lung Health? *Chest* **2015**, *148*, 596–606. [CrossRef] [PubMed]
59. Sharma, P.; Murthy, P.; Bharath, M.M.S. Chemistry, Metabolism, and Toxicology of Cannabis: Clinical Implications. *Iran. J. Psychiatry* **2012**, *7*, 149–156. [PubMed]
60. Flachenecker, P.; Henze, T.; Zettl, U.K. Nabiximols (THC/CBD Oromucosal Spray, Sativex®) in Clinical Practice—Results of a Multicenter, Non-Interventional Study (MOVE 2) in Patients with Multiple Sclerosis Spasticity. *Eur. Neurol.* **2014**, *71*, 271–279. [CrossRef]
61. Abu-Sawwa, R.; Scutt, B.; Park, Y. Emerging Use of Epidiolex (Cannabidiol) in Epilepsy. *J. Pediatr. Pharmacol. Ther.* **2020**, *25*, 485–499. [CrossRef]
62. Badowski, M.E.; Yanful, P.K. Dronabinol oral solution in the management of anorexia and weight loss in AIDS and cancer. *Ther. Clin. Risk Manag.* **2018**, *14*, 643–651. [CrossRef]
63. Savage, S.R.; Romero-Sandoval, A.; Schatman, M.; Wallace, M.; Fanciullo, G.; McCarberg, B.; Ware, M. Cannabis in Pain Treatment: Clinical and Research Considerations. *J. Pain* **2016**, *17*, 654–668. [CrossRef]
64. Chung, M.; Kim, H.K.; Abdi, S. Update on cannabis and cannabinoids for cancer pain. *Curr. Opin. Anesthesiol.* **2020**, *33*, 825–831. [CrossRef]
65. Dhopeshwarkar, A.; Mackie, K. CB2 Cannabinoid Receptors as a Therapeutic Target—What Does the Future Hold? *Mol. Pharmacol.* **2014**, *86*, 430–437. [CrossRef]
66. Woodhams, S.G.; Chapman, V.; Finn, D.P.; Hohmann, A.G.; Neugebauer, V. The cannabinoid system and pain. *Neuropharmacology* **2017**, *124*, 105–120. [CrossRef] [PubMed]
67. Soliman, N.; Haroutounian, S.; Hohmann, A.G.; Krane, E.; Liao, J.; Macleod, M.; Segelcke, D.; Sena, C.; Thomas, J.; Vollert, J.; et al. Systematic review and meta-analysis of cannabinoids, cannabis-based medicines, and endocannabinoid system modulators tested for antinociceptive effects in animal models of injury-related or pathological persistent pain. *Pain* **2021**, *162*, S26–S44. [CrossRef] [PubMed]
68. Bennett, M.I.; Rayment, C.; Hjermstad, M.; Aass, N.; Caraceni, A.; Kaasa, S. Prevalence and aetiology of neuropathic pain in cancer patients: A systematic review. *Pain* **2012**, *153*, 359–365. [CrossRef] [PubMed]
69. Massey, R.L.; Kim, H.K.; Abdi, S. Brief review: Chemotherapy-induced painful peripheral neuropathy (CIPPN): Current status and future directions. *Can. J. Anesth. Can. Anesth.* **2014**, *61*, 754–762. [CrossRef] [PubMed]
70. Burgos, E.; Gómez-Nicola, D.; Pascual, D.; Martín, M.I.; Nieto-Sampedro, M.; Goicoechea, C. Cannabinoid agonist WIN 55,212-2 prevents the development of paclitaxel-induced peripheral neuropathy in rats. Possible involvement of spinal glial cells. *Eur. J. Pharmacol.* **2012**, *682*, 62–72. [CrossRef] [PubMed]

71. Rahn, E.J.; Deng, L.; Thakur, G.A.; Vemuri, K.; Zvonok, A.M.; Lai, Y.Y.; Makriyannis, A.; Hohmann, A.G. Prophylactic cannabinoid administration blocks the development of paclitaxel-induced neuropathic nociception during analgesic treatment and following cessation of drug delivery. *Mol. Pain* **2014**, *10*, 27. [CrossRef]
72. Wu, J.; Hocevar, M.; Bie, B.; Foss, J.F.; Naguib, M. Cannabinoid Type 2 Receptor System Modulates Paclitaxel-Induced Microglial Dysregulation and Central Sensitization in Rats. *J. Pain* **2019**, *20*, 501–514. [CrossRef]
73. King, K.M.; Myers, A.M.; Soroka-Monzo, A.J.; Tuma, R.F.; Tallarida, R.J.; Walker, E.A.; Ward, S.J. Single and combined effects of Δ9 -tetrahydrocannabinol and cannabidiol in a mouse model of chemotherapy-induced neuropathic pain. *Br. J. Pharmacol.* **2017**, *174*, 2832–2841. [CrossRef]
74. Rahn, E.J.; Makriyannis, A.; Hohmann, A.G. Activation of cannabinoid CB1 and CB2 receptors suppresses neuropathic nociception evoked by the chemotherapeutic agent vincristine in rats. *Br. J. Pharmacol.* **2007**, *152*, 765–777. [CrossRef]
75. Deng, L.; Guindon, J.; Vemuri, V.K.; Thakur, G.A.; White, F.A.; Makriyannis, A.; Hohmann, A.G. The maintenance of cisplatin- and paclitaxel-induced mechanical and cold allodynia is suppressed by cannabinoid CB_2 receptor activation and independent of CXCR4 signaling in models of chemotherapy-induced peripheral neuropathy. *Mol. Pain* **2012**, *8*, 71. [CrossRef]
76. Harris, H.M.; Sufka, K.J.; Gul, W.; ElSohly, M.A. Effects of Delta-9-Tetrahydrocannabinol and Cannabidiol on Cisplatin-Induced Neuropathy in Mice. *Planta Med.* **2016**, *82*, 1169–1172. [CrossRef] [PubMed]
77. Mecs, L.; Tuboly, G.; Toth, K.; Nagy, E.; Nyari, T.; Benedek, G.; Horvath, G. Peripheral antinociceptive effect of 2-arachidonoyl-glycerol and its interaction with endomorphin-1 in arthritic rat ankle joints. *Clin. Exp. Pharmacol. Physiol.* **2010**, *37*, 544–550. [CrossRef] [PubMed]
78. Schreiber, A.K.; Neufeld, M.; Jesus, C.H.A.; Cunha, J.M. Peripheral antinociceptive effect of anandamide and drugs that affect the endocannabinoid system on the formalin test in normal and streptozotocin-diabetic rats. *Neuropharmacology* **2012**, *63*, 1286–1297. [CrossRef] [PubMed]
79. Karbarz, M.J.; Luo, L.; Chang, L.; Tham, C.-S.; Palmer, J.A.; Wilson, S.J.; Wennerholm, M.L.; Brown, S.M.; Scott, B.P.; Apodaca, R.L.; et al. Biochemical and Biological Properties of 4-(3-phenyl-[1,2,4] thiadiazol-5-yl)-piperazine-1-carboxylic acid phenylamide, a Mechanism-Based Inhibitor of Fatty Acid Amide Hydrolase. *Anesth. Analg.* **2009**, *108*, 316–329. [CrossRef]
80. Cravatt, B.F.; Demarest, K.; Patricelli, M.P.; Bracey, M.H.; Giang, D.K.; Martin, B.R.; Lichtman, A.H. Supersensitivity to anandamide and enhanced endogenous cannabinoid signaling in mice lacking fatty acid amide hydrolase. *Proc. Natl. Acad. Sci. USA* **2001**, *98*, 9371–9376. Available online: https://www.pnas.org/doi/abs/10.1073/pnas.161191698 (accessed on 1 August 2022). [CrossRef] [PubMed]
81. Kamimura, R.; Hossain, M.Z.; Unno, S.; Ando, H.; Masuda, Y.; Takahashi, K.; Otake, M.; Saito, I.; Kitagawa, J. Inhibition of 2-arachydonoylgycerol degradation attenuates orofacial neuropathic pain in trigeminal nerve-injured mice. *J. Oral Sci.* **2018**, *60*, 37–44. [CrossRef]
82. Desroches, J.; Guindon, J.; Lambert, C.; Beaulieu, P. Modulation of the anti-nociceptive effects of 2-arachidonoyl glycerol by peripherally administered FAAH and MGL inhibitors in a neuropathic pain model. *Br. J. Pharmacol.* **2008**, *155*, 913–924. [CrossRef]
83. Khasabova, I.A.; Chandiramani, A.; Harding-Rose, C.; Simone, D.A.; Seybold, V.S. Increasing 2-arachidonoyl glycerol signaling in the periphery attenuates mechanical hyperalgesia in a model of bone cancer pain. *Pharmacol. Res.* **2011**, *64*, 60–67. [CrossRef]
84. Noyes, R.; Brunk, S.F.; Baram, D.A.; Canter, A. Analgesic effect of delta-9-tetrahydrocannabinol. *J. Clin. Pharmacol.* **1975**, *15*, 139–143. [CrossRef]
85. Noyes, R., Jr.; Brunk, S.F.; Avery, D.H.; Canter, A. The analgesic properties of delta-9-tetrahydrocannabinol and codeine. *Clin. Pharmacol. Ther.* **1975**, *18*, 84–89. [CrossRef]
86. Johnson, J.R.; Lossignol, D.; Burnell-Nugent, M.; Fallon, M.T. An Open-Label Extension Study to Investigate the Long-Term Safety and Tolerability of THC/CBD Oromucosal Spray and Oromucosal THC Spray in Patients With Terminal Cancer-Related Pain Refractory to Strong Opioid Analgesics. *J. Pain Symptom Manag.* **2013**, *46*, 207–218. [CrossRef] [PubMed]
87. Lichtman, A.H.; Lux, E.A.; McQuade, R.; Rossetti, S.; Sanchez, R.; Sun, W.; Wright, S.; Kornyeyeva, E.; Fallon, M.T. Results of a Double-Blind, Randomized, Placebo-Controlled Study of Nabiximols Oromucosal Spray as an Adjunctive Therapy in Advanced Cancer Patients with Chronic Uncontrolled Pain. *J. Pain Symptom Manag.* **2018**, *55*, 179–188.e1. [CrossRef] [PubMed]
88. Bar-Lev Schleider, L.; Mechoulam, R.; Lederman, V.; Hilou, M.; Lencovsky, O.; Betzalel, O.; Shbiro, L.; Novack, V. Prospective analysis of safety and efficacy of medical cannabis in large unselected population of patients with cancer. *Eur. J. Intern. Med.* **2018**, *49*, 37–43. [CrossRef] [PubMed]
89. Wang, L.; Hong, P.J.; May, C.; Rehman, Y.; Oparin, Y.; Hong, C.J.; Hong, B.Y.; AminiLari, M.; Gallo, L.; Kaushal, A.; et al. Medical cannabis or cannabinoids for chronic non-cancer and cancer related pain: A systematic review and meta-analysis of randomised clinical trials. *BMJ* **2021**, *374*, n1034. [CrossRef]
90. Lynch, M.E.; Cesar-Rittenberg, P.; Hohmann, A.G. A Double-Blind, Placebo-Controlled, Crossover Pilot Trial With Extension Using an Oral Mucosal Cannabinoid Extract for Treatment of Chemotherapy-Induced Neuropathic Pain. *J. Pain Symptom Manag.* **2014**, *47*, 166–173. [CrossRef]
91. Wang, T.; Collet, J.-P.; Shapiro, S.; Ware, M.A. Adverse effects of medical cannabinoids: A systematic review. *CMAJ* **2008**, *178*, 1669–1678. [CrossRef]
92. Machado Bergamaschi, M.; Helena Costa Queiroz, R.; Waldo Zuardi, A.; Alexandre, S.; Crippa, J. Safety and Side Effects of Cannabidiol, a Cannabis sativa Constituent. *Curr. Drug Saf.* **2011**, *6*, 237–249. [CrossRef]

93. Campeny, E.; López-Pelayo, H.; Nutt, D.; Blithikioti, C.; Oliveras, C.; Nuño, L.; Maldonado, R.; Florez, G.; Arias, F.; Fernández-Artamendi, S.; et al. The blind men and the elephant: Systematic review of systematic reviews of cannabis use related health harms. *Eur. Neuropsychopharmacol. J. Eur. Coll. Neuropsychopharmacol.* **2020**, *33*, 1–35. [CrossRef]
94. Volkow, N.D.; Baler, R.D.; Compton, W.M.; Weiss, S.R.B. Adverse Health Effects of Marijuana Use. *N. Engl. J. Med.* **2014**, *370*, 2219–2227. [CrossRef]
95. Freeman, T.P.; Hindocha, C.; Green, S.F.; Bloomfield, M.A.P. Medicinal use of cannabis based products and cannabinoids. *BMJ* **2019**, *365*, l1141. [CrossRef]
96. Powell, D.; Pacula, R.L.; Jacobson, M. Do medical marijuana laws reduce addictions and deaths related to pain killers? *J. Health Econ.* **2018**, *58*, 29–42. [CrossRef] [PubMed]
97. Mayor, S. WHO proposes rescheduling cannabis to allow medical applications. *BMJ* **2019**, *364*, l574. [CrossRef] [PubMed]
98. Maharajan, M.K.; Yong, Y.J.; Yip, H.Y.; Woon, S.S.; Yeap, K.M.; Yap, K.Y.; Yip, S.C.; Yap, K.X. Medical cannabis for chronic pain: Can it make a difference in pain management? *J. Anesth.* **2020**, *34*, 95–103. [CrossRef] [PubMed]

Journal of
Clinical Medicine

MDPI

Article

Sensory Thresholds and Peripheral Nerve Responses in Chronic Tension-Type Headache and Neuropsychological Correlation

Rosalinda Romero-Godoy [1,2,*], Sara Raquel Romero-Godoy [3], Manuel Romero-Acebal [3] and Mario Gutiérrez-Bedmar [4,5,6,*]

1 Department of Nursing and Physiotherapy, University of Balearic Islands, 07122 Palma, Spain
2 Cognitive Affective Neuroscience & Clinical Psychology Research Group, Institute of Health Science Research (IUNICS-IdISBa), ECYCS Research Group, University of Balearic Islands, 07120 Palma, Spain
3 Neurology Department, Virgen de la Victoria University Hospital, 29010 Malaga, Spain; sararaquelrogo@gmail.com (S.R.R.-G.); mromeroa@uma.es (M.R.-A.)
4 Preventive Medicine and Public Health Department, School of Medicine, University of Malaga, 29010 Malaga, Spain
5 Biomedical Research Institute of Malaga (IBIMA), 29010 Malaga, Spain
6 CIBERCV Cardiovascular Diseases, Carlos III Health Institute, 28029 Madrid, Spain
* Correspondence: r.romero@uib.es (R.R.-G.); bedmar@uma.es (M.G.-B.)

Abstract: Chronic tension-type headache (CTTH) is a common disease with no fully defined pathophysiological processes. We designed a study to value electrophysiological responses in these patients and their correlation with possible psychopathological manifestations in order to deepen understanding of central and peripheral mechanisms of CTTH. In 40 patients with CTTH and 40 healthy controls, we used electrical stimulation to determine sensory threshold (SPT) and pain perception threshold (PPT) and the characteristics of the electrophysiological sensory nerve action potential (SNAP): initial sensory response (ISR) and supramaximal response (SMR). We then calculated the intensity differences between thresholds (IDT), namely SPT-PPT, ISR-SMR and SMR-PPT, and correlated these IDTs with psychological characteristics: trait and state anxiety, depression, and emotional regulation. The SPT, together with the ISR and SMR thresholds, were higher ($p < 0.01$) in CTTH patients. The SMR-PPT IDT was smaller and correlated with significantly higher indicators of depression, state and trait anxiety, and poorer cognitive reappraisal. CTTH patients have less capacity to recognize non-nociceptive sensory stimuli, greater tendency toward pain facilitation, and a poor central pain control requiring higher stimulation intensity thresholds to reach the start and the peak amplitude of the SNAP. This is consistent with relative hypoexcitability of the Aβ nerve fibers in distant regions from the site of pain, and therefore, it could be considered a generalized dysfunction with a focal expression. Pain facilitation is directly associated with psychological comorbidity.

Keywords: chronic tension-type headache; electrical nerve stimulation; sensory threshold; pain threshold; central sensitization; peripheral sensitization; Aβ fiber excitability

Citation: Romero-Godoy, R.; Romero-Godoy, S.R.; Romero-Acebal, M.; Gutiérrez-Bedmar, M. Sensory Thresholds and Peripheral Nerve Responses in Chronic Tension-Type Headache and Neuropsychological Correlation. *J. Clin. Med.* **2022**, *11*, 1905. https://doi.org/10.3390/jcm11071905

Academic Editors: Markus W. Hollmann, Casandra I. Montoro Aguilar and Carmen María Galvez Sánchez

Received: 12 March 2022
Accepted: 27 March 2022
Published: 29 March 2022

1. Introduction

Tension-type headache is the most frequent form of headache and a hard-to-treat disease with an estimated prevalence of between 30% and 78% throughout the lifetime of the people who suffer it [1], with an estimated incidence of chronic tension-type headache (CTTH) of between 2% and 3% in the general population [2] that causes considerable functional limitations and have significant personal and economic repercussions [3,4].

The pathophysiological mechanisms of CTTH have yet to be fully defined but are thought to be due both to hypersensitivity in pericranial structures and local nerve receptors [5–8] and deregulation or hypersensitization in central nervous system (CNS) pain modulation pathways [6–10]. These alterations may be interlinked in a self-activating loop that perpetuates cranial pain [11–13] (Figure 1).

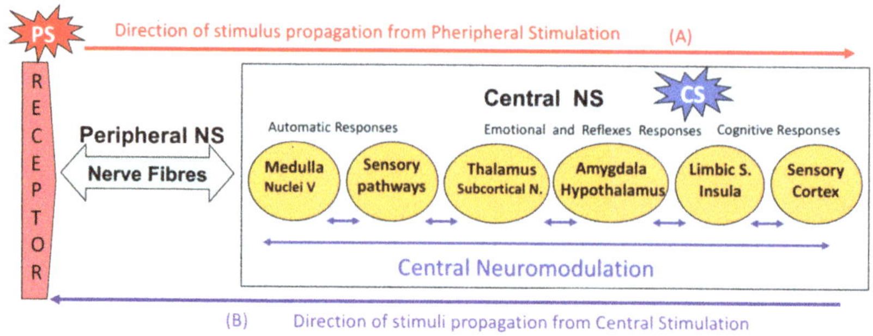

Figure 1. Diagram showing the physiology of craniofacial sensitivity, sensory perception of pain, and pain modulation.

As show in Figure 1, sensory perception is a central nervous system process that can be activated by (A) a stimulus that activates receptors or peripheral nerves (peripheral generator) or (B) a nerve impulse initiated in central nerve system circuits (central generator).

(A) A peripheral stimulus (PS) activates external (skin) or internal (fascia, muscles, viscera) neuroreceptors that stimulate nerve fibers. Large-diameter, myelinated nerve fibers (Aα and Aβ) are more easily excitable than small nerve fibers (Aδ and C).
The nerve fibers carry the stimulus to the CNS. Large-diameter, myelinated nerve fibers (Aβ) conduct signals more rapidly than small nerve fibers (Aδ and C).
The first stimuli to reach the spinal cord come from large-diameter, myelinated nerve fibers, which then control the input from the remaining fibers in the dorsal horn of the spinal cord ("gate control").
If signals from the small fibers are particularly intense (intense stimulus) and/or selective, they will override the gate-control mechanism.
Once in the spinal cord (CNS), the nerve impulses travel along the lemniscal pathways or posterior funiculi to suprasegmental structures.
In the head and neck, sensory stimuli travel directly to the trigeminal sensory nucleus in the brain stem.
The impulses reach subcortical structures (thalamus, subcortical nuclei) and then the amygdala and hypothalamus, triggering the emotional reaction and its vegetative response, which in turn is a sensory modulation mechanism.
From the thalamus, impulses travel to cortical structures, such as the limbic cortex, insula cortex, and somatosensory association cortex, generating the sensory cognitive response that perceives the sensation. The sensation is in turn appraised and linked to a prior experience, and this may generate a conditioned response
All these CNS structures are interrelated and constitute the central neuromodulation mechanism.

(B) The circuit can be reversed: an impulse (central stimulus, CS) can be generated primarily in sensory-related CNS structures (central sensory nuclei, psycho-emotional regulation circuits, sensory cortex, etc.), which will trigger perception.
Central hyperstimulation due to functional alterations in pain perception circuits would lead not only to an abnormal, exaggerated perception of pain but also to peripheral tissue hypersensitivity. This stimulates nerve fibers (peripheral hypersensitization), which in turn feed back to the CNS to generate secondary central hypersensitization.
Both mechanisms can be found in chronic pain processes, making it difficult to define the origin of the self-activation loop [13–15].

Stimuli can reach the peripheral nervous system (PNS) from outside (exteroception) or inside (interoception) the body. Excitability is the physiological capacity of the membrane of a nerve fiber to generate an action potential when stimulated. Large-diameter, myelinated nerve fibers (Aα and Aβ) are more excitable and transmit nerve impulses more rapidly than small and unmyelinated fibers (Aδ and C) [16,17]. The excitability of the membrane of a nerve fiber can depend on the intensity and frequency of the stimuli it receives so that a preceding stimulus can cause a transient state of initial hypoexcitability that transitions to hyperexcitability. This peripheral modulation of axonal membrane excitability is more accentuated in large-diameter, myelinated nerve fibers [14,18].

The CNS may be stimulated extrinsically from peripheral nerves or intrinsically by stimuli generated in the CNS itself. Depending on the quality of the stimulus and the type of synapse involved, this will either activate or inhibit the nerve pathways, circuits, and neural networks and modulate CNS activity. The processing of nerve impulses travelling along the spinal cord, brain stem, and brain leads to the perception and evaluation of sensation, setting in motion certain responses that can be reflexive, automatic, or voluntary and are either conditioned or unconditioned or unconscious or conscious [19,20] (Figure 1).

During processing, the sensory impulse leaves an "imprint" or sensory memory that can be accompanied by an emotional component [5,21]. Responses to successive exposure to the same stimulus will be influenced by this sensory and emotional imprint and can facilitate or inhibit the stimulus. This is the process of central sensitization, in which hypersensitization is determined by facilitation and hyposensitization by inhibition. This process is not limited to physical and/or biochemical functional changes in the CNS but can also modulate excitability in peripheral nerve fibers [5,6,15,22–25].

Sensitization, therefore, can be generated from external or internal sensory impulses in the neural circuits involved in the sensory and/or emotional regulation of pain, thus activating a sensation or feeling with a sensitive sensory response that is the same or similar to the response that would have been elicited by an external stimulus [5,6,21,26]. This is consistent with the notion of pain as a sensory and emotional experience "associated with actual or potential tissue damage" [27].

We hypothesized that CTTH may involve primary functional alterations in the central pain modulation circuits that facilitate the perception of pain, promoting in turn peripheral hypersensitivity that causes changes in neuronal excitability and leads to and enhances central hypersensitization. To test this hypothesis, we applied electrical stimulation to healthy volunteers and patients with CTTH to elicit subjective non-nociceptive pain responses and objective responses related to neuronal excitability. We correlated these with various psychological parameters, including anxiety, depression, and emotional regulation, in order to identify probable differences and associations with psychopathological comorbidity.

2. Materials and Methods

2.1. Participants

Forty subjects with a diagnosis of CTTH (age range 30–65 years, median 50.35, SD 10.12) and another forty healthy controls (HC) with no headache (age range 23–59 years, median 40.65, SD 10.51) were included in the study. Subjects with CTTH were recruited from the Neurology Department of the Virgen de la Victoria University Hospital in Malaga (Spain). The study was approved by the Ethics Committee of the University of Malaga. All subjects participated voluntarily and signed an informed consent form before inclusion. This study complies with the ethical criteria defined in the Declaration of Helsinki of 2014 and Organic Act March 2018, of 5 December, on the Protection of Personal Data and Guarantee of Digital Rights.

The diagnosis was made by a neurologist specialized in headache, following the criteria of the International Classification of Headache Disorders [1]. The electrophysiology study was performed by a specialist in clinical neurophysiology. Psychometric data were collected by a clinical neuropsychologist. All raters were blinded to the results of the other investigators. The data were analyzed by an independent evaluator.

The inclusion criteria for subjects with CTTH and healthy controls were: aged between 20–65 years and no psychotropic drugs or analgesics taken in the 72 h prior to the study.

Individuals diagnosed with a CNS or PNS disorder or who might present technical skin and/or subcutaneous tissue issues that could make it difficult to stimulate or register sensory responses were excluded [28]. Patients with more than one type of headache (such as chronic tension-type headache and migraine) were not included.

2.2. Materials

2.2.1. Electrophysiology Study

The electrophysiology study was performed with a Sierra Wave electromyography system, version 7 (Cadwell, WA, USA), with integrated electrical neurostimulator and disposable surface electrodes and dermal temperature probe from the same brand.

2.2.2. Questionnaires

The following questionnaires (Figure 2) were used to collect psychological variables:

Beck Depression Inventory—II (BDI—II) to determine the existence and severity of depression symptoms [29,30];

State—Trait Anxiety Inventory (STAI) to evaluate anxiety as a temporary state (state anxiety) or as a personal characteristic (trait anxiety) [31,32];

Emotion Regulation Questionnaire (ERQ) to separately assess cognitive reappraisal or regulation prior to an emotional experience and expressive suppression after an emotional experience [33,34];

Positive and Negative Affect Schedule (PANAS) to evaluate the subject's emotional recognition, as a positive or negative affect, either as a trait or a state (trait or state positive affect, trait or state negative affect) [35,36].

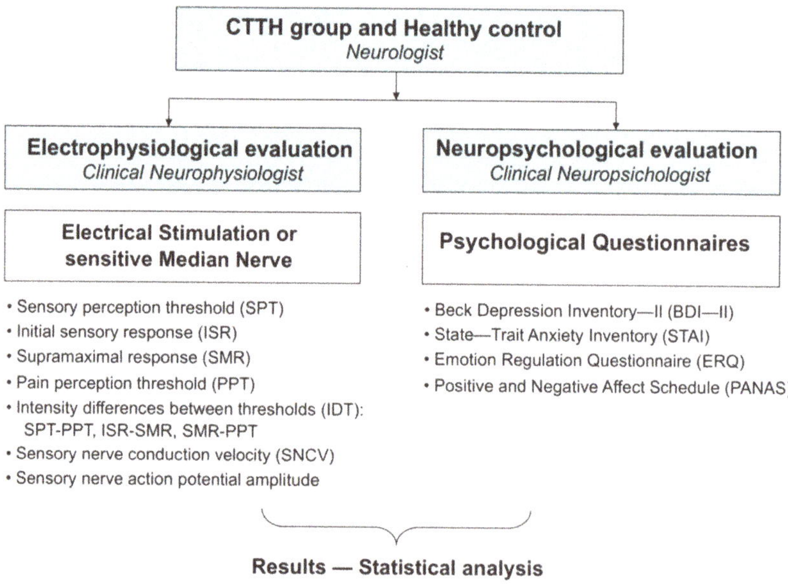

Figure 2. Methodological scheme.

2.3. Methods

Antidromic stimulation of the right median nerve was performed by applying an electrical stimulus to the anterior flexure of the wrist and collecting the sensory response in the second finger of the hand. The position of the recording, reference, ground, and stimulation electrodes remained unchanged throughout the procedure in order to achieve a reliable and reproducible recording [12,16,37–39].

The characteristics of the study and the subjective parameters to be collected were explained to all subjects. The following subjective responses reported by the subject were evaluated: the sensory perception threshold (SPT) or intensity at which the subject first recognized the applied stimulus and the pain perception threshold (PPT) or intensity at which the subject begins to recognize the stimulus as painful. The following objective responses observed during electrophysiology tests were evaluated: initial sensory response (ISR) or intensity at which the start of a detectable SNAP is observed and supramaximal response (SMR) or intensity at which the SNAP reaches its peak amplitude (Figure 2).

The intensity differences between thresholds (IDT) were determined in the following parameters: SPT-PPT, ISR-SMR, and SMR-PPT (Figure 2).

The electroneurographic parameters sensory nerve conduction velocity (SNCV) and SNAP amplitude were measured in m/s and μV, respectively, to determine normality according to the reference values (Figure 2).

The study was performed with the subject at rest, lying on an examination table (in position at least 15 min before the examination). The room temperature was maintained at 23–25 °C, and the skin temperature, measured with a temperature probe held by the patient, was between 30 and 32 °C. The electrical stimulus consisted of a quadrangular pulse lasting 0.1 ms, which was increased in increments of 1 mA until the perception threshold was reached and the initial SNAP obtained, after which it was increased in 2 mA increments until the remaining thresholds and responses had been obtained. The forced choice method was used to correctly measure the SPT and PPT, increasing and decreasing the intensity on at least 3 occasions to pinpoint the exact intensity generated by the sensation evaluated [40,41]. To determine ISR and SMR, 5 μV gains per division were used. ISR was defined as the minimum intensity needed to obtain a detectable SNAP without amplification. SMR was defined as the intensity needed to obtain an SNAP whose amplitude did not increase after applying a stimulus that was 20% more intense than the threshold. The stimuli were applied at intervals of between 25 and 55 s to avoid the expectation phenomenon [16].

2.4. Statistical Analysis

Data from the experimental and control groups were analyzed descriptively. The quantitative, psychological, and electrophysiological variables were expressed as mean and standard deviation (SD). The Kolmogorov–Smirnov normality test was used to test the normality of the distribution of quantitative data, and the Levene test was used to verify the equality of variances of all levels of each factor. Following this, the psychological and electrophysiological variables from both groups (CTTH and HC) were compared using the independent samples *t*-test in the case of normally distributed quantitative variables and the Mann–Whitney U test in the case of non-normally distributed variables.

Pearson's linear correlation coefficient was used to test for linear correlations between electrophysiological variables in the experimental and control groups separately. The linear correlation coefficients between psychological and electrophysiological variables were also calculated in each group.

Logistic regression analysis was performed to determine the capacity of the most sensitive electrophysiological variables to classify the data. The default variable input method was used. The effect was controlled by age and gender, taking age and sex as independent variables and SPT, ISR, and SMR as dependent variables and analyzing the relationship between each variable using the Pearson chi-squared goodness-of-fit test.

The diagnostic accuracy of electrophysiological variables that differed significantly between the HC and CTTH groups was evaluated with Receiver Operating Characteristic (ROC) curves, using cut-off points with the highest specificity and sensitivity.

Statistical analysis was performed on IBM SPPS Statistics v.27 (IBM, Armonk, NY, USA). A 95% confidence interval was used in all tests, and significance was set at $p < 0.05$.

3. Results

3.1. Differences in Subjective and Objective Electrophysiological Responses between Subjects with Chronic Tension-Type Headache and Healthy Controls

Table 1 and Figures 3 and 4 compare the stimulus intensity values for the defined response thresholds and the intensity values between the IDTs analyzed. Significant differences were observed between groups (HC and CTTH) in the subjective SPT response ($p < 0.001$) and the electrophysiological ISR ($p < 0.001$) and SMR ($p < 0.001$) responses, all of which were higher in the CTTH group vs. HCs. No differences were found between groups with respect to the subjective PPT response ($p = 0.372$). The only IDT in which a significant difference was observed was ISR-SMR ($p < 0.001$), which was greater in CTTH subjects. The SPT-PPT IDT ($p = 0.090$) and the SMR-PPT IDT ($p = 0.302$) did not differ between groups, and there were no significant differences in the electrophysiological SNCV parameters ($p = 0.526$) or SNAP amplitude ($p = 0.613$).

Table 2 shows the correlations between subjective SPT and PPT responses, electrophysiological ISR and SMR responses, and IDTs between the CTTH patients and HCs.

The logistic regression study showed that the statistically significant differences observed between groups in SPT, ISR, and SMR are independent of the age and gender effect ($X^2 = 10.276$, $p = 0.246$), thus proving the goodness-of-fit null hypothesis and showing that the model is capable of correctly classifying 80% of the subjects.

Table 1. Electrical stimuli intensity response thresholds and intensity difference between thresholds in CTTH ($n = 40$) and healthy controls ($n = 40$).

	Healthy Controls (in mA)		CTTH (in mA)		*p*
	MD ± SD	Median	MD ± SD	Median	
SPT **	5.38 ± 1.34	5.00	7.49 ± 2.45	7.25	<0.001 [b]
ISR **	9.70 ± 3.33	8.75	13.19 ± 5.15	11.75	<0.001 [a]
SMR **	19.66 ± 4.08	19.00	24.93 ± 3.33	25.00	<0.001 [b]
PPT	36.65 ± 10.92	35.50	39.24 ± 14.58	36.50	0.372 [a]
SPT-PPT IDT	31.28 ± 10.94	30.00	31.75 ± 13.36	29.25	0.090 [a]
ISR-SMR IDT **	9.96 ± 2.11	10.00	11.74 ± 3.59	11.50	<0.01 [b]
SMR-PPT IDT	16.99 ± 10.93	16.00	14.31 ± 12.08	12.00	0.302 [a]

Quantitative variables are expressed as mean ± standard deviation and median. CTTH, chronic tension-type headache; IDT, intensity difference between thresholds; ISR, initial sensory response; PPT, pain perception threshold; SMR, supramaximal response; SPT, sensory perception threshold. [a] *t*-test, [b] Mann–Whitney U-test. ** $p < 0.01$.

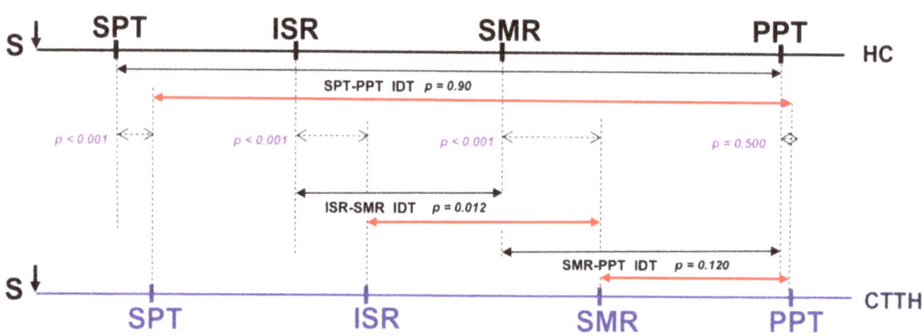

Figure 3. Comparison of sensory responses to electrical stimuli in CTTH patients and healthy controls. CTTH, chronic tension-type headache; HC, healthy control; IDT, intensity difference between thresholds; ISR, initial sensory response; PPT, pain perception threshold; S, stimulus; SMR, supramaximal response; SPT, sensory perception threshold.

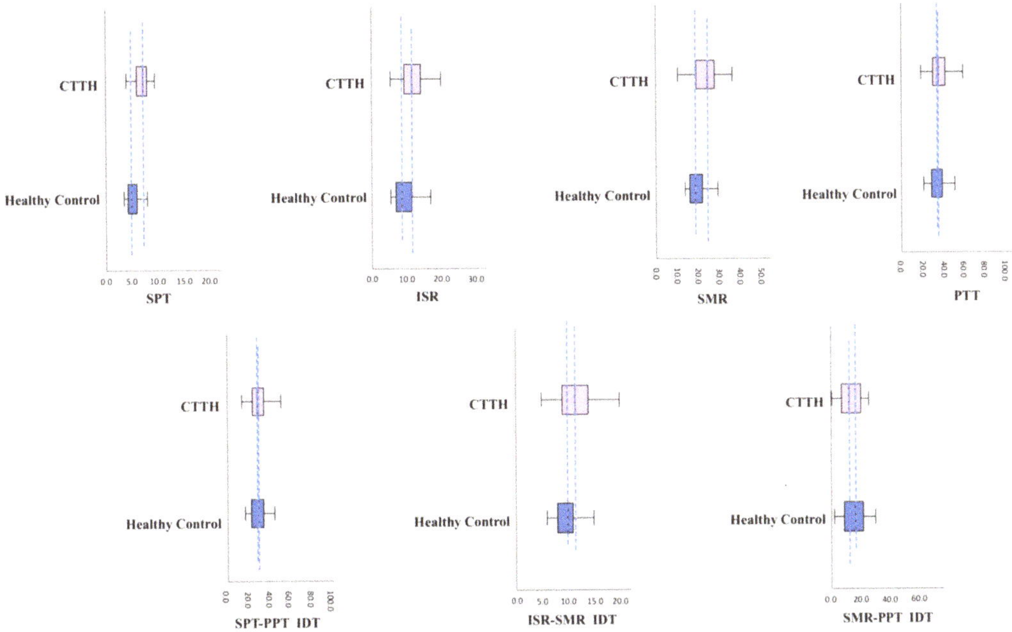

Figure 4. Box plots comparing subjective and objective electrophysiological responses and IDTs between healthy controls and CTTH patients. IDT, intensity difference between thresholds; ISR, initial sensory response; PPT, pain perception threshold; SMR, supramaximal response; SPT, sensory perception threshold.

Table 2. Correlation between subjective and objective electrophysiological responses and IDTs in healthy controls and CTTH.

		ISR	SMR	PPT	SPT-PPT IDT	ISR-SMR IDT	SMR-PPT IDT
SPT	HC	0.602 **	0.644 **				
	CTTH	0.575 **	0.557 **	0.558 **	0.426 **	0.324 **	0.332 *
ISR	HC		0.856 **			0.453 **	
	CTTH		0.897 **	0.418 **	0.351 *	0.415 **	
SMR	HC					0.580 **	
	CTTH			0.562 **	0.511 **	0.774 **	
PPT	HC				0.992 **		0.930 **
	CTTH				0.988 **	0.559 **	0.862 **
SPT-PPT IDT	HC						0.952 **
	CTTH					0.551 **	0.879 **

Data expressed as the Pearson correlation coefficient. CTTH, chronic tension-type headache; HC, healthy controls; IDT, intensity difference between thresholds; ISR, initial sensory response; PPT, pain perception threshold; SMR, supramaximal response; SPT, sensory perception threshold. * $p < 0.05$, ** $p < 0.01$.

The ROC curve showed that the SPT (90% sensitivity and 63% specificity), ISR (82.5% sensitivity and 58% specificity), and SMR (70% sensitivity and 72.5% specificity) responses were diagnostically accurate (Figure 5).

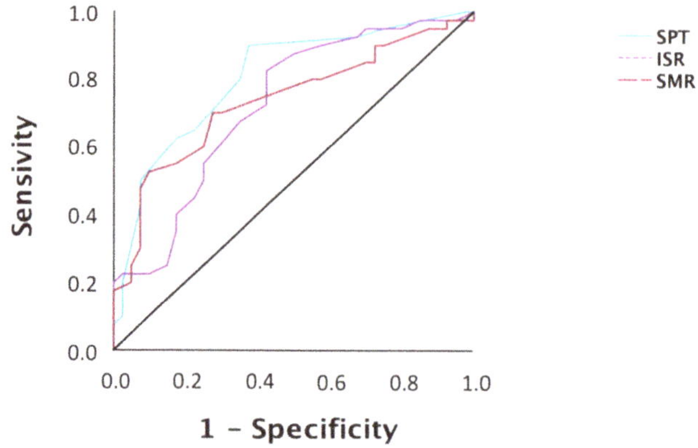

Figure 5. ROC curve of subjects with or without CTTH.

3.2. Psychological Differences between Subjects with Chronic Tension-Type Headache and Healthy Controls

Table 3 shows the differences in psychological questionnaire scores between the CTTH group and HCs. In HCs, these scores were within reference limits for the healthy population. Scores for state anxiety ($p < 0.001$), trait anxiety ($p < 0.001$), depression ($p < 0.001$), and state negative affect ($p < 0.001$) were significantly higher in the CTTH group vs. HCs, while score for state positive affect ($p < 0.001$) and trait positive affect ($p = 0.020$) and cognitive reappraisal ($p < 0.005$) were significantly lower in the CTTH group vs. HCs.

Table 3. Psychological differences between subjects with CTTH and healthy controls according to their questionnaire scores.

	Healthy Controls (n = 40)	CTTH (n = 40)	p
State anxiety **	20.20 ± 11.90	35.80 ± 14.25	<0.001 [a]
Trait anxiety **	19.33 ± 9.21	30.90 ± 11.61	<0.001 [a]
Depression **	7.53 ± 5.42	16.13 ± 9.58	<0.001 [a]
State positive affect **	31.58 ± 7.19	25.18 ± 7.23	<0.001 [a]
Trait positive affect *	33.00 ± 6.01	29.25 ± 7.97	0.020 [a]
State negative affect **	18.08 ± 5.99	25.40 ± 8.70	<0.001 [a]
Trait negative affect	18.58 ± 5.88	21.35 ± 6.84	0.055 [a]
Cognitive reappraisal *	4.71 ± 1.38	4.05 ± 1.33	0.033 [a]
Expressive suppression	3.26 ± 1.42	3.93 ± 1.64	0.055 [a]

Quantitative variables are expressed as mean ± standard deviation. The data express the numerical score obtained on the questionnaires. CTTH, chronic tension-type headache. [a] *t*-test, * $p < 0.05$, ** $p < 0.01$.

3.3. Correlations between Electrophysiological and Psychological Variables

In the control group, a positive correlation was observed between trait positive affect and PPT (r = 0.338, $p = 0.033$) and also between PPT-related intervals: SPT-PPT (r = 0.344, $p = 0.030$) and SMR-PPT (r = 0.379, $p = 0.016$).

In the CTTH group, a positive correlation was observed between PPT and the psychological variable trait positive affect (r = 0.306, $p = 0.055$) and a negative correlation between the SMR-PPT interval and the psychological variables trait negative affect (r = −0.315, $p = 0.047$), state anxiety (r = −0.360, $p = 0.022$), trait anxiety (r = −0.431, $p = 0.005$), and depression (r = −0.368, $p = 0.019$). The SMR-PPT interval only presented a significant positive correlation with respect to cognitive reappraisal (r = 0.324, $p = 0.042$) (Figure 6).

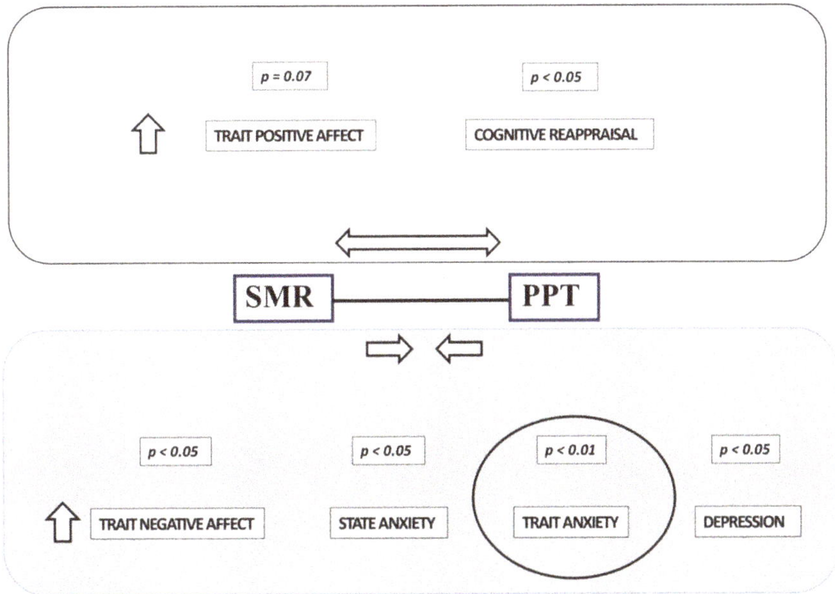

Figure 6. Correlation between pain facilitation and neuropsychological variables.

4. Discussion

The SPT indicates the degree of subjective non-nociceptive sensory discrimination. Physiologically, it is determined by the activation of large-diameter, myelinated nerve fibers (Aα and Aβ) that are more susceptible to excitation and that rapidly transmit the impulse to the CNS, where it is initially recognized (Figure 1) [10,12,15].

In our study, the SPT was significantly higher in patients with CTTH compared to healthy controls (Figures 3 and 4). In patients with CTTH, this has been previously observed in both trigger points [42,43] and other body areas [44–46] and could be due to a lower capacity for subjective sensory discrimination due to an alertness/attention deficit in the CNS (central dysmodulation) or hypoexcitability in Aα and Aβ nerve fibers, which are more excitable and conduct nerve impulse more rapidly (peripheral dysmodulation) [40].

The ISR and SMR are objective parameters related to nerve excitability. Both responses are recorded by stimulating Aβ fibers. The ISR objectively indicates the activation of a sufficient number Aβ sensory nerve fibers to evoke a sensory potential capable of being detected in the electrophysiological study, while the SMR indicates the activation of all the sensory fibers in the nerve. Although small nerve fibers (Aδ and C), which are associated with thermal and pain sensitivity, can be activated at the SMR intensity, they do not contribute to the SNAP observed in conventional electrophysiology [47].

The stimulus intensity required to reach the ISR and SMR was higher in subjects with CTTH compared to HCs, which suggests that Aβ nerve fibers in subjects with CTTH are less susceptible to excitability compared to healthy individuals (Figures 3 and 4). Studies have shown that hyperstimulation of a nerve can determine the hypoexcitability of its fibers, with the larger, myelinated Aβ nerves being the most easily modulated [5,14,18,40].

We were unable to observe the degree of excitability of Aδ and C fibers since they are not expressed in SNAPs. However, we, like other authors, have assumed that they are either not hypoexcited or less hypoexcited than large-diameter fibers [14,18,40].

The hypoexcitability of Aβ fibers was observed at a point distant from trigger points that are potentially hypersensitive in patients with CTTH, suggesting that it may be a diffuse event. We evaluated this finding in the median sensitive nerve because of its higher sensibility and stability response recording; the evaluation of this sensitive response in other sensitive nerve in lower limbs may be of interest in other new studies.

When the intensity of the electrical stimulus is increased, a PPT is reached, in which the sensory interpretation changes from non-nociceptive to painful. The PPT is an indicator of the capacity to recognize and modulate pain perception on a psychosensorial level and is determined by activation of the Aδ and C fibers (already achieved by delivering the intensity needed to achieve an SMR) and by the successive steps, connections, and regulations that occur from the time the painful sensory impulse enters the CNS until it reaches the somatosensory perceptive and associative cortex (Figure 1).

Other authors [46,48] have also failed to observe any differences in PPT between subjects with CTTH and healthy controls, and this has also been reported in other types of patients with idiopathic pain symptoms, such as fibromyalgia or local regional pain syndrome [49–51]. This, however, is a controversial finding since other authors contend that patients with CTTH have a lower PPT [52–56].

We attempted to resolve this issue by evaluating the SMR-PPT IDT. This interval indicates the intensity increase required from excitation of all the sensory fibers of the nerve until pain is perceived; we have therefore called it the "pain permeability interval". Although the differences observed were not significant, this interval is shorter in subjects with CTTH compared to healthy controls (Figures 3 and 4), leading us to believe that an alteration in central pain regulation circuits facilitates central pain perception.

If there is indeed a central, generalized pain facilitation mechanism, we need to consider why cranial pain in patients with CTTH is localized instead of generalized as it is in fibromyalgia. Although this is a questionable assumption, one possible explanation is that the frontotemporal cranial structures, which receive their sensory innervation from the trigeminal nerve, have more direct access to the CNS and less input modulation than in body areas where access is through the spinal cord gate-control filter [13,42,43,57,58].

According to the central sensitization theory of chronic pain, competent nociceptive stimuli can trigger neuroplasticity processes in the central circuits that transmit, modulate, and perceive pain; thus, the perception of a particular pain is either facilitated and perpetuated permanently or elicited with a far lower intensity pain stimulus [5,6]. This theory is based on the hypothesis that external nociceptive stimuli are the primary drivers of these changes due to myofascial contraction or alteration and local biochemical and inflammatory changes. This leads to secondary hypersensitization in central circuits, which in turn triggers peripheral adaptation responses in sensory receptors and local pericranial myofascial territories (trigger points) that cause and perpetuate the situation [5,6,22,52,56,59–61]. In our study, we found that subjects with CTTH presented a significantly lower permeability for pain, so we believe that the primary cause for hypersensitization is central dysmodulation.

On a neuropsychological level, we found significantly higher rates of state anxiety and trait anxiety, significantly higher rates of depression, and a far lower capacity for emotional regulation in patients with CTTH compared to healthy controls (Table 3). These neuropsychological alterations are closely related to their extremely short "pain permeability interval" (Figures 3 and 4), leading us to believe that central dysmodulation mechanisms together with neuropsychological alterations play an important role in the origin of pain perception facilitation in subjects with CTTH.

We did not find any correlation between the higher SPT observed in subjects with CTTH and any particular psychopathological or emotional regulation trait, which suggests to us that this lower discrimination sensitivity to sensory perception is an independent defining trait of the psychological variables found in subjects with CTTH and that this could be related to attention span or sensory avoidance in these subjects, a hypothesis that could be explored in subsequent studies.

Studies have shown that the CNS acts as the primary sensory trigger in circuits that transmit, modulate, perceive and evaluate feelings and that these can precede the functional and structural modifications that occur as an organic expression of such feelings in peripheral areas, where, by a process of sustained activation (such as gestures, postures, muscle, or myofascial tone), they bring about functional and structural modifications that may in turn act as the causal mechanisms of a process of hypersensitization and pain re-entry facilitation [15,20,21,26].

Some authors have observed that people with chronic pain, specifically patients with CTTH, present a greater psychopathological burden in the form of anxiety, depression, or emotional management difficulties [10,15,62–64]. These are frequently linked to other comorbidities that cause chronic pain, such as fibromyalgia, osteoarticular pain, oral and facial pain, abdominal pain, postoperative pain, or neurovegetative alterations, such as irritable bowel syndrome, tachycardia, etc. [5,6,15,63].

Neuropsychological alterations may be secondary to or influenced by a persistent painful life experience although their primary or secondary link to CTTH is controversial and should be explored in future studies. However, it is evident that their presence worsens and/or perpetuates CTTH symptoms [15].

To summarize, CTTH is associated with primary central pain facilitation that can set in motion by a particular painful experience that can then lead to hypersensitivity in peripheral tissue structures. These alterations lead to sensory hyperstimulation that may induce a relative hypoexcitability of Aβ fibers and further facilitates the input of pain sensations in the CNS, mediated peripherally by Aδ and C fibers. This re-entry loop perpetuates the painful experience and reinforces central hypersensitization. The close correlation with psychopathological alterations, such as anxiety, depression, or lack of emotional control, can be an expression of the cause itself or a consequence of the sustained painful life experience, thus helping to perpetuate and reinforce the pain [64–68].

Despite the fact that the diagnosis of CTTH is clinical, it would be necessary to evaluate these patients in both neurophysiological and neuropsychological aspects to better define the profile of each one and adapt the best therapeutic management to avoid the perpetuation and reinforce sensitization.

5. Conclusions

The nervous system is an integrated, dynamic macro-complex in which all functions are interdependent, synchronized, and reciprocal and modulated by plasticity mechanisms. Therefore, chronic processes can be difficult to isolate or disassociate from a physiological perspective. This study helps show that the primary cause of pain perception dysmodulation in patients with CTTH might be a primary predisposition in the CNS, which leads to secondary peripheral hypersensitization and hypoexcitability of Aβ fibers. Greater pain facilitation is closely associated with a greater psychological comorbidity burden of anxiety, depression, and emotional disturbance. We believe that our findings can improve the conceptual understanding of CTTH and help clinicians achieve a more effective and sustained therapeutic response.

Author Contributions: Conceptualization, R.R.-G., S.R.R.-G., M.R.-A. and M.G.-B.; methodology, R.R.-G., S.R.R.-G., M.R.-A. and M.G.-B.; validation R.R.-G., S.R.R.-G., M.R.-A. and M.G.-B., formal analysis, R.R.-G. and M.R.-A.; investigation, R.R.-G., S.R.R.-G., M.R.-A. and M.G.-B.; resources, R.R.-G., S.R.R.-G., M.R.-A. and M.G.-B.; data curation, R.R.-G. and M.R.-A.; writing—original draft preparation, R.R.-G., S.R.R.-G., M.R.-A. and M.G.-B.; writing—review and editing, R.R.-G., S.R.R.-G., M.R.-A. and M.G.-B.; visualization, R.R.-G., S.R.R.-G., M.R.-A. and M.G.-B.; supervision, R.R.-G., S.R.R.-G., M.R.-A. and M.G.-B. All authors have read and agreed to the published version of the manuscript.

Funding: This research received no external funding.

Institutional Review Board Statement: The study was approved by the Ethics Committee of the University of Malaga. All subjects participated voluntarily and signed an informed consent form before inclusion. This study complies with the ethical criteria defined in the Declaration of Helsinki of 2014 and Organic Act March 2018, of 5 December, on the Protection of Personal Data and Guarantee of Digital Rights.

Informed Consent Statement: Informed consent was obtained from all subjects involved in the study.

Data Availability Statement: Not applicable.

Conflicts of Interest: The authors declare no conflict of interest.

References

1. Headache Classification Committee of the International Headache Society (IHS). The International Classification of Headache Disorders, 3rd edition. *Cephalalgia* **2018**, *38*, 1–211. [CrossRef] [PubMed]
2. Bendtsen, L.; Jensen, R. Tension-type headache: The most common, but also the most neglected, headache disorder. *Curr. Opin. Neurol.* **2006**, *19*, 305–309. [CrossRef] [PubMed]
3. Linde, M.; Gustavsson, A.; Stovner, L.J.; Steiner, T.J.; Barré, J.; Katsarava, Z.; Lainez, J.M.; Lampl, C.; Lantéri-Minet, M.; Rastenyte, D.; et al. The cost of headache disorders in Europe: The Eurolight project. *Eur. J. Neurol.* **2012**, *19*, 703–711. [CrossRef] [PubMed]
4. Ashina, S.; Buse, D.C.; Bjorner, J.B.; Bendtsen, L.; Lyngberg, A.C.; Jensen, R.H.; Lipton, R.B. Health-related quality of life in tension-type headache: A population-based. *Scand. J. Pain* **2021**, *21*, 778–787. [CrossRef]
5. Latremoliere, A.; Woolf, C.J. Central sensitization: A generator of pain hypersensitivity by central neural plasticity. *J. Pain* **2009**, *10*, 895–926. [CrossRef]
6. Woolf, C.J. Central sensitization: Implications for the diagnosis and treatment of pain. *Pain* **2011**, *152*, S2–S15. [CrossRef]
7. Ashina, S.; Bendtsen, L.; Ashina, M.; Magerl, W.; Jensen, R. Generalized hyperalgesia in patients with chronic tension-type headache. *Cephalalgia* **2006**, *26*, 940–948. [CrossRef]
8. Fernández-de-Las-Peñas, C.; Plaza-Manzano, G.; Navarro-Santana, M.J.; Olesen, J.; Jensen, R.H.; Bendtsen, L. Evidence of localized and widespread pressure pain hypersensitivity in patients with tension-type headache: A systematic review and meta-analysis. *Cephalalgia* **2021**, *41*, 256–273. [CrossRef]
9. Gatchel, R.J.; Peng, Y.B.; Peters, M.L.; Fuchs, P.N.; Turk, D.C. The biopsychosocial approach to chronic pain: Scientific advances and future directions. *Psychol. Bull.* **2007**, *133*, 581–624. [CrossRef]
10. Salomons, T.V.; Nusslock, R.; Detloff, A.; Johnstone, T.; Davidson, R.J. Neural emotion regulation circuitry underlying anxiolytic effects of perceived control over pain. *J. Cogn. Neurosci.* **2015**, *27*, 222–233. [CrossRef]
11. Caamaño-Barrios, L.H.; Galán-Del-Río, F.; Fernández-de-Las-Peñas, C.; Plaza- Manzano, G.; Arendt-Nielsen, L.; Ortega-Santiago, R. Widespread Pressure Pain Sensitivity over Nerve Trunk Areas in Women with Frequent Episodic Tension-Type Headache as a Sign of Central Sensitization. *Pain Med.* **2020**, *21*, 1408–1414. [CrossRef]
12. Sang, C.N.; Max, M.B.; Gracely, R.H. Stability and Reliability of Detection Thresholds for Human A-Beta and A-Delta Sensory Afferents Determined by Cutaneous Electrical Stimulation. *J. Pain Symptom Manag.* **2003**, *25*, 64–73. [CrossRef]
13. Chichorro, J.G.; Porreca, F.; Sessle, B. Mechanisms of craniofacial pain. *Cephalalgia* **2017**, *37*, 613–626. [CrossRef]
14. Burke, D.; Kiernan, M.C.; Bostock, H. Excitability of human axons. *Clin. Neurophysiol.* **2001**, *112*, 1575–1585. [CrossRef]
15. Wilhelmsen, I. Biological sensitisation and psychological amplification: Gateways to subjective health complaints and somatoform disorders. *Psychoneuroendocrinology* **2005**, *30*, 990–995. [CrossRef]
16. Pasluosta, C.; Kiele, P.; Stieglitz, T. Paradigms for restoration of somatosensory feedback via stimulation of the peripheral nervous system. *Clin. Neurophysiol.* **2018**, *129*, 851–862. [CrossRef]
17. Valls-Solé, J. Electromiografía y Electrodiagnóstico Neurológico: Fundamentos, Consideraciones Anatómicas y Fisiológicas. In *Manual de Electromiografía Clínica*, 3rd ed.; Gutiérrez-Rivas, E., Jiménez, M.D., Pardo, J., Romero-Acebal, M., Eds.; Ergon: Madrid, Spain, 2021; pp. 9–18.
18. Bostock, H.; Cikurel, K.; Burke, D. Threshold tracking techniques in the study of human peripheral nerve. *Muscle Nerve* **1998**, *21*, 137–158. [CrossRef]
19. Woolf, C.J. What is this thing called pain? *J. Clin. Investig.* **2010**, *120*, 3742–3744. [CrossRef]
20. Ossipov, M.H.; Dussor, G.O.; Porreca, F. Central modulation of pain. *J. Clin. Investig.* **2010**, *120*, 3779–3787. [CrossRef]
21. Bechara, A.; Damasio, A.R. The somatic marker hypothesis: A neural theory of economic decision. *Games Econ. Behav.* **2005**, *52*, 336–372. [CrossRef]
22. Fernández-de-las-Peñas, C.; Schoenen, J. Chronic tension-type headache: What is new? *Curr. Opin. Neurol.* **2009**, *22*, 254–261. [CrossRef]
23. Woolf, C.J. Central sensitization: Uncovering the relation between pain and plasticity. *Anesthesiology* **2007**, *106*, 864–867. [CrossRef]
24. Basbaum, A.I.; Bautista, D.M.; Scherrer, G.; Julius, D. Cellular and molecular mechanisms of pain. *Cell* **2009**, *139*, 267–284. [CrossRef]
25. Costigan, M.; Scholz, J.; Woolf, C.J. Neuropathic pain: A maladaptive response of the nervous system to damage. *Annu. Rev. Neurosci.* **2009**, *32*, 1–32. [CrossRef]
26. Damasio, A.R. The somatic marker hypothesis and the possible functions of the prefrontal cortex. *Philos. Trans. R. Soc. Lond. B Biol. Sci.* **1996**, *351*, 1413–1420. [CrossRef]
27. Raja, S.N.; Carr, D.B.; Cohen, M.; Finnerup, N.B.; Flor, H.; Gibson, S.; Keefe, F.J.; Mogil, J.S.; Ringkamp, M.; Sluka, K.A.; et al. The revised International Association for the Study of Pain definition of pain: Concepts, challenges, and compromises. *Pain* **2020**, *161*, 1976–1982. [CrossRef]
28. Tursky, B.; Watson, P.D. Controlled physical and subjective intensities of electric shock. *Psychophysiology* **1964**, *1*, 151–162. [CrossRef] [PubMed]

29. Beck, A.T.; Steer, R.A.; Brown, G.K. *Manual for the Beck Depression Inventory-II*; Psychological Corporation: San Antonio, TX, USA, 1996.
30. Sanz, J.; Perdigón, A.L.; Vázquez, C. The spanish adaptation of Beck's Depression Inventory-II (BDI-II): 2. Psychometric properties in the general population. *Clín. Y Salud* **2003**, *14*, 249–280.
31. Spielberger, C.; Gorsuch, R.; Lushene, R. *STAI Manual for the State-Trait Anxiety Inventory*; Consulting Psychologist Press: Palo Alto, CA, USA, 1970.
32. Spielberger, C.; Gorsuch, R.; Lushene, R. *Cuestionario de Ansiedad Estado-Rasgo Manual*, 4th ed.; TEA Ediciones SA: Madrid, Spain, 1993.
33. Gross, J.J.; John, O.P. Individual differences in two emotion regulation processes: Implications for affect, relationships, and well-being. *J. Pers. Soc. Psychol.* **2003**, *85*, 348–362. [CrossRef]
34. Cabello, R.; Salguero, J.M.; Fernández-Berrocal, P.; Gross, J.J. A Spanish adaptation of the Emotion Regulation Questionnaire. *Eur. J. Psychol. Assess.* **2013**, *29*, 234–240. [CrossRef]
35. Watson, D.; Clark, L.A.; Tellegen, A. Development and validation of brief measures of positive and negative affect: The PANAS scales. *J. Pers. Soc. Psychol.* **1988**, *54*, 1063–1070. [CrossRef]
36. Serafini, K.; Malin-Mayor, B.; Nich, C.; Hunkele, K.; Carroll, K.M. Psychometric properties of the Positive and Negative Affect Schedule (PANAS) in a heterogeneous sample of substance users. *Am. J. Drug Alcohol Abus.* **2016**, *42*, 203–212. [CrossRef]
37. Basser, P.J.; Roth, B.J. New currents in electrical stimulation of excitable tissues. *Annu. Rev. Biomed. Eng.* **2000**, *2*, 377–397. [CrossRef]
38. Rattay, F. The basic mechanism for the electrical stimulation of the nervous system. *Neuroscience* **1999**, *89*, 335–346. [CrossRef]
39. Rubinstein, J.T. Analytical theory for extracellular electrical stimulation of nerve with focal electrodes. II. Passive myelinated axon. *Biophys. J.* **1991**, *60*, 538–555. [CrossRef]
40. Gracely, R.H. Pain measurement. *Acta Anaesthesiol. Scand.* **1999**, *43*, 897–908. [CrossRef]
41. Sekuler, R.; Nash, D.; Armstrong, R. Sensitive, objective procedure for evaluating response to light touch. *Neurology* **1973**, *23*, 1282–1291. [CrossRef]
42. Schepelmann, K.; Dannhausen, M.; Kotter, I.; Schabet, M.; Dichgans, J. Exteroceptive suppression of temporalis muscle activity in patients with fibromyalgia, tension-type headache, and normal controls. *Electroencephalogr. Clin. Neurophysiol.* **1998**, *107*, 196–199. [CrossRef]
43. Tataroglu, C.; Kanik, A.; Sahin, G.; Ozge, A.; Yalcinkaya, D.; Idiman, F. Exteroceptive suppression patterns of masseter and temporalis muscles in central and peripheral headache disorders. *Cephalalgia* **2002**, *22*, 444–452. [CrossRef]
44. Le Bars, D.; Dickenson, A.H.; Besson, J.M. Diffuse noxious inhibitory controls (DNIC). I. Effects on dorsal horn convergent neurons in the rat. *Pain* **1979**, *6*, 283–304. [CrossRef]
45. Le Bars, D.; Dickenson, A.H.; Besson, J.M. Diffuse noxious inhibitory controls (DNIC): II. Lack of effects on non-convergent neurons, supraspinal involvement and theoretical implications. *Pain* **1979**, *6*, 305–327. [CrossRef]
46. Pielsticker, A.; Haag, G.; Zaudig, M.; Lautenbacher, S. Impairment of pain inhibition in chronic tension-type headache. *Pain* **2005**, *118*, 215–223. [CrossRef]
47. Romero-Godoy, R.; Romero-Godoy, J.; Gitiérrez-Gutiérrez, G.; Romero-Acebal, M. Fibras nerviosas finas y sistema nervioso autónomo. In *Manual de Electromiografía Clínica*, 3rd ed.; Gutiérrez-Rivas, E., Jiménez, M.D., Pardo, J., Romero-Acebal, M., Eds.; Ergon: Madrid, Spain, 2021; pp. 359–369.
48. Flor, H.; Diers, M.; Birbaumer, N. Peripheral and electrocortical responses to painful and non-painful stimulation in chronic pain patients, tension headache patients and healthy controls. *Neurosci. Lett.* **2004**, *361*, 147–150. [CrossRef]
49. Lautenbacher, S.; Rollman, G.B. Possible deficiences of pain modulation in fibromyalgia. *Clin. J. Pain* **1997**, *13*, 189–196. [CrossRef]
50. Kosek, E.; Hansson, P. Modulatory influence on somatosensory perception from vibration and heterotopic noxious conditioning stimulation (HNCS) in fibromyalgia patients and healthy subjects. *Pain* **1997**, *70*, 41–51. [CrossRef]
51. Leffler, A.S.; Hansson, P.; Kosek, E. Somatosensory perception in a remote pain-free area and function of diffuse noxious inhibitory controls (DNIC) in patients suffering from long-term trapezius myalgia. *Eur. J. Pain* **2002**, *6*, 149–159. [CrossRef]
52. Jensen, R. Pathophysiological mechanisms of tension-type headache: A review of epidemiological and experimental studies. *Cephalalgia* **1999**, *19*, 602–621. [CrossRef]
53. Schoenen, J.; Bottin, D.; Hardy, F.; Gerard, P. Cephalic and extracephalic pressure pain thresholds in chronic tension-type headache. *Pain* **1991**, *47*, 145–149. [CrossRef]
54. Langemark, M.; Jensen, K.; Jensen, T.S.; Olesen, J. Pressure pain thresholds and thermal nociceptive thresholds in chronic tension-type headache. *Pain* **1989**, *38*, 203–210. [CrossRef]
55. Bendtsen, L.; Jensen, R.; Olesen, J. Decreased pain detection and tolerance thresholds in chronic tension-type headache. *Arch. Neurol.* **1996**, *53*, 373–376. [CrossRef]
56. Hole, K.; Berge, O.G. Regulation of pain sensitivity in the central nervous system. *Cephalalgia* **1981**, *1*, 51–59. [CrossRef] [PubMed]
57. Pielsticker, A.; Lautenbacher, S. Disturbances in pain perception in primary headaches (migraine, tension-type headache and cluster headache). In *The Pathophysiology of Pain Perception*; Lautenbacher, S., Fillingim, R.B., Eds.; Plenum: New York, NY, USA, 2004; pp. 43–57.
58. Milanov, I.; Bogdanova, D. Trigemino-cervical reflex in patients with headache. *Cephalalgia* **2003**, *23*, 35–38. [CrossRef] [PubMed]
59. Fernández-de-las-Peñas, C.; Cuadrado, M.L.; Arendt-Nielsen, L.; Simons, D.G.; Pareja, J.A. Myofascial trigger points and sensitization: An updated pain model for tension-type headache. *Cephalalgia* **2007**, *27*, 383–393. [CrossRef] [PubMed]

60. Fernández-de-Las-Peñas, C.; Ge, H.Y.; Arendt-Nielsen, L.; Cuadrado, M.L.; Pareja, J.A. The local and referred pain from myofascial trigger points in the temporalis muscle contributes to pain profile in chronic tension-type headache. *Clin. J. Pain* **2007**, *23*, 786–792. [CrossRef]
61. Do, T.P.; Heldarskard, G.F.; Kolding, L.T.; Hvedstrup, J.; Schytz, H.W. Myofascial trigger points in migraine and tension-type headache. *J. Headache Pain* **2018**, *19*, 84. [CrossRef]
62. Torelli, P.; Abrignani, G.; Castellini, P.; Lambru, G.; Manzoni, G.C. Human psyche and headache: Tension-type headache. *Neurol. Sci.* **2008**, *29*, S93–S95. [CrossRef]
63. Aaseth, K.; Grande, R.B.; Leiknes, K.A.; Benth, J.Š.; Lundqvist, C.; Russell, M.B. Personality traits and psychological distress in persons with chronic tension-type headache. The Akershus study of chronic headache. *Acta Neurol. Scand.* **2011**, *124*, 375–382. [CrossRef]
64. Haratian, A.; Amjadi, M.M.; Ghandehari, K.; Hatamian, H.; Kiani, S.; Habibi, M; : Aghababaei, Z; Ataei, M. Emotion Regulation Difficulties and Repetitive Negative Thinking in Patients With Tension Headaches and Migraine. *Casp. J. Neurol. Sci.* **2020**, *6*, 147–155. [CrossRef]
65. Zebenholzer, K.; Lechner, A.; Broessner, G.; Lampl, C.; Luthringshausen, G.; Wuschitz, A.; Obmann, S.M.; Berek, K.; Wöber, C. Impact of depression and anxiety on burden and management of episodic and chronic headaches—A cross-sectional multicentre study in eight Austrian headache centres. *J. Headache Pain* **2016**, *17*, 15. [CrossRef]
66. Everaert, J.; Joormann, J. Emotion regulation difficulties related to depression and anxiety: A network approach to model relations among symptoms, positive reappraisal, and repetitive negative thinking. *Clin. Psychol. Sci.* **2019**, *7*, 1304–1318. [CrossRef]
67. Cooney, R.E.; Joormann, J.; Eugène, F.; Dennis, E.L.; Gotlib, I.H. Neural correlates of rumination in depression. *Cogn. Affect. Behav. Neurosci.* **2010**, *10*, 470–478. [CrossRef]
68. Chuen Yee Lo, B.; Lau, S.; Cheung, S.H.; Allen, N.B. The impact of rumination on internal attention switching. *Cogn. Emot.* **2012**, *26*, 209–223. [CrossRef]

Journal of
Clinical Medicine

MDPI

Article

Psychiatric Comorbidity and Emotional Dysregulation in Chronic Tension-Type Headache: A Case-Control Study

Rosalinda Romero-Godoy [1,2,*], Sara Raquel Romero-Godoy [3], Manuel Romero-Acebal [3] and Mario Gutiérrez-Bedmar [4,5,6,*]

1 Department of Nursing and Physiotherapy, University of Balearic Islands, 07122 Palma, Spain
2 Cognitive Affective Neuroscience Clinical Psychology Research Group, Institute of Health Science Research (IUNICS-IdISBa), ECYCS Research Group, University of Balearic Islands, 07120 Palma, Spain
3 Neurology Department, Virgen de la Victoria University Hospital, 29010 Malaga, Spain
4 Preventive Medicine and Public Health Department, School of Medicine, University of Málaga, 29010 Malaga, Spain
5 Biomedical Research Institute of Malaga-IBIMA, 29010 Malaga, Spain
6 CIBERCV Cardiovascular Diseases, Carlos III Health Institute, 28029 Madrid, Spain
* Correspondence: r.romero@uib.es (R.R.-G.); bedmar@uma.es (M.G.-B.)

Citation: Romero-Godoy, R.; Romero-Godoy, S.R.; Romero-Acebal, M.; Gutiérrez-Bedmar, M. Psychiatric Comorbidity and Emotional Dysregulation in Chronic Tension-Type Headache: A Case-Control Study. *J. Clin. Med.* **2022**, *11*, 5090. https://doi.org/10.3390/jcm11175090

Academic Editors: Markus W. Hollmann, Casandra I. Montoro Aguilar and Carmen María Galvez Sánchez

Received: 18 July 2022
Accepted: 25 August 2022
Published: 30 August 2022

Abstract: Background: Chronic tension-type headache (CTTH) is frequently associated with a psychiatric comorbidity of depression and anxiety. Most studies focus their attention on this association, and only few link CTTH with psycho-affective emotional regulation disorders. Objective: To evaluate the association of CTTH with anxiety, depression, positive and negative affectivity, and emotional management in CTTH patients with neither a previous diagnosis of psychiatric disorder nor use of psychoactive drugs or abuse of analgesics. Design: Case-control study. Methods: Validated scores for state and trait anxiety, depression, positive and negative state and trait affect, cognitive reappraisal, and expressive suppression were assessed in 40 subjects with CTTH and 40 healthy subjects. Associations between CTTH and psychological status were assessed through linear multivariate regression models. Results: CTTH was associated with higher scores for depression (Beta = 5.46, 95% CI: 1.04–9.88), state and trait anxiety (Beta = 12.77, 95% CI: 4.99–20.56 and Beta = 8.79, 95% CI: 2.29–15.30, respectively), and negative state affect (Beta = 5.26, 95% CI: 0.88–9.64). Conclusions: CTTH is directly associated with depression, anxiety, and negative affectivity signs despite the absence of a previously diagnosed psychiatric disorder or psychopharmacological intake. The recognition of these comorbid and psycho-affective disorders is essential to adapt the emotional management of these patients for better control.

Keywords: chronic tension-type headache; depression; anxiety; negative affect; emotion regulation; comorbidity

1. Introduction

The International Association for the Study of Pain defines pain as: "An unpleasant sensory and emotional experience associated with, or resembling that associated with, actual or potential tissue damage". This allows considering it as a singular psychophysical perception due to factors that may vary both interpersonally and individually in the same person over time and according to their physical, psychological, and social circumstances [1].

Tension-type headache, as defined by the latest revision of the International Headache Society (IHS), is a pathological disorder that fulfills the criteria of an essential pain without an organic basis or underlying structural damage [2]. It is the most common type of headache and is one of the most prevalent diseases globally, being the second in terms of global disease burden [3].

According IHS criteria, Chronic tension-type headache (CTTH) occurs with a frequency of more than 15 days a month or more than 180 days a year and persisting for more than 3 months [2]. It has been estimated that CTTH affects 2–3% of the general population [4], and it causes a significant functional limitation as well as a major impact on the quality of life [5–9].

CTTH is commonly associated with comorbidity of anxiety and depression [10–15]. Anxiety and depression are common neuropsychiatric disorders in our society, as well as in chronic pain pathologies [16], and their diagnostic clinical criteria are defined according to the Diagnostic and Statistical Manual of Mental Disorders (DSM V) [17]. Their prevalence in the Spanish population, according to the National Institute of Statistics (INE), are estimated to be 5.3% for depression and 5.8% for anxiety [18]. They are generally associated with emotional expression disorders and, at the same time, involve a disturbance in the processing and regulation of negative thinking material [19]; a reduction of negative thought material inhibition with less use of cognitive reappraisal and greater use of expressive suppression [7,20], as well as a greater faculty for rumination and difficulty in removing non-relevant negative thoughts from memory [21–23], have both been observed in subjects with high levels of depression. The rumination of negative thoughts generates a state of permanent tension that can contribute to the genesis of tension-type headaches. Thus, high levels of repetitive negative thinking have been associated not only with an emotional regulation deficit but also with the presence of tension headaches [23]. This situation may stay and become chronic, setting up a functional disturbance known as catastrophizing pain, that may persist even following the disappearance of the triggering factors [24].

The objective of our study was to evaluate the association of anxiety, depression, and positive and negative traits of affectivity and emotional management with patients with CTTH without a previous diagnosis of psychopathological disorder or consumption of psychotropic drugs or abuse of analgesics in order to consider a baseline situation without these influences, understand their conditions, and establish the most appropriate therapies for them.

2. Materials and Methods

2.1. Study Design and Participants Selection

The design of the present study was a case-control study. Forty subjects with a diagnosis of CTTH and another forty healthy controls (HC) with no headache were included. Cases were recruited from the Neurology Department of the Virgen de la Victoria University Hospital in Malaga (Spain). The CTTH diagnosis was made by a neurologist skilled in headaches, following International Classification of Headache Disorders criteria. Psychometric and socio-demographic data were collected by a clinical neuropsychologist.

Following a convenience-sampling method, controls were recruited among relatives or friends of patients who attended other departments of the same hospital for reasons other than neurological diseases. Controls were evaluated by a clinical interview with the clinical neurologist and neuropsychologist to avoid inter-observer error. Those who had any other illness or chronic disease, including any type of headache, were excluded.

The inclusion criteria for subjects with CTTH and HC were as follows: age between 20–69 years, with normal cognitive capacity for understanding and performing the neuropsychological tests as well as being informed and helped by the neuropsychologist.

Participants were excluded if they met any of the following criteria: having more than one type of headache (such as chronic tension-type headache and migraine), another chronic pain disease, chronic consumption of psychopharmacological and/or analgesic medication or taking any type of them at least 72 h prior to data collection, and clinical diagnosis or recognition of any neuropsychological disorder.

Cases in this study were incident cases since the Neurology Department of the Virgen de la Victoria University Hospital is a reference center for these pathologies, and all cases included were for the first time evaluated and diagnosed with CTTH.

The Ethics Committee of the University of Malaga approved this study (code number: S1033; date: 14 June 2010).

2.2. Psychological Status Measurement

The following questionnaires were used to collect psychological variables:

Beck Depression Inventory–II (BDI–II), to determine depression symptoms' existence and severity, consisting of 21 items. The scoring scale is as follows: 0–9 (normal), 10–18 (mild depression), 19–29 (moderate depression), and 30–63 (severe depression), with an alpha coefficient of 0.87 [25,26].

State–Trait Anxiety Inventory (STAI), to evaluate anxiety as a temporary state (state anxiety) or as a personal characteristic (trait anxiety), consisting of 20 items each, with a Cronbach's α coefficient ranging from 0.82 to 0.92. Anxiety is considered as a state with scores over 20.54 $\pm$ 10.56 for males and 23.3 $\pm$ 11.93 for females, and a trait for scores over 20.19 $\pm$ 8.89 for males and 24.99 $\pm$ 10.05 for females [27,28].

Emotion Regulation Questionnaire (ERQ), to separately assess cognitive reappraisal or regulation before an emotional experience and expressive suppression after an emotional experience. This test consists of 10 items: 6 items assess cognitive reappraisal, with a score of 4.73 $\pm$ 1.03 for men and 4.85 $\pm$ 1.0 for women and a Cronbach's α coefficient of 0.79, and 4 items assess expressive suppression, with a score of 3.80 $\pm$ 1.22 for men and 3.15 $\pm$ 1.24 for women and a Cronbach's α coefficient of 0.75 [29,30].

Positive and Negative Affect Schedule (PANAS), to evaluate subject's emotional recognition of positive or negative affect, either as a trait or a state (trait or state positive affect, trait or state negative affect). It consists of 20 items each for both trait and state. A score of 30.23 $\pm$ 6.16 for males and 30.37 $\pm$ 6.08 for females denotes positive affect with a Cronbach's α coefficient of 0.87–0.89, and a score of 20.61 $\pm$ 6.54 for males and 22.69 $\pm$ 6.83 for females denotes negative affect with a Cronbach's α coefficient of 0.89–0.91 [31,32].

2.3. Covariate Assessment

During a face-to-face interview, the following variables were collected: age, sex, body mass index (BMI), background (if they were of urban or rural background), low socio-economic status (collected by asking subjects their yearly income and comparing it with the average Spanish salary), tertiary education (subjects were asked if they had completed a given level of studies), physical activity (subjects were asked whether or not they engaged in daily physical activity), smoking (subjects were asked if they had a daily smoking habit), and dietary intake of alcohol and coffee/tea (subjects were asked if they had a daily intake habit of both).

2.4. Statistical Analysis

Sample size was calculated based on the previously published study by Holroyd et al. [12] in which differences in mean scores between CTTH patients and controls were 4.1 (pooled standard deviation (SD) = 6.5) for BDI and 10.7 (pooled SD = 9.8) on the Trait Anxiety Scale of the STAI. To detect group differences with a significance level of 0.05 and a power of 0.80, 40 participants per group are necessary for BDI scores and only 14 participants per group for STAI scores. The final sample size was $n = 80$ (40 participants per group).

Characteristics of cases and controls were described as means and standard deviations (SDs) for continuous variables and percentages for categorical variables. Group comparisons were carried out using the Mann–Whitney test, Welch's test, or Fisher's exact test as appropriate.

Adjusted mean scores of psychological variables for levels of categorical socio-demographic variables were estimated and compared with analysis of variance. Associations between psychological variables and continuous socio-demographic variables were assessed through multivariate linear regression models.

To estimate the association between CTTH and psychological status, we adjusted a multivariate linear regression model for each psychological variable as the dependent variable. These linear models included the presence of CTTH as an independent variable and were adjusted by age, sex, and potential confounding variables to avoid any confusion bias. Potential confounders were included in the model when they were associated with CTTH or the dependent variable at a level of statistical significance of $p < 0.25$ [33] and without multicollinearity.

All statistical tests were two-sided and p values < 0.05 were considered statistically significant. All statistical analyses were conducted using Stata version 17.0 (StataCorp LLC, College Station, TX, USA).

3. Results

3.1. Participants' Characteristics

Table 1 shows the sociodemographic characteristics of the study sample (CTTH vs. HC). We observed that patients with CTTH were older (50.6 years vs. 40.6 years; $p < 0.001$), had higher BMI (26.9 Kg/m^2 vs. 23.0 kg/m^2; $p < 0.001$), did less daily physical activity (17.5% vs. 52.5%; $p = 0.002$), had a lower educational level (15% vs. 70%; $p < 0.001$), and consumed less alcohol (2.5% vs. 22.5%; $p = 0.014$) and coffee or tea (30.0% vs. 60%; $p = 0.013$).

Table 1. Characteristics of CTTH patients and healthy controls.

Characteristic	CTTH	HC	*p* Value
n	40	40	
Age (years)	50.6 (10.5)	40.6 (10.5)	**<0.001** [a]
Sex (% women)	87.5	67.5	0.059 [c]
Smoking (%)	10.0	17.5	0.518 [c]
Background (% urban)	75.0	82.5	0.586 [c]
Low socio-economic status (%)	30.0	22.5	0.612 [c]
Body Mass Index (kg/m^2)	26.9 (4.4)	23.0 (2.2)	**<0.001** [b]
Physical activity (%)	17.5	52.5	**0.002** [c]
Tertiary education (%)	15.0	70.0	**<0.001** [c]
Dietary intake			
Alcohol (%)	2.5	22.5	**0.014** [c]
Coffee or tea (%)	30.0	60.0	**0.013** [c]

Data given as mean (standard deviation) or %. Statistically significant results are shown in bold ($p < 0.05$). CTTH: chronic tension-type headache. HC: healthy control. [a] Mann–Whitney test; [b] Welch's test; [c] Fisher's exact test.

3.2. Psychopathological Characteristics of the Participants

We observed, employing the same psychometric inventories, depression symptoms in 40% of HC, practically all of them with mild intensity (35.5%); in the group of CTTH patients, depression symptoms were observed in 72.5%, with mild (35%) or moderate (25.5%) intensity. State anxiety symptoms were observed in 87.5% of the CTTH patients and in 27.5% of HC; trait anxiety was observed in 75% of the CTTH patients and in 32.5% of HC (Figure 1).

3.3. Socio-Demographic Characteristics Associated with Psychological Status

Tables 2 and 3 show the associations between socio-demographic variables and psychological variables in the sample.

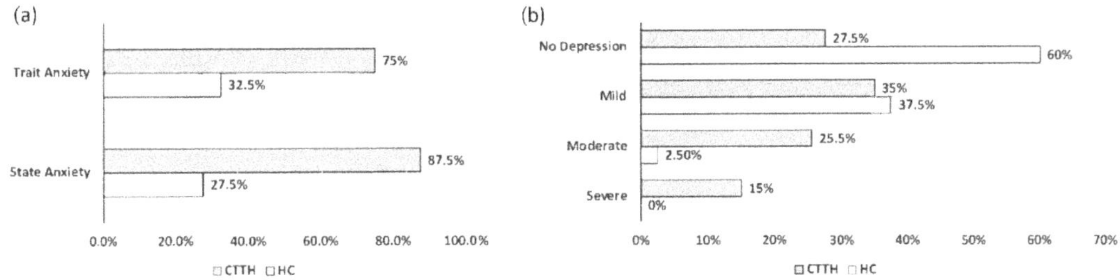

Figure 1. Presence of anxiety (**a**) and level of depression (**b**). CTTH: chronic tension-type headache. HC: healthy control.

Table 2. Adjusted [a] scores for Depression, State and Trait Anxiety, Cognitive Reappraisal and Expressive Suppression by socio-demographic variables.

Socio-Demographic Variables	*Psychological Variables*									
	Depression		**State Anxiety**		**Trait Anxiety**		**Cognitive Reappraisal**		**Expressive Suppression**	
	Adjusted Mean	p [b]	**Adjusted Mean**	p [b]	**Adjusted Mean**	p [b]	**Adjusted Mean**	p [b]	**Adjusted Mean**	p [b]
Sex [c]										
Men (n = 18)	12.0	0.915	23.2	0.138	24.4	0.785	4.2	0.560	4.8	**<0.001**
Women (n = 62)	11.8		29.4		25.3		4.4		3.3	
Background										
Urban (n = 17)	11.6	0.629	27.7	0.726	24.1	0.162	4.5	0.203	3.5	0.421
Rural (n = 63)	12.8		29.2		28.7		4.0		3.8	
Tertiary education										
Yes (n = 34)	7.6	**0.001**	20.8	**0.001**	21.5	**0.037**	4.5	0.708	3.1	**0.011**
No (n = 46)	14.9		33.3		27.7		4.3		4.0	
Low socio-economic status										
Yes (n = 21)	15.7	**0.019**	33.5	0.053	28.5	0.129	4.1	0.257	4.4	**0.001**
No (n = 59)	10.4		26.0		23.9		4.5		3.3	
Physical activity										
Yes (n = 28)	9.2	0.069	23.3	0.054	21.4	0.051	5.1	**0.001**	3.2	0.079
No (n = 52)	13.2		30.5		27.1		4.0		3.8	
Smoking										
Yes (n = 11)	11.9	0.980	28.2	0.967	23.7	0.672	5.0	0.132	4.0	0.312
No (n = 69)	11.8		28.0		25.3		4.3		3.5	
Alcohol intake										
Yes (n = 10)	11.3	0.841	28.3	0.631	21.0	0.252	4.4	0.982	3.6	0.914
No (n = 70)	11.9		25.8		25.7		4.4		3.6	
Coffee or Tea intake										
Yes (n = 36)	8.8	**0.007**	22.2	**0.002**	22.2	0.055	4.5	0.447	3.4	0.219
No (n = 44)	14.3		32.8		27.5		4.3		3.8	
Age (years)	0.129 [d]	0.152 [e]	−0.112 [d]	0.464 [e]	0.222 [d]	0.065 [e]	−0.007 [d]	0.618 [e]	0.049 [d]	**0.001** [e]
Body Mass Index (Kg/m^2)	1.089 [f]	**<0.001** [e]	0.901 [f]	0.059 [e]	1.136 [f]	**0.002** [e]	−0.108 [f]	**0.015** [e]	0.086 [f]	0.053 [e]

[a] Adjusted for age and sex; [b] F test; [c] Adjusted for age; [d] Coefficient of a linear regression model with sex as covariate; [e] Student's T-test; [f] Coefficient of a linear regression model with age and sex as covariate. Statistically significant results are shown in bold ($p < 0.05$).

Table 3. Associations of socio-demographic characteristics with scores for State/Trait Positive and Negative Affect.

Socio-Demographic Variables	*Psychological Variables*							
	State Positive Affect		Trait Positive Affect		State Negative Affect		Trait Negative Affect	
	Adjusted Mean [a]	p [b]	Adjusted Mean [a]	p [b]	Adjusted Mean [a]	p [b]	Adjusted Mean [a]	p [b]
Sex [c]								
Men (n = 18)	28.4	0.999	29.6	0.337	20.0	0.339	20.7	0.617
Women (n = 62)	28.4		31.6		22.2		19.8	
Background								
Urban (n = 17)	29.0	0.157	32.0	**0.034**	21.5	0.669	19.9	0.818
Rural (n = 63)	26.0		27.8		22.5		20.3	
Tertiary education								
Yes (n= 34)	32.4	**<0.001**	33.3	**0.039**	17.8	**0.001**	18.4	0.109
No (n = 46)	25.4		29.5		24.6		21.1	
Low socio-economic status								
Yes (n = 21)	24.0	**0.003**	29.2	0.167	25.2	**0.027**	20.5	0.644
No (n = 59)	29.9		31.8		20.5		19.8	
Physical activity								
Yes (n = 28)	32.2	**0.002**	33.4	**0.048**	19.3	0.065	19.8	0.909
No (n = 52)	26.3		29.9		23.1		20.0	
Smoking								
Yes (n = 11)	25.9	0.264	32.2	0.616	22.0	0.916	21.2	0.498
No (n = 69)	28.8		31.0		21.7		19.8	
Alcohol intake								
Yes (n = 10)	29.4	0.656	33.0	0.385	21.2	0.842	20.1	0.956
No (n = 70)	28.2		30.9		21.8		19.9	
Coffee or Tea intake								
Yes (n = 36)	30.4	**0.049**	31.4	0.798	18.6	**0.003**	18.3	**0.049**
No (n = 44)	26.7		30.9		24.3		21.3	
Age (years)	−0.126 [d]	0.114 [e]	−0.091 [d]	0.217 [e]	0.045 [d]	0.592 [e]	−0.010 [d]	0.881 [e]
Body Mass Index (Kg/m^2)	−0.309 [f]	0.215 [e]	−0.373 [f]	0.106 [e]	0.619 [f]	**0.018** [e]	0.626 [f]	**0.002** [e]

[a] Adjusted for age and sex; [b] F test; [c] Adjusted for age; [d] Coefficient of a linear regression model with sex as covariate; [e] Student's t-test; [f] Coefficient of a linear regression model with age and sex as covariates. Statistically significant results are shown in bold ($p < 0.05$).

Scores for depression (Table 2) were positively associated with low socio-economic status (p = 0.019) and BMI (p = 0.007), and negatively associated with tertiary education (p = 0.001) and coffee or tea intake (p = 0.007). State anxiety scores were inversely associated with tertiary education (p = 0.001) and coffee or tea intake (p = 0.002). Low educational level and BMI were directly associated with trait anxiety scores (p = 0.037 and p = 0.002, respectively). We found higher scores for cognitive reappraisal among subjects who do physical activity (p = 0.001) and those with lower BMI (p = 0.015). Scores for expressive suppression were higher in men of older age (p < 0.001 and p = 0.001 respectively), subjects with low socio-economic status (p = 0.001), and subjects without tertiary education (p = 0.001).

Concerning affect variables (Table 3) scores for state positive affect were positively associated with tertiary education (p < 0.001), physical activity (p = 0.002) and coffee or tea intake (0.049), and negatively associated with low socio-economic status (p = 0.003). Trait positive affect scores were higher in subjects from urban areas (p = 0.034), and those who do physical activity (p = 0.048) and with tertiary education (p = 0.039). Scores for state negative affect were higher in subjects without tertiary education and daily coffee intake (p = 0.001 and p = 0.003, respectively), and with low socio-economic status and higher BMI (p = 0.027

and $p = 0.018$, respectively). Finally, subjects without daily coffee intake and higher BMI show higher scores for trait negative affect ($p = 0.049$ and $p = 0.002$, respectively).

3.4. Association between CTTH and Psychological Parameters

Table 4 shows associations between CTTH and psychological variables. It is observed that patients with CTTH are more prone to depression (regression coefficient (Beta) = 5.46, 95% Confidence Interval (95% CI): 1.04–9.88), state and trait anxiety (Beta = 12.77, 95% CI: 4.99–20.56 and Beta = 8.79, 95%CI: 2.29–15.30, respectively), and state negative affect (Beta = 5.26, 95% CI: 0.88–9.64). We observed negative associations with cognitive reappraisal and state positive affect, although only borderline significances were found ($p = 0.098$ and $p = 0.074$, respectively).

Table 4. Associations (multivariate analysis [a]) between CTTH and psychological parameters.

Dependent Variable	Non-Standardized Regression Coefficient for CTTH (95% Confidence Interval)	*p*
Depression [b]	**5.46 (1.04, 9.88)**	**0.016**
State Anxiety [b]	**12.77 (4.99, 20.56)**	**0.002**
Trait Anxiety [b,c]	**8.79 (2.29, 15.30)**	**0.009**
Cognitive Reappraisal [c,d]	−0.69 (−1.51, 0.13)	0.098
Expressive Suppression [b]	0.02 (−0.77, 0.81)	0.962
State Positive Affect [b,c]	−3.82 (−8.02, 0.37)	0.074
Trait Positive Affect [b,c]	−2.56 (−6.82, 1.69)	0.234
State Negative Affect [b]	**5.26 (0.88, 9.64)**	**0.019**
Trait Negative Affect	1.90 (−1.83, 5.64)	0.312

[a] Linear multivariate regression models adjusted by sex, age (years), tertiary education (dichotomous), body mass index (Kg/m^2), alcohol consumption (dichotomous), and coffee or tea consumption (dichotomous); [b] Additionally adjusted by low socio-economic status (dichotomous); [c] Additionally adjusted by background (rural/urban); [d] Additionally adjusted by smoking (dichotomous). Statistically significant results are shown in bold ($p < 0.05$).

4. Discussion

Even though CTTH patients in our study were not previously diagnosed with depressive and/or anxiety disorders, we found a significant increase in depression and anxiety symptoms as comorbid conditions compared to HC.

According to INE sources, the incidence of depression and anxiety in the general Spanish population is 5.7 and 5.8%, respectively [18]. However, these numbers are supposedly estimated following criteria of prevalence in patients who come to the psychiatric consulting and, probably, the apparently healthy general population has a higher frequency of these psychopathologies [34].

For this reason, we preferred to use BDI–II and STAI inventories to achieve a more adequate assessment of depression and anxiety symptoms, both in CTTH patients and in HC subjects, despite the fact that a diagnosis of previous depressive and/or anxiety disorders was not present in either group. Thus, with this specific evaluation, we observed higher symptoms of depression and anxiety in both the HC and CTTH groups than expected by the INE [18] (Figure 1).

In the HC group, the prevalence of mild depression symptoms was estimated to be 40%, whereas in CTTH subjects the prevalence was 72.5%, being mild in 37.5% and moderate in 25.5%; this implies that depression symptoms appear in CTTH almost twice as frequently when compared to healthy subjects and that they are expressed with greater severity. In the HC subjects, the presence of state and trait anxiety symptoms were observed in 27.5% and 32.5%, respectively, while in CTTH subjects exhibited higher state and trait anxiety traits (87.5% and 75.5%, respectively); therefore, patients with CTTH have anxiety symptoms 2.5–3 times more frequently than healthy subjects. These findings have also been previously reported by numerous authors, most of them using psychometric assessment tests similar to those used in our study [9,11–13]. However, there are few references on the possible condition of dysregulation in affective and emotional expression in these patients [23] and if they do, they consider it not to be interrelated [35].

In our study we have assessed both the presence of depression and anxiety symptoms as well as affective and emotional regulation in CTTH patients without a recognized psychopathological disorder, considering that possible psycho-emotional disturbances would be causal determinants and/or influence the course of this disorder [36,37]. We observed that CTTH is associated not only with depression and anxiety, but also with a negative affect state, which implies that these subjects tend to have an emotional situation where emotions with a negative tendency predominate (such as anger, contempt, disgust, guilt, fear) [38]. This fact has also been previously appreciated, considering that high levels of negative thinking are associated with a greater emotional regulation deficit [23].

Repetitive negative thinking (whether ruminating on events that have already occurred, uncertainty, or fear of an unknown future due to excessive worry) makes people face situations with a greater state of anxiety and mood disturbance [39], reinforcing pain [40,41]. However, less negative affect conditions imply situations of greater calmness and serenity [31].

One of the main triggering and/or perpetuating factors in CTTH may be the influence of a greater negative affect that these patients have [23,42]. In our study we have found an increase in the negative state affect without a significant increase in the negative trait affect. This is a singular finding and not well-explained since it should be expected that both trait and state negative affects would be increased. This fact is not duly referenced by other authors and could be due to the characteristics of our sample, as participants might be without recognized chronic psychopathological conditions, or due to the limited number of evaluated patients.

When in confirmed psychiatric disorders, the relationship between negative affect and emotional dysregulation does not always occur, appearing in those individuals with borderline personality disorder (BPD) but not in dysthymic [43]. BPD patients have more frequent chronic headaches, and the inverse also holds [44].

A higher frequency of CTTH has been observed in patients with alexithymia (difficulty differentiating emotions) [35], however these findings could be influenced by sample characteristics, since it is not specified whether individuals in that study had a psychopathological disorder nor is it specified if they were receiving psychopharmacological or analgesic treatment that could influence emotional dysregulation [45]. It should also be considered that 55–70% of patients who come to the clinic due to headaches usually have a chronic use of medication, and most of them have an overuse or abuse [46].

We also observed that CTTH patients have a lower level of positive affective state and cognitive reappraisal. However, a larger sample would be necessary to assess whether these findings have a definitive relevance.

CTTH patients usually do symptomatic management of their symptoms with frequent consumption of psychoactive drugs due to anxiety, depression, and other psychiatric comorbidities, as well as chronic overuse of analgesics for pain [47,48] without approaching a global or multimodal physiopathological spectrum of the disease; this generates a pharmacological dependence that influences the chronification and poor control of their symptoms [49]. The use or overuse of psychoactive drugs and analgesics can alter affective states acutely during intake, during withdrawal, or as a result of chronic use [50,51].

Currently, the management of CTTH focuses especially on the symptomatic pharmacological treatment of pain, anxiety and depression comorbidity, and their repercussions (with analgesics, anxiolytics and muscle relaxants, and antidepressants); it may also be associated with other types of pharmacological and non-pharmacological options, such as: physiotherapy (electrotherapy, myofascial trigger point treatment, cervical manipulation) [52–54], psychological therapy (biofeedback, relaxation techniques) [55], or botulinum toxin [56], with uncertain efficacy in the medium and long terms. We believe that re-education and emotional support techniques that reinforce positive affect can contribute to a sustained supportive benefit for these patients; it has been observed that it is possible to re-educate negative thinking, and this implies better coping with pain, preventing pain chronification and catastrophizing conditions [24,57–59].

An important implication of our findings is the need for adding or combining psychological interventions with the management of CTTH rather than pharmacotherapy alone since a possible bidirectional relationship between CTTH and psychological comorbidities could lead to more drug dependency in these patients. Nonpharmacological therapies such as progressive muscle relaxation and deep breathing exercise have shown effectiveness in regard to pain severity, frequency, and functional status among patients with CTTH [60]. Prospective studies are needed to confirm this bidirectional relationship. This study helps in guiding a better management and treatment of CTTH, showing the importance of psychological work directed at attitude, life perspective, and the ability to face situations in a more positive and resolute way [24,57,59].

The present findings should be interpreted in the context of several limitations. First, it is possible that the small sample size may have led to no significant differences being found. Future studies with larger sample sizes and more data may support our results. Second, the neuropsychological evaluation of the CTTH patients and HC subjects was done with neuropsychological inventories and not by a psychiatric assessment, without considering other possible neuropsychiatric comorbidities in them. Third, CTTH subjects who were taking psychoactive drugs were not compared with those who were not; to assess the differences between them, it would be of interest for following studies to compare the data obtained in this analysis with other CTTH subjects with consumption of psychoactive drugs and/or analgesics overuse and assess possible differences. Finally, we have not assessed the severity of the headache and its possible relationship with neuropsychiatric symptoms.

The current study has several strengths, including that it was evaluating a special sample without previous psychopathological diagnosis, psychopharmacological treatment, or analgesic overuse or recent intake in order to consider their basal states without these determinants. The diagnosis and selection were done by a neurologist with special experience in headaches, and psychometric data were collected, face-to-face, by a trained clinical neuropsychologist. Consistent validation questionnaires in Spanish were used to assess the symptoms of depression, anxiety, affective state, and emotional management, both in the sample of CCTH and in the control group to obtain comparable results.

5. Conclusions

There is a high degree of association with depression and/or anxiety symptoms in CTTH subjects despite the lack of previously diagnosed psychiatric disorders or psychopharmacological intake and there is a high score of negative affectivity in them as a cause or manifestation of these disturbances. The recognition of these comorbid and psycho-affective disorders is essential to adapt the management of these patients for better control.

Author Contributions: Conceptualization, R.R.-G., S.R.R.-G., M.R.-A. and M.G.-B.; methodology, R.R.-G., S.R.R.-G., M.R.-A. and M.G.-B.; formal analysis, M.G.-B.; investigation, R.R-G., S.R.R.-G., M.R.-A. and M.G.-B.; resources, R.R.-G.; S.R.R.-G., M.R.-A. and M.G.-B.; data curation, R.R-G. and M.G.-B.; writing—original draft preparation, R.R.-G.; S.R.R.-G., M.R.-A. and M.G.-B.; writing—review and editing, R.R-G.; S.R.R.-G., M.R.-A. and M.G.-B.; visualization, R.R.-G.; S.R.R.-G., M.R.-A. and M.G.-B.; supervision, R.R-G. and M.G.-B.; project administration, R.R.-G. and M.G.-B. All authors have read and agreed to the published version of the manuscript.

Funding: This research received no external funding.

Institutional Review Board Statement: The study was approved by the Ethics Committee of the University of Malaga (code number: S1033; date: 14 June 2010). All subjects participated voluntarily and signed an informed consent form before inclusion. This study complies with the ethical criteria defined in the Declaration of Helsinki of 2014 and Organic Act 3/2018, of 5 December, on the Protection of Personal Data and Guarantee of Digital Rights.

Informed Consent Statement: Informed consent was obtained from all subjects involved in the study.

Data Availability Statement: The data presented in this study are available on request from the corresponding authors.

Conflicts of Interest: The authors declare no conflict of interest. The authors alone are responsible for the content and writing of the article.

References

1. Raja, S.N.; Carr, D.B.; Cohen, M.; Finnerup, N.B.; Flor, H.; Gibson, S.; Keefe, F.J.; Mogil, J.S.; Ringkamp, M.; Sluka, K.A.; et al. The revised International Association for the Study of Pain definition of pain: Concepts, challenges, and compromises. *Pain* **2020**, *161*, 1976–1982. [CrossRef] [PubMed]
2. Headache Classification Committee of the International Headache Society (IHS). The International Classification of Headache Disorders, 3rd edition. *Cephalalgia* **2018**, *38*, 1–211. [CrossRef] [PubMed]
3. GBD 2016 Disease and Injury Incidence and Prevalence Collaborators. Global, regional, and national incidence, prevalence, and years lived with disability for 328 diseases and injuries for 195 countries, 1990–2016: A systematic analysis for the Global Burden of Disease Study 2016. *Lancet* **2017**, *390*, 1211–1259. [CrossRef]
4. Bendtsen, L.; Jensen, R. Tension-type headache: The most common, but also the most neglected, headache disorder. *Curr. Opin. Neurol.* **2006**, *19*, 305–309. [CrossRef]
5. Linde, M.; Gustavsson, A.; Stovner, L.J.; Steiner, T.J.; Barré, J.; Katsarava, Z.; Lainez, J.M.; Lampl, C.; Lantéri-Minet, M.; Rastenyte, D.; et al. The cost of headache disorders in Europe: The Eurolight project. *Eur. J. Neurol.* **2012**, *19*, 703–711. [CrossRef] [PubMed]
6. Chowdhury, D. Tension type headache. *Ann. Indian Acad. Neurol.* **2012**, *15*, S83–S88.
7. Nichols, V.P.; Ellard, D.R.; Griffiths, F.E.; Kamal, A.; Underwood, M.; Taylor, S.J.C. The lived experience of chronic headache: A systematic review and synthesis of the qualitative literature. *BMJ Open* **2017**, *7*, e019929. [CrossRef]
8. Steiner, T.J.; Antonac, F.; Jensen, R.; Lainez, M.J.; Lanteri-Minet, M.; Valade, D. Recommendations for headache service organization and delivery in Europe. *J. Headache Pain* **2011**, *12*, 419–426. [CrossRef]
9. Peñacoba-Puente, C.; Fernández-de-Las-Peñas, C.; González-Gutierrez, J.L.; Miangolarra-Page, J.C.; Pareja, J.A. Interaction between anxiety, depression, quality of life and clinical parameters in chronic tension-type headache. *Eur. J. Pain* **2008**, *12*, 886–894. [CrossRef]
10. Zebenholzer, K.; Lechner, A.; Broessner, G.; Lampl, C.; Luthringshausen, G.; Wuschitz, A.; Obmann, S.M.; Berek, K.; Wöber, C. Impact of depression and anxiety on burden and management of episodic and chronic headaches—A cross-sectional multicentre study in eight Austrian headache centres. *J. Headache Pain* **2016**, *17*, 15. [CrossRef]
11. Mongini, F.; Rota, E.; Deregibus, A.; Ferrero, L.; Migliaretti, G.; Cavallo, F.; Mongini, T.; Novello, A. Accompanying symptoms and psychiatric comorbidity in migraine and tension-type headache patients. *J. Psychosom. Res.* **2006**, *61*, 447–451. [CrossRef] [PubMed]
12. Holroyd, K.A.; Stensland, M.; Lipchik, G.L.; Hill, K.R.; O'Donnell, F.S.; Cordingley, G. Psychosocial correlates and impact of chronic tension-type headaches. *Headache* **2000**, *40*, 3–16. [CrossRef]
13. Song, T.J.; Cho, S.J.; Kim, W.J.; Yang, K.I.K.; Yun, C.H.; Chu, M.K. Anxiety and Depression in Tension-Type Headache: A Population-Based Study. *PLoS ONE* **2016**, *11*, e0165316. [CrossRef]
14. Beghi, E.; Bussone, G.; D'Amico, D.; Cortelli, P.; Cevoli, S.; Manzoni, G.C.; Torelli, P.; Tonini, M.C.; Allais, G.; De Simone, R.; et al. Headache, anxiety and depressive disorders: The HADAS study. *J. Headache Pain* **2010**, *11*, 141–150. [CrossRef] [PubMed]
15. Zwart, J.A.; Dyb, G.; Hagen, K.; Ødegård, K.J.; Dahl, A.A.; Bovim, G.; Stovner, L.J. Depression and anxiety disorders associated with headache frequency. The Nord-Trøndelag Health Study. *Eur. J. Neurol.* **2003**, *10*, 147–152. [CrossRef] [PubMed]
16. Gatchel, R.J.; Peng, Y.B.; Peters, M.L.; Fuchs, P.N.; Turk, D.C. The biopsychosocial approach to chronic pain: Scientific advances and future directions. *Psychol. Bull.* **2007**, *133*, 581–624. [CrossRef]
17. American Psychiatric Association. *Diagnostic and Statistical Manual of Mental Disorders*, 5th ed.; American Psychiatric Publishing: Washington, DC, USA, 2013.
18. Instituto Nacional de Estadística. Encuesta Europea de Salud en España. 2020. Available online: https://www.ine.es/prensa/eese_2020.pdf (accessed on 10 July 2022).
19. Hu, T.; Zhang, D.; Wang, J.; Mistry, R.; Ran, G.; Wang, X. Relation between emotion regulation and mental health: A meta-analysis review. *Psychol. Rep.* **2014**, *114*, 341–362. [CrossRef]
20. Kim, J.; Cho, S.J.; Kim, W.J.; Yang, K.I.; Yun, C.H.; Chu, M.K. Insomnia in tension-type headache: A population-based study. *J. Headache Pain* **2017**, *18*, 95. [CrossRef]

21. Cooney, R.E.; Joormann, J.; Eugène, F.; Dennis, E.L.; Gotlib, I.H. Neural correlates of rumination in depression. *Cogn. Affect. Behav. Neurosci.* **2010**, *10*, 470–478. [CrossRef]
22. Chuen Yee Lo, B.; Lau, S.; Cheung, S.H.; Allen, N.B. The impact of rumination on internal attention switching. *Cogn. Emot.* **2012**, *26*, 209–223. [CrossRef]
23. Haratian, A.; Amjadi, M.M.; Ghandehari, K.; Hatamian, H.; Kiani, S.; Habibi, M.; Aghababaei, Z.; Ataei, M. Emotion Regulation Difficulties and Repetitive Negative Thinking in Patients with Tension Headaches and Migraine. *Casp. J. Neurol. Sci.* **2020**, *6*, 147–155.
24. Pulvers, K.; Hood, A. The role of positive traits and pain catastrophizing in pain perception. *Curr. Pain Headache Rep.* **2013**, *17*, 330. [CrossRef] [PubMed]
25. Beck, A.T.; Steer, R.A.; Brown, G.K. *Manual for the Beck Depression Inventory-II*; Psychological Corporation: San Antonio, TX, USA, 1996.
26. Sanz, J.; Perdigón, A.L.; Vázquez, C. The Spanish adaptation of Beck's Depression Inventory–II (BDI–II): 2. Psychometric properties in the general population. *Clínica Y Salud* **2003**, *14*, 249–280.
27. Spielberger, C.; Gorsuch, R.; Lushene, R. *STAI Manual for the State-Trait Anxiety Inventory*; Consulting Psychologist Press: Palo Alto, CA, USA, 1970.
28. Spielberger, C.; Gorsuch, R.; Lushene, R. *Cuestionario de Ansiedad Estado-Rasgo. Manual*, 4th ed.; TEA Ediciones SA: Madrid, Spain, 1993.
29. Gross, J.J.; John, O.P. Individual differences in two emotion regulation processes: Implications for affect, relationships, and well-being. *J. Pers. Soc. Psychol.* **2003**, *85*, 348–362. [PubMed]
30. Cabello, R.; Salguero, J.M.; Fernández-Berrocal, P.; Gross, J.J. A Spanish adaptation of the Emotion Regulation Questionnaire. *Eur. J. Psychol. Assess.* **2013**, *29*, 234–240.
31. Watson, D.; Clark, L.A.; Tellegen, A. Development and validation of brief measures of positive and negative affect: The PANAS scales. *J. Pers. Soc. Psychol.* **1988**, *54*, 1063–1070. [CrossRef]
32. Sandín, B.; Chorot, P.; Lostao, L.; Joiner, T.E.; Santed, M.A.; Valiente, R.M. Escalas PANAS de Afecto Positivo y Negativo: Validación factorial y convergencia estructural. *Psicothema* **1999**, *11*, 37–51.
33. Hosmer, D.W.; Lemeshow, S.; Sturdivant, R.X. *Applied Logistic Regression*, 3rd ed.; John Wiley & Sons: Hoboken, NJ, USA, 2013.
34. Heckman, B.D.; Holroyd, K.A. Tension-type headache and psychiatric comorbidity. *Curr. Sci. Inc.* **2006**, *10*, 439–447. [CrossRef]
35. Yücel, B.; Kora, K.; Ozyalçín, S.; Alçalar, N.; Ozdemir, O.; Yücel, A. Depression, automatic thoughts, alexithymia, and assertiveness in patients with tension-type headache. *Headache* **2002**, *42*, 194–199. [CrossRef]
36. Koechlin, H.; Coakley, R.; Schechtery, N.; Werner, C.; Kossowsky, J. The role of emotion regulation in chronic pain: A systematic literature review. *J. Psychosom. Res.* **2018**, *107*, 38–45. [CrossRef] [PubMed]
37. Salomons, T.V.; Nusslock, R.; Detloff, A.; Johnstone, T.; Davidson, R.J. Neural emotion regulation circuitry underlying anxiolytic effects of perceived control over pain. *J. Cogn. Neurosci.* **2015**, *27*, 222–233. [CrossRef] [PubMed]
38. Watson, D.; Clark, L.A.; Tellegen, A. Desarrollo y validación de medidas breves de afecto positivo y negativo: Las escalas PANAS. *Rev. Pers. Y Psicol. Soc.* **1988**, *54*, 1063–1070. [CrossRef]
39. Gross, J.J. Antecedent- and response-focused emotion regulation: Divergent consequences for experience, expression, and physiology. *J. Pers. Soc. Psychol.* **1998**, *74*, 224–237. [CrossRef] [PubMed]
40. Thompson, T.; Keogh, E.; French, C.C.; Davis, R. Anxiety sensitivity and pain: Generalisability across noxious stimuli. *Pain* **2008**, *134*, 187–196. [CrossRef] [PubMed]
41. Esteve, M.R.; Camacho, L. Anxiety sensitivity, body vigilance and fear of pain. *Behav. Res. Ther.* **2008**, *46*, 715–727.
42. Wang, J.; Huang, Q.; Li, N.; Tan, G.; Chen, L.; Zhou, J. Triggers of migraine and tension-type headache in China: A clinic-based survey. *Eur. J. Neurol.* **2013**, *20*, 689–696. [CrossRef]
43. Bradley, B.; DeFife, J.A.; Guarnaccia, C.; Phifer, J.; Fani, N.; Ressler, K.J.; Westen, D. Emotion dysregulation and negative affect: Association with psychiatric symptoms. *J. Clin. Psychiatry* **2011**, *72*, 685–691. [CrossRef]
44. Saper, J.R.; Lake, A.E. Borderline Personality Disorder and the Chronic Headache Patient: Review and Management Recommendations. *Headache* **2008**, *42*, 663–674. [CrossRef]
45. Lutz, J.; Gross, R.T.; Vargovichb, A.M. Difficulties in emotion regulation and chronic pain-related disability and opioid misuse. *Addict. Behav.* **2018**, *87*, 200–205. [CrossRef]
46. Rapoport, A.; Stang, P.; Gutterman, D.L.; Cady, R.; Markley, H.; Weeks, R.; Saiers, J.; Fox, A.W. Analgesic rebound headache in clinical practice: Data from a physician survey. *Headache* **1996**, *36*, 14–19. [CrossRef]
47. Da Silva, A.N.; Lake, A.E. 3rd. Clinical aspects of medication overuse headaches. *Headache* **2014**, *54*, 211–217. [CrossRef] [PubMed]
48. Schnider, P.; Aull, S.; Feucht, M.; Mraz, M.; Travniczek, A.; Zeiler, K.; Wessely, P. Use and abuse of analgesics in tension-type headache. *Cephalalgia* **1994**, *14*, 162–167. [CrossRef] [PubMed]
49. Nauser, J.W.; Nelson, C.I.; Gross, R.T.; Vargovich, A.M. Pain Experiences and Their Relation to Opioid Misuse Risk and Emotion Dysregulation. *Pain Res. Manag.* **2020**, *2020*, 7234625. [CrossRef] [PubMed]
50. Baker, T.B.; Japuntich, S.J.; Hogle, J.M.; McCarthy, D.E.; Curtin, J.J. Pharmacologic and Behavioral Withdrawal from Addictive Drugs. *Curr. Dir. Psychol. Sci.* **2006**, *15*, 232–236. [CrossRef]
51. Koob, G.F.; Le Moal, M. Drug abuse: Hedonic homeostatic dysregulation. *Science* **1997**, *278*, 52–58. [CrossRef]

52. Do, J.K.; Kwon, D.R. Efficacy of cranial microcurrent stimulation in patients with tension-type headache: A prospective, randomised, double-blinded, sham-controlled clinical trial. *Int. J. Clin. Pr.* **2021**, *75*, e14437. [CrossRef]
53. Cumplido-Trasmonte, C.; Fernández-González, P.; Alguacil-Diego, I.M.; Molina-Rueda, F. Manual therapy in adults with tension-type headache: A systematic review. Terapia manual en adultos con cefalea tensional: Revisión sistemática. *Neurologia* **2021**, *36*, 537–547. [CrossRef]
54. Fernández-de-Las-Peñas, C.; Florencio, L.L.; Plaza-Manzano, G.; Arias-Buría, J.L. Clinical Reasoning Behind Non-Pharmacological Interventions for the Management of Headaches: A Narrative Literature Review. *Int. J. Environ. Res. Public Health* **2020**, *17*, 4126. [CrossRef] [PubMed]
55. Lee, H.J.; Lee, J.H.; Cho, E.Y.; Kim, S.M.; Yoon, S. Efficacy of psychological treatment for headache disorder: A systematic review and meta-analysis. *J. Headache Pain* **2019**, *20*, 17. [CrossRef]
56. Freund, B.; Rao, A. Efficacy of Botulinum Toxin in Tension-Type Headaches: A Systematic Review of the Literature. *Pain Pr.* **2019**, *19*, 541–551. [CrossRef]
57. Roditi, D.; Robinson, M.E.; Litwins, N. Effects of coping statements on experimental pain in chronic pain patients. *J. Pain Res.* **2009**, *2*, 109–116. [CrossRef] [PubMed]
58. Thorn, B.E.; Pence, L.B.; Ward, L.C.; Kilgo, G.; Clements, K.L.; Cross, T.H.; Davis, A.M.; Tsui, P.W. A randomized clinical trial of targeted cognitive behavioral treatment to reduce catastrophizing in chronic headache sufferers. *J. Pain* **2007**, *8*, 938–949. [CrossRef] [PubMed]
59. Wenzel, A. Cognitive reappraisal. In *Process Based CBT. The Science and Core Clinical Competencies of Cognitive Behavioral Therapy*; Hayes, S.C., Hofmann, S.G., Eds.; New Harbinger Publications, Inc: Oakland, CA, USA, 2008; pp. 325–337.
60. Gopichandran, L.; Srivastsava, A.K.; Vanamail, P.; Kanniammal, C.; Valli, G.; Mahendra, J.; Dhandapani, M. Relaxation and Deep Breathing Exercise on Pain, Disability, and Sleep Among Patients with Chronic Tension-Type Headache. *Holist. Nurs. Pract.* **2021**. ahead of print. [CrossRef] [PubMed]

Journal of
Clinical Medicine

MDPI

Review

Dry Needling in Physical Therapy Treatment of Chronic Neck Pain: Systematic Review

Manuel Rodríguez-Huguet [1,2,*], Maria Jesus Vinolo-Gil [1] and Jorge Góngora-Rodríguez [3]

1 Department of Nursing and Physiotherapy, University of Cádiz, 11009 Cádiz, Spain; mariajesus.vinolo@uca.es
2 Clinical Management Unit Rehabilitation, University Hospital of Puerta del Mar, 11009 Cádiz, Spain
3 Department of Physiotherapy, Osuna School University, University of Sevilla, 41640 Sevilla, Spain; jorgemgr@euosuna.org
* Correspondence: manuel.rodriguez@uca.es

Abstract: Chronic Neck Pain (CNP) is one of the main causes of disability worldwide, and it is necessary to promote new strategies of therapeutic approach in the treatment of chronic pain. Dry needling (DN) is defined as an invasive physiotherapy technique used in the treatment of neuromusculoskeletal disorders. The purpose of this review was to assess the effectiveness of invasive techniques in treatment of CNP. The search focused on randomized clinical trials, and according to the selection criteria, eight studies were obtained. In conclusion, DN can be an effective treatment option for CNP, positive outcomes were achieved in the short-term and in the follow-up performed between three and six months, and this technique may offer better outcomes than a placebo intervention based on the application of simulated DN.

Keywords: chronic pain; dry needling; neck pain; physical therapy

Citation: Rodríguez-Huguet, M.; Vinolo-Gil, M.J.; Góngora-Rodríguez, J. Dry Needling in Physical Therapy Treatment of Chronic Neck Pain: Systematic Review. *J. Clin. Med.* **2022**, *11*, 2370. https://doi.org/10.3390/jcm11092370

Academic Editors: Carmen María Galvez Sánchez, Casandra I. Montoro Aguilar and Markus W. Hollmann

Received: 23 March 2022
Accepted: 21 April 2022
Published: 23 April 2022

1. Introduction

Cervical pain, or neck pain, can be defined as that unpleasant sensory and emotional experience associated with actual or potential tissue damage that affects the cervical region [1,2]. It may range from the suboccipital line to the level of the spine of the scapula [1,2]. Therefore, this condition is one of the main causes of disability worldwide, with a prevalence above 30% [1,3,4], which entails significant socioeconomic costs [1,4–7]. It becomes persistent in half of the cases, which exhibit chronic symptoms and recurrent pain episodes [3] that can extend beyond six months [5]. However, the updated classification of chronic pain allows us to understand chronic neck pain (CNP) as a primary entity that is not associated with a specific etiology, and lasts with functional limitation and emotional affectation for more than three months [8].

Studies indicate a female predominance in terms of the distribution by sex of neck pain, and in the age range of 35–49 years [9], especially from the age of 45 [10]. Typically, research indicates that the risk of neck pain is linked to physical and psychosocial factors, and may be related to lack of movement, sustained postures, and office work [11,12].

Usually, neck pain is nonspecific. This way, it is not attributable to fractures, trauma, or any other specific recognizable pathology (such as infectious, vascular, or oncological conditions). Therefore, examination and clinical analysis can rule out the warning signs that may relate the cases to specific systemic origins [1,3,5,13]. The assessment of patients with neck pain involves determining: (a) pain intensity by means of pain assessment scales (VAS or NPRS); (b) associated functionality or disabilities (Neck Disability Index, NDI) [14]; and (c) mobility of the cervical region (Range of Motion, ROM) [5]. Furthermore, in the complete evaluation of the neck, it is convenient to attend to the neurological assessment based on myotomes, dermatomes, and reflexes [15–17].

In addition, the assessment of patients with CNP should necessarily objectify comorbidities and associated symptoms [18], such as anxiety, depression, stress (DASS

Scale) [19–22], and sleep disorders (Pittsburgh Sleep Quality Index) [20]. At present, it is essential to deepen the investigation of new strategies of therapeutic approach in the treatment of chronic pain, especially motivated by the low efficacy of the available pharmacological treatments. Therefore, it becomes convenient to look for alternatives that are effective and tolerable for patients [7,13].

In regard to physical therapy in the management of neck pain, the effect of conventional treatments is limited. Electrotherapy modalities (transcutaneous electrical nerve stimulation) could improve symptoms in CNP, but the evidence in this regard is not conclusive [23], and passive mobilization or manipulative therapy is no better than an exercise program [24].

Dry needling (DN) is defined as a minimally invasive physiotherapy technique used in the treatment of neuromusculoskeletal disorders [25–27]. Needling the most painful point of the muscle is also contemplated in traditional Chinese medicine acupuncture, where it is described as Ah Shi needling [28,29]. Its goal is to restore the physiological state of the tissue, reduce pain levels, and increase mobility through the application of mechanical stimuli caused by the insertion of acupuncture needles. These techniques are typical of physiotherapy, in which the physical agents pass through patient's skin [25–27]. With respect to the classification of the needling technique, the purpose of classifying it as "dry" is to emphasize the condition of the physical agent, i.e., in this type of technique, there is neither pharmacological substances nor chemical agents introduced nor any fluid extracted [25,27,30].

Regarding the DN techniques, it is possible to define two modalities based on the depth of needle insertions [26,30]. The first is superficial DN, which confers analgesia by hyperstimulation. In this case, the needle goes through the skin and the subcutaneous cellular tissue without reaching the muscle. The other modality is deep DN, which functions directly on myofascial trigger points, since the needle penetrates the muscle tissue and has the ability to produce a local twitch response [26,30,31]. Local twitch response is an involuntary contraction reaction of the muscles to the mechanical stimulus of the puncture [31].

Thus, DN could be a treatment option for myofascial trigger points (hypersensitive areas of muscle fibers associated with motor abnormalities) [27]. However, precision during needling and the performance of the procedure seems to be essential for its correct development, with the ability of the physiotherapists being vital to perform the treatment properly [25,32]. The mechanism of action of DN is related to the effects achieved on myofascial trigger points [27]. The persistence of these points can favor the phenomenon of central sensitization. Therefore, it is possible to apply these invasive physiotherapy techniques in chronic pathologies [33], and it can be recommended for the treatment of CNP [27].

The present study arises from the need to deepen knowledge about the treatment of CNP through physiotherapy techniques. The goal was to assess the effectiveness of invasive techniques—specifically DN—in pain levels, and their relationship with other measurement variables, in order to establish action guidelines for the physiotherapeutic approach to CNP. Therefore, the main objective is to do a systematic evaluation of the effectiveness of dry needling in the treatment of chronic neck pain.

2. Materials and Methods

The present study is a systematic review addressing the topic being assessed in order to meet the effectiveness of dry needling in the treatment of chronic neck pain. The search focused on randomized clinical trials in order to obtain results that might indicate the most appropriate invasive physiotherapy intervention modalities in the treatment of CNP. The present work was conducted following the Preferred Reporting for Systematic Reviews and Meta-Analyses (PRISMA) guidelines, establishing the research approach through the PICO question format, namely: the selected population was the one that suffered from CNP (P = population); the intervention was invasive physical therapy treatment with DN

(I = intervention) in comparison to other treatment modalities, or absence of treatment as control (C= comparison); and the main variable of the study was pain, which could be related to cervical mobility, quality of life, and other associated aspects (O = outcomes).

The bibliographic search was conducted in PubMed, Web of Science, Scopus, and Cochrane Library as reference databases within health sciences, and PEDro, as a specific database of evidence-based knowledge within physiotherapy. The search was conducted between October 2021 and March 2022. The descriptors "chronic neck pain" and "dry needling" were entered using the Boolean operator "AND" in databases. Therefore, the formula used was ""chronic neck pain" AND "dry needling"". The search was focused on these terms in order to analyze the updated evidence easily accessible to the health professional. It would be possible to include more combined terms; however, the intention was to show the results that the reader could quickly find. The research does not apply terms such as arthritis, fibromyalgia, or whiplash, since the search focuses on chronic neck pain and a primary origin not associated with trauma or systemic cause.

The following selection criteria were established so that the search was limited to clinical trials and prospective studies. This review includes only randomized clinical trials, and the randomization minimizes selection bias and favors similarity between groups [34,35].

Those studies included assessments of neck pain as one of the main study variables. Chronic pain is currently defined according to the new classification of World Health Organization [8], and the inclusion criteria establish the selection of patients with chronic neck pain exclusively. The selected studies start from subjects with chronic neck pain not associated with a traumatic origin. Interventions dedicated to physical therapy treatment were also inclusion criteria, and studies that focused on traditional Chinese medicine acupuncture were excluded.

The studies discarded were those with repeated references, articles in languages other than Spanish or English, systematic reviews, study projects, case reports, studies of other pathologies or non-physiotherapeutic techniques or not conducted in humans, and those that were not considered relevant. The articles resulting from the search guidelines were analyzed in detail, and the selection of articles included investigations that had valid measurement instruments.

The methodological quality of the studies was assessed through the score they achieved in the PEDro scale. PEDro is Physiotherapy Evidence Database, and this database is the main reference for finding out the most up-to-date evidence in physiotherapy, and for assessing the effects of interventions and treatments. The PEDro scale includes 11 items that allow assessing the methodological quality of randomized clinical trials with a final score range of 0 to 10; the items included in the PEDro scale can be seen in Appendix A. The PEDro scale has excellent reliability for use in systematic reviews of randomized clinical trials [36]. The scores were obtained from the PEDro database and later revised.

Two independent reviewers performed the search and screened the articles; these reviewers applied inclusion/exclusion criteria, and later, another reviewer supervised the systematic review, quality assessment, and data extraction. The authors decided to make a qualitative analysis due to heterogeneity in outcome measurement precluding statistical integration with guarantees.

3. Results

According to the search and selection criteria previously established in the method of the present study, eleven studies are obtained. The PRISMA flow diagram (Figure 1) illustrates the conduction and selection stages of the systematic review.

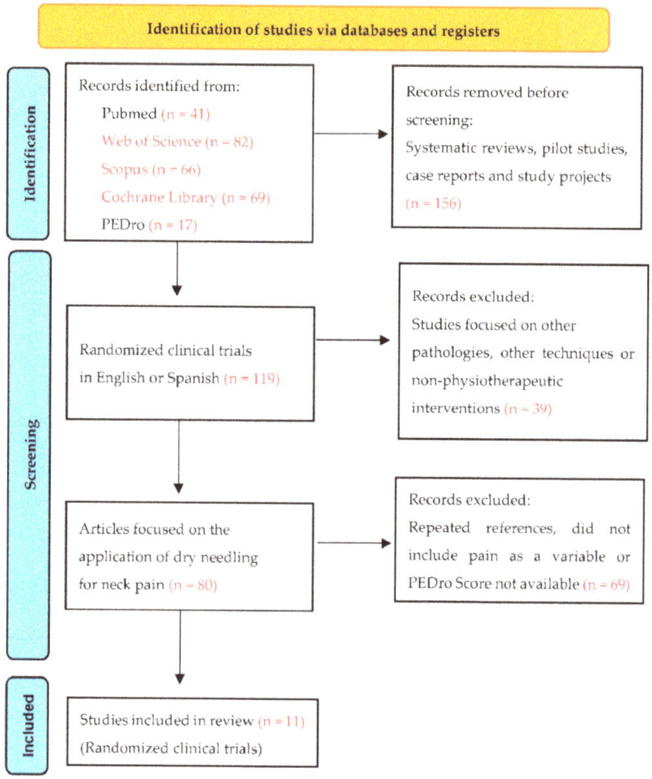

Figure 1. PRISMA flow diagram. Identification of the results obtained from the databases.

Table 1 presents the characteristics of the clinical trials based on the application of DN in the treatment of CNP assessed (the sample was composed of 807 individuals with CNP). All included articles were randomized clinical trials. In addition, it indicates the methodological quality of these studies based on their score obtained in the PEDro scale. This scale assesses the level of recommendation of scientific articles based on their methodological quality, establishing a score between zero and ten. All the selected studies obtained a minimum score of five, and most of them reached a score of seven or eight points, which is a high recommendation level. This table also indicates the outcomes measures in the studies and the assessment time. PEDro score details of each randomized clinical trial selected are available in Appendix A. On the other hand, Appendix B includes specific details of each article, such as countries where studies were conducted, or the type of clinical center. Moreover, this table indicates the outcomes measurements and the assessment time of each randomized clinical trial selected.

Table 1. Characteristics of the clinical trials included in the systematic review.

Author (Year)	Participants and Groups	PEDro Score	Outcomes Measurements	Assessment Time
Irnich et al. (2002)	N = 36	6/10	Pain ROM	Immediate post-intervention (15–30 min after treatment)
Llamas-Ramos et al. (2014)	N = 94 (47/47)	8/10	Pain PPT ROM Disability	3 post-intervention evaluations: 1 day, 1 week, and 2 weeks after the last treatment session

Table 1. *Cont.*

Author (Year)	Participants and Groups	PEDro Score	Outcomes Measurements	Assessment Time
Cerezo-Téllez et al. (2016)	N = 130 (65/65)	6/10	Pain PPT ROM Strength NDI	6 post intervention evaluations: After 2 sessions; after full treatment; 15, 30, 90, and 180 days
Sobhani et al. (2017)	N = 39 (13/13/13)	5/10	Pain Catastrophism ROM NDI	1 post-intervention evaluation
Manafnezhad et al. (2019)	N = 70 (35/35)	6/10	Pain NDI PPT	Evaluation prior to each session and final evaluation 1 week after the last session
Gallego-Sendarrubias et al. (2020)	N = 101 (47/54)	7/10	Pain PPT ROM NDI	3 post-intervention evaluations: an evaluation after each session and one month after completion
Stieven et al. (2020)	N = 116 (58/58)	8/10	Pain NDI Perceived effects Catastrophism Sleep quality Self-efficacy	3 post-intervention evaluations: at 1, 3, and 6 months
Gattie et al. (2021)	N = 77 (37/40)	7/10	NDI Pain Perceived effects	3 post-intervention evaluations: 4 weeks, at 6 months, and 1 year
Leon-Hernandez et al. (2021)	N = 40 (20/20)	7/10	Pain PPT NDI Kinesiophobia	2 post-intervention evaluations: 1 week and 1 month
Stieven et al. (2021)	N = 44 (15/14/15)	8/10	PPT Pain	Immediate post-intervention evaluation and at 10 min
Valiente-Castrillo et al. (2021)	N = 60 (21/20/19)	8/10	Pain NDI Kinesiophobia Catastrophism Depression Anxiety Fear Pain Pain Attitudes	3 post-intervention evaluations: at the end of the full treatment, at 1 month, and at 3 months

Abbreviations. PPT: Pressure Pain Threshold; ROM: Range of Motion; NDI: Neck Disability Index.

The intensity of pain (VAS or NPRS scales) was the most assessed variable in the studies [29,37–46], followed by disability (NDI or NPQ scales) [37–45], and the pressure pain threshold (PPT) [37,39,41,42,45,46]. Five of the studies had assessed the cervical range of motion (ROM) [29,37,39,40,42], and other variables had also been included to a lesser extent, such as strength [39], perceived effects [43,44], self-efficacy [43], level of catastrophism [38,40,43], sleep quality [43], kinesiophobia [38,45], anxiety [38], depression [38], fear of pain [38], or attitude towards pain [38]. The length of follow-up varied between immediate post-intervention evaluation [29,46] and one year [44].

Table 2 shows the data referring to the intervention protocols (DN treatment and alternative treatment) of each of the clinical trials included in this systematic review, and the results of each study.

Table 2. Interventions, procedures, and results of the clinical trials based on the application of DN in the treatment of CNP.

Author (Year)	DN Interventions Protocols	Alternative Treatment	Results
Irnich et al. (2002)	1 session DN trapezius, splenius, levator scapula, semispinalis, sternocleidomastoid, scalenus, and paravertebral muscles (LTR: Yes)	1 session: needle acupuncture at distant point/sham laser acupuncture	There are no differences between DN and sham laser acupuncture
Llamas-Ramos et al. (2014)	2 sessions in 2 weeks: DN upper trapezius (LTR: Yes)	2 sessions in 2 weeks: trigger point manual therapy (compression, stretching, and friction massage)	↓ Pain ↑ PPT ↑ ROM ↓ Disability
Cerezo-Téllez et al. (2016)	4 sessions in 2 weeks: DN multifidus, splenius, upper trapezius, and levator scapula (LTR: Yes) + passive stretching	4 sessions in 2 weeks: Passive stretching	↓ Pain ↑ PPT ↑ ROM ↑ Strength ↓ NDI
Sobhani et al. (2017)	5 sessions in 10 days: bilateral DN upper trapezius and levator scapulae (LTR: not specified) + passive stretching	5 sessions in 10 days: manual therapy (ischemic trigger point compression)/kinesiotaping on trigger points	↓ Pain ↓ Catastrophism ↑ ROM ↓ NDI
Manafnezhad et al. (2019)	3 sessions, 1 per week: DN upper trapezius (LTR: Yes)	3 sessions, 1 per week: Shock waves in upper trapezius	↓ Pain ↓ NDI ↑ PPT
Gallego-Sendarrubias et al. (2020)	2 sessions with 1 week interval: DN trapezius and levator scapulae (LTR: Yes) + manual therapy	2 sessions with 1 week interval: sham DN + manual therapy	↓ Pain ↑ PPT ↑ ROM ↓ NDI
Stieven et al. (2020)	4–6 sessions in 4 weeks: DN upper trapezius, middle trapezius, multifidus, splenius, and levator scapulae (LTR: Yes) + manual therapy (cervical and thoracic mobilization) and exercise	4–6 sessions in 4 weeks: manual therapy (cervical and thoracic mobilization) and exercise	↓ Pain
Gattie et al. (2021)	7 sessions in 4 weeks: DN trapezius, levator scapulae, splenius capitis, semispinalis, spinalis capitis, multifidus, and suboccipital muscles (LTR: Yes) + manual therapy + exercise	7 sessions in 4 weeks: sham DN + manual therapy + exercise	There are no differences between DN and sham DN
Leon-Hernandez et al. (2021)	2 sessions, 1 per week: DN upper trapezius (LTR: Yes) + 15 min of percutaneous needle electrical stimulation (low frequency versus high frequency)		↓ Pain (There are no differences between DN modalities)
Stieven et al. (2021)	1 session unilateral DN upper trapezius (LTR: Yes)	1 session: myofascial release or sham DN	↑ PPT ↓ Pain
Valiente-Castrillo et al. (2021)	6 sessions in 2 weeks: DN upper trapezius, levator scapulae, splenius, and multifidus (LTR: Yes) + self-stretching + 3 sessions 30′ therapy education for one of the experimental groups	10 sessions in 2 weeks: 15 min TENS and 15 min Microwave + self-stretching	↓ Pain ↓ NDI ↓ Kinesiophobia ↓ Catastrophism ↓ Depression ↓ Anxiety ↓ Fear Pain ↑ Pain Attitudes

Abbreviations. DN: Dry Needling; LTR: Local Twitch Response; PPT: Pressure Pain Threshold; ROM: Range of Motion; NDI: Neck Disability Index.

The sample assessed was composed of 807 individuals with CNP, of which 398 had received physical therapy treatment with DN alone [37,41,46] or in combination with other complementary interventions [38–40,42–45]; 373 had received alternative treatment with different modalities based on manual therapy, such as stretching [37–40,42–44,46], therapeutic exercises [43,44], shock waves [41], kinesiotaping [40], transcutaneous electrical nerve stimulation (TENS) [38], microwave [38], or simulated DN [44,46]; and 36 received three treatments options (DN, needle acupuncture at distant point, and sham laser acupuncture with a 1 week wash-out period between the interventions) [29].

Treatments based on the isolated intervention of DN [41,46], including post-needling stretching [38–40], or combined with other therapies [38,42–44] were proposed in comparison to other treatment modalities, including placebo treatments using sham DN [29,42,46]. The intervention protocols ranged from a single treatment session [29,46] to a four-week treatment with up to seven sessions [44]. All the studies collected were randomized clinical trials, which entailed high methodological quality and in-depth analyses that allowed making comparisons and drawing significant conclusions.

The duration of the intervention in the trials was variable; likewise, the follow-up time indicates differences between investigations. Studies indicated positive effects on pain [37–43,46], NDI [38–42], ROM [37,39,40,42], PPT [37,39,41,42,46], strength [39], and other psychological factors such as kinesiophobia, catastrophic thinking, anxiety, depression, fear of pain, or attitude towards pain [38,40].

4. Discussion

The present review examined the most recent evidence available on the use and benefits of DN in physical therapy treatment for CNP.

Pain intensity was the most studied variable. Depending on the study, the VAS scale or the NPRS scale were used, both of which showed high reproducibility and validity for short- and long-term assessments of CNP [39,41,45]. Focusing on pain, the shorter-term outcomes were found in the study conducted by Stieven et al. [46], who demonstrated the immediate effects of a single-session treatment. That study showed that a single application of unilateral DN at the level of the upper trapezius or a myofascial release treatment of that musculature could generate a superior response than a placebo intervention, with pain reduction and increased PPT.

Along the same lines, Sobhani et al. [40] performed a treatment of five sessions distributed over ten days, collecting the outcomes at the end of the intervention. These authors observed a decrease in the intensity of pain, a reduction in the NDI and catastrophic thoughts, and increased mobility. Disability is one of the important variables to assess in CNP, and usually the NDI scale is used, but it is also possible to use other scales [37]. Manafnezhad et al. [41] found similar effects in the follow-up performed one week after the intervention and after three weeks of treatment at the rate of one session per week.

On the other hand, it was possible to find the outcomes achieved by carrying out a long-term follow-up of up to one year (Gattie et al. [44]), also in comparison to a placebo-type sham DN treatment. These authors did not observe differences between DN treatment and placebo. Alternatives interventions based on placebo could suggest that the use of placebo could have a place within the treatments. In the same way, Irnich et al. [29] compared the effects of DN intervention versus traditional acupuncture treatment and sham laser treatment in the same group of patients.

Most studies performed intermediate follow-ups ranging from three to six months [38,39,43], with four to six treatment sessions distributed over two to four weeks or one-month follow-up after two sessions with a one-week interval [42]. Regarding the periodicity of the follow-ups, it is worth highlighting the study conducted by Cerezo-Téllez et al. [39], whose analysis included up to six post-intervention assessments.

Upper trapezius and levator muscles are the most frequent locations to DN intervention [40–42,46]; usually, the treatment of studies includes DN in this musculature, and combine with other neck or back muscles [38,39,43,44]. Another aspect to analyze would be the performance of the technique unilaterally or bilaterally, although this would be related to the lateral predominance of the symptoms and to the proprioceptive control at the cervical level, as in cases in which there is a structural alteration [47].

In general, the applications of DN techniques were performed following the action protocols described by Travell and Simons [38,39,42], with rapid needle entry and exit movements under the principles of the Hong's technique, in which the needle is retracted into the subcutaneous tissue and then redirected to another region of the trigger point without leaving the tissue [37–39] by means of the therapists' wrist flexion and extension movements [41]. The procedure affected the musculature bilaterally [40], for one to two minutes [41], seeking to trigger local spasm reactions [38,39,42,43]. In many cases, DN was accompanied by ischemic compression or post-needling stretching [38–40,42,43,45].

The mechanism of action of DN can be determined based on chemical and neurophysiological changes associated with mechanical effects derived from the stimulus provided by invasive therapy on soft tissue [41], which modifies the activation and perpetuation of myofascial trigger points [42]; usually, the DN intervention causes a local twitch response [29,38,39,41,43,44]. The methodology proposed in the assessed studies focused on DN interventions on the myofascial trigger points of the upper trapezius and the levator scapulae muscles [40–42,46], and, to a lesser extent, on splenium, multifidus, or middle trapezius, among others [38,39,43,44].

In the studies that performed placebo interventions with sham DN [42,44,46], sham needles were used to simulate the puncture without penetrating the skin [42,44]. Therefore, three of the studies apply sham DN as a placebo treatment option, making it necessary to delve into the conditions of this intervention. In addition, the alternative treatment was performed by means of stretching [38,39], therapeutic physical exercises [43,44], or manual therapy techniques (myofascial treatment or cervical and thoracic mobilization) [40,42–44,46], or by means of instrumental techniques, such as TENS and microwaves [38], kinesiotaping [40], and waves shock [41].

The research of Leon-Hernandez et al. [45] stands out for the comparison between two treatment modalities based on the percutaneous needle electrical stimulation after application of the DN. In these treatments, the DN of the upper trapezius is performed (with local twitch response), and then a low or high frequency current is applied. This option shows that DN can be combined with associated electrotherapy and can obtain similar results regardless of the stimulation frequency.

Specifically, in the comparison between DN interventions and alternative treatments, it should be noted that the results may be favorable to invasive treatments [38,39,42]. However, the differences may be slight [43], or the beneficial effects achieved may be similar to those produced by the control treatment [40,41].

In general, it highlights the relationship of the treatment proposals of the trials with therapeutic exercise, and this reinforces the need to direct physiotherapy to a relationship between passive techniques and active movement. Exercise has positive effects on pain and functionality, and it should be oriented according to the interests and individual goals of the patient, and could be combined with instrumental techniques [48,49]. Is it possible to achieve the same effects with manual stimulation of the treatment points? [50].

The positive outcomes that support the success of DN with respect to the study variables in CNP are in line with the conclusions of other previous reviews that considered this type of intervention useful [51]. In addition, the changes achieved are in line with what has been observed in other related pathologies, such as headache [52,53]. In the same way, it would be possible to point out that these effects could help reduce over-medicalization, and represent a non-pharmacological treatment option [7], which will also reduce the socioeconomic costs associated with neck pain.

The results found show us that the research that relates the DN intervention with CNP is growing, with most of the available articles being recent. The limitations of the present review were due to the differences in the articles analyzed in terms of treatment protocols and lengths of follow-up. With a view to future clinical trials, it would be interesting to have tools that assess objective changes in muscle function or performance, with greater presence of strength tests and novel tools, such as electromyographic control. Consequently, it would also be convenient to study other aspects, such as the relationship between the results achieved with DN and the size of the needles or the duration of the session, and, above all, the type of employment of the patients, because the effect could be limited in work with static positions or head-down postures [11,48].

5. Conclusions

In conclusion, it is possible to point out that DN can be an effective treatment option for CNP. The studies assessed indicated that positive outcomes were achieved in the short-term and in the follow-up performed between three and six months, although the effects seemed to be limited in very long-term follow-ups, such as one year.

DN may offer better outcomes than a placebo intervention based on the application of simulated DN. This way, further research on this topic should be conducted. The recommended length of DN treatment for CNP would range from four to six sessions, distributed over two to four weeks.

The physiotherapy treatment based on the application of DN is mainly focused on performing the technique on the upper trapezius and the levator scapulae muscles following the procedures described by Travell and Simons. This intervention is normally performed bilaterally. It can be accompanied by stretching and combined with other techniques of manual therapy and therapeutic exercises. In addition to having effects on the intensity of CNP, DN treatments have had positive effects on other related variables such as ROM, NDI, or PPT.

Further studies are needed to combine the monitoring of short-and long-term variables, preferably in comparison to placebo interventions. Those studies will allow determining the changes induced at the structural and functional levels of the affected musculature, such as changes in the levels of strength or in the patterns of muscle activation derived from the interventions.

The variability among studies could make it difficult to determine conclusions.

Author Contributions: Conceptualization, M.R.-H. and J.G.-R.; methodology, M.R.-H., J.G.-R. and M.J.V.-G.; software, J.G.-R.; validation, J.G.-R.; formal analysis, J.G.-R. and M.J.V.-G.; investigation, J.G.-R. and M.R.-H.; resources, M.R.-H.; data curation, J.G.-R.; writing—original draft preparation, J.G.-R.; writing—review and editing, M.R.-H. and M.J.V.-G.; visualization, J.G.-R.; supervision, M.R.-H. and M.J.V.-G.; project administration, M.R.-H. All authors have read and agreed to the published version of the manuscript.

Funding: This research received no external funding.

Institutional Review Board Statement: Not applicable.

Informed Consent Statement: Not applicable.

Data Availability Statement: Not applicable.

Conflicts of Interest: The authors declare no conflict of interest.

Appendix A

Appendix A indicates the PEDro Scale score details of each randomized clinical trial included in the systematic review.

The PEDro Scale assesses the following sections: eligibility criteria were specified; subjects were randomly allocated to groups (in a crossover study, subjects were randomly allocated an order in which treatments were received); allocation was concealed; the groups were similar at baseline regarding the most important prognostic indicators; there was blinding of all subjects; there was blinding of all therapists who administered the therapy; there was blinding of all assessors who measured at least one key outcome; measures of at least one key outcome were obtained from more than 85% of the subjects initially allocated to groups; all subjects for whom outcome measures were available received the treatment or control condition as allocated, or, where this was not the case, data for at least one key outcome was analyzed by "intention to treat"; the results of between-group statistical comparisons are reported for at least one key outcome; the study provides both point measures and measures of variability for at least one key outcome.

Table A1. PEDro Score.

Author (Year)	PEDro Scale Score Details
Irnich et al. (2002)	Eligibility criteria: Yes; Random allocation: Yes; Concealed allocation: Yes; Baseline comparability: No; Blind subjects: No; Blind therapists: No; Blind assessors: Yes; Adequate follow-up: Yes; Intention-to-treat analysis: No; Between-group comparisons: Yes; Point estimates and variability: Yes.
Llamas-Ramos et al. (2014)	Eligibility criteria: Yes; Random allocation: Yes; Concealed allocation: Yes; Baseline comparability: Yes; Blind subjects: No; Blind therapists: No; Blind assessors: Yes; Adequate follow-up: Yes; Intention-to-treat analysis: Yes; Between-group comparisons: Yes; Point estimates and variability: Yes.
Cerezo-Téllez et al. (2016)	Eligibility criteria: Yes; Random allocation: Yes; Concealed allocation: No; Baseline comparability: Yes; Blind subjects: No; Blind therapists: No; Blind assessors: Yes; Adequate follow-up: Yes; Intention-to-treat analysis: No; Between-group comparisons: Yes; Point estimates and variability: Yes.
Sobhani et al. (2017)	Eligibility criteria: No; Random allocation: Yes; Concealed allocation: No; Baseline comparability: Yes; Blind subjects: No; Blind therapists: No; Blind assessors: Yes; Adequate follow-up: No; Intention-to-treat analysis: No; Between-group comparisons: Yes; Point estimates and variability: Yes.
Manafnezhad et al. (2019)	Eligibility criteria: Yes; Random allocation: Yes; Concealed allocation: No; Baseline comparability: Yes; Blind subjects: No; Blind therapists: No; Blind assessors: Yes; Adequate follow-up: Yes; Intention-to-treat analysis: No; Between-group comparisons: Yes; Point estimates and variability: Yes.
Gallego-Sendarrubias et al. (2020)	Eligibility criteria: Yes; Random allocation: Yes; Concealed allocation: Yes; Baseline comparability: Yes; Blind subjects: Yes; Blind therapists: No; Blind assessors: No; Adequate follow-up: Yes; Intention-to-treat analysis: Yes; Between-group comparisons: No; Point estimates and variability: Yes.
Stieven et al. (2020)	Eligibility criteria: Yes; Random allocation: Yes; Concealed allocation: Yes; Baseline comparability: Yes; Blind subjects: No; Blind therapists: No; Blind assessors: Yes; Adequate follow-up: Yes; Intention-to-treat analysis: Yes; Between-group comparisons: Yes; Point estimates and variability: Yes.
Gattie et al. (2021)	Eligibility criteria: Yes; Random allocation: Yes; Concealed allocation: Yes; Baseline comparability: Yes; Blind subjects: No; Blind therapists: No; Blind assessors: No; Adequate follow-up: Yes; Intention-to-treat analysis: Yes; Between-group comparisons: Yes; Point estimates and variability: Yes.
Leon-Hernandez et al. (2021)	Eligibility criteria: Yes; Random allocation: Yes; Concealed allocation: No; Baseline comparability: Yes; Blind subjects: Yes; Blind therapists: No; Blind assessors: Yes; Adequate follow-up: Yes; Intention-to-treat analysis: No; Between-group comparisons: Yes; Point estimates and variability: Yes.
Stieven et al. (2021)	Eligibility criteria: No; Random allocation: Yes; Concealed allocation: Yes; Baseline comparability: Yes; Blind subjects: No; Blind therapists: No; Blind assessors: Yes; Adequate follow-up: Yes; Intention-to-treat analysis: Yes; Between-group comparisons: Yes; Point estimates and variability: Yes.
Valiente-Castrillo et al. (2021)	Eligibility criteria: Yes; Random allocation: Yes; Concealed allocation: Yes; Baseline comparability: Yes; Blind subjects: No; Blind therapists: No; Blind assessors: Yes; Adequate follow-up: Yes; Intention-to-treat analysis: Yes; Between-group comparisons: Yes; Point estimates and variability: Yes.

Appendix B

Appendix B show more characteristics of each randomized clinical trial included in the systematic review.

Table A2. Specific details of studies.

Author (Year)	Country and Clinical Center
Irnich et al. (2002)	Germany—Department of Physical Medicine and Rehabilitation and the Interdisciplinary Pain Unit at the University of Munich
Llamas-Ramos et al. (2014)	Spain—Alcalá de Henares University
Cerezo-Téllez et al. (2016)	Spain—Primary Health Care Centers at Alcalá de Henares Health Area
Sobhani et al. (2017)	Iran—Baqiyatallah University of Medical Sciences
Manafnezhad et al. (2019)	Iran—Tabriz University of Medical Sciences
Gallego-Sendarrubias et al. (2020)	Spain—San Carlos Clinic Hospital
Stieven et al. (2020)	Brazil—Physiotherapy private clinic in Porto Alegre
Gattie et al. (2021)	United States—Concord Hospital and Franciscan Health physical therapy clinics
Leon-Hernandez et al. (2021)	Spain—La Salle University, Madrid
Stieven et al. (2021)	Brazil—Physiotherapy private clinic in Porto Alegre
Valiente-Castrillo et al. (2021)	Spain—Infanta Sofía University Hospital

References

1. Bier, J.D.; Scholten-Peeters, W.G.; Staal, J.B.; Pool, J.; van Tulder, M.W.; Beekman, E.; Knoop, J.; Meerhoff, G.; Verhagen, A.P. Clinical Practice Guideline for Physical Therapy Assessment and Treatment in Patients With Nonspecific Neck Pain. *Phys. Ther.* **2018**, *98*, 162–171. [CrossRef] [PubMed]
2. Climent, J.M.; Bagó, J.; García-López, A. Patología dolorosa de columna: Cervicalgia, dorsalgia y lumbalgia. *FMC Form. Médica Contin. Atención Primaria* **2014**, *21*, 9–35. [CrossRef]
3. Cohen, S.P. Epidemiology, diagnosis, and treatment of neck pain. In *Mayo Clinic Proceedings*; Elsevier Ltd.: Amsterdam, The Netherland, 2015; Volume 90, pp. 284–299.
4. Cohen, S.P.; Hooten, W.M. Advances in the diagnosis and management of neck pain. *BMJ* **2017**, *358*, j3221. [CrossRef] [PubMed]
5. Blanpied, P.R.; Gross, A.R.; Elliott, J.M.; Devaney, L.L.; Clewley, D.; Walton, D.M.; Sparks, C.; Robertson, E.K. Clinical practice guidelines linked to the international classification of functioning, disability and health from the orthopaedic section of the American physical therapy association. *J. Orthop. Sports Phys. Ther.* **2017**, *47*, A1–A83. [CrossRef] [PubMed]
6. Liu, R.; Kurihara, C.; Tsai, H.T.; Silvestri, P.J.; Bennett, M.I.; Pasquina, P.F.; Cohen, S.P. Classification and treatment of chronic Neck pain: A longitudinal cohort study. *Reg. Anesth. Pain Med.* **2017**, *42*, 52–61. [CrossRef]
7. George, S.Z.; Lentz, T.A.; Goertz, C.M. Back and neck pain: In support of routine delivery of non-pharmacologic treatments as a way to improve individual and population health. *Transl. Res.* **2021**, *234*, 129–140. [CrossRef]
8. Treede, R.-D.; Rief, W.; Barke, A.; Aziz, Q.; Bennett, M.I.; Benoliel, R.; Cohen, M.; Evers, S.; Finnerup, N.B.; First, M.B.; et al. A classification of chronic pain for ICD-11. *Pain* **2015**, *156*, 1003. [CrossRef]
9. Hoy, D.G.; Protani, M.; De, R.; Buchbinder, R. The epidemiology of neck pain. *Best Pract. Res. Clin. Rheumatol.* **2010**, *24*, 783–792. [CrossRef]
10. Lin, I.H.; Chang, K.H.; Liou, T.H.; Tsou, C.M.; Huang, Y.C. Progressive shoulder-neck exercise on cervical muscle functions in middle-aged and senior patients with chronic neck pain. *Eur. J. Phys. Rehabil. Med.* **2018**, *54*, 13–21. [CrossRef]
11. Ye, S.; Jing, Q.; Wei, C.; Lu, J. Risk factors of non-specific neck pain and low back pain in computer-using office workers in China: A cross-sectional study. *BMJ Open* **2017**, *7*, e014914. [CrossRef]
12. Kim, R.; Wiest, C.; Clark, K.; Cook, C.; Horn, M. Identifying risk factors for first-episode neck pain: A systematic review. *Musculoskelet. Sci. Pract.* **2018**, *33*, 77–83. [CrossRef] [PubMed]
13. Côté, P.; Yu, H.; Shearer, H.M.; Randhawa, K.; Wong, J.J.; Mior, S.; Ameis, A.; Carroll, L.J.; Nordin, M.; Varatharajan, S.; et al. Non-pharmacological management of persistent headaches associated with neck pain: A clinical practice guideline from the Ontario protocol for traffic injury management (OPTIMa) collaboration. *Eur. J. Pain* **2019**, *23*, 1051–1070. [CrossRef] [PubMed]
14. Andrade Ortega, J.A.; Martínez, A.D.D.; Ruiz, R.A. Validación de una versión Española del Índice de Discapacidad Cervical. *Med. Clin.* **2008**, *130*, 85–89. [CrossRef] [PubMed]
15. Riew, K.D. Variations in cervical myotomes and dermatomes. *Spine J.* **2019**, *19*, 1143–1145. [CrossRef]
16. Furukawa, Y.; Miyaji, Y.; Kadoya, A.; Kamiya, H.; Chiba, T.; Hokkoku, K.I.; Hatanaka, Y.; Imafuku, I.; Miyoshi, K.; Sonoo, M. Determining C5, C6 and C7 myotomes through comparative analyses of clinical, MRI and EMG findings in cervical radiculopathy. *Clin. Neurophysiol. Pract.* **2021**, *6*, 88–92. [CrossRef]
17. Hakimi, K.; Spanier, D. Electrodiagnosis of cervical radiculopathy. *Phys. Med. Rehabil. Clin. N. Am.* **2013**, *24*, 1–12. [CrossRef]
18. Malfliet, A.; Coppieters, I.; Van Wilgen, P.; Kregel, J.; De Pauw, R.; Dolphens, M.; Ickmans, K. Brain changes associated with cognitive and emotional factors in chronic pain: A systematic review. *Eur. J. Pain* **2017**, *21*, 769–786. [CrossRef]

19. Yavuz, B.G.; Aydinlar, E.I.; Dikmen, P.Y.; Incesu, C. Association between somatic amplification, anxiety, depression, stress and migraine. *J. Headache Pain* **2013**, *14*, 53. [CrossRef]
20. Yalinay Dikmen, P.; Yavuz, B.G.; Aydinlar, E.I. The relationships between migraine, depression, anxiety, stress, and sleep disturbances. *Acta Neurol. Belg.* **2015**, *115*, 117–122. [CrossRef]
21. Peres, M.F.P.; Mercante, J.P.P.; Tobo, P.R.; Kamei, H.; Bigal, M.E. Anxiety and depression symptoms and migraine: A symptom-based approach research. *J. Headache Pain* **2017**, *18*, 1–8. [CrossRef]
22. Seidel, S.; Beisteiner, R.; Manecke, M.; Aslan, T.S.; Wöber, C. Psychiatric comorbidities and photophobia in patients with migraine. *J. Headache Pain* **2017**, *18*, 1–4. [CrossRef] [PubMed]
23. Martimbianco, A.L.C.; Porfírio, G.J.M.; Pacheco, R.L.; Torloni, M.R.; Riera, R. Transcutaneous electrical nerve stimulation (TENS) for chronic neck pain. *Cochrane Database Syst. Rev.* **2019**, *2019*, 1465–1858. [CrossRef] [PubMed]
24. Ganesh, G.S.; Mohanty, P.; Pattnaik, M.; Mishra, C. Effectiveness of mobilization therapy and exercises in mechanical neck pain. *Physiother. Theory Pract.* **2015**, *31*, 99–106. [CrossRef] [PubMed]
25. Mayoral-del-Moral, O.; Torres-Lacomba, M. Fisioterapia invasiva y punción seca. Informe sobre la eficacia de la punción seca en el tratamiento del síndrome de dolor miofascial y sobre su uso en Fisioterapia. *Cuest. Fisioter.* **2009**, *38*, 206–217.
26. Capó-Juan, M.A. Síndrome de dolor miofascial cervical. Revisión narrativa del tratamiento fisioterápico. *An. Sist. Sanit. Navar.* **2015**, *38*, 105–116. [CrossRef]
27. Mayoral-del-Moral, O.; Salvat-Salvat, I. Punción seca de los puntos gatillo miofasciales. In *Fisioterapia Invasiva*; Valera-Garrido, F., Minaya-Muñoz, F., Eds.; Elsevier: Barcelona, Spain, 2017; pp. 297–312. ISBN 978-84-9113-099-4.
28. Li, X.; Wang, R.; Xing, X.; Shi, X.; Tian, J.; Zhang, J.; Ge, L.; Zhang, J.; Li, L.; Yang, K. Acupuncture for Myofascial Pain Syndrome: A Network Meta-Analysis of 33 Randomized Controlled Trials. *Pain Physician* **2017**, *20*, E883–E902.
29. Irnich, D.; Behrens, N.; Gleditsch, J.M.; Stör, W.; Schreiber, M.A.; Schöps, P.; Vickers, A.J.; Beyer, A. Immediate effects of dry needling and acupuncture at distant points in chronic neck pain: Results of a randomized, double-blind, sham-controlled crossover trial. *Pain* **2002**, *99*, 83–89. [CrossRef]
30. Mayoral-del-Moral, O. Fisioterapia invasiva del síndrome de dolor miofascial. *Fisioterapia* **2005**, *27*, 69–75. [CrossRef]
31. Perreault, T.; Dunning, J.; Butts, R. The local twitch response during trigger point dry needling: Is it necessary for successful outcomes? *J. Bodyw. Mov. Ther.* **2017**, *21*, 940–947. [CrossRef]
32. Dommerholt, J.; Mayoral-del-Moral, O.; Gröbli, C. Trigger Point Dry Needling. *J. Man. Manip. Ther.* **2006**, *14*, 70–87. [CrossRef]
33. Shah, J.P.; Thaker, N. Punción seca segmentaria en el dolor musculoesquelético. In *Fisioterapia Invasiva*; Valera-Garrido, F., Minaya-Muñoz, F., Eds.; Elsevier: Barcelona, Spain, 2017; pp. 335–356. ISBN 978-84-9113-099-4.
34. Lim, C.Y.; In, J. Randomization in clinical studies. *Korean J. Anesthesiol.* **2019**, *72*, 221–232. [CrossRef] [PubMed]
35. Rosenberger, W.F.; Uschner, D.; Wang, Y. Randomization: The forgotten component of the randomized clinical trial. *Stat. Med.* **2019**, *38*, 1–12. [CrossRef] [PubMed]
36. Maher, C.G.; Sherrington, C.; Herbert, R.D.; Moseley, A.M.; Elkins, M. Reliability of the PEDro scale for rating quality of randomized controlled trials. *Phys. Ther.* **2003**, *83*, 713–721. [CrossRef] [PubMed]
37. Llamas-Ramos, R.; Pecos-Martín, D.; Gallego-Izquierdo, T.; Llamas-Ramos, I.; Plaza-Manzano, G.; Ortega-Santiago, R.; Cleland, J.; Fernández-de-las-Peñas, C. Comparison of the short-term outcomes between trigger point dry needling and trigger point manual therapy for the management of chronic mechanical neck pain: A randomized clinical trial. *J. Orthop. Sports Phys. Ther.* **2014**, *44*, 852–861. [CrossRef] [PubMed]
38. Valiente-Castrillo, P.; Martín-Pintado-Zugasti, A.; Calvo-Lobo, C.; Beltran-Alacreu, H.; Fernández-Carnero, J. Effects of pain neuroscience education and dry needling for the management of patients with chronic myofascial neck pain: A randomized clinical trial. *Acupunct. Med.* **2021**, *39*, 91–105. [CrossRef] [PubMed]
39. Cerezo-Téllez, E.; Torres-Lacomba, M.; Fuentes-Gallardo, I.; Perez-Muñoz, M.; Mayoral-Del-Moral, O.; Lluch-Girbés, E.; Prieto-Valiente, L.; Falla, D. Effectiveness of dry needling for chronic nonspecific neck pain: A randomized, single-blinded, clinical trial. *Pain* **2016**, *157*, 1905–1917. [CrossRef] [PubMed]
40. Sobhani, V.; Shamsoddini, A.; Khatibi-Aghda, A.; Mazloum, V.; Kia, H.H.; Emami Meybodi, M.K. Effectiveness of dry needling, manual therapy, and Kinesio Taping for patients with chronic myofascial neck pain: A single-blind clinical trial. *Trauma Mon.* **2017**, *22*. [CrossRef]
41. Manafnezhad, J.; Salahzadeh, Z.; Salimi, M.; Ghaderi, F.; Ghojazadeh, M. The effects of shock wave and dry needling on active trigger points of upper trapezius muscle in patients with non-specific neck pain: A randomized clinical trial. *J. Back Musculoskelet. Rehabil.* **2019**, *32*, 811–818. [CrossRef]
42. Gallego-Sendarrubias, G.M.; Rodríguez-Sanz, D.; Calvo-Lobo, C.; Martín, J.L. Efficacy of dry needling as an adjunct to manual therapy for patients with chronic mechanical neck pain: A randomised clinical trial. *Acupunct. Med.* **2020**, *38*, 244–254. [CrossRef]
43. Stieven, F.; Ferreira, G.; Wiebusch, M.; de Araújo, F.; da Rosa, L.; Silva, M. Dry Needling Combined With Guideline-Based Physical Therapy Provides No Added Benefit in the Management of Chronic Neck Pain: A Randomized Controlled Trial. *J. Orthop. Sports Phys. Ther.* **2020**, *50*, 447–454. [CrossRef]
44. Gattie, E.; Cleland, J.A.; Pandya, J.; Snodgrass, S. Dry Needling Adds No Benefit to the Treatment of Neck Pain: A Sham-Controlled Randomized Clinical Trial With 1-Year Follow-up. *J. Orthop. Sports Phys. Ther.* **2021**, *51*, 37–45. [CrossRef] [PubMed]

45. Leon-Hernandez, J.V.; Calvo-Lobo, C.; Martin-Pinado-Zugasti, A.; Fernandez-Carnero, J.; Beltran-Alacreu, H. Effectiveness of Dry Needling with Percutaneous Electrical Nerve Stimulation of High Frequency Versus Low Frequency in Patients with Myofascial Neck Pain. *Pain Physician* **2021**, *24*, 135–143.
46. Stieven, F.; Ferreira, G.; de Araújo, F.; Angellos, R.; Silva, M.; da Rosa, L. Immediate Effects of Dry Needling and Myofascial Release on Local and Widespread Pressure Pain Threshold in Individuals With Active Upper Trapezius Trigger Points: A Randomized Clinical Trial. *J. Manipulative Physiol. Ther.* **2021**, *44*, 95–102. [CrossRef] [PubMed]
47. Reddy, R.S.; Tedla, J.S.; Dixit, S.; Abohashrh, M. Cervical proprioception and its relationship with neck pain intensity in subjects with cervical spondylosis. *BMC Musculoskelet. Disord.* **2019**, *20*, 1–7. [CrossRef] [PubMed]
48. Iqbal, Z.A.; Alghadir, A.H.; Anwer, S. Efficacy of Deep Cervical Flexor Muscle Training on Neck Pain, Functional Disability, and Muscle Endurance in School Teachers: A Clinical Trial. *Biomed Res. Int.* **2021**, *2021*, 7190808. [CrossRef] [PubMed]
49. Iversen, V.M.; Vasseljen, O.; Mork, P.J.; Fimland, M.S. Resistance training vs general physical exercise in multidisciplinary rehabilitation of chronic neck pain: A randomized controlled trial. *J. Rehabil. Med.* **2018**, *50*, 743–750. [CrossRef]
50. Kim, M.; Kim, J. Effects of Acupressure on Pain, Flexibility, and Substance P in Middle-Age Women with Chronic Neck Pain. *J. Altern. Complement. Med.* **2021**, *27*, 160–167. [CrossRef]
51. Callejas-Marcos, I.; Torrijos-Bravo, A.; Torres-Chica, B.; Ortiz-Gutiérrez, R.M. Eficacia de la punción seca en la cervicalgia en comparación con otras técnicas de fisioterapia: Una revisión sistemática. *Rehabilitación* **2019**, *53*, 189–197. [CrossRef]
52. Gildir, S.; Tüzün, E.H.; Eroğlu, G.; Eker, L. A randomized trial of trigger point dry needling versus sham needling for chronic tension-type headache. *Medicine* **2019**, *98*, e14520. [CrossRef]
53. Pourahmadi, M.; Mohseni-Bandpei, M.A.; Keshtkar, A.; Koes, B.W.; Fernández-De-Las-Peñas, C.; Dommerholt, J.; Bahramian, M. Effectiveness of dry needling for improving pain and disability in adults with tension-type, cervicogenic, or migraine headaches: Protocol for a systematic review. *Chiropr. Man. Therap.* **2019**, *27*, 1–11. [CrossRef]

Journal of
Clinical Medicine

MDPI

Review

The Unhappy Shoulder: A Conceptual Review of the Psychosomatics of Shoulder Pain

Matthias Vogel [1,*], Marius Binneböse [1], Hannah Wallis [1], Christoph H. Lohmann [2], Florian Junne [1], Alexander Berth [2] and Christian Riediger [2]

[1] Department of Psychosomatic Medicine and Psychotherapy, Otto-von Guericke-University of Magdeburg, 39120 Magdeburg, Germany
[2] Department of Orthopedic Surgery, Otto-von Guericke-University of Magdeburg, 39120 Magdeburg, Germany
* Correspondence: matthias.vogel@med.ovgu.de; Tel.: +49391-6714200; Fax: +49391-6714202

Abstract: Introduction: Chronic pain is a multifaceted disorder genuinely entangled with psychic and psychosomatic symptoms, which are typically involved in the processes of chronification. The impingement syndrome of the shoulder is no exception to this rule, but several studies have shown respective peculiarities among those with pain and impingement of the shoulder. Notably, chronic pain is a lateralized experience, and, similarly, its psychosomatic correlates may be attached to the hemispheres functionally. Aim: The present review therefore gives an overview of the respective findings, with regard not only to psychopathology, but also to personality factors and psychologic trauma, since the latter are reportedly associated with chronic pain. Moreover, we acknowledge symmetry as a possible pathogenic factor. Methods: This narrative review followed the current standards for conducting narrative studies. Based on prior findings, our research strategy included the relevance of psychotraumatologic and symmetrical aspects, as well as comorbidity. We retrieved the relevant literature reporting on the impact of psychopathology as well as personality features on shoulder pain, as published up to January 2022 from the Medline database (1966–2022). Study selecton: We included numerous studies, and considered the contextual relevance of studies referring to the neuropsychosomatics of chronic pain. Results: Pain-specific fears, depression, and anxiety are important predictors of shoulder pain, and the latter is generally overrepresented in those with trauma and PTSD. Moreover, associations of shoulder pain with psychological variables are stronger as regards surgical therapies as compared to conservative ones. This may point to a specific and possibly trauma-related vulnerability for perioperative maladaptation. Additionally, functional hemispheric lateralization may explain some of those results given that limb pain is a naturally lateralized experience. Not least, psychosocial risk factors are shared between shoulder pain and its physical comorbidities (e.g., hypertension), and the incapacitated state of the shoulder is a massive threat to the function of the human body as a whole. Conclusions: This review suggests the involvement of psychosomatic and psychotraumatologic factors in shoulder impingement-related chronic pain, but the inconclusiveness and heterogeneity of the literature in the field is possibly suggestive of other determinants such as laterality.

Keywords: shoulder; impingement; chronic pain; functional hemispheric lateralization; psychosomatic; negative affect

Citation: Vogel, M.; Binneböse, M.; Wallis, H.; Lohmann, C.H.; Junne, F.; Berth, A.; Riediger, C. The Unhappy Shoulder: A Conceptual Review of the Psychosomatics of Shoulder Pain. *J. Clin. Med.* **2022**, *11*, 5490. https://doi.org/10.3390/jcm11185490

Academic Editors: Markus W. Hollmann, Casandra I. Montoro Aguilar and Carmen María Galvez Sánchez

Received: 10 June 2022
Accepted: 14 September 2022
Published: 19 September 2022

1. Introduction

The term impingement of the shoulder refers to a chronic and painful dysfunction of the shoulder causing pain at the elevation and internal rotation of the humerus. The prevalence of shoulder impingement syndrome (SIS) differs between age cohorts and was reported to range from 4.7–46.7% in terms of 1-year prevalence [1]. Similarly, McBeth [2] estimated that 20–33% of the general population were likely to report shoulder pain. Moreover, shoulder pain is among the leading causes of disability, and the third ranking condition of chronic pain. SIS is multifactorial and associated with a variety of disorders, e.g., diabetes, arterial hypertension, and thyroid disorders, as well as adiposity. In the general population, lesions of the rotator cuff (85%) and/or impingement syndromes [3] represent the most frequent causes of shoulder pain. SIS is a chronic, regional pain syndrome and based on the mechanical irritation of subacromial structures. The corresponding pain manifests mostly at the abduction of the limb from 70°–120° (i.e., the so-called "painful arc", and clinical hallmark), at working overhead, and when lying on the affected side of the body [3]. The theory of impingement posits that mechanical conflicts between different structures of the joint would lead to shoulder pain, the second to third ranking musculoskeletal disorder [4]. Mostly, its symptomatic course develops in the fifth decade and the age peak lies between 40 and 60 years. Dependent on the precipitating factors, impingement syndromes are classified as primarily extrinsic, secondarily extrinsic, intrinsic, and inner impingement [5]. Glenohumeral osteoarthritis (secondarily extrinsic) and rotator cuff tear (intrinsic) are two common causes of shoulder pain, and the manifestation in the shoulder is the third ranking of osteoarthritis [6]. Regarding the subacromial impingement, ref. [7] a contact between the rotator cuff and the acromion causes damage to the rotator cuff, which may in turn confine the subacromial space. As a result, the mobility of the joint is compromised, even to the extent of total immobility as possibly suffered from in frozen shoulder. The structures mainly involved in the respective mechanical irritation are the supraspinatus tendon and the bursa subacromialis, causing irritation of the acromion and the coracoacromial ligamentum. Besides immobilization, conservative treatment is based on pain-relieving medication, physical therapy, as well as steroid injections. Even under such conservative therapeutic regimes, an operation (e.g., acromioplasty) takes place in 30% of the cases due to the lack of pain relief. Unfortunately, however, the operation does not always successfully [8] establish the desired relief of pain, either.

A similar paradox is known with respect to arthroplasty, especially of the knee, where 25% of patients tend to be unsatisfied with the results of the operation [9]. Among the explanations for this are the associations between osteoarthritis and psychopathology, esp. negative affect [10], personality [11], and trauma [12]. Besides negative affect, the psychologic suffering associated with chronic pain involves specific fears such as catastrophizing, which contribute to central sensitization and hyperalgesia, as well as to allodynia by means of heightened awareness directed to the sensation of pain. Negative affect is an umbrella term for anxiety and depression, and neuroticism reflects the tendency to experience aversive emotional states, especially negative affect [13]. Differently phrased, neuroticism resembles emotional lability and, thus, a source of complication when coping with illness. In addition, neuroticism generates unstable mood thus causing emotional lability, which is often expressed as a depressed or anxious mood, including worries about health-related issues. Negative affect is linked to chronic pain, e.g., of the knee [12], the back [14], and the shoulder [15]. Moreover, negative affect predicts worse outcomes and less satisfaction with therapies for chronic pain, such as arthroplasty [10], and is possibly a predisposition for posttraumatic stress disorder (PTSD), a connection described in the frame of the diathesis–stress model of PTSD [16], which may be of relevance for invasive therapies performed in people with posttraumatic symptoms. Negative affect was shown to rise in those with postoperative pain after total knee arthroplasty (TKA) and is deemed capable of inducing specific (i.e., pain-related) fears [12,17]. Moreover, as far as TKA is concerned, dissociative symptoms may qualify as negative affect in that they are possibly capable of inducing pain catastrophizing, thus ultimately increasing the perception of pain [12]. Dissociation is understood as posttraumatic symptomatology, and several dissociative symptoms [18] are required for the diagnosis of PTSD (i.e., amnesia, hypermnesia, derealization). Interestingly, with respect to chronic pain, PTSD itself conveys a heightened risk [19], possibly based on the activation of a clinical psychopathologic cascade initiated by negative affect and dissociation. Negative affect and neuroticism are also associated with a variety of physical illnesses, e.g., osteoarthritis [20], hypertension, and diabetes [21].

In addition to its associations with those disorders, negative affect may be a function of the right hemisphere [22]. Considering the lateralized manner in which peripheral pain is inherently organized, those anatomic underpinnings of peripheral pain possibly influence its associations with psychopathology.

A growing body of literature suggests psychosomatic and psychic comorbidity to modulate the subjective experience of shoulder pain, as well. Against this background, psychosomatic comorbidity complicates the adaptation to shoulder disorders, calling for complex and integrated approaches to their treatment. The present review gives an integrative overview of the respective findings that are suggestive of a link between the algofunction (i.e., the combined status regarding pain and function of the shoulder) related to frozen shoulder and psychiatric or psychosomatic syndromes, as well as the potential role of shoulder surgery as a crystallization point for posttraumatic psychopathology. Moreover, we strive to strengthen the hypothesis of the lateralization of psychosomatic correlates of pain.

2. Methods

The present review follows the recommendations for a narrative review [23]. Hence, we intended to depict not only the extent, but also the range and nature, of these studies, especially with respect to the extent to which the respective findings are integratable in a conceptual frame derived from research on other pain sites. In particular, we were interested in weighing the findings against the background of psychosomatic and psychotraumatologic concept formation. We searched Medline (1966–2022), as of January 2022. Our search strategy included the following terms mapped to the appropriate MeSH subject headings: ("childhood trauma" OR "PTSD" OR "dissociation" OR "amnesia" OR "derealisation" OR "depersonalization") AND ("surgery" OR "postoperative maladaptation" OR "perioperative maladaptation" OR "depression and anxiety" OR "posttraumatic distress" OR "perioperative negative affectivity" OR "somatization"). The following terms were also included: ("comorbidity", "personality", "borderline", and emotional lability). Additional terms used in the search were "lateralized", "hemisphere", and "contralateral", in order to account for the fundamental principles of central pain processing.

To be included in the review, papers needed to measure or focus on specific dimensions of psychological influence on shoulder pain. Peer-reviewed journal papers were included if they were: written in English, involved human participants, and described a measure for psychological influence. Quantitative, qualitative, and mixed-method studies were included in order to consider different aspects of measuring psychological influence. In particular, we sought to identify psychosomatic and further etiologic concepts which are suitable for the integration of physical and psychic symptoms alike. Among those concepts is that of lateralization, referring to the central processing of pain that not only includes the activation of the contralateral hemisphere, but also the functional lateralization of mood, potentially causing syndromes such as anxiety to take side with contralateral peripheral pain for anatomic reasons.

3. Results

After duplicates were removed, a total of >499 citations were identified. After exclusion based on title/abstract and following assessment of eligibility based on full texts, we considered 48 studies eligible for this review. Our Medline search revealed a heterogenous set of endpoints and independent variables reflecting psychological disturbances. Although the hospital anxiety and depression scale was often reported, other measures of anxiety and depression were also deployed. In addition, specific fears such as pain catastrophizing and kinesiophobia are reported as predictors of the algofunction by three studies. Another important approach to the study question was the analysis of patient expectations as exemplified by Oh et al. [24]. Fewer studies reported personality characteristics as predictors of the algofunction in shoulder impingement. Table A1 (see Appendix A) gives an overview of those studies. As we hypothesized, the literature reviewed here was in line with the assumption of a posttraumatic pathway of maladaptation after shoulder surgery, and, in addition, the findings did not contradict the assumption of a lateralized pattern of association between shoulder pain and psychiatric syndromes. To make matters even more complex, central sensitization may not only involve lateralization, but also affect patterns of immunologic response. Thus, the present review could mark a new field of study with respect to the (psycho-)dynamics of shoulder pain.

4. Discussion

4.1. Psychosocial Correlates of Chronic Shoulder Pain

In clinical settings, the perception of patients with shoulder pain is often characterized by the impression of neurotic alignment, tenseness, and a lower pain threshold [25]. Moreover, the more peculiar the patient is in terms of the emotional presentation, the longer the duration, and the greater the severity of his or her disability was found to be [26]. Since shoulder impingement syndromes are among the top representatives of causes for chronic pain, the associations of chronic pain with psychosomatic features are likewise manifest in shoulder impingement, as well. Accordingly, Cho et al. [27] reported the preoperative association between depression and joint dysfunction as well as quality of life, all of them assessed preoperatively. Similarly, as for the prospective perspective, Dekker et al. [28] found higher scores on the hospital anxiety and depression scale connected to less postoperative satisfaction after 6 months. Park et al. [29] found early (up to 6 months) postoperative pain and the range of motion (RoM) affected by the preoperative presence of anxiety and depression. They concluded that psychological factors would delay the recovery as far as shoulder disorders are concerned. In addition, Cho et al. [30] showed the prediction of the joint function by preoperative depression scores, highlighting the functional influence of depression. Similarly, Martinez-Calderon et al. [31], in their review on psychosomatic influences on shoulder pain, report a relationship between depression, anxiety, emotional distress, and shoulder pain. On this note, depression and anxiety also predicted shoulder pain after 3 months in Debeer et al.'s [32] study, and this study showed improvement in psychological well-being to be linked to less physical pain, whereas the opposite, i.e., prediction of more pain by psychological deterioration, was not shown. This finding is interesting because it may point to a "somato-genic" nature of psychosocial findings in relation to shoulder pain and corresponds to the assumption of pain lateralization [22].

The fear avoidance model of chronic pain posits pain to be modulated by sensory amplification as a result of the attention drawn to its perception by specific fears, mostly pain catastrophizing. As a result, kinesiophobia, that is, the fear of motion and re-injury, rises and makes withdrawal from social and work-related contexts act as a contraphobic compromise, relieving from fear on the one hand, but leading to chronification on the other, especially as regards surgical treatments [12,33]. Less participation and activity, however, prompt less healthy lifestyles and increase the burden of pain. Accordingly, kinesiophobia predicted shoulder pain in Debeer et al.'s study [30], and, in addition, the authors report kinesiophobia to be more stable in men than in women over the study period. Likewise, Martinez-Calderon et al. [30] showed an association between preoperative concerns, fear avoidance, and chronic shoulder pain. In their recent review, DeBaets et al. [33] conclude fear avoidance to predict treatment outcomes only when the treatment was surgical, whereas, otherwise, outcome expectancies and self-efficacy predicted the respective outcomes. This finding begs the question of how much the operative setting poses a specific challenge for coping resources different from conservative settings. DeBaets et al.'s [33] conclusion might therefore be in line with the suggestion of a posttraumatic pathway of postoperative maladaptation after total knee arthroplasty that is hypothesized to result from prior traumatization, setting the stage for re-traumatization by the operation [12].

Moreover, Menendez et al. [34] found psychological factors (i.e., pain catastrophizing and insufficient coping) linked to shoulder pain, and report the same regarding social circumstances such as (un-)employment. In a prospective study, Thorpe et al. [35] identified a cluster of patients with surgery for rotator cuff repair, characterized by restricted psychological health, and whose pain and function of the shoulder were worse than in those without psychological problems. Potter et al. [36], however, found mild and moderate psychological distress not to correlate with the one-year outcomes of arthroscopic rotator cuff repair. Contrarily, Cho et al. [26] report a postoperative decrease in psychologic symptoms along with increased quality of life within a 12-month follow-up. Thus, as much as shoulder pain may induce depression, its reduction might act as an antidepressant. Counterintuitively, however, pain and injury of the dominant shoulder (limb) are associated with less hysteria and hypochondriasis [37]. The same authors highlight the relevance of the dominant upper limb for ambulation, body care, and movement [37]. As regards the impinged shoulder, this translates to dependency on others for daily activities and personal needs, shorter walking range, as well as less speed, and the authors underscore the finding of heightened hysteria as well as hypochondriasis in those with a lesion of the non-dominant limb, who are therefore considered to have a higher somatic awareness. However, this finding might reflect the more general fact that unilateral pain leads to the activation of the contralateral hemisphere. Ji et al. [38] have supposed a differential pattern of nociception in the left and right amygdala, and, in humans, the right hemispheric lateralization of amygdala function is linked to negative emotions [39]. Not least, shoulder disorders are heavily associated with problems returning to work, especially if coinciding with depression and anxiety. Thus, financial problems and disadvantageous prospects in the labor market often affect those with shoulder disorders disproportionately [40].

Considering the aforementioned involvement of specific fears and negative affect in the pathogenesis and maintenance of chronic pain, associations of shoulder pain with psychiatric disorders are to be expected. Accordingly, Bot et al. [41] found prevalences of depression (21%), anxiety (26%), schizophrenia (24%), as well as dementia (29%) elevated in candidates for shoulder arthroplasty. Apart from being, partly excessively, overrepresented, those entities were, except for schizophrenia, also linked to a higher risk of adverse events, including anemic states and longer institutionalized treatment for shoulder pain. Vice versa, depression increases the risk of rotator cuff tear and rotator cuff repair surgery remarkably [42]. That aside, psychiatric comorbidity is linked to increased cost and opioid use in relation to shoulder rotator cuff repair [43]. In addition to psychiatric disorders, sleep problems are present in 70–89% of the patients with rotator cuff tendinopathy [44]. Karels et al. [45] found somatization, kinesiophobia, and pain catastrophizing to predict the persistence of complaints over a 6-month follow-up, and classify their findings as corroborating the fear avoidance model. Similarly, Engebretsen et al. [46] report the association between pain-specific fears and shoulder pain, but [47] no significant effect of self-efficacy on either disability or on return to work. Several studies [48–51] report coping styles, in particular avoidant coping, to be associated with pain and disability of the shoulder.

The understanding of psychosomatic reactions to shoulder pain is connected to the question of causality, given that depression or anxiety could be a reaction to shoulder pain. This stance, however, is called into question by reports of non-linearity of the relationship between the extent of shoulder pain and depression [52]. As Badcock et al. [52] hypothesize, ceiling effects may preclude a further worsening impact of an increased load of depressive symptoms. Furthermore, these authors report the levels of disability to modulate those of depression, e.g., through problems sleeping. However, affective disorders and personality disorders are linked to arthritis, leading some authors to speculate about an essential relationship between those phenomena that, according to this stance, may be the symptoms of a single entity rather than representing different entities [24].

4.2. Recovery Expectancies

Another avenue of research investigates outcome expectancies in relation to the factual outcomes of therapy. On this note, Oh et al. [15] report outcome expectancies associated with the preoperative dysfunction of the joint, and Henn III et al. found preoperative positive expectations linked to more favorable postoperative results [53] after a 1 year follow-up. Likewise, Martinez-Calderon et al. [30] could show high levels of self-efficacy, resilience and expectations of recovery to be linked to levels of pain and disability albeit based on heterogenous studies involving different end-points and measures. Chester et al. [54], studying non-surgically managed shoulder pain, report that the prediction of pain (1/2 year) was best by the initial levels of shoulder pain, but strongly mediated by positive recovery expectations and optimism. Interestingly, the positive nature of the expectation may outweigh pain as a predictor. Accordingly, O'Malley et al. [55] found expectations to contribute to the short-term (3 months) functional outcome of shoulder disorders, explaining the interplay of functional improvements with functional expectations in terms of a specific capacity of negative expectations to undermine functional outcomes. In addition, Chester et al. [56] reported self-efficacy as a factor protective against shoulder pain. In addition, Henn III et al. [53], investigating a sample with primary surgical repair of a chronic rotator cuff tear, found positive expectations associated with the actual outcome with respect to function, even after controlling for a set of confounding variables including age, gender, smoking, workers' compensation status, symptom duration, number of previous operations, number of comorbidities, tear size, and repair technique.

Notably, Bandura [57] understood expectations of self-efficacy as the extent to which an individual will strive to cope with a certain health condition. Therefore, expectations may be linked to more or less favorable ways of coping, prevailing mood, sickness behavior, and compliance, and thus impact the course of a disease effectively. That said, a patient´s motivation for treatment is largely guided by her or his expectancies. The motivation for treatment comprises a cognitive, as well as an affective, component [58], the latter being the subjective suffering and the secondary gain from illness, and the former referring to the disease-related concept. The individual connotation of these components may be inclined to more or less predominance of medical, psychic, or social factors, as far as symptoms and expected treatments are concerned. In osteoarthritis, illness perception is predictive of disability, especially the perception of the level of perceived control and consequences of osteoarthritis (OA) [16]. In turn, as disability progresses and the prognosis deteriorates, particularly the judgement of the individual affection with OA in terms of the number of symptoms, the belief about their negative impact, and chronicity, grows ever more pessimistic. Hence, poor illness perceptions seem to function as a self-fulfilling prophecy.

4.3. *Higher-Order Factors: Temperament, Personality, and Posttraumatic Pathways*

In that same sense, expectations reflect the tendencies that constitute the personality. For example, Basat et al. [59] found depressive temperament (operationalized as having withdrawn, the presence of self-blaming features, and the absence of steadiness) linked to a worse algofunctional outcome during a follow-up of almost 2 years. Likewise, Bru et al. [60] reported neuroticism and extraversion as well as trait anxiety correlated to pain ratings and concluded from their cross-sectional, retrospective study that personality traits would be more involved in shoulder pain than in back pain (p. 491), and Chiaramonte et al. report an association between primary adhesive capsulitis and perfectionism, novelty seeking (negative), and harm avoidance [61]. Not least, another study [62] found the effect of pain catastrophizing on joint function (though not pain) moderated by optimism.

With respect to such findings, however, Coronado et al. [62] also note the tendency of weakness that the associations between the outcomes of rotator cuff repair and psychological variables display, and the bias towards the study of surgical treatments in that respect as opposed to conservative therapies. Likewise, Sheikhzadeh et al. [63] in their formidable review have shown that psychosocial factors unfold their potential to predict pain in a more clear-cut manner with respect to surgical therapies as opposed to conservative ones. This result is in line with research highlighting the traumatic and interpersonal potential of surgery based on the suggestion that the violation of bodily integrity might bear the risk of re-traumatization for the traumatized [12].

Likewise, as to the link between chronic pain and psychological trauma, shoulder disorders are also overrepresented in veterans or (other) individuals with PTSD [61]. On this note, Wang et al. proposed a substantial overlap between pain, PTSD, and emotional factors, including strong feelings of anger, hatred, and aggression. Interestingly, some authors [33] note that the muscles of the back and the shoulder would be the first to react to tension [64].

4.4. How Are the Shoulder and the Psyche Connected?

The upper limb is especially characterized by dexterity, motion, and sensibility, all of which are at stake when the shoulder is functionally disabled and painful [65]. Mitchell et al. [66] suggest upper-limb injuries to compromise the function of the limb and, along with that, also to hamper psychosocial well-being. Surprisingly, however, as these authors further report, long-term outcomes are similar for those treated with amputation or limb salvage. Other authors find only a weak correlation and conclude there is no such thing as a "frozen shoulder personality" [31]. Notwithstanding, the comorbid conditions of diabetes and arterial hypertension are both linked to personality on genetic [67], clinical [68,69], and therapeutic [70] levels. Thus, the frequent coincidence of shoulder impingement, diabetes mellitus, and arterial hypertension may be rooted at least partly in shared psychosocial factors, which possibly promote their common manifestation [71]. For example, neuroticism is associated with higher levels of hypochondriasis, and may affect dietary habits and other aspects of illness behavior [72]. Generally, patients with the comorbidity of mental disorders and painful physical symptoms display higher levels of emotional distress, poorer physical functioning, and lower rates of help seeking [73].

As to the mechanisms linking psychiatric symptoms and shoulder pain, the elements of the fear avoidance model, precisely fear avoidance beliefs such as kinesiophobia and pain catastrophizing, are likely involved in the dynamics of the chronification of shoulder pain. Accordingly, there [30] was a relationship between emotional distress, depression, anxiety, preoperative concerns, and fear avoidance as well as chronic shoulder pain. However, these authors highlight the weakness of this association, as well as the presence of several biases. Moreover, the more widespread the pain, the more robust the association with psychological variables, leading the authors to conclude that generalized pain involving the shoulder is more bio-psycho-social than pain restricted to the shoulder only. Likewise, Sarquis et al. [74] found shoulder pain to be most disabling when embedded in a state of generalized pain, involving other sites as well. In line with this theorizing, knee pain especially predicts the spreading of pain [48]. For the sake of the full picture, it seems noteworthy that traditional and complementary methods (e.g., acupuncture) play only a minor role in the treatment of shoulder pain. Notwithstanding, integrative approaches are potentially promising as they effectively mitigate pain and improve states of negative affectivity, as well [75].

4.5. Comorbidity

Due to its complex anatomy, which involves not only the rotator cuff, but also capsulo-ligamentous structures as well as their chronic inflammation, fibrosis, and contracture, the shoulder unfolds a complicated and multifaceted etiopathology of its chronic affection with pain. Aspects of lifestyle, increasing load, immunological factors, as well as psychological features, not to mention hormonal and possibly genetic factors, all adjust the risk of SIS [76,77], and the profile of comorbidities of shoulder pain may serve to illustrate this stance. As regards the physical comorbidities, they apparently share some of the associative patterns between psychological factors and physical disease. Depression, anxiety, and neuroticism are overrepresented not only in those with shoulder pain, but also in those with arterial hypertension and diabetes [78].

One should nevertheless bear in mind that, while certain labilizing traits may have beneficial effects on one disorder, they may still be a deteriorating factor in another one [79,80].

Exemplifying this statement, neuroticism may confer a greater potential of health-related anxiety, promoting a healthier lifestyle and greater levels of adhesion with respect to cardiovascular disease [81]. Contrarily, neuroticism is not considered protective, but a vulnerability factor, when it comes to arthritis-related pain [82].

4.6. The Shoulder and the Knee: Key to Bipedalism

The knee is of even more importance and relevance for chronic pain than the shoulder. Reasons for the knee to bear complications include reduced participation, walking distance, and speed [83]. Yet, even more importantly, the knee is well-nigh key to bipedalism. The shoulder mirrors these qualities as it is also a peculiar joint with specific anatomy and function, is linked to chronic pain, and, once disordered, threatens the individual participation fundamentally. Both joints are essential underpinnings of the human two-legged mobility and our upright gait, and hence their pathologies have the potential of seriously crippling the body's functional capabilities. This argument may help understand the psychological impact of those entities on general well-being. In addition, both entities are embedded in a pattern of physical morbidity that adds to the individual's burden, hampering adaptive coping even more.

Not least [57], coping represents a competency depending on the individual's psychic presentation, not only as far as mood disorders are concerned, but also with respect to the fundamental organization of the psyche as reflected in the individual's personality. Thus, there may be a complex interaction between these dispositions and shoulder pain.

4.7. A Note on Centralized Pain and the Lateralized Nature of Pain and Its Psychosocial Correlates

In the nineteenth century, English physician John Spender elaborated a new classification of the initial symptoms of OA including changes in velocity and tension of the heart's action, vasomotor changes, and specific neural symptoms [83]. The suggestion implied by this description was that the CNS could be functionally involved in the pathogenesis of OA. Contemporarily, this theory is revived insofar as there is the proposal of low-grade infection regulated top-down by a setpoint, as Morris et al. [84] state, that adjusts the neural, hormonal, inflammatory, and immune tone. The synovium and other joint structures are innervated by sympathetic and sensory fibers projecting to the thalamus and diencephalon. The higher the autonomic tone, the fewer anti-inflammatory effects of the parasympathicus are being brought to bear [84]. On the contrary, total knee arthroplasty is apparently associated with increased levels of circulating noradrenaline and adrenaline [85]. This high sympathetic tone leads to increased output of neutrophils and inflammatory monocytes from the bone marrow, cytokine production, and a heightened cell-mediated immune response [84].

Contemporarily, chronic pain is understood as centralized in the sense that pain would be intensified by central nervous processes and dysfunctions. Apart from pain, these processes often coincide with problems sleeping and memorizing, as well as fatigue, anxiety, or depression [86].

Independently from states of chronic pain, research suggests psychopathologic syndromes such as depression or anxiety to be functionally attached to the hemispheres, suggesting the psychosomatic epiphenomena of chronic pain to possibly be organized in a lateralized manner [32], not unlike the inherently lateralized pattern of limb pain. Hence, some of the repeatedly reported associations between lateralized chronic (shoulder) pain and psychopathology may reflect not only processes of sensitization, but also those of lateralization. Were this the case, then laterality might codetermine maladaptive patterns of adjustment based on differential left and right pathways of neural transmission [87]. Quite obviously, a purely peripheral concept of, e.g., osteoarthritis cannot explain the above outlined pattern of comorbidity. Moreover, centralized pain is less responsive to opioid treatments, further underscoring the clinical significance of this distinction. On the contrary, an unrecognized systematic pattern of association between lateralized pain and psychic as well as psychosomatic epiphenomena may contribute to the heterogeneity and inconclusiveness of the associations reported regarding, e.g., shoulder pain and psychopathology. On this note, a recent review weighed the significance of the reported associations by counting [63] the instances in which a psychological construct proved capable of the prediction of shoulder pain, or not. This illustrative and informative procedure may nevertheless omit the role of supra-ordinate factors such as laterality. In addition to other lateralized functions of the CNS, its neuroimmunomodulatory impact on the immune system may also indeed be a lateralized activity [88], with differences between the hemispheres pertaining to, e.g., the activation of macrophages involved in phagocytosis, inflammation, cytokine production, and antigen presentation, and to T cell activity affecting not only cellular, but also humoral, immunity. Moreover, with respect to traditional medicine there is the puzzling finding of beneficial effects of contralateral acupuncture on shoulder pain [75]. These are known to unfold on peripheral, spinal, and supraspinal levels [89,90], and they apparently rely on lateralization in terms of mirror symmetry, as well. Acupuncture is thus influential with respect to the antagonization of central sensitization, e.g., by means of segmental inhibition, or the activation of opioid or adrenergic receptors. The precise mechanism by which contralateral acupuncture is capable of mitigating limb pain, however, is unknown, but it likely involves neuroplastic processes of supraspinal origin [91], especially in connection with the anterior cingulate cortex [91]. Although promising, those alternative and complementary methods have nevertheless received only little attention in the literature on shoulder disorders.

5. Conclusions

The purpose of the present review was to summarize findings on the psychosomatics of shoulder pain, regarding psychopathologic syndromes and factors of the personality, and to connect them with specific psychosomatic, as well as psychotraumatologic, concept formation. As others did before, we underscore the frequent coincidence of psychopathology in relation to shoulder pain. Not unlike the knee, which—when painful—is robustly associated with a variety of mood and cognitive changes, and with higher-order factors such as neuroticism, shoulder pain is also entangled with psychopathology. A similar observation can be made regarding the physical comorbidities of shoulder pain, i.e., arterial hypertension and diabetes mellitus, which display a similar pattern of association with psychiatric syndromes. The present review demonstrates the complexity of psychosocial epiphenomena of chronic pain and of their interaction with shoulder pain, in particular, as well as the necessity of an integrated neuropsychosocial understanding and of a holistic treatment of pain.

6. Limitations

The present review summarizes the findings on the psychological and psychosomatic implications of shoulder pain. In doing so, it focusses on the interface between lateralized pain and the respective anatomy including the lateralization of pain afferents as well as the peculiarities of psychological trauma and its role in the chronification of pain. We discuss the included studies in accordance with these foci.

Funding: This research received no external funding.

Institutional Review Board Statement: Not applicable.

Informed Consent Statement: Not applicable.

Data Availability Statement: Not applicable.

Acknowledgments: The authors would like to thank Jörg Frommer for leading the group to a fruitful and interdisciplinary cooperation. We also thank Christopher Coutts for language editing.

Conflicts of Interest: The authors declare no conflict of interest.

Appendix A.

Table A1. Characteristics of the included studies.

First Author (Ref.)	Year	No. of Partici-Pants	Mean Age (Years)	Duration of Symtpoms	Psychological Factor	Outcome Measure: Pain Intensity	Outcome Measure: Disability	Data Collection (Follow-Up)	Study Design
Badcock et al. [52]	2002	2606 (304 with unilateral shoulder pain) (142 completed the follow-up)	47.7	≥1 year to ≤3 years	Anxiety (HADS-A); depressive symptoms (HADS-D); emotional distress (HADS)	Pain intensity (5-point Likert scale)	Disability (disability question-naire)	24 months	Longitudinal (prospective cohort study)
Bijsterbosch et al. [26]	2009	384 (241 completed all follow-ups)	59 (SD 7.5)	N/A	Illness perception (IPQ-R)	Pain intensity score modification of articular index for the assessment of osteoar-thritis	Disability (HAQ)	6 years	Longitudinal (prospective cohort study)
Bot et al. [41]	2014	348.842	69 (SD 15)	N/A	Diagnosis of depression, anxiety, schizophrenia, dementia	N/A	N/A	N/A	Retrospective cohort study
Cho et al. [30]	2015	58 (47 completed the follow-up)	57 (SD 8)	25 months (SD 36)	Anxiety (HADS-A); depressive symptoms (HADS-D); sleep disturbance (PSQI)	Pain intensity (VAS)	Disability (ASES)	12 months	Longitudinal (prospective cohort study)
Debeer et al. [32]	2021	72	53 (SD 7)	8 months	Anxiety and depressive symptoms (HADS), kinesophobia (TSK-11)	Pain intensity (VAS, SPADI)	Disability (SPADI)	3 months	Longitudinal (prospective cohort study)
Dekker et al. [28]	2016	86 (44 completed all follow-ups)	53.6 (de-pressed) 56.2 (non-depressed)	>3 months	Depressive symptoms (HADS)	Pain intensity (VAS, OSS)	Disability (OSS)	6 months	Longitudinal retrospective cohort study
Karels et al. [45]	2007	748 474 completed all follow-ups)	43.5 (SD 11.4)	≥3 months	Kinesophobia (TSK-11); depressive symptoms, anxiety, somatization, distress (4DSQ); catastrophizing (CSQ)	N/A	Disability (DASH)	6 months	Longitudinal (prospective cohort study)
Menendez et al. [34]	2015	139	58.1 (SD 14.3)	18.7 months (SD 26.8)	Depressive symptoms (PHQ-2); catastrophizing (PCS); self-efficacy (PSEQ)	Pain intensity (SPADI)	Disability (SPADI)	-	Cross-sectional cohort study
Oh et al. [15]	2012	174 (128 included)	58.8 (SD 8.2)	N/A	Preoperative expectations and concerns	Pain intensity (SF-36)	Disability (SST, Constant-Murley score)	Pre- and postopera-tive	Prospective cohort study
Potter et al. [36]	2015	269 (85 included)	62 (SD 2)	N/A	Distress (DRAM)	Pain intensity (VAS, ASES)	Disability (SST, ASES)	1 year	Prospective cohort study
Thorpe et al. [35]	2018	184 (124 completed all follow- ups)	54	N/A	Depressive symptoms and anxiety (DASS), catastrophizing (PCS); self-efficacy (PSEQ); kinesophobia (TSK-11)	Pain intensity (ASES)	Disability (ASES)	12 months	Longitudinal (prospective cohort study)
Koorevaar et al. [25]	2016	315	Not re-ported	40 (32)	Distress, depression, anxiety, and somatization	N/A	Function (DASH score)	12 months	Longitudinal (prospective cohort study)
Engebretsen et al. [47]	2010	104	48 (10.7)	N/A	HSCL-10, VAS	SPADI	SPADI	12 months	Prospective cohort study
Engebretsen et al. [46]	2015	200	49.8 (10.9)	N/A	Hopkins Symptom Check List	SPADI	SPADI	None	Cross-sectional cohort study

Table A1. *Cont.*

First Author (Ref.)	Year	No. of Partici-Pants	Mean Age (Years)	Duration of Symtpoms	Psychological Factor	Outcome Measure: Pain Intensity	Outcome Measure: Disability	Data Collection (Follow-Up)	Study Design
Wolfensberger et al. [49]	2016	158	47.1 (11.1)	5.5–15 months	HADS, PCS, TSK	DASH, brief pain inventory	DASH, patient Global Impression of Change measure	No follow-up	Retrospective
Badcock et al. [52]	2002	2606	47.7	N/A	HADS, PCS, TSK	VAS	N/A	2 years	Prospective cohort study
Henn III et al. [53]	2007	125	56.2 ± 11.4	16.0 ± 25.9 months	SF 36, MODEMS (partly)	DASH	DASH	1 year	Prospective, cross-sectional
Chester et al. [56]	2019	1030	57 (15.44)	N/A	Selected criteria	DASH	DASH	6 months	Prospective, cross-sectional
O'Malley et al. [55]	2004	199	51.6 (±15.7)	N/A	Patient Shoulder Expectancy Fulfillment, SF-12	FLEX-SF	FLEX-SF	3 months	Prospective, cross-sectional
Sarquis et al. [74]	2016	1410	20–59 years	N/A	SF-36, BSI-18	Questions about muscu-loskeletal pain	-	-	Prospective, cross-sectional
Zhang et al. [75]	2016	80	45.0 (7.4)		SF-36	DASH	DASH, Constant-Murley score	2 months	Prospective cohort study

ASES: American Shoulder and Elbow Surgeons (ASES) Society standardized shoulder assessment form; BSI: brief symptom inventory; CSQ: coping strategy questionnaire; DASH: disabilities of the arm, shoulder and hand questionnaire; DASS: depression anxiety stress scale; Disabilities of the Arm, Shoulder and Hand (DASH) questionnaire, DRAM: the Distress and Risk Assessment Method; FLEX-SF: Flexilevel Scale of Shoulder Function; HADS: hospital anxiety and depression rating scale; HAQ: health assessment questionnaire; HSCL: Hopkins Symptoms Check List; IPQ: illness perception questionnaire; MODEMS: Musculoskeletal Outcomes Data Evaluation and Management System; OSS: Oxford shoulder score; PCS: pain catastrophizing scale; PHQ: patient health questionnaire; PSEQ: pain self-efficacy questionnaire; PSQI: Pittsburgh sleep quality index; SF (−12/−36): short form (−12/−36) questionnaire; SPADI: Shoulder Pain and Disability Index, SST: simple shoulder test; TSK: Tampa scale of kinesiophobia; VAS: visual analogue scale; 4DSQ: the Four-Dimensional Symptom Questionnaire.

References

1. Luime, J.J.; Koes, B.W.; Hendriksen, I.J.M.; Burdorf, A.; Verhagen, A.P.; Miedema, H.S.; Verhaar, J.A.N. Prevalence and incidence of shoulder pain in the general population: A systematic review. *Scand. J. Rheumatol.* **2004**, *33*, 73–81. [CrossRef] [PubMed]
2. McBeth, J.; Jones, K. Epidemiology of chronic musculoskeletal pain. *Best Pract. Res. Clin. Rheumatol.* **2007**, *21*, 403–425. [CrossRef] [PubMed]
3. Garving, C.; Jakob, S.; Bauer, I.; Nadjar, R.; Brunner, U.H. Impingement Syndrome of the Shoulder. *Deutsches Ärzteblatt International* **2017**, *114*, 765–776. [CrossRef] [PubMed]
4. Kinge, J.M.; Knudsen, A.K.; Skirbekk, V.; Vollset, S.E. Musculoskeletal disorders in Norway: Prevalence of chronicity and use of primary and specialist health care services. *BMC Musculoskelet. Disord.* **2015**, *16*, 75. [CrossRef]
5. Pandey, V.; Willems, W.J. Rotator cuff tear: A detailed update. *Asia-Pacific J. Sports Med. Arthrosc. Rehabil. Technol.* **2015**, *2*, 1–14. [CrossRef]
6. Tirabassi, J.; Aerni, G. Shoulder Conditions: Glenohumeral Joint Osteoarthritis and Adhesive Capsulitis. *FP Essent.* **2020**, *491*, 17–21.
7. De la Serna, D.; Navarro-Ledesma, S.; Alayón, F.; López, E.; Pruimboom, L. A Comprehensive View of Frozen Shoulder: A Mystery Syndrome. *Front. Med.* **2021**, *8*, 663703. [CrossRef]
8. Karjalainen, T.; Jain, N.B.; Page, C.M.; Lähdeoja, T.A.; Johnston, R.V.; Salamh, P.; Kavaja, L.; Ardern, C.; Agarwal, A.; Vandvik, P.O.; et al. Subacromial decompression surgery for rotator cuff disease. *Cochrane Database Syst. Rev.* **2019**, *2019*, CD005619. [CrossRef]
9. Riddle, D.L.; Wade, J.B.; Jiranek, W.A.; Kong, X. Preoperative pain catastrophizing predicts pain outcome after knee arthroplasty. *Clin. Orthop. Relat. Res.* **2010**, *468*, 798–806. [CrossRef]
10. Hirschmann, M.T.; Testa, E.; Amsler, F.; Friederich, N.F. The unhappy total knee arthroplasty (TKA) patient: Higher WOMAC and lower KSS in depressed patients prior and after TKA. *Knee Surg. Sports Traumatol. Arthrosc.* **2013**, *21*, 2405–2411. [CrossRef]
11. Biskin, R.S.; Frankenburg, F.R.; Fitzmaurice, G.M.; Zanarini, M.C. Pain in patients with borderline personality disorder. *Pers. Ment. Health* **2014**, *8*, 218–227. [CrossRef] [PubMed]

12. Vogel, M.; Meyer, F.; Frommer, J.; Walter, M.; Lohmann, C.H.; Croner, R. Unwillingly traumatizing: Is there a psycho-traumatologic pathway from general surgery to postoperative maladaptation? *Scand. J. Pain* **2020**, *21*, 238–246. [CrossRef] [PubMed]
13. Rusting, C.L.; Larsen, R.J. Extraversion, neuroticism, and susceptibility to positive and negative affect: A test of two theoretical models. *Pers. Individ. Differ.* **1997**, *22*, 607–612. [CrossRef]
14. De Raad, B. *The Big Five Personality Factors: The Psycholexical Approach to Personality*; Hogrefe & Huber Publishers: Göttingen, Germany, 2000.
15. Gilj, A.; Goodman, A.D.; Mulcahey, M.K. Psychological factors affecting outcomes after elective shoulder surgery. *J. Am. Acad. Orthop. Surg.* **2018**, *26*, e98–e104. [CrossRef]
16. Elwood, L.S.; Mott, J.; Williams, N.L.; Lohr, J.M.; Schroeder, D.A. Attributional style and anxiety sensitivity as maintenance factors of posttraumatic stress symptoms: A prospective examination of a diathesis–stress model. *J. Behav. Ther. Exp. Psychiatry* **2009**, *40*, 544–557. [CrossRef] [PubMed]
17. Vancleef, L.M.G.; Vlaeyen, J.W.S.; Peters, M.L. Dimensional and componential structure of a hierarchical organization of pain-related anxiety constructs. *Psychol. Assess.* **2009**, *21*, 340–351. [CrossRef]
18. American Psychiatric Association. *Diagnostic and Statistical Manual of Mental Disorders*, 5th ed.; American Psychiatric Association: Arlington, VA, USA, 2013. [CrossRef]
19. Kind, S.; Otis, J.D. The Interaction between Chronic Pain and PTSD. *Curr. Pain Headache Rep.* **2019**, *23*, 91. [CrossRef]
20. Tan, V.; Jinks, C.; Chew-Graham, C.; Healey, E.L.; Mallen, C. The triple whammy anxiety depression and osteoarthritis in long-term conditions. *BMC Fam. Pract.* **2015**, *16*, 163. [CrossRef]
21. Weston, S.J.; Graham, E.K.; Turiano, N.A.; Aschwanden, D.; Booth, T.; Harrison, F.; James, B.D.; Lewis, N.A.; Makkar, S.R.; Mueller, S.; et al. Is Healthy Neuroticism Associated with Chronic Conditions? A Coordinated Integrative Data Analysis. *Collabra Psychol.* **2020**, *6*, 42. [CrossRef]
22. Vogel, M.; Binneböse, M.; Lohmann, C.H.; Junne, F.; Berth, A.; Riediger, C. Are Anxiety and Depression Taking Sides with Knee-Pain in Osteoarthritis? *J. Clin. Med.* **2022**, *11*, 1094. [CrossRef]
23. Green, B.N.; Johnson, C.D.; Adams, A. Writing narrative literature reviews for peer-reviewed journals: Secrets of the trade. *J. Chiropr. Med.* **2006**, *5*, 101–117. [CrossRef]
24. Oh, J.H.; Yoon, J.P.; Kim, J.Y.; Kim, S.H. Effect of expectations and concerns in rotator cuff disorders and correlations with preoperative patient characteristics. *J. Shoulder Elb. Surg.* **2012**, *21*, 715–721. [CrossRef]
25. Koorevaar, R.C.T.; Riet, E.V.; Gerritsen, M.J.J.; Madden, K.; Bulstra, S.K. The Influence of Preoperative and Postoperative Psychological Symptoms on Clinical Outcome after Shoulder Surgery: A Prospective Longitudinal Cohort Study. *PLoS ONE* **2016**, *11*, e0166555. [CrossRef]
26. Bijsterbosch, J.; Scharloo, M.; Visser, A.W.; Watt, I.; Meulenbelt, I.; Huizinga, T.W.J.; Kaptein, A.A.; Kloppenburg, M. Illness perceptions in patients with osteoarthritis: Change over time and association with disability. *Arthritis Care Res.* **2009**, *61*, 1054–1061. [CrossRef]
27. Cho, C.-H.; Song, K.S.; Hwang, I.; Warner, J.J.P. Does Rotator Cuff Repair Improve Psychologic Status and Quality of Life in Patients with Rotator Cuff Tear? *Clin. Orthop. Relat. Res.* **2015**, *473*, 3494–3500. [CrossRef] [PubMed]
28. Dekker, A.P.; Salar, O.; Karuppiah, S.V.; Bayley, E.; Kurian, J. Anxiety and depression predict poor outcomes in arthroscopic subacromial decompression. *J. Shoulder Elb. Surg.* **2016**, *25*, 873–880. [CrossRef]
29. Park, J.H.; Rhee, S.-M.; Kim, H.S.; Oh, J.H. Effects of Anxiety and Depression Measured via the Hospital Anxiety and Depression Scale on Early Pain and Range of Motion After Rotator Cuff Repair. *Am. J. Sports Med.* **2021**, *49*, 314–320. [CrossRef] [PubMed]
30. Cho, C.-H.; Jung, S.-W.; Park, J.-Y.; Song, K.-S.; Yu, K.-I. Is shoulder pain for three months or longer correlated with depression, anxiety, and sleep disturbance? *J. Shoulder Elb. Surg.* **2013**, *22*, 222–228. [CrossRef] [PubMed]
31. Martinez-Calderon, J.; Struyf, F.; Meeus, M.; Luque-Suarez, A. The association between pain beliefs and pain intensity and/or disability in people with shoulder pain: A systematic review. *Musculoskelet. Sci. Pract.* **2018**, *37*, 29–57. [CrossRef] [PubMed]
32. Debeer, P.; Commeyne, O.; De Cupere, I.; Tijskens, D.; Verhaegen, F.; Dankaerts, W.; Claes, L.; Kiekens, G. The outcome of hydrodilation in frozen shoulder patients and the relationship with kinesiophobia, depression, and anxiety. *J. Exp. Orthop.* **2021**, *8*, 85. [CrossRef]
33. De Baets, L.; Matheve, T.; Meeus, M.; Struyf, F.; Timmermans, A. The influence of cognitions, emotions and behavioral factors on treatment outcomes in musculoskeletal shoulder pain: A systematic review. *Clin. Rehabil.* **2019**, *33*, 980–991. [CrossRef] [PubMed]
34. Menendez, M.E.; Baker, D.K.; O Oladeji, L.; Fryberger, C.T.; McGwin, G.; A Ponce, B. Psychological Distress Is Associated with Greater Perceived Disability and Pain in Patients Presenting to a Shoulder Clinic. *J. Bone Jt. Surg.* **2015**, *97*, 1999–2003. [CrossRef] [PubMed]
35. Thorpe, A.M.; O'Sullivan, P.B.; Mitchell, T.; Hurworth, M.; Spencer, J.; Booth, G.; Goebel, S.; Khoo, P.; Tay, A.; Smith, A. Are Psychologic Factors Associated with Shoulder Scores After Rotator Cuff Surgery? *Clin. Orthop. Relat. Res.* **2018**, *476*, 2062–2073. [CrossRef] [PubMed]
36. Potter, M.Q.; Wylie, J.; Granger, E.K.; Greis, P.E.; Burks, R.T.; Tashjian, R.Z. One-year Patient-reported Outcomes After Arthroscopic Rotator Cuff Repair Do Not Correlate with Mild to Moderate Psychological Distress. *Clin. Orthop. Relat. Res.* **2015**, *473*, 3501–3510. [CrossRef]
37. Gagliese, L.; Schiff, B.B.; Taylor, A. Differential Consequences of Left- and Right-Sided Chronic Pain. *Clin. J. Pain* **1995**, *11*, 207. [CrossRef]

38. Ji, G.; Neugebauer, V. Hemispheric Lateralization of Pain Processing by Amygdala Neurons. *J. Neurophysiol.* **2009**, *102*, 2253–2264. [CrossRef]
39. Yoshimura, S.; Ueda, K.; Suzuki, S.-I.; Onoda, K.; Okamoto, Y.; Yamawaki, S. Self-referential processing of negative stimuli within the ventral anterior cingulate gyrus and right amygdala. *Brain Cogn.* **2009**, *69*, 218–225. [CrossRef] [PubMed]
40. Pichené-Houard, A.; Paysant, J.; Claudon, L.; Paris, N.; Michel, B.; Jacquot, A.; Martinet, N.; Sirveaux, F.; Wild, P. Predictive factors for the duration until return to work after surgery for work-related rotator cuff syndrome: A prospective study of 92 workers. *Am. J. Ind. Med.* **2021**, *64*, 1028–1039. [CrossRef]
41. Bot, A.G.; Menendez, M.E.; Neuhaus, V.; Ring, D. The influence of psychiatric comorbidity on perioperative outcomes after shoulder arthroplasty. *J. Shoulder Elb. Surg.* **2014**, *23*, 519–527. [CrossRef]
42. Kuo, L.-T.; Chen, H.-M.; Yu, P.-A.; Chen, C.-L.; Hsu, W.-H.; Tsai, Y.-H.; Chen, K.-J.; Chen, V.C.-H. Depression increases the risk of rotator cuff tear and rotator cuff repair surgery: A nationwide population-based study. *PLoS ONE* **2019**, *14*, e0225778. [CrossRef]
43. DiBartola, A.C.; Cvetanovich, G.L. Editorial Commentary: Mental Health Comorbidities Are Associated with Increased Cost, Opioid Use, and Inferior Outcomes After Shoulder Rotator Cuff Repair. *Arthrosc. J. Arthrosc. Relat. Surg.* **2020**, *36*, 2661–2663. [CrossRef]
44. Wong, W.K.; Li, M.Y.; Yung, P.S.-H.; Leong, H.T. The effect of psychological factors on pain, function and quality of life in patients with rotator cuff tendinopathy: A systematic review. *Musculoskelet. Sci. Pract.* **2020**, *47*, 102173. [CrossRef]
45. Karels, C.; Bierma-Zeinstra, S.; Burdorf, A.; Verhagen, A.; Nauta, A.; Koes, B. Social and psychological factors influenced the course of arm, neck and shoulder complaints. *J. Clin. Epidemiol.* **2007**, *60*, 839–848. [CrossRef]
46. Engebretsen, K.; Grotle, M.; Bautz-Holter, E.; Ekeberg, O.; Brox, J. Determinants of the shoulder pain and disability index in patients with subacromial shoulder pain. *J. Rehabil. Med.* **2010**, *42*, 499–505. [CrossRef] [PubMed]
47. Engebretsen, K.; Grotle, M.; Bautz-Holter, E.; Ekeberg, O.M.; Brox, J.I. Predictors of Shoulder Pain and Disability Index (SPADI) and work status after 1 year in patients with subacromial shoulder pain. *BMC Musculoskelet. Disord.* **2010**, *11*, 218. [CrossRef]
48. Laslett, L.L.; Otahal, P.; Hensor, E.M.; Kingsbury, S.R.; Conaghan, P.G. Knee Pain Predicts Subsequent Shoulder Pain and the Association Is Mediated by Leg Weakness: Longitudinal Observational Data from the Osteoarthritis Initiative. *J. Rheumatol.* **2016**, *43*, 2049–2055. [CrossRef] [PubMed]
49. Wolfensberger, A.; Vuistiner, P.; Konzelmann, M.; Plomb-Holmes, C.; Léger, B.; Luthi, F. Clinician and Patient-reported Outcomes Are Associated with Psychological Factors in Patients with Chronic Shoulder Pain. *Clin. Orthop. Relat. Res.* **2016**, *474*, 2030–2039. [CrossRef] [PubMed]
50. George, S.Z.; Wallace, M.R.; Wu, S.S.; Moser, M.W.; Wright, T.W.; Farmer, K.W.; Borsa, P.A.; Parr, J.J.; Greenfield, W.H.; Dai, Y.; et al. Biopsychosocial influence on shoulder pain. *Pain* **2015**, *156*, 148–156. [CrossRef]
51. George, S.Z.; Wu, S.S.; Wallace, M.R.; Moser, M.W.; Wright, T.W.; Farmer, K.W.; Greenfield, W.H.; Dai, Y.; Li, H.; Fillingim, R.B. Biopsychosocial Influence on Shoulder Pain: Influence of Genetic and Psychological Combinations on Twelve-Month Postoperative Pain and Disability Outcomes. *Arthritis Care Res.* **2016**, *68*, 1671–1680. [CrossRef]
52. Badcock, L.J.; Lewis, M.; Hay, E.M.; McCarney, R.; Croft, P.R. Chronic shoulder pain in the community: A syndrome of disability or distress? *Ann. Rheum. Dis.* **2002**, *61*, 128–131. [CrossRef]
53. Henn, R.F.; Kang, L.; Tashjian, R.Z.; Green, A. Patients'Preoperative Expectations Predict the Outcome of Rotator Cuff Repair. *J. Bone Jt. Surg.* **2007**, *89*, 1913–1919. [CrossRef]
54. Chester, R.; Jerosch-Herold, C.; Lewis, J.; Shepstone, L. Psychological factors are associated with the outcome of physiotherapy for people with shoulder pain: A multicentre longitudinal cohort study. *Br. J. Sports Med.* **2016**, *52*, 269–275. [CrossRef]
55. O'Malley, K.J.; Roddey, T.S.; Gartsman, G.M.; Cook, K.F. Outcome Expectancies, Functional Outcomes, and Expectancy Fulfillment for Patients with Shoulder Problems. *Med. Care* **2004**, *42*, 139–146. [CrossRef] [PubMed]
56. Chester, R.; Khondoker, M.; Shepstone, L.; Lewis, J.S.; Jerosch-Herold, C. Self-efficacy and risk of persistent shoulder pain: Results of a Classification and Regression Tree (CART) analysis. *Br. J. Sports Med.* **2019**, *53*, 825–834. [CrossRef]
57. Bandura, A. Self-efficacy. In *Encyclopedia of Human Behavior*; Ramachaudran, V.S., Ed.; New York Academic Press: New York, NY, USA, 1994; Volume 4, pp. 71–81.
58. OPD Task Force. *Operationalized Psychodynamic Diagnostics OPD-2: Manual of Diagnosis and Treatment Planning*; Hogrefe: Cambridge, MA, USA; Toronto, ON, Canada, 2008.
59. Basat, H.; Armangil, M.; Yoğun, Y. Effect of affective temperament on outcome of rotator cuff surgery. *Orthop. Traumatol. Surg. Res.* **2019**, *105*, 1549–1553. [CrossRef]
60. Bru, E.; Mykletun, R.J.; Svebak, S. Neuroticism, extraversion, anxiety and type a behaviour as mediators of neck, shoulder and lower back pain in female hospital staff. *Personal. Individ. Differ.* **1993**, *15*, 485–492. [CrossRef]
61. Chiaramonte, R.; Bonfiglio, M.; Chisari, S. A significant relationship between personality traits and adhesive capsulitis. *Rev. Assoc. Med. Bras.* **2020**, *66*, 166–173. [CrossRef]
62. Coronado, R.A.; Seitz, A.L.; Pelote, E.; Archer, K.R.; Jain, N.B. Are Psychosocial Factors Associated with Patient-reported Outcome Measures in Patients with Rotator Cuff Tears? A Systematic Review. *Clin. Orthop. Relat. Res.* **2018**, *476*, 810–829. [CrossRef]
63. Sheikhzadeh, A.; Wertli, M.M.; Weiner, S.S.; Rasmussen-Barr, E.; Weiser, S. Do psychological factors affect outcomes in musculoskeletal shoulder disorders? A systematic review. *BMC Musculoskelet. Disord.* **2021**, *22*, 560. [CrossRef] [PubMed]

64. Wang, S.-J.; Rushiti, F.; Sejdiu, X.; Pacolli, S.; Gashi, B.; Salihu, F.; Modvig, J. Survivors of war in northern Kosovo (III): The role of anger and hatred in pain and PTSD and their interactive effects on career outcome, quality of sleep and suicide ideation. *Confl. Health* **2012**, *6*, 4. [CrossRef]
65. Tintle, L.S.M.; Baechler, L.M.F.; Nanos, C.G.P.; A Forsberg, L.J.; Potter, M.B.K. Traumatic and Trauma-Related Amputations. *J. Bone Jt. Surg.* **2010**, *92*, 2934–2945. [CrossRef] [PubMed]
66. Mitchell, S.L.; Hayda, R.; Chen, A.T.; Carlini, A.R.; Ficke, J.R.; MacKenzie, E.J. The Military Extremity Trauma Amputation/Limb Salvage (METALS) Study. *J. Bone Jt. Surg.* **2019**, *101*, 1470–1478. [CrossRef] [PubMed]
67. Zhang, F.; Baranova, A.; Zhou, C.; Cao, H.; Chen, J.; Zhang, X.; Xu, M. Causal influences of neuroticism on mental health and cardiovascular disease. *Qual. Life Res.* **2021**, *140*, 1267–1281. [CrossRef] [PubMed]
68. Lee, S.-F.; Li, C.-P. Personality as a predictor of HbA1c level in patients with type 2 diabetes mellitus. *Medicine* **2021**, *100*, e26590. [CrossRef] [PubMed]
69. Popiołek, L.; Siga, O.; Dzieża-Grudnik, A.; Popiołek, I.; Moląg, M.; Królczyk, J.; Grodzicki, T.; Walczewska, J.; Rutkowski, K. Personality traits and hypertension-mediated organ damage. *Psychiatr. Polska* **2019**, *53*, 1003–1020. [CrossRef] [PubMed]
70. Seto, A.; Han, X.; Price, L.L.; Harvey, W.F.; Bannuru, R.R.; Wang, C. The role of personality in patients with fibromyalgia. *Clin. Rheumatol.* **2019**, *38*, 149–157. [CrossRef]
71. Hemingway, H.; Marmot, M. Evidence based cardiology: Psychosocial factors in the aetiology and prognosis of coronary heart disease: Systematic review of prospective cohort studies. *BMJ* **1999**, *318*, 1460–1467. [CrossRef]
72. Esposito, C.M.; Ceresa, A.; Buoli, M. The Association between Personality Traits and Dietary Choices: A Systematic Review. *Adv. Nutr. Int. Rev. J.* **2021**, *12*, 1149–1159. [CrossRef]
73. Demyttenaere, K.; Bonnewyn, A.; Bruffaerts, R.; Brugha, T.; De Graaf, R.; Alonso, J. Comorbid painful physical symptoms and depression: Prevalence, work loss, and help seeking. *J. Affect. Disord.* **2006**, *92*, 185–193. [CrossRef]
74. Sarquis, L.M.; Coggon, D.; Ntani, G.; Walker-Bone, K.; Palmer, K.T.; Felli, V.; Harari, R.; Barrero, L.; Felknor, S.A.; Gimeno, D.; et al. Classification of neck/shoulder pain in epidemiological research. *Pain* **2016**, *157*, 1028–1036. [CrossRef]
75. Zhang, H.; Sun, J.; Wang, C.; Yu, C.; Wang, W.; Zhang, M.; Lao, L.; Yi, M.; Wan, Y. Randomised Controlled Trial of Contralateral Manual Acupuncture for the Relief of Chronic Shoulder Pain. *Acupunct. Med.* **2016**, *34*, 164–170. [CrossRef]
76. Meislin, R.J.; Sperling, J.W.; Stitik, T.P. Persistent shoulder pain: Epidemiology, pathophysiology, and diagnosis. *Am. J. Orthop.* **2005**, *34* (Suppl. S12), 5–9.
77. Kim, S.K.; Nguyen, C.; Jones, K.B.; Tashjian, R.Z. A genome-wide association study for shoulder impingement and rotator cuff disease. *J. Shoulder Elb. Surg.* **2021**, *30*, 2134–2145. [CrossRef]
78. Irvine, M.J.; Garner, D.M.; Olmsted, M.P.; Logan, A.G. Personality differences between hypertensive and normotensive individuals: Influence of knowledge of hypertension status. *Psychosom. Med.* **1989**, *51*, 537–549. [CrossRef]
79. Čukić, I.; Weiss, A. Personality and diabetes mellitus incidence in a national sample. *J. Psychosom. Res.* **2014**, *77*, 163–168. [CrossRef] [PubMed]
80. Debeer, P.; Franssens, F.; Roosen, I.; Dankaerts, W.; Claes, L. Frozen shoulder and the Big Five personality traits. *J. Shoulder Elb. Surg.* **2014**, *23*, 221–226. [CrossRef] [PubMed]
81. Gale, C.R.; Čukić, I.; Batty, G.; McIntosh, A.; Weiss, A.; Deary, I. When Is Higher Neuroticism Protective Against Death? Findings from UK Biobank. *Psychol. Sci.* **2017**, *28*, 1345–1357. [CrossRef] [PubMed]
82. Bucourt, E.; Martaillé, V.; Mulleman, D.; Goupille, P.; Joncker-Vannier, I.; Huttenberger, B.; Reveillere, C.; Courtois, R. Comparison of the Big Five personality traits in fibromyalgia and other rheumatic diseases. *Jt. Bone Spine* **2017**, *84*, 203–207. [CrossRef]
83. Vogel, M.; Krippl, M.; Frenzel, L.; Riediger, C.; Frommer, J.; Lohmann, C.; Illiger, S. Dissociation and Pain-Catastrophizing: Absorptive Detachment as a Higher-Order Factor in Control of Pain-Related Fearful Anticipations Prior to Total Knee Arthroplasty (TKA). *J. Clin. Med.* **2019**, *8*, 697. [CrossRef]
84. Morris, J.L.; Letson, H.L.; Gillman, R.; Hazratwala, K.; Wilkinson, M.; McEwen, P.; Dobson, G.P. The CNS theory of osteoarthritis: Opportunities beyond the joint. *Semin. Arthritis Rheum.* **2019**, *49*, 331–336. [CrossRef]
85. Hall, G.M.; Peerbhoy, D.; Shenkin, A.; Parker, C.J.; Salmon, P. Hip and knee arthroplasty: A comparison and the endocrine, metabolic and inflammatory responses. *Clin. Sci.* **2000**, *98*, 71–79. [CrossRef]
86. Clauw, D.J.; Hassett, A.L. The role of centralised pain in osteoarthritis. *Clin. Exp. Rheumatol.* **2017**, *35* (Suppl. S107), 79–84. [PubMed]
87. Berretz, G.; Wolf, O.T.; Güntürkün, O.; Ocklenburg, S. Atypical lateralization in neurodevelopmental and psychiatric disorders: What is the role of stress? *Cortex* **2020**, *125*, 215–232. [CrossRef] [PubMed]
88. Sumner, R.C.; Parton, A.; Nowicky, A.V.; Kishore, U.; Gidron, Y. Hemispheric lateralisation and immune function: A systematic review of human research. *J. Neuroimmunol.* **2011**, *240*, 1–12. [CrossRef]
89. Shi, Y.; Yao, S.; Shen, Z.; She, L.; Xu, Y.; Liu, B.; Liang, Y.; Jiang, Y.; Sun, J.; Wu, Y.; et al. Effect of Electroacupuncture on Pain Perception and Pain-Related Affection: Dissociation or Interaction Based on the Anterior Cingulate Cortex and S1. *Neural Plast.* **2020**, *2020*, 8865096. [CrossRef] [PubMed]
90. Lyu, Z.; Guo, Y.; Gong, Y.; Fan, W.; Dou, B.; Li, N.; Wang, S.; Xu, Y.; Liu, Y.; Chen, B.; et al. The Role of Neuroglial Crosstalk and Synaptic Plasticity-Mediated Central Sensitization in Acupuncture Analgesia. *Neural Plast.* **2021**, *2021*, 8881557. [CrossRef] [PubMed]
91. Yi, M.; Zhang, H.; Lao, L.; Xing, G.-G.; Wan, Y. Anterior Cingulate Cortex is Crucial for Contra- but Not Ipsi-Lateral Electro-Acupuncture in the Formalin-Induced Inflammatory Pain Model of Rats. *Mol. Pain* **2011**, *7*, 61. [CrossRef]

Journal of
Clinical Medicine

MDPI

Article

Differences in Postural Balance, Pain Sensitivity and Depression between Individuals with Acute and Chronic Back Pain

José Antonio Mingorance [1,2,*], Pedro Montoya [1], José García Vivas Miranda [3] and Inmaculada Riquelme [1,2]

1 Research Institute on Health Sciences (IUNICS-IdISBa), University of the Balearic Islands, 07122 Palma de Mallorca, Spain; pedro.montoya@uib.es (P.M.); inma.riquelme@uib.es (I.R.)
2 Department of Nursing and Physiotherapy, University of the Balearic Islands, 07122 Palma de Mallorca, Spain
3 Laboratory of Byosystems, Institute of Physics, Federal University of Bahia, Salvador 40170-115, Brazil; vivasm@gmail.com
* Correspondence: josea.mingorance@uib.es; Tel.: +34-971-171-310

Abstract: To compare differences in postural balance, pain and depression in patients with chronic and acute low back pain, twenty patients with chronic and twenty patients with acute low back pain from the Edward Francis Small Hospital (Banjul, Gambia), as well as 20 age-matched healthy controls participated in the study. A modified Romberg test was used to assess postural balance during one minute with closed eyes. Body sway in the anteroposterior and mediolateral axes was video-recorded during test performance and further analyzed with an open source software for movement analyses (CvMob). Pain sensitivity was assessed by means of pressure pain thresholds and depression by a self-report questionnaire (PHQ-9). As results, patients with chronic low back pain displayed higher body sway in the anteroposterior and mediolateral axes, as well as faster body sway than patients with acute low back pain and healthy controls. Nevertheless, group differences disappeared when depression was introduced as a covariate, indicating a major role of depression in postural balance deficits of patients with pain disorders. As conclusions, the assessment of postural balance and depression should be implemented in the clinical routine for the design of tailored interventions in pain conditions.

Keywords: proprioception; postural balance; acute pain; chronic pain; depression

Citation: Mingorance, J.A.; Montoya, P.; Vivas Miranda, J.G.; Riquelme, I. Differences in Postural Balance, Pain Sensitivity and Depression between Individuals with Acute and Chronic Back Pain. *J. Clin. Med.* **2022**, *11*, 2700. https://doi.org/10.3390/jcm11102700

Academic Editors: Carmen María Galvez Sánchez, Casandra I. Montoro Aguilar and Markus W. Hollmann

Received: 23 March 2022
Accepted: 6 May 2022
Published: 10 May 2022

1. Introduction

Postural balance is compromised in patients with chronic pain, such as complex regional pain syndrome [1], fibromyalgia [2], neck [3,4] and low back pain [5,6]. One possible explanation is that these deficits could be due to central processes involved in pain experience. Indeed, it has been shown that altered postural balance in patients with chronic low back pain could be associated with changes in motor cortex organization [7]. Accordingly, several studies have reported that an alteration in motor control may have causative impact on the emergence and maintenance of chronic pain [8–13].

The transition from acute to chronic pain is determined by many pain features and individual characteristics [14]. In this sense, depression has been considered one of the main risk factors for pain chronification [15–17]. Thus, it has been reported that depression can predict the persistence of pain in muscle-skeletal injuries [18], contributes to the transition towards chronic pain [19–21], and is associated with postural instability in neurological disorders such as stroke [14] and Parkinson disease [20], as well as in the elderly [22].

The impairment of postural balance in chronic pain conditions is clinically relevant due to its association with the risk of falls and functional restrictions in daily life [21]. Determining whether postural dysfunction is present in acute and chronic pain, as well as examining its relationship with the presence of depression, could contribute to improve the treatment and diagnosis of pain in several pain conditions [3]. The present study aimed at exploring potential deficits in postural balance associated to pain duration, pain sensitivity and depression in individuals suffering from acute or chronic low back pain. For this purpose, pressure pain sensitivity at a painful and a non-painful body location, self-reports of depression and several parameters of static body sway in patients with acute or chronic low back pain were compared to healthy individuals. We hypothesized that postural balance would be impaired in individuals with chronic pain as compared to acute pain patients and healthy controls, and that deficits in postural balance would be modulated by depression.

2. Materials and Methods

2.1. Participants

Individuals with chronic and acute low back pain were identified by medical doctors at the Edward Francis Hospital (Banjul, Gambia) in summer of 2016. Chronic pain was defined as pain lasting more than 3 months. Inclusion criteria were: [1] age between 25 and 50 years, and [2] diagnosis of low back pain at the acute or chronic phase. The selected patients were informed of the aim and methods of the study and invited to participate by signing the informed consent. The protocol was approved by the Research and Ethics Committee of The Republic of the Gambia. Participants were excluded from the study if they had not signed the informed consent or if a diagnosis of neurological disorders were included in the hospital medical report.

The mean low back pain point prevalence in Africa is 32% [23]. A sample size calculation was performed taking into account the Banjul's population of 33,000 inhabitants, and by using the GRANMO sample size calculator (GRANMO: http://www.imim.es/) with a power of 0.9 and alpha of 0.05. According to these parameters, it was estimated that a sample of 20 participants per group would be required to detect significant differences. Forty people with low back pain accepted to participate and were included in the study: 20 patients with acute low back pain [15 females, mean age = 37.9 (1.32)], and 20 patients with chronic low back pain [12 females, mean age = 40.8 (1.44)]. Twenty age-matched healthy individuals with no pain [15 females, mean age = 40.8 (1.63)] were also recruited and included in the study. Group comparisons for age, body mass index, height, weight and pain duration are displayed in Table 1.

Table 1. Displays the sociodemografic data of the three groups of participants.

	Chronic Pain (n = 20)	Group Acute Pain (n = 20)	Control (n = 20)	
	Mean (SD)	**Mean (SD)**	**Mean (SD)**	**Significance Level**
Age (years)	40.8 (1.44)	37.9 (1.32)	40.75 (1.63)	0.28
Pain duration (months)	29.1 (2.54)	1.07 (0.07)	0	$p < 0.001$
BMI	21.97 (1.54)	19.81 (0.75)	21.11 (0.81)	0.38
Height (centimeters)	167.65 (2.01)	170.5 (2.11)	171.45 (1.71)	0.36
Weight (kilograms)	61.2 (3.97)	58.1 (2.56)	60.25 (1.84)	0.75
Gender (women)	n = 10	n = 9	n = 10	0.98

2.2. Assessments

Postural balance, pressure pain sensitivity and level of depression were assessed in all participants in one session at the Edward Francis Hospital.

Pain sensitivity was assessed by using a standard algometer and was defined as the necessary pressure (expressed in Newtons) to cause a painful sensation. Algometry was applied at two bilateral body locations following a pseudorandom sequence: great trochanters (defined by low back pain patients was a painful body location) and epicondyles (non-painful body location). Algometry has been found to be non-invasive, efficient and reliable [24] in the exploration of pathophysiological mechanisms involved in muscle pain syndromes [25] and is considered as a neurophysiological marker of central somatosensory processing [26].

Depression was assessed by the PHQ-9 scale of The Patient Health Questionnaire. This self-report questionnaire is considered as a good screening tool for depression in primary care [24].

Postural balance was assessed by asking participants to perform the modified Romberg test for one minute and with their eyes closed. This task has proven to be an objective measure of balance in an upright position [27]. The task performance was recorded on video with a standard webcam (©Logitech, Lausanne, Switzerland) at a rate of 30 frames per second and located two meters above ground level. For recording purposes, participants used a headband (located at the level of the parietal lobe) that contains two marks separated 5 cm from each other. Participants were asked to remain in an orthostatic position with their feet apart (at shoulder width) and with arms extended along the body [17]. The balancing of the body in the mediolateral and anteroposterior axes was processed through the use of an open source software (CvMob) developed for computer vision purposes [27]. The standard deviation of body sway in each plane (mediolateral and anteroposterior), as well as speed of body sway (cm/sec) were obtained as balance parameters. It has been shown that the measurement and analysis of body sway through this procedure are reliable and produce results similar to those provided by posturography [27].

2.3. Statistical Analyses

The assumption of normality in all variables was previously assessed with the Kolmogorov-Smirnov test. Analyses of variance (ANOVAs) were used to test group differences (between-subject factor GROUP: chronic pain vs. acute pain vs. healthy controls) in postural balance, pressure pain sensitivity and level of depression. An additional within-subjects factor BODY LOCATION (epicondyle vs. greater trochanter) was used to analyze pressure pain sensitivity. Finally, the within-subjects factor AXIS (anteroposterior vs. mediolateral) was also used to analyze balance parameters (standard deviations and speed of body sway). Greenhouse–Geisser corrections were applied for the violation of sphericity assumptions in the ANOVAs. Bonferroni corrections were applied for post-hoc comparisons. Pearson correlations were used to explore the associations of body sway parameters with depression and pressure pain. Statistical analyses were performed using the SPSS software. A p-value of 0.05 was used for statistical significance.

3. Results

There were no significant group differences in age, gender, height, weight or body mass index ($p > 0.29$). As expected, significant differences in pain duration ($F(2,57) = 125.65$, $p < 0.001$) revealed that patients with chronic pain had longer pain duration than patients with acute pain or healthy controls (all $p < 0.001$).

Figures 1 and 2 display means and typical errors of pressure pain measures for the three groups in epicondyles and greater trochanters. Significant effects of GROUP (in epicondyles $F(2,57) = 50.66$, $p < 0.001$ and in greater trochanters $F(2,57) = 50.66$, $p < 0.001$), BODY LOCATION (in epicondyles $F(1,57) = 12.07$, $p < 0.001$ and in greater trochanters $F(2,57) = 13.56$, $p < 0.001$) and GROUP × BODY LOCATION were found (in epicondyles $F(2,57) = 6.76$, $p = 0.002$ and in greater trochanters $F(2,57) = 7.66$, $p = 0.003$). Post-hoc comparisons indicated that pain thresholds in epicondyles and greater trochanters were lower in patients with chronic and acute low back pain than in healthy controls for both body locations ($p < 0.001$), and that there were no significant differences between patients with chronic and acute low back pain ($p > 0.40$). In addition, post-hoc comparisons revealed that pain sensitivity at the greater trochanter was lower than at the epicondyle (both $p < 0.001$) in healthy controls, while there were no differences between both body locations in patients with chronic or acute pain for both body locations ($p > 0.19$).

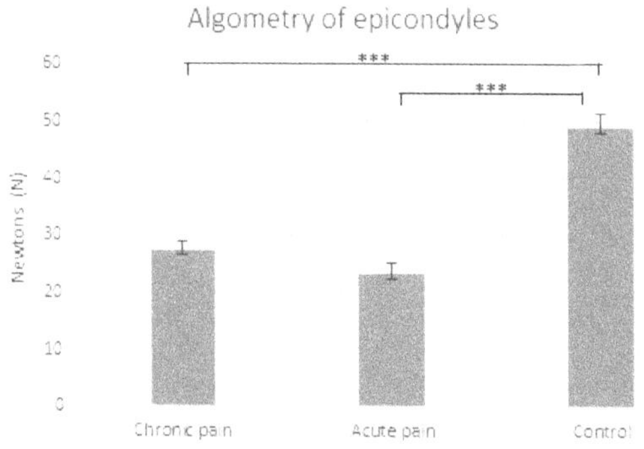

Figure 1. Means and typical errors of pressure pain thresholds (in Newtons) averaged for epicondyles in the three groups (chronic pain vs. acute pain vs. control). *** $p < 0.001$.

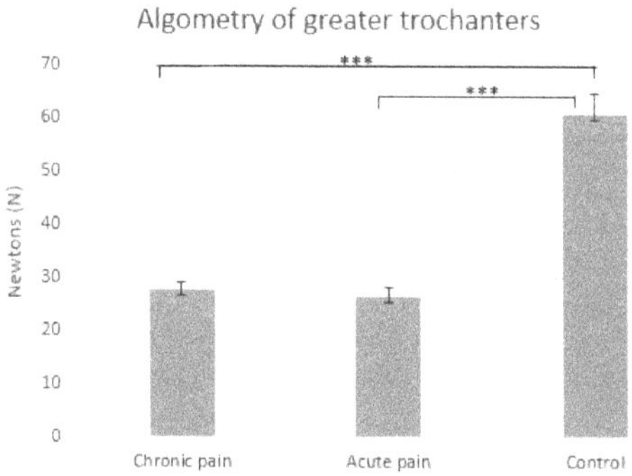

Figure 2. Means and typical errors of pressure pain thresholds (in Newtons) averaged for greater trochanters in the three groups (chronic pain vs. acute pain vs. control). *** $p < 0.001$.

Figure 3 displays mean depression scores in the three groups. Significant effects due to GROUP ($F(2,57) = 51.54$ ($p < 0.001$) were found. Post-hoc comparisons indicated that patients with chronic low back pain displayed higher scores compared to patients with acute pain ($p < 0.001$) and healthy controls ($p < 0.001$), and that patients with acute pain reported higher depression scores than healthy controls ($p < 0.007$.

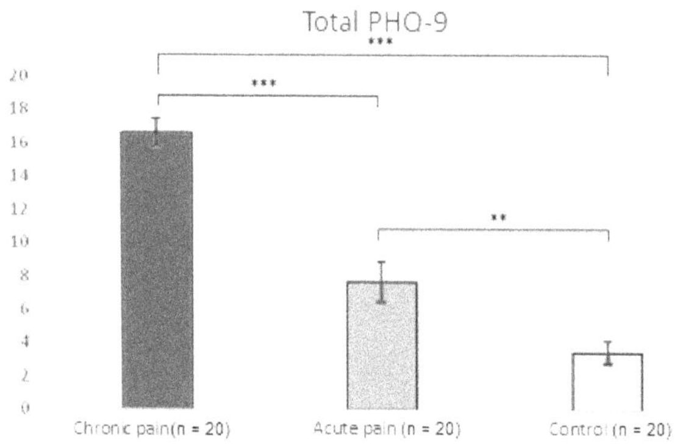

Figure 3. Means and typical errors of depression scores in the three groups (chronic pain vs. acute pain vs. control). ** $p < 0.01$, *** $p < 0.001$).

Figure 4 shows the pattern of body sway in one typical individual from each group. It can be observed that patients with chronic and acute low back pain display higher variability of body sway as compared to healthy controls. A significant effect due to GROUP was found ($F(2,57) = 15.48$, $p < 0.001$), which indicates that body displacements in the anteroposterior and mid-lateral axes displayed greater variability in patients with chronic low back pain than in patients with acute pain ($p < 0.001$) and healthy controls ($p = 0.002$), whereas no significant differences were found between patients with acute pain and healthy controls ($p = 0.19$). No significant differences were found due to AXIS ($F(1,57) = 2.98$, $p = 0.09$) or to GROUP × AXIS ($F(2,57) = 1.91$, $p = 0.16$).

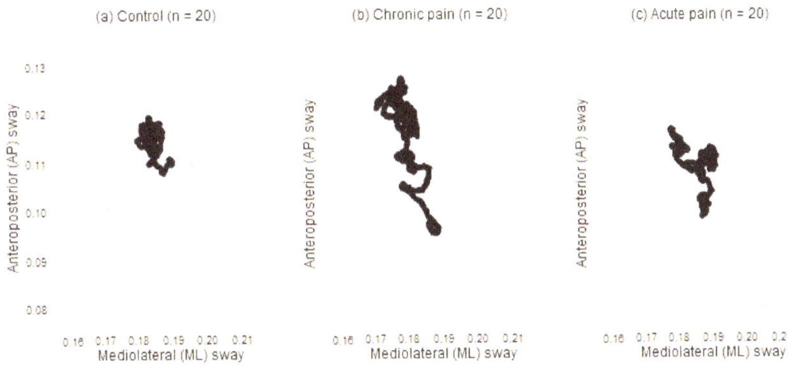

Figure 4. Pattern of body sway in typical individuals from each group. (**a**) Healthy controls, (**b**) patient with chronic low back pain, (**c**) patient with acute low back pain.

The ANOVA on speed of body sway yielded a significant effect due to GROUP ($F(2,57) = 9.71$, $p < 0.001$), showing that body sway was faster in patients with chronic low back pain than in patients with acute pain ($p = 0.001$) and healthy controls ($p = 0.002$), and that there were no significant differences between patients with acute pain and healthy controls ($p = 0.95$).

Finally, significant positive correlations were found between depression scores and body sway parameters (standard deviation of anteroposterior and mediolateral sway, as well as speed of body sway) (all $r > 0.30$, all $p < 0.02$), indicating that impaired body sway parameters were associated with higher depression. No significant correlations were found between body sway parameters and pain sensitivity measures. Considering these results, additional analyses of covariance (ANCOVAs) were performed on body sway parameters controlling for the effects of depression. There were significant effects due to GROUP in body sway through the mid-lateral axis ($p = 0.005$), but not in body sway through the anteroposterior axis or in speed of body sway.

4. Discussion

The aim of the present study was to analyze differences on postural balance, pain sensitivity and depression due to chronic and acute low back pain. In particular, we measured the variability of the body sway in the anteroposterior and mediolateral axes, as well as body sway velocity, pain sensitivity at the greater trochanter (painful body location in low back pain) and epicondyle (a usually non-painful body location), and self-reports of depression. Our data revealed that patients with chronic low back pain had poorer postural balance (greater variability and faster body sway velocity) and enhanced depression than patients with acute low back pain, and that the latter were similar to healthy controls in postural balance. In addition, we observed that both groups of patients with acute and chronic low back pain had greater sensitivity to pain than healthy controls. Finally, we found that depression, but not pain sensitivity, accounted for the deficits in postural balance.

These findings are in agreement with previous literature that shows that patients with chronic pain have deficits in postural balance [3,4,9] and, therefore, a greater risk of falls than healthy controls [21]. Indeed, alterations on postural control such as larger sway areas, greater center of gravity displacement or increased EMG activity have been previously described [4–12] in patients with chronic low back pain, suggesting some process of reorganization of the central nervous system in response to the chronification of pain [25]. Thus, the fact that only patients with chronic, but not with acute low back pain displayed deficits in postural balance seems to be in agreement with this interpretation. Furthermore, the significant relationship between postural balance deficits and enhanced depression scores seems to provide additional evidence of some type of neural adaptation induced by a central sensitization that goes beyond enhanced pain sensitivity [9].

In the present study, we further observed that both groups of patients with low back pain had enhanced pain sensitivity at painful and non-painful body locations as compared to healthy controls. Chronic low back pain has been associated with widespread changes in somatosensory sensitivity (included enhanced pain sensitivity at locations distinct from painful body regions), pointing to significant brain plasticity and central sensitization [28]. The fact that patients with acute low back pain also showed an enhancement of pain sensitivity at painful and non-painful body locations suggested that maintaining pain for a few days (as in acute low back pain) may also lead to relevant changes in brain processing of pain.

Depression, and not pain sensitivity, was the main factor that influenced postural balance in the present study. Moreover, we found higher levels of depression in patients with chronic pain compared to those with acute pain and healthy controls. These findings are partially in agreement with previous studies that show that altered postural control in patients with chronic pain could be strongly associated with pain-related symptoms [2,8]. Depression and pain are very comorbid and higher levels of depression have been associated with increased clinical sensitivity to pain and functional disability [19]. Furthermore, previous studies have shown that depression is related to deficits in visual and proprioceptive integration [22], can affect the performance of the sensorimotor task and the effectiveness of fall prevention [20], and is associated with a deteriorated balance in neurological conditions such as stroke [14] or Parkinson disease [20]. Therefore, the strong association observed in our study between balance parameters and depression further confirms the role of mood as a key component for postural control and supports the evaluation of depression in clinical routine to adapt the physical intervention in patients with musculoskeletal pain. The link between depression and chronic pain works in both directions [29] It has been shown that emotional disorders, such as depression, are common comorbid conditions that exacerbate the severity and persistence of chronic pain [30]. Pain and depression have been shown to be highly intertwined and can exacerbate physical and psychological symptoms [29,30] Moreover, it has been observed that the serotonergic and norepinephrine system plays a very important role in this comorbidity and that the brain structures that encode pain are also involved in mood, so the use of serotonergic antidepressants and norepinephrine may be useful to mitigate the pain [30,31]. Although more research is needed to analyze the neuroplastic mechanisms that link pain chronification and balance disorders, our findings suggested that the evaluation of postural balance, along with pain sensitivity and depression, could provide powerful indicators for the transition of acute pain to chronic pain.

Our findings should be analyzed taking into account some methodological limitations. One of the major limitation of the present study is that postural balance was measured through the video recording of head movements. Although this method has been previously validated, other direct and indirect measurements of postural control such as posturography (usually recorded by force platforms), electromyography (EMG) or even electroencephalography (EEG) recordings from motor cortices would be helpful to confirm these findings. A second important limitation was that the effects of chronic and acute pain on postural balance were based on a cross-sectional study with a relatively small sample of patients. A larger sample of patients with all possible pain duration intervals could have contributed to a better understanding of the changes that occur in the postural balance associated with the transition from acute to chronic pain. Although in our study there were no sex differences in sensitivity to pain and depression, other studies have shown changes in these variables with respect to gender [32–34]. The small sample size may also explain this fact. Another major shortcoming was the lack of data on the current pain perception, apart from pain sensitivity and depression measures. No other psychosocial factors related to pain were collected, such as catastrophizing, pain vigilance, perceived health quality, the impact of pain on social life, or functional disability caused by pain. Finally, the fact that the existence of neurological disorders was only obtained from the clinical records of the patients and was not directly confirmed by the experimenters, could be also considered a relevant shortcoming of the study.

5. Conclusions

The findings of this study provided empirical evidence that patients with chronic low back pain had worse postural balance and enhanced depression than patients with acute low back pain. In contrast, patients with acute and chronic low back pain showed a similar enhancement in pain sensitivity. Finally, we found that depression, but not enhanced pain sensitivity, accounted for the deficits in postural balance. All these findings revealed the different relevance of postural balance, pain sensitivity and depression in the transition from acute to chronic pain conditions. Further investigation of the neurophysiological mechanisms involved in the association between these variables could help to better understand the chronification of pain and improve clinical assessment and intervention of chronic and acute low back pain.

Author Contributions: Conceptualization, J.A.M., P.M., J.G.V.M. and I.R.; Data curation, J.A.M. and J.G.V.M.; Formal analysis, P.M. and J.G.V.M.; Investigation, J.A.M. and I.R.; Methodology, J.A.M., J.G.V.M. and I.R.; Project administration, P.M. and I.R.; Software, J.G.V.M.; Supervision, P.M.; Writing—original draft, J.A.M., P.M. and I.R.; Writing—review & editing, J.A.M. and I.R. All authors have read and agreed to the published version of the manuscript.

Funding: This research was funded by grants from the Spanish State Secretariat for Research, Development and Innovation and European Regional Development Funds (#PSI2017-88388-C4-1-R) to P.M., grant PID2020-114967GA-I00 funded by MCIN/AEI/10.13039/501100011033 to I.R., and the support of the National Council of Technological and Scientific Development, CNPq, Brazil (Grant number: 307828/2018-2).

Institutional Review Board Statement: The study was conducted according to the guidelines of the Declaration of Helsinki, and approved by the Research and Ethics Committee of The Republic of the Gambia on 20 July 2016 with the code 01082016.

Informed Consent Statement: Informed consent was obtained from all subjects involved in the study.

Data Availability Statement: The data presented in this study are available on request from the corresponding author.

Conflicts of Interest: The authors declare no conflict of interest.

References

1. Bank, P.J.; Peper, C.L.; Marinus, J.; Beek, P.J.; van Hilten, J.J. Motor dysfunction of complex regional pain syndrome is related to impaired central processing of proprioceptive. *J. Pain* **2013**, *14*, 1460–1474. [CrossRef] [PubMed]
2. Muto, L.H.; Sauer, J.F.; Yuan, S.L.; Sousa, A.; Mango, P.C.; Marques, A.P. Postural control and balance self-efficacy in women with fibromyalgia. Are there differences? *Eur. J. Phys. Med. Rehabil.* **2015**, *51*, 149–154.
3. Stanton, T.R.; Leake, H.B.; Chalmers, K.J.; Moseley, G.L. Evidence of impaired proprioception in chronic idiopathic neck pain: Systematic review and meta-analysis. *Phys. Ther.* **2016**, *96*, 876–887. [CrossRef]
4. Moreira, C.; Bassi, A.R.; Brandao, M.P.; Silva, A.G. Do patients with chronic neck pain have distorted body image and tactile dysfunction? *Eur. J. Phys.* **2017**, *19*, 215–221. [CrossRef]

5. Leinonen, V.; Kankaanpää, M.; Luukkonen, M.; Kansanen, M.; Hänninen, O.; Airaksinen, O.; Taimela, S. Lumbar paraspinal muscle function, perception of lumbar position, and postural control in disc herniation-related back pain. *Spine* **2003**, *28*, 842–848. [CrossRef]
6. Tsigkanos, C.; Gaskell, L.; Smirniotou, A.; Tsigkanos, G. Static and dynamic balance deficiencies in chronic low back pain. *J. Back Musculoskelet.* **2016**, *29*, 887–893. [CrossRef]
7. Wand, B.M.; O'Connell, N.E. Chronic non-specific low back pain–subgroups or a single mechanism? *BMC Musculoskel. Dis.* **2008**, *25*, 9–11.
8. Ruhe, A.; Fejer, R.; Walker, B. Center of pressure excursion as a measure of balance performance in patients with non-specific low back pain compared to healthy controls: A systematic review of the literature. *Eur. Spine J.* **2011**, *20*, 358–368. [CrossRef]
9. Claeys, K.; Brumagne, S.; Dankaerts, W.; Kiers, H.; Janssens, L. Decreased variability in postural control strategies in young people with non-specific low back pain is associated with altered proprioceptive reweighting. *Eur. J. Appl. Physiol.* **2011**, *111*, 115–123. [CrossRef]
10. Mok, N.W.; Brauer, S.G.; Hodges, P.W. Hip strategy for balance control in quiet standing is reduced in people with low back pain. *Spine* **2004**, *29*, 107–112. [CrossRef]
11. Sipko, T.; Kuczynski, M. Intensity of chronic pain modifies postural control in low back patients. *Eur. J. Pain* **2013**, *17*, 612–620. [CrossRef] [PubMed]
12. Massé-Alarie, H.; Flamand, V.H.; Moffet, H.; Schneider, C. Corticomotor control of deep abdominal muscles in chronic low back pain and anticipatory postural adjustments. *Exp. Brain Res.* **2012**, *218*, 99–109. [CrossRef] [PubMed]
13. Keogh, E.; Book, K.; Thomas, J.; Giddins, G.; Eccleston, C. Predicting pain and disability in patients with hand fractures: Comparing pain anxiety, anxiety sensitivity and pain catastrophizing. *Eur. J. Pain.* **2010**, *14*, 446–451. [CrossRef] [PubMed]
14. Bosco, M.A.; Gallinati, J.L.; Clark, M.E. Conceptualizing and treating comorbid chronic pain and Posttraumatic Stress Disorder. *Pain Res. Treat.* **2013**, *2013*, 174728.
15. Guo, Y.; Wang, Y.; Sun, Y.; Wang, J.Y. A Brain Signature to Differentiate Acute and Chronic Pain in Rats. *Front. Comput. Neurosci.* **2016**, *10*, 41. [CrossRef]
16. García-Pastor, C.; Álvarez-Solís, G.A. The Romberg test. *Rev. Mex. Neuroci.* **2014**, *15*, 31–35.
17. Gea, J.; Muñoz, M.A.; Costa, I.; Ciria, L.F.; Miranda, J.G.; Montoya, P. Viewing pain and happy faces elicited similar changes in postural body sway. *PLoS ONE* **2014**, *9*, e104381.
18. Holley, A.L.; Wilson, A.C.; Palermo, T.M. Predictors of the transition from acute to persistent musculoskeletal pain in children and adolescents: A prospective study. *Pain* **2017**, *18*, 794–801. [CrossRef]
19. Berubé, M.; Choinière, M.; Laflamme, Y.G.; Gélinas, C. Acute to chronic pain transition in extremity trauma: A narrative review for future preventive interventions. *Int. J. Orthop Trauma Nurs.* **2016**, *23*, 47–59. [CrossRef]
20. Hassan, A.; Vallabhajosula, S.; Zahodne, L.B.; Bowers, D.; Okun, M.S.; Fernández, H.H.; Hass, C.J. Correlations of apathy and depression with postural instability in Parkinson disease. *J. Neurol. Sci.* **2014**, *338*, 162–165. [CrossRef]
21. Kwan, M.M.; Lin, S.I.; Close, J.C.; Lord, S.R. Depressive symptoms in addition to visual impairment, reduced strength and poor balance predict falls in older Taiwanese people. *Age Ageing* **2012**, *41*, 606–612. [CrossRef] [PubMed]
22. Deschamps, T.; Thomas-Ollivier, V.; Sauvaget, A.; Bulteau, S.; Fortes-Bourbousson, M.; Vachon, H. Balance characteristics in patients with major depression after a two-month walking exercise program. *Gait Posture* **2015**, *42*, 590–593. [CrossRef] [PubMed]
23. Louw, Q.A.; Morris, L.D.; Grimmer-Somers, K. The prevalence of low back pain in Africa: A systematic review. *BMC Musculoskelet. Disord.* **2007**, *8*, 105. [CrossRef]
24. Dobscha, S.K.; Corson, K.; Perrin, N.A.; Hanson, G.C.; Leibowitz, R.Q.; Doak, M.N.; Dickinson, K.C.; Sullivan, M.D.; Gerrity, M.S. Collaborative care for chronic pain in primary care: A cluster randomized trial. *JAMA* **2009**, *301*, 1242–1252. [CrossRef] [PubMed]
25. Sá, S.; Silva, A.G. Repositioning error, pressure pain threshold, catastrophizing and anxiety in adolescents with chronic idiopathic neck pain. *Musculoskelet. Sci. Pract.* **2017**, *30*, 18–24. [CrossRef] [PubMed]
26. Backonja, M.M.; Attal, N.; Baron, R.; Bouhassira, D.; Drangholt, M.; Dyck, P.J.; Edwards, R.R.; Freeman, R.; Gracely, R.; Haanpaa, M.H.; et al. Value of quantitative sensory testing in neurological and pain disorders: NeuPSIG consensus. *Pain* **2013**, *154*, 1807–1819. [CrossRef]
27. Peña, N.; Credicio, B.C.; Nogueria, L.P.; Salles, R.M.; Souza, L.G.; Vale, M.; Cavalcanti, M.; Bomfim, J.P.; Vivas, J.G. Free instrument for measurements of motion. *Rev. Bras. Ensino Fís.* **2013**, *3*, 1–5.
28. Puta, C.; Schulz, B.; Schoeler, S.; Magerl, W.; Gabriel, B.; Gabriel, H.H.; Miltner, W.H.; Weiss, T. Somatosensory Abnormalities for Painful and Innocuous Stimuli at the Back and at a Site Distinct from the Region of Pain in Chronic Back Pain Patients. *PLoS ONE* **2013**, *8*, e58885. [CrossRef]
29. Ishak, W.W.; Wen, R.Y.; Naghdechi, L.; Vanle, B.; Dang, J.; Knosp, M.; Dascal, J.; Marcia, L.; Gohar, Y.; Eskander, L.; et al. Pain and Depression: A Systematic Review. *Harv. Rev. Psychiatry* **2018**, *26*, 352–363. [CrossRef]
30. Bonilla, H.; Sánchez, J.A.; Estevez, M.M.; Molina, T.; Cortes, J.L.; Alfaro, A. Depression and Pain: Use of Antidepressants. *Curr. Neuropharmacol.* **2022**, *20*, 384–402. [CrossRef] [PubMed]
31. Obata, H. Analgesic Mechanisms of Antidepressants for Neuropathic Pain. *Int. J. Mol. Sci.* **2017**, *18*, 11. [CrossRef] [PubMed]

32. Bartley, E.J.; Fillingim, R.B. Sex differences in pain: A brief review of clinical and experimental findings. *Br. J. Anaesth.* **2013**, *111*, 52–58. [CrossRef] [PubMed]
33. Dance, A. Why the sexes don't feel pain the same way. *Nature* **2019**, *567*, 448–450. [CrossRef] [PubMed]
34. Salk, R.H.; Hyde, J.S.; Abramson, L.Y. Gender differences in depression in representative national samples: Meta-analyses of diagnoses and symptoms. *Psychol. Bull.* **2017**, *143*, 783–822. [CrossRef]

Journal of
Clinical Medicine

MDPI

Review

The Link between Fibromyalgia Syndrome and Anger: A Systematic Review Revealing Research Gaps

Carmen M. Galvez-Sánchez [1,*], Gustavo A. Reyes del Paso [1], Stefan Duschek [2] and Casandra I. Montoro [1,*]

[1] Department of Psychology, Faculty of Humanities and Educational Sciences, University of Jaén, 23071 Jaén, Spain; greyes@ujaen.es

[2] Department of Psychology, Institute of Psychology, UMIT-University for Health Sciences, Medical Informatics and Technology, 6060 Hall in Tyrol, Austria; stefan.duschek@umit.at

* Correspondence: cgalvez@ujaen.es (C.M.G.-S.); imontoro@ujaen.es (C.I.M.)

Abstract: Anger has been associated with increased pain perception, but its specific connection with Fibromyalgia Syndrome (FMS) has not yet been established in an integrated approach. Therefore, the present systematic review focuses on exploring this connection, and based on this connection, delimiting possible gaps in the research, altogether aimed at improving FMS clinical intervention and guiding future research lines. Anger is considered a basic negative emotion that can be divided into two dimensions: anger-in (the tendency to repress anger when it is experienced) and anger-out (the leaning to express anger through verbal or physical means). The current systematic review was performed based on the guidelines of the PRISMA and Cochrane Collaborations. The Prospective Register of Systematic Reviews (PROSPERO) international database was forehand used to register the review protocol. The quality of chosen articles was assessed and the main limitations and research gaps resulting from each scientific article were discussed. The search included PubMed, Scopus, and Web of Science databases. The literature search identified 13 studies eligible for the systematic review. Levels of anger-in have been shown to be higher in FMS patients compared to healthy participants, as well as patients suffering from other pain conditions (e.g., rheumatoid arthritis). FMS patients had also showed higher levels of state and trait anxiety, worry and angry rumination than other chronic pain patients. Anger seems to amplify pain especially in women regardless FMS condition but with a particularly greater health-related quality of life´s impact in FMS patients. In spite of the relevance of emotions in the treatment of chronic pain, including FMS, only two studies have proposed intervention programs focus on anger treatment. These two studies have observed a positive reduction in anger levels through mindfulness and a strength training program. In conclusion, anger might be a meaningful therapeutic target in the attenuation of pain sensitivity, and the improvement of the general treatment effects and health-related quality of life in FMS patients. More intervention programs directed to reduce anger and contribute to improve well-being in FMS patients are needed.

Keywords: fibromyalgia syndrome; anger; pain; intervention; health-related quality of life

Citation: Galvez-Sánchez, C.M.; Reyes del Paso, G.A.; Duschek, S.; Montoro, C.I. The Link between Fibromyalgia Syndrome and Anger: A Systematic Review Revealing Research Gaps. *J. Clin. Med.* **2022**, *11*, 844. https://doi.org/10.3390/jcm11030844

Academic Editor: Sabrina Ravaglia

Received: 26 December 2021
Accepted: 2 February 2022
Published: 5 February 2022

1. Introduction

There is controversy on the conceptualization of anger [1]. Although there exists a theoretical mismatch about the nature and definition of anger, its complex and dynamic conceptualization is recognized [2–4]. In this sense, anger is considered one of the basic emotions together with fear, disgust, sadness, happiness, and surprise [1,4,5]. Anger may be both, a state and a personality trait [1,6]. Furthermore, anger is mainly expressed in two basic dimensions: anger towards others or outside (also called anger-out), and anger towards oneself or within (which is also known as anger-in, anger turned inward, or unexpressed anger). On purpose, these two basic dimensions have been deeply studied in relation to anger management (i.e., as anger-in (the tendency to repress anger when it is experienced) and anger-out (the leaning to express anger through verbal or physical forms)) [7], and the sensitivity to both, acute and chronic pain [8].

Related to the neurological correlates of anger, several brain structures have been involved in both anger and aggression, including those related with emotion regulation (i.e., the amygdala) [1,5]. For instance, studies focus on human brain imaging have reported greater activity in anterior cingulate cortex and orbitofrontal cortex when individuals are asked to recall past experiences that made them feel angry [5,9]. Historically, studies of anger and aggression have been conducted to explore the involvement of subcortical structures in emotion [1]. Among these structures, the hypothalamus has been one of the earliest and leading associated to anger and aggressive behavior, and based on it a neural circuit for anger and aggression has been frequently proposed [1].

In addition, the neurotransmitter serotonin has also been proposed to play a relevant role in the regulation of anger and aggression [1,9]. In fact, the serotonin deficiency hypothesis (that is, the causal role of diminished serotonin in anger and aggression) is widely supported by the scientific evidence. This evidence shows clearly that aggression is inversely related to serotonergic activity [1,5].

Chronic pain patients usually experience anger [10,11]. Nonetheless, it tends to be underestimated due to the denial and negative social connotation of this emotion [12], especially in women [13]. A possible explanation for anger denial can be related to the social norms and religious values which are assumed to repress its expression [14]. Chronic pain patients, compared to healthy controls, have frequently reported higher levels of anger suppression and/or hostility, which in turn have been related to increased pain and disability [10,11,15]. Kerns et al. [16] reported that the internalization of angry feelings explained a considerable part of the variance in pain intensity, perceived interference and reported frequency of pain behaviors in chronic pain patients. Gaskin et al. [17] revealed that state anger may be a significant predictor of the affective pain. Anger-in has also significantly been associated with depression and pain, whereas anger-out has been linked to greater disability in chronic pain patients [10].

One of the prototypical chronic pain conditions is fibromyalgia syndrome (FMS), which is characterized by generalized and persistent non-inflammatory musculoskeletal pain. Accompanying symptoms frequently comprise depression, anxiety, fatigue, insomnia, morning stiffness, and cognitive impairments (i.e., memory and attention problems, concentration difficulties, mental slowness, etc.) [18,19]. Moreover, a high percentage of FMS patients generally exhibited negative affect, which encompass alexithymia, catastrophizing, neuroticism [20–23] and deficit in health-related quality of life [21,22,24]. Its prevalence is stablished at 2 to 4% in the general population, and seems to be more frequent in women than in men [18]. However, recent studies reveal a possible gender bias which leads healthcare professionals to overestimate FMS prevalence in women simultaneously is underestimated in men [25,26]. Nowadays, there is not a specific treatment for FMS. Therefore, research should contribute to the clinical practice.

Regarding the empirical investigation of the role of anger in FMS, the available literature is scarce. Several authors have pointed out that FMS patients tend to experience higher levels of anger, in comparison with rheumatoid arthritis (RA) patients and healthy controls [27–29]. In the same line, RA patients are considered to be more prone to experience anger (trait anger) in addition to readily express it, while anger is rather internalized and suppressed by FMS patients [30]. Inhibited anger has been linked to greater intense pain than uninhibited anger [31,32], this being, in fact, more common in FMS patients [20,27]. On this detail, physiological arousal has been proposed as a mechanism that underlies the effect of anger in pain intensity due to effortful suppression, and the counterintuitive rise of the accessibility of angry thoughts and feelings after suppression [7,33]. Additionally, both enhanced [27,34] and reduced [35,36] pain has been reported after anger expression (measured by the 'Anger Expression Inventory', experimental emotion-induction tasks, etc.) [34,35]. These mixed findings may be explained by the trait-by-state matching model [37]. This model proposes a reduction of anger and its negative consequences such as pain by the matching of a general style to express anger with actual anger-expressive behavior [36]. Oppositely, according to the same model, the lack of anger expression in high trait anger-out individuals intensifies anger and pain [36]. Furthermore, higher pain and anger has been linked to poorer health and quality of life in FMS [24].

Due to the fact that social constraints discourage the expression of anger, overall, in women [13], frequent mismatches may arise between the urge to express anger and its actual expression [38]. Furthermore, given that anger is associated with negative clinical outcomes in FMS, it can be argued that its addressing in clinical practice might be beneficial for optimizing treatment and improving health-related quality of life of these patients. However, fewer studies exploring the beneficial effects of its intervention have been conducted. Based on the above reviewed literature, the present systematic review focuses on exploring the connection between anger and FMS and, based on it, delimiting possible gaps in the research, altogether aimed at improving FMS clinical intervention and guiding future research on this topic.

2. Materials and Methods

2.1. Search Strategy

Accordingly, to the guidelines of the Cochrane Collaboration and the Preferred Reporting Items for Systematic Reviews and Meta-Analyses (PRISMA), the current systematic review was conducted [39]. The Prospective Register of Systematic Reviews (PROSPERO) international database was forehand used to register the review protocol (registration ID: CRD42021226843). The search terms included: "fibromyalgia" and "anger". The terms were extracted from the Medical Subject Headings (MeSH). The PICO question was: Which is the relation between fibromyalgia and anger and the possible gaps on the -based on it- lines of research?

Two researchers (C.M.G.-S. and C.I.M.) independently searched the PubMed, Scopus, and Web of Science (WOS) databases. In case of exist any discrepancy, it was solved by consensus between authors. All articles were independently screened by the two researchers previously mentioned (C.M.G.-S. and C.I.M.), who also selected the studies which fulfill the inclusion criteria for the subsequent full text analysis. In addition, the titles and abstracts of the articles were revised to eliminate irrelevant research according to the review objectives; later, the selected articles were analyzed in depth. In accordance with the inclusion and exclusion criteria, the full texts of relevant articles were screened to reach a final set of articles to be included in the revision. C.M.G.-S. and C.I.M. decided whether to include or exclude the different studies that arose in the preliminary screened and any discrepancies were solved by all authors, who made the final judgement regarding the inclusion of each research. In the PRISMA flowchart (Figure 1) the screening and selection processes are shown for better comprehension. Before data extraction and quality assessment, C.M.G.-S. and C.I.M. revised the final set of articles to verify their eligibility for this systematic review. The last search was performed on 26 November 2021.

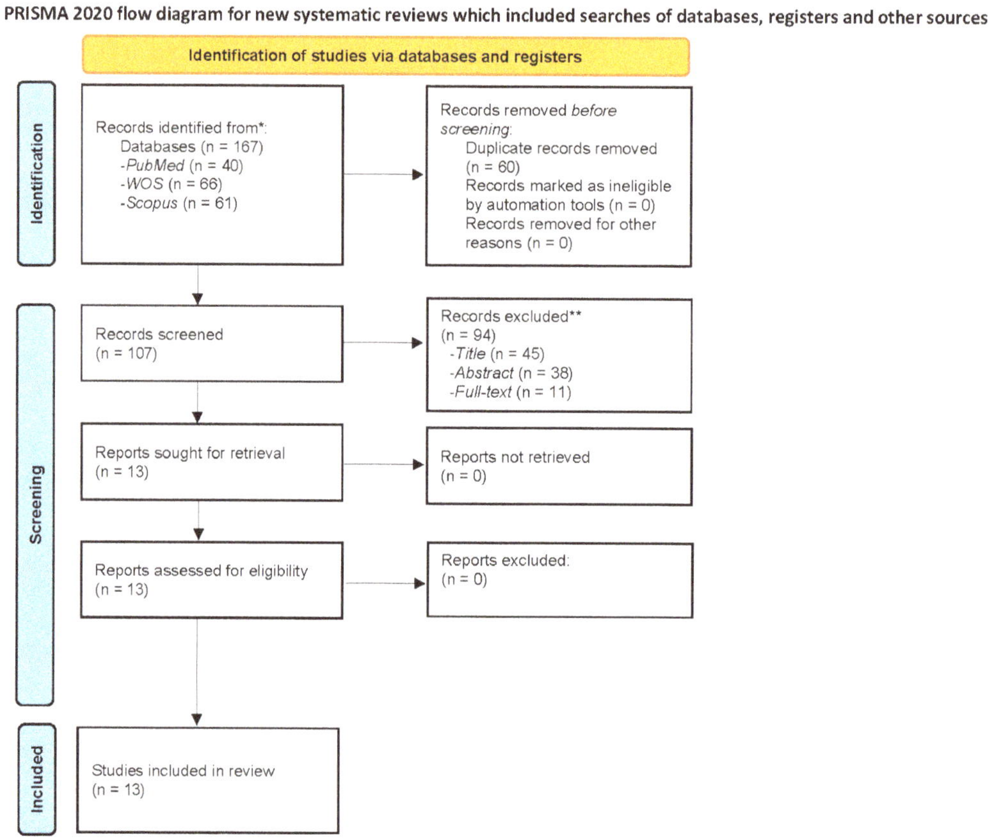

Figure 1. Flow diagram of FMS and anger.

2.2. Eligibility Criteria

The inclusion criteria comprise: (1) peer-reviewed original studies of FMS and anger, (2) adult patients (≥18 years old) with an official diagnosis of FMS (American College of Rheumatology official criteria); and (3) English-written articles. Likewise, articles were excluded if they were (1) review article or meta-analysis; (2) comment, editorial, case report, letter, or meeting/congress abstract; and (3) non-English publication.

2.3. Data Extraction and Quality Assessment

C.M.G.-S. and C.I.M., independently extracted the characteristic, methodologies and main results of each article; solving any discrepancies between all authors. To elaborate the Table 1, the following data was retrieved: first author, study name, country, year of publication, study design, sample size (participant age and sex), total of participants in each study group, and the diagnostic criteria of FMS. The studies details can be consulted in Table 1. The other two authors (G.A.R.d.P. and S.D.) reviewed all the data to guarantee the quality and precision of the extraction.

With the objective to assess the quality of the selected articles, both C.M.G.-S. and C.I.M. independently assessed and explored the limitations of each study. As in previous occasions, any discrepancies in the analysis of limitations were discussed by all authors, who made the final decision together.

2.4. Data Synthesis

Considering the purpose of this systematic review, the authors checked the main objectives of each study, the methodology, and if there were or not healthy control groups included. The clinical relevance of the main findings and the principal limitations of each research were also determined (See Table 1 for more detail). The analysis of the characteristics of each study and their quality and limitations—following the guidelines of the Cochrane Collaboration and the Preferred Reporting Items for Systematic Reviews and Meta-Analyses (PRISMA)—were made to better knowledge of the connection between FMS and anger and to stablish possible research gaps; the last with the objective to improve FMS clinical intervention and guide future research lines.

3. Results

3.1. Literature Search and Study Characteristics

A total of 167 articles were identified among all database searches, and 107 were finally chosen for screening. The detailed inclusion process may be reviewed in the PRISMA flow chart (Figure 1). Finally, 24 full-text articles were analyzed to assess their eligibility for the current systematic review. Only 13 articles fulfilled the inclusion criteria, therefore, they were included in the data extraction (Table 1) and quality assessment processes.

The selected studies were published between 2000 and 2019. Within the 13 studies, 11 were cross-sectional [20,24,27–30,40–45], 1 longitudinal [46], and 1 was a clinical trial [47]. Of the total of selected studies, nine studies were conducted in Europe [24,27,29,40–42,44–46], one in the United States of America [28], two in Brazil [43,47] and one in Israel [30]. The 13 selected studies include a total of 1511 participants, of which 902 are women with FMS (age range: 40–58 years old) and 595 women belong to the control groups: 151 women with another chronic pain disorder: 71 RA patients (age range: 45–46 years old), 50 chronic low back pain patients (age mean: 47 years old), 30 osteoporosis and/or osteoarthritis patients (age mean: 59 years old) and 444 healthy women (age range: 38–52 years). In total, only 14 men (9 men with FMS and 5 healthy men) participated particularly in one of the studies [24].

Table 1. Characteristics of relevant eligible studies regarding FMS and Anger.

First Author (Publication Year), Study Name, Country	Objective	Study Design	Sample Size [Mean ± Age (SD)]	FMS Diagnostic Criteria	Instruments	Variables and Results
Amir et al., 2000 [30]. Coping styles, anger, social support, and suicide risk of women with Fibromyalgia Syndrome. Israel.	To examine some personal dispositions in FMS patients.	Cross-sectional.	N = 220 female participants. 51 FMS patients (48.96 ± 8.41). 51 RA patients (46.25 ± 13.61). 50 CLBP patients (47.12 ± 11.61). 50 HW (45.66 ± 13.11).	1990 ACR.	Coping Inventory for Stressful Situations. STAXI. Suicide Risk Scale. Social Support Scale.	CP patients: similar personality traits. High coping style of avoidance and anger (especially: state anger and anger-in). FMS patients: not significant differences from the other patient groups on any variables. Not have a characteristic personality pattern.
Sayar et al., 2004 [27]. Alexithymia and anger in patients with Fibromyalgia. Turkey.	To delineate the relevance of the personality construct alexithymia and anger-in in patients with FMS.	Cross-sectional.	N = 112 female participants. 50 FMS patients (40.50 ± 8.80). 20 RA patients (45.60 ± 14.90). 42 HW (38.80 ± 10.40).	1990 ACR.	FIQ. BDI. BAI. STAXI. VAS. TAS.	FMS patients: higher anger-in than in RA patients. Anger-out and anxiety predicted the level of pain severity. In spite of anger-in is higher in FMS, it is the behavioral expression of anger, together with anxiety, that predicts the pain severity.
Shelley-Tremblay et al., 2009 [28]. The effects of sucrose consumption on left-frontal asymmetry and anger in persons with Fibromyalgia Syndrome. United States of America.	To determine whether FMS patients differ from age-matched healthy normal controls in their reaction to 75 g of sucrose by measuring the time course of self-report and electrophysiological responses.	Cross-sectional.	N = 18 female participants. 8 FMS patients (48.05 ± 6.14). 10 HW (47.05 ± 7.08).	1990 ACR.	Demographic Questionnaire. FIQ. HADS. POMS. Carbohydrate Addict's Scale. Sucrose test meal beverage. Apparatus: Biopac MP30. Scan 4.2. An Accu-Chek Advantage.	FMS patients: higher levels of depression, anger, and other indicators of distress at all time points and increased rLFA than HW. Correlation between anger an increased rLFA.

Table 1. *Cont.*

First Author (Publication Year), Study Name, Country	Objective	Study Design	Sample Size [Mean ± Age (SD)]	FMS Diagnostic Criteria	Instruments	Variables and Results
Van Middendorp et al., 2010 [44]. The effects of anger and sadness on clinical pain reports and experimentally-induced pain thresholds in women with and without fibromyalgia. Netherlands.	To examine the effects of experimentally induced anger and sadness on self-reported clinical and experimentally-induced pain in a sample of women with and without fibromyalgia.	Cross-sectional.	N = 121 female participants. 62 FMS patients (46.30 ± 10.80). 59 HW (48.90 ± 11.40).	1990 ACR.	PANAS-X. VAS. Emotion induction procedure: autobiographical recall procedure. Experimentally-induced pain (electrical pain induction) measures: Sensory threshold. Pain threshold. Pain tolerance.	FMS patients: anger and sadness amplify pain in women with and without FMS. A stronger emotion-induced pain response was associated with more emotional reactivity. Anger and sadness reactivity to the emotion inductions were associated with greater increases in clinical pain responses. No convincing evidence was found for a larger sensitivity to anger and sadness in women with FMS than in women without FMS, or for a larger sensitivity to anger than to sadness in FMS.
Van Middendorp et al., 2010 [29]. Effects of anger and anger regulation styles on pain in daily life of women with fibromyalgia: a diary study. Netherlands.	To examine, among patients with fibromyalgia, whether anger during everyday life amplifies pain and whether general and situational anger inhibition and anger expression modulate the anger–pain link.	Cross-sectional.	N = 333 female participants. 333 FMS patients (47.00 ± 12.01).	1990 ACR.	Diary. SECS. Daily anger questions. VAS.	FMS patients: state anger predicted higher end-of-day pain in half of the patients, but lower pain in one-quarter of patients. State anger inhibition was unrelated to pain. Trait anger inhibition was related to more pain. Lowest pain level among patients with high trait anger expression who actually expressed their anger in an anger-arousing situation.

Table 1. *Cont.*

First Author (Publication Year), Study Name, Country	Objective	Study Design	Sample Size [Mean ± Age (SD)]	FMS Diagnostic Criteria	Instruments	Variables and Results
González-Roldán et al., 2013 [41]. Altered psychophysiological responses to the view of others' pain and anger faces in fibromyalgia patients. Spain.	To examined brain activity, corrugator muscle electromyography (EMG), and heart rate (HR) responses to others' faces expressing pain in patients with fibromyalgia.	Cross-sectional.	N = 40 female participants. 20 FMS patients (53.40 ± 8.10). 20 HW (52.70 ± 9.90).	1990 ACR.	Semistandardized interview. BDI. STAI. PANAS. EHI. WHYMPI (only in FMS). Emotional Face Task. Psychophysiological Recordings: Corrugator EMG activity, HR, and EEG signals.	FMS patients: greater cardiac deceleration to all facial expressions than pain-free controls, and enhanced N100 amplitudes to pain and anger faces in comparison with neutral faces. Greater theta power in response to pain and anger faces, as well as more reduced alpha power than pain-free controls to all faces.
Amutio et al., 2015 [46]. Mindfulness training for reducing anger, anxiety, and depression in Fibromyalgia patients. Spain.	To verify whether the application of a mindfulness-based training program was effective in modifying anger, anxiety, and depression levels in a group of women diagnosed with FMS.	Longitudinal Study.	N = 32 female patients. 32 FMS patients (51.82 ± 10.18): 14 experimental group and 18 control group (waiting list).		BDI. STAI. STAXI-2. Mindfulness intervention program.	FMS patients: a significant reduction of anger (trait) levels, internal expression of anger, state anxiety, and depression as well as a significant increase in internal control of anger. Mindfulness-based treatment was effective after 7 weeks. Results were maintained 3 months after the end of the intervention.
Ricci et al., 2016 [42]. Worry and anger rumination in Fibromyalgia Syndrome. Italy.	(1) To investigate the psychological profile of patients with FMS as compared to patients with other chronic pain syndromes (CP) and healthy subjects (HS) and (2) To examine the associations between anxiety, depression, worry and angry rumination in FMS patients.	Cross-sectional.	N = 90 female participants. 30 FMS patients (54.00 ± 12.00). 30 (59.00 ± 13.00) women with other type of CP (osteoporosis and osteoarthritis). 30 HW (age not specified).	1990 and 2010 ACR.	Socio-demographic information form. STAI. PSWQ. BDI-I. ARS.	FMS patients: higher levels of state and trait anxiety, worry and angry rumination than CP patients and HS. Worry and angry rumination were strongly associated in FMS.

Table 1. *Cont.*

First Author (Publication Year), Study Name, Country	Objective	Study Design	Sample Size [Mean ± Age (SD)]	FMS Diagnostic Criteria	Instruments	Variables and Results
Di Tella et al., 2017 [40]. Alexithymia, not fibromyalgia, predicts the attribution of pain to anger-related facial expressions. Italy.	To test the hypothesis that the attribution of pain to emotional facial expressions (other than pain) is greater in patients with FMS.	Cross-sectional.	N = 123 female participants. 41 FMS patients (50.80 ± 10.20). 82 HW (51.70 ± 8.40).	Expert rheumatologist.	HADS. TAS-20. Emotional Pain Estimation and Emotional Pain Ascription Task: modified version of the Ekman 60 Faces Test.	FMS patients: not increased attribution of pain to facial expressions of emotions. Alexithymic individuals demonstrated no specific problem in the recognition of basic emotions, but attributed significantly more pain to angry facial expression.
Offenbaecher et al., 2017 [24]. Struggling with adversities of life: the role of forgiveness in patients suffering from Fibromyalgia. Germany.	(1) To compare the magnitude and direction of associations between forgiveness and pain, mental and physical health, quality of life, and anger in a sample of FMS participants and healthy controls, and (2) To compare FMS and controls on mean levels of these variables.	Cross-sectional	N = 254 participants. 173 FMS patients (161 women and 9 men) (58.00 ± 8.80). 81 HP (76 women and 5 men) (47.20 ± 14.20).	Not specified.	Initial survey. Demographic questions: age, education, religion, sex and marital status. Two questions about the degree of religiosity and spirituality. Forgiveness of self and others scales. HADS. SF-12. SF-16. STAI-II. VAS. Regional pain scale.	FMS patients: higher pain and anger and poorer health and quality of life. Lower levels of both forgiveness of self and others.

Table 1. *Cont.*

First Author (Publication Year), Study Name, Country	Objective	Study Design	Sample Size [Mean ± Age (SD)]	FMS Diagnostic Criteria	Instruments	Variables and Results
El Tassa et al., 2018 [43]. Mood states, depressive symptoms, and physical function in women with Fibromyalgia. Brazil.	To investigate the relationship between mood states, depressive symptoms, and physical performance in women with FMS.	Cross-sectional case-control study.	N = 45 female participants. 28 FMS patients (44.80 ± 5.50). 17 HW (43.40 ± 4.70).	ACR 1990.	BRUMS. BDI. HAQ. VAS. Threshold painful sensibility: dial algometer. Physical Function: 6-min Walk Test; Sit and Reach Test; 8-ft Up Go Test; and 30-s Chair Stand Test. Knee flexion and extension maximum isometric voluntary contractions (MIVC).	FMS patients: tension and anger showed a positive correlation with tests that demand strength in knee extension.
Andrade et al., 2019 [47]. Acute effect of strength training on mood of patients with fibromyalgia syndrome. Brazil.	To analyze the acute effect of strength training (ST) sessions on the mood states of patients with fibromyalgia.	Clinical trial.	N = 28 female participants. 28 FMS patients (51.88 ± 10.22).	1990 and 2016 ACR.	Sociodemographic and clinical data: self-reported instrument. BRUMS. Strength training program.	FMS patients: the ST practice had positive effects on the patients' mood states after a single session. Reductions in anger, mental confusion, mood depression, fatigue, and tension, due to ST program.

Table 1. *Cont.*

First Author (Publication Year), Study Name, Country	Objective	Study Design	Sample Size [Mean ± Age (SD)]	FMS Diagnostic Criteria	Instruments	Variables and Results
Toussaint et al., 2019 [45]. Anger rumination mediates differences between fibromyalgia patients and healthy controls on mental health and quality of life. Germany.	To examine differences between fibromyalgia patients and healthy controls on anger rumination, mental health and quality of life and tested anger rumination as a mediator of patient-control differences in mental health and quality of life.	Cross-sectional.	N = 116 female participants. 58 FMS patients (58.80 ± 8.80). 58 HW (47.00 ± 14.20).	Having an FMS diagnosis (any criteria specified).	Socio-demographics data: age, sex, and educational level. ARS. HADS. SF-12. SF-16.	FMS patients: higher anger rumination scales and depression and anxiety and lower on quality of life. All anger rumination scales were related to poorer mental health and quality of life. Patient–control differences on mental health and quality of life were mediated by anger rumination. The only subscale with mediating effects was anger memories.

Abbreviations: ACR: American College of Rheumatology's Criteria; ARS: Anger Rumination Scale; BAI: Beck Anxiety Inventory; BDI: Beck Depression Inventory; BRUMS: Brunel Mood Scale; CLBP: Chronic Lower Back Pain; CP: chronic pain syndromes; EHI: Edinburgh Handedness Inventory; EEG: Electroencephalogram; EMG: Electromyography; FIQ: Fibromyalgia Impact Questionnaire; FMS: Fibromyalgia Syndrome; HADS: Hospital Anxiety and Depression Scale; HAQ: Health Assessment Questionnaire; HP: Healthy Participants; HR: Heart Rate; HW: Healthy Women; PANAS: Positive and Negative Affect Schedule; PANAS-X: Positive and Negative Affect Schedule-Expanded Form; POMS: Profile of Mood States; PSWQ: Penn State Worry Questionnaire; SECS: Self-Expression and Control Scale; SF-12: 12-item Quality of Life Scale; SF-16: 16-item Quality of Life Scale; STAXI: State-Trait Anger Expression Inventory; STAXI-2: State-Trait Anger Expression Inventory; STAI: Spielberger State Anxiety Inventory; STAI-II: State-Trait Anger Inventory-II; RA: Rheumatoid Arthritis; TAS-20: Toronto Alexithymia Scale; VAS: Visual Analogue Scale; WHYMPI: West Haven-Yale Multidimensional Pain Inventory.

3.2. FMS and Anger

The current systematic review has an explorative nature and the selected studies included experimental tasks, descriptive studies, and interventions or treatments studies (such as mindfulness and strength training programs), among other designs to evaluate, treat (to reduce or to learn how to better cope with anger) or elicit an anger response, or analyze the attentional negative bias to anger.

3.2.1. Anger in the Context of Personality Research

A predominant coping style of avoidance and anger, especially a high state anger and anger-in, was found in chronic pain patients [30]. In the same line, anger-in tend to be higher in FMS patients in comparison with healthy participants [24,27–29] and RA patients [27]. On purpose, anger-in and the anxiety scores foretold the level of pain severity in FMS patients [27]. However, it is interesting to note that in spite of anger-in is higher in patients who suffer from FMS, it is the behavioral expression of anger, along with anxiety, which predicts the pain severity in these patients [27].

Related to personality patterns, chronic patients seem to share some similar personality traits [30]. Several authors state that FMS patients do not significant differ from the other chronic pain patient groups (i.e., chronic lower back pain and RA patients) on personality traits [30]. In the case of anger as personality trait, anger seems not to be a characteristic personality trait in FMS patients [30].

3.2.2. The Association between Anger and Other Relevant Variables in FMS

On the other hand, different researches studied the relationships between anger and clinical, emotional and/or physiological variables. In the physiological aspect, Shelley-Tremblay et al. [28] observed that FMS patients exhibited greater levels of depression and anger, among other indicators of distress as well as increased relative left-frontal activation (rLFA) than healthy participants. An association between anger and increased rLFA has been also suggested [28]. Furthermore, in a study conducted by González-Roldán et al. [41] FMS patients showed greater cardiac deceleration to all facial expressions compared to pain-free controls, and enhanced N100 amplitudes to pain and anger faces in comparison with neutral faces; supporting the presence of an attentional bias in FMS patients that would contribute to the automatic encoding of pain-related and unpleasant bodily information. Moreover, in the same study, a greater theta power was observed in response to pain and anger faces, along with more reduced alpha power than pain-free controls to all faces; pointing out that a higher recruitment of attentional resources and a more elaborated stimulus encoding seem to characterize the brain processing of pain and anger faces in FMS patients [41].

Regarding clinical, cognitive, and emotional variables, van Middendorp et al. [29] were the first authors to analyze both the general tendency to regulate anger (trait anger regulation) and its actual regulation in anger-arousing situations (state anger regulation). In this study, state anger predicted higher end-of-day pain in the almost half of the FMS patients (in 166 of 333 FMS patients), but lower pain in one-quarter of patients [29]. However, while state anger inhibition was unrelated to pain [29], trait anger inhibition was related to higher levels of pain [29]. Lower pain levels among FMS patients scoring high in trait anger expression (who actually expressed their anger in an anger-arousing situation) were also found [29].

Altogether, anger and sadness seem to amplify pain in women with and without FMS [44]. In fact, a stronger emotion-induced pain response was linked to more emotional reactivity [44]. Nevertheless, no conclusive evidence was found for a larger sensitivity to anger and sadness in female FMS patients than in women without FMS, or for a larger sensitivity to anger than to sadness in female FMS patients [44]. Likewise, anger and sadness were confirmed to be general risk factors for pain amplification [44], which emphasizes the need to implement emotion regulation techniques in clinical practice in order to reduce emotional pain sensitization in FMS patients [44].

Moreover, FMS patients exhibit higher levels of state and trait anxiety, worry, and angry rumination than other chronic pain patients (e.g., osteoporosis and osteoarthritis) [42,45] and healthy participants [42]. Simultaneously, worry and angry rumination has been strongly associated within the FMS group [42]. All anger rumination scales have been associated with a poor mental health and quality of life [45]. Moreover, the reported differences on mental health and quality of life between FMS patients and healthy participants have proposed to be mediated by anger rumination [45]. Additionally, in the study of Offenbaecher et al. [24], FMS showed higher pain and anger and poorer health and quality of life, which in turn were associated to lower levels of both, forgiveness of self and forgiveness of others [24].

It has also been observed that people with FMS who score high in alexithymia (difficulties in identifying and describing subjective feelings together with external-oriented thinking) attributed more pain to faces that express anger in facial recognition tasks compared to the rest of basic emotions [40].

3.2.3. Interventions Aimed at Reducing or Better Coping Anger in FMS

Concerning physical activity, tension and anger showed a positive association with tests that require strength in knee extension in female FMS patients [43]. The mood states have been demonstrated to be also factors which may favor or impair motor performance [43]. El Tassa et al. [43] using the Profile of Mood States (POMS) instrument, authors reported that the greater success in physical performance is generally manifested by factors such as greater values of vigor (positive factors) and lower values of tension, depression, fatigue, confusion, and anger (usually associated with a physical depressed state). This study highlights a likely association among mood states (i.e., anger), depressive symptoms, and physical function (particularly physical function by field-based fitness tests). However, the lack of further studies at this regard should be accounted for.

Lastly, only two studies [46,47] have proposed and examined anger intervention programs. Amutio et al. [46] developed a mindfulness-based program intervention which resulted in a considerable decrease of anger (trait) levels (measured by the State-Trait Anger Expression Inventory), internal expression of anger, state anxiety, and depression together with an important increase in internal control of anger in the FMS compared to the FMS control group (waiting list) [46]. The mindfulness-based treatment was effective after seven weeks and its benefits were long lasting three months after the end of the intervention program [46]. Similarly, Andrade et al. [47] developed a strength training program to improve the mood state of FMS patients. The strength training program had a positive impact on the patients' mood state after a single session [47]. Reductions in levels of anger (state), mental confusion, depression, fatigue, and tension due to the strength training program were also reported [47].

3.3. *Quality of Selected Studies*

C.M.G.-S. and C.I.M., performed a detailed evaluation of each study and any discrepancy was resolved by discussion with the rest of the authors. Due to the homogeneity of the selected manuscripts, the analysis was focus on the limitations of each study.

The main limitations of studies included the specification of two different diagnostic criteria for FMS in the same research [42,47] (for instance the 1990 and 2010 criteria [42] or the 1990 and 2016 criteria) [47]. In both studies [42,47] it is not clear on which diagnostic criteria the study based on. Although the 1990 ACR criteria was replaced by the 2010 criteria and nowadays new diagnostic proposals were undertaken (i.e., 2016 criteria), the major part of healthcare practitioners continue employing digital palpation or 1990 ACR criteria, in which is difficult to control the level of pressure exerted, and over or underdiagnosis seems to appear [18,19,48–50]. Additionally, it has been pointed out that the 1990 criteria and 2016 proposal entail different measures of FMS [51]. The 1990 criteria emphasize peripheral allodynia (tender points), whereas the 2016 emphasized the central pain perception and distress [51]. Therefore, it is important to inform about the used FMS diagnostic criteria.

Other limitations found were: (1) the non-specification of the diagnostic criteria used at all [24,45]; (2) the non-report of the mean and standard deviation of the age of healthy participants [42]; (3) the low sample size (<20 participants) [28]; and (4) the non-clarification of how the sample size was calculated [24,27–30,40,41,43,44,46]. In fact, only three studies reported the procedure for the determination of the sample size [42,45,47]. The previous analysis also reveals the need to overcome the research gap referred to the variety of methodological designs. It would be recommendable to perform similar methodological studies to draw stronger conclusions. In addition, it is necessary to evaluate differentially anger as a state and trait in order to better know its characteristics. Unfortunately, only few studies measured state and trait anger [24,27,30,41,42,46].

As is pointed in the discussion, the reported limitations need to be overcome in future studies to better understand the relation between FMS and anger, establish the possible gaps of this research and optimize the FMS intervention.

4. Discussion

The studies reviewed about anger have been heterogenous. To a better clarification and understanding, in the current discussion it will be presented the three main directions in this review: studies related to (1) personality traits in FMS, (2) the relationships between anger and other variables in FMS, and (3) interventions focused on reducing or managing anger in FMS (see Figure 2, elaborated by authors, for more detail and comprehension).

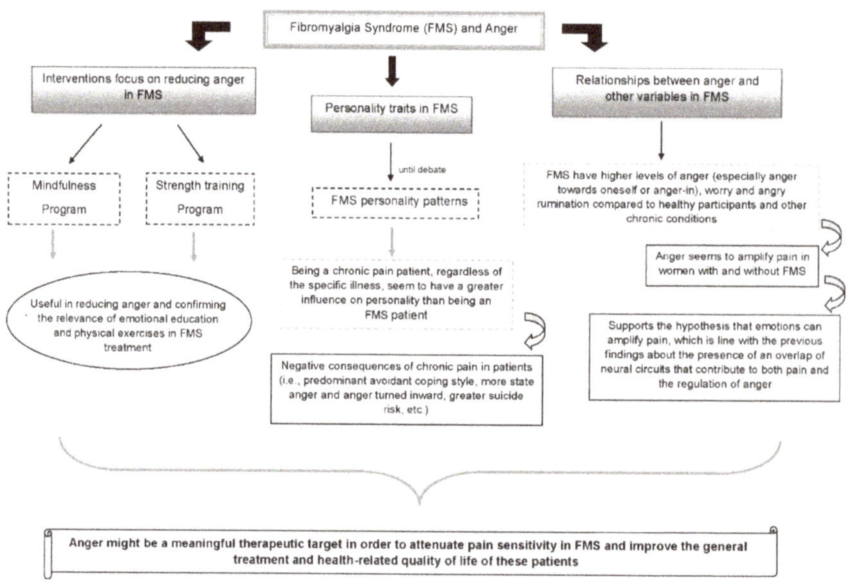

Figure 2. FMS and Anger.

4.1. Anger in the Context of Personality Studies

Firstly, the question about whether exist or no a personality trait pattern in FMS remains under debate, and therefore its possible components, including anger, are also under debate.

The absence of an FMS personality pattern [30] has been explained through different mechanisms. Firstly, it is well-known that it may be not relevant to research about "permanent" personality traits since they are uncovered by the standard measures [52]. In addition, personality traits are always influenced or interact with the environment, and this interaction is required to be analyzed in personality research [52].

Given the previous ideas, some authors state that being a chronic pain patient, regardless of the specific chronic pain illness, seems to have a greater influence on personality [30]. It can be argued that suffering from a chronic illness might be more relevant than suffering specifically from a pain disease. It is likely that these personality characteristics are the result of the chronic condition and its coping [23]. Therefore, future research should also study the factors associated with the personality traits themself instead of the existence or non-existence of the traits per se.

In spite of not existing or being under debate the existence or not of a FMS personality patterns, it has been confirmed that the presence of chronic pain has negative consequences in patients (e.g., predominant avoidant coping style, more state anger and anger-in, greater suicide risk, etc.) [30].

In the case of anger, its presence in pain patients has been assumed since a few decades ago [53,54]. Specially, with regard to anger-in, some clinicians consider this as a normal reaction to not so regular situation [30]. The tendency of showing anger-in might be related to the fear of losing support from friends and relatives [27]. Moreover, anger-in could affect both, mental and physical health and contribute to reduction of health-related quality of life of these patients [55]. At the same time, it is possible that the behavioral expression of anger leads to increased pain sensitivity by provoking sympathetic activation [27]. Anger also can become chronic. In this sense, chronic angry emotional reactions are often maladaptive since they are associated with predominant chronic sympathetic activation and interpersonal disruption [55].

In conclusion, although, as indicated above, a pain-prone personality seems not to exist and the personality patterns reported in several research result from facing to a chronic stress situation such as chronic pain, chronic pain patients and healthy participants are supposed to significantly differ in personality, indicating that the specific disease seems not to determine the pattern since it depends on the chronicity of the same [30]. Nonetheless, it should be noted the relevance to include the emotional factors for better approaching aimed at getting better health outcomes in the diagnosis, treatment, and prevention of FMS [23,50,56].

4.2. The Relationships between Anger and Clinical, Emotional and Cognitive Variables in FMS

Secondly, referring to the relation between anger and clinical, emotional, and cognitive variables in FMS (i.e., clinical pain, anxiety, depression, etc.), the majority of the studies has focused on the level of anger per se more than in the associations between clinical, cognitive and emotional FMS variables and anger; or the impact of anger in FMS patients; which should not be overlooked as another important research gap.

Most of the analyzed studies in this review report that women [24,27,28,30] and men [24] with FMS have higher levels of anger (especially anger-in compared to healthy participants [24,27–30] and RA patients) [27]. Nonetheless, one study found no convincing evidence of increased sensitivity to anger in women with FMS [29].

Regarding the physiological aspects, frequently, researchers have analyzed the association between brain physiology and mood through power spectra electroencephalography (EEG) analyses, specifically within the alpha power band (8–12 Hz) [57]. Alpha waves are usually related to a wakeful relaxed state, particularly visible in occipital regions when the eyes are closed, whereas cortical deactivation seems to be linked to an increase in alpha amplitude in response to a specific stimulus or task [58]. Furthermore, lower relative right hemisphere compared to left hemisphere EEG oscillations, especially in the frontal lobes, is associated with behavioral approach-oriented emotions including anger and positive mood states [57]. Relatively greater right, in comparison with left frontal EEG asymmetry seems to be also associated with negative emotions (i.e., depression and anxiety) [28]. This indicates, as Harmon-jones [59] suggests, that the motivational direction component (approach/withdraw) is the key peculiarity that determines the relative left or right frontal activation, instead of the valence component (positive/negative).

Based on previous findings, Shelley-Tremblay et al. [28], showed a significant correlation between anger-hostility and rLFA -limited to the frontomedial sites- in FMS patients. Apart from these results, in the study of Shelley-Tremblay et al. [28] healthy and FMS participants exhibited a steadily increase in distress. Nevertheless, while the healthy participants reported the distress as a more withdrawal-related depression response, FMS patients experienced the distress as an approach-related, anger response. These results might be suggesting the possibility of a unique pattern of response to negative events in FMS patients [28], which need to be more deeply investigated.

Moreover, previous research indicate that a carbohydrate-face diet might improve chronic and idiopathic post-prandial mood symptoms in FMS patients [28]. On purpose, the Carbohydrate Addict's Scale scores (a 17-binary forced-choice items questionnaire, to determine carbohydrate cravers, and therefore, the presence of a low carbohydrate diet), correlated with post-prandial rLFA in FMS [28]. This association is consistent with the showed appetitive approach-related motivation in the presence of negative affect in FMS patients [28]. FMS patients might ingest sweets to cope with negative physical and emotional feelings [28]. In fact, eating disorders, including greater levels of emotional eating, have been reported in FMS patients [60,61]. Based on the finding of a tiding between rLFA and positive reinforcement and anger [28], the ingestion of sweets by FMS patients may be self-reinforcing, yet tend to increase not only emotional but also physical symptoms [28]. This hypothesis needs to be consistently studied, since if it is confirmed, positive implications for FMS treatment recommendations might surface [28].

The research of Shelley-Tremblay [28] also found no evidence regarding a positive bolster in mood after consuming glucose in FMS patients. In fact, since 0 and 60 min to post-prandial high alpha oscillations arose. A possible explanation for self-medication with carbohydrates can be gain ability to be concentrated on immediate task demands, and not the improvement of mood itself [28]. Once again, our review indicates a research gap in this case of the effects of consumption of carbohydrates and glucose in FMS. In addition, in age-matched controls, the negative association observed between frontal alpha power and blood glucose may detail a decrease in frontal cortical activity associated to lessen blood glucose [28]. However, the lack of this association in FMS patients likely identify a cortical-associated alpha rhythm structures or processes disruption [28]. The presence of altered alpha, and its possible relation to thalamic abnormalities, is in line to several previous studies that stated the role of a thalamic dysfunction in FMS symptoms and etiology [62–64].

Psychophysiological responses to pain copying in chronic pain patients have also been studied [41]. It is well-known that suffering from FMS is related to a vulnerability to the effects of negative mood and a pattern of selective processing or cognitive attentional bias to the encoding of pain-related information [65–67]. In addition, it is further known that altered affective processing might be involved in the development and maintenance of pain and other affective symptoms related to FMS [20,68–70]. In this context, brain and cardiac activity elicited by viewing facial expressions of pain and anger in others is suggested to be impaired in FMS patients [41], showing an attentional negative bias which has even so far proposed as an assessment and treatment psychobiological marker in FMS. An increased mobilization of attention resources to pain and anger faces, along with a reduced allocation of attention to happy faces as well as an enhanced defensive reaction have characterized information processing in FMS [41,71].

Regarding psychological variables in FMS, behavioral expression of anger, along with anxiety, seems to be the best predictors of pain severity in FMS patients [27]. Furthermore, van Middendorp et al. [29] reported that state anger predicted higher end-of-day pain in half of the FMS patients, but lower pain in one-quarter of these patients. While state anger inhibition was not associated with pain in this study, trait anger inhibition was associated with higher pain [29]. Lower pain level among patients with high trait anger expression were also found, indicating that anger and a general leaning to inhibit anger predicts heightened pain in the everyday life of female FMS patients [29]. These results are in line with former research which demonstrated the pain-enhancing effects of anger-in, in anger induction experiments, mostly in persons who generally experience high levels of anger [12,34,72]. The current evidence suggests that the experience of both, anger and/or sadness amplify pain in women with and without FMS [44], which is congruent with the suggested presence of an overlap of neural circuits that are involved not only in pain but also in the regulation of anger [73]. As anger expression usually predicts less pain [29], the use of therapeutic emotional expression techniques in the treatment of clinical population including FMS may be beneficial [74–76].

Other negative emotions have been reported along with anger as a maladaptive distress copying style in FMS patients, for instance, rumination [42,45]. In this sense, rumination with anger has been significantly linked to poorer mental health and general health-related quality of life in patients with FMS [42,45]. In FMS patients, worry and rumination might be acting as coping strategies to deal with the negative emotional experience, although paradoxically an emotional well-being is not obtained [42]. The relationship between anger expression and health consequences is probably not linear. Ruminating and anger [77] and the mere expression of anger without cognitive processing [77] have been proposed to be maladaptive coping strategies themselves and might be mediating factor of the above relationship (see the Multiple Systems Model of Angry Rumination developed by Denson [78]). Altogether, these findings provide insights supporting the expression of one's anger as a protector against rumination, as well as a factor in solving an emotionally problematic situation, lessen anger intensity and pain.

The relation between negative affect and daily pain in chronic pain patients has been well-established [79,80]. Negative emotions seem to be experienced with more intensity in FMS patients compared to the general population [20]. Accordingly, to the strong emotions neurophysiologic pain highlight, a greater associated pain processing in FMS is likely observed [72].

Di Tella et al. [40] reported that FMS patients who scored high in alexithymia attributed more pain to faces that express anger in facial recognition tasks. Alexithymia, instead of FMS per se, seems to play a relevant role in understanding the reported differences in pain attribution to anger-related facial expressions [40]. Anger processing might contribute to explain the specific significance attribution of pain to angry faces in FMS [40]. FMS patients usually exhibit high levels of alexithymia, a personality disposition affecting emotional self-awareness [50,56,71,81–85]. Alexithymia may be conceptualized as a cognitive style characterized by a problem in identifying and describing subjective feelings, and low externally oriented thinking [86,87]. Furthermore, the involvement of anterior cingulate cortex (ACC) in alexithymia has been suggested in several studies [88–90], reinforcing the idea that an altered ACC activity compromised functioning in persons who experience high levels of alexithymia [91]. Alexithymia is associated with a delayed preparation to process biologically prepotent events as measured by the orienting complex (N2/P3a); delayed preparation is even stronger for angry faces [91]. Based on the fact that ACC is considered as the principal source of these neurophysiological components, these results are in line with the hypothesis concerning the impairment in ACC functioning in alexithymia by indexing its delayed contribution around 300 ms [91]. Empirical evidence also supports ACC reactivity is positively associated with the anger intensity [92]. More ACC activation was reported when the face depicted anger with a greater intensity [91].

Another research framework is related to forgiveness in chronic pain in general and FMS in particular. Forgiveness has been linked to pain, anger, and psychological distress in chronic pain patients [93]. Forgiving oneself and others may be included in the psychosocial care of FMS patients to potentiate enhanced mental health and quality of life and reduced anger [24]. In this sense, FMS patients usually exhibited lower levels of forgiveness not only of self but also of others [24]. The inclusion of forgiveness as a therapeutic target may facilitate FMS patients use it as a coping strategy to better deal with symptoms (both psychological and physical), and improve the general well-being [24]. Forgiveness, which is considered both a state and a trait, is a multidimensional construct that refers to oneself or others [94]. In the field of well-being promotion studies, the trait forgiveness (in face of its momentary state) is of a considerable interest due to its influence over time and situations and general greater positive psychological impact [95]. In healthy participants, forgiveness has been associated with a variety of psychological well-being indicators such as reduced anger, along with lower depression and anxiety [24,96–98]. Forgiveness has been also related to reduced sympathetic arousal, enhanced parasympathetic tone, and physical health and longevity [96–98]. In addition, in several studies using a heterogeneous sample of pain patients with various etiologies, locations, and pain duration and extension, forgiveness has been related to less time spending in avoiding or fighting again pain, reduced pain intensity and pain interference, as well as greater levels of mental health [99]. It is necessary to promote protective psychological mechanisms such as forgiveness in the wake of facilitate its potential to relieve symptoms of pain and psychological distress. This may reduce anger, promote emotional well-being, and improve quality of life in FMS patients [24]. Without detriment to the above, more studies are necessary to evaluate the anger intervention, as a state, since as a trait it is difficult to modify.

4.3. Interventions Focus on Reducing or Managing Anger in FMS

Although the findings reviewed support the undoubted clinical relevance of anger in FMS, only two studies [46,47] have up to date applied a treatment for it. Amutio et al. [46] observed that mindfulness was effective in reducing anger (trait) in FMS patients. Authors conclude that due to the prevalence of negative emotions in FMS and the problems to manage them [28,29,65–67], mindfulness seems to be a good therapeutic strategy for managing negative emotions. Mindfulness leads chronic pain patients to experience awareness and acceptance of the sensations and feelings related to their symptoms whereas they continue physically and mentally active and focus on their daily life and values [46]. Mindfulness can be conceptualized as being focus on experiences in the present moment [100]. Two basic components of mindfulness are self-regulation of attention and acceptance of one's own experiences in a non-evaluative way (in other words, a non-reactive awareness) [101]. In consequence, mindfulness seems to be a potent pathway to learn and apply new non-reactive models of responding to the emotional suffering and tolerate pain (without suffering) associated with different disorders, including FMS [46]. However, more studies are required to document the effectiveness of mindfulness programs in the reduction and management of anger in FMS patients.

Regarding physical activity in FMS patients, tension and anger showed a positive correlation with tests that demand strength in knee extension [43]. In addition, stressful interpersonal events [102], general negative affect [103], and anger in daily life [44] increase pain sensitivity and the reactivity of pain-relevant physiologic and muscle tension [36,104]. Nevertheless, more research is required to investigate whether a possible negative mood state (i.e., depressive, with predominance of anger, etc.) in the chronic pain population, influences the accomplishment of certain physical tasks (i.e., walking, running, etc.) or even tasks that reflect the activities of the daily life (i.e., doing housework, shopping, etc.) [43]. The findings of El Tassa et al. [43] clearly reveal that some components of mood states (i.e., tension and anger) are associated with the physical function of women with FMS. However, this is still a research line little explored [43]. On purpose, to relieve the physical and psychological symptoms and, in consequence, the general health of FMS patients, it is well-known that physical exercise is proposed as a valid alternative treatment since past years [47,105–108]. Between the several types of physical exercise, the most effective treatment option to reduce common symptoms of FMS has been strength training [109–114]. In the clinical trial performed by Andrade et al. [47] a reduction was reported in anger levels in FMS by a strength training program. Although these results demonstrate acute health positive outcomes to physical exercise in FMS patients [47], as it occurs with the above-mentioned study [46], more research is still needed to confirm these conclusions.

The previous results support that FMS patients who express their anger have a better clinical profile (i.e., lower level of clinical pain) [42,44]. It has also been confirmed that the psychological intervention could be also focus on developing a healthy expression of anger to reduce its negative impact on FMS patients [42,44,46,115]. It is important to note that FMS treatment guidelines emphasize the importance of patient psychoeducation and self-care strategies for the management of symptoms, and advise for the need of integrating non-pharmacologic with pharmacologic treatments [116]. Based on previous studies, both reducing anger and expressing it in a proper and healthy way seems to be useful in FMS treatment. In special, it is advisable to conduct more studies to evaluate whether specific anger reduction improves different clinical variables (i.e., a moderation analysis to check what effect has anger on the effectiveness of treatment in the rest of the clinical parameters) and whether is better express and/or reduce anger. Up to date, it seems that both (reduction and proper anger expression) are positive for FMS patients, but the remain question is if the effects of both entail equal benefits. Nevertheless, as it has been become aware along this review, more studies on the subject, in general, are needed to draw stronger conclusions. Although the majority of analyzed studies have been focus on assessing anger instead of treat it, and considering the relation between anger and the rest of aforementioned explained variables (i.e., pain, anxiety, depression, alexithymia, attentional bias, low forgiveness, altered psychophysiological responses, low health-related quality of life, etc.), it is recommendable to develop and evaluate treatment programs to instruct patients about how manage anger and, as a result, relieve their symptoms.

To summarize, this review points out some important future lines of research, such as, the circumstances in which certain personality traits are elicited rather than the existence or non-existence of the traits per se; the pattern of reactions to negative events in FMS patients; the presence of emotional eating disorders in FMS patients; the relation of anger reduction with general and positive health parameters instead of negative variables; the expression, management and levels of anger in male FMS patient; the consumption of carbohydrates and glucose in FMS, and its effects; and the possible associations among mood states (i.e., anger), physical function (particularly with reference to physical function by field-based fitness tests), etc. Regarding treatment, it is necessary to design more treatments and to develop research to assess if specific anger reduction improves different clinical parameters (i.e., anxiety, depression, pain, fatigue, insomnia, rumination, worry, coping strategies, health-related quality of life, etc.).

5. Conclusions

To the best of our knowledge, this systematic review is the first to be conducted on the relationship between FMS and anger. Anger-in tends to be higher in FMS patients compared to healthy participants and RA patients. FMS patients also exhibit greater levels of state and trait anxiety, worry and angry rumination than other chronic pain patients. Anger seems to amplify pain in women in general, especially those with FMS and affects more the health-related quality of life of FMS patients. In spite of the relevance of emotions in the treatment of chronic pain, including FMS, only two studies have proposed intervention programs focus on anger treatment, indicating a positive reduction in anger levels through mindfulness and a strength training program, respectively. Additionally, this systematic review highlights some important research gaps, as well as the need to study anger and state anger in general more than focus on anger due its overall temporal and situational consistency. Considering the influence of negative emotions on chronic pain (for example, anger, sadness, etc.) it is vital that anger is studied more deeply in FMS in order to provide insights directed to improve the diagnosis, treatment, and quality of life of these patients. More research is also needed on the anger subject in men with FMS since gender differences (i.e., in coping strategies, symptoms, treatment adherence, etc.) are relevant in chronic disease and treatment need to be personalized. In addition, FMS patients are likely to present with anger in clinical practice. Therefore, skills for handling with angry patient are essential for primary care providers at all levels.

Author Contributions: Conceptualization, C.M.G.-S. and C.I.M.; methodology, C.M.G.-S. and C.I.M.; validation, C.M.G.-S. and C.I.M.; formal analysis, C.M.G.-S., G.A.R.d.P., S.D. and C.I.M.; investigation, C.M.G.-S., G.A.R.d.P., S.D. and C.I.M.; resources, C.M.G.-S. and C.I.M.; data curation, C.M.G.-S. and C.I.M.; writing—original draft preparation, C.M.G.-S. and C.I.M.; writing—review and editing, C.M.G.-S., G.A.R.d.P., S.D. and C.I.M.; visualization, C.M.G.-S., G.A.R.d.P., S.D. and C.I.M.; supervision, C.M.G.-S. and C.I.M.; project administration, C.M.G.-S. and C.I.M. All authors have read and agreed to the published version of the manuscript.

Funding: This research received no external funding.

Institutional Review Board Statement: Not applicable.

Informed Consent Statement: Not applicable.

Conflicts of Interest: The authors declare no conflict of interest.

References

1. Gilam, G.; Hendler, T. Deconstructing Anger in the Human Brain. *Behav. Neurobiol. Schizophr. Its Treatment.* **2015**, *30*, 257–273. [CrossRef]
2. Averill, J.R. Studies on anger and aggression: Implications for theories of emotion. *Am. Psychol.* **1983**, *38*, 1145–1160. [CrossRef] [PubMed]
3. Berkowitz, L. On the formation and regulation of anger and aggression: A cognitive-neoassociationistic analysis. *Am. Psychol.* **1990**, *45*, 494–503. [CrossRef]
4. Berkowitz, L.; Harmon-Jones, E. Toward an Understanding of the Determinants of Anger. *Emotion* **2004**, *4*, 107–130. [CrossRef] [PubMed]
5. Bear, M.F.; Connors, B.W.; Paradiso, M.A. *Neuroscience: Exploring the Brain*; Wolter Kluwer: Philadelphia, PA, USA, 2016.
6. Trost, Z.; Vangronsveld, K.; Linton, S.J.; Quartana, P.J.; Sullivan, M.J. Cognitive dimensions of anger in chronic pain. *Pain* **2012**, *153*, 515–517. [CrossRef]
7. Spielberger, C.D.; Jacobs, G.; Russel, S.; Crane, R.S. Assessment of anger: The state-trait anger scale. In *Advances in Personality Assessment*; Butcher, J.N., Spielberger, C.D., Eds.; Hillsdale: Lawrence Erlbaum, NJ, USA, 1983; Volume 2, pp. 159–186.
8. Bruehl, S.; Burns, J.W.; Chung, O.Y.; Ward, P.; Johnson, B. Anger and pain sensitivity in chronic low back pain patients and pain-free controls: The role of endogenous opioids. *Pain* **2002**, *99*, 223–233. [CrossRef]
9. Alia-Klein, N.; Gan, G.; Gilam, G.; Bezek, J.; Bruno, A.; Denson, T.F.; Hendler, T.; Lowe, L.; Mariotti, V.; Muscatello, M.R.; et al. The feeling of anger: From brain networks to linguistic expressions. *Neurosci. Biobehav. Rev.* **2020**, *108*, 480–497. [CrossRef] [PubMed]
10. Okifuji, A.; Turk, D.C.; Curran, S.L. Anger in chronic pain: Investigations of anger targets and intensity. *J. Psychosom. Res.* **1999**, *47*, 1–12. [CrossRef]
11. Janssen, S.; Spinhoven, P.; Brosschot, J.F. Experimentally induced anger, cardiovascular reactivity, and pain sensitivity. *J. Psychosom. Res.* **2001**, *51*, 479–485. [CrossRef]
12. Fernandez, E.; Turk, D.C. The scope and significance of anger in the experience of chronic pain. *Pain* **1995**, *61*, 165–175. [CrossRef]
13. Porter, L.S.; Stone, A.A.; Schwartz, J.E. Anger expression and ambulatory blood pressure: A comparison of state and trait measures. *Psychosom. Med.* **1999**, *61*, 454–463. [CrossRef] [PubMed]
14. Corbishley, M.; Hendrickson, R.; Beutler, L. Behavior, affect, and cognition among psychogenic pain patients in group ex-pressive psychotherapy. *J. Pain Symptoms Manag.* **1990**, *5*, 241–248. [CrossRef]
15. Moldofsky, H.; Chester, W. Pain and mood patterns in patients with rheumatoid arthritis: A Prospective study. *Psychosom. Med.* **1970**, *32*, 309–318. [CrossRef] [PubMed]
16. Kerns, R.D.; Rosenberg, R.; Jacob, M.C. Anger expression and chronic pain. *J. Behav. Med.* **1994**, *17*, 57–67. [CrossRef] [PubMed]
17. Gaskin, M.; Greene, A.; Robinson, M.; Geisser, M. Negative affect and the experience of chronic pain. *J. Psychosom. Res.* **1992**, *36*, 707–713. [CrossRef]
18. Wolfe, F.; Clauw, D.J.; Fitzcharles, M.-A.; Goldenberg, D.L.; Katz, R.S.; Mease, P.; Russell, A.S.; Russell, I.J.; Winfield, J.B.; Yunus, M.B. The American College of Rheumatology Preliminary Diagnostic Criteria for Fibromyalgia and Measurement of Symptom Severity. *Arthritis Care Res.* **2010**, *62*, 600–610. [CrossRef]
19. Wolfe, F.; Smythe, H.A.; Yunus, M.B.; Bennett, R.M.; Bombardier, C.; Goldenberg, D.L.; Tugwell, P.; Campbell, S.M.; Abeles, M.; Clark, P.; et al. The american college of rheumatology. Criteria for the classification of fibromyalgia. Report of the Multicenter Criteria Committee. *Arthritis Rheum.* **1990**, *33*, 160–172. [CrossRef]
20. van Middendorp, H.; Lumley, M.A.; Jacobs, J.W.; van Doornen, L.J.; Bijlsma, J.W.; Geenen, R. Emotions and emotional approach and avoidance strategies in fibromyalgia. *J. Psychosom. Res.* **2008**, *64*, 159–167. [CrossRef]
21. Galvez-Sánchez, C.M.; Montoro, C.I.; Duschek, S.; Del Paso, G.A.R. Pain catastrophizing mediates the negative influence of pain and trait-anxiety on health-related quality of life in fibromyalgia. *Qual. Life Res.* **2020**, *29*, 1871–1881. [CrossRef]
22. Galvez-Sánchez, C.M.; Montoro, C.I.; Duschek, S.; del Paso, G.A.R. Depression and trait-anxiety mediate the influence of clinical pain on health-related quality of life in fibromyalgia. *J. Affect. Disord.* **2020**, *265*, 486–495. [CrossRef]

23. Montoro, C.I.; del Paso, G.A.R. Personality and fibromyalgia: Relationships with clinical, emotional, and functional variables. *Pers Individ* **2015**, *85*, 236–244. [CrossRef]
24. Offenbaecher, M.; Dezutter, J.; Kohls, N.; Sigl, C.; Vallejo, M.A.; Rivera, J.; Bauerdorf, F.; Schelling, J.; Vincent, A.; Hirsch, J.K.; et al. Struggling With Adversities of Life: The Role of Forgiveness in Patients Suffering from Fibromyalgia. *Clin. J. Pain* **2017**, *33*, 528–534. [CrossRef]
25. Wolfe, F.; Walitt, B.; Perrot, S.; Rasker, J.J.; Häuser, W. Fibromyalgia diagnosis and biased assessment: Sex, prevalence and bias. *PLoS ONE* **2018**, *13*, e0203755. [CrossRef] [PubMed]
26. Srinivasan, S.; Maloney, E.; Wright, B.; Kennedy, M.; Kallail, K.J.; Rasker, J.J.; Häuser, W.; Wolfe, F. The Problematic Nature of Fibromyalgia Diagnosis in the Community. *ACR Open Rheumatol.* **2019**, *1*, 43–51. [CrossRef]
27. Sayar, K.; Gulec, H.; Topbas, M. Alexithymia and anger in patients with fibromyalgia. *Clin. Rheumatol.* **2004**, *23*, 441–448. [CrossRef] [PubMed]
28. Shelley-Tremblay, J.; Ernst, A.; Kline, J.P. The effects of sucrose consumption on left-frontal asymmetry and anger in persons with Fibromyalgia Syndrome. *J. Musculoskelet. Pain* **2009**, *17*, 334–349. [CrossRef]
29. van Middendorp, H.; Lumley, M.A.; Moerbeek, M.; Jacobs, J.W.; Bijlsma, J.W.; Geenen, R. Effects of anger and anger regulation styles on pain in daily life of women with fibromyalgia: A diary study. *Eur. J. Pain* **2010**, *14*, 176–182. [CrossRef] [PubMed]
30. Amir, M.; Neumann, L.; Bor, O.; Shir, Y.; Rubinow, A.; Buskila, D. Coping Styles, Anger, Social Support, and Suicide Risk of Women with Fibromyalgia Syndrome. *J. Musculoskelet. Pain* **2000**, *8*, 7–20. [CrossRef]
31. Quartana, P.J.; Burns, J.W. Painful consequences of anger suppression. *Emotion* **2007**, *7*, 400–414. [CrossRef]
32. Quartana, P.J.; Yoon, K.L.; Burns, J.W. Anger Suppression, Ironic Processes and Pain. *J. Behav. Med.* **2007**, *30*, 455–469. [CrossRef]
33. Burns, J.W.; Quartana, P.J.; Bruehl, S. Anger inhibition and pain: Conceptualizations, evidence and new directions. *J. Behav. Med.* **2008**, *31*, 259–279. [CrossRef] [PubMed]
34. Bruehl, S.; Chung, O.Y.; Burns, J.W. Anger Expression and Pain: An Overview of Findings and Possible Mechanisms. *J. Behav. Med.* **2006**, *29*, 593–606. [CrossRef] [PubMed]
35. Burns, J.W.; Kubilus, A.; Bruehl, S. Emotion induction moderates effects of anger management style on acute pain sensitivity. *Pain* **2003**, *106*, 109–118. [CrossRef]
36. Burns, J.W. Arousal of negative emotions and symptom-specific reactivity in chronic low back pain patients. *Emotion* **2006**, *6*, 309–319. [CrossRef]
37. Engebretson, T.O.; Matthews, K.A.; Scheier, M.F. Relations between anger expression and cardiovascular reactivity: Reconciling inconsistent findings through a matching hypothesis. *J. Pers Soc. Psychol.* **1989**, *57*, 513–521. [CrossRef]
38. Brosschot, J.F.; Thayer, J.F. Anger inhibition, cardiovascular recovery, and vagal function: A model of the link between hostility and cardiovascular disease. *Ann. Behav. Med.* **1998**, *20*, 326–332. [CrossRef]
39. Page, M.J.; McKenzie, J.E.; Bossuyt, P.M.; Boutron, I.; Hoffmann, T.C.; Mulrow, C.D.; Shamseer, L.; Tetzlaff, J.M.; Akl, E.A.; Brennan, S.E.; et al. The PRISMA 2020 statement: An updated guideline for reporting systematic reviews. *BMJ* **2021**, *372*, n71. [CrossRef]
40. Di Tella, M.; Enrici, I.; Castelli, L.; Colonna, F.; Fusaro, E.; Ghiggia, A.; Romeo, A.; Tesio, V.; Adenzato, M. Alexithymia, not fibromyalgia, predicts the attribution of pain to anger-related facial expressions. *J. Affect. Disord.* **2018**, *227*, 272–279. [CrossRef]
41. González-Roldán, A.M.; Muñoz, M.A.; Cifre, I.; Sitges, C.; Montoya, P. Altered Psychophysiological Responses to the View of Others' Pain and Anger Faces in Fibromyalgia Patients. *J. Pain* **2013**, *14*, 709–719. [CrossRef]
42. Ricci, A.; Bonini, S.; Continanza, M.; Turano, M.; Puliti, E.; Finocchietti, A.; Bertolucci, D. Worry and anger rumination in fibromyalgia syndrome. *Reumatismo* **2016**, *68*, 195–198. [CrossRef]
43. El Tassa, K.O.M.; Leite, N.; Goes, S.M.; Homann, D.; Rodacki, A.L.F.; Titski, A.C.K.; Stefanello, J.M.F. Mood States, Depressive Symptoms, and Physical Function in Women with Fibromyalgia. *J. Exerc. Physiol. Online* **2018**, *21*, 119–132.
44. Van Middendorp, H.; Lumley, M.A.; Jacobs, J.W.G.; Bijlsma, J.W.J.; Geenen, R. The effects of anger and sadness on clinical pain reports and experimentally-induced pain thresholds in women with and without fibromyalgia. *Arthritis Care Res.* **2010**, *62*, 1370–1376. [CrossRef] [PubMed]
45. Toussaint, L.; Sirois, F.; Hirsch, J.; Kohls, N.; Weber, A.; Schelling, J.; Vajda, C.; Offenbäecher, M. Anger rumination mediates differences between fibromyalgia patients and healthy controls on mental health and quality of life. *Pers Ment. Heal.* **2019**, *13*, 119–133. [CrossRef]
46. Amutio, A.; Franco, C.; de Pérez-Fuentes, M.C.; Gázquez, J.J.; Mercader, I. Mindfulness training for reducing anger, anxiety, and depression in fibromyalgia patients. *Front Psychol.* **2015**, *5*, 1572. [CrossRef] [PubMed]
47. Andrade, A.; Steffens, R.D.A.K.; Sieczkowska, S.M.; Coimbra, D.R.; Vilarino, G.T. Acute effect of strength training on mood of patients with fibromyalgia syndrome. *Reumatismo* **2019**, *71*, 141–147. [CrossRef]
48. Wolfe, F.; Clauw, D.J.; Fitzcharles, M.A.; Goldenberg, D.L.; Häuser, W.; Katz, R.L.; Mease, P.J.; Russell, A.S.; Russell, I.J.; Walitt, B. 2016 Revisions to the 2010/2011 fibromyalgia diagnostic criteria. *Semin. Arthritis Rheum.* **2016**, *46*, 319–329. [CrossRef]
49. Galvez-Sánchez, C.M.; Del Paso, G.A.R. Diagnostic Criteria for Fibromyalgia: Critical Review and Future Perspectives. *J. Clin. Med.* **2020**, *9*, 1219. [CrossRef]
50. Galvez-Sánchez, C.M.; Duschek, S.; del Paso, G.A.R. Psychological impact of fibromyalgia: Current perspectives. *Psychol. Res. Behav. Manag.* **2019**, *12*, 117–127. [CrossRef]

51. Ahmed, S.; Aggarwal, A.; Lawrence, A. Performance of the American College of Rheumatology 2016 criteria for fibromyalgia in a referral care setting. *Rheumatol. Int.* **2019**, *39*, 1397–1403. [CrossRef]
52. Suls, J.; David, J.P.; Harvey, J.H. Personality and Coping: Three Generations of Research. *J. Pers.* **1996**, *64*, 711–735. [CrossRef]
53. Tschannen, T.A.; Duckro, P.N.; Margolis, R.B.; Tomazic, T.J. The Relationship of Anger, Depression, and Perceived Disability Among Headache Patients. *Headache J. Head Face Pain* **1992**, *32*, 501–503. [CrossRef]
54. Affleck, G.; Tennen, H.; Urrows, S.; Higgins, P. Individual differences in the day-to-day experience of chronic pain: A prospective daily study of rheumatoid arthritis patients. *Health Psychol.* **1991**, *10*(6), 419–426. [CrossRef]
55. Greenwood, K.; Thurston, R.; Rumble, M.; Waters, S.J.; Keefe, F.J. Anger and persistent pain: Current status and future directions. *Pain* **2003**, *103*, 1–5. [CrossRef]
56. Davydov, D.M.; Galvez-Sánchez, C.M.; Montoro, C.I.; de Guevara, C.M.L.; Reyes del Paso, G.A. Personalized behavior management as a replacement for medications for pain control and mood regulation. *Sci. Rep.* **2021**, *11*, 20297. [CrossRef] [PubMed]
57. Coan, J.; Allen, J.J. Frontal EEG asymmetry as a moderator and mediator of emotion. *Biol. Psychol.* **2004**, *67*, 7–50. [CrossRef] [PubMed]
58. Kimura, M.; Mori, T.; Suzuki, H.; Endo, S.; Kawano, K. EEG changes in odor effects after the stress of long monotonous work. *J. Int. Soc. Life Inform. Sci.* **2001**, *19*, 271–274.
59. Harmon-Jones, E. Contributions from research on anger and cognitive dissonance to understanding the motivational functions of asymmetrical frontal brain activity. *Biol. Psychol.* **2004**, *67*, 51–76. [CrossRef]
60. Elkfury, J.L.; Antune, L.C.; Angoleri, L.D.M.; Sipmann, R.B.; de Souza, A.; Torres, I.L.D.S.; Caumo, W. Dysfunctional eating behavior in fibromyalgia and its association with serum biomarkers of brain plasticity (BDNF and S100B): An exploratory study. *Arch. Endocrinol. Metab.* **2021**, *65*, 713–722. [CrossRef]
61. Carnes, A.; Alcántara, A.; Bueno, M.; Castan, E.; Lecube, A. Fibromyalgia and eating disorders in morbid obesity. *Endocrinología y Nutrición* **2014**, *61*, 555–556. [CrossRef]
62. Schmidt-Wilcke, T.; Luerding, R.; Weigand, T.; Jurgens, T.; Schuierer, G.; Leinisch, E. Striatal grey matter increased in patients suffering from fibromyalgia A voxel based morphometry study. *Pain* **2007**, *132*, S109–S116. [CrossRef]
63. Chen, J.J.H.; Wang, J.Y.; Chang, Y.M.; Su, S.Y.; Chang, C.T.; Sun, S.S.; Kao, C.H.; Lee, C.C. Regional cerebral blood flow between primary and concomitant fibromyalgia patients: A possible way to differentiate concomitant fibromyalgia from the primary disease. *Scand. J. Rheumatol.* **2007**, *36*, 226–232. [CrossRef] [PubMed]
64. Wik, G.; Wik, G.; Fischer, H.; Bragee, B.; Finer, B.; Fredrikson, M. Functional anatomy of hypnotic analgesia: A PET study of patients with fibromyalgia. *Eur. J. Pain* **1999**, *3*, 7–12. [CrossRef]
65. Aldrich, S.; Eccleston, C.; Crombez, G. Worrying about chronic pain: Vigilance to threat and misdirected problem solving. *Behav. Res. Ther.* **2000**, *38*, 457–470. [CrossRef]
66. Asmundson, G.J.; Kuperos, J.L.; Norton, G.R. Do patients with chronic pain selectively attend to pain-related information? Preliminary evidence for the mediating role of fear. *Pain* **1997**, *72*, 27–32. [CrossRef]
67. Vlaeyen, J.W.S.; Linton, S.J. Fearavoidance and its consequences in chronic musculoskeletal pain: A state of the art. *Pain* **2000**, *85*, 317–332. [CrossRef]
68. Bartley, E.J.; Rhudy, J.L.; Williams, A.E. Experimental Assessment of Affective Processing in Fibromyalgia. *J. Pain* **2009**, *10*, 1151–1160. [CrossRef]
69. Montoya, P.; Sitges, C.; García-Herrera, M.; Izquierdo, R.; Truyols, M.; Blay, N.; Collado, D. Abnormal Affective Modulation of Somatosensory Brain Processing Among Patients With Fibromyalgia. *Psychosom. Med.* **2005**, *67*, 957–963. [CrossRef]
70. Sitges, C.; García-Herrera, M.; Pericás, M.; Collado, D.; Truyols, M.; Montoya, P. Abnormal brain processing of affective and sensory pain descriptors in chronic pain patients. *J. Affect. Disord.* **2007**, *104*, 73–82. [CrossRef]
71. Montoro, C.I.; Duschek, S.; Reyes del Paso, G.A. Alexithymia in fibromyalgia síndrome. *Pers. Individ.* **2016**, *102*, 170–179. [CrossRef]
72. Rainville, P.; Bao, Q.V.; Chretien, P. Pain-related emotions modulate experimental pain perception and autonomic responses. *Pain* **2005**, *118*, 306–318. [CrossRef]
73. Bruehl, S.; Burns, J.W.; Chung, O.Y.; Chont, M. Pain-related effects of trait anger expression: Neural substrates and the role of endogenous opioid mechanisms. *Neurosci. Biobehav. Rev.* **2009**, *33*, 475–491. [CrossRef] [PubMed]
74. Smyth, J.M.; Stone, A.A.; Hurewitz, A.; Kaell, A. Effects of writing about stressful experiences on symptom reduction in patients with asthma or rheumatoid arthritis: A randomized trial. *J. Am. Med. Assoc.* **1999**, *281*, 1304–1309. [CrossRef] [PubMed]
75. Pennebaker, J.W.; Zech, E.; Rimé, B. Disclosing and sharing emotion: Psychological, social, and health consequences. In *Handbook of Bereavement Research: Consequences, Coping, and Care*; Stroebe, M.S., Hansson, R.O., Stroebe, W., Schut, H., Eds.; American Psychological Association: Washington, DC, USA, 2001.
76. Gillis, M.E.; Lumley, M.A.; Mosley-Williams, A.; Leisen, J.C.C.; Roehrs, T. The health effects of at-home written emotional disclosure in fibromyalgia: A randomized trial. *Ann. Behav. Med.* **2006**, *32*, 135–146. [CrossRef] [PubMed]
77. Bushman, B.J.; Bonacci, A.M.; Pedersen, W.C.; Vasquez, E.A.; Miller, N. Chewing on it can chew you up: Effects of rumination on triggered displaced aggression. *J. Pers. Soc. Psychol.* **2005**, *88*, 969–983. [CrossRef]
78. Denson, T.F. The Multiple Systems Model of Angry Rumination. *Pers. Soc. Psychol. Rev.* **2012**, *17*, 103–123. [CrossRef]
79. Zautra, A.; Smith, B.; Affleck, G.; Tennen, H. Examinations of chronic pain and affect relationships: Applications of a dynamic model of affect. *J. Consult. Clin. Psychol.* **2001**, *69*, 786–795. [CrossRef]

80. Staud, R.; Robinson, M.E.; Vierck, C.J., Jr.; Cannon, R.C.; Mauderli, A.P.; Price, D.D. Ratings of experimental pain and pain-related negative affect predict clinical pain in patients with fibromyalgia syndrome. *Pain* **2003**, *105*, 215–222. [CrossRef]
81. Castelli, L.; Tesio, V.; Colonna, F.; Molinaro, S.; Leombruni, P.; Bruzzone, M.; Fusaro, E.; Sarzi-Puttini, P.; Torta, R. Alexithymia and psychological distress in fibromyalgia: Prevalence and relation with quality of life. *Clin. Exp. Rheumatol.* **2012**, *30*, 70–77.
82. Di Tella, M.; Castelli, L. Alexithymia in Chronic Pain Disorders. *Curr. Rheumatol. Rep.* **2016**, *18*, 41. [CrossRef]
83. Di Tella, M.; Ghiggia, A.; Tesio, V.; Romeo, A.; Colonna, F.; Fusaro, E.; Torta, R.; Castelli, L. Pain experience in Fibromyalgia Syndrome: The role of alexithymia and psychological distress. *J. Affect. Disord.* **2017**, *208*, 87–93. [CrossRef]
84. Ghiggia, A.; Romeo, A.; Tesio, V.; Di Tella, M.; Colonna, F.; Geminiani, G.C.; Fusaro, E.; Castelli, L. Alexithymia and de-pression in patients with fibromyalgia: When the whole is greater than the sum of its parts. *Psychiatry Res.* **2017**, *255*, 195–197. [CrossRef] [PubMed]
85. Galvez-Sánchez, C.M.; del Paso, G.A.R.; Duschek, S. Cognitive Impairments in Fibromyalgia Syndrome: Associations With Positive and Negative Affect, Alexithymia, Pain Catastrophizing and Self-Esteem. *Front. Psychol.* **2018**, *9*, 377. [CrossRef] [PubMed]
86. Sifneos, P.E. *Short-Term Psychotherapy and Emotional Crisis*; Harvard University Press: Cambridge, MA, USA, 1972.
87. Taylor, G.J.; Bagby, R.M.; Parker, J.D.A. *Disorders of Affect Regulation: Alexithymia in Medical and Psychiatric Illness*; Cambridge University Press: Cambridge, MA, USA, 1999.
88. Aftanas, L.; Varlamov, A.; Reva, N.; Pavlov, S. Disruption of early event-related theta synchronization of human EEG in alexithymics viewing affective pictures. *Neurosci. Lett.* **2003**, *340*, 57–60. [CrossRef]
89. Berthoz, S.; Artiges, E.; Poline, J.-B.; Rouquette, S.; Consoli, S.M.; Martinot, J.-L.; Van De Moortele, P.-F. Effect of Impaired Recognition and Expression of Emotions on Frontocingulate Cortices: An fMRI Study of Men With Alexithymia. *Am. J. Psychiatry* **2002**, *159*, 961–967. [CrossRef]
90. Kano, M.; Fukudo, S.; Gyoba, J.; Kamachi, M.; Tagawa, M.; Mochizuki, H.; Itoh, M.; Hongo, M.; Yanai, K. Specific brain pro-cessing of facial expressions in people with alexithymia: An H2 15O-PET study. *Brain* **2003**, *126*, 1474–1484. [CrossRef]
91. Vermeulen, N.; Luminet, O.; Corneille, O. Alexithymia and the automatic processing of affective information: Evidence from the affective priming paradigm. *Cogn. Emot.* **2006**, *20*, 64–91. [CrossRef]
92. Blair, R.J.R.; Morris, J.S.; Frith, C.; Perrett, D.; Dolan, R. Dissociable neural responses to facial expressions of sadness and anger. *Brain* **1999**, *122 (Pt. 5)*, 883–893. [CrossRef]
93. Carson, J.W.; Keefe, F.J.; Goli, V.; Fras, A.M.; Lynch, T.R.; Thorp, S.R.; Buechler, J.L. Forgiveness and chronic low back pain: A preliminary study examining the relationship of forgiveness to pain, anger, and psychological distress. *J. Pain* **2005**, *6*, 84–91. [CrossRef]
94. Worthington, E.L., Jr.; Lavelock, C.; van Oyen Witvliet, C. Measures of forgiveness: Self-report, physiological, chemical, and behavioral indicators. In *Measures of Personality and Social Psychological Constructs*; Boyle, G.J., Saklofske, D.H., Matthews, G., Eds.; Academic Press: Oxford, UK, 2014; pp. 474–502.
95. Toussaint, L.; Shields, G.; Dorn, G.; Slavich, G.M. Effects of lifetime stress exposure on mental and physical health in young adulthood: How stress degrades and forgiveness protects health. *J. Health Psychol.* **2016**, *21*, 1004–1014. [CrossRef]
96. Whited, M.C.; Wheat, A.L.; Larkin, K.T. The influence of forgiveness and apology on cardiovascular reactivity and recovery in response to mental stress. *J. Behav. Med.* **2010**, *33*, 293–304. [CrossRef]
97. Witvliet, C.V.; Ludwig, T.E.; Vander Laan, K.L. Granting forgiveness or harboring grudges: Implications for emotion physiology, and health. *Psychol. Sci.* **2001**, *12*, 117–123. [CrossRef] [PubMed]
98. Toussaint, L.L.; Owen, A.D.; Cheadle, A. Forgive to Live: Forgiveness, Health, and Longevity. *J. Behav. Med.* **2011**, *35*, 375–386. [CrossRef] [PubMed]
99. Rippentrop, E.A.; Altmaier, E.M.; Chen, J.J.; Found, E.M.; Keffala, V. The relationship between religion/spirituality and physical health, mental health, and pain in a chronic pain population. *Pain* **2005**, *116*, 311–321. [CrossRef] [PubMed]
100. Kabat-Zinn, J. *Full Catastrophe Living: Using the Wisdom of your Body and Mind to Face Stress, Pain and Illness*; Delacorte: New York, NY, USA, 1990.
101. Bishop, S.R.; Lau, M.; Shapiro, S.; Carlson, L.; Anderson, N.D.; Carmody, J.; Segal, Z.V.; Abbey, S.; Speca, M.; Velting, D.; et al. Mindfulness: A proposed operational definition. *Clin. Psychol. Sci. Pract.* **2004**, *11*, 230–241. [CrossRef]
102. Parrish, B.P.; Zautra, A.J.; Davis, M.C. The role of positive and negative interpersonal events on daily fatigue in women with fibromyalgia, rheumatoid arthritis, and osteoarthritis. *Health Psychol.* **2008**, *27*, 694–702. [CrossRef]
103. Zautra, A.J.; Johnson, L.M.; Davis, M.C. Positive Affect as a Source of Resilience for Women in Chronic Pain. *J. Consult. Clin. Psychol.* **2005**, *73*, 212–220. [CrossRef]
104. Rainville, P.; Bechara, A.; Naqvi, N.; Damasio, A.R. Basic emotions are associated with distinct patterns of cardiorespiratory activity. *Int. J. Psychophysiol.* **2006**, *61*, 5–18. [CrossRef]
105. Brosseau, L.; A Wells, G.; Tugwell, P.; Egan, M.; Wilson, K.G.; Dubouloz, C.-J.; Casimiro, L.; A Robinson, V.; McGowan, J.; Busch, A.; et al. Ottawa Panel Evidence-Based Clinical Practice Guidelines for Aerobic Fitness Exercises in the Management of Fibromyalgia: Part 1. *Phys. Ther.* **2008**, *88*, 857–871. [CrossRef]
106. Brosseau, L.; A Wells, G.; Tugwell, P.; Egan, M.; Wilson, K.G.; Dubouloz, C.-J.; Casimiro, L.; A Robinson, V.; McGowan, J.; Busch, A.; et al. Ottawa Panel Evidence-Based Clinical Practice Guidelines for Strengthening Exercises in the Management of Fibromyalgia: Part 2. *Phys. Ther.* **2008**, *88*, 873–886. [CrossRef]

107. Kelley, G.A.; Kelley, K.S.; Jones, D.L. Efficacy and Effectiveness of Exercise on Tender Points in Adults with Fibromyalgia: A Meta-Analysis of Randomized Controlled Trials. *Arthritis* **2011**, *2011*, 125485. [CrossRef]
108. Busch, A.J.; Webber, S.; Richards, R.S.; Bidonde, J.; Schachter, C.L.; A Schafer, L.; Danyliw, A.; Sawant, A.; Bello-Haas, V.D.; Rader, T.; et al. Resistance exercise training for fibromyalgia. *Cochrane Database Syst. Rev.* **2013**, *2013*, CD010884. [CrossRef] [PubMed]
109. Kingsley, J.D.; McMillan, V.; Figueroa, A. The Effects of 12 Weeks of Resistance Exercise Training on Disease Severity and Autonomic Modulation at Rest and After Acute Leg Resistance Exercise in Women with Fibromyalgia. *Arch. Phys. Med. Rehabil.* **2010**, *91*, 1551–1557. [CrossRef] [PubMed]
110. Andrade, A.; Vilarino, G.T.; Serafim, T.T.; Júnior, A.A.P.; Souza, C.A.; Sieczkowska, S.M. Modulation of Autonomic Function by Physical Exercise in Patients with Fibromyalgia Syndrome: A Systematic Review. *PM&R* **2019**, *11*, 1121–1131. [CrossRef]
111. Andrade, A.; Steffens, R.D.A.K.; Sieczkowska, S.M.; Tartaruga, L.A.P.; Vilarino, G.T. A systematic review of the effects of strength training in patients with fibromyalgia: Clinical outcomes and design considerations. *Adv. Rheumatol.* **2018**, *58*, 36. [CrossRef] [PubMed]
112. Andrade, A.; Sieczkowska, S.M.; Vilarino, G. Resistance Training Improves Quality of Life and Associated Factors in Patients With Fibromyalgia Syndrome. *PM&R* **2019**, *11*, 703–709. [CrossRef]
113. Gavi, M.B.R.O.M.; Vassalo, D.V.; Amaral, F.T.; Macedo, D.C.; Gava, P.L.; Dantas, E.M.; Valim, V. Strengthening exercises improve symptoms and quality of life but do not change autonomic modulation in fibromyalgia: A randomized clinical trial. *PLoS ONE* **2014**, *9*, 8. [CrossRef]
114. Ericsson, A.; Palstam, A.; Larsson, A.; Löfgren, M.; Bileviciute-Ljungar, I.; Bjersing, J.; Gerdle, B.; Kosek, E.; Mannerkorpi, K. Resistance exercise improves physical fatigue in women with fibromyalgia: A randomized controlled trial. *Arthritis Res. Ther.* **2016**, *18*, 176. [CrossRef]
115. Castelli, L.; Tesio, V. Commentary: Mindfulness training for reducing anger, anxiety, and depression in fibromyalgia patients. *Front. Psychol.* **2016**, *7*, 740. [CrossRef]
116. Menzies, V. CE: Fibromyalgia syndrome: Current considerations in symptom management. *Am. J. Nurs.* **2016**, *116*, 24–32. [CrossRef]

Journal of
Clinical Medicine

MDPI

Article

Fibromyalgia Syndrome and Cognitive Decline: The Role of Body Mass Index and Clinical Symptoms

Cristina Muñoz Ladrón de Guevara [1,*], Gustavo A. Reyes del Paso [1], María José Fernández Serrano [2] and Casandra I. Montoro [1,*]

[1] Department of Psychology, University of Jaén, 23071 Jaén, Spain; greyes@ujaen.es
[2] Department of Methodology for Behavioral Science, University of Granada, 18071 Granada, Spain; mjfser@ugr.es
* Correspondence: cmladron@ujaen.es (C.M.L.d.G.); imontoro@ujaen.es (C.I.M.)

Abstract: The high prevalence of obesity and overweight in fibromyalgia (FM) may be an important factor in the well-known cognitive deficits seen in the disorder. This study analyzed the influence of body mass index (BMI) and primary clinical symptoms of FM (pain, fatigue, insomnia, anxiety, and depression) on attention, memory, and processing speed in FM. Fifty-two FM patients and thirty-two healthy participants completed cognitive tasks assessing selective, sustained, and divided attention; visuospatial and verbal memory; and information processing speed. Furthermore, they were evaluated in terms of the main clinical symptoms of the disorder. FM patients showed a marked reduction of cognitive performance in terms of selective, sustained, and divided attention; visuospatial memory; and processing speed, but no group differences were observed in verbal memory. BMI negatively affects sustained and selective attention, verbal memory, and processing speed and is the main predictor of performance in these basic cognitive domains. Our findings confirm the presence of cognitive deficits with respect to attention and visual memory, as well as slower processing speed, in FM. Moreover, the results support a role of BMI in the observed cognitive deficits. Interventions increasing physical activity and promoting cognitive stimulation could be useful for strengthening cognitive function in FM patients.

Keywords: body mass index; clinical pain; cognitive decline; fibromyalgia

Citation: Muñoz Ladrón de Guevara, C.; Reyes del Paso, G.A.; Fernández Serrano, M.J.; Montoro, C.I. Fibromyalgia Syndrome and Cognitive Decline: The Role of Body Mass Index and Clinical Symptoms. *J. Clin. Med.* **2022**, *11*, 3404. https://doi.org/10.3390/jcm11123404

Academic Editor: Giuseppe Lanza

Received: 10 May 2022
Accepted: 11 June 2022
Published: 14 June 2022

1. Introduction

Fibromyalgia (FM) is defined as a chronic pain syndrome of unknown etiology characterized by diffuse, widespread, and non-inflammatory musculoskeletal pain, which is accompanied by symptoms such as morning stiffness, fatigue, mood disorders, sleep disturbances, and cognitive impairment; it predominantly affects middle-aged adult women, that is, women over 50 years of age [1–3]. One of the most common complaints reported by FM patients is cognitive alterations [4–7]. Specifically, these cognitive complaints have been suggested to affect 50–80% of FM patients and include memory loss that extends to the capacity to recall names, conversations, words and quotations, problems expressing thoughts, difficulty in adequately remembering directions and scheduled activities, and a kind of "fog" that prevents sufferers from perceiving daily events clearly [8–10]. These cognitive problems, together with the experience of pain, limit the daily life activities of FM patients and cause a great deal of discomfort [11,12]. In fact, patients report that they are among the most deleterious symptoms of the disease, due to their negative impact on functional capacity, working life, and quality of life [13–15].

Despite patients' complaints, cognitive dysfunction in FM has received relatively less clinical and empirical support/attention compared with clinical pain symptoms; however, more studies have appeared in recent years, with current evidence indicating the presence of cognitive deficits in several neuropsychological domains [13,16]. Although short- and long-term implicit and working memory deficits, as well as slowness to complete complex cognitive tasks (i.e., executive control and emotional recognition tasks) have been confirmed [9,13,16–22], the results remain controversial. While most studies point to general deficits in information processing speed; selective and sustained attention; and visuospatial, verbal, and semantic memory in FM patients compared to healthy participants [5,13,18,23–29], others observed no substantial cognitive deficits in association with FM [27,30–34].

In addition, there is no consensus on the factors influencing the cognitive impairments seen in FM, although the intensity of clinical pain has been proposed as one such factor. Several studies have shown an inverse association between clinical pain levels and cognitive performance in FM patients (e.g., [16,19,28,31,35–40]). However, it is important to note that not all studies demonstrated this association [10,23,41,42].

Other factors proposed to explain the presence of cognitive impairments in FM include medication intake, mood and emotional alterations (i.e., depression and anxiety), and fatigue and sleep problems. However, while some studies have reported a significant relationship between depression and/or anxiety, and cognitive deficits in FM [25,38,42–44], others suggested that cognitive deficits are independent of comorbid depression and/or anxiety disorders [5,6,16,28,29,39]. The situation is similar for fatigue and/or sleep disorders, i.e., some studies have supported the notion that these factors influence cognitive performance [27,28,45], while others have not [19,29,39,40,46,47].

Body mass index (BMI) may also influence cognitive performance, especially when meeting the threshold for obesity (i.e., BMI > 25 kg/m^2; [48–51]. Indeed, this has been demonstrated in the general population [52–54]. However, although overweight and obesity are highly prevalent in FM [55,56], to the best of our knowledge, only two studies have attempted to elucidate the relationship between BMI and cognitive impairment in FM. The first one, performed by Soriano-Maldonado et al. [57], revealed strong associations between aerobic fitness, attention, working memory, delayed recall, and verbal learning in FM, while no associations were observed between parameters used to assess overweight (BMI, body fat percentage, fat mass index, and waist circumference) and cognitive ability. Contrarily, Muñoz Ladrón de Guevara et al. [16] found a negative influence of BMI on performance in a cognitive test measuring components of executive function (updating, inhibitory control, switching, decision-making, self-regulation, and planning) in FM patients.

Given that findings regarding the negative association between BMI and cognitive function in FM are limited to executive function components, and taking into account the equivocal results regarding the deficits in basic cognitive processes (attention, memory, and processing speed) seen in FM, the aims of the present study were to: (1) test for deficits in basic cognitive processes in FM, in the domains of attention (selective, sustained, and divided attention), memory (verbal and visuospatial), and information processing speed; and (2) explore the association between BMI and these basic cognitive processes. The role of clinical variables such as pain, anxiety, depression, fatigue, sleep problems (insomnia), and medication use on the cognitive performance of FM patients will be also explored.

2. Materials and Methods

2.1. Participants

The study was part of a larger project assessing cognition and emotional processing in FM [16,21,58]. In total, 52 patients diagnosed with FM and 32 healthy participants took part in the study. Given the higher prevalence of FM in women compared to men and with the aim of avoiding possible gender-related confounding, only women were included in the study. Patients were recruited through the Fibromyalgia Associations of Jaén and Úbeda (Spain). All of the patients met the American College of Rheumatology criteria for the diagnosis of FM [3]. Healthy participants were recruited through local advertisements. Exclusion criteria for all participants included metabolic abnormalities, neurological disorders (e.g., traumatic head injury), and severe somatic (e.g., cancer) or psychiatric (e.g., drug dependency, psychosis) diseases. The sociodemographic and clinical data are shown in Table 1. Patients did not differ from healthy participants in terms age or years of education but showed a trend toward a higher BMI.

Table 1. Means (M) and standard deviations (SD) of the clinical and sociodemographic data of fibromyalgia (FM) patients and healthy controls. Results of group comparisons (t or $\chi 2$) are also displayed.

	FM (N = 52) M ± SD or n (%)	Healthy Controls (N = 32) M ± SD or n (%)	t [82]/$\chi 2$	*p*
Age (y)	51.25 ± 8.67	52.94 ± 6.59	−0.95	0.35
Years of education	9.27 ± 3.52	10.59 ± 3.64	−1.65	0.10
BMI	28.29 ± 4.49	26.49 ± 4.36	1.80	0.075
Depression (SCID), n, %	22 (42.30)	2 (6.25)	12.62	<0.0001
Anxiety Disorders * (SCID), n, %	25 (48.08)	7 (21.88)	5.77	0.016
Antidepressant use, n, %	27 (51.92)	2 (6.26)	18.28	<0.0001
Anxiolytic use, n, %	35 (67.31)	8 (25.00)	14.19	<0.0001
Non-opioid analgesic use, n, %	45 (86.54)	8 (25.00)	32.22	<0.0001
Opiate use, n, %	23 (44.23)	0 (0.00)	16.49	<0.0001
State anxiety (STAI)	30.92 ± 11.92	17.19 ± 9.60	5.51	<0.0001
Trait anxiety (STAI)	35.29 ± 9.34	17.56 ± 10.24	8.14	<0.0001
Depression (BDI)	21.90 ± 12.56	4.47 ± 5.67	7.39	<0.0001
Fatigue (FSS)	50.56 ± 12.35	19.88 ± 11.14	11.92	<0.0001
Insomnia (COS)	29.73 ± 7.43	17.09 ± 7.52	7.91	<0.0001
Sensory pain (MPQ)	35.59 ± 18.39	12.38 ± 3.85	8.52	<0.0001
Affective pain (MPQ)	5.92 ± 4.50	0.71 ± 0.72	8.10	<0.0001
Evaluative pain (MPQ)	3.27 ± 1.03	2.29 ± 1.38	3.33	<0.01
Miscellaneous (MPQ)	9.25 ± 5.90	4.14 ± 2.56	5.16	<0.0001

* Note: Anxiety disorders include panic disorder, generalized anxiety disorder, phobias and adjustment disorder; n = number of participants. Non-opioid analgesic use includes the following analgesic drugs: non-steroidal anti-inflammatory drugs, 29 patients; paracetamol, 34 patients; metamizole, 7 patients; anticonvulsants, 10 patients; tramadol, 20 patients; and codeine, 4 patients.

2.2. Clinical Assessments

The clinical history and sociodemographic data of the patients were obtained via a semi-structured interview. The Structured Clinical Interview for Axis I Disorders of the Diagnostic and Statistical Manual of Mental Disorders (SCID [59]) was used to check for psychiatric disorders, especially anxiety and depression. Clinical pain was quantified using the Spanish version of the McGill Pain Questionnaire (MPQ [60]). The following four scales from the MPQ were applied: sensory pain (score range: 0–84), affective pain (score range: 0–22), evaluative pain (score range: 0–4), and miscellaneous pain (score range: 0–30). The internal consistency (Cronbach's α) of the Spanish version of the MPQ ranges from 0.66 to 0.80 [61]. Depressive symptoms were assessed using the Spanish version of the Beck Depression Inventory (BDI [62]; score range: 0–63; Cronbach's α = 0.95). Levels of anxiety were assessed using the State-Trait Anxiety Inventory (STAI [63]; score range: 0–60 for both scales; Cronbach´s α = 0.93 for state anxiety and 0.87 for trait anxiety). Fatigue was assessed using the Spanish version of the Fatigue Severity Scale (FSS [64]; score range: 9–63; Cronbach´s α = 0.88). Insomnia was measured using the Oviedo Sleep Quality Questionnaire (COS [65]; score range: 9–45; Cronbach´s α = 0.77).

2.3. Cognitive Assessment

The ***d2 Attention test*** (d2 [66]) was used for the measurement of sustained and selective attention. The d2 consists of a cancellation task in which participants must discriminate between (target stimuli) and cancel (non-target stimuli) visually similar stimuli. It consists of 658 items divided into 14 rows, each consisting of 47 characters. Specifically, it has 16 different types of characters, i.e., the letters "d" and "p", each with one, two, three or four small quotation marks. The target stimulus is the letter "d" with two quotation marks ("") that appear together (above or below the letter "d") or separately. The letter "d" accompanied by one, three, or four consecutive quotation marks and the letter "p" (regardless of the number of quotation marks) act as distractor stimuli. The duration of the entire test ranges from 8 to 10 min. The participant has 20 s to respond to each of the test rows. The d2 variables indexing performance are as follows: the number of stimuli or items attempted in the 14 rows (TR_d2); total test effectiveness (d2_TOT), calculated as the total number of items attempted in the 14 rows (TR) minus the total number of omissions and commissions; and the concentration index (d2_CON), calculated as the number of items correctly marked minus the number of errors of commission.

The ***Trail Making Test*** (TMT [67]) was used for measuring divided attention and information processing speed. The TMT is a subtest of the Delis–Kaplan Executive Function System (D-KEFS [67]) battery. It consists of a set of five conditions composed of visual stimuli (letters and numbers), preceded by a test trial. The conditions are as follows: Condition 1 (visual scan; participants must identify the three numbers that appear on the answer sheet), Condition 2 (number sequencing; participants must line up numbers 1 to 16 in ascending order while ignoring the letters), Condition 3 (letter sequencing; participants must line up letters A to P in alphabetical order while ignoring the numbers), Condition 4 (switching between numbers and letters; participants must connect numbers and letters in alphanumeric order (numbers in ascending order and letters in alphabetical order, i.e., 1-A, 2-B...until reaching 16-P)) and Condition 5 (motor speed; participants must draw a dotted line). The stimuli that comprise each of these five conditions appear in a larger area than in the original version of the TMT, such that there is more interference [67]. For all five conditions, the examiner instructs the participants to respond as quickly and precisely as possible. Performance on Condition 4 was taken as a measure of divided attention [68] and performance on Conditions 2 and 3 as a measure of information processing speed [42,69].

The ***Rey–Osterrieth Complex Figure Test*** (ROCF [70]) was used to measure visuospatial memory. The ROCF consists of three conditions: copying, immediate recall, and delayed recall. In the first condition, the ROCF figure is presented, and the participants are asked to copy it. Immediately thereafter, in the second condition, participants have to remember and draw the figure without any visual guidance, and after a 30 min delay (third condition), the figure must be drawn once again. The scores vary according to the scoring system used (maximum = 36 points) but are typically based on evaluations related to location, accuracy, and organization (18 items). Each ROCF condition takes 5 min to complete, and the total test time is approximately 40 min. Copy accuracy (first condition: copy execution) and copy reproduction from memory (delayed; third condition: memory execution) were taken as performance measures.

The ***Five-digit test*** (5DT [71]) was used for measuring information processing speed. This test consists of four conditions presented in order of difficulty (the least difficult first). In each condition, a series of 50 stimuli framed by small rectangles (each rectangle contains one to five digits or asterisks) are presented. In Condition 1 (reading), the participant is asked to read the digits, while in Condition 2 (counting) the asterisks have to be counted. In Condition 3 (interference), the digits must be counted while ignoring the numerical values (note that the number of digits in the boxes does not correspond to their numerical values). Finally, in Condition 4 (alternation), the criteria are identical to those in Conditions 1 and 2 (reading, counting), but participants must switch from the primary to the secondary criterion (i.e., from counting to reading) according to a visual cue. Test performance was indexed by the spent taken (information processing speed) to complete each condition [72]; shorter times indicate better performance.

The ***Test de Aprendizaje Verbal Español-Complutense*** (TAVEC [73]) was used to measure verbal memory. In the first condition of the TAVEC, the evaluator reads aloud a list of 16 words (List A; also called the shopping list) five times, and participants must immediately recall as many words as possible (immediate free memory). Following this, the evaluator reads aloud a new list (List B; interference list), which the participant must also reproduce. After a 20 min of break, a third list of 44 words is read out. This list includes all words from List A and several from List B, as well as some distractor words not included in either previous list. The participant must decide whether each word belongs to List A (recognition task). The performance indices are the total number of words recalled during the five trials (RI_AT), total number of words recalled in the short-term recall trial (RL_CP), and total number of words recalled in the long-term recall trial (RL_LP).

2.4. Procedure

All participants were evaluated individually in two sessions approximately 2 h in duration separated by 1 week. In the first session, a clinical psychologist recorded the patients' clinical history, sociodemographic data (including weight and height), and medication intake and determined whether they met any of exclusion criteria. Subsequently, the SCID was conducted, during which the questionnaires previously described in the clinical assessment section were completed. In addition, in order to detect possible simulated memory impairment, participants completed the 15-item Rey Memory Test [70]; none of the participants met the criterion for impairment (score < 6). The cognitive tests were performed during the second session. The tests were presented in a fixed order, alternating between verbal and nonverbal tasks. There was a 5 min break after the completion of each cognitive task. The study was approved by the Human Research Ethics Committee of the University of Jaén and all participants gave written informed consent.

2.5. Statistical Analysis

Group differences in cognitive performance were tested for by multivariate analysis of variance (MANOVA), including BMI as a covariate and then by univariate ANOVA models (also including BMI as a covariate). The effects of medication use and comorbid depression and anxiety disorders were subjected to stratified analyses in the FM group only, using MANOVA models comparing patients using and not using analgesics, anxiolytics, opioids, and antidepressants, as well as patients with and without depressive and anxiety disorders (with BMI as a covariate). The effect sizes are indicated by adjusted eta squared (η_p^2) values.

Associations between clinical variables and cognitive performance were only analyzed in the FM group. Firstly, to reduce the number of correlations performed (and thus limit type I error), we performed a multiple correlation analysis (the correlation coefficient (R) indicates the existence of an association, but not its direction (positive or negative), between the predictor variables (anxiety [STAI], depression [BDI], fatigue [FSS], insomnia [COS], and the four clinical pain variables [MPQ]) and each cognitive domain (selective attention and sustained attention [d2_TR, d2_CON, d2_TOT of the d2 Attention test], divided attention [Condition 4 of the TMT], visuospatial memory [copying and memory conditions of the ROFC], verbal memory [RI_AT, RL_CP, RL_LP of the TAVEC], and information processing speed [Conditions 2 and 3 of the TMT, and Conditions 1–4 of the 5DT]). Secondly, multiple regression analyses using the stepwise method were conducted, with BMI and the clinical variables as predictors and the cognitive parameters as dependent variables. The adjusted R^2 was used to evaluate the changes in predictions associated with each new block.

3. Results

3.1. Demographic and Clinical Variables

FM patients reported higher rates of depression and anxiety, and of self-reported clinical pain, depression, anxiety, fatigue and insomnia, than healthy participants. Additionally, FM patients used more opioid and non-opioid analgesics, anxiolytics, and antidepressants than healthy participants (Table 1).

Group Comparisons

The MANOVA revealed a significant main effect of group on general cognitive performance ($F[15, 67] = 2.20$, $p = 0.015$, $\eta_p^2 = 0.33$), but no main effect of BMI ($F[15, 67] = 1.69$, $p = 0.075$, $\eta_p^2 = 0.27$).

Table 2 displays the means and standard deviations of the cognitive parameters. Univariate analysis showed significant group differences in all performance variables, except information processing speed (Condition 2 of both the TMT and 5DT) and all TAVEC verbal memory conditions; the FM patients showed poorer performance than the healthy participants. A significant main effect of BMI was also observed on selective and sustained attention (d2_TR, d2_CON, d2_TOT), information processing speed (Condition 2 of the TMT and Conditions 2–4 of the 5DT), and verbal memory (RI_AT, RL_CP, and RL_LP conditions of the TAVEC). Higher BMI was associated with poorer cognitive performance for these conditions.

Table 2. Means (M) and standard deviations (SD) of cognitive performance parameters for the FM patients and healthy controls: F, p and η_p^2 values indicating the main effects of group and body mass index (BMI) are also presented.

Test	FM N = 52 M ± SD	Healthy Controls N = 32 M ± SD	F[1, 81] for Group	p for Group	η_p^2 for Group	F[1, 81] for BMI	p for BMI	η_p^2 for BMI
d2_TR	347.56 ± 77.45	407.63 ± 91.95	7.46	<0.01	0.08	7.85	<0.01	0.09
d2_CON	111.08 ± 47.87	150.22 ± 36.69	12.55	<0.01	0.13	4.99	0.028	0.06
d2_TOT	313.23 ± 81.17	385.47 ± 86.77	11.42	<0.01	0.12	8.90	<0.01	0.10
TMT Condition 2	53.38 ± 26.99	45.25 ± 17.76	0.97	0.328	0.01	8.38	<0.01	0.10
TMT Condition 3	75.62 ± 43.02	51.75 ± 25.28	6.39	0.013	0.07	2.10	0.151	0.03
TMT Condition 4	159.60 ± 67.49	122.03 ± 53.55	5.89	0.017	0.07	0.98	0.326	0.01
ROCF copying condition	29.30 ± 6.40	33.83 ± 3.01	12.42	<0.01	0.13	0.53	0.470	0.01
ROCF memory condition	15.77 ± 6.16	20.36 ± 6.44	8.60	<0.01	0.10	2.13	0.148	0.03
5DT Condition 1	23.90 ± 6.94	19.72 ± 3.05	9.05	<0.01	0.10	0.52	0.473	0.01
5DT Condition 2	27.52 ± 9.26	23.72 ± 4.14	3.19	0.078	0.04	4.19	0.044	0.05
5DT Condition 3	46.67 ± 18.10	36.41 ± 6.10	6.80	0.011	0.08	8.29	<0.01	0.09
5DT Condition 4	62.19 ± 22.69	49.91 ± 13.03	4.84	0.031	0.06	15.39	<0.0001	0.16
TAVEC RI_AT	50.31 ± 9.65	53.44 ± 10.78	0.90	0.346	0.01	5.03	0.028	0.06
TAVEC RL_CP	10.88 ± 2.83	10.97 ± 3.08	0.012	0.726	0.00	6.07	0.016	0.07
TAVEC RL_LP	11.12 ± 2.76	11.66 ± 2.75	0.15	0.695	0.00	6.33	0.014	0.07

Note: d2 = d2 Attention test; D-KEFS = Delis–Kaplan Executive Function Test Battery Trail Making Test; ROCF = Rey–Osterrieth Complex Figure Test; 5FDT = Five-Digit Test; TAVEC = Test de Aprendizaje Verbal Español-Complutense.

The MANOVAs performed to compare cognitive performance between FM patients with and without depression or anxiety disorders (SCID) did not reveal a significant main effect of the presence of depression (F[15, 35] = 0.69, p = 0.775, η_p^2 = 0.23), but there was a trend toward better performance by patients with anxiety disorders (F(15, 35) = 1.96, p = 0.051, η_p^2 = 0.46). However, in univariate analysis, the effect of the presence of anxiety disorders was non-significant for all measured cognitive variables. Moreover, in multivariate analysis, there was no main effect of medication use (F[15, 35] = 1.00, p = 0.476, η_p^2 = 0.30 for anxiolytics;

F[15, 35] = 0.57, p = 0.875, η_p^2 = 0.20 for analgesics; F[15, 35] = 1.17, p = 0.339, η_p^2 = 0.33 for antidepressants; and F[15, 35] = 0.52, p = 0.914, η_p^2 = 0.18 for opioids).

3.2. *Associations between Clinical Variables and Cognitive Performance*

3.2.1. Exploratory Multiple Correlation Analysis

Exploratory multiple correlation analysis revealed an association between BMI and selective and sustained attention (d2 Attention test [d2_TR, d2_CON and d2_TOT]; R = 0.46, p = 0.009) and information processing speed (TMT Conditions 2 and 3 and 5DT Conditions 1–4; R = 0.52, p = 0.021). In addition, the different pain indices (MPQ) were associated with visuospatial memory (ROCF copying and memory conditions; R = 0.48, p = 0.001 for sensorial pain; R = 0.46, p = 0.003 for affective pain; and R = 0.49, p = 0.001 for miscellaneous pain). No other associations were observed in the multiple correlation analysis.

3.2.2. Regression Analysis

Table 3 shows the results of the multiple regression analysis performed to determine the ability of BMI and the clinical variables to predict cognitive performance. Regarding selective and sustained attention, BMI negatively predicted performance in the d2_TR, d2_CON and d2_TOT conditions. Regarding information processing speed, BMI (in the first model) and sensorial pain (in the second model) were positively associated with the time taken to perform TMT Condition 2; moreover, the time taken to perform Conditions 3 and 4 of the 5DT was positively predicted by BMI. With respect to visuospatial memory, memory execution (ROCF) was negatively predicted by sensorial pain (MPQ). Regarding verbal memory, the RI_AT TAVEC condition was positively predicted by state anxiety (STAI), and the RI_CP TAVEC condition was negatively predicted by BMI. Finally, state anxiety was positively associated (in the first model) with sensorial pain and negatively related (in the second model) to the RI_LP TAVEC condition.

Table 3. Results of multiple regression analysis performed to determine the ability of clinical factors and BMI to predict cognitive performance in FM patients.

Cognitive Test	Model	Predictor	β	r^2	t	p
d2_TR	Model 1	BMI	−0.42	0.17	−3.24	0.002
d2_CON	Model 1	BMI	−0.28	0.08	−2.08	0.043
d2_TOT	Model 1	BMI	−0.42	0.18	−3.28	0.002
TMT Condition 2	Model 1	BMI	0.38	0.15	2.94	0.005
	Model 2	BMI	0.35	0.11	2.85	0.006
		Sensorial Pain (MPQ)	0.33		2.67	0.010
5DT Condition 3	Model 1	BMI	0.32	0.10	2.35	0.023
5DT Condition 4	Model 1	BMI	0.49	0.24	3.92	<0.0001
ROCF memory condition	Model 1	Sensorial Pain (MPQ)	−0.46	0.21	−3.65	<0.01
TAVEC RI_AT	Model 1	State anxiety (STAI)	0.32	0.10	2.38	0.021
TAVEC RL_CP	Model 1	BMI	−0.28	0.08	−2.02	0.048
TAVEC RL_LP TAVEC	Model 1	State anxiety (STAI)	0.30	0.09	2.18	0.034
	Model 2	State anxiety (STAI)	0.35	0.08	2.65	0.011
		Sensorial Pain (MPQ)	−0.29		−2.19	0.033

Note: d2 = d2 Attention test; D-KEFS = Delis–Kaplan Executive Function Test Battery Trail Making Test; ROCF = Rey–Osterrieth Complex Figure Test; 5DT = Five Digit Test; TAVEC = Test de.

4. Discussion

This study explored the cognitive domains of attention, memory, and information processing speed in FM patients using a neuropsychological test battery that comprehensively assesses selective, sustained, and divided attention, visuospatial and verbal memory, and cognitive processing speed. In addition, we explored the influence of BMI and clinical variables such as pain, anxiety, depression, fatigue, insomnia, and medication use on the cognitive performance of these patients.

Compared to healthy participants, FM patients showed lower performance in the domains of selective and sustained attention, divided attention, processing speed, and visuospatial memory. These results support the notion of markedly impaired attention, visuospatial memory, and information processing speed in FM and are in accordance with previous studies [5,18,23,28,29,74,75]. However, in opposition to our preceding findings [58] no group differences were observed in verbal memory (as measured by the TAVEC). Although at first glance the lack of differences in verbal memory between FM and healthy participants may seem striking, the literature on this matter is in fact inconsistent. Indeed, and in accordance with the present findings, Castel et al. [30,76] did not find differences in verbal memory (as measured by the TAVEC) between FM patients and controls. These discrepant results may be explained in part by differences in the dependent variables (i.e., TAVEC conditions) selected to index verbal memory performance. In the present study, we selected three measures of immediate free recall, as well as measures of short- and long-term recall, while in our previous study [58], two measures of immediate free recall, errors of omission, false-positive responses, and an index of discrimination were used. It is also important to mention that, in the present study, the effect of BMI was controlled for in the group comparisons, and that BMI significantly affected verbal memory performance (see below a further discussion of this issue). In conclusion, not all studies have demonstrated differences in verbal memory between FM and healthy participants (e.g., [27,30,32,76] for negative results). More research is needed to shed light on the verbal memory performance of FM patients.

Significant effects of BMI on selective and sustained attention, information processing speed, and verbal memory were also found in this study; higher BMI was associated with lower performance in these cognitive domains. By contrast, BMI did not significantly affect divided attention or visuospatial memory. Correlation and regression analysis confirmed that higher BMI was associated with lower performance in FM. Specifically, higher BMI predicted slower processing speed, less sustained and selective attention, and poorer verbal memory. However, BMI was not associated with variables indexing divided attention and visuospatial memory.

The findings regarding BMI are of special importance, as obesity and overweight are often seen in FM [55]. A higher BMI has been related to more severe FM and to the occurrence of musculoskeletal pain in the general population [55,77]. The complex relationships between obesity and pain may be mediated by mechanical overload and multiple proinflammatory and neurohormonal mechanisms [78]. In agreement with a recent review by D'Onghia et al. [55] revealing a high prevalence of obesity in European FM patients, the mean BMI in our FM sample was 28.29 kg/m^2 (class 1 obesity; [51]). Moreover, higher rates of pain complaints and chronic pain have been reported among individuals with obesity [79].

Obesity has been cited a risk factor for poor cognitive performance in the general population [80], especially in the domains of attention/vigilance, visual and verbal memory, information processing speed, and executive function [53,54,81–84]. Our results confirm the role of BMI in cognitive deficits in FM, including not only complex cognitive functions (i.e., executive function) as reported in a previous study (see Muñoz Ladrón de Guevara et al. [16]), but also more basic cognitive processes such as sustained and selective attention, verbal memory, and processing speed. The precise mechanisms linking cognitive performance and obesity have not yet been identified, although altered brain structure, blood–brain barrier and leptin regulation, poorer cerebrovascular function and blood flow cerebral perfusion, arterial hypertension, oxidative stress, and inflammation have also been implicated [80,85–92].

Against this background, the mechanisms underlying the relationship between obesity and pain might explain the detrimental effect of BMI on cognitive performance in FM. Several pronociceptive and antinociceptive pathways have suggested to have an important role in the relation between obesity and pain sensitivity, particularly the presence of inflammatory markers such as interleukin-6 (IL-6) and C-reactive protein (CRP) [93]. Interestingly, Okifuji et al. [56] found that, in women with FM, CRP was positively associated with BMI. Additionally, higher CRP levels have been associated with poor memory, attention, and processing speed in clinical samples [94].

Similarly, elevated levels of leptin (a hormone synthesized in adipose tissue and produced in excess in obese subjects) have been associated with body pain in healthy postmenopausal women with a BMI > 25 kg/m^2 and in FM patients whose average weight was 81.17 kg/m^2 [95]. Peripheral leptin penetrates the cerebrospinal fluid and central nervous system and interacts with the hypothalamus and hippocampus [96,97], which are thought to be altered in FM [98,99]. The involvement of the hippocampus in memory processes is well known, and leptin has been implicated in memory impairment in obese populations [85]. From a behavioral perspective, physical inactivity and a sedentary lifestyle may be contributing factors. Physical inactivity is frequent in FM, which promotes obesity and impaired cognitive performance [100,101]. Increased physical activity, specifically an increase in aerobic capacity, is one of the most effective methods for treating FM [102]. Several studies have shown an association between aerobic exercise and improvements in attention, processing speed, executive function, and memory in the general population [103,104].

Regarding the effect of clinical factors on the cognitive performance of FM patients, our results showed a negative association between the different pain components (sensorial, affective, and miscellaneous) and visuospatial memory. Regression analysis confirmed the association for sensorial pain. These findings corroborate the well-known interfering effect of pain on cognitive function in FM [16,19,28,29,36,39,47].

Although our FM patients with and without a diagnosis of depression or anxiety did not differ in cognitive performance, the regression analysis showed that state anxiety was a positive predictor of some TAVEC verbal memory variables. This association of cognitive improvement with state anxiety is striking, as other studies either suggested a negative influence of anxiety on working memory, attention, and general cognitive function [42,43,105], or no effect of anxiety [16,19,28,29,39]. This result is difficult to explain, but it is possible that higher state anxiety promotes greater arousal, where increased activation can lead to improved performance [106,107]. Finally, our non-significant results for fatigue, insomnia, and medication use (for all four types of drugs) are in line with previous studies suggesting a minor role of these factors in the cognitive impairment seen in FM patients [40,47,108].

A limitation of the present study was the relatively small size of the patient sample, as well as the smaller number of participants in the healthy group relative to the FM patient group. This might have limited the statistical power of the group comparisons. Nevertheless, our sample size was comparable to or larger than those in most other studies in this field [25–27,40,108]. Additionally, another limitation of this study pertains to the lack of information about the possible influence of medication on the assessed variables; this could have been explored by comparing patients grouped according to the use of particular medications or combinations thereof. The sample size was insufficient to form such patient subgroups, although previous studies did not suggest substantial effects of medication on cognitive performance in FM [40]. Nonetheless, it is important to highlight that previous literature has reported some side effects on cognition and weight associated to the medication use. For instance, an increase of greater cognitive deterioration [109] and significant weight gain [110,111] have been associated to anticonvulsants use in adults. Furthermore, factors such as fatigue, mental effort, and distraction during performance of the tests were not controlled for, similar to most other studies. These factors can impact the cognitive performance of FM patients [23,112]. Likewise, given the inverse association revealed in this study between the experience of clinical pain and cognitive performance in FM, and the lack of research evaluating differences between FM severity subgroups on these factors, it should be considered as a future line of research. Finally, although the relevance of BMI to the cognitive performance of our FM patients is clear, possible mediating mechanisms, such as physical exercise and general level of fitness, were not measured and should be considered in future research.

5. Conclusions

In conclusion, our findings confirm the presence of deficits in cognitive basic processes, such as selective, sustained, and divided attention; visuospatial memory; and information processing speed (but not verbal memory), in FM patients. Moreover, BMI negatively affected the cognitive performance of our patients. In light of the high prevalence of overweight and obesity in FM [55], our findings suggest the need for interventions to reduce the body weight of these patients. In particular, tailored physical exercise is strongly recommended for FM. Interventions improving physical capacity, disability, and fatigue could increase cognitive performance directly, as well as indirectly via the associated reduction in body weight. Finally, given the empirical support for the presence of cognitive deficits in FM, neuropsychological rehabilitation programs for these patients are recommended.

Author Contributions: Conceptualization, G.A.R.d.P., M.J.F.S. and C.I.M.; methodology, G.A.R.d.P., C.M.L.d.G., M.J.F.S. and C.I.M.; validation, G.A.R.d.P., C.M.L.d.G., M.J.F.S. and C.I.M.; formal analysis, G.A.R.d.P., C.M.L.d.G. and C.I.M.; investigation, G.A.R.d.P., C.M.L.d.G. and C.I.M.; resources, G.A.R.d.P.; data curation, C.M.L.d.G. and M.J.F.S.; writing—original draft preparation, C.M.L.d.G.; writing—review and editing, G.A.R.d.P. and C.I.M.; visualization, G.A.R.d.P., C.M.L.d.G., M.J.F.S. and C.I.M.; supervision, G.A.R.d.P. and C.I.M.A; project administration, G.A.R.d.P.; funding acquisition, G.A.R.d.P. All authors have read and agreed to the published version of the manuscript.

Funding: This research was supported by a grant from the Spanish Ministry of Science and Innovation co-financed by FEDER funds (RTI2018-095830-B-I00/ AEI/10.13039/501100011033).

Institutional Review Board Statement: All subjects gave their informed consent for inclusion before they participated in the study. They were free to leave the experiment at any time. The study was conducted in accordance with the Declaration of Helsinki and in accordance with the recommendations of national and international ethics guidelines, Psychologist Code of Ethics, American Psychological Association, Code of Good Research Practices of author´s institution and the Spanish Law 5/2018 of 5 December and was approved by the Ethics Committee of University of Jaén. The study did not involve any invasive procedure, and it did not carry any risk to the participants' mental or physical health, thus not requiring ethics approval according to the Spanish law BOE 14/2007.

Informed Consent Statement: All the data have been collected from adults who have voluntarily participated in the research and have given informed consent as subjects for this study.

Data Availability Statement: The authors claim that this manuscript describes an original research work which has not been preregistered. The data presented in this study are available on request from authors. The data are not publicly available due to compliance with privacy laws.

Conflicts of Interest: The authors declare no conflict of interest.

References

1. Queiroz, L.P. Worldwide epidemiology of fibromyalgia. *Curr. Pain Headache Rep.* **2013**, *17*, 356. [CrossRef] [PubMed]
2. Wolfe, F.; Clauw, D.J.; Fitzcharles, M.-A.; Goldenberg, D.L.; Katz, R.S.; Mease, P.; Russell, A.S.; Russell, I.J.; Winfield, J.B.; Yunus, M.B. The American College of Rheumatology preliminary diagnostic criteria for fibromyalgia and measurement of symptom severity. *Arthritis Care Res.* **2010**, *62*, 600–610. [CrossRef] [PubMed]
3. Schaefer, C.; Mann, R.; Masters, E.T.; Cappelleri, J.C.; Daniel, S.R.; Zlateva, G.; McElroy, H.J.; Chandran, A.; Adams, E.H.; Assaf, A.R.; et al. The comparative burden of chronic widespread pain and fibromyalgia in the United States. *Pain Pract.* **2016**, *16*, 565–579. [CrossRef] [PubMed]
4. Bartkowska, W.; Samborski, W.; Mojs, E. Cognitive functions, emotions and personality in woman with fi-bromyalgia. *Anthropol. Anz.* **2018**, *75*, 271–277. [CrossRef]

5. Galvez-Sánchez, C.M.; de la Coba, P.; Colmenero, J.M.; Reyes Del Paso, G.A.; Duschek, S. Attentional function in fibromyalgia and rheumatoid arthritis. *PLoS ONE* **2021**, *16*, e0246128. [CrossRef]
6. Glass, J.M.; Park, D.C.; Minear, M.; Crofford, L.J. Memory beliefs and function in fibromyalgia patients. *J. Psychosom. Res.* **2005**, *58*, 263–269. [CrossRef]
7. Teodoro, T.; Edwards, M.J.; Isaacs, J.D. A unifying theory for cognitive abnormalities in functional neurologi-cal disorders, fibromyalgia and chronic fatigue syndrome: Systematic review. *J. Neurol. Neurosurg. Psychiatry* **2018**, *89*, 1308–1319. [CrossRef]
8. Arnold, L.M.; Crofford, L.J.; Mease, P.J.; Burgess, S.M.; Palmer, S.C.; Abetz, L.; Martin, S.A. Patient perspectives on the impact of fibromyalgia. *Patient Educ. Couns.* **2008**, *73*, 114–120. [CrossRef]
9. Can, S.S.; Gencay-Can, A.; Gunendi, Z. Validity and reliability of the clock drawing test as a screening tool for cognitive impairment in patients with fibromyalgia. *Compr. Psychiatry* **2012**, *53*, 81–86. [CrossRef]
10. Katz, R.S.; Heard, A.R.; Mills, M.; Leavitt, F. The prevalence and clinical impact of reported cognitive difficulties (fibrofog) in patients with rheumatic disease with and without fibromyalgia. *J. Clin. Rheumatol.* **2004**, *10*, 53–58. [CrossRef]
11. Schmidt-Wilcke, T.; Wood, P.; Lürding, R. Schmerz und Aufmerksamkeit: Kognitive Defizite bei Fibrom-yal giepatienten. *Schmerz* **2010**, *24*, 46–53. [CrossRef] [PubMed]
12. Williams, D.A.; Clauw, D.J.; Glass, J.M. Perceived cognitive dysfunction in fibromyalgia syndrome. *J. Musculoskelet. Pain* **2011**, *19*, 66–75. [CrossRef]
13. Kravitz, H.M.; Katz, R.S. Fibrofog and fibromyalgia: A narrative review and implications for clinical practice. *Rheumatol. Int.* **2015**, *35*, 1115–1125. [CrossRef] [PubMed]
14. Mease, P.J.; Arnold, L.M.; Choy, E.H.; Clauw, D.J.; Crofford, L.J.; Glass, J.M.; Martin, S.A.; Morea, J.; Simon, L.; Strand, C.V.; et al. OMERACT Fibromyalgia Wor-king Group. Fibromyalgia syndrome module at OMERACT 9: Domain construct. *J. Rheumatol.* **2009**, *36*, 2318–2329. [CrossRef]
15. Schaefer, C.; Chandran, A.; Hufstader, M.; Baik, R.; McNett, M.; Goldenberg, D.; Gerwin, R.; Zlateva, G. The comparative bur-den of mild, moderate and severe fibromyalgia: Results from a cross-sectional survey in the United States. *Health Qual. Life Outcomes* **2011**, *9*, 71. [CrossRef]
16. Muñoz Ladrón de Guevara, C.; Fernández-Serrano, M.J.; Reyes Del Paso, G.A.; Duschek, S. Executive function impairments in fibromyalgia syndrome: Relevance of clinical variables and body mass index. *PLoS ONE* **2018**, *13*, e0196329.
17. Ambrose, K.R.; Gracely, R.H.; Glass, J.M. Fibromyalgia dyscognition: Concepts and issues. *Reumatismo* **2012**, *64*, 206–215. [CrossRef]
18. Cherry, B.J.; Zettel-Watson, L.; Shimizu, R.; Roberson, I.; Rutledge, D.N.; Jones, C.J. Cognitive performance in women aged 50 years and older with and without fibromyalgia. *J. Gerontol. B Psychol. Sci. Soc. Sci.* **2014**, *69*, 199–208. [CrossRef]
19. Duschek, S.; Werner, N.S.; Winkelmann, A.; Wankner, S. Implicit memory function in fibromyalgia syn-drome. *Behav. Med.* **2013**, *39*, 11–16. [CrossRef]
20. Gelonch, O.; Garolera, M.; Valls, J.; Castellà, G.; Varela, O.; Rosselló, L.; Pifarre, J. The effect of depressive symp-toms on cognition in patients with fibromyalgia. *PLoS ONE* **2018**, *13*, e0200057. [CrossRef]
21. Muñoz Ladrón de Guevara, C.; Reyes Del Paso, G.A.; Fernández-Serrano, M.J.; Duschek, S. Facial emotion recognition and executive functions in fibromyalgia. *Pain Med.* **2021**, *22*, 1619–1629. [CrossRef] [PubMed]
22. Tesio, V.; Torta, D.M.E.; Colonna, F.; Leombruni, P.; Ghiggia, A.; Fusaro, E.; Geminiani, G.C.; Torta, R.; Castelli, L. Are fibromyalgia patients cognitively impaired? Objective and subjective neuropsychological evidence: Cognitive impairment in FM. *Arthritis Care Res.* **2015**, *67*, 143–150. [CrossRef] [PubMed]
23. Bar-On Kalfon, T.; Gal, G.; Shorer, R.; Ablin, J.N. Cognitive functioning in fibromyalgia: The central role of effort. *J. Psychosom. Res.* **2016**, *87*, 30–36. [CrossRef] [PubMed]
24. Dick, B.; Eccleston, C.; Crombez, G. Attentional functioning in fibromyalgia, rheumatoid arthritis, and musculoskeletal pain patients. *Arthritis Rheum.* **2002**, *47*, 639–644. [CrossRef]
25. Dick, B.D.; Verrier, M.J.; Harker, T.K.; Rashiq, S. Disruption of cognitive function in fibromyalgia syndrome. *Pain* **2008**, *139*, 610–616. [CrossRef]
26. Harker, K.T.; Klein, R.M.; Dick, B.; Verrier, M.J.; Rashiq, S. Exploring attentional disruption in fibromyalgia using the attentional blink. *Psychol. Health* **2011**, *26*, 915–929. [CrossRef]
27. Kim, S.-H.; Kim, S.-H.; Kim, S.-K.; Nam, E.J.; Han, S.W.; Lee, S.J. Spatial versus verbal memory impairments in patients with fibromyalgia. *Rheumatol. Int.* **2012**, *32*, 1135–1142. [CrossRef]
28. Montoro, C.I.; Duschek, S.; Muñoz Ladrón de Guevara, C.; Fernández-Serrano, M.J.; Reyes del Paso, G.A. Ab-errant cerebral blood flow responses during cognition: Implications for the understanding of cognitive deficits in fibromyalgia. *Neuropsychology* **2015**, *29*, 173–182. [CrossRef]
29. Reyes Del Paso, G.A.; Montoro, C.I.; Duschek, S. Reaction time, cerebral blood flow, and heart rate responses in fibromyalgia: Evidence of alterations in attentional control. *J. Clin. Exp. Neuropsychol.* **2015**, *37*, 414–428. [CrossRef]
30. Castel, A.; Cascón-Pereira, R.; Boada, S. Memory complaints and cognitive performance in fibromyalgia and chronic pain: The key role of depression. *Scand. J. Psychol.* **2021**, *62*, 328–338. [CrossRef]
31. Grace, G.M.; Nielson, W.R.; Hopkins, M.; Berg, M.A. Concentration and memory deficits in patients with fibromyalgia syndrome. *J. Clin. Exp. Neuropsychol.* **1999**, *21*, 477–487. [CrossRef] [PubMed]

32. Leavitt, F.; Katz, R.S. Normalizing memory recall in fibromyalgia with rehearsal: A distraction-counteracting effect. *Arthritis Rheum.* **2009**, *61*, 740–744. [CrossRef] [PubMed]
33. Miró, E.; Lupiáñez, J.; Hita, E.; Martínez, M.P.; Sánchez, A.I.; Buela-Casal, G. Attentional deficits in fibromyalgia and its relationships with pain, emotional distress and sleep dysfunction complaints. *Psychol. Health* **2011**, *26*, 765–780. [CrossRef] [PubMed]
34. Walitt, B.; Roebuck-Spencer, T.; Bleiberg, J.; Foster, G.; Weinstein, A. Automated neuropsychiatric measurements of information processing in fibromyalgia. *Rheumatol. Int.* **2008**, *28*, 561–566. [CrossRef]
35. Bell, T.; Trost, Z.; Buelow, M.T.; Clay, O.; Younger, J.; Moore, D.; Crowe, M. Meta-analysis of cognitive performance in fibromyalgia. *J. Clin. Exp. Neuropsychol.* **2018**, *40*, 698–714. [CrossRef]
36. Galvez-Sánchez, C.M.; Muñoz Ladrón de Guevara, C.; Montoro, C.I.; Fernández-Serrano, M.J.; Duschek, S.; Reyes del Paso, G.A. Cognitive deficits in fibromyalgia syndrome are associated with pain responses to low intensity pressure stimulation. *PLoS ONE* **2018**, *13*, e0201488. [CrossRef]
37. Karp, J.F.; Reynolds, C.F., 3rd; Butters, M.A.; Dew, M.A.; Mazumdar, S.; Begley, A.E.; Lenze, E.; Weiner, D.K. The relationship between pain and mental flexibility in older adult pain clinic patients. *Pain Med.* **2006**, *7*, 444–452. [CrossRef]
38. Munguía-Izquierdo, D.; Legaz-Arrese, A.; Moliner-Urdiales, D.; Reverter-Masía, J. Neuropsicología de los pacientes con síndrome de fibromialgia: Relación con dolor y ansiedad. *Psicothema* **2008**, *20*, 427–431.
39. Reyes Del Paso, G.A.; Pulgar, A.; Duschek, S.; Garrido, S. Cognitive impairment in fibromyalgia syndrome: The impact of cardiovascular regulation, pain, emotional disorders and medication: Cognitive impairment in fibromyalgia syndrome. *Eur. J. Pain* **2012**, *16*, 421–429. [CrossRef]
40. Verdejo-García, A.; López-Torrecillas, F.; Calandre, E.P.; Delgado-Rodríguez, A.; Bechara, A. Executive function and decision-making in women with fibromyalgia. *Arch. Clin. Neuropsychol.* **2009**, *24*, 113–122. [CrossRef]
41. Emad, Y.; Ragab, Y.; Zeinhom, F.; El-Khouly, G.; Abou-Zeid, A.; Rasker, J.J. Hippocampus dysfunction may explain symptoms of fibromyalgia syndrome. A study with single-voxel magnetic resonance spectroscopy. *J. Rheumatol.* **2008**, *35*, 1371–1377. [PubMed]
42. Wu, Y.-L.; Huang, C.-J.; Fang, S.-C.; Ko, L.-H.; Tsai, P.-S. Cognitive impairment in fibromyalgia: A meta-analysis of case–control studies. *Psychosom. Med.* **2018**, *80*, 432–438. [CrossRef] [PubMed]
43. Gelonch, O.; Garolera, M.; Valls, J.; Rosselló, L.; Pifarré, J. Executive function in fibromyalgia: Comparing subjective and objective measures. *Compr. Psychiatry* **2016**, *66*, 113–122. [CrossRef]
44. Suhr, J.A. Neuropsychological impairment in fibromyalgia: Relation to depression, fatigue, and pain. *J. Psychosom. Res.* **2003**, *55*, 321–329. [CrossRef]
45. Pidal-Miranda, M.; González-Villar, A.J.; Carrillo-de-la-Peña, M.T.; Andrade, E.; Rodríguez-Salgado, D. Broad cognitive complaints but subtle objective working memory impairment in fibromyalgia patients. *PeerJ* **2018**, *6*, e5907. [CrossRef] [PubMed]
46. Ranum, R.M.; Toussaint, L.L.; Whipple, M.O.; Vincent, A. Predictive bidirectional relations between pain, fatigue, and dyscognition in fibromyalgia. *Mayo Clin. Proc. Innov. Qual. Outcomes* **2022**, *6*, 143–147. [CrossRef]
47. Weiß, S.; Winkelmann, A.; Duschek, S. Recognition of facially expressed emotions in patients with fibromyalgia syndrome. *Behav. Med.* **2013**, *39*, 146–154. [CrossRef]
48. Cournot, M.; Marquié, J.C.; Ansiau, D. Relation between body mass index and cognitivefunction in healthy middle-aged men and women. *Neurology* **2006**, *67*, 1208–1214. [CrossRef]
49. Dahl, A.K.; Hassing, L.B.; Fransson, E.I.; Gatz, M.; Reynolds, C.A.; Pedersen, N.L. Body mass index acrossmidlife and cognitive change in late life. *Int. J.* **2013**, *37*, 296–302.
50. O'Brien, P.D.; Hinder, L.M.; Callaghan, B.C.; Feldman, E.L. Neurological consequences of obesity. *Lancet Neurol.* **2017**, *16*, 465–477. [CrossRef]
51. WHO Consultation on Obesity; Division of Noncommunicable Diseases; Programme of Nutrition, Family and Reproductive Health. *Obesity: Preventing and Managing the Global Epidemic: Report of a WHO Consultation on Obesity, Geneva, 3–5 June 1997*; World Health Organization: Geneva, Switzerland, 1998.
52. Callaghan, B.C.; Reynolds, E.L.; Banerjee, M.; Chant, E.; Villegas-Umana, E.; Gardner, T.W.; Votruba, K.; Giordani, B.; Pop-Busui, R.; Pennathur, S. The preva-lence and determinants of cognitive deficits and traditional diabetic complications in the severely obese. *Diabetes Care* **2020**, *43*, 683–690. [CrossRef] [PubMed]
53. Gameiro, F.; Perea, M.V.; Ladera, V.; Rosa, B.; García, R. Executive functioning in obese individuals waiting for clinical treatment. *Psicothema* **2017**, *29*, 61–66. [PubMed]
54. Restivo, M.R.; McKinnon, M.C.; Frey, B.N.; Hall, G.B.; Syed, W.; Taylor, V.H. The impact of obesity on neuropsychological functioning in adults with and without major depressive disorder. *PLoS ONE* **2017**, *12*, e0176898. [CrossRef] [PubMed]
55. D'Onghia, M.; Ciaffi, J.; Lisi, L.; Mancarella, L.; Ricci, S.; Stefanelli, N.; Meliconi, R.; Ursini, F. Fibromyalgia and obesity: A com-prehensive systematic review and meta-analysis. *Semin. Arthritis Rheum.* **2021**, *51*, 409–424. [CrossRef] [PubMed]
56. Okifuji, A.; Bradshaw, D.H.; Olson, C. Evaluación de la obesidad en la fibromialgia: Biomarcadores neuroendocrinos, síntomas y funciones. *Clin. Rheumatol.* **2009**, *8*, 475–478. [CrossRef]
57. Soriano-Maldonado, A.; Artero, E.G.; Segura-Jiménez, V.; Aparicio, V.A.; Estévez-López, F.; Álvarez-Gallardo, I.C.; Munguía-Izquierdo, D.; Casimiro-Andújar, A.J.; Delgado-Fernández, M.; Ortega, F.B. Association of physical fitness and fatness with cognitive function in women with fibromyalgia. *J. Sports Sci.* **2016**, *34*, 1731–1739. [CrossRef]

58. Galvez-Sánchez, C.M.; Reyes Del Paso, G.A.; Duschek, S. Cognitive impairments in fibromyalgia syndrome: Associations with positive and negative affect, alexithymia, pain catastrophizing and selfesteem. *Front. Psychol.* **2018**, *9*, 377. [CrossRef]
59. First, M.; Spitzer, R.; Gibbon, M.; Williams, J. *Entrevista Clínica Estructurada para los Trastornos del Eje I del DSM-IV (SCIDI)*; Masson: Barcelona, Spain, 1999.
60. Lázaro, C.; Bosch, F.; Torrubia, R.; Baños, J.-E. The development of a Spanish questionnaire for assessing pain: Preliminary data concerning reliability and validity. *Eur. J. Psychol. Assess.* **1994**, *10*, 145–151.
61. Masedo, A.I.; Esteve, R. Some empirical evidence regarding the validity of the Spanish version of the McGill Pain Questionnaire (MPQ-SV). *Pain* **2000**, *85*, 451–456. [CrossRef]
62. Sanz, J.; Navarro, M.E.; Vázquez, C. Adaptación española del Inventario para la Depresión de Beck-II (BDI-II): I. Propiedades psicométricas en estudiantes universitarios. *Análisis Y Modif. Conducta* **2003**, *29*, 239–288.
63. Spielberger, C.D.; Gorsuch, R.L.; Lushene, R.E. *Cuestionario de Ansiedad Estado-Rasgo (STAI): Manual*; TEA Ediciones: Madrid, Spain, 1986.
64. Bulbena, A.; Berrios, G.E.; De Larrinoa, F. *Medición Clínica en Psiquiatría y Psicología*; Masson: Barcelona, Spain, 2000.
65. Bobes, J.; González, M.P.; Sáiz, P.A.; Bascarán, M.T.; Iglesias, C.; Fernández, J.M. Propiedades psicométricas del cuestionario Oviedo de sueño. *Psicothema* **2000**, *12*, 107–112.
66. Brickenkamp, R. *Aufmerksamkeits-Belastungs-Test (Test d2)*; Hogrefe: Göttingen, Germany, 1962.
67. Delis, D.C.; Kaplan, E.; Kramer, J.H. *Delis-Kaplan Executive Function System (D-KEFS)*; The Psychological Corporation: San Antonio, TX, USA, 2001.
68. Spreen, S.; Strauss, E. *A Compendium of Neuropsychological Test: Administration, Norms and Commentary*; Oxford University Press: New York, NY, USA, 1991.
69. Reitan, R.M. Validity of the trail making test as an indicator of organic brain damage. *Percept. Mot. Ski.* **1958**, *8*, 271–276. [CrossRef]
70. Rey, A. *L'examen Clinique en Psychologie (The Clinical Examination in Psychology)*; Presse Universitaires de France: Paris, France, 1964.
71. Sedó, M. *Test de los Cinco Dígitos*; TEA Ediciones: Madrid, Spain, 2007.
72. de Paula, J.J.; Oliveira, T.D.; Querino, E.H.G.; Malloy-Diniz, L.F. The Five Digits Test in the assessment of older adults with low formal education: Construct validity and reliability in a Brazilian clinical sam-ple. *Trends Psychiatry Psychother.* **2017**, *39*, 173–179. [CrossRef] [PubMed]
73. Benedet, M.J.; Alejandre, M.A. *TAVEC: Test de Aprendizaje Verbal. España-Complutense*; TEA Ediciones: Madrid, Spain, 1998.
74. Roldán-Tapia, L.; Cánovas-López, R.; Cimadevilla, J.; Valverde, M. Cognition and perception deficits in fibromyalgia and rheumatoid arthritis. *Reumatol. Clín.* **2007**, *3*, 101–109. [CrossRef]
75. Veldhuijzen, D.S.; Sondaal, S.F.V.; Oosterman, J.M. Intact cognitive inhibition in patients with fibromyalgia but evidence of declined processing speed. *J. Pain* **2012**, *13*, 507–515. [CrossRef]
76. Castel, A.; Cascón, R.; Salvat, M.; Sala, J.; Padrol, A.; Pérez, M. Cognitive performance and memory complaints in chronic patients: With fibromyalgia versus without fibromyalgia. *Rev. Soc. Española Dolor* **2008**, *15*, 358–370.
77. Somers, T.J.; Wren, A.A.; Keefe, F.J. Understanding chronic pain in older adults: Abdominal fat is where it is at. *Pain* **2011**, *152*, 8–9. [CrossRef]
78. Schwartz, M.W.; Seeley, R.J.; Zeltser, L.M.; Drewnowski, A.; Ravussin, E.; Redman, L.M.; Leibel, R.L. Obesity pathogenesis: An endocrine society scientific statement. *Endocr. Rev.* **2017**, *38*, 267–296. [CrossRef]
79. Okifuji, A.; Hare, B. The association between chronic pain and obesity. *J. Pain Res.* **2015**, *8*, 399–408. [CrossRef]
80. Nguyen, J.C.D.; Killcross, A.S.; Jenkins, T.A. Obesity and cognitive decline: Role of inflammation and vascular changes. *Front. Neurosci.* **2014**, *8*, 375. [CrossRef]
81. Baskaran, C.; Animashaun, A.; Rickard, F.; Toth, A.T.; Eddy, K.T.; Plessow, F.; Bredella, M.A.; Misra, M. Memory and executive function in adolescent and young adult females with moderate to severe obesity before and after weight loss surgery. *Obes. Surg.* **2021**, *31*, 3372–3378. [CrossRef] [PubMed]
82. Calvo, D.; Galioto, R.; Gunstad, J.; Spitznagel, M.B. Uncontrolled eating is associated with reduced executive functioning: Uncontrolled eating and cognitive function. *Clin. Obes.* **2014**, *4*, 172–179. [CrossRef] [PubMed]
83. Qavam, S.E.; Anisan, A.; Fathi, M.; Pourabbasi, A. Study of relationship between obesity and executive functions among high school students in Bushehr, Iran. *J. Diabetes Metab. Disord.* **2015**, *14*, 79. [CrossRef] [PubMed]
84. Sargénius, H.L.; Lydersen, S.; Hestad, K. Neuropsychological function in individuals with morbid obesity: A cross-sectional study. *BMC Obes.* **2017**, *4*, 6. [CrossRef] [PubMed]
85. Arnoldussen, I.A.; Kiliaan, A.J.; Gustafson, D.R. Obesity and dementia: Adipokines interact with the brain. *Eur. Neuropsychopharmacol.* **2014**, *24*, 1982–1999. [CrossRef]
86. Chan, J.S.; Yan, J.H.; Payne, V.G. The impact of obesity and exercise on cognitive aging. *Front. Aging Neurosci.* **2013**, *5*, 97. [CrossRef]
87. Freeman, L.R.; Haley-Zitlin, V.; Rosenberger, D.S.; Granholm, A.C. Damaging effects of a high-fat diet to the brain and cognition: A review of proposed mechanisms. *Nutr. Neurosci.* **2014**, *17*, 241–251. [CrossRef]
88. Frisardi, V.; Solfrizzi, V.; Seripa, D.; Capurso, C.; Santamato, A.; Sancarlo, D.; Vendemiale, G.; Pilotto, A.; Panza, F. Metabolic-cognitive syndrome: A cross-talk between metabolic syndrome and Alzheimer's disease. *Ageing Res. Rev.* **2010**, *9*, 399–417. [CrossRef]

89. Gonzales, M.M.; Takashi, T.; Eagan, D.E.; Tanaka, H.; Vaghasia, M.; Haley, A.P. Indirect effects of elevated body mass index on memory performance through altered cerebral metabolite concentrations. *Psychosom. Med.* **2012**, *74*, 691. [CrossRef]
90. Greenwood, C.E.; Winocur, G. High-fat diets, insulin resistance and declining cognitive function. *Neurobiol. Aging* **2005**, *26*, 42–45. [CrossRef]
91. Smith, E.; Hay, P.; Campbell, L.; Trollor, J.N. A review of the association between obesity and cognitive function across the lifespan: Implications for novel approaches to prevention and treatment. *Obes. Rev.* **2011**, *12*, 740–755. [CrossRef] [PubMed]
92. Wolf, P.A.; Beiser, A.; Elias, M.F.; Au, R.; Vasan, R.S.; Seshadri, S. Relation of obesity to cognitive function: Importance of central obesity and synergistic influence of concomitant hypertension. The Framingham Heart Study. *Curr. Alzheimer Res.* **2007**, *4*, 111–116. [CrossRef] [PubMed]
93. Bluher, M.; Fasshauer, M.; Tonjes, A.; Kratzsch, J.; Schon, M.R.; Paschke, R. Association of interleukin-6,C-reactive protein, interleukin-10 and adiponectin plasma concentrations with measures of obesity, insulin sensitivity and glucose metabolism. *Exp. Clin. Endocrinol. Diabetes* **2005**, *113*, 534–537. [CrossRef] [PubMed]
94. Bulzacka, E.; Boyer, L.; Schurhoff, F.; Godin, O.; Berna, F.; Brunel, L.; Andrianarisoa, M.; Aouizerate, B.; Capdevielle, D.; Chereau-Boudet, I.; et al. Fond Chronic peripheral inflammation is associated with cognitive impairment in schizophrenia: Results from the multicentric FACE-SZ dataset Schizophr. *Schizophr. Bull.* **2016**, *42*, 1290–1302. [CrossRef]
95. Younger, J.; Kapphahn, K.; Brennan, K.; Sullivan, S.D.; Stefanick, M.L. Association of Leptin with body pain in women. *J. Womens Health* **2016**, *25*, 752–760. [CrossRef]
96. Peiser, C.; McGregor, G.P.; Lang, R.E. Binding and internalization of leptin by porcine choroid plexus cells in culture. *Neurosci. Lett.* **2000**, *283*, 209–212. [CrossRef]
97. Zlokovic, B.V.; Jovanovic, S.; Miao, W.; Samara, S.; Verma, S.; Farrell, C.L. Differential regulation of leptin transport by the choroid plexus and blood-brain barrier and high affinity transport systems for entry into hypothalamus and across the blood-cerebrospinal fluid barrier. *Endocrinology* **2000**, *141*, 1434–1441. [CrossRef]
98. Murga, I.; Guillen, V.; Lafuente, J.V. Cerebral magnetic resonance changes associated with fibromyalgia syndrome. Cambios en la resonancia magnética cerebral asociados al síndrome de fibromialgia. *Med. Clín.* **2017**, *148*, 511–516. [CrossRef]
99. Neeck, G. Neuroendocrine and hormonal perturbations and relations to the serotonergic system in fibromyalgia patients. *Scand. J. Rheumatol.* **2000**, *29*, 8–12. [CrossRef]
100. Esteban-Cornejo, I.; Tejero-Gonzalez, C.M.; Sallis, J.F.; Veiga, O.L. Physical activity and cognition in adolescents: A systematic review. *J. Sci. Med. Sport* **2015**, *18*, 534–539. [CrossRef]
101. Jacobsen, S.; Holm, B. Muscle strength and endurance compared to aerobic capacity in primary fibromyalgia syndrome. *Clin. Exp. Rheumatol.* **1992**, *10*, 419–420. [PubMed]
102. Häuser, W.; Ablin, J.; Fitzcharles, M.-A.; Littlejohn, G.; Luciano, J.V.; Usui, C.; Walitt, B. Fibromyalgia. *Nat. Rev. Dis. Primers* **2015**, *1*, 15022. [CrossRef] [PubMed]
103. Angevaren, M.; Aufdemkampe, G.; Verhaar, H.J.J.; Aleman, A.; Vanhees, L. Physical activity and enhanced fit-ness to improve cognitive function in older people without known cognitive impairment. *Cochrane Database Syst. Rev.* **2008**, *16*, CD005381. [CrossRef]
104. Smith, P.J.; Blumenthal, J.A.; Hoffman, B.M.; Cooper, H.; Strauman, T.A.; Welsh-Bohmer, K.; Browndyke, J.; Sherwood, A. Aerobic exercise and neurocognitive performance: A meta-analytic review of randomized controlled trials. *Psychosom. Med.* **2010**, *72*, 239–252. [CrossRef]
105. Miró, E.; Martínez, M.P.; Sánchez, A.I.; Prados, G.; Lupiáñez, J. Men and women with fibromyalgia: Relation between attentional function and clinical symptoms. *Br. J. Health Psychol.* **2015**, *20*, 632–647. [CrossRef]
106. Humphreys, M.S.; Revelle, W. Personality, motivation, and performance: A theory of the relationship between individual differences and information processing. *Psychol. Rev.* **1984**, *91*, 153. [CrossRef]
107. Tracy, J.I.; Mohamed, F.; Faro, S.; Tiver, R.; Pinus, A.; Bloomer, C.; Pyrros, A.; Harvan, J. Harvan The effect of autonomic arousal on attentional focus. *Neuroreport* **2000**, *11*, 4037–4042. [CrossRef]
108. Park, D.C.; Glass, J.M.; Minear, M.; Crofford, L.J. Cognitive function in fibromyalgia patients. *Arthritis Rheum.* **2001**, *44*, 2125–2133. [CrossRef]
109. Nivitha, M.; Narayanan, J.; Chitra, V. A Review on the Cognitive Impairment caused by Anti-epileptics and their Management. *NVEO-Nat. Volatiles Essent. Oils J. NVEO* **2021**, *8*, 12905–12919.
110. Ackerman, S.; Nolan, L.J. Bodyweight gain induced by psychotropic drugs: Incidence, mechanisms and management. *CN Drugs* **1998**, *9*, 135–151. [CrossRef]
111. Allison, D.B.; Mentore, J.L.; Heo, M.; Chandler, L.P.; Cappelleri, J.C.; Infante, M.C.; Weiden, P.J. Antipsychotic-induced weight gain: A comprehensive research synthesis. *Am. J. Psychiatry* **1999**, *156*, 1686–1696. [CrossRef] [PubMed]
112. Glass, J.M. Cognitive dysfunction in fibromyalgia and chronic fatigue syndrome: New trends and future directions. *Curr. Rheumatol. Rep.* **2006**, *8*, 425–429. [CrossRef] [PubMed]

Journal of
Clinical Medicine

MDPI

Article

Test–Retest Reliability and Concurrent Validity of the 3 m Backward Walk Test under Single and Dual-Task Conditions in Women with Fibromyalgia

Juan Luis Leon-Llamas [1], Santos Villafaina [1,2,*], Alvaro Murillo-Garcia [1], Francisco Javier Domínguez-Muñoz [1] and Narcis Gusi [1,3]

1 Grupo de Investigación Actividad Física y Calidad de Vida (AFYCAV), Facultad de Ciencias del Deporte, Universidad de Extremadura, 10003 Caceres, Spain
2 Departamento de Desporto e Saúde, Escola de Saúde e Desenvolvimento Humano, Universidade de Évora, 7004-516 Évora, Portugal
3 International Institute for Innovation in Aging, University of Extremadura, 10003 Caceres, Spain
* Correspondence: svillafaina@unex.es

Abstract: Background: Previous studies have reported good test–retest reliability for the 3 m backward test (3MBWT) in different populations. However, reliability of the 3MBWT has not been studied in fibromyalgia (FM) under single and dual-task conditions; Methods: A total of 21 women with FM participated in this study. Participants completed the Revised Fibromyalgia Impact Questionnaire and two physical fitness tests: the 3MBWT and the Timed Up and Go (TUG). The dual-task condition consisted of subtracting two by two while performing the test, starting from a random number less than 100; Results: Values showed that the 3MBWT can be considered reliable under single and dual-task conditions when measured with both a manual stopwatch and a Chronopic automatic stopwatch. A strong concurrent validity was shown of 3MBWT and TUG results in the test and retest and the different devices. The relationship between the performance of the 3MBWT in test and retest conditions under single and dual-task conditions measured with different devices and the impact of the disease were high; Conclusions: The 3MBWT is a reliable tool under the single and dual-task conditions in women with FM. It shows higher reliability values when time is taken using a Chronopic. This test also shows high concurrent validity with the TUG test. Its performance is related to the impact of the disease.

Keywords: reproducibility; assessment; chronic pain; activities of daily living; mobility

Citation: Leon-Llamas, J.L.; Villafaina, S.; Murillo-Garcia, A.; Domínguez-Muñoz, F.J.; Gusi, N. Test–Retest Reliability and Concurrent Validity of the 3 m Backward Walk Test under Single and Dual-Task Conditions in Women with Fibromyalgia. *J. Clin. Med.* **2023**, *12*, 212. https://doi.org/10.3390/jcm12010212

Academic Editors: Carmen María Galvez Sánchez, Casandra I. Montoro Aguilar and Markus W. Hollmann

Received: 14 November 2022
Revised: 20 December 2022
Accepted: 24 December 2022
Published: 27 December 2022

1. Introduction

Fibromyalgia (FM) is a chronic disease that is characterized by chronic widespread, diffuse, and persistent musculoskeletal pain, often accompanied by other symptoms, such as fatigue, sleep disorders, mood disturbance, anxiety, depression, cognitive problems, low physical activity, and balance problems [1–3]. All these symptoms have an important influence on the activities of daily living [4] and tend to reduce the health-related quality of life in this population [5]. It is estimated that FM affects 0.2% to 6.6% of the general population and mainly women over 50 years old [6].

One of the ten most debilitating symptoms of FM is balance impairments, which is experienced by 45% of this population [7]. Moreover, people with FM usually report nonspecific postural balance disorder, an increased prevalence of falls [8], a reduced performance in mobility [9–11], a higher risk of falling [12–14], and, therefore, a lower performance on balance tests [12,14]. In addition, gait disturbances [15] that are influenced by attention and executive function [16] have been also detected.

One of the most important objectives that a rehabilitation or training program should follow is to increase the individual's performance to minimize the risks associated with the condition. Therefore, previous studies have evaluated the physical fitness of people with FM using different tests to assess flexibility [17], endurance [10], strength [10,17–19], balance [9], or mobility [11,17]. Among the physical fitness tests used to assess functional mobility, the Timed Up and Go test (TUG) has been used in different populations [20,21], including FM [9,11,17]. This test involves walking forward, balance, and turning tasks. Nevertheless, walking backward, which is not contemplated in the TUG test, is more complex and requires higher neuromuscular and proprioceptive control [22]. Moreover, it is a task that can occur in everyday life situations, such as opening a door, avoiding an obstacle, or backing up to a chair [23]. Additionally, walking backward is considered a more sensitive measure for assessing mobility and balance deficits [24,25]. In this regard, Carter et al. [23] proposed the 3 m walking backward test (3MBWT). This is a clinical tool developed in healthy older adults to identify the risk of falling that appears to be more accurate or equal to other existing tests such as TUG, Five Times Sit-to-Stand, and Four Square Step Test. Regarding the 3MBWT, it has shown high test–retest reliability and validity in the stroke population [26], community-dwelling older adults [27], multiple sclerosis [28,29], and patients with advanced knee osteoarthritis [30]. However, this test has yet to be studied in people with FM. Interestingly, it could become an important clinical tool due to the characteristics of this population since it is essential to perform a functional assessment of mobility and balance to aid in diagnosing and managing the disease.

Due to the similarities to real-life conditions and activities of daily living requirements [31], previous studies have included a simultaneous cognitive task (dual-task paradigm). Therefore, assessing these activities is essential in clinical and ecological settings since they require significant attention and executive processes [31]. In this regard, people with FM have exhibited a considerable impairment in dual-task performance compared to healthy controls [32–34]. Furthermore, the reliability of the chair stand test [18], 10-m walking test [11], TUG [11], and arm curl test [18] under dual-task conditions have been explored for people with FM. Nevertheless, the reliability of walking backward while performing a cognitive task has yet to be assessed. This issue is crucial since healthcare professionals and researchers can better understand an individual's symptoms and develop a more effective treatment plan to address their specific needs.

To our knowledge, previous investigations have not explored the reliability and validity of the 3MBWT in people with FM. Therefore, this study aimed to analyze the test–retest reliability of the 3MBWT under single and dual-task conditions. As a secondary objective, we also aimed to evaluate the test–rest reliability using different instruments (stopwatch and Chronopic). Lastly, we also aimed to assess the concurrent validity of the TUG and 3MBWT as well as the relationship between the 3MBWT test and the impact of the disease. We hypothesized that good test–retest reliability values would be obtained with both Chronopic and stopwatch, with higher scores when using a Chronopic, as previous studies suggested [9,11]. Additionally, a high concurrent validity between the 3MBWT and TUG test would be obtained considering the results reported in previous research [26–29], and a significant correlation between the 3MBWT and the impact of the disease would be observed.

2. Materials and Methods

2.1. Participants

Twenty-one women with FM were enrolled in this cross-sectional study. The sample size and statistical power were calculated using the PASS software (version 11.0; PASS; Kaysville, Utah). In this regard, with two samples per participant, there is a 98% power to detect an intra-class correlation of 0.95 under the alternative hypothesis when the intraclass correlation under the null hypothesis is 0.75, using an F-test with a significance level of 0.05.

The participants fulfilled the following inclusion criteria for this study: (a) to be a female between 35 and 65 years old, (b) to be diagnosed with FM by a rheumatologist according to the criteria established by the American College of Rheumatology [35], and (c) to understand the physical fitness protocols. Participants were excluded if they: (a) were pregnant, (b) were enrolled in another clinical trial or research that could impact the results, and (c) had any condition where exercise is contraindicated.

All the participants gave written informed consent. The Research Ethics Committee of the University of Extremadura approved the protocols of the current study (approval reference: 51/2021).

2.2. Procedure

The Spanish version of the Revised Fibromyalgia Impact Questionnaire (FIQR) was administered [36]. This instrument is composed of 21 items divided into three domains (function, overall impact, and symptoms). The maximum score is 100, which corresponds to the worst overall impact. In addition, age and anthropometric measurements were acquired using a Tanita Body Composition Analyzer BC-418 MA (Tanita Corp., Tokyo, Japan).

The 3MBWT and (2) the TUG were performed under single and dual-task conditions. The dual-task condition consisted of subtracting two by two (a random number lower than 100) while performing the physical fitness tests.

The 3 m Backward Walk Test (3MBWT) was performed according to the procedure proposed by Carter et al. [23]. A distance of three meters was measured with black tape establishing the start and finish. Participants were asked to place their heels on the start mark. Then, they had to walk backward as fast and safely as possible at the "go" signal. Running was not allowed, and they could look behind themselves if they wished.

In the Timed Up and Go (TUG) test, participants had to get up from a chair without armrests, walk a distance of 3 m without running, turn around a cone, walk back to the chair, and sit down [37].

Simultaneous stopwatch and automatic timer records were obtained. For the TUG, the Chronopic (Chronojump, BoscoSystem®, Barcelona, Spain) time was obtained using a DIN A4-sized contact platform placed on the back of the chair, which was used to open and close the circuit to obtain the test time [9,11]. For the 3MBWT a DIN A2-sized contact platform on the start line combined with a photocell on the end line was used. Physical tests were repeated after seven days to avoid learning effect [11,18,38,39]. Participants performed three trials for each condition (single and dual-task), and the order of TUG test and 3MBWT was randomized.

2.3. Statistical Analysis

Statistical analysis was conducted using the Statistical Package for the Social Sciences (SPSS, version 24.0; IBM Corp., Armonk, NY, USA) software. Based on data provided by the Shapiro–Wilk test, parametric tests were employed. The statistical significance was established at the $p \leq 0.05$ level. To estimate the intraclass correlation coefficient (ICC) and its 95% confidence intervals of the 3MBWT in the single and dual-task conditions at test and retest times, the 3,1 (Two-way mixed effects, consistency, single rater/measurement) model was used following the recommendations by Weir [40] and Koo [41]. Regarding the ICC classification, an ICC value lower than 0.50 indicates "poor" reliability, an ICC value between 0.50 and 0.75 indicates "moderate" reliability, an ICC value between 0.75 and 0.90 indicates "good" reliability, and an ICC value higher than 0.90 indicates "excellent" reliability. This ICC classification was interpreted according to the guideline proposed by Koo [41].

The standard error of measurement (SEM) was calculated using the following formula:

$$\text{SEM} = \text{SD} \times \sqrt{1 - \text{ICC}} \quad (1)$$

The minimal detectable change (MDC) was obtained according to the formula:

$$\text{MDC} = 1.96 \times \text{SEM} \times \sqrt{2} \quad (2)$$

The SEM and MDC were expressed as a percentage according to the following formula, SEM% or MCD% = (SEM or MCD/mean) × 100, where the mean is the average of the test and retest.

To identify the level of agreement between the test and retest, and the measuring devices in the 3MBWT under single and dual-task conditions, Bland–Altman plots were performed [42].

The Pearson's product–moment correlation coefficient (r) was used to explore the concurrent validity comparing the 3MBWT and the TUG. Finally, the relationship between 3MBWT and the impact of the disease was also analyzed through the total value of the FIQR. Cohen's recommendations [43] were followed to interpret the correlation coefficient. A score ≥ 0.5 was strong, moderate if the score was between 0.5 and 0.35, and poor if the score was ≤0.35.

3. Results

A total of 21 women with FM from a local association participated in this study. The main characteristics of the participants are shown in Table 1.

Table 1. Descriptive characteristics of the participants.

Variables (N = 21)	Mean (SD)
Age (years)	52.48 (5.99)
Height (cm)	160.10 (0.07)
Weight (kg)	73.50 (14.37)
BMI (kg/m^2)	28.67 (5.53)
FIQR	59.68 (22.07)
FIQR-Function	16.06 (7.74)
FIQR-Overall impact	10.71 (6.90)
FIQR-Symptoms	32.90 (9.77)
Falls in the last six months (number)	0.95 (1.20)

Abbreviations: N, sample; SD, standard deviation; BMI, body mass index, FIQR, Fibromyalgia Impact Questionnaire Revised.

Table 2 shows the relative reliability (ICC) and absolute reliability (SEM and MDC) of the performance obtained in the 3MBWT, under the single and dual-task conditions in both test and retest with the different devices. Following the recommendations by Koo et al. [41], the 95% confidence intervals of the ICC were used to interpret the reliability values. Regarding the single condition, "poor" to "good" and "moderate" to "excellent" reliability values were obtained for the stopwatch and Chronopic, respectively. On the other hand, in the dual-task condition, the reliability values for the stopwatch were "moderate" to "excellent" and for the Chronopic were "good" to "excellent".

Table 2. Reliability of the 3MBWT under single and dual-task conditions.

Variables		Test	Retest	ICC (95% CI)	SEM	%SEM	MDC	%MDC
3MBWT (s)	Stopwatch	2.90 (0.87)	2.85 (1.13)	0.71 (0.283–0.882)	0.54	18.73	1.49	51.92
	Chronopic	2.80 (0.88)	2.75 (1.09)	0.85 (0.619–0.937)	0.38	13.75	1.06	38.11
3MBWT DT (s)	Stopwatch	3.21 (0.95)	2.81 (1.10)	0.89 (0.718–0.954)	0.34	11.29	0.94	31.31
	Chronopic	3.06 (1.03)	2.90 (1.03)	0.93 (0.817–0.970)	0.27	9.14	0.76	25.35

Abbreviations: 3MBWT, 3 m backward test; s, seconds; SD, standard deviation; ICC, intraclass correlation coefficient; CI, confidence interval; SEM, standard error of measurement; MDC, minimal detectable change; DT, dual-task.

Reliability values obtained by comparing the different devices in both the single and dual-task conditions in the test and retest are shown in Table 3. Taking into account the 95% confidence intervals of the ICC, a reliability value of "good" to "excellent" was obtained for the test, and an "excellent" value was obtained for the retest in the single and dual-task condition.

Table 3. Reliability of the 3MBWT under single and dual-task conditions using stopwatch and Chronopic in the test and retest.

Variables		Stopwatch Mean (SD)	Chronopic Mean (SD)	ICC (95% CI)
3MBWT (s)	Test	2.90 (0.87)	2.80 (0.88)	0.92 (0.811–0.969)
	Retest	2.85 (1.13)	2.75 (1.09)	0.974 (0.937–0.990)
3MBWT DT (s)	Test	3.21 (0.95)	3.06 (1.03)	0.91 (0.779–0.964)
	Retest	2.81 (1.10)	2.90 (1.03)	0.974 (0.937–0.990)

Abbreviations: 3MBWT, 3 m backward test; s, seconds; SD, standard deviation; ICC, intraclass correlation coefficient; CI, confidence interval; DT, dual-task.

Figure 1 shows the Bland–Altman plots of the times obtained by stopwatch and Chronopic in test and retest in the single and dual-task conditions, and the times obtained between the two devices in both the single and dual-task conditions in the test and retest, respectively.

Table 4 shows the concurrent validity analysis results of 3MBWT and TUG test. All correlation values obtained were classified as strong [43] in the test and retest and the different devices.

Table 4. Concurrent validity between 3MBWT and TUG under single and dual-task conditions, in test and retests, with stopwatch and Chronopic.

		Stopwatch	
		Test Condition	Retest Condition
	Variables	TUG	TUG
Single	3MBWT	0.735 ***	0.831 ***
Dual	3MBWT	0.679 ***	0.875 ***
		Chronopic	
		Test Condition	Retest Condition
	Variables	TUG	TUG
Single	3MBWT	0.834 ***	0.794 ***
Dual	3MBWT	0.845 ***	0.906 ***

Abbreviations: 3MBWT, 3-m backward test; TUG, timed up and go. *** p-value < 0.001.

Finally, the relationship between the performance of the 3MBWT in test and retest conditions under single and dual-task conditions measured with different devices and the impact of the disease were strong, excepting the 3MBWT in test condition under single condition measured with a stopwatch (r: 0.488), which was moderate. In analyzing the dimensions that make up the FIQR questionnaire, strong correlations were obtained between the "symptoms" dimension and all the conditions and devices. Similarly, strong correlations were also obtained between the dimension "overall impact" except for the single and dual-task conditions in the test period, measured with the stopwatch and the Chronopic, respectively, where moderate correlations were reported. As for the dimension "function," only moderate correlations were found in the single condition in the retest and test periods, measured with a stopwatch and Chronopic, respectively. Results are shown in Table 5.

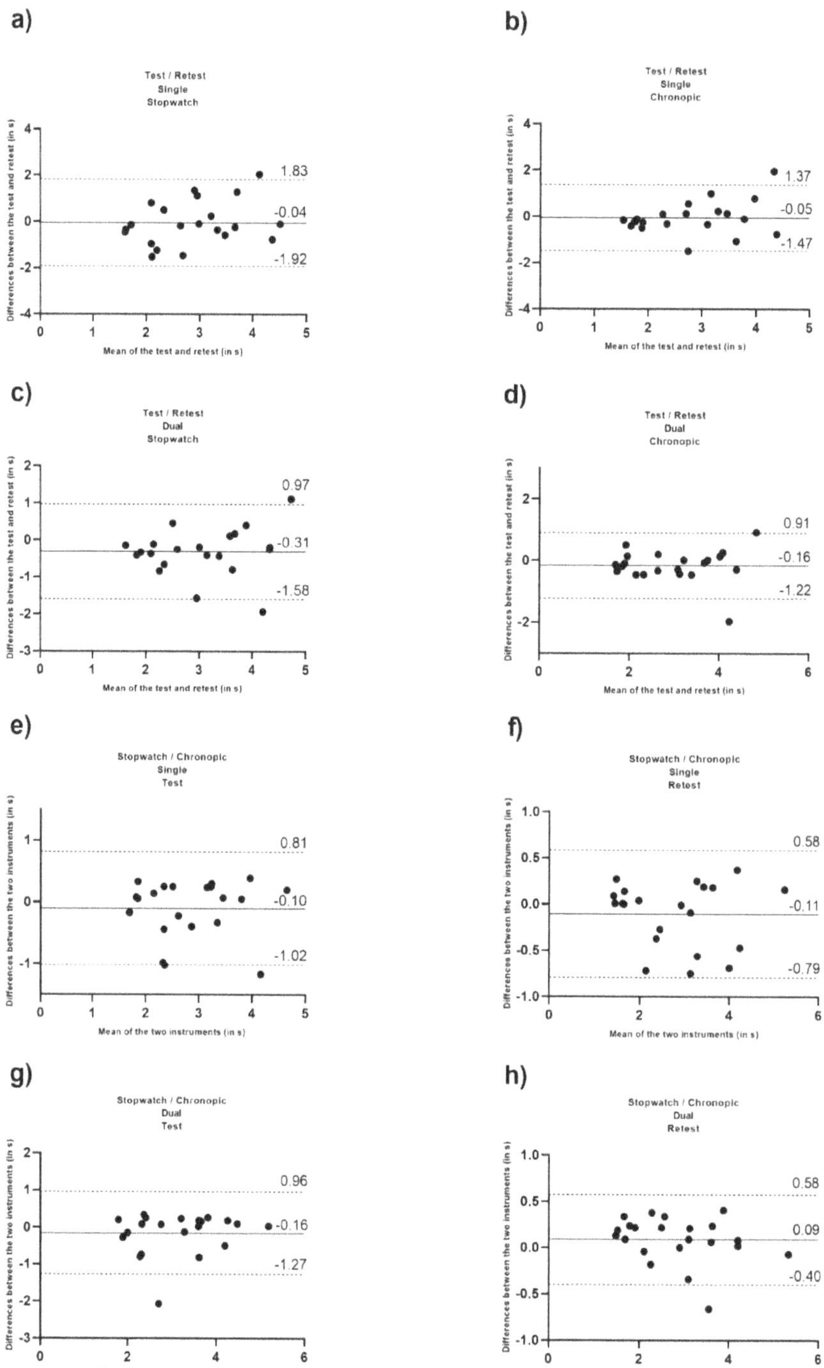

Figure 1. (**a**) differences between test and retest vs. the mean of the two measurements under the single condition using a stopwatch; (**b**) differences between test and retest vs. the mean of the two measurements

under the single condition using a Chronopic; (**c**) differences between test and retest vs. the mean of the two measurements under the dual-task condition using a stopwatch; and (**d**) differences between test and retest vs. the mean of the two measurements under the dual-task condition using a Chronopic; (**e**) differences between stopwatch and Chronopic vs. the mean of the two measurements under the single condition in test; (**f**) differences between stopwatch and Chronopic vs. the mean of the two measurements under the single condition in retest; (**g**) differences between stopwatch and Chronopic vs. the mean of the two measurements under the dual-task condition in test; and (**h**) differences between stopwatch and Chronopic vs. the mean of the two measurements under the dual-task condition in retest.

Table 5. Correlation between 3MBWT and FIQR under single and dual-task conditions, in test and retest, with stopwatch and Chronopic.

	Stopwatch Variables	FIQR	FIQR-Function	FIQR-Overall impact	FIQR-Symptoms
Single	3MBWT (test)	0.488 *	0.273	0.488 *	0.543 *
	3MBWT (retest)	0.659 ***	0.461 *	0.652 **	0.663 ***
Dual	3MBWT (test)	0.527 *	0.396	0.513 *	0.514 *
	3MBWT (retest)	0.614 ***	0.389	0.630 **	0.634 **
	Chronopic Variables	FIQR	FIQR-Function	FIQR-Overall impact	FIQR-Symptoms
Single	3MBWT (test)	0.654 ***	0.448 *	0.558 **	0.729 ***
	3MBWT (retest)	0.577 ***	0.325	0.624 **	0.604 **
Dual	3MBWT (test)	0.532 *	0.356	0.444 *	0.607 **
	3MBWT (retest)	0.636 ***	0.394	0.631 **	0.679 ***

Abbreviations: 3MBWT, 3-m backward test; FIQR, fibromyalgia impact questionnaire revised. * p-value < 0.05; ** p-value < 0.01; *** p-value < 0.001.

Figure 1 Bland–Altman plots of the times obtained by stopwatch and Chronopic in test and retest under the single and dual-task conditions and Bland–Altman plots of the times obtained between the two devices under the single and dual-task conditions in the test and retest.

4. Discussion

This study aimed to investigate the test–retest reliability and concurrent validity of the 3MBWT in women with FM under single and dual-task conditions. We also aimed to investigate the agreement between a manual stopwatch and a Chronopic automatic stopwatch. In order to provide clinical and objective directions, the SEM, MDC, and Bland–Altman plots were reported. Generally, good reliability values were obtained for the 3MBWT test when measured with a stopwatch and Chronopic in both single and dual-task conditions. Similarly, the 3MBWT and the TUG achieved good concurrent validity. Lastly, performance between 3MBWT and the impact of the disease were analyzed, and consistent relationships were found between both.

In the present study, walking backward has been analyzed because it is a complex task that requires high neuromuscular and proprioceptive control [22]. Walking backward usually occurs in activities of daily living, such as opening a door, avoiding an obstacle, or backing up to a chair [23]. Therefore, it is a sensitive measure for assessing mobility and balance deficits [24,25]. In people with FM, performing a functional assessment of mobility and balance is essential to manage the disease. However, one of the main tests used to evaluate these characteristics in this population is the TUG [9,11,17]. However, this test does not include backward gait. In this sense, we consider it relevant to analyze the psychometric properties of the 3MBWT in people with FM since previous studies have focused on other populations obtaining good reliability and validity values [26–29]. Therefore, the 3MBWT is a tool that can be used elsewhere in the clinical and research context. Moreover, due to the fact that more than one task is performed at the same time in activities of daily living, and the impairment in dual-task ability detected on people with FM [32,44,45], we decided to incorporate the dual-task paradigm in this cross-sectional study.

Results showed that the 3MBWT could be considered reliable under single and dual-task conditions when measured with both a stopwatch and a Chronopic. However, it is necessary to consider the ICC fluctuation range [41]. Nevertheless, the data presented in the Bland–Altman plots (Figure 1) showed that most of the 3MBWT values were close to the mean of the test–retest differences in both single and dual-task conditions, having a bias close to zero and a reduced variability seeing the limits of agreement. Therefore, there is a high level of agreement between the test–retest measures evaluated in the 3MBWT since the values obtained provide consistent results. The reported ICC in the single condition with a stopwatch (0.71, 95% CI 0.283–0.882) is lower than those reported in previous studies that investigated test–retest reliability in stroke [26] (0.985, 95% CI 0.973–0.992), community-dwelling older adults [27] (0.940, 95% CI 0.90–0.96), and primary total knee arthroplasty [46] (0.942).

Our findings might be due to the symptomatology of FM [47], characterized by widespread pain and fatigue, which can fluctuate in intensity and severity over time [48,49]. For this reason, a person's symptoms and level of functioning can vary daily and affect the physical fitness performance. In this regard, previous studies highlighted what can affect performance in physical fitness tests [50,51]. The same rationale can also affect cognitive function [52], including attention, memory, and information processing. These factors may have contributed to the variability of results between the test and retest. Nevertheless, the ICC values obtained in the present study are acceptable, so the test analyzed seems to be stable enough to be used in the characterization of people with FM.

The optimal time interval between tests may vary depending on the construct being measured, the stability of the construct over time, and the target population [53]. For this study, a seven-day period was selected, the same as previous studies conducted in people with FM [11,18,38,39], to minimize the impact of potential confounding variables, such as recovery or learning effects [54]. However, other studies have used shorter test–retest times to assess test–retest reliability on the 3MBWT [26–29]. In addition, the tests (TUG and 3MBWT), as well as the conditions (single and dual-task), were randomized to ensure that the order of administration may not bias the results. In this way, obtaining more accurate and reliable results is possible by eliminating biases and reducing the influence of external factors that may affect the results.

As expected, the ICC values were slightly higher when using Chronopic versus stopwatch, since the use of a manual stopwatch adds human variability to the measurement by the evaluator [9,55]. Therefore, using an automatic timer can be a cost-effective alternative to assess performance in the 3MBWT in both single and dual conditions. However, although the ICC values obtained by the stopwatch are slightly lower than those obtained by the Chronopic, our data suggest that the use of a manual stopwatch could be also very useful for this test, since it yields relatively good reliability values in both single (0.71, 95% CI 0.283–0.882) and dual-task conditions (0.89, 95% CI 0.718–0.954) (see Table 2). Similarly, the lower ICC obtained in the single and dual-task conditions in the test performance was probably due to human error experienced when using a manual stopwatch. This may be suggested since the scores between the stopwatch and the Chronopic differed slightly, unlike the values obtained in the new test. Nevertheless, the ICC values obtained are classified as good to excellent (see Table 3).

Our study also provided the SEM and MDC values of the 3MBWT under all conditions and devices. These values are important for interpreting the results of the 3MBWT, because they can help clinicians and researchers to determine if there are meaningful changes in the performance of this test. Furthermore, the estimate of random variation in the data (SEM) and the minimum detectable change (MDC) are both lower when the Chronopic is used. Previous research has also observed this trend assessing test–retest reliability under the single condition in TUG and 30 s chair stand test [9,55]. Bland–Altman plots were also reported for a more comprehensive analysis of the results, showing bias and limits of agreement.

In our study, the TUG test was used to test the validity of the 3MBWT since it is a tool frequently used in clinical practice [56,57], showing high reliability in FM in both single [9] and dual-task conditions [11]. Although the TUG test does not contemplate walking backward, as previous studies did [26–29], in the present study we have used the TUG test to conduct the concurrent validity. Moreover, this test has obtained the highest relationship values in most cases [26,27,29]. Significant correlations between 3MBWT and TUG tests were obtained, which can be considered relevant since the TUG test comprises movements that can occur in activities of daily living, including walking, turning, and sitting [37]. In addition, correlation analyses showed a strong correlation in the single condition between the 3MBWT and TUG test measured with a stopwatch, as in previous studies in stroke [26], community-dwelling older adults [27], and adults [23]. In our study, the correlation in single conditions between 3MBWT and TUG measured through the automatic timer also showed strong correlation values. Similarly, the correlation in the dual-task conditions also obtained strong values in the test and retest measured by a stopwatch and a Chronopic.

Our results also found a positive correlation between the 3MBWT performance and the impact of FM obtained through the FIQR questionnaire. Strong to moderate correlations were found between FIQR total score and the performance obtained in single and dual-task conditions using manual stopwatch and Chronopic. Additionally, correlations between FIQR dimensions and 3MBWT have been reported. In this line, the strongest correlations were found in the symptoms dimension, followed by overall impact, where moderate correlations were also found. However, function dimension did not show significant correlation with 3MBWT performance in most cases. These findings could indicate that performance on the 3MBWT does not correlate well with the actions included in the function dimension by including activities that are not highly associated with walking backward (i.e., combing hair, preparing food, shopping) but do correlate with symptomatology and overall impact. Nevertheless, future studies should corroborate this hypothesis.

Previous studies have highlighted the importance of assessing backward gait in older adults [24,25], showing a reduction in performance in different parameters when comparing to young and middle-aged adults. In this regard, during backward gait, greater neuromuscular and proprioceptive control is required, in addition to faster and more frequent balance corrections due to the elimination of visual feedback [22,58]. Additionally, it has been shown that walking backward shows greater or equal sensibility than walking forward, and it is strongly related to the risk of falling [23]. In this sense, assessing backward gait, via the 3MBWT, in FM may be of interest to clinicians to observe changes in mobility and balance due to the balance impairment manifested in this population [59]. Thus, a previous study [60] conducted a physical exercise intervention based on walking backward in community-dwelling older adults. Given these reasons and the strong relationships between the impact of the disease and the performance obtained in the 3MBWT, this test can be used as a useful tool in FM populations to assess exercise-based interventions.

The present study has some limitations. In this regard, the relatively small sample size did not allow us to generalize results to all women with FM. Moreover, only women were included in this cross-sectional study. Thus, results cannot be extrapolated to men with this disease. Therefore, it would be interesting to extend the sample with different age ranges, which allow us to establish cut-off points.

5. Conclusions

The results obtained from this study show that the 3MBWT is a reliable tool under the single and dual-task conditions in women with FM. It shows higher reliability values when time is taken using a Chronopic. This test also shows high concurrent validity with the TUG test, and its performance is related to the impact of the disease. These results may help clinicians and researchers in the assessment of balance and functional mobility and to interpret the effect of interventions in this population.

Author Contributions: Conceptualization, J.L.L.-L., F.J.D.-M. and N.G.; Data curation, A.M.-G. and F.J.D.-M.; Formal analysis, J.L.L.-L., A.M.-G. and F.J.D.-M.; Investigation, S.V.; Methodology, S.V. and N.G.; Project administration, N.G.; Supervision, S.V.; Validation, A.M.-G. and N.G.; Visualization, J.L.L.-L.; Writing—original draft, J.L.L.-L. and S.V.; Writing—review and editing, A.M.-G., F.J.D.-M. and N.G. All authors have read and agreed to the published version of the manuscript.

Funding: The author J.L.L.-L. was supported by a grant from the Spanish Ministry of Education, Culture, and Sport (FPU18/05655). The author S.V. was supported by a grant from the Universities Ministry of Spain and the European Union (NextGenerationUE) "Ayuda del Programa de Recualificación del Sistema Universitario Español, Modalidad de ayudas Margarita Salas para la formación de jóvenes doctores" (MS-03). The author A.M.-G. was supported by a grant from the Spanish Ministry of Education, Culture and Sport (FPU17/03130). In the framework of the Spanish National R+D+i Plan, the current study was co-funded by the Spanish Ministry of Sciences and Innovation (reference PID2019-107191RB-I00/AEI/10.13039/501100011033). This study was also funded by the Research Grant for Groups (GR21176) funded by the Junta de Extremadura and the European Regional Development Fund (ERDF/FEDER) "a way of doing Europe". This study was supported by the Biomedical Research Networking Center on Frailty and Healthy Aging (CIBERFES) and FEDER funds from the European Union (CB16/10/00477) "a way of doing Europe".

Institutional Review Board Statement: The study was conducted according to the guidelines of the Declaration of Helsinki and approved by the Research Ethics Committee of the University of Extremadura (approval reference: 51/2021).

Informed Consent Statement: Informed consent was obtained from all subjects involved in the study.

Data Availability Statement: Data are available under reasonable request to the corresponding author.

Acknowledgments: The authors are very grateful to the Extremadura Association of Fibromyalgia (AFIBROEX) in Cáceres for helping recruit the participants for this study.

Conflicts of Interest: The authors declare no conflict of interest. The funders had no role in the design of the study; in the collection, analyses, or interpretation of data; in the writing of the manuscript, or in the decision to publish the results.

References

1. Wolfe, F.; Clauw, D.J.; Fitzcharles, M.A.; Goldenberg, D.; Katz, R.; Mease, P.; Russell, A.; Russell, J.; Winfield, J.; Yunus, M. The American College of Rheumatology preliminary diagnostic criteria for fibromyalgia and measurement of symptom severity. *Arthritis Care Res.* **2010**, *62*, 600–610. [CrossRef] [PubMed]
2. Macfarlane, G.J.; Kronisch, C.; Dean, L.E.; Atzeni, F.; Häuser, W.; Fluß, E.; Choy, E.; Kosek, E.; Amris, K.; Branco, J.; et al. EULAR revised recommendations for the management of fibromyalgia. *Ann. Rheum. Dis.* **2017**, *76*, 318–328. [CrossRef] [PubMed]
3. Collado-Mateo, D.; Gallego-Diaz, J.M.; Adsuar, J.; Domínguez-Muñoz, F.J.; Olivares, P.R.; Gusi, N. Fear of falling in women with fibromyalgia and its relation with number of falls and balance performance. *BioMed Res. Int.* **2015**, *2015*, 589014. [CrossRef] [PubMed]
4. Gaudreault, N.; Boulay, P. Cardiorespiratory fitness among adults with fibromyalgia. *Breathe* **2018**, *14*, e25–e33. [CrossRef] [PubMed]
5. Hoffman, D.L.; Dukes, E.M. The health status burden of people with fibromyalgia: A review of studies that assessed health status with the SF-36 or the SF-12. *Int. J. Clin. Pract.* **2008**, *62*, 115–126. [CrossRef] [PubMed]
6. Marques, A.P.; Santo, A.d.S.d.E.; Berssaneti, A.A.; Matsutani, L.A.; Yuan, S.L.K. Prevalence of fibromyalgia: Literature review update. *Rev. Bras. Reumatol.* **2017**, *57*, 356–363. [CrossRef]
7. Bennett, R.M.; Jones, J.; Turk, D.C.; Russell, I.J.; Matallana, L. An internet survey of 2596 people with fibromyalgia. *BMC Musculoskelet. Disord.* **2007**, *8*, 27.
8. Jones, K.D.; Horak, F.B.; Winters, K.S.; Morea, J.M.; Bennett, R.M. Fibromyalgia is associated with impaired balance and falls. *J. Clin. Rheumatol. Pract. Rep. Rheum. Musculoskelet. Dis.* **2009**, *15*, 16. [CrossRef]
9. Collado-Mateo, D.; Domínguez-Muñoz, F.J.; Adsuar, J.C.; Merellano-Navarro, E.; Olivares, P.R.; Gusi, N. Reliability of the timed up and go test in fibromyalgia. *Rehabil. Nurs. J.* **2018**, *43*, 35–39. [CrossRef]
10. Villafaina, S.; Borrega-Mouquinho, Y.; Fuentes-García, J.P.; Collado-Mateo, D.; Gusi, N. Effect of Exergame Training and Detraining on Lower-Body Strength, Agility, and Cardiorespiratory Fitness in Women with Fibromyalgia: Single-Blinded Randomized Controlled Trial. *Int. J. Environ. Res. Public Health* **2020**, *17*, 161. [CrossRef]
11. Murillo-Garcia, A.; Villafaina, S.; Leon-Llamas, J.L.; Sánchez-Gómez, J.; Domínguez-Muñoz, F.J.; Collado-Mateo, D.; Gusi, N. Mobility Assessment under Dual Task Conditions in Women with Fibromyalgia: A Test-Retest Reliability Study. *PM&R* **2021**, *13*, 66–72.

12. Jones, K.D.; King, L.A.; Mist, S.D.; Bennett, R.M.; Horak, F.B. Postural control deficits in people with fibromyalgia: A pilot study. *Arthritis Res. Ther.* **2011**, *13*, 1–13. [CrossRef] [PubMed]
13. Meireles, S.A.; Antero, D.C.; Kulczycki, M.M.; Skare, T.L. Prevalence of falls in fibromyalgia patients. *Acta Ortop. Bras.* **2014**, *22*, 163–166. [CrossRef] [PubMed]
14. Lomas-Vega, R.; Rodríguez-Almagro, D.; Peinado-Rubia, A.B.; Zagalaz-Anula, N.; Molina, F.; Obrero-Gaitán, E.; Ibáñez-Vera, A.J.; Osuna-Pérez, M.C. Joint Assessment of Equilibrium and Neuromotor Function: A Validation Study in Patients with Fibromyalgia. *Diagnostics* **2020**, *10*, 1057. [CrossRef]
15. Rasouli, O.; Stensdotter, A.-K.; Van der Meer, A.L.H. TauG-guidance of dynamic balance control during gait initiation in patients with chronic fatigue syndrome and fibromyalgia. *Clin. Biomech.* **2016**, *37*, 147–152. [CrossRef]
16. Yogev-Seligmann, G.; Hausdorff, J.M.; Giladi, N. The role of executive function and attention in gait. *Mov. Disord. Off. J. Mov. Disord. Soc.* **2008**, *23*, 329–342. [CrossRef] [PubMed]
17. Martín-Martínez, J.P.; Villafaina, S.; Collado-Mateo, D.; Pérez-Gómez, J.; Gusi, N. Effects of 24-week exergame intervention on physical function under single-and dual-task conditions in fibromyalgia: A randomized controlled trial. *Scand. J. Med. Sci. Sports* **2019**, *29*, 1610–1617. [CrossRef] [PubMed]
18. Leon-Llamas, J.L.; Villafaina, S.; Murillo-Garcia, A.; Collado-Mateo, D.; Domínguez-Muñoz, F.J.; Sánchez-Gómez, J.; Gusi, N. Strength assessment under dual task conditions in women with fibromyalgia: A test–retest reliability study. *Int. J. Environ. Res. Public Health* **2019**, *16*, 4971. [CrossRef]
19. Martín-Martínez, J.P.; Collado-Mateo, D.; Domínguez-Muñoz, F.J.; Villafaina, S.; Gusi, N.; Pérez-Gómez, J. Reliability of the 30 s Chair Stand Test in Women with Fibromyalgia. *Int. J. Environ. Res. Public Health* **2019**, *16*, 2344. [CrossRef]
20. Bennell, K.; Dobson, F.; Hinman, R. Measures of physical performance assessments: Self-Paced walk test (SPWT), stair climb test (SCT), Six-Minute walk test (6MWT), chair stand test (CST), timed up & go (TUG), sock test, lift and carry test (LCT), and car task. *Arthritis Care Res.* **2011**, *63*, S350–S370.
21. Renata, D.; Donadio, M.V.F. Timed'Up & Go'test in children and adolescents. *Rev. Paul. Pediatr.* **2013**, *31*, 377–383.
22. Thomas, M.A.; Fast, A. One step forward and two steps back: The dangers of walking backwards in therapy. *Am. J. Phys. Med. Rehabil.* **2000**, *79*, 459–461. [CrossRef] [PubMed]
23. Carter, V.; Jain, T.; James, J.; Cornwall, M.; Aldrich, A.; De Heer, H.D. The 3-m backwards walk and retrospective falls: Diagnostic accuracy of a novel clinical measure. *J. Geriatr. Phys. Ther.* **2019**, *42*, 249–255. [CrossRef] [PubMed]
24. Fritz, N.E.; Worstell, A.M.; Kloos, A.D.; Siles, A.B.; White, S.E.; Kegelmeyer, D.A. Backward walking measures are sensitive to age-related changes in mobility and balance. *Gait Posture* **2013**, *37*, 593–597. [CrossRef]
25. Laufer, Y. Effect of age on characteristics of forward and backward gait at preferred and accelerated walking speed. *J. Gerontol. Ser. A Biol. Sci. Med. Sci.* **2005**, *60*, 627–632. [CrossRef]
26. Kocaman, A.A.; Arslan, S.A.; Uğurlu, K.; Kırmacı, Z.İ.K.; Keskin, E.D. Validity and Reliability of The 3-Meter Backward Walk Test in Individuals with Stroke. *J. Stroke Cerebrovasc. Dis.* **2021**, *30*, 105462. [CrossRef]
27. Özden, F.; Özkeskin, M.; Bakırhan, S.; Şahin, S. The test–retest reliability and concurrent validity of the 3-m backward walk test and 50-ft walk test in community-dwelling older adults. *Ir. J. Med. Sci.* **2021**, *191*, 921–928. [CrossRef]
28. Kirmaci, Z.İ.K.; Adiguzel, H.; Erel, S.; Neyal, A.M.; Neyal, A.; Ergun, N. Validity and reliability of the 3-meter backward walk test in patients with multiple sclerosis. *Mult. Scler. Relat. Disord.* **2022**, *63*, 103842. [CrossRef]
29. Bilek, F.; Demir, C.F. Validity and reliability of the 3-meter backward walk test in mildly disabled persons with multiple sclerosis. *Mult. Scler. Relat. Disord.* **2022**, *58*, 103532. [CrossRef]
30. Nalbant, A.; Unver, B.; Karatosun, V. Test–retest reliability of the L-Test in patients with advanced knee osteoarthritis. *Physiother. Theory Pract.* **2021**, *38*, 2983–2987. [CrossRef]
31. Juan, I.P.; Ustárroz, J.T.; Sala, M.G. Paradigmas de ejecución dual: Aspectos conceptuales. *Rev. Neurol.* **2021**, *72*, 357–367.
32. Villafaina, S.; Collado-Mateo, D.; Domínguez-Muñoz, F.J.; Fuentes-García, J.P.; Gusi, N. Impact of adding a cognitive task while performing physical fitness tests in women with fibromyalgia: A cross-sectional descriptive study. *Medicine* **2018**, *97*, e13791. [CrossRef] [PubMed]
33. Villafaina, S.; Polero, P.; Collado-Mateo, D.; Fuentes-García, J.P.; Gusi, N. Impact of adding a simultaneous cognitive task in the elbow's range of movement during arm curl test in women with fibromyalgia. *Clin. Biomech.* **2019**, *65*, 110–115. [CrossRef] [PubMed]
34. Sempere-Rubio, N.; López-Pascual, J.; Aguilar-Rodríguez, M.; Cortés-Amador, S.; Espí-López, G.; Villarrasa-Sapiña, I.; Serra-Añó, P. Characterization of postural control impairment in women with fibromyalgia. *PLoS ONE* **2018**, *13*, e0196575. [CrossRef]
35. Wolfe, F.; Clauw, D.J.; Fitzcharles, M.-A.; Goldenberg, D.L.; Häuser, W.; Katz, R.L.; Mease, P.J.; Russell, A.S.; Russell, I.J.; Walitt, B. 2016 Revisions to the 2010/2011 fibromyalgia diagnostic criteria. *Semin. Arthritis Rheum.* **2016**, *46*, 319–329. [CrossRef] [PubMed]
36. Salgueiro, M.; García-Leiva, J.M.; Ballesteros, J.; Hidalgo, J.; Molina, R.; Calandre, E.P. Validation of a Spanish version of the revised fibromyalgia impact questionnaire (FIQR). *Health Qual. Life Outcomes* **2013**, *11*, 132. [CrossRef]
37. Podsiadlo, D.; Richardson, S. The timed "Up & Go": A test of basic functional mobility for frail elderly persons. *J. Am. Geriatr. Soc.* **1991**, *39*, 142–148.
38. Adsuar, J.C.; Olivares, P.R.; Parraca, J.A.; Hernández-Mocholí, M.A.; Gusi, N. Applicability and test-retest reliability of isokinetic shoulder abduction and adduction in women fibromyalgia patients. *Arch. Phys. Med. Rehabil.* **2013**, *94*, 444–450. [CrossRef]

39. Carbonell-Baeza, A.; Alvarez-Gallardo, I.; Segura-Jiménez, V.; Castro-Pinero, J.; Ruiz, J.; Delgado-Fernández, M.; Aparicio, V. Reliability and feasibility of physical fitness tests in female fibromyalgia patients. *Int. J. Sports Med.* **2015**, *36*, 157–162. [CrossRef]
40. Weir, J.P. Quantifying test-retest reliability using the intraclass correlation coefficient and the SEM. *J. Strength Cond. Res.* **2005**, *19*, 231–240.
41. Koo, T.K.; Li, M.Y. A guideline of selecting and reporting intraclass correlation coefficients for reliability research. *J. Chiropr. Med.* **2016**, *15*, 155–163. [CrossRef]
42. Bland, J.M.; Altman, D. Statistical methods for assessing agreement between two methods of clinical measurement. *Lancet* **1986**, *327*, 307–310. [CrossRef]
43. Cohen, J. *Statistical Power Analysis for the Social Sciences*; Lawrence Erlbaum Associates: Mahwah, NJ, USA, 1988.
44. Villafaina, S.; Gusi, N.; Rodriguez-Generelo, S.; Martin-Gallego, J.d.D.; Fuentes-García, J.P.; Collado-Mateo, D. Influence of a cell-phone conversation on balance performance in women with fibromyalgia: A cross-sectional descriptive study. *BioMed Res. Int.* **2019**, *2019*, 5132802. [CrossRef] [PubMed]
45. Radunović, G.; Veličković, Z.; Rašić, M.; Janjić, S.; Marković, V.; Radovanović, S. Assessment of gait in patients with fibromyalgia during motor and cognitive dual task walking: A cross-sectional study. *Adv. Rheumatol.* **2021**, *61*, 53. [CrossRef] [PubMed]
46. Unver, B.; Sevik, K.; Yarar, H.A.; Unver, F.; Karatosun, V. Reliability of 3-m backward walk test in patients with primary total knee arthroplasty. *J. Knee Surg.* **2020**, *33*, 589–592. [CrossRef] [PubMed]
47. Mezhov, V.; Guymer, E.; Littlejohn, G. Central Sensitivity and Fibromyalgia. *Intern. Med. J.* **2021**, *51*, 1990–1998. [CrossRef]
48. Estévez-López, F.; Segura-Jiménez, V.; Álvarez-Gallardo, I.C.; Borges-Cosic, M.; Pulido-Martos, M.; Carbonell-Baeza, A.; Aparicio, V.A.; Geenen, R.; Delgado-Fernández, M. Adaptation profiles comprising objective and subjective measures in fibromyalgia: The al-Ándalus project. *Rheumatology* **2017**, *56*, 2015–2024. [CrossRef]
49. Doerr, J.M.; Fischer, S.; Nater, U.M.; Strahler, J. Influence of stress systems and physical activity on different dimensions of fatigue in female fibromyalgia patients. *J. Psychosom. Res.* **2017**, *93*, 55–61. [CrossRef]
50. Carbonell-Baeza, A.; Aparicio, V.A.; Sjöström, M.; Ruiz, J.R.; Delgado-Fernández, M. Pain and functional capacity in female fibromyalgia patients. *Pain Med.* **2011**, *12*, 1667–1675. [CrossRef]
51. De Gier, M.; Peters, M.L.; Vlaeyen, J.W. Fear of pain, physical performance, and attentional processes in patients with fibromyalgia. *Pain* **2003**, *104*, 121–130. [CrossRef]
52. Kalfon, T.B.-O.; Gal, G.; Shorer, R.; Ablin, J.N. Cognitive functioning in fibromyalgia: The central role of effort. *J. Psychosom. Res.* **2016**, *87*, 30–36. [CrossRef] [PubMed]
53. Streiner, D.L.; Norman, G.R.; Cairney, J. *Health Measurement Scales: A Practical Guide to Their Development and Use*; Oxford University Press: Oxford, MI, USA, 2015.
54. Dutil, É.; Bottari, C.; Auger, C. Test-retest reliability of a measure of independence in everyday activities: The ADL profile. *Occup. Ther. Int.* **2017**, *2017*, 3014579. [CrossRef] [PubMed]
55. Collado-Mateo, D.; Madeira, P.; Dominguez-Muñoz, F.J.; Villafaina, S.; Tomas-Carus, P.; Parraca, J.A. The automatic assessment of strength and mobility in older adults: A test-retest reliability study. *Medicina* **2019**, *55*, 270. [CrossRef] [PubMed]
56. Kear, B.M.; Guck, T.P.; McGaha, A.L. Timed Up and Go (TUG) test: Normative reference values for ages 20 to 59 years and relationships with physical and mental health risk factors. *J. Prim. Care Community Health* **2017**, *8*, 9–13. [CrossRef] [PubMed]
57. Bohannon, R.W. Reference values for the timed up and go test: A descriptive meta-analysis. *J. Geriatr. Phys. Ther.* **2006**, *29*, 64–68. [CrossRef]
58. Hoogkamer, W.; Meyns, P.; Duysens, J. Steps forward in understanding backward gait: From basic circuits to rehabilitation. *Exerc. Sport Sci. Rev.* **2014**, *42*, 23–29. [CrossRef]
59. Núñez-Fuentes, D.; Obrero-Gaitán, E.; Zagalaz-Anula, N.; Ibáñez-Vera, A.J.; Achalandabaso-Ochoa, A.; López-Ruiz, M.d.C.; Rodríguez-Almagro, D.; Lomas-Vega, R. Alteration of Postural Balance in Patients with Fibromyalgia Syndrome—A Systematic Review and Meta-Analysis. *Diagnostics* **2021**, *11*, 127. [CrossRef]
60. Maritz, C.A.; Pigman, J.; Grävare Silbernagel, K.; Crenshaw, J. Effects of Backward Walking Training on Balance, Mobility, and Gait in Community-Dwelling Older Adults. *Act. Adapt. Aging* **2020**, *45*, 202–216. [CrossRef]

Journal of
Clinical Medicine

MDPI

Article

The Effects of Body Composition Characteristics on the Functional Disability in Patients with Degenerative Lumbar Spinal Stenosis

Yesull Kim [1,2], Chanhong Lee [1], Hyunji Oh [1], Ji-Seon Son [1,2] and Aram Doo [1,2,*]

[1] Department of Anesthesiology and Pain Medicine, Jeonbuk National University Medical School and Hospital, Jeonju 54907, Republic of Korea; blackcaat@naver.com (Y.K.); kyjrevol@naver.com (C.L.); hyunj4885@naver.com (H.O.); sjs6803@jbnu.ac.kr (J.-S.S.)

[2] Research Institute of Clinical Medicine of Jeonbuk National University-Biomedical Research Institute of Jeonbuk National University Hospital, Jeonju 54907, Republic of Korea

* Correspondence: ardoo@jbnu.ac.kr; Tel.: +82-63-250-1241; Fax: +82-63-250-1240

Abstract: Several research studies suggest that obese patients are at a higher risk of developing lumbar spinal disorder, including degenerative lumbar spinal stenosis (LSS), compared to normal-weight individuals. However, there are few investigations of how obesity affects functional disability in activities of daily living (ADL) in patients who were diagnosed with LSS. This prospective observational study aimed to determine if an association exists between body composition parameters, such as body fat and skeletal muscle, and functional disability in ADL of LSS patients. In the results of the current study, there were significant differences in percent body fat between the mild/moderate and severe disability groups. However, there were no differences in skeletal muscle mass or index between the two groups. Furthermore, we found a positive linear relationship between percent body fat and functional disability in male sex. This study suggests that increased percent body fat predicts potential severe functional disability in ADL in LSS patients. Body composition analysis may provide useful information for predicting the disease severity of various lumbar spinal disorders in clinical practice.

Keywords: body composition; fat; function; low back pain; obesity

Citation: Kim, Y.; Lee, C.; Oh, H.; Son, J.-S.; Doo, A. The Effects of Body Composition Characteristics on the Functional Disability in Patients with Degenerative Lumbar Spinal Stenosis. *J. Clin. Med.* **2023**, *12*, 612. https://doi.org/10.3390/jcm12020612

Academic Editor: Misao Nishikawa

Received: 20 December 2022
Revised: 2 January 2023
Accepted: 6 January 2023
Published: 12 January 2023

1. Introduction

Spinal pain is a growing concern in aging populations with increasing life expectancy worldwide. Degenerative lumbar spinal stenosis (LSS) frequently causes typical symptoms, including neurologic intermittent claudication, sciatica and low back pain. In addition, vague leg symptoms, such as paresthesia, weakness and altered sensation, may exist [1,2]. These characteristic manifestations may lead to functional disabilities in activities of daily living (ADL), decreased quality of life and increased social isolation, especially in older adults.

Functional disability in ADL may be a representative of the disease severity of LSS, because it means how the spinal pain and neurologic deficit affects the patients' daily life. It has been reported that the greater the intensity of symptoms, the worse the functional disability [3]. Furthermore, evaluating functional disability in ADL may help to establish the treatment plan and even predict the post-surgical outcome for patients with LSS [4]. Radiologic imaging, such as magnetic resonance imaging (MRI), is used to decide the severity of LSS with more clarity, but it is greatly limited. It is well known that the correlation between the functional status and the severity of radiologic findings is often unmatched [5,6]. Despite the importance of functional disability in ADL in LSS patients, there are no clear predictive factors associated with it.

Obesity has been increasingly investigated as a potential predictor for the development of various lumbar spinal disorders, but the results are inconsistent, and the causal relationships are also unclear [7–13]. Several researches suggested that obese patients were at a higher risk of developing lumbar spinal disorder, including LSS, compared to normal-weight individuals [10,11]. Other studies reported that obesity was associated with the severity of the lumbar intervertebral disc degeneration and even with the less functional improvement after surgery in LSS patients [8,14,15]. However, there are few investigations of how obesity (increased body fat) affects functional disability in ADL in patients who were diagnosed with LSS.

The aim of the current study was to determine if an association exists between body composition characteristics and functional disability in ADL of LSS patients, especially to understand which body fat parameters could accurately predict it. We further expected that other body composition parameters related to the amount of skeletal muscle also affect it. Additionally, the therapeutic effects of epidural steroid injection of LSS patients were evaluated.

2. Materials and Methods

This prospective observational study was approved by the Institutional Review Board of the author's hospital and registered with the WHO International Clinical Trials Registry Platform (KCT0006046). This manuscript adheres to the applicable STROBE guidelines. After obtaining written informed consent, a total of 72 consecutive patients who visited our pain clinic in a tertiary care hospital due to LSS were enrolled in the study. Inclusion criteria were as follows: (1) age >40 years; (2) clinical LSS symptoms (radiculopathy +/− low back pain) more than 3 months; (3) symptom intensity with numeric rating scale (NRS; 0–10) of 4 or more; (4) radiologic confirmation of LSS through magnetic resonance imaging (MRI). Patients with a literacy problem or language difficulties; a history of psychotic disorder or drug abuse; chronic opioid usage over 3 months; a concomitantly complicated spinal disease, including epidural lipomatosis; ligament ossification or diffuse idiopathic skeletal hyperostosis; a definite indication for prompt surgery, such as cauda equina syndrome; a history of previous spinal surgery; orthopedic metal implants in any body region; and cardiac pacemaker or implantable cardioverter-defibrillator (ICD) were excluded from the study.

2.1. Evaluation of Functional Disability in ADL and Group Allocation

The functional disability in ADL was evaluated using a validated Korean version of the Oswestry Disability Index (ODI) [16]. All participants were asked to complete the self-reported ODI questionnaire in their first visit to our department. ODI is a widely used, self-reported questionnaire for assessing a patient's functional disability in ADL in patients with lumbar spinal pain. ODI consists of 10 items that are disease-associated health status measurements of how pain affects functional disability in ADL in patients with lumbar spinal pain. Each item is rated on a 6-point scale that ranges from 0 to 5, and the global score is added and multiplied by 2. Therefore, the global score ranges from 0 to 100. The higher the global score, the greater the functional disability in ADL. We divided participants into two groups, the mild to moderate disability group (ODI $\leq$ 40) and the severe disability group (ODI > 40), as previous studies suggested [17].

2.2. Body Composition Analysis Using Bioelectrical Impedance Analysis (BIA)

All participants underwent body composition measurement using a body composition analyzer (Inbody S10®, Biospace, Seoul, Republic of Korea), according to the manufacturer's guidelines, at their first visits to our department. Inbody S10® provides various information for body composition through BIA methods. Patients were asked to take a rest in the supine position on a nonconductive table for at least 10 min before measurements. The skin surface where the electrode would be placed was cleansed with an alcohol swab before application, in keeping with standard practice. Then, the surface electrodes were attached to both fingers (thumb and middle finger) and ankles, according to the manufacturer's instructions.

Body composition parameters, such as body fat mass (kg), percent body fat (%), skeletal muscle mass (kg) and skeletal muscle index (kg/m^2), were recorded.

2.3. Outcome Measures

Other demographic factors that may be associated with functional disability in ADL, including age, sex, comorbid disease, radiologic severity of LSS (degree of stenosis and number of stenotic segment) and duration of symptoms, were also evaluated. The degree of spinal canal stenosis was categorized from A to D, according to the previous method of classification by Schizas et al. [18] using MRI. That of foraminal stenosis was categorized as mild, moderate or severe stenosis.

We also measured the cross-sectional area (CSA) of the psoas and multifidus muscles, using T1-weighted axial MRI images at the midpoint of the L3/4 intervertebral disc. Using picture archiving and communication system imaging measurement software (Infinitt healthcare, Seoul, Republic of Korea), the CSA of the multifidus and the psoas muscles were measured, as presented in Figure 1. All measurements were independently analyzed by two pain physicians who were blinded to patients' characteristics, and a consensus had to be found. In case of disagreement with a difference of more than 15%, images were reviewed together and discussed until the consensus was gained.

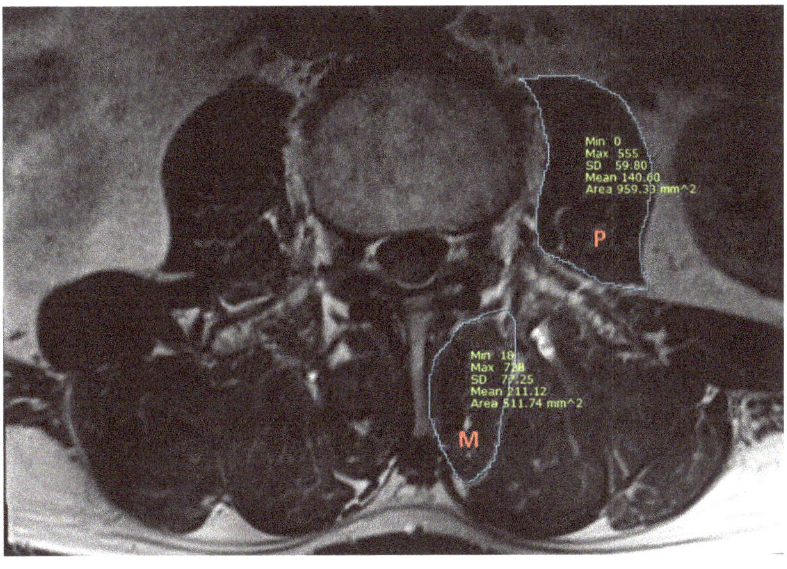

Figure 1. A representative magnetic resonance image for the measurement of cross-sectional area (mm^2) of the psoas and multifidus muscles. P, psoas muscle; M, multifidus muscle.

2.4. Epidural Steroid Injection Procedure

All participants received a target-specific transforaminal epidural steroid injection in the involved spinal segment judged from the patients' symptoms and MRI findings at their first visits. All procedures were performed with guidance with a fluoroscope (ARCADIS Orbic®; Siemens AG, Erlangen, Germany) by an experienced pain physician. The patients were placed in a prone position, and standard sterile preparation was conducted. Using the ipsilateral oblique view on the fluoroscopy to obtain a traditional "safety triangle" image [19], a 22-gauge spinal needle was introduced just inferior to the pedicle using the tunnel vision technique. After reaching the intervertebral foramen, the final position of the needle tip was adjusted using the anteroposterior and lateral fluoroscopic view. After confirming appropriate epidural contrast uptake, 5 mL of 0.6 % lidocaine containing 5 mg dexamethasone was administered. For the multi-level procedure at two or more sites, 5 mL of drug was used at each level, with a divided dose of dexamethasone not to exceed a total dose of 5 mg. The number of epidural blocks during 4 weeks and the degree of pain relief using the changes of NRS at the first visit and 4-weeks follow-up were recorded.

The body composition parameters, including body fat mass (kg), percent body fat (%), skeletal muscle mass (kg), skeletal muscle index (kg/m^2) and other demographic characteristics, were compared between the mild/moderate and severe disability groups. The primary outcomes were the differences of the body composition parameters between the two groups. Secondary outcomes included epidural block-related therapeutic effects in the two groups.

2.5. Sample Size Determination and Statistical Analysis

Sample size was predetermined by the *t*-test sample size calculation, using IBM SPSS Statistics for Windows, version 27, based on the assumption that the minimum detectable difference between the two groups in percent body fat was 10%. A total of 64 patients were required, with a significance level of 0.05 ($\alpha = 0.05$) and a power of 80% ($\beta = 0.20$). Considering the predicted dropout rate, the total sample size was increased to 72.

All descriptive data are expressed as the number of patients, mean ± SD, and median [interquartile range]. Continuous variables were analyzed by a two-tailed *t*-test or Mann—Whitney rank-sum test after a normality test. The χ^2 test was used to compare categorical variables. Linear regression analysis was performed to verify the relationships between body composition parameters and the ODI scores. A *p*-value of less than 0.05 was considered statistically significant. All statistical analyses were performed using IBM SPSS Statistics for Windows, version 27.

3. Results

3.1. Study Participants and Patient Characteristics

Among the 72 participants enrolled, 63 patients (29 in the mild/moderate group and 34 in the severe disability group) completed the study. The CONSORT flow diagram is shown in Figure 2. The average ODI score was 26.9 and 55.6 in the mild/moderate and severe disability groups, respectively ($p < 0.001$). Patient demographics, including age, sex, body weight, body mass index (BMI) and radiologic severity of LSS, were compared between the two groups. No significant differences of these parameters were observed between the two groups (Table 1).

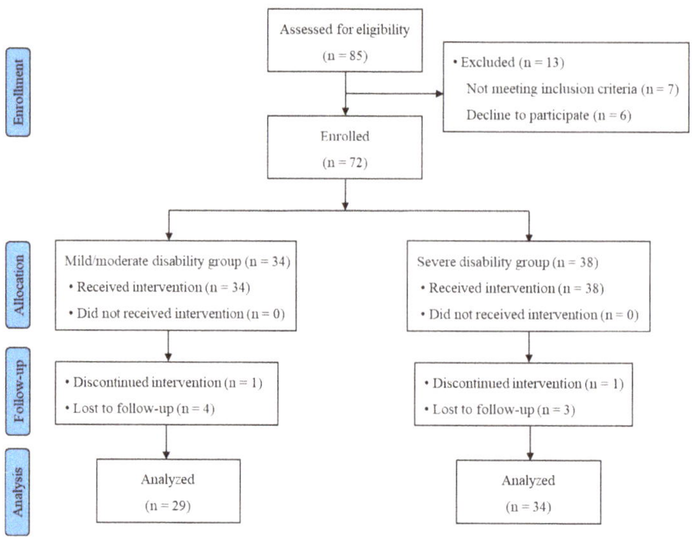

Figure 2. Subject flow diagram.

Table 1. Patient demographics.

	Mild/Moderate Disability (n = 29)	Severe Disability (n = 34)	*p* Value
Age (years)	68.0 (63.5–73.0)	69.5 (60.0–76.0)	0.879
Sex (M/F)	14/15	11/23	0.198
Body weight (kg)	60.7 ± 10.7	63.6 ± 11.9	0.301
BMI (kg/m^2)	23.6 ± 2.8	25.1 ± 3.2	0.053
Underlying metabolic diseases			
Hypertension	10 (34.5%)	7 (20.6%)	0.216
Diabetes mellitus	5 (17.2%)	4 (11.8%)	0.721
Hyperlipidemia	4 (13.8%)	3 (8.8%)	0.694
Radiologic severity of LSS			
Degree of spinal canal stenosis			
Grade A/B/C/D	14/3/5/2	8/7/10/2	0.143
Degree of foraminal stenosis			
Mild/Moderate/Severe	4/6/11	0/3/9	0.374
Number of stenotic segment			
1/2/3 or more	1.5 (1.0–2.0)	1.0 (1.0–2.0)	0.605
Duration of symptom (months)	12.0 (5.3–57.0)	6.0 (2.0–27.0)	0.173
Type of analgesic medications			
NSAIDs	7 (24.1%)	10 (29.4 %)	0.638
Acetaminophen/tramadol combinations	4 (13.8%)	9 (26.5%)	0.215
Opioids	1 (3.4%)	2 (5.9%)	1.000
Total ODI score	26.9 ± 9.8	55.6 ± 11.4	<0.001 *

Data are presented as median (interquartile range), numbers, mean ± standard deviations, or numbers (percentages). Mild/moderate disability was defined as Oswestry disability score (ODI) ≤40. Severe disability was ODI > 40. * $p < 0.05$ by two-tailed *t*-test.

3.2. Study Outcomes

Body composition parameters and cross-sectional areas of the spinal muscles of the two groups are shown in Table 2. Percent body fat (%) was significantly higher in the severe disability group compared to the mild/moderate group in each sex ($p = 0.016$ in male and $p = 0.004$ in female). The proportion of obese patients (percent body fat ≥17% in men and ≥32 % in women) was compared, and it was significantly higher in the severe disability group compared to the mild/moderate group only in females ($p = 0.028$ by chi-square test).

Table 2. Body composition parameters by bioimpedance analysis and cross-sectional areas of the psoas and multifidus muscles.

	Mild/Moderate Disability (n = 29)	Severe Disability (n = 34)	*p* Value
Number of patients			
Male	14	11	
Female	15	23	
BMI (kg/m^2)			
Male	23.8 ± 2.8	25.3 ± 2.5	0.161
Female	23.4 ± 2.9	25.0 ± 3.5	0.149
Body fat mass (kg)			
Male	10.1 ± 4.8	15.4 ± 6.1	0.014 *
Female	17.4 ± 8.7	21.0 ± 6.0	0.237
Percent body fat (%)			
Male	14.6 ± 6.0	23.2 ± 9.4	0.016 *
Female	27.4 ± 7.4	34.5 ± 6.0	0.004 *
No. of obese patients (%) †			
Male	7 (50.0%)	8 (66.7%)	0.414
Female	5 (31.3%)	16 (73.3%)	0.028 ‡

Table 2. *Cont.*

	Mild/Moderate Disability (n = 29)	Severe Disability (n = 34)	*p* Value
Skeletal muscle mass (kg)			
Male	32.1 ± 3.4	30.4 ± 4.7	0.320
Female	20.8 ± 2.8	21.1 ± 3.2	0.763
Skeletal muscle index (kg/m^2)			
Male	9.3 ± 1.3	9.6 ± 0.9	0.678
Female	7.3 ± 1.4	7.1 ± 1.0	0.624
CSA of psoas (mm^2)			
Male	1147.3 ± 119.8	539.9 ± 145.5	<0.001 *
Female	879.4 ± 219.2	619.9 ± 175.1	0.020 *
CSA of multifidus (mm^2)			
Male	676.0 (540.5–804.1)	398.3 (324.4–510.6)	<0.001 §
Female	575.1 ± 178.0	459.3 ± 93.4	0.146

Data are presented as numbers, means ± standard deviations and median (interquartile range). BMI, body mass index; CSA, cross-sectional area. * $p < 0.05$ by two-tailed *t*-test. † Obese patients were judged from percent body fat ≥ 32% in women and ≥17% in men. ‡ $p < 0.05$ by Chi-square test. § $p < 0.05$ by Mann–Whitney rank-sum test.

The linear regression analysis revealed that percent body fat was positively correlated to the ODI score in males (r = 0.554 and p = 0.005). However, there was no statistically significant relationship between them in females (r = 0.331 and p = 0.052) (Figure 3).

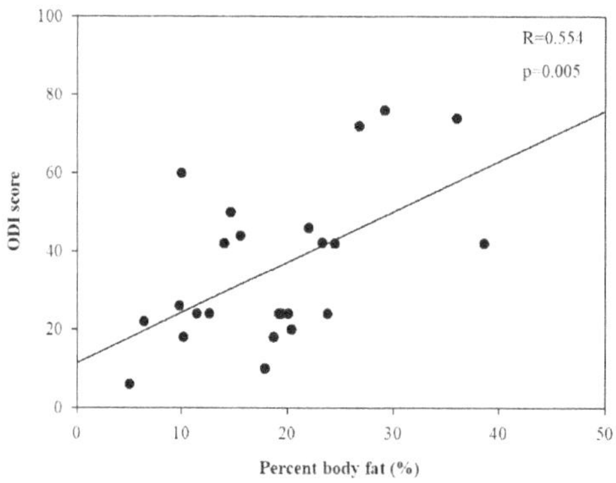

(**A**) Male

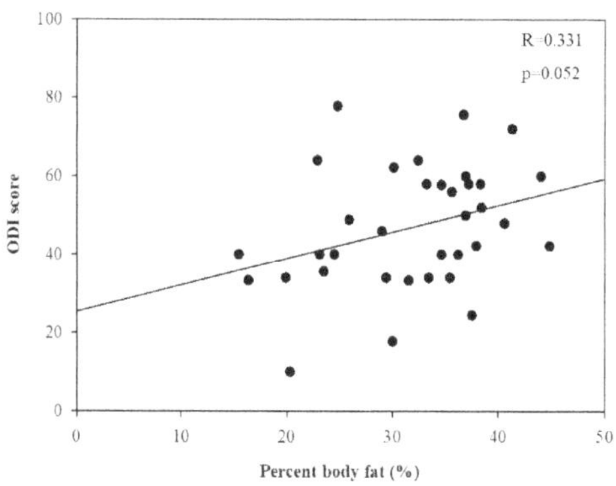

(**B**) Female

Figure 3. Relationships between percent body fat (%) and Oswestry disability index score.

Meanwhile, there were no significant differences in the body composition parameters related to skeletal muscle, including skeletal muscle mass (kg) and skeletal muscle index (kg/m^2), between the two groups. However, the CSA of the spinal muscles, such as psoas and multifidus, were significantly different between the two groups in each sex. The CSAs of psoas muscles were significantly smaller in the severe disability groups compared to the mild/moderate group in each sex ($p < 0.001$ in male and $p = 0.020$ in female) (Table 2). In further analysis, there were significant linear relationships between the CSA of psoas and multifidus muscles and the ODI score (Figure 4A,B).

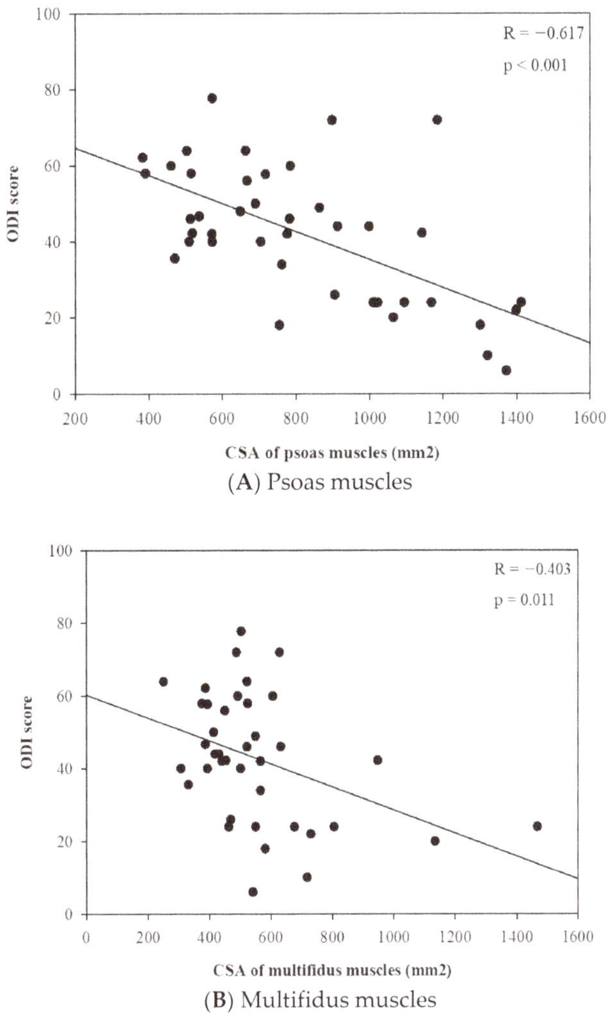

Figure 4. Relationships between cross-sectional area (CSA) of psoas and multifidus muscles (mm^2) and Oswestry disability index score.

The epidural block procedure-related pain-relieving effect is shown in Table 3. The NRS score at 4 weeks following the first epidural block was significantly lower in the mild/moderate disability group compared to the severe disability group ($p < 0.001$). The patients in the severe disability group experienced a smaller pain-relieving effect from the epidural block compared to the mild/moderate disability group (45.1% vs. 25.2%, $p = 0.002$).

Table 3. Epidural block-related profile.

	Mild/Moderate Disability (n = 29)	Severe Disability (n = 34)	p Value
NRS (0–10) at first visit	6.0 (5.0–7.8)	7.0 (6.0–8.0)	0.041 *
NRS (0–10) at 4-wks follow-up	3.2 ± 1.3	5.4 ± 2.1	<0.001 †
Pain relief (%) during 4 weeks	45.1 ± 20.0	25.2 ± 4.6	0.002 †
Number of epidural blocks during 4 weeks	2.0 (1.0–2.0)	1.5 (1.0–2.0)	0.155

NRS, Numeric rating scale. * $p < 0.05$ by Mann–Whitney rank-sum test. † $p < 0.05$ by two-tailed t-test.

4. Discussion

The current study demonstrated that LSS patients with severe disability in ADL (ODI score > 40) had a significantly higher fat mass and percent body fat compared to subjects with mild to moderate disability. The higher the percentage of body fat, the greater the functional disability in ADL, with a linear relationship. As previous studies suggested that radiologic imaging is limited for evaluating disease severity [5,6], radiologic severity of LSS was comparable between the mild/moderate and severe disability groups in this study. Meanwhile, LSS patients with severe disability experienced a smaller therapeutic effect from repeated epidural blocks compared to those with mild/moderate disability. This result suggests that evaluating functional disability in LSS patients potentially helps to predict the response to conservative treatment, such as epidural blocks, and to establish more effective treatment options promptly. Many studies suggested that overweight and obesity was positively related to the development of lumbar spinal diseases [10–13]. However, the precise mechanisms of the association are little known, and the causal relationships are also unclear. Some studies believe that excessive mechanical overload might affect the development of degenerative spinal disease [10,12]. Others suggests that obesity might be the result of the limited daily activity caused by spinal pain [20]. Despite numerous studies, there are few investigations of how obesity affects functional disability in patients who were diagnosed with LSS.

Fanuele et al. revealed that general and spinal disease-associated functional status was significantly worse in overweight and obese patients compared to normal weight individuals in a large population-based cross-sectional survey [21]. However, they declared the possible inaccuracy of self-reported BMI as one of the limitations of the study. BMI is a commonly used tool for clarifying obesity in most studies [8,10,11,14,21]. It is a simple, traditional and easily applicable method to judge body fatness in clinical practice. However, BMI, which is body weight in kilograms divided by height in meters squared, is not the accurate measurement of body fat. It cannot distinguish between body fat and lean body mass nor reflect accurate body fat mass and distribution. BMI might over- or underestimate body fat, and it can be different according to sex, age, ethnicity and individual variations [22,23].

The current study proved that percent body fat was a better predictor for functional disability in LSS patients than BMI was, even though the mechanism of association between percent body fat and functional disability in ADL in LSS patients remains unclear. Although percent body fat was significantly different between the mild/moderate and severe disability group, the BMI was similar in the two groups. Therefore, we suggest that the body composition analysis could be used as a part of a supplementary diagnostic tool for predicting the functional status of LSS patients in clinical practice. BIA is a reliable, inexpensive, fast and bed-side applicable tool for measuring body composition. It allows estimating the composition of various body compartments, such as body fat, fat-free mass, body water or body cell mass in both healthy and ill subjects [24–26]. BIA has also been recently applied to evaluate nutritional or metabolic status, as well as body hydration status, in patients with various entities of diseases [27]. BIA might be able to expand its role for predicting the severity or the prognosis of various painful musculoskeletal disorders, and further investigations in a large population should be performed.

The current study also aimed to evaluate whether the severe disability of LSS patients was associated with the skeletal muscle parameters of BIA, such as skeletal muscle mass or index. However, we cannot find those associations. Indeed, sarcopenia has been focused on as associated with decreased function in ADL in older patients, with further association with several musculoskeletal disease entities [28]. Furthermore, the importance of the paraspinal muscle has been investigated in the clinical progress of various musculoskeletal diseases of the lumbar spine. Structural change, such as atrophy or fat infiltration in the multifidus and paraspinal muscles, has been observed in patients with chronic low back pain [28–31]. In the current study, skeletal muscle parameters of BIA were not beneficial enough for predicting the functional disability of LSS patients, but radiologic measures of psoas and multifidus muscles seem to have the potential to predict it. A future study of a large population should be performed to explain these associations clearly.

These are limitations of this study. First, this study was limited to a relatively small number of participants of a single hospital. Second, the causality of the patients' LSS and their body composition characteristics were not discussed. Third, the long-term effect of high percent body fat or reduction of body fat on LSS was not evaluated in this study. The effects of physical or surgical weight reduction on the improvement of patients' symptoms and function are still inconclusive [32,33]. Further observational cohort studies can be conducted.

5. Conclusions

In conclusion, this study suggests that increased percent body fat predicts potential severe functional disability in ADL in LSS patients. BIA may provide useful information for predicting the severity or the prognosis of various lumbar spinal disorders in clinical practice.

Author Contributions: Conceptualization, A.D. and J.-S.S.; methodology, A.D. and J.-S.S.; formal analysis, A.D. and Y.K.; investigation, A.D., C.L. and H.O.; data curation, H.O.; writing—original draft preparation, Y.K.; writing—review and editing, A.D. and Y.K. All authors have read and agreed to the published version of the manuscript.

Funding: This research received no external funding.

Institutional Review Board Statement: The study was conducted according to the guidelines of the Declaration of Helsinki and approved by the Institutional Review Board of Jeonbuk National University Hospital (CUH 2018-11-037, date of approval: 2 January 2019).

Informed Consent Statement: Informed consent was obtained from all subjects involved in the study.

Conflicts of Interest: The authors declare no conflict of interest.

References

1. Amundsen, T.; Weber, H.; Lilleas, F.; Nordal, H.J.; Abdelnoor, M.; Magnaes, B. Lumbar spinal stenosis. Clinical and radiologic features. *Spine* **1995**, *20*, 1178–1186. [CrossRef] [PubMed]
2. Kirkaldy-Willis, W.H.; Paine, K.W.; Cauchoix, J.; McIvor, G. Lumbar spinal stenosis. *Clin. Orthop. Relat. Res.* **1974**, *24*, 30–50. [CrossRef]
3. Lin, S.I.; Lin, R.M.; Huang, L.W. Disability in patients with degenerative lumbar spinal stenosis. *Arch. Phys. Med. Rehabil.* **2006**, *87*, 1250–1256. [CrossRef] [PubMed]
4. Kim, G.U.; Park, J.; Kim, H.J.; Shen, F.; Cho, J.; Chang, B.S.; Lee, C.K.; Chun, H.J.; Yeom, J.S. Definitions of unfavorable surgical outcomes and their risk factors based on disability score after spine surgery for lumbar spinal stenosis. *BMC Musculoskelet. Disord.* **2020**, *21*, 288. [CrossRef] [PubMed]
5. Zeifang, F.; Schiltenwolf, M.; Abel, R.; Moradi, B. Gait analysis does not correlate with clinical and MR imaging parameters in patients with symptomatic lumbar spinal stenosis. *BMC Musculoskelet. Disord.* **2008**, *9*, 89. [CrossRef] [PubMed]

6. Sirvanci, M.; Bhatia, M.; Ganiyusufoglu, K.A.; Duran, C.; Tezer, M.; Ozturk, C.; Aydogan, M.; Hamzaoglu, A. Degenerative lumbar spinal stenosis: Correlation with Oswestry Disability Index and MR imaging. *Eur. Spine J.* **2008**, *17*, 679–685. [CrossRef] [PubMed]
7. Dario, A.B.; Ferreira, M.L.; Refshauge, K.; Sanchez-Romera, J.F.; Luque-Suarez, A.; Hopper, J.L.; Ordonana, J.R.; Ferreira, P.H. Are obesity and body fat distribution associated with low back pain in women? A population-based study of 1128 Spanish twins. *Eur. Spine J.* **2016**, *25*, 1188–1195. [CrossRef]
8. Samartzis, D.; Karppinen, J.; Chan, D.; Luk, K.D.; Cheung, K.M. The association of lumbar intervertebral disc degeneration on magnetic resonance imaging with body mass index in overweight and obese adults: A population-based study. *Arthritis Rheum.* **2012**, *64*, 1488–1496. [CrossRef]
9. Dario, A.B.; Loureiro Ferreira, M.; Refshauge, K.; Luque-Suarez, A.; Ordonana, J.R.; Ferreira, P.H. Obesity does not increase the risk of chronic low back pain when genetics are considered. A prospective study of Spanish adult twins. *Spine J.* **2017**, *17*, 282–290. [CrossRef]
10. Knutsson, B.; Sandén, B.; Sjödén, G.; Järvholm, B.; Michaëlsson, K. Body Mass Index and Risk for Clinical Lumbar Spinal Stenosis: A Cohort Study. *Spine* **2015**, *40*, 1451–1456. [CrossRef]
11. Su, C.A.; Kusin, D.J.; Li, S.Q.; Ahn, U.M.; Ahn, N.U. The Association between Body Mass Index and the Prevalence, Severity, and Frequency of Low Back Pain: Data from the Osteoarthritis Initiative. *Spine* **2018**, *43*, 848–852. [CrossRef] [PubMed]
12. Han, T.S.; Schouten, J.S.; Lean, M.E.; Seidell, J.C. The prevalence of low back pain and associations with body fatness, fat distribution and height. *Int. J. Obes. Relat. Metab. Disord.* **1997**, *21*, 600–607. [CrossRef] [PubMed]
13. Samartzis, D.; Karppinen, J.; Mok, F.; Fong, D.Y.; Luk, K.D.; Cheung, K.M. A population-based study of juvenile disc degeneration and its association with overweight and obesity, low back pain, and diminished functional status. *J. Bone Joint Surg. Am.* **2011**, *93*, 662–670. [CrossRef] [PubMed]
14. Azimi, P.; Yazdanian, T.; Shahzadi, S.; Benzel, E.C.; Azhari, S.; Nayeb Aghaei, H.; Montazeri, A. Cut-off Value for Body Mass Index in Predicting Surgical Success in Patients with Lumbar Spinal Canal Stenosis. *Asian Spine J.* **2018**, *12*, 1085–1091. [CrossRef] [PubMed]
15. Elsamadicy, A.A.; Adogwa, O.; Vuong, V.D.; Mehta, A.I.; Vasquez, R.A.; Cheng, J.; Karikari, I.O.; Bagley, C.A. Patient Body Mass Index is an Independent Predictor of 30-Day Hospital Readmission After Elective Spine Surgery. *World Neurosurg.* **2016**, *96*, 148–151. [CrossRef]
16. Kim, D.Y.; Lee, S.H.; Lee, H.Y.; Lee, H.J.; Chang, S.B.; Chung, S.K.; Kim, H.J. Validation of the Korean version of the oswestry disability index. *Spine* **2005**, *30*, E123–E127. [CrossRef]
17. Fairbank, J.C.; Pynsent, P.B. The Oswestry Disability Index. *Spine* **2000**, *25*, 2940–2952; discussion 2952. [CrossRef]
18. Schizas, C.; Theumann, N.; Burn, A.; Tansey, R.; Wardlaw, D.; Smith, F.W.; Kulik, G. Qualitative grading of severity of lumbar spinal stenosis based on the morphology of the dural sac on magnetic resonance images. *Spine* **2010**, *35*, 1919–1924. [CrossRef]
19. Bogduk, N. Lumbar transforaminal injection of corticosteroids. In *International Spine Intervention Society Practice Guidelines for Spinal Diagnostic and Treatment Procedures*; International Spinal Intervention Society: San Francisco, CA, USA, 2004; p. 187.
20. Lake, J.K.; Power, C.; Cole, T.J. Back pain and obesity in the 1958 British birth cohort: Cause or effect? *J. Clin. Epidemiol.* **2000**, *53*, 245–250. [CrossRef]
21. Fanuele, J.C.; Abdu, W.A.; Hanscom, B.; Weinstein, J.N. Association between obesity and functional status in patients with spine disease. *Spine* **2002**, *27*, 306–312. [CrossRef]
22. Batsis, J.A.; Mackenzie, T.A.; Bartels, S.J.; Sahakyan, K.R.; Somers, V.K.; Lopez-Jimenez, F. Diagnostic accuracy of body mass index to identify obesity in older adults: NHANES 1999-2004. *Int. J. Obes.* **2016**, *40*, 761–767. [CrossRef] [PubMed]
23. Gallagher, D.; Heymsfield, S.B.; Heo, M.; Jebb, S.A.; Murgatroyd, P.R.; Sakamoto, Y. Healthy percentage body fat ranges: An approach for developing guidelines based on body mass index. *Am. J. Clin. Nutr.* **2000**, *72*, 694–701. [CrossRef] [PubMed]
24. Kyle, U.G.; Bosaeus, I.; De Lorenzo, A.D.; Deurenberg, P.; Elia, M.; Manuel Gómez, J.; Lilienthal Heitmann, B.; Kent-Smith, L.; Melchior, J.C.; Pirlich, M.; et al. Bioelectrical impedance analysis-part II: Utilization in clinical practice. *Clin. Nutr.* **2004**, *23*, 1430–1453. [CrossRef]
25. Andreoli, A.; Garaci, F.; Cafarelli, F.P.; Guglielmi, G. Body composition in clinical practice. *Eur. J. Radiol.* **2016**, *85*, 1461–1468. [CrossRef] [PubMed]
26. Roubenoff, R.; Dallal, G.E.; Wilson, P.W. Predicting body fatness: The body mass index vs estimation by bioelectrical impedance. *Am. J. Public Health* **1995**, *85*, 726–728. [CrossRef]
27. Mulasi, U.; Kuchnia, A.J.; Cole, A.J.; Earthman, C.P. Bioimpedance at the bedside: Current applications, limitations, and opportunities. *Nutr. Clin. Pract.* **2015**, *30*, 180–193. [CrossRef] [PubMed]
28. Marcus, R.L.; Addison, O.; Dibble, L.E.; Foreman, K.B.; Morrell, G.; Lastayo, P. Intramuscular adipose tissue, sarcopenia, and mobility function in older individuals. *J. Aging Res.* **2012**, *2012*, 629637. [CrossRef]
29. Goubert, D.; Oosterwijck, J.V.; Meeus, M.; Danneels, L. Structural Changes of Lumbar Muscles in Non-specific Low Back Pain: A Systematic Review. *Pain Physician* **2016**, *19*, E985–E1000.

30. Goubert, D.; De Pauw, R.; Meeus, M.; Willems, T.; Cagnie, B.; Schouppe, S.; Van Oosterwijck, J.; Dhondt, E.; Danneels, L. Lumbar muscle structure and function in chronic versus recurrent low back pain: A cross-sectional study. *Spine J.* **2017**, *17*, 1285–1296. [CrossRef]
31. Shahidi, B.; Hubbard, J.C.; Gibbons, M.C.; Ruoss, S.; Zlomislic, V.; Allen, R.T.; Garfin, S.R.; Ward, S.R. Lumbar multifidus muscle degenerates in individuals with chronic degenerative lumbar spine pathology. *J. Orthop. Res.* **2017**, *35*, 2700–2706. [CrossRef]
32. Chen, L.H.; Weber, K.; Mehrabkhani, S.; Baskaran, S.; Abbass, T.; Macedo, L.G. The effectiveness of weight loss programs for low back pain: A systematic review. *BMC Musculoskelet. Disord.* **2022**, *23*, 488. [CrossRef]
33. Lidar, Z.; Behrbalk, E.; Regev, G.J.; Salame, K.; Keynan, O.; Schweiger, C.; Appelbaum, L.; Levy, Y.; Keidar, A. Intervertebral disc height changes after weight reduction in morbidly obese patients and its effect on quality of life and radicular and low back pain. *Spine* **2012**, *37*, 1947–1952. [CrossRef]

MDPI
St. Alban-Anlage 66
4052 Basel
Switzerland
www.mdpi.com

Journal of Clinical Medicine Editorial Office
E-mail: jcm@mdpi.com
www.mdpi.com/journal/jcm

www.ingramcontent.com/pod-product-compliance
Lightning Source LLC
Chambersburg PA
CBHW040815250926
51850CB00007BA/1177
* 9 7 8 3 0 3 6 5 8 6 4 4 1 *